WITH MUSKET, CANNON
AND SWORD

With Musket, Cannon and Sword

Battle Tactics of Napoleon and His Enemies

BRENT NOSWORTHY

SARPEDON

New York

Published in the United States by
SARPEDON
166 Fifth Avenue
New York, NY 10010

First published in Great Britain in 1996 as
"Battle Tactics of Napoleon and His Enemies"
by Constable and Co. Ltd, London.

ISBN 1-885119-27-5

Library of Congress Cataloging-in-Publication Data

Nosworthy, Brent
    With musket, cannon and sword : battle tactics of Napoleon and
his enemies / by Brent Nosworthy.
        p.   cm.
Includes bibliographical references and index.
ISBN 1-88519-27-5
    1. France—History, Military—1789–1815. 2. Napoleonic Wars,
1800–1815—Campaigns—Europe. 3. Napoleon I, Emperor of the French,
1769–1821—Military leadership. 4. Military art and science—
Europe—History.   I. Title.
DC151.N67   1996
940.2´7—dc20   96-6161
                                                                          CIP

10 9 8 7 6 5 4 3 2 1

MANUFACTURED IN THE UNITED STATES OF AMERICA

I would like to dedicate this book to my family
—Mom, Alice, Enerria and Tristan—
all of whom exhibited extreme patience and understanding
during the thousands of hours it was necessary to closet
myself away in my workroom.

This book is also dedicated to all my friends,
especially Angel, David, Fred and Simon, who never
failed to provide much needed encouragement.
It is also dedicated to my "sister" Xiomara, who has
taught me the meaning of true friendship.

CONTENTS

ILLUSTRATIONS

PLATES

Acknowledgements

I would like to thank Steve Carpenter, Paul Gagnon, William Keyser, Jean Lochet, Stefan Patejak, Brian Pieper, Carl Paradis, Roger Kennedy, George Nafziger, Larry O'Donnel, Jean-Guy Ratté and Emmanual Vovsi for supplying me with a number of interesting military historical works. Many thanks are also extended to Lou Giorgino and Frank Rella for editorial assistance.

This is also an appropriate occasion to thank heartily the staff of the Rare Book Room of the McCellan Library, McGill University, Montreal, the New York Public Library, especially those at the 43rd Street Annexe and the Bibliothèque Nationale de Quebec, Montreal.

Introduction

THOSE STRUGGLING TO ARRIVE at a genuine understanding of warfare in any historical period can never afford to limit their examination to formal doctrine treated in isolation, no matter how thoroughly or conscientiously conducted. After looking at the complete repertoire of theoretical practices, they must then focus on what actually occurred on the battlefield. No treatment of tactics or combat can ever be complete unless it considers the events within a number of actual battles. Given the volume of currently available works which provide accounts of well-known Napoleonic battles, this might strike some as a superfluous effort. However, although these accounts are useful from a purely narrative point of view, they infrequently provide the detail needed to understand tactical-level events on the battlefield.

The traditional approach used to dissect and analyse battles which explains 'what' occurred during a particular contest has unfortunately largely ignored the 'how' and the 'why'. Typically, a description of a battle tells us what forces were present on either side, the lie of the land, and the dispositions of both armies, followed by a description of the events as they unfolded. However, the great majority of these descriptions are very general in nature: 'the forces under so-and-so's command charged forward and after three attempts took the redoubt.' Occasionally a modicum of detail is added, and we might learn, for example, that the offensive force consisted of the 32nd, 44th and 52nd regiments, and that they were 'in column'.

If we accept that the study of history should be more than a prosaic list of dates and facts, then this principle must be applied to military history as well. Surely it is as important to know why a French column broke at Austerlitz or, conversely, why British infantry were able to withstand repeated cavalry assaults at Waterloo as it is to know simply that these events occurred. The more general descriptions which curiously avoid these types of explanations are as common as they are devoid of any meaningful detail. After reading many of these battle accounts, one is left with the distinct impression the author *purposely* left out lower-level details, as if their inclusion were not only irrelevant, but even harmful, obscuring an overall understanding of the larger events. Tactical minutiae such as 'the cavalry already at the gallop deployed into line by fours' is rarely, if ever, to be found in these types of accounts.

The usual rationale for this filtration of detail is the conviction that the outcome of battles was the result of more 'important' factors such as the troops' morale, their leadership, as well as grand tactical and strategic planning, rather than purely tactical issues and events. Essentially, this argument rates each type of factor according to the extent to which it influenced the result of the contest. In other words, how often did each prove to be the 'deciding factor' in the outcome of an engagement? At first glance, this appears to be a plausible and even the most objective method of assessing each type of event or factor operative during a battle. The problem, however, is that by focusing on so-called 'deciding factors', the complex intertwining of forces and lesser events taking place prior to the resolution of the contest tends to be pushed to the background and ignored.

One of the best ways of illustrating the limitations of this approach and how it actually provides a distorted view of combat is to apply this type of analysis to another category of physical contest, one of which the average reader probably has some direct experience, if only as a spectator. This is professional boxing. Fortunately, this will not take us far afield, since boxing, like combat, pits two opponents against one another, each attempting to impose his will upon the other through the skilful use of physical force.

Consider the case where a boxing match involves two equally matched contestants with very similar styles and boxing skills. The match continues through a number of hard-fought rounds, until one boxer 'puts his opponent away' simply because, being in better physical condition, he was able to outlast his adversary. However, let us say that until the last round the match was basically a draw with both opponents frequently scoring with punches to the head and body as they moved continuously about the ring. Using the 'decisive factor' argument, someone might argue that the countless number of body and eye feints, foot movements, jabs, parries, etc. are not really that important, since what ultimately decided the fight was physical conditioning. Taking this argument to its logical extremity, one could even conclude that feints, body movements, fancy footwork, etc. can never be important since the 'decisive' action is always delivered by the fists.

Obviously, no one with any familiarity with boxing would take this argument seriously, since it is recognized that all of the boxer's actions form a broad repertoire of movements which work together to wear down the opponent and set up an opportunity to deliver the final blow. Top physical conditioning, the ability to 'out-think' one's opponent, a devastating knockout right cross are all major components in a boxer's arsenal. But they all work together in an orchestrated set of physical movements which also include and rely upon constant footwork and minor body movements. This is actually very similar to the complex set of dynamics present on any battlefield. The difference, of course, is that battles are made up of a far greater number of movements and other actions, and are influenced by very many more factors. Nevertheless, regardless of the number and diversity of factors and events, they all are part of the same overall process, that is the battle being fought.

Another method of assessing the importance of an event or factor on the battlefield, and one that should be used to supplement the 'decisive factor' criterion, is to attempt to determine to what extent a factor or occurrence makes up the processes and events constituting the entire battle. In other words, each factor is evaluated not only on the extent to which it *decided* the battle but also the degree to which it made up the actions within that conflict. With the addition of this second consideration, tactical considerations no longer can be relegated to a minor role, but must be perceived as of the utmost importance, since everything that occurs is ultimately manifested on a tactical level.

A battle is made up of a large number of troop movements, firefights, feints and a myriad other tactical events. A battalion here and there may 'ploy' into column to bypass difficult ground before returning into line; another battalion may meet a cavalry threat by doubling its ranks, while its neighbour forms a square, and so on.

Even large-scale events must be implemented on a tactical level. A commander feints an attack on the enemy's left flank while bringing his main force to bear on the opposite wing. Obviously, this is a 'grand tactical' action. Nevertheless, in order for this to be accomplished, the men in the main assault must ploy into columns, march forward, manoeuvre around obstacles and then return to line, when near the enemy, to deliver a volley. The grand tactical measure of attacking the flank consists of a number of minor steps or phases all of which are tactical in nature. The same is true for any other conceivable grand tactical operation.

This observation applies to many other elements or dimensions at work during a battle. Consider the troop's morale, often cited as an important factor in determining the outcome of any conflict. A body of infantry is attacked by adversaries much more determined to stand and fight. The defending forces, seeing the enemy's determination, become increasingly nervous; here and there men in the ranks begin to fire, despite their officers' proscriptions to the contrary. Some of the men begin to seek shelter at the back of the line, so that many of the files are now ten to fifteen men deep, and gaps begin to appear along the line. Finally, as the enemy approaches within point-blank range, the whole gives way as the men flee to the rear.

True, in this case, the attackers are victorious because the defenders lacked sufficient will to resist. Yet, to have any effect at all, the low morale has to manifest itself on a tactical level, in this case in disorganized 'battle fire' which, beginning at too long a range, disordered the formation and made it impossible for the officers to order a pre-emptive rush at the attackers during the final moments. Since the result of a significant alteration of the troops' morale is to positively or negatively affect their performance, changes in morale, when they have any effect, *always* take effect on a tactical level. This is equally true with other types of large-scale issues or forces. We could say tactical-level events and actions are the 'molecules' out of which almost all other higher-level forces are made up. They provide the mechanism that allows all other factors to interact with one another, thus moulding the events on the field of battle.

The all too common historian's abhorrence of tactical issues and the resulting unwillingness to examine battlefield events at the 'microscopic' level has meant that the complex mixture of lower-level events making up any contest have remained largely unnoticed and thus uncommented upon. A great many of the descriptions of Napoleonic era battles amount to little more than self-fulfilling prophecies. Tactical-level issues perceived from the very beginning as unimportant are ignored and thus filtered out of the examination of the battle's events. The resulting accounts, not surprisingly, mention little of these concerns, thereby strongly reinforcing the notion to the reader that low-level events are indeed insignificant.

To rectify this deficiency, there is a pressing need to re-examine many of the battles of the era and piece together a more detailed picture of the events as they unfolded during these engagements. Only when these more detailed accounts are assembled can the nature, role and import of less obvious factors and dynamics be accurately assessed. The first chapter of this present work, therefore, is devoted to a detailed examination of the Battle of Lodi, Kellerman's charge at Marengo and the Battle of Sedyman. These have been selected because they allow an interesting insight into what was occurring on the battlefield on the lowest of levels. These three accounts attempt to include all the tactical-level events only to the degree that they are mentioned in eye-witness accounts or other primary sources. No effort is made to explain or elaborate upon each of these tactical practices since that is the purpose of the remainder of this present work.

PART I

BACKGROUND

CHAPTER 1

Tactics in Three Napoleonic Battles

BATTLE OF LODI (10 MAY 1796)

ALTHOUGH THE BATTLE OF LODI is chiefly known for the seemingly reckless rush of a massive French infantry column across the Adda River, when a detailed account of this day's events is reconstructed, a more complex picture begins to emerge, one which shows both sides employing a series of tactical measures.

After the loss at Fombio, 8 May 1796, the Austrians under Beaulieu were forced to fall back towards the Adda. The Austrians showed a brave front throughout this movement and the retreat was not a rout. Reaching the town of Lodi, they initially attempted to make a stand on the near side of the river. The main town was on the 'French' side of the river, while there were only woods and a few isolated buildings on the 'Austrian' side.

Bonaparte and the French advance guard neared Lodi at nine o'clock in the morning. Quickly, all nearby French cavalry was ordered to attack the Austrian outposts that had been hastily set up to guard the approaches to the town. This impromptu effort was supported by four pieces of light artillery which had been quickly attached to a team of coach horses supplied by some recently arrived nobility of Pliasance. Swiftly, the *ad hoc* force succeeded in capturing an Austrian gun and pushing in the outposts. Beaulieu's resolve to defend the town in force was unsettled by this sudden success, and he ordered the Austrian army to evacuate Lodi. A single infantry battalion from the Austrian Nadasti regiment and two cavalry

3

squadrons were left behind to hold out against the French, while the main body of the Austrians immediately began to cross the single bridge over the Adda.

As these first tentative probes were underway, Bonaparte made plans for the main offensive effort and ordered the main body of the French army to hasten forward. Responding to their commander's orders, Augereau's division, which had halted at Borghetto, and Masséna's, in a nearby town, both hastened forward.[1]

Meanwhile, back in Lodi, a brisk cannonade broke out on both sides, which appears once again to have caught the Austrians off guard. Mixing pusillanimity with foolish optimism, Beaulieu committed a second strategic error. He failed to destroy the one object which would have certainly slowed down the French advance. Still resolved to maintain a footing on the near side of the Adda, the defenders had been unwilling to dismantle the bridge, the most effective delaying tactic available under the circumstances. The earnestness of the French cannonade, however, soon convinced Beaulieu and his staff of the impossibility of maintaining their position in the town. The last of the Austrian troops were soon ordered to hurry across and rejoin the main Austrian force. Once across, Major Malcamp, who commanded the retiring Austrian force, positioned several cannons on the bridge facing the French across the river. To ensure a cross fire, additional guns were placed to the left and right of the bridge along the bank. Bonaparte on his part employed a similar tactic, placing his artillery in a battery along the near bank and personally supervised the placement of two pieces.[2] In an account penned some time after the battle, Bonaparte calculated that Beaulieu had positioned as many as thirty artillery pieces on the bridge and along the bank, though this was probably a gross exaggeration and is at odds with other contemporary accounts. Bonaparte goes on to mention that the mutually inflicted cannonade was 'very brisk' and continued for 'several hours'.[3]

It was at this point that a sizeable portion of the French army arrived on the scene. Beaumont's cavalry and some supporting artillery were ordered to cross the Adda at a ford half a league above Lodi. Once across, it was to work its way back towards the bridge at Lodi and bear down on the Austrian right flank. Unfortunately, the French cavalry encountered unexpected difficulties and suffered costly delays crossing the ford. As it turned out, this deprived them of participating in the main brunt of the battle. Fortunately for Bonaparte and the French, the infantry elements encountered no such obstacles. As they reached Lodi in dribs and drabs, Bonaparte immediately started to organize these troops into a single, closed order column. General Dupas and a composite battalion of carabiniers were placed at the head of the column and were followed by a composite battalion of grenadiers. One account has Bonaparte and his generals organizing the massive column while harassed by a 'tremendous' fire from Austrian artillery.[4] Grivet, writing in the 1860s, on the other hand, writes that the column was formed under the relative protection of a rampart overlooking the river.[5]

Regardless of where it was formed, Bonaparte and his generals led their column to the bridge. The Austrians were ready and, almost as soon as the head of the column set foot on the bridge, the Austrian artillerymen discharged their pieces which had been loaded with canister. Enfiladed by the Austrian artillery positioned on either side of the bridge, not to mention having to sustain the pieces directly in front of them, the French suffered heavy losses and fell back. Twice more the column attempted to advance across the bridge, but each time it suffered the same fate. Bonaparte and his staff sensed the gravity of the moment. The column was reinforced with fresh troops, and Bonaparte and six generals (Berthier, Masséna, Cervoni, Dallemagne, *chef de brigade* Lannes, and *chef de bataillon* Dupas) placed themselves at the front of the column.

Fortunately for the French, the brisk and almost continuous fire from the artillery on both sides momentarily produced a thick pall of smoke, which obscured the French column's movements from their adversaries on the far shore. Bonaparte was in his typical form and at no loss as to how to seize this opportunity. For a fourth time the French infantry rushed forward in closed column. The Austrians, their vision still obscured by the dense smoke, did not see the French advance until it was too late.[6] Taken by this momentary surprise, panic spread through the Austrian ranks and the men recoiled backwards.

Apparently, one of the causes of the Austrian defeat was an unthinking application of the prevalent artillery doctrine by their gunners in front and on the sides of the bridge. Round shot ('cannonballs') was used when the enemy was still at long and medium ranges, while canister was resorted to during the final moments. This made perfect sense if the enemy had advanced in the traditional formation, that is in *line*. However, forced to advance over a narrow bridge, the French infantry was in a very lengthy column. Had the Austrian gunners had a moment to reflect, they would have realized that they should have used round shot to plough holes throughout the entire length of the advancing French column. Instead, they followed the conventional wisdom, designed for the open battlefield, and inflicted heavy casualties, but only at the head of the column.[7]

Although the front of the column was successfully stymied, the remainder survived to press on and, as the column neared the far bank, many of the carabiniers and grenadiers on the sides of the column jumped into the river. Wading through the water, they reached the far shore, where they spread out on both sides of the bridge in extended order and fought as skirmishers. The remainder of the heavy column managed to make its way over the bridge, where it marched directly towards the Austrian line, which had retired some distance from the bank. Fortunately for the advancing French forces, the undulating nature of the ground afforded partial protection from Austrian musket fire and so they were able to form a substantial bridgehead relatively unmolested. As the French column moved away from the banks of the Adda, it divided into a number of smaller platoon-sized closed columns. The battalion of carabiniers remained in the centre with the platoons from the grenadier battalion in its rear fanning out to the right and to the left. The whole was preceded by numerous skirmishers. The confident demeanour of the advancing French, the effect of the well-placed artillery on the Lodi side of the river, and Beaumont's cavalry now at last bearing down on the right flank ensured the success of the French bridgehead.[8]

The Austrian cavalry, forced into inactivity up to this point, attempted to turn the situation around and advanced to charge the oncoming French infantry. The latter, however, sensing success, 'were not easily intimidated'. Meanwhile, additional French divisions led by generals Rusca, Augereau and Bayrand arrived and entered into the fray. The Austrians, unnerved by the unexpected French success at Lodi bridge, threatened by the French cavalry on their right flank and the flood of new French reinforcements, finally began an unchecked retreat. The French, however, were unable to mount an effective pursuit. Many of the rank and file had marched more than ten leagues, and night was falling fast. The battle finally ended, and the Austrians lost about twenty pieces of cannon and 2,000 or 3,000 men, who were either *hors de combat* (i.e., casualties – dead or wounded) or taken prisoner.[9]

This expanded account of the day's action shows that what has been typically recounted as simply several precipitous rushes across the narrow Lodi bridge, when looked at in its entirety was tactically more diverse than has usually been portrayed. A quick recapitulation of the tactical events demonstrates this.

The French began the assault on the town by combining light artillery with the available cavalry. Later both sides lined the bank on either side of the Adda with all available artillery to produce a convergent fire upon the bridge's exits. The actual assault delivered by a French closed infantry column was formed from élite grenadiers and carabiniers. The Austrians repeatedly repelled the massive column firing canister when the French reached the halfway point across the bridge; this was not as effective as if they had fired round shot at the narrow columns on the bridge. After each repulse, Bonaparte and his generals threw themselves in front of the men and frantically worked at restoring the formation and the men's confidence. Seizing the opportunity afforded by a lull in the wind with the attendant thick 'fog' of smoke produced by the seemingly incessant artillery fire, Bonaparte rallied his men a third time and was able to approach the Austrians on the far side unobserved until almost the last moment, when it was too late to fire the artillery. Meanwhile, many of the French infantry in the column on the bridge jumped into the river on either side, where they began to fight as skirmishers. Once on the far side, the main body fragmented into a number of platoon-sized columns which systematically fanned out so that the force occupied a frontage more consistent with normal fighting requirements.

Clearly, the battle of Lodi illustrates the first criterion needed to demonstrate the importance of tactical practices and tactical-level events during the resolution of any military confrontation. These low-level events and practices are found to occur repeatedly throughout the entire engagement rather than only infrequently or sporadically. In this particular confrontation, at the very least, tactics have the same importance as minor movements such as feints and body movements in boxing. Although not necessarily the 'deciding factor', their importance lies in their frequency of occurrence as well as the degree to which they set up the major events which did decide the issue.

MARENGO (4 JUNE 1800)

One might argue that the Battle of Lodi was necessarily a tactical affair, since almost all of the main action occurred on or in the immediate vicinity of a single bridge. With the exception of the cavalry, which only belatedly took part in the action, almost all of the combatant forces were within several hundred paces of the bridge's entrance and exit, and it is hardly surprising that low-level events could determine the final outcome.

This argument, however, cannot be applied to the next battle we will examine: the Battle of Marengo. Although initially only affecting the French advance guard, this historic confrontation ultimately involved two entire armies, took over eight hours to be resolved and at its height stretched over ten square miles. Nevertheless, when a detailed picture of this conflict is assembled, once again the constant ebb and flow of tactical manoeuvring is observed throughout the conflict. Despite the size of the engagement, the entire combat finally was dramatically resolved as a result of a single tactical blow which would snatch a hard-earned victory from the Austrians and hand it to a French force which up to that point had suffered a continuum of reverses throughout the day and was on the brink of total defeat.

Prior to the outbreak of the engagement, Napoleon had believed that the Austrians would continue to retreat and took no steps to concentrate his forces for a major engagement. During the night the Austrians had thrown three bridges across the Bormida and managed to surprise Gardanne's advance guard. Gradually, Victor's division and several other elements to the rear made their way forward and a lengthy battle line developed.

Unlike many of the engagements familiar to posterity, the French fought in a traditional linear formation, with two extended infantry lines in the centre and cavalry on either flank. It was the Austrians' turn to utilize column formations. The earlier attacks in front of Marengo saw the Austrians advance in heavy columns, which for the most part were unsuccessful.

Though unsupported for hours, Victor and Gardanne's infantry put up stiff resistance and were only slowly beaten back. Heavily outnumbered, they seized every opportunity to stop and renew a stubborn defensive. The French displayed a mastery of formal military techniques that had proved to be beyond the capabilities of earlier revolutionary armies. At one point during the retreat, for example, the 72nd Demi-brigade was completely surrounded by numerous Austrian cavalry and was simultaneously charged in the front and the rear. True to the highest professional standards of the eighteenth century, its third rank faced about and warded off the cavalry in the rear while the front two ranks held off those attacking the front.[10]

Despite their determination, the French were forced back in a series of retreats, and the Austrians continued to make headway, especially on the French left. By 3 p.m. the entire French line was now forced to fall back towards San Giuliano.[11] The retrograde movement on Victor's side of the line began to be precipitous. Monnier's division, having only entered the fray in the afternoon, was still relatively fresh, and retreat on this side much more gradual. The result was that over the next several hours the front line of the French army assumed a somewhat concave configuration, with Monnier's division on the right the most advanced, and Victor's shattered formations on the left very much closer to San Giuliano in the rear. Lannes' division ran diagonally between these two extremes.

The Austrians followed closely along the entire length of their line. Independent bodies of Austrian cavalry started to circle various French battalions, but were still successfully held at bay.[12] The Austrian artillery in front of the advancing Austrian infantry proved to be considerably more effective. Subjected to quickly fired canister, many of the French units began to lose their cohesiveness, and the field quickly became littered with the dead, wounded, fugitives and discarded equipment.[13]

Before the battle started, Desaix's division had been ordered to advance towards Rivalta and Novi. However, Desaix, hearing the artillery, halted his men and ordered them to march to the sound of the guns. He and his staff entered San Giuliano at around 4 o'clock; his division arrived on the battlefield a half hour later.[14]

From the Austrian perspective the battle appeared to have been won. There was now a torrential flow of French fugitives and disordered units towards the rear. The skirmishers in particular had become disorganized, many losing track of their parent battalion. Joseph Petit who had been a participant at the battle with the French Horse Guard estimated that by 4 o'clock there remained but six thousand men still capable of fighting. Of the over fifteen thousand originally engaged, a third were now casualties.[15] Only six French guns along the front lines remained operational. The whole affair had totally surprised the French and there were none of the preparations usually taken before a set piece action. One result was a shortage of carriages and wagons to carry off the wounded and dying. A considerable portion of the infantry acted as beasts of burden carrying their fallen comrades off the battlefield. And, of course, this provided an opportunity for many of the less brave to flee this scene of what now appeared to be the inevitable French defeat all the more quickly. There was, moreover, a general shortage of officers. In addition to those lost to casualties, many had left their post, falling victim to hunger, thirst and sheer fatigue.

Many of the wounded crawled or were carried to the wooded areas on the edges and to the rear of the battlefield. Unfortunately, however, both shot and canister from the Austrian guns cut through the trees and the vines in these areas, and many of the wounded were crushed to death by the falling branches and tree trunks.[16]

The defeated French forces, especially on the left, flowed toward the natural back door to the battlefield: the San Giuliano defile where the greatest efforts were being made to reform the scattered formations. Bordered on one side by a wood and on the other by a densely packed vineyard, the defile lent itself to a determined resistance.

It was at this point that Desaix's division finally arrived at around 4.30 in the afternoon, initially deploying behind Victor's men, near the extreme left of the French army's rather serpentine battle line. A great many fugitives were milling about this area, and potentially this could have had a disastrous effect on Desaix's men. Bonaparte and Berthier, accompanied by other general officers and members of the staff, energetically rode up and down along the line exhorting the men to return to or remain with their formations and continue the fight. Bonaparte and his generals realized that the French army, having already suffered a series of reverses that day, was incapable of sustaining another setback. Every precaution was taken to place the remaining troops in the best possible position.

The remnants of the original fighting force and the newly arrived troops were formed up along two lines. Desaix's division was positioned in front, that is, west of San Giuliano. Slightly undulating ground would conceal Desaix's men from the Austrians as they approached. A portion of Desaix's front line advanced so that an echelon refusing its right was formed, i.e. the elements on the left were in front, those on the right were rearward. On the left, the

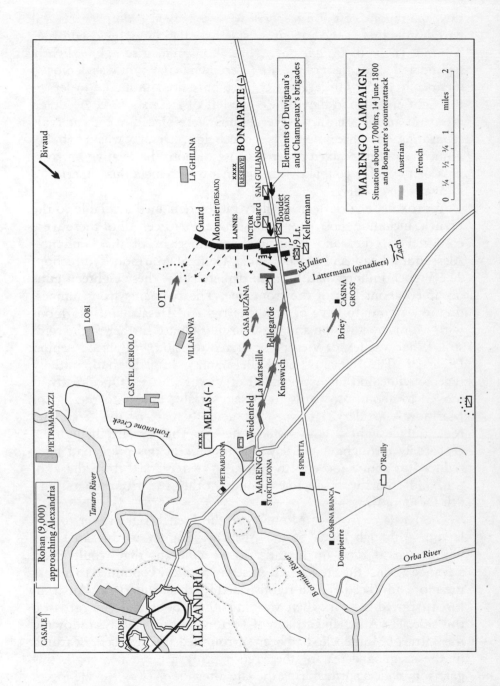

The Battle of Marengo, 14 June 1800

three battalions of the 9th *légère* were in mixed order, the central battalion in line flanked on either side by a battalion in closed-order column. The 30th *de ligne* of two battalions, remained in line slightly behind and to the right of the 9th *légère*, while the 59th was deployed identically to the 9th *légère*, i.e. three battalions in mixed order, to the right and behind the 30th.[17] The left of Desaix's force occupied a portion of the vineyard; several guns were placed in the intervals separating the three tiers of the echelon. Desaix was probably induced to utilize mixed order because of both the relative narrowness of the defile coupled with the enemy's tremendous superiority in available cavalry.

Approximately fourteen artillery pieces remained available to the French, including those supplied by Desaix's force. All of these were collected together and positioned to the right of the Giuliano–Alessandria road and placed under General Marmont's direction. The French infantry had been so depleted that these eighteen guns occupied about half of the front line. The remnants from Lannes' division appear to have been to the right of Desaix and Marmont with Monnier's division and the Consular Guard further to the right still. What was left of Victor's shattered division was placed behind Desaix.[18] The remains of Kellermann's brigade had initially regrouped behind the extreme left of Victor's forces. Once ready, it moved to about 200 yards to Desaix's right, that is to the left of Marmont's artillery.[19] It was not actually part of this first line, remaining a slight distance behind the line. Thrown into the fighting repeatedly throughout the day, the brigade at this point had been reduced to about 400 effectives (only 156 remained from the 2nd, 6th, and 20th cavalry regiments and another 250 from the 1st and 8th Dragoons).[20]

The battle in front of Monnier on the French right never totally let up. Although much of the Austrian infantry in this area had withdrawn to form up in the massive columns that would soon advance against the French left, Austrian artillery continued to harass the more advanced French right. Aided by this artillery fire Austrian forces started to work their way into the woods and vineyards on this side. The Austrian garrison of Tortona during the days following the Battle of Montebello had been surrounded and besieged. Learning of the seeming defeat of the French army around Marengo, this garrison made a sortie during the late afternoon. Thus, hostile forces were now active both in the front and the rear of the French army.

The grenadiers of the Consular Guard repulsed earlier during their abortive assault in front of Castel-Ceriolo, had succeeded in regrouping and took their place to Monnier's right. Many men from the Austrian Legion of Bussi had scoured the ground after that defeat and collected whatever French Consular Guard grenadier caps they could find. The same men now stood in front of the grenadiers taunting the latter by twirling these caps on their sabres.

It took about an hour for the French to deploy their forces for what was to be their final effort. The troops forming in the relatively open ground in the defile were particularly vulnerable to the often point blank Austrian artillery fire: 'Every discharge mowed down whole ranks. Their ricochet bullets carried away with them men and horses. They received death amidst them in this manner, without moving a step, except to close their ranks over the dead bodies of their comrades.'[21] The cannonballs even reached Murat and Victor's cavalry still attempting to reform in the rear.

The Austrian cannonade continued to about 5 o'clock when their main body neared the new French line of battle. It is only with difficulty that we can reconstruct what happened along the entirety of the battle front. Quite naturally, posterity has focused on what proved to be the decisive action of the day, and there are a number of accounts of Desaix and Kellermann's action against Zack's column. Evelyn Wood, a late nineteenth-century British general and military historian has pieced together probably the most detailed picture of those events, which changed the outcome of the day's action in what appeared to be a matter of moments.

Unaware of the arrival of French reinforcements and their opponents' frantic preparations, the main body of the Austrians approached in a series of columns marching along the Guilano–Alessandria road, their bands playing. Confident that the battle had already been won, the common sense precaution of sending scouts out in front of the main body had been ignored. The Austrians were unable to see Desaix's men masked behind a small stretch of slightly rising ground and were momentarily startled when they unexpectedly came into view. The first brigade in the Austrian column under Wallis' command, suspecting an ambush, quickly retired. Zack exhorted the next brigade, Latterman's grenadiers, to stand firm, which they did. Marmont's guns began to fire from the very first moments of the confrontation. After twenty minutes of this lively cannonade, Desaix ordered the 9th *légère* forward. Unfortunately, at almost this very moment Desaix was killed, apparently shot in the back by one of his own men. His aides-de-camp were not present at this tragic moment and the loss was only discovered when a soldier attempted to take the dead man's coat.

What followed represents one of the most dramatic and most significant sudden changes of fortune in military history. Of equal importance, it demonstrates just how so-called 'lower-level' tactical issues at certain critical moments could have as much influence on the overall flow of events as more commonly recognized 'high-level' considerations, such as a grand tactical movement, troops' morale, etc. The advancing French infantry moved into the path of Marmont's fire and the guns had to be momentarily silenced. The Austrian infantry now unleashed what Kellermann was later to recall as a 'tremendous discharge'. So powerful was this single volley that the French line instantly began to waver. Groups of infantrymen started to take refuge behind the more stalwart among them and the line started to bend. This was the last stage before a linear formation would break, the men running away to save themselves. The Austrians fired another volley and began to advance forward at the double. However, this advance was not performed in the most orderly fashion but 'in disorder, and in confidence of victory'. Though the general area appears to have been partially obscured by dust and smoke, both Marmont and Kellermann observed this turn of events and realized all hopes depended upon the French line holding its position. Both were now to take action, totally independently of one another, the combined effects of which would snatch away the hard-earned Austrian victory.

Though in the process of preparing to move forward, Marmont's artillery still managed to fire four rounds of canister into the massive Austrian column, at the moment it was beginning its disorganized charge forward. Kellerman, meanwhile, had started to take his own action, ordering his cavalry to advance in all haste past Marmont's guns on his right. His men quickly gained the Austrian column's flank. Without stopping, Kellermann ordered his men, then apparently in an open column of troops, to wheel to the right thus instantly forming line. A moment later the charge was sounded. Only an imperfect cavalry line was formed, with the 2nd and 20th Regiments slightly in advance of the other regiments struggling to catch up. Nevertheless, seldom in history has there been a more successful cavalry charge. The Austrians were caught completely off guard. Not only did they not see the French cavalry approach, being totally preoccupied with the French infantry they were hoping to crush, but they were defenceless (or so it would seem to them), having nothing but empty muskets and no longer in completely closed order. The Austrians went from elation over expected victory to sudden dread and confusion when faced with this new, deadly adversary. Not surprisingly, there proved no will to resist and the Austrians showed themselves incapable of defending themselves with a strong show of bayonets, something they most surely would have attempted if not so totally caught off guard. It is probably not out of place to quote Kellermann's own recollections of this monumental moment:

> Desaix held back the enemy's tirailleurs on their main body, but at the aspect of the formidable column of 6,000 Hungarian grenadiers, our troops hesitated. I was advancing in line, even with them, on the right of the road, being rather concealed by some vineyards, and observing everything which passed. It was no doubt, at this instant, that Desaix received his death wound, for after a tremendous discharge from the enemy, I perceived our line waver. It bends and is on the point of giving way – the Austrians pursue in haste – they are in disorder, and in confidence of victory: I perceive this – I am in the midst of them, and they have laid down their arms. All this in less time than it has taken me to write these half-dozen lines – thus did 200 men cause 6,000 grenadiers to lay down their arms.[22]

The results were staggering. Everyone in the column immediately surrendered. Though the French boasted of taking 6,000 prisoners, they acquired approximately 2,000 men. Among them was General Zack, who had taken over command from General Melas who had earlier been forced to retire off the field. Also captured were six stands of colours and four artillery pieces.[23]

BATTLE OF SEDYMAN (7 OCTOBER 1798)

The Battle of Marengo demonstrates most clearly that even the largest and most critical of engagements could be decided, at least occasionally, by tactical-level events, such as when Kellermann initiated his impromptu charge against the large column of victorious

Austrian infantry. Of course, this was the exception rather than the rule. A great majority of other Revolutionary and Napoleonic battles were decided by other factors, like the quality of leadership and grand tactical efforts and capabilities.

This often has been interpreted to demonstrate the relative unimportance or irrelevance of tactical issues. However, when stepping back and looking at the continuum of conflict during the entire period, one is struck by the relative equality of tactical ability among most of the major western European contestants.

This is not to suggest that throughout the period there was an absolute or constant equality among combatants. Minor and transient advantages appeared throughout these wars. In the early Revolutionary period, French forces enjoyed a tactical advantage when they startled their opponents with assaults formed from dense columns preceded by swarms of annoying skirmishers. The French under Napoleon enjoyed even clearer tactical advantages during the 1805 campaign when they adopted a larger, deeper mixed order formation to meet the expected threat posed by irregular Russian horsemen, and then again the next year when they utilized the *carré oblique* (oblique square) to counter the even greater problems anticipated from the Prussian cavalry. Later in this work an effort will be made to show that the British infantry enjoyed a tactical advantage of sorts throughout the Peninsular War and the Hundred Days. However, these isolated advantages were never so great as to create an insurmountable advantage where the entire engagement was won or lost purely on this tactical level. Throughout the history of warfare, and this certainly applies to warfare during the age of the musket, one army or another periodically unearths some tactical development giving it a momentary advantage, such as Frederick the Great's manoeuvre system developed between 1748 and 1756, or the massive use of attack columns and skirmishers by the French Revolutionary armies in the early 1790s. However, in the hyper-competitive military environment that has characterized the European military intellectual tradition at least as far back as the late sixteenth century, whatever tactical advantages do appear invariably are transient. Sooner or later, and usually sooner, the other side simply adopts the same or a similar set of tactics, or devises some original, but effective, counter-measure.

The same cannot be said of the tactical prowess of western European armies when compared to their near-eastern or Asian counterparts during the same period. From the early eighteenth century, a vast differential in tactical capabilities arose between the armies of the west, who were busy forging new fighting methods based on the characteristics and capabilities of the musket and socket bayonet, and those of the east, whose fighting methods remained largely unchanged. This difference in tactical capabilities dominated the nature of the struggle whenever these two types of forces met, especially by Napoleonic times. This was certainly the case whenever French forces took the field against their Turkish and Mameluke foes during the Egyptian campaign, 1798–1801. Whether one looks at the major battles during this campaign such as the Battles of the Pyramids or Heliopolis, or smaller contests such as the battles of Sedyman or Chebr-Keis, one finds that the Europeans' use of ordered formations, disciplined musket fire, and adroit use of artillery made the crushing defeat inflicted on their disorganized foes inevitable. A quick review of the Battle of Sedyman demonstrates this most convincingly.

On the morning of 7 October 1798 Desaix with his division found himself confronted by Mourad-Bey's army. This latter force consisted of about 5–6,000 horsemen and a body of infantry corps guarding the entrenchments around Sedyman, supported by four pieces of artillery. Initially, 'platoons' of skirmishers were spread out over the plain in front of the French army.[24] As the enemy horsemen descended from the irregular hills around Sedyman, Desaix ordered the various scouts and skirmishers to return to their demi-brigades, and his force was quickly drawn up into a number of battalion squares capped by two smaller squares, each of 180 men, on either side of the row of French battalion squares.[25] In a letter written soon after this affair Donzelot told Berthier that these two smaller squares were placed 'in the angles' at either extreme of the row of squares to produce a *feu croisé*.[26] This means the battalion squares were replaced *en échiquier* (checker board pattern) to allow for a cross fire to be delivered against any who ventured near them, while simultaneously minimizing the chances of hitting the friendly infantry in the adjoining formation.

At first, the Mamelukes were reluctant to charge the small but prepared French force. However, after about two hours, the Mamelukes finally began their assault. The warriors uttering their 'horrible cries', their music playing, the entire mounted force came on 'at the speed of scouts'. As was their wont, the Mamelukes attacked in an

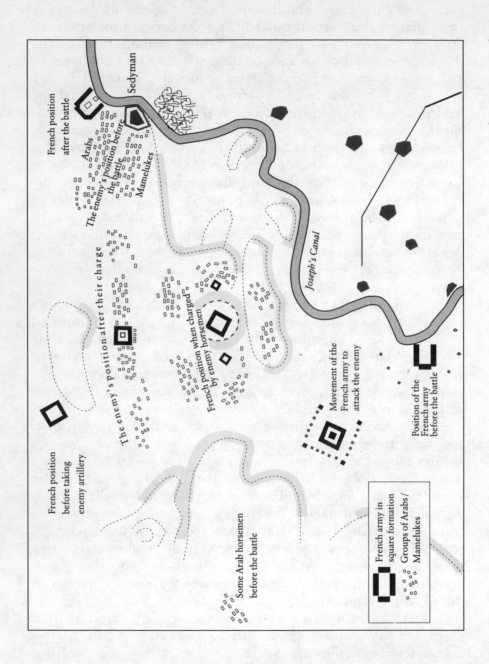

Sedyman

French position after the battle

Arabs

The enemy's position before the battle

Mamelukes

Joseph's Canal

The enemy's position after their charge

French position when charged by enemy horsemen

Movement of the French army to attack the enemy

Position of the French army before the battle

French position before taking enemy artillery

Some Arab horsemen before the battle

French army in square formation

Groups of Arabs / Mamelukes

The Battle of Sedyman

irregular fashion. Unlike European cavalry who always attempted to maintain ordered formations even in the final moments at the gallop, Asiatic horsemen emphasized speed and individual skill with their weapons. No attempt, therefore, was made to adhere to any formalized formation.

The French apparently awaited the attack with the greatest possible sang-froid. In a possibly apocryphal account, Desaix says that when he gave his troops permission to fire, with the enemy still between fifty to a hundred paces away, the grenadiers of the 61st Demi-brigade replied with cockiness, 'Only at 20 paces, my General.'[27] The attack fell on the French forces at two different points. A large Mameluke force attempted to charge a small square on the extreme right, made up of men from the 21st Demi-brigade commanded by a Captain Vallette. Another body of Asiatic horsemen circled around and threatened the rear of the square formed from men of the 98th Demi-brigade. The attack against the 98th, though furious, was unsuccessful. Here, the French infantry with its controlled fire was able to keep the Mameluke horsemen at bay long enough to frustrate their attack and finally to dampen their spirits. At first, though, the situation was uncertain. Horsemen who were knocked off their horses or those whose horses were killed from under them attempted to go under the French defences by crawling along the ground on their stomachs. When close enough, they started to slash at the unguarded legs of the French infantrymen who out of necessity had to keep their bayonets up high. Others, still mounted, discharged their firearms, muskets or pistols from well within point blank range. Then, rather than momentarily retreating to reload their firelocks, they threw their weapons at the infantrymen along the periphery of the square in front of them. Daggers, battle axes, and even articles of personal armour were hurled as well. Nevertheless, the effects of file fire soon took its toll and the Mameluke horsemen were sent back, frustrated and demoralized.[28]

The assault on Captain Vallette's small square on the right resulted in quite a different conclusion. The irregular horsemen managed to approach very near to the square, and following their comrades' examples elsewhere on the battlefield, a veritable cloud of missiles was directed at the French soldiers while the dismounted worked their way under the hedge rows of bayonets. In this case, some Mamelukes managed to work their way into the French ranks, and as was the case with Turkish horsemen against Russian infantry, death and destruction instantly spread everywhere, with entire limbs lopped off in single strokes. Within seconds about forty French infantry lay dead or seriously wounded.[29] The remainder of the men in the tiny square would certainly have met the same fate had it not been for the intervention of the other French infantrymen in the adjoining squares. Fortunately, these squares had been positioned so as to protect each other with mutually supporting fire. The successful Mamelukes were immediately fired upon by nearby French infantry and artillery firing canister and were quickly driven off.

The destruction of Captain Vallette's small square is a clear example of determined cavalry breaking completely a prepared infantry square. As such it deserves some attention. The few personal accounts that have come down to us offer two different, and mutually exclusive explanations as to why the square was destroyed. The 'official' version, that is the one Desaix offered Bonaparte in a letter written after the battle and repeated throughout the early nineteenth century, was that the men in this small square 'nourished' their fire too long. Desaix says that Vallette ordered his men to 'Fire at 10 paces and then cross [charge with] the bayonet' and the men carried out these orders. Allowed to approach well within a stone's throw of the defenders, the horsemen were able to do more damage throwing their weapons and armour than by firing their sundry assortment of firearms. The result was that sufficient gaps appeared as the infantrymen were knocked down by the assorted projectiles.[30] However, General Friant in a letter to a certain Captain Binot dated the 19 vendémiaire Year VII, that is, 10 October 1798, provides quite a different account. According to Friant, the problem was not that the French infantry in Vallette's square withheld their fire too long. Quite the opposite – they gave in to their natural impulses and the fire was begun at too long a range. In other words, they did not withhold their fire long enough.[31]

Given these conflicting accounts, and the credentials of those offering each of these, it is impossible to decide with any certainty which of these versions described the events as they actually occurred. Desaix's version probably strikes us as suspicious, being of the self-flattering variety: essentially he implies the destruction of the square occurred because the French infantrymen here were too brave, or followed their doctrine to an extreme. Friant, on the other hand, describes a problem that we know plagued infantry throughout the entire age of the musket. Infantry which began its fire at too long a range was frequently broken. In any case, with the dispersion of the Mameluke assault on the right, the Mameluke attack came to an end. The *pas de charge* was now beaten and the French began their offensive, in turn. The four pieces of Mameluke artillery, despite the excellent target offered by the advancing French columns, was insufficient to repel the French infantry in their orderly formations. The enemy entrenchment, cannon and baggage soon were in French hands.[32]

On this day, and basically throughout the entire Egyptian campaign, the French used a technique that the great heavyweight boxer, Muhammed Ali, in our own day has dubbed as the 'rope a dope' tactic. The enemy, very much superior in size, was allowed to attack. Once his energy and cohesion was spent the French assumed the attack, and completely overthrew the enemy whose lack of formalized tactics and indiscipline made effective defence difficult if not impossible. The same fate befell the enemies of the French at Chebr-Keis, Samhoùd, Heliopolis, and the Battle of the Pyramids.

Having looked at three different battles in great detail, it is apparent that tactics did indeed play a more significant role in these affairs than has been generally recognized. The use of tactics on the battlefield was ubiquitous. What appears at a higher level of abstraction as a unified action was in actuality a collection of low-level tactical events. In our three examples, the combatants are seen to be continuously moving, manoeuvring, or employing some sort of tactical device. However, the true importance of tactics does not arise simply because of its frequency of occurrence, but also because of its impact upon the results of the contest. Kellerman's charge at Marengo, for example, illustrates most dramatically that tactical-level events occasionally had a determinative effect on the outcome of the engagement. Of even greater significance, the Egyptian campaign demonstrates that whenever the differential between two armies' tactical capabilities was sufficiently large, the result of any engagement was exclusively determined by the capabilities of the tactically superior force. Tactical-level events and practices are only reduced to secondary importance as a parity of tactical capabilities is reached. Then, given the near equality of both protagonists' fighting methods, the resolution of the conflict must devolve on other factors or series of considerations.

Unfortunately, historians and military analysts have frequently failed to make this observation. Noticing that in one case a battle is decided because of the higher morale of one side, in another because of better preparations, they have tended to focus on these individual issues and have consistently ignored the very framework within which all events had to occur. As a result this generally has provided about the same level of accuracy or awareness as the man standing atop a high and craggy mountain who, looking only at the ground immediately below him, concludes that all of the surrounding countryside must be flat.

CHAPTER 2

The Emergence of Tactics

Although the overall approach to the study of warfare had originally been known as the 'art of war', by the mid-eighteenth century, the term 'tactics' started to gain increasing acceptance. In its original sense, the term simply referred to the understanding of the principles of the movement of troops around the field of battle. At this early stage, 'tactics' pertained only to the methods used to deploy the army into its initial position prior to the engagement, as well as those used to manipulate troops around unfavourable terrain once the action began.

The more modern implication of the term, the movement and *use* of troops in order to secure an advantage over the enemy, only gradually emerged as the term was increasingly used during the latter half of the eighteenth century. And it was only by Napoleonic times that writers could take for granted that the average military reader was familiar with the term, which started to gain more of an all-encompassing sense, referring to the study of all aspects of combat on the battlefield, at least when considering not more than several regiments.

Writing several decades after the conclusion of the Napoleonic Wars, Marshal Marmont, a distinguished French veteran of these wars, asserted that tactics is the 'art of handling troops upon the field of battle, and of manoeuvring them without confusion . . . it is the science of the application of manoeuvres'. Marmont, however, felt that the purview of tactics went beyond simply the mechanistic study of motion and use of organized manoeuvres. It included the use of these movements and their combinations to deceive and outwit the enemy. In Marmont's eyes, the purpose of tactics was, by skilful movement, to bring to bear a superior force against the enemy at a critical point on the battlefield. Usually this was achieved by concealing movements and thus intentions so as to arrive unexpectedly at the critical point in the conflict. According to Marmont:

> Tactical talent consists in causing the unexpected arrival, upon the most accessible and the most important positions, of means which destroy the equilibrium, and give the victory; to execute, in a word, with promptness, movements which disconcert the enemy, and for which he is entirely unprepared.[1]

A. H. Bülow, a radical Prussian military thinker contemporary to Marmont, compared the skilful use of tactics to fencing. Like fencing, a battle was a struggle between two antagonists, each of whom attempted a series of thrusts and attacks while forced to counter the actions of their opponent. Similarly, the successful use of the 'art of war' meant that: 'It is important to draw your antagonist's attention to one part, while, collecting your strength, you attack him in another, where he is open. This, in fencing, is called a feint; in war, a demonstration.'[2] To achieve these ends, a commander had to have developed more than a modicum of *coup d'oeil*, that is, the ability to judge distances, especially with an eye to manoeuvring formations.

However, there was also a growing recognition that to achieve acceptable performance on the battlefield tactics had also to include preparatory and training elements. John Mitchell, a general in the British infantry in the 1830s, for example, when providing his definition of tactics, focused primarily on this preparatory aspect, explaining that in his view tactics was:

> [the] science that shows how the individual soldier is to be trained . . . and includes everything that is, or should be, taught on the drill-ground, in order to render the soldier, whether acting individually or in mass, as formidable a combatant as may be consistent with his moral and physical powers.[3]

Mitchell then went on to describe what he felt was the essential curriculum for this training. An effective programme had to include how the army was to form up to support all of its elements and to best use its weaponry. It was also necessary to instruct the men how to deploy in column, line and squares, as well as how to reduce or change the direction of an extended front when necessary. And probably the most important was the ability to march and advance to the attack while preserving 'perfect order'.

TACTICS VERSUS GRAND TACTICS

During the last century, it has become accepted practice to differentiate 'tactics' from 'grand tactics'. By convention, tactics has come to be applied to the movement or use of force on a small level, usually within one or several functional units. This was typically a battalion, but could also have been a regiment or even a brigade if the component battalions were working together as a single tactical unit. 'Grand tactics' refers to the coordinated use of larger-sized blocks, such as divisions and corps. The distinction between tactics and grand tactics, however, did not exist as a self-conscious boundary or demarcation during either the linear or Napoleonic periods. There has been a change in perspective among those studying warfare during this period. Historians looking back at the eighteenth century and the Napoleonic period have been largely uninterested in low-level tactical phenomena, which had come to be perceived as no longer relevant since by this time musket technology was obsolete. Tactics and 'grand tactics' increasingly came to be perceived as separate and somehow self-contained. This distinction allowed 'minor' tactical elements to be segregated from higher level 'grand tactical' elements and then conveniently set aside.

The military men who had actually employed these tactical and grand tactical systems had a fundamentally different perspective from the historians who would follow them. All of these systems, techniques and procedures had a pragmatic application and were intended for use on the battlefield. None were theoretical, at least in the same way they would be to later generations. 'Minor tactics,' rather than being perceived as inconsequential and irrelevant, was viewed as the foundations upon which all higher level concepts and procedures had to be based. There was an intuitive understanding that techniques at either the high end or the low end were not self-contained, but somehow were part of a continuum, where to be effective each component had to be compatible with the other elements surrounding it. Napoleon and his generals could never view what we call 'grand tactical' designs as separate and self-contained ideas. In order to be practical, they had to be achieved using the lower-level tactical elements that were available.

This can be clearly demonstrated by several examples occurring during the linear and Napoleonic periods. For example, there has been a tendency to view Frederick the Great's use of the 'oblique attack', probably his most notable innovation, as purely a high-level grand-tactical conception. However, on a purely conceptual level, there was little new about Frederick's oblique attack. Commanders had attempted to outflank the opposing forces since time immemorial. Frederick's innovation was not the concept of attacking the enemy's flank, but the way it was executed. The Prussian secret manoeuvres developed between 1748 and 1756 allowed the Prussians to quickly shift their infantry laterally using the 'march by lines' manoeuvre.[4] Once in their new lateral position, the infantry advanced in echelon, a new formation itself made possible by the newly acquired manoeuvring proficiency. In other words, Frederick's new grand tactics was made possible by and was completely dependent upon low-level tactical techniques, i.e. the simultaneous quarter-wheel by platoons.

The French army under Napoleon, like the Prussians under Frederick the Great, were able to defeat their enemy using a repertoire of powerful grand tactical innovations. As we will see in Chapter 8, all of these grand tactical capabilities were equally dependent upon tactical-level innovations that had been developing in the background.

A MODERN DEFINITION OF TACTICS

An examination of the military literature of the period yields a diverse set of views on the newly emerging conception of tactics. The very diversity of opinion encountered among military experts demonstrates that even at the close of the Napoleonic period the notion of 'tactics' was still in its formative stages. Like the blind men in Plato's cave, all of these authors described essentially the same set of nebulous, still evolving conceptions, but from very different points of view. Still in the process of transformation, it is not unnatural that each author would focus on that aspect of tactics that best meshed with his own particular background or perspective. Since the goal of the present work is to explore the tactical systems used during this period, their origins and how they varied army to army, it is possibly not inappropriate to take advantage of historical hindsight and apply a more modern, more encompassing definition of tactics to the material under study.

All tactical systems, whether those used at Armageddon, Waterloo or in the Gulf War, are made up of two fundamental elements: the positioning and repositioning of troops, and the use of available weaponry, in other words: 'movement' and 'force'. Based on this observation, tactics can be defined as the development of formal systems of troop movement and the use of available weaponry to derive a localized advantage over the enemy during combat. At first glance, the study of tactics appears to be a very complex area, one which necessarily encompasses numerous elements and a truly wide array of different types of issues. Trying to digest all of these would be an onerous undertaking indeed, if these were examined only in the order they were encountered, and dealt with as a seemingly end-less stream of unrelated topics. It is important that any study of tactics, regardless of the period in question, be preceded by a prelimi-nary phase where a systematic attempt is made to discover the logical structure or natural relationships that exist between the elements or components that make up the discipline of tactics. Fortunately, in the case of tactics everything within this discipline can be grouped together into several major categories, according to its ultimate func-tion or purpose. These categories are: methods of organizing troops on the battlefield, how troops are moved, the most effective use of available weaponry, and the ability to react efficaciously to situations encountered on the battlefield.

The reliance upon a primitive small arm such as the arquebus and its successor, the musket, had created a need for large, highly organ-ized formations. It was only natural, therefore, that in the period under examination the first requirement of any tactical system was to address the manner in which troops were arranged prior to and during the conflict. Obviously, during the linear and Napoleonic periods, this area dealt with the various *formations* that could be used: the use of lines, columns, how the cavalry were to be deployed in relationship to infantry, where were the best places for the artillery, and so on. If the first stage of any tactical system is to define the 'units of force', that is, the basic building blocks, the next must concern itself with devising means of allowing these to move effectively. The reliance upon rigid pre-defined formations throughout the musket era meant that it was necessary to rely on highly formalized techniques to deploy the army on to the battlefield prior to the start of the conflict and move troops from position to position once the engagement had begun. Once the basic formations had been established it was necessary to assemble the repertoire of drills and manoeuvres that would serve, in turn, as the basis of all movement.

The third tactical area concerned itself with discovering the most efficient means of utilizing the weaponry at hand. In the case of infantry, this took the form of the 'manual of arms' which was the regimented procedure used to load, present and fire the muskets, as well as the particular fire system used to deliver this fire in a controlled and organized fashion. Similar considerations applied to both of the other two arms: cavalry and artillery.

The fourth and last dimension of tactics is the development of methods to efficiently respond to various 'tactical' situations that commonly recur on the battlefield. The most common situations in this area were how the infantry should conduct itself when enemy cavalry made a sudden appearance, how both infantry and cavalry were to advance when seeking to engage the enemy, how infantry or cavalry would attack artillery, the best way of employing artillery in various situations, etc. By piecing together the various tenets and practices in all four of these areas, a fairly accurate picture can be assembled of the tactical doctrine developed by the major armies during the period.

However, this picture, though very comprehensive, provides only a theoretical view of the various systems then in use, being limited almost entirely to what the troops were *trained* to do on the parade ground. A deeper, more incisive understanding of how troops sought to fight during that period, or for that matter during any other period, can be achieved only by extending the analysis to include two other largely ignored but extremely important 'dimensions' of any tactical system. The first of these 'dimensions' can be said to *precede* the development of any specific tactical procedure or practice; the second always *follows* its introduction, only manifesting itself in the crucible of battle. The creation and development of any tactical procedure, such as a manoeuvre or a way of responding to a specific situation, rarely came about simply because of the caprice of some military ideologue. A tactical technique or practice was the response to a perceived need, and reflected the desire to improve upon the existing methods to achieve at least a temporary advantage over the opponent. The process of assembling tactics, however, was never an open-ended affair. Each new tactical iteration had to meet a number of requirements.

It is relatively easy for anyone looking back at the past to understand that the physical characteristics of the weaponry in use has always played a large, if not decisive, role in shaping the nature of the tactical systems that could be used. Any method the infantry used to defend itself against enemy cavalry, for example, had to be based upon a realistic assessment of how quickly the infantrymen's muskets could be fired. Even the nature of the formations, down to the smallest minutiae, such as the depth (number of ranks) and width (number of files) of the formations as well as the distance between the rank and files, was heavily shaped by performance capabilities of the infantryman's flintlock musket and the average physical attributes of the men in the formation. However, to be effective not only did each tactical practice have to mesh with the weaponry being used, it also had to take into account both the physical and psychological capabilities of the men who were expected to perform these tactical procedures. These less tangible considerations were just as much at work in determining which tactics were successful and which would prove to be impractical as more concrete influences such as the characteristics of the available weaponry.

In order for any tactical procedure to be of use, it has to be 'do-able' under the extremely stressful conditions that inevitably arise on the battlefield. Here, 'do-able' goes beyond the physical limitations of the weaponry, but refers also to what the average soldier could do or endure once he found himself in the thick of the fighting. The long continuum of European wars provided ample opportunity for the more reflective among the military to observe that when it came to the effect on the men performing the manoeuvre or technique, *not all tactics were created equal*. On a purely psychological level, those tactics which proved the most successful on the battlefield were those that tended to impart a positive psychological effect on those employing them, and a negative impact on those against whom it was being directed. Several examples should be considered:

Frederick the Great's development of the organized charge at speed, the dominant theoretical model for cavalry versus cavalry actions until well past the end of the Napoleonic Wars, clearly illustrates the importance of the psychological dimension of tactics. Frederick realized that the charge at speed bolstered the morale of the advancing force, while the enemy, seeing a dense, highly ordered formation rushing upon them, more often than not panicked and fled. The efficacy of this tactic lay in its ability to destroy the opponent's will to stand and fight rather than cause the latter's total physical destruction.

The techniques utilized by the infantry when called upon to defend itself against enemy cavalry is another excellent example of how the psychological ramifications of a procedure were exploited to achieve the tactic's objective. Infantry, for example, would usually withhold fire until the enemy cavalry had approached to a close range. This was as much a recognition of the fear it imparted to the onrushing cavalry and the simultaneous controlling effect on the defending infantry as it was an awareness of the infantryman's inability to reload and fire rapidly and effectively under these conditions. Once again, the effect on what we could call the soldier's 'psyche' was not only acknowledged when putting together this tactic, but exploited and used as a driving force or principle. Even though there still had not emerged a formal awareness of the workings of the human mind – what we today know as psychology – nevertheless, competent officers with field experience intuitively recognized the existence of many psychological processes and how they impacted on the troops' performance in combat.

These observations force the following conclusion. All tactical practices and procedures are actually made up of two layers. The outer layer, the one which is normally associated with the term 'tactics', consists of a set of overt instructions. This is the 'doctrine' which is self-consciously employed by the officers and inculcated into the troops through near-constant training. For example, in such-and-such a situation, the battalion is to stop, the ranks close up, the first rank kneels, and the two last ranks are to begin firing by ranks when the enemy horse has closed to thirty paces. The tactics here are defined by a series of steps to be performed in a specific situation. Unfortunately, most historical works studying tactics of previous periods have limited their scope to this first layer. The resulting descriptions amount to 'catalogues' of the various tactical systems then in use, i.e. the formations, manoeuvres and a limited number of situational procedures.

Underneath the more obvious procedural level of each tactic, however, lurked the physical and psychological requirements that had to be met in order for the tactical to be feasible. Though we can be certain that the great majority of those in the military were not consciously aware of these factors, simply regarding each procedure as a series of steps it was their duty unfailingly to perform, the more perspicacious among experienced officers at least intuitively understood the importance of such factors. Not only were these psychological considerations taken into account when applying a tactic in the field, but the more competent among those in authority had understood and exploited these dynamics when designing the tactic in the first place. It is this type of awareness that makes works by such authorities as Tielke, Warnery, Nolan, Frederick the Great, Fortuné de Brack, and Bland so interesting to posterity.

PRACTICE VERSUS THEORY

Tactics, by its very nature, is a complex admixture of sophisticated theoretical doctrine and mundane but necessary training and procedures rehearsed daily on the parade ground. Unfortunately, because much of tactics, or at least that portion of this science which deals with the timing and delivery of force, is purely conceptual, there has been a tendency to concentrate exclusively on those aspects that can be easily quantified, such as the initial deployments of the troops prior to the start of a battle, the movement of troops, and any pre-formulated manoeuvres that were used. Even some very notable works such as Colin's *L'infanterie au XVIIIe siècle: La tactique* and Quimby's *The Background of Napoleonic Warfare* have virtually confined themselves to the manoeuvres the troops habitually practised on the parade ground and review field. The problem with this type of approach is that, even though it can clearly show what the troops were trained to perform, it rarely unravels many of the mysteries of what they actually did when in actual combat.

It is all too easy for those living almost two hundred years later to forget that the ultimate arbiters of these forces, designs and manoeuvres, as well as the objects affected by these processes were flesh and blood. The best tactical system was only as good as the collection of individuals undertaking its execution. Conversely, any tactical system was only feasible to the extent that it could be performed by the average soldier under conditions typically encountered on the battlefield.

Even an ideal theoretical system, modelled on the capabilities of the average combatant, could never be guaranteed to succeed in every instance. The vagaries of circumstance which inevitably arose during any protracted engagement would give truth to Robert Burns' frequently quoted saying: 'the best laid schemes o' mice an' men gang aft agley.' Phrased in modern and less poetical terms: regardless of the soundness and practicality of any tactical system, there was always some difference between the way it had been envisioned on a theoretical level and the way it could be implemented on the field of battle.

There are a number of reasons why there was and always will be a discrepancy between what the troops prepare for prior to the start of a campaign and what they are able to put into practice in the field. The most obvious is that the reality encountered on the battlefield imposes a set of operating conditions on officers and their men never encountered during a peacetime environment. Manoeuvres conducted on parade ground or review field were performed under optimal conditions, and were uncontested. During a peacetime manoeuvre, there was no external force attempting either to obstruct the movement or destroy the personnel performing the manoeuvre. On the battlefield the reverse was true. The enemy, if competently led, did everything in its power to hamper every motion of one's own troops, by attempting to inflict casualties on them, placing obstacles through its own troop movements, and unfolding its own plans which would demand some sort of response.

Many manoeuvres and procedures were difficult enough to perform even on the relative serenity of the parade ground. However, the noise, smoke and general confusion of that battlefield complicated matters still further. The cannons' roar and the crackle of the musketry made orders difficult and often impossible to hear. Enough smoke was generated that on relatively windless days officers and men more than a few feet away became totally obscured, and one end of a formation was invisible to the other. Even more debilitating, however, was the psychological impact of combat on the individual soldier. The ability to concentrate and follow orders calmly was greatly lessened, and soldiers could even experience difficulties performing simple physical activities, if overcome by their involuntary responses to the threats surrounding them. The casualties suffered by the men also negatively affected their ability to perform rehearsed actions. As men fell, the officers had to attempt to redress the formation, filling up empty files as they became vacant. The dead and wounded on the ground obstructed movement, and some of the still healthy men had to be detached to carry their seriously wounded comrades back to whatever medical facilities existed in the rear. And, if the casualties were heavy enough, morale would be lowered further undermining any remaining willingness and capability to move and fight.

Another factor which frequently reduced the effectiveness of the intended tactics and plans is obvious upon reflection, but has rarely been examined in any detail. An officer's plans could, and probably would, be affected by his opponent's actions and plans. In other words, the actions of those on one side almost always had to be modified because of the actions and tactics of those they were fighting against. Combat was, is, and always will be truly a complex interplay of dynamic systems.

A simple example demonstrates the nature of this interaction. Let's say that a French brigade commander was ordered to attack the enemy Austrian line. His army's doctrine called for a speedy advance up to about twenty to thirty paces from the defenders, where his men were to deliver battalion fire, followed by a spirited attack with lowered bayonets. The defending Austrians, however, are commanded by a daring officer who decides to pre-empt the French assault as soon as he sees the latter are forty to fifty paces away from his own position. He orders his own men to shoulder arms and advance, presumably at a slow pace in order to retain the best possible order. This situation could easily throw the advancing French force into confusion. Originally the attackers, the French unexpectedly discover that the enemy is also assuming the offensive. Finding themselves in this unexpected situation the men in the ranks might become sufficiently confused to stop on their own accord and deliver fire, or the commanding officer might even order them to halt and do the same. In either case, this would result in a modification of the original plans due to the enemy's actions and tactics.

This type of interaction, or interference, happened continuously on the battlefield, and tended to influence or modify what was being undertaken, how it was being conducted or performed, as well as the ultimate outcome. In many respects, this interaction between opposing tactics was a struggle of wills or a conflict of 'styles'. Each side attempted to impose its style, that is its methods of warfare, on the other.

If both sides relied on the same set of tactics and combat methods, as was the case during any tactically stable period where the general repertoire of options was essentially the same for all combatants, then the conflict was dependent on who had the better commander, who had the highest morale, or who was better trained. However, whenever a combatant introduced a radically novel or even a relatively new tactical system, another factor was introduced. Warfare was no longer simply the ability to inflict greater casualties on your opponent than he could upon you, to outlast him in a crisis or perform traditional procedures faster or more effectively. It now became a struggle as to whose tactical system would dominate, whose plans would unfold as desired and expected, versus who would be consigned continually to play catchup, constantly modifying their original plans to meet some new, unexpected and almost always undesirable contingency.

All of these considerations, when taken collectively, have important implications to anyone trying to understand the evolution of tactics or the combat experience and events which occurred at specific battles. Following the lead of the pragmatically oriented professional, military historians must similarly expand the study of tactics beyond the scholarly exegesis of the formal doctrine or cataloguing routines and procedures. Tactics can never be considered simply the collection of formal doctrine and routine procedures practised assiduously during peacetime. It is just as much how the soldier armed with his training responded in the crucible of battle.

In the chapters that follow two basic questions will be examined. The first is how did the basic properties of the weaponry in use shape and define the conduct of warfare on the Napoleonic battlefield. The second is how did tacticians, once they recognized these constraints, evolve a set of tactics and grand tactics that best utilized the way human beings were able to handle these weapons in combat.

CHAPTER 3

The Psychological Basis of Tactics

THE CONSCIOUS RECOGNITION that tactical procedures could profoundly influence human 'sentiment' was not at all apparent to the great majority of military men up to the mid-eighteenth century. Tactics, though clearly viewed as important, was approached from a purely mechanistic perspective. Its purpose was to allow the rank and file to perform the prescribed routines more effectively, in order to bring a preponderance of force to bear at a critical moment. Rarely were tactical practices seen as contributing to a man's will to fight or affecting his performance beyond the routine called for by the procedure. If we listened simply to the declared values of this age, we would believe that a man's resolution to fight, especially under adverse circumstances and ill fortune, was solely proportionate to his 'courage', an attribute that was somehow connected to his innermost qualities. According to this view, a soldier's performance was a reflection of his character, which many denizens of the eighteenth century believed was, in turn, largely a function of his society's 'national characteristics.' Tactics was only the means of harnessing these existing virtues; it was not considered a *psychotropic* mechanism able to influence the soldier's performance in a more extended sense.

Perusing the various manuals and treatises of this early period, one is struck by their starkness of treatment. Almost without exception they are extremely mechanistic in both approach and content, limiting themselves to routinized procedures such as the drill, manual of arms, the position of troops in formation, and a few very simple 'evolutions', as the precursors of manoeuvres were then called. What they did *not* provide is just as illuminating. In these early works, there is almost no 'situational analysis.' Little attempt is made to explain what the troops are to do in various types of commonly occurring situations. No effort is made to provide a rationale for whatever is prescribed or why it is effective and when it should be used. However, even during this early period the more astute among military men noticed that the soldier's 'sentiment', and hence his ability to perform, was not only affected by the larger events surrounding the group as a whole but was also influenced by some of the more trivial details, such as what the men were doing when they encountered a particular situation.

Starting in the late 1720s, a nascent recognition started to develop – at first very slowly, but later with increasing frequency of expression – that the potential effect of tactics could extend beyond the purely mechanical dimension. The Chevalier de Folard in his writings, for example, reasoned that the dense, solid column of infantry would buoy the morale of the friendly infantry conducting the charge as much as it would intimidate the enemy infantry in front of it. Twenty years later, caught up in the general conflagration that has become known in the English-speaking world as the Wars of Austrian Succession, Frederick the Great realized that the compact, highly organized cavalry formation closing upon the enemy at speed would have a positive effect on the troopers' morale in direct proportion to the negative effect it imposed on their adversaries.

To this newer variety of tactician, the creation of a tactical system was rarely, if ever, simply a *mechanical* assembly of a series of steps or actions. Nor was it strictly limited to simply determining how to inflict the most casualties among the enemy or figuring out how to allow the men to move the most quickly. When charged with creating a new system or improving upon existing practices, these innovative military thinkers realized, if only on an intuitive level, they could never afford totally to lose sight of how the rank and file tended to feel and respond while performing the tactical procedure under battlefield conditions.

Truly effective tactics would not only allow the troops to fire more effectively or move more quickly round the battlefield, they could also influence the way the soldiers thought and felt as well. It was gradually recognized that the ability to resist an opponent's actions was not simply the result of the courage or determination of the individuals making up a particular formation. Increasingly, military thinkers were becoming aware that the soldiers' morale and hence their continued collective performance could also be influenced by minute detail, such as how the men were organized, and especially the tasks they were called upon to perform as the events of the battlefield unfolded. Prior to 1750, this recognition was as rare as it was fragmentary in the few cases where it did occur. However, in the relative plethora of works which started to appear immediately before and after the Seven Years' War, observations regarding the relationship between tactics and human nature and how each affected the men's feelings became more common.

The frequency with which wars erupted throughout the seventeenth and eighteenth centuries provided tacticians with no lack of opportunity to observe how their men reacted to the full range of situations encountered on the field of battle. As a result, the more reflective and observant among the martial analysts were able to extract from this massive body of collective empirical experience a number of 'principles' of human behaviour.

Although the main charge of the present work is to describe the individual tactics which were used during the Napoleonic era, it would be profitable to piece together what was known about human responses to commonly occurring combat situations in order to understand the psychological foundations, if any, upon which they were based.

GLIMPSE OF THE ATTACKING LINE

Ordinarily, the combat experience began when the two sides were still beyond the effective range of the available weaponry. If the defending lines were deployed facing open ground, the men in these lines would see the enemy force approaching from a considerable distance. When the plain was expansive and the weather dry, the defenders would first become aware of the enemy's movement by the dust cloud rising slightly above the horizon in the distance. Veteran troops were able to judge not only the direction of the enemy's movement, but also whether the troops in the distance were cavalry or infantry by the intensity and height of these clouds. Obviously, the dust thrown up by a large body of cavalry was thicker and rose higher than that caused by infantry. On a sunny day, a glitter would also be seen as the sun's rays were reflected off the enemy's arms. It was brightest when the enemy headed in their direction, and it became less intense whenever the enemy faced away.[1] Only at about 2,000 metres could a soldier discern the enemy with the naked eye. At this distance, it was only possible to make out groups of men, such as a company or platoon, without being able to tell if it was infantry or cavalry. This distinction could only be made at 1,200 metres or closer, while the movements of individual soldiers only became visible at 600 metres.[2] As the events unfolded, the senior officers in the defending force would strain their eyes to follow the enemy's movement, calculating their own movements and actions if there was anything to do other than stand and wait.

Ironically, this task was actually made easier with the proliferation of skirmishers on the battlefield during the 1790s and early 1800s. Experienced officers along the defending lines had begun to learn to use the very movement of the enemy skirmishers as an effective means of assessing the terrain separating the two forces. The officers would pay careful attention to the skirmishers as they advanced across the fields towards them. The men would appear to rise and fall, as well as occasionally disappear as they crossed undulations, depressions and various otherwise 'hidden' obstacles. This was a useful trick if the defenders had arrived at their defensive position before being able to scout the land in front of them before deploying. By the height of the Napoleonic Wars, veteran officers confronted with enemy skirmishers in front of their defensive lines would sometimes drive away these skirmishers simply to observe their retreat and use this same method to evaluate the terrain behind the skirmishers' initial position.[3]

As the defenders looked on, the attacking force would continue its advance. In earlier days, both cavalry and infantry would begin their assault more or less simultaneously. However, by the Napoleonic wars this practice had largely fallen into disuse. Now, the infantry was often committed first to soften the enemy, the cavalry being held back until the defender showed signs of weakness.

THE DYNAMICS OF THE ASSAULT

In the first phases of the assault, the psychological advantage was initially with the attacking force. General Mitchell's comments about the effect of the advance on the psyche of British infantry was actually applicable to all reliable troops throughout the musket era:

> The assailants ... derive a sort of wild courage from the very circumstance of advancing: the mere idea of attacking is 'spirit stirring,' and animates ... soldiers with a species of enthusiasm.[4]

William Müller, writing in England around 1810 pointed out that the troops moving forward by definition left the dead and wounded behind and thus derived an additional advantage. The individual soldier while advancing, even when forced to perform the most deliberate of cadenced marches, was less aware of the events in the ranks beside and behind him than when he and his comrades were forced to remain motionless and await the enemy's initiative.[5]

The spirit of the defender, on the other hand, was more likely to cool at this initial stage. If they were well commanded, the defending troops would be prohibited from firing until the last moments and would thus be forced to remain motionless for what seemed an interminable period. So, there was nothing to do but wait, and watch the enemy coming ever closer. The defender, moreover, was also denied the true picture of the events as they unfolded. The attacker's wounded and dead were left behind and hidden from the defenders as the men in the advancing formation struggled to tighten their ranks. And, of course, once the muskets began to fire and clouds of smoke started to rise there was almost no chance of sensing the other side's casualties, even if the other side stopped to return fire.[6]

As the attackers approached, the individual defenders became increasingly nervous and in all but the most seasoned and steady troops there would be an inevitable 'flutter and hurry' as the soldiers struggled to load and deliver their pieces.[7]

In a large-scale action, it was almost certain that the enemy artillery would eventually start to play on the defending line. When this happened, the reports of the artillery and the sound of the balls flying through the air would make the men flinch. Every now and then soldiers would be struck down by a cannon ball that found its way into the formation, and it was not uncommon for a cannon ball to take out a complete file of men at a single stroke. Captain Charles François of the French 30th *régiment de ligne*, for example, recounts how his regiment took numerous direct hits as it advanced against the Great Redoubt at the Battle of Borodino, occasionally resulting in the destruction of several files at a time.[8] Whenever round shot (i.e. solid 'cannon balls') ploughed through the ranks, the defending soldiers would see mangled limbs being strewn through the air and hear the screams and groans as the wounded thrashed about on the ground. As the attackers neared, this effect only increased as both the reports of the cannons and their accuracy increased as the range between the guns and their targets gradually diminished.[9] According to one veteran of the Peninsular Wars, enduring a cannonade was 'one of the greatest trials of patience – viz. to look on passively at a cannonade which was pretty lively'.[10]

It was even more trying to endure ricochet fire. When fired at long and even medium range the cannon balls would be visible to the naked eye. One British observer compared round shot ricocheting off the ground as similar to the balls bowled at cricket. And if uneven ground separated both sides, many rounds would ricochet before reaching their target. If the men in the line were fortunate enough to notice these bounding balls, they were often able to open the ranks and get out of the way, though short-sighted men weren't always as lucky.[11] Skirmishers and officers outside the actual formation, once they saw the oncoming cannon ball, had an easier time removing themselves from harm's way than troops in the ranks who were encumbered by those tightly packed around them. If round shot could be seen and sometimes avoided, canister fire was a sudden affair which reminded many of a severe hail-storm of the kind 'which knocks the leaves off the trees'.[12]

Those subjected to musket fire had to endure a similar experience. It was extremely nerve-racking to be subjected to even small arms fire. One officer described the sound as reminding him of 'buzzing of bees'.[13] When the firing became truly brisk, many soldiers in their letters and memoirs also used the hail metaphor to describe intense musket fire. Though there was a tendency for untrained soldiers to duck or cower when hearing this sound, practice and doctrine required everyone to ignore these sights and sounds and remain completely erect at all times. Veteran officers explained to their men that they could only hear shells or balls that had passed them, thus shells and bullets were harmless once heard. This advice, however, was of little comfort for those caught in firefight who on all sides caught sight of death and mayhem. An anonymous subaltern in the British army during the Peninsular Wars recounts how his commander advised the men how to comport themselves when under fire:

> It is therefore necessary to acquaint you that the whizzing of the balls is apt to cause a disagreeable sensation; but this, gentlemen, arises from the mistaken idea, for the moment you hear that sound the danger is past. You will not, therefore, show a bad example to the men by ducking.

Though the term 'ducking' or 'duck' is commonly used today, it was fairly new in the period of which we are writing. The practice of the men in the ranks covering their heads presumably to reduce the chances of being hit by musket fire had become fairly common during the American War of Independence. The motion of the men's heads reminded observers of 'the characteristic movement of ducks, and hence the term "ducking"[14] your heads and flinching your bodies, for that is unsoldier-like, and may cause a panic in the troops; but always keep the head up, the body erect, and even in danger show a pleasing and determined aspect, which may command respect and admiration in your men, and animate them to that glory which Britons have a right to anticipate.'[15]

If the enemy had succeeded in getting close enough, their fire would be felt, and the defenders would begin to take casualties. Complete files could become *hors de combat* and gaps would eventually appear along the line. The NCOs and officers struggled desperately to take men from the rear ranks and throw them into these voids. Men on the flanks would be pushed inward, so that the battalion's front gradually contracted, leaving ever larger intervals between it and its neighbour. Of course, the sight of an approaching enemy also had a profound effect on the defenders. The sight of the glittering arms covering the battlefield in front of them, the masses of dense columns marching towards their position, could undermine the will of even brave men. And, these psychological pressures would only increase as the battle unfolded, as noise, confusion and casualties mounted.

During the eighteenth century, the defenders would see the enemy forces stretching across a wide expanse in what may have appeared as one continuous line. The small intervals between regiments and battalions would not have been that noticeable at a longer range. However, by the height of the Napoleonic Wars these long lines would mostly have been replaced by clumps of men representing the dense battalion columns which had become increasingly popular among most combatant nations. As the hostile army advanced over the ground separating the two combatants, its formations would expand and contract creating the impression that they had a life of their own. If the defenders were inexperienced, not well led, or lacking in motivation there was a good chance that the defending infantry would eventually give in to their natural instincts and begin to fire. The act of loading and firing repeatedly relieved the men's nervousness: '. . . he [the infantryman] is ignorant of its true value; he loads and fires in haste and confusion, in hopes of hiding himself under the cover of its smoke, or of drowning his fears under its noise.'[16] When this happened, especially when the fire was delivered at too long a distance, at 300 paces or so, the attackers gained a distinct advantage. The confusion among the defending ranks and the loss of their first and most effective fire, now worked to the attacker's favour and aided his efforts to work his way closer. It was in this situation, when the defenders had begun firing prematurely, that the attacker had the best opportunity to advance up to point blank range and threaten to resolve the whole affair with the points of their bayonets. The defenders, discouraged by the ineffectiveness of their fire and feeling there was little else they could throw against the oncoming enemy, who appeared to display the greater courage and determination, would be the most likely to start to waver and then ultimately to break.

This was the most likely course of events when the defender began to fire prematurely during the attacker's advance. If, however, the defending infantry, instead of giving in to these natural impulses, managed to restrain itself and withhold its fire until the moment chosen by its officers, the attacker's initial advantage in morale would gradually start to diminish. After arriving within the limits of the 'psychologically' effective range of the musket, about 200–300 paces, the tension would mount as each second passed without a response from the defender. The attacking infantry knew that their interests were best served if the enemy waiting in front of them broke down and started to fire at a longer, rather than a shorter, range. The realization that the withheld fire 'would be very unpleasant when it came' started to play on the advancing infantryman's psyche. As time passed and the defenders remained motionless, the attacker's 'ardour would begin to cool' and the first seeds of hesitation would start to manifest itself in the ranks of the oncoming force.[17] When the defender displayed this type of courage and determination, the attacking body would often stop and begin firing, despite the most determined efforts of their officers to renew the assault. If this happened, especially when the two forces were still at only a medium range, a prolonged but relatively ineffective firefight usually occurred. Though causing a lot of noise, smoke and general confusion, these types of affairs were usually not decisive and lasted until one side ran out of ammunition or decided to settle the affair with cold steel.

Probably the best description of this sensation and the results they produced among an attacking force, is provided by Colonel Bugeaud in his description of a French assault on a British position he participated in during the Peninsular War:

> The men became excited, called out to one another, and increased the speed of their march; the column became a little confused. The English remained quite silent with ordered arms, and from their steadiness appeared to be a long red wall ... Very soon we got nearer, crying 'Vive l'Empereur! En avant! A la baionette!' Shakos were raised on the muzzles of muskets, the march became a run, the ranks fell into confusion, the agitation became a tumult; shots were fired as we advanced. The English line remained silent, still and unmoved, with ordered arms, even when we were no more than 300 yards distant, and it appeared the storm was about to break. The contrast was striking; in our innermost thoughts, we all felt that the enemy was taking a long time in firing, and this fire, held for so long, would be very unpleasant when it came. Our ardour cooled. The moral power of a steadiness which nothing can shake ... overcame our minds. At this moment of painful expectation, the English wall shouldered arms; an indescribable feeling would fix many of our men to the spot; they began an uncertain fire. The enemy's steady, concentrated volleys swept our ranks; decimated, we turned round seeking to recover our equilibrium; then three formidable cheers broke the silence of our opponents; at the third they were on us, pushing our disorganized flight.[18]

Before a formation broke and fled, the men would gradually lose their nerve and the cohesiveness of the formation would dissolve. Individuals along the ranks would slink to the rear of the formation, trying to find safety behind those in front. Gradually, sometimes suddenly, depending upon circumstances, entire files would become vacant, so that gaps appeared along the line. Of course, the NCOs and officers in the *serre-file* behind the line did everything in their power to keep the men in their proper position in the ranks, but in grave or grossly confusing situations, such as an extended firefight, the more timid succeeded in gaining the rear of the formation. In the eighteenth century, the French military writer Henri-François de Bombelles observed that in these situations the four rank line of his time degenerated to a quasi-line eight men deep.[19] He was referring to the amorphous de facto 'formations' that tended to evolve during a fiercely fought contest. At Mollwitz, some of the battalions were observed to stand 'forty to eighty men deep'[20] while De Ligne claims some battalions at Leuthen were a hundred men deep.[21] Columns were not exempt from this type of disorder. In a severe crisis, the front companies would try to scurry backwards along the flanks, and the same vertical elongation found in lines also occurred.[22] If a column had been advancing, this tendency often prevented the officers from being able to deploy it into line. The men in the rear companies would frequently refuse to leave the perceived safety of the column and remain huddled behind those in front.

CONTACT VERSUS NO CONTACT

Although there was a decided tendency for one side or the other to stop and begin to fire, it was not uncommon for an attacking force to be able to advance close enough that it appeared to both sides that the conflict would only be resolved with the thrust of the bayonet. Nevertheless, it is probably difficult for the modern mind to conceive how the attackers could continue to attack, once the defenders began to fire at anything closer than medium range. It is natural to assume that the danger of being hit with musket fire increased directly as the distance between the attacker and defender decreased. However, Colonel Bugeaud in his perspicacious notes to young officers, assures us that once a firefight had begun at a relatively long range, casualties would actually drop off in the final moments as the two groups of combatants neared one another. If the defender had begun firing at long range, let's say at around 300 paces, their volleys would initially cause increasing casualties as the attackers advanced. This increase of casualties continued until the attacker was about 100 to 150 paces away and then the rate of casualties would actually start to decline. As the attackers approached, the individual defenders would tend to become increasingly nervous and there would be an increasing degree of confusion as the soldiers struggled to load and deliver their pieces. Casualties during the last moments tended to be 'trifling at the moment of grappling with the enemy'. The result was that, if the attackers managed to reserve their fire until they reached close quarters, and the defenders had already begun to fire, the attackers stood an extremely good chance of overthrowing the defending line.[23]

Although the Napoleonic Wars are full of instances of opposing infantry closing to extremely close ranges, after the wars it was often said by French veterans that the Battle of Amstetten was the only example where both sides actually clashed with the bayonet in open terrain.[24] This observation about the extreme rarity of two groups of opposing infantry making contact in open terrain, incidentally, concurs with the conclusion generally drawn by those studying linear warfare which preceded this period. In this latter case, the battle of Moys is the only known case where opposing bodies of infantry crossed bayonets on open terrain.[25] It was generally recognized that in open ground, regardless of the determination of both sides, one side or the other would inevitably break before the attacker and defender were able to cross bayonets. This is not to say that no one in an open field was ever killed or wounded by the bayonet: there were many such casualties. However, these did not occur because both sides stood their ground and engaged in hand-to-hand combat. Almost always bayonet wounds were inflicted during the pursuit after one side turned their backs and attempted to flee. The affair at Maida (4 July 1806) offers a perfect example. The French had succeeded in advancing very close – too close one could say.

Hand-to-hand combat could only occur as soon as something on the battlefield changed the soldier's focus from his being part of a group to that of an individual fighter. As long as the battalion remained in open terrain, there was an insurmountable tendency for each individual soldier to identify with the formation as a whole. From the soldier's perspective, his continued safety depended upon the cohesion of his unit. Although the battalion might stand even though some of its men attempted to flee to the rear, on open ground, the most resolute of soldiers was immediately compelled to retire as soon as the formation itself started to dissolve. Regardless of a soldier's courage or foolhardiness, individuals deserted by the remainder of their unit could never stand up to an enemy formation which remained intact. And, since a formation on one side or the other invariably broke before the opposing groups closed to hand-to-hand fighting, those that would have been otherwise inclined to stand and fight were drawn along in the sudden but irreversible torrent to the rear. A slightly different set of psychological dynamics was at work in broken terrain. By necessity, the rigid relationship of the ranks and files within the formation became disordered as the men spread out to work their way around the obstacles. As men climbed over a ditch or crossed through a hamlet, though they continued to sense they were part of a group, they no longer saw themselves as part of a tight, neatly defined formation. To a large degree, the sense of security supplied by an ordered formation under normal conditions was now replaced by the physical nature of the ground or obstacles around them. A man standing behind a tree saw his safety not in there being men directly to his front and rear or to his left and right, but instead because there was a physical object directly in front of him which could stop not only a bayonet but even a bullet or canister. As a soldier placed his safety in physical objects around him, he correspondingly placed less importance on a formation. The focus was shifted from the safety in numbers to safety resulting from his own particular situation and actions. Moreover, men positioned behind a hedge or in a house would sense the openness surrounding their small 'island' of shelter. To move back, was to move back into a wide open ground. If the men in the broken terrain were not in formation, there was no way to move on to clear terrain, except in complete and uncontrolled flight. In this way the disposition or motions of the group no longer dictated so absolutely the actions of individuals, and hand-to-hand fighting could occur.

Blakeney, who served with the British in the Peninsula, describes such an occurrence, as well as the reasons why the mêlée was unavoidable:

> . . . Next morning the French seeing us thus thought we had retired and left Portuguese to guard the heights. With dreadful shouts, they leaped over that wall before which they had stood,

when guarded by the British. We were scarce able to withstand their fury. To retreat was impossible; all behind being ploughed land, rendered knee deep by the rain. There was not a moment to hesitate. To it we fell, pell-mell, British and French mixed together. It was a trial of strength in single combat; every man had his opponent, many had two . . .

The British and French, unable to see each other during the last moments, had unexpectedly advanced to very close quarters. Both sides were unable to retire: the French because of the wall they had just jumped over, the British because of the relative impassibility of the ploughed land behind them.

The ever colourful Captain Coignet describes another bayonet fight he participated in at Marengo:

An Austrian division coming up from the right wing charged us with bayonets. We ran up also and crossed bayonets with them. We overcame them, and I received a small cut in the right eyelid, as I was parrying a thrust from a grenadier. I did not miss him, but the blood blinded my eyes.[26]

However, this occurred at the end of the day after Kellerman's charge and the destruction and capture of the large Austrian column. Unfortunately, Coignet does not provide additional details, but this mêlée almost certainly occurred because the forces involved were sufficiently disorganized that individual actions became possible or because of some obstacle encountered, such as the vineyard or the woods on the flanks, etc.

Of course, a large number of sources were used to assemble this picture of what was known about the psychology of eighteenth-century combat. It is certainly not being suggested, however, that there was anyone during the period of which we speak, even the most experienced and thoughtful of officers, who had worked out the typical occurrence of events to this level of detail. At the time of which we speak there were no comprehensive 'psychological' treatises, military authors only dealt with these matters as they came to mind or were encountered and observed within their own personal experience. There were a few men, however, such as Frederick the Great and Maurice de Saxe who not only had an overall insight into the importance of orchestrating the men's feelings during combat, but also were in a position to utilize this knowledge to create more effective tactical systems and practices.

In the next several chapters, we trace the story of how Napoleonic tactics evolved and how this type of knowledge was used.

CHAPTER 4

Infantry Tactics I:
Opposing Doctrines on Infantry Attack and Defence

DURING THE ERA in which the musket dominated the European battlefield, man's theories about human nature were neither as formalized nor extensive as they are today. A rigorous and methodical study of the workings of the human mind, what today we call 'psychology', did not exist. Nevertheless, despite this absence of a modern theoretical framework, the rudimentary awareness that combatants' feelings and responses were somehow causally connected to the circumstances encountered, and that these could be influenced by training and what they were required to perform in each type of situation, began gradually to take hold. This understanding, though both primitive and fragmentary, when coupled with the more generally recognized capabilities of the available weaponry – musket, sword and cannon – was the driving force moulding the development of fighting practices throughout the entire period and it predetermined the direction these innovations could take.

To a very large degree, this accounts for the unexpectedly high degree of similarity found among most tactical practices encountered throughout most of the eighteenth century. True, we encounter aberrations here and there, such as Folard's heavy columns proposed in the 1720s and the Russian infantry techniques created to hold off an implacable mounted enemy. Nevertheless, when we consider the full panorama of tactical developments in the European theatre leading up to the Napoleonic period, we are forced to concede that there was far more similarity than substantial difference. And, in by far the great majority of cases where differences are found, it was more a variation in the method of implementation than an indication of a fundamentally different goal or overall philosophy. This basic similarity in tactical systems was no coincidence: common problems tend to engender common solutions. Military men throughout western Europe had the same basic building blocks at their disposal and essentially the same human material. It can hardly be surprising, therefore, that they often came up with similar solutions.

There was, however, one important area where there was much less agreement. This was the role of small arms fire during infantry operations, both on the attack or the defence. We could even say that much of the development of infantry tactics and fighting methods during the eighteenth century was driven by the effort to discover the most effective method of utilizing infantry firepower. Although replete with many local variations and differences, infantry tactical doctrine during the eighteenth century can be divided into two general philosophies. The first was imbued with a pronounced aggressive offensive spirit and was typified by the *à prest* assault, which was the French version of the quick advance with shouldered muskets minimizing the role of firepower while on the attack. The opposite school felt that the most efficacious use of infantry demanded that at least a modicum of firepower be used even while on the offensive. This difference in basic philosophy also applied to defensive infantry tactics. There were those who believed that small arms fire should be used to cause casualties among the attacker and disorder his ranks, while others strongly believed that it was far better to withhold defensive fire until the last possible moment when it would be the most destructive.

EIGHTEENTH-CENTURY ANTECEDENT

Much of the modern literature that deals with warfare during the Napoleonic Age tends to give the impression, if only by the omission of explanations to contrary, that the quick assault with lowered bayonets, so strongly associated with French infantry during both the Revolutionary and Napoleonic periods, somehow originated with the adoption of attack columns early in the Revolutionary Wars. The few works that have sought to trace the roots of 'Napoleonic Warfare', such as Quimby's *The Background of Napoleonic Warfare* and Colin's *L'infanterie au XVIIIe siècle: La tactique*, usually attribute the origins of this practice to the aggressive offensive philosophy advocated by the *ordre profond* school of tactics which grew out of the Chevalier de Folard's writings in the late 1720s.[1] In actual fact, this method of quick attack was part of a much more pervasive philosophy of offensive tactics that pre-dated the division of French tactical theory into *ordre profond* and *ordre mince* schools by at least thirty-five years and certainly was never limited to the French army. To a greater degree than has been commonly recognized, the principles of the aggressive assault were only a relatively minor mutation of existing tactical doctrine. They can easily be traced to French infantry as far back as the 1690s and were probably discovered even earlier in the seventeenth century.

As just mentioned, throughout the entire flintlock era there were two main schools of thought regarding how an attack should be conducted by infantry. One side argued that the quick assault, performed without stopping to deliver fire was the most effective. The other view held that any advance without periodically stopping to fire was doomed to failure because the casualties inflicted by the defenders as they awaited the assault would never be returned. All offensive tactics were ultimately based on one of these two fundamental approaches, or the attempt to combine these opposite schools, such as the Dutch school and later the Prussian attempt during Frederick William's reign to fire while advancing. Given this reliance of Revolutionary and Napoleonic armies upon these established methods and principles, it is probably not out of place to provide a short survey of the most common approaches to offensive tactics in use during the eighteenth century.

THE A PREST METHOD

Almost throughout the era of the musket the pre-eminent philosophy underlying offensive tactics employed by the French infantry and others was what was occasionally referred to in the early eighteenth century as the *à prest* advance, or quickly delivered assault. This is not to say that there had been no continued evolution in offensive tactics after this point; there was. However, the most general philosophy underlying how infantry was to deliver the assault essentially remained the same. French tactics were consistently imbued with an unmistakable offensive spirit. Whenever possible, the French infantry were to assume an offensive role and attack the enemy, rather than await the enemy's assault. The French marshal Puységur noting his experiences during the Nine Years' War and the War of Spanish Succession observed that French commanders had found this to be an effective means of dealing with the often commented upon tendency of French troops to fight ferociously in the initial efforts only to have their spirits dampened if the engagement became prolonged.

According to the *à prest* doctrine, the attack began with a large-scale action and, unless there were special circumstances to warrant the contrary, the entire first line of infantry began its march forward at the same time, as did the cavalry, typically stationed on either flank of the infantry. The second line to the rear followed the first and strove to maintain the interval between them that had been established as they deployed. This was important, since if this distance became too great, the second line would be unable to support the first should the latter be overthrown or encounter difficulties.[2] The infantry advanced in as orderly a fashion as terrain and circumstances would permit. The march began with a deliberate gait until the last fifty to seventy paces. At this point, the infantry line would stop temporarily as the officers quickly urged the ranks closer together. In the days before cadenced marching, the ranks were often left about thirteen feet apart up until this point when they were closed to one or two feet. As soon as all was ready, the march resumed. However, the pace was speeded up and the men advanced *à prest*, that is with a quickened step. Following the established doctrine, French officers would prohibit their men from beginning to fire until they ordered them to do so during the final moments of the assault.[3] In fact, some French military men ordered their men to charge the attack home without ever firing at all. During the 1690s, this was the practice of Monsieur de Greder, the proprietary colonel of the regiment Maurice de Saxe would later command. His men, still armed with the cumbersome matchlock, were forbidden to even light their coils of match prior to the beginning of the assault, and thus were physically unable to do so, even if they wanted to. Once his men were twenty-five to seventy-five paces from the enemy, he would personally lead the final charge in front of the regiment.[4]

According to Catinat, another French marshal who commanded the Army of Italy during part of the 1690s, this tactic provided the attacker with a psychological advantage during the final moments of the attack. If the defenders fired at the attacker at any time during the last hundred paces of the approach, they were incapable of fire during the final seconds, which was precisely the time in which having any type of psychological edge was extremely critical. The knowledge that they were defenceless, at least in terms of fire combat, and the realization that the approaching enemy still retained its capability to fire would almost certainly demoralize the defenders as they fought their fears and did their best simply to stand their ground. The attackers, on the other hand, having not yet delivered their fire became all the more confident realizing they had the ability to fire on a now defenceless enemy.[5] The theoretical counter to this tactic was for the defender to simply withhold its fire until the very last second. The defender would then never find themselves denuded of their fire, and therefore would never become quite as demoralized as the attacker hoped. The possibility that this potential countermeasure might be used, led most officers favouring the *à prest* assault to believe that the attacking force should withhold its fire during the advance, until twenty to thirty paces from the enemy, stop and deliver fire, and then run into the enemy before the latter could recover from the blow or return the fire. If this was executed properly, the defenders would be incapacitated and thrown in temporary confusion by this murderous volley, fired literally at point blank range, and would most likely be unable to fire in the three or four seconds the attackers needed to cross the last distance. Faced with an onrushing foe, the clouds of smoke from the recent 'battalion fire' (the whole offensive formation firing at once) and, even more importantly, the necessarily heavy casualties from the point blank fire, the defenders would almost certainly break before actual contact was made.

This was the theory behind the *à prest* method of attack, and was clearly the forefather of Chevalier de Folard's aggressive offensive philosophy put forward in the 1720s, as well as the French use of closed columns so frequently resorted to during the Revolutionary Wars. When creating the *ordre profond* school of offensive tactics, Folard had not invented a new approach to the use or non-use of firearms during the assault; rather, his innovation was the creation of a new medium for the quickly delivered attack where the fire was withheld: a heavy, closed column was now to be employed, instead of the traditional line. This distinction, unfortunately, has been lost on military historians for the last hundred and sixty years. The use of this method of aggressive attack was certainly not limited to French infantry, and was, in fact, probably the dominant offensive philosophy during the whole of the eighteenth century. At the beginning of the eighteenth century, for example, one finds similar tactics being occasionally used by the Bavarians, as well as the Swedes under Charles XII, who was especially fond of aggressive tactics. The Swedish version of this tactic was known as *ga-pa* or a 'go on' assault, and was codified into the Swedish 1701 infantry regulations.[6] The Russians, forced to fight the Swedish during the Great Northern War (1700–1721), employed similar assault tactics, which they referred to as a 'go through' attack. These remained at the heart of Russian offensive doctrine throughout the musket period, being heartily advocated and frequently used by Suvarov in the Italian campaigns of the late 1790s. Even the British and Dutch, who utilized a different set of offensive tactics when attacking an enemy in relatively open terrain, advocated such tactics when assaulting strong points such as an entrenchment, parapet or *abatis*.[7]

THE 'DUTCH' METHOD OF ATTACK

Those commanders who used the *à prest* method of attack or some derivative version tended to relegate the use of fire combat to strictly defensive situations. However, as early as the Thirty Years' War some efforts were made to employ small arms in a more offensive role. Gustavus Adolphus, for example, experimented with a primitive form of 'platoon fire.'[8] However, the nature of the weaponry, matchlocks, and the clumsy manual of arms then in use made reliance on this relatively complicated firing system impractical in the face of battle. The introduction of the flintlock near the end of the seventeenth century stimulated some military authorities to re-evaluate the traditional methods of delivering fire, such as *feu de rang* or 'rank fire' (which at this time referred to a type of caracole fire), and look for new methods that could exploit the properties of the new weaponry then in the process of being introduced.

It appears that the Dutch were the first to devise and then use a practical method of 'platoon firing'. In any case, military writers of the 1750s attributed this tactic to the Dutch and referred to the tactics as the 'Dutch school' or 'Dutch method'.[9] The significance of this new method of delivering fire was that it allowed an attacker periodically to deliver a series of volleys while advancing towards the enemy. This represented a fundamentally different offensive philosophy: the defender's fire was not to be ignored but to be returned, in the hopes of reducing his will to stand and fight.

One of the best descriptions of the rationale for this offensive tactic was provided by the Marquis de Santa-Cruz, a Spanish military authority and tactician. Santa-Cruz believed that when an attacking force neared an enemy that was determined to resist and making use of well timed volleys, the attacker was at a distinct disadvantage if he simply attempted to ignore the fire and rush in and settle the matter with cold steel, i.e. the lowered bayonet. The men advancing would become increasingly dismayed, when faced with the terrible buzzing and whistling of the musket balls and unsettling sight of the wounded and dead falling to the ground as the successive volleys took their toll. Any recruits or less experienced men in the formation were particularly affected by the ordeal. Many of the attackers, quickly brought to a state of extreme agitation, would begin to fire despite their officers' wishes. These shots, totally unaimed, ended up being directed 'as much at the sky as the earth'. The result was that when and if the attackers made it to twenty or thirty paces from the defenders, who remained relatively composed, their numbers were diminished through casualties and desertion, and whatever forces did remain were no longer in order. In this state of affairs, the defenders could easily send the attackers reeling back if they retained sufficient presence of mind to counterattack with lowered bayonets at the right moment.[10] To counteract this possibility, the Dutch devised a method of assault in which the attacking force periodically stopped and a portion of the formation delivered a volley, before stepping off once again.

Under the Stuarts, the British had operated within the French school of thought. However, after the Glorious Revolution of 1688, the British increasingly fell under the influence of the Dutch, especially after the outbreak of the War of Spanish Succession, which saw these two nations allied to fight Louis XIV and his numerous French armies. Not surprisingly, as early as 1709 at the Battle of Malplaquet (11 September 1709), we find the British using a version of platoon firing while on the offensive. Although the memoirs of Captain Robert Parker provide a description of the firing system employed by the Royal Regiment of Ireland (the 18th Foot) during this battle, a later description by Richard Kane 'A New System Of Military

Discipline for a Battalion of Foot', published in 1745 is even more detailed. The attacking battalions of infantry would advance at a deliberate pace towards the enemy until they were fired upon by the enemy within effective range. This was judged to be when they were between fifty and a hundred paces. At this point, if they had been fired upon, the colonel would order the battalion to halt and begin the firing process. The first part of the battalion to fire, called the 'first firing', made ready, delivered its fire when given the order by the colonel and then quickly reloaded. Meanwhile, the men in the next 'firing' prepared to fire. If as a result of the 'first firing' the enemy broke, the battalion would be ordered to resume their march and chase the enemy. On the other hand, if the enemy continued to hold its ground the second firing would be ordered to deliver its fire. The third firing would then automatically begin its preparations to fire, while the second firing started to reload.

The colonel could continue this process of ordering each successive firing to deliver its fire until the enemy started to give way. However, it was much more likely that after a few volleys, the battalion would be made to march forward again. After advancing a suitable distance, the battalion would most likely be brought to a halt a second time so that several new volleys could be brought to bear, using the same procedure as during the first round. Should the enemy continue to stand after the next series of volleys the attacking formation would resume its forward motion and, once close enough, attempt to charge in with lowered bayonets. If at any point the enemy finally broke, the colonel would halt the battalion, if it was in motion, and have it resume firing. Most probably this would take the form of battalion fire where all the men fired at once, to inflict the most damage on the retiring enemy while it was still in range. Or, the battalion might continue its platoon firing. In any case, an experienced officer would not let the battalion chase the enemy, since this would necessarily lead to the disordering of the formation, which could prove extremely dangerous if there were other enemy formations in the area.[11]

In the fire system just described, the attacking force periodically had to come to a full stop in order that a portion of its front could let off a volley. However, certain 'Germanic' armies, such as the Dutch and Prussians, utilized a slightly more sophisticated firing technique that allowed the advancing infantry to fire while it continued its advance. When using this method, the attacking battalion never really came to a full stop while any of its men delivered their fire.

The attacking formation would march with shouldered arms until it had approached close enough to inflict meaningful casualties upon the defenders. Bland, in his description of this 'Dutch Method' of attack, estimates this distance to be around sixty paces. While marching, the men in the battalion advanced with 'recovered arms'. A few moments later the platoon furthest to the right in the battalion would quickly advance in front of the battalion until its rear rank was even with the front rank elsewhere along the front. At this point, its men would halt, kneel, lock, present and fire. The battalion meanwhile would continue to advance, albeit 'as slow as the foot can fall' so that the battalion's cohesion would not be lost. Another reason for this slow and deliberate gait was to allow the men who had just fired to reload while they continued to advance. As soon as the platoon on the right had fired, the one on the left flank would spring forward and fire. Then it became the turn of the second platoon from the right, followed by that of the second platoon on the left etc., until the two platoons in the centre had participated in the fire combat.

As soon as all the platoons had reloaded, the battalion would switch from the slow, deliberate method of marching to a more normal pace. At some point, the platoons in the battalion would recommence the 'alternate fire' just described, so that it was expected that the defenders would be subjected to two or three complete fires by the time the attackers were twenty paces or so distant. At this point, like the British they would deliver a 'whole fire', that is 'battalion fire' before rushing in with lowered bayonets. Bland informs us that this method often caused the defenders to break after a single round of firing, and even when the attackers had to advance to close range usually there were few casualties inflicted on the advancing forces.

Despite these virtues, this Dutch method of alternate firings while advancing was difficult to perform and demanded the highest possible level of discipline and training among those attempting to employ it. Not only did the infantrymen have to be completely expert in loading under battle conditions, the officers, especially those commanding platoons, had to be thoroughly familiar with the series of commands and the firing process. There was, however, an even more serious danger. As the advancing battalion continued to fire it had a higher vulnerability to a counterattack by the defensive line than did the other methods of attacking. Once the advancing battalion was close enough, if it continued to fire by alternate platoons, the enemy could attempt to surprise it by a quick and sudden motion. If successful, many of the attackers still concentrating on the process of reloading:

> . . . will be apt to give away, from a notion of their being then defenseless; the consequence of which may throw a pannick [sic] into the whole, and involve them in the same misfortune: therefore, unless it is managed with great conduct, it may very easily turn to their disadvantage.[12]

It would seem that infantry in most armies were unable to perform this complicated tactic under battlefield conditions. The general opinion was that only the Dutch troops possessed sufficient discipline to fire while advancing effectively.

MECHANICS OF THE ADVANCE

Despite these differences in the role of firepower during the assault, there were a great many other aspects of the infantry advance that almost everyone agreed upon. Whether the *à prest* or the Dutch method of attack was followed, the infantry were to advance with shouldered muskets; the musket with bayonet attached leaning against the left shoulder.[13] Prior to the introduction of cadenced marching, around 1750, most of the advance was conducted at a very slow pace to avoid hopelessly disordering the formation.[14] Although cadenced marching allowed the commander to order a faster advance than had previously been possible, it was still important to advance only as quickly as order permitted. This principle held true throughout the Napoleonic Wars. During the struggle for Pratzen Heights at Austerlitz, for example, witnessing the conflict from the Austro-Russian side Count von Stutterheim noted that the two large French infantry masses moving on to the heights advanced 'with great coolness, and at a slow pace . . .'[15] On the other hand, instances were known where the attacking force was brought to the quick pace while still three or four hundred paces away from the enemy. The exact range at which the men would be ordered to begin an assault varied from army to army and even from commander to commander. The French tended to place their officers slightly in front of the advancing ranks. This was to inspire their men, and lead them forward into battle. Midway through the eighteenth century, the Prussians started to place many of their officers slightly to the rear of the formation. The reasons were twofold: the officers were less of a target to enemy marksmen, and, probably even more importantly, the officers and NCOs once in the rear were well placed to stop those who lost heart and tried to find safety to the rear.

Among the British, Dutch and Prussians the strictest silence was required of the men. It had long been observed when the men started to talk amongst themselves, their concentration on marching was lessened and the formation would gradually become disordered. Officers positioned in front of the formation had to slow down periodically and turn around to see that the proper distances and silences were maintained.[16] The order between the ranks and files in a formation was called its 'dressing', and an ordered battalion was referred to as being 'dressed'. To maintain order within the formation during the march, it was important that everyone in each file followed directly behind the file leader. Throughout the advance, the junior officers devoted most of their energies to making sure that the ranks and files remained 'dressed'. Despite these efforts, the ranks and files within any formation would gradually become increasingly disordered as the movement continued. Inevitably, the formation would become so disordered that it would become necessary to stop and 'dress' the battalion. The men would halt and the officers and NCOs would order the men to fall in behind their file leaders and align with the flank men at either side of each rank. The frequency with which a formation had to be stopped and dressed depended upon the terrain being passed over, the experience of the soldiers and how fast they were required to march. Troops taking casualties were also forced to dress much more frequently than their counterparts, who advanced unchallenged.

As the battalion continued its advance, its senior officers kept a watchful eye not only on the enemy but also on the other friendly formations participating in the same assault. In the days of strict linear warfare this was to ensure that the battalion always retained its alignment with the battalions to its left and right along the same line. However, even with the disappearance of general assaults in lengthy lines, the issue of multi-battalion alignment never totally lost its relevancy. By 1805–1806, for example, the French started to manoeuvre the infantry division keeping all or most of their battalions in several tiers of closed-order battalion columns. In this type of situation, it was very important that a proper lateral distance (equivalent to one 'interval') was always maintained from the neighbour on either side. If the battalion columns crowded too close together it became very difficult to quickly deploy into line, should this become necessary.

The infantrymen were strictly forbidden to fire until commanded to do so by their officers. In the early eighteenth century, very often this meant withholding fire until very close to the enemy. However, with the increased availability of gun powder, from the Seven Years' War onward, it became increasingly popular to stop and deliver fire at various stages during the assault. When the battalion had advanced to within a hundred paces of the enemy, the NCOs and officers would start to tighten up the formation, preparatory to the final assault. The files would be brought closer together, although care had to be taken that enough room remained for the soldiers to be able to march, fire and load easily.[17] The distance between the ranks would also be reduced to two feet or a pace. To bring the ranks closer was to invite confusion: the ranks in the rear would bump into those in the front, the men would start to curse and complain and the concentration required for the attack be irreparably lost.[18]

The initial approach would have been made with a deliberate step in order to retain the best possible order along the line. As we have seen, if the infantry were to use an *à prest* attack, the pace would be quickened somewhere between seventy and a hundred paces of the enemy, in the last moments the men often charging at the run. The officers, initially positioned a little in front of the formation, would now melt in with the first rank. In the French army, for example, it was customary at this point for the officers to place only half their body sticking out of the front rank. This precaution allowed them to still see along the length of the line but prevented the enemy from attacking them independently of the remainder of the formation.[19]

Those practising the continued use of deliberate volleys would continue at the slower pace. Of course, even here after the last volley at between twenty and thirty paces, the men would be ordered to make a spirited bayonet charge. This last part of the advance was conducted at the run, since this was considered to have the most terrifying effect on the enemy.[20] At the very last moments, the attackers were to lower their bayonets and lunge at their adversaries directly in front of them.

When we think of the Napoleonic period, or for that matter the entire period in which the flintlock was in use, we conjure up images of drums beating as they accompanied the infantry into the thick of battle. In actual fact, throughout the entire flintlock period, music supplied by drums, hautboys, flutes and trumpets was found on the battlefield and served several roles. There existed a tradition over many centuries of using music to maintain or even buoy up the morale of the troops. During the linear period, the general deployment of an army was a much lengthier affair, and musicians were often ordered to strike up once a portion of the line was deployed and forced to remain in position while the remainder of the army continued to move into position, or the commanders assayed the situation and decided their course of action.[21] The music served to distract the soldiers as they were played upon by any enemy artillery that might be in range. By the mid-eighteenth century, there was an attempt to use martial music to achieve two other ends: to help the rank and file maintain an even cadenced march, and to serve as an alternate method of communicating orders from the battalion commander to his men.

The Prussians and their stunning series of successes during the Silesian Wars had popularized the use of both cadenced marching and the cadenced manual of arms. A drum beat delivered at the appropriate tempo was thought to assist marching, since it could signal the men just how fast to march as well as when to begin the next foot motion. Around the same time, the Prussians, British and a little later the French experimented with the drum to communicate commands from the battalion commander to his men.[22] In actual practice, musical instruments appear to have had much more limited application on the battlefield. Many experienced officers felt that drum rolls and the airs of a flute were not particularly useful and even possibly harmful once the action began. The music after all distracted the men, and made the commands more difficult to hear. Charles XII of Sweden during the Great Northern War, for example, forbade music during the attack, arguing that the loud sounds of both drums and trumpets made it very difficult for the men to be able to hear orders.[23]

The use of drums to help the soldiers march in cadence, so popular in theoretical works around the mid-eighteenth century, also proved to be less effective than was initially anticipated. There were several reasons for this. For the music to be completely effective in this role, each musician would have had to have the same timing as all the others in that line. Of course, in practice, this was never accomplished, and the rhythm for the musicians at one part of the line would be slightly different to those elsewhere. This resulted in a slight variance in the cadence which inevitably resulted in the line becoming disordered. Ironically, even if the musicians managed to completely synchronize their tempo, the laws of physics offered another obstacle. The time required by sound waves to reach the outlying troops meant that they reached various parts of any extended line at slightly different points in time. Sound travels at approximately 300 yards per second. So at battalion widths of 150 yards, men at the extremity of the battalion in line would respond slightly later than those in the middle, next to the drummers. Although this delay was only about a quarter of a second, this, when coupled with other problems described above, would generate disorder within the ranks as they marched.[24]

DEFENSIVE TACTICS UP TO 1757

The tactical doctrine available to the defender was shaped by very similar considerations. In the classical linear period, the defender would also tend to deploy his infantry along two lengthy lines; the second about 300 paces behind the first. Obviously, the defending forces, if properly led, would be positioned to exploit whatever advantages were offered by the terrain. The officers attached to each battalion would do their best to ensure that the ranks and files were orderly and the men resolute. The men remained silent throughout the enemy's advance, so as to be able to hear their officers' orders. The commander of the defending forces, or other high-ranking officers commanding a wing or a brigade, had two choices, to await the enemy without flinching until the last possible moment or to commence firing once the enemy had advanced to within seventy to eighty paces.

There were advantages and disadvantages to both doctrines of defence, and history has afforded many examples of competent commanders utilizing each of these opposing tactics. Those who advocated the use of firepower felt that it was desirable to begin firing as soon as the enemy had advanced to within sixty to eighty paces. They argued that the casualties thus inflicted would demoralize the attackers and, even more importantly, begin to cause confusion among the oncoming ranks. It must be remembered that by this point most attackers would be advancing *à prest*, that is at the 'quick march'. In the days prior to cadenced marching, the ranks would quickly become confused, even when moving as little as fifty paces. The distance between many of the files could open up, causing gaps to appear, or as happened even more frequently, the men would crowd together in the centre of the formation causing the intervals between the battalions to be enlarged. Consequently, the additional disorder caused by men falling to the ground or left behind as a result of the close range fire significantly increased the attacker's susceptibility to a counter-charge.[25] In such a counter-charge, those who used this defensive doctrine felt the defender held the upper hand. The previously stationary defending ranks remained in perfect order until the counter-charge was ordered. It was believed that in this situation the attacking forces, seeing the ordered infantry quickly coming towards them and sensing their own confusion, would turn around and flee.

There were those who felt these advantages were only theoretical, and that the defending ranks while firing repeatedly became just as disordered as the advancing enemy. Those adhering to this school of thought felt that given the type of muskets then in use, only one fire could be effectively delivered during the time the enemy traversed the last fifty paces or so. Any additional volleys would only provide a fraction of the shots delivered by the first. These factors considered, it was best for the defending ranks to withhold their fire until the last possible moment when the attacker had advanced to point-blank range, that is, about twenty paces. They argued that this minimized the disorder among the defenders while it almost certainly ensured the maximum disorder possible among the attackers. A fire delivered at so close a range was hardly likely to miss and a great number of casualties could be expected. The resulting confusion among the advancing men would be tremendous. As soon as the single volley was delivered, the first rank, if it had been kneeling, would stand up, and the defenders were ordered to counter-charge. The short distance separating the two opposing forces guaranteed that the defenders reached the attackers while the latter were still recoiling from the shock of the volley which had just been delivered, but the confusion among the defending ranks from the movement was simultaneously minimized.

To some degree, the types of volley system used by an army determined which of these two basic offensive systems were used when forced to defend. The British, Dutch and Prussian infantry were able to perform platoon firing effectively, so not surprisingly these systems were often used in defensive situations. The French, on the other hand, during this early period still relied on 'fire by ranks' and tended to reserve platoon firing on the defensive for when they were positioned behind some fortified position, such as an entrenchment.[26]

CHAPTER 5

Infantry Tactics II:
Late Eighteenth-Century Developments

TYPES OF FIRE SYSTEMS

DEPENDING UPON THE CRITERIA used in the evaluation, one could either conclude that the methods of delivering fire during the Napoleonic age had stagnated, differing little from those in the classical linear period, or that this area like so many others was in a dynamic state of continuous change. If one concentrates solely on the mechanical aspects of the fire delivery systems then in use the necessary conclusion would have to be that indeed there was little new. None of the major fire systems in use at the beginning of the nineteenth century were newly invented. With one possible exception, all had been conceived of at least half a century previously, and most had seen at least limited use in previous wars. This is not surprising since the flintlock's capabilities changed little during its career, and the most effective methods of delivering fire were quickly discovered after its general introduction to most western European armies during the 1687–1710 period. A glance at contemporary literature, shows that 'platoon fire', 'fire by ranks', 'battalion fire' and 'fire by files', not to mention 'firing in skirmisher order' were the most common methods of delivering fire during the Napoleonic Wars. With the possible exception of 'fire by files', all of these were documented during the early eighteenth century. Platoon fire and derivatives such as 'divisional firing' etc. can be traced at least as far back as the Dutch army in the last quarter of the seventeenth century, while 'fire by ranks' and 'battalion fire' can be traced to the French army of the same period.[1] One of the fire systems most frequently encountered during the Napoleonic Wars was 'fire by files' or *feu de deux rangs* (fire by two ranks) as it was called in France. This firing procedure was officially adopted in France by the 1776 infantry regulations.[2] However, writing more than thirty years earlier Maurice de Saxe (*Mes rêveries* was published in 1757 but written in 1732) provided a description of both firing in skirmisher order and what appears to be a predecessor to the 'fire by files' method.[3]

Nevertheless, the impression that the methods used to deliver infantry firepower had stagnated by the Napoleonic period is somewhat illusory. The American tactician Duane, writing during the height of the Napoleonic Wars, on the contrary concluded that no other aspect of warfare had recently gone through such repeated transformations as the philosophy underlying the proper use of small arms fire. Seeking to sum up all the various changes concerning the use of small arms fire, Duane concluded:

> Of all the branches of tactics, none has undergone a greater variety of changes, none has been so ill digested and completed in its exercises, as the mode of fire. It has been a matter of dispute among the most distinguished officers for a century; each endeavouring to bring it into perfection in their own way: by charging carefully – by charging with given proportions of powder – by ramming down – by dispensing with the ramrod, and depending upon the weight of the ball & the shock of the butt against the ground: then came the principal of extension, or giving a long line of fire – then the order of formation, in 2, 3, 4 ranks – then volley firing, firing by sub-divisions and platoons: kneeling of the 1st rank and last, the execution of the greatest number of discharges of firelock in a minute, as Guibert very truly says, increasing the noise, smoke and confusion of action.[4]

Actually, both views are equally correct in their assessment. Looking only at the mechanical level, there indeed had been little change: the purely procedural aspects of the various fire delivery systems, for the most part, had been discovered and codified by the 1730s. Nevertheless, there continued to be fervent experimentation with a number of related issues, such as the importance of 'well-directed' fire versus sheer volume of fire, how much powder to use for each charge, and so on. These developments, when considered collectively, would later substantially increase the effectiveness of musket fire under battle conditions.

THE 'QUICK FIRE' PHILOSOPHY

Three mid-eighteenth century innovations would ultimately have a profound effect on the way infantry attacked its enemy or defended itself on the battlefield: the increased availability of gunpowder allowing each soldier to be supplied with many more cartridges, the adoption of cadenced marching, and the introduction of a cadenced manual of arms, the last two made possible by regular drilling and instruction demanded by Frederick William of Prussia. Frederick William required his infantry to untiringly practise loading and firing their muskets, a procedure known to the military as the 'manual of arms'. Through this seemingly endless rehearsal, Frederick William and Leopold of Anhalt-Dessau were able to effect a most important innovation: each step in the manual of arms was cadenced, in other words, everyone performed each step at exactly the same moment. It was this ability, rather than simply performing the loading procedure more quickly that made Prussian infantry firepower *appear* so awesome. However, this capability as it applied to offensive doctrine was largely ignored by his son, Frederick the Great, for almost the first two decades of his reign. When Frederick first went to war in 1740, following the example of Charles XII of Sweden, he required his infantry whenever possible to assume the offensive and quickly advance towards the enemy without stopping to fire. In adopting these tactics, Frederick placed himself squarely in the French/Swedish tactical school and clearly broke from his father's predilection for the Dutch method of attack which called for the advancing lines to periodically stop and execute well delivered volleys to attempt to break the enemy's will to continue to stand and resist.[5]

However, as Frederick's enemies learned from the Prussian example and improved the discipline and training in their own armies, these aggressive tactics proved less and less successful. As a result, within several years of the opening of the Seven Years' War Frederick was forced to concede that when attacking an enemy prepared to fight, it was usually necessary first to soften the defending line by stopping and administering several well-delivered volleys. Frederick once commented that after a fifteen-minute firefight, the Austrian ranks, would start to 'shake and jumble'; it was then that they were most susceptible to a forceful onslaught.[6]

The feasibility of Frederick's quick fire methods were based partly on the Prussian adoption of rigorous infantry training and the cadenced manual of arms. They were also indebted to the increased availability of gunpowder around the mid-eighteenth century. Prior to this, ammunition had been very much more restricted and the average infantry was sent into battle with usually less than twenty-five cartridges. This was significantly less than the fifty to sixty cartridges carried by soldiers during the Seven Years' War. The quality of gunpowder that existed in the early eighteenth century was considerably poorer than that which would become available fifty years later. This meant a musket would invariably become fouled after about thirty discharges, and this was one of the reasons for limiting the supply during the early period. Better quality powder also meant that infantry could fire more shots and hence more cartridges were distributed. The original lack of cartridges had created strong psychological pressure on the infantrymen to withhold their fire until it was really needed. Musket fire had to be used very much more sparingly than later when it was common for infantrymen to be equipped with four to six times this amount. Prior to the increased availability of gunpowder neither officer nor man would ever have been tempted to stop and engage in a long range firefight, unless forced to do so because of other circumstances.

One of the reasons usually attributed to the success of Prussian infantry was its ability to 'outshoot' the opposing infantry, or more accurately, to give the impression that it was outshooting its opponents. Once again, the legacy of Frederick William's training came to the fore, and the Prussian infantry was able to deliver relatively ordered volleys much more quickly than its counterpart in other western European armies. The ability to fire five times a minute, so closely associated with the Prussian infantry, soon became the watchword at military training camps throughout Europe. The Austrians and the other German states were the first to emulate the Prussian example; they were quickly followed by the British. This new tactic of firing as quickly as possible was known in the English-speaking world as 'quick fire'.[7] In this case, the infantry would dispense with ramming the charge properly down the barrel or even ramming it at all. Instead, the soldier would bang the butt of his musket repeatedly on the ground to shake the cartridge sufficiently down the barrel. To facilitate this, the man would enlarge the diameter of the vent leading into the barrel near the priming pan. This allowed some of the powder to fall into this pan, and thus simultaneously charged and primed the pieces.[8] Though it was obvious that this practice reduced the effectiveness of the charge and caused frequent 'flare backs', it also reduced the amount of time needed to reload, and thus sped up the rate of fire.

On the surface, the adoption of 'quick fire' did not appear to have any effect on the methods of delivering systems then in use. The same type of volley firing continued to be used, or so it seemed; they simply had to be performed more quickly than before the concept of 'quick firing' came into vogue. For example, the British infantry before and after the Seven Years' War continued to espouse platoon firing as the best method of delivering volley fire. The French infantry, originally relying on 'fire by ranks,' followed the British example during the 1751–1753 period. In actual fact, however, the adoption of 'quick fire' had the most profound effect on how volley fire was performed. Subtly, the methods of delivering fire began to change. Although the British after the Seven Years' War continued to use platoon firing, just as they had prior to the outbreak of hostilities in 1740, notable differences between the old and new methods of platoon firing had emerged.

Prior to 1740, the volley mechanism was orchestrated so that the colonel remained completely in control of the fire, which *on purpose* was to be quite sparse. In other words, the troops would be ordered to stop, a portion of the men typically would deliver a single volley and then recommence their advance. There was no emphasis on the speed at which the volleys were delivered, and engaging in a prolonged firefight was eschewed. The colonel actually gave each 'division', which for firing purposes was about one third of the battalion, the order to fire. In this earlier version of platoon firing, the next division to fire was not ordered to fire immediately after the preceding division,[9] but had to await the colonel's command. Every step in the process had been designed to allow the colonel to retain control over each action in the firing procedure. The advent of the Prussian 'quick fire' philosophy quickly changed all this. The emphasis on speed meant that the divisions were now required to deliver fire as quickly as possible in succession. To accomplish this staccato-like effect, the colonel no longer controlled exactly when each division was to fire, and the authority to designate the exact moment to fire was transferred to the officer commanding the division. This transformation in the way platoon fire was executed had two profound effects. The first was intentional: a dramatic increase in the rate of fire, believed to inflict proportionately higher casualties among the enemy. The second effect, though just as important, was not as obvious: by reducing the time separating the individual 'firings' and pressuring the men to reload and present their arms as quickly as possible, the 'coefficient of confusion', among the ranks, so to speak, was also dramatically increased.

In the earlier system, where each firing was ordered to fire once before moving, there had been a noticeable pause before the next delivered its fire. Consequently, it was much easier to control the men. Someone firing out of turn would stand out and be subjected to immediate discipline and the fire, therefore, remained controlled. With the emphasis on quick fire, where each firing could discharge as little as four or five seconds after its predecessor (three firings – each attempting to fire four or five times a minute), after several volleys, the formal groupings would start to blur. A division or platoon might begin to fire a second or two early, and a sense of continuous fire would arise. The men, reloading as fast as they could would each start to fire as soon as they were ready and the officers would lose control. The fire, which had started off as regular volleys, would soon devolve into disorganized and uncontrolled individual fire. When this happened, the officers were no longer able readily to stop the firing and resume the advance, and the firefight devolved into a prolonged affair. Despite these shortcomings, the frequent success of the Prussians during the Seven Years' War added credibility to the Prussians' advocacy of the quick firing doctrine. Authorities in other western European armies began increasingly to cite this as a reason for the ascendancy of the Prussian infantry over their enemies. The infantry in other German states, and then the British, followed the Prussian lead with many of its officers experimenting with quick fire techniques. The result was that by 1790, the Prussian infantry of the Seven Years' War was still regarded as the ideal model and the quick firing philosophy remained almost unquestioned. Of course, in those armies such as the French where the *à prest* doctrine was employed on the offensive, quick fire doctrine was relegated to defensive applications.

Probably one of the most enthusiastic proponents of the quick fire philosophy in the British service was William Müller whose major work, the three-volume *The Elements of the Science of War*, was published in London in 1811. Müller argued that trained troops with ordinary ramrods required eleven seconds to reload, provided that the soldier omitted several steps in the manual of arms and allowed the powder to fall into the vent by itself. Troops equipped with conical iron ramrods could reload even more quickly: in about eight to nine seconds. Consequently, those using ordinary ramrods could fire about four to five times a minute and those with conical ramrods, five to six. Armed with these observations, Müller set out to devise a method of delivering volleys that would utilize this quick fire capability. Müller advocated dividing each company within the battalion into four divisions. Observing that nine seconds were required to reload, Müller reasoned that each division could be ordered to fire every twelve seconds. If these were staggered, this meant that a part of the company was delivering fire every three seconds, that is, the company was delivering some fire twenty times each minute. Müller conceded that a more rapid succession of volleys, theoretically possible by dividing the company into a greater number of smaller subunits, was in practice not feasible. Battle conditions called for at least three seconds between volleys. As one division fired its volley, the men in the next division had to stand with lowered arms. If the men in the second division, stood with presented arms while the first were ordered to fire, its men would also fire, and this meant the second division could only be ordered to present their arms after the first had fired. For the fire to be effective, the order to fire could only be given about one and a half seconds after the men presented their weapons, otherwise, most of the men would not be able even to point their musket in the enemy's general direction as they fired.[10]

RATE OF FIRE

This increased emphasis on speed of firing naturally leads us to the question: how fast could an experienced infantryman fire his musket under battlefield conditions? Many military men even during Napoleon's time accepted the Prussian claim of five rounds per minute, although there was no shortage of those who challenged the infantry's ability to deliver this high rate of fire whenever a firefight had to be maintained for more than one or two minutes. Fortunately for posterity, Duane conducted a number of experiments to test the efficacy and characteristics of musket and artillery fire under various circumstances. One of the experiments was designed specifically to measure how quickly a musket could be fired by an experienced infantryman. Two men from a light infantry company were positioned a hundred paces from a target. One was instructed to fire with his knapsack on; the other was allowed to remove it. Although both men were to 'level' their muskets at the target, they were not to actually 'aim', and they were to fire as fast as they could.

As it turned out, both men were able to fire the eighteen rounds they had been provided with in five minutes. At this point, out of ammunition, the two waited for additional rounds to be brought up, and during this halt, the muskets' barrels had a chance to partially cool. Given the delay, the observers gave up trying to keep track of the time and now a sergeant was allowed to hand the cartridges to the men as soon as they began to reload after each fire. The observers noted that the two men started to fire about twenty-five per cent more quickly as a result. As the men started to fire anew, the barrels started to heat up once again, and gradually became too hot to touch. The two men continued firing, however. One man reloaded his musket by holding it by the sling whilst the other held the small of the stock while reloading. By the time one had fired thirty-seven rounds and the other thirty-five, the observers felt there was now a danger of an explosion while reloading and the experiment was brought to an end.

This experiment determined how many rounds could be got off in quick succession, but it had failed to address the issue of maximum rate of fire. A similar experiment was conducted using a very experienced soldier who was now pushed back to 121 paces from the target. Once the command to fire was given, he was able to loose the first three rounds in a minute, with a total of thirty-six rounds in thirteen minutes. The observers noted that the time taken to fire the last eighteen rounds was the same as the first: six and a half minutes. The infantrymen, though firing quickly, continued to reload properly and was required to ram down the cartridge with two 'smart' strokes. Despite the emphasis on speed, the shots were fairly accurate; fifteen rounds struck the target while the remainder struck near the target. As in the first experiment the barrel began to heat up with the repeated firings. After the twenty-fifth shot, the barrel became too hot to be held by hand, and the infantryman continued to reload holding the musket by its sling.[11]

The conclusions to be drawn from this series of experiments are straightforward. Although a veteran soldier might be able to unleash five rounds in the first minute or so, his average would very quickly decrease to about three per minute for any extended time. Moreover, this rate could only be kept up for about eight minutes when the barrel would become too hot for the gun to be loaded using the formal cadenced manual of arms. As will be seen elsewhere, firefights lasting up to three hours were not unheard of. However, Duane's experiences strongly suggest that during these extended firefights a much lower average rate of fire must have prevailed.

FIRING BY FILES

That the new emphasis on volume of fire led to a more frequent breakdown of orderly volleys did not go completely unnoticed. Many, however, sought a means of addressing this problem without rejecting the new emphasis on a higher rate of fire that underlay this tendency in the first place. In France where, as in the remainder of Europe, the infantry continued to deploy along three ranks, the various traditional methods of delivering fire continued to be employed. During the closing years of the *ancien régime*, a series of formal tests had demonstrated that the fire of the third rank was ineffective.[12] Obstructed by the first two ranks most of the muskets in the third rank were fired harmlessly in the air. To put the soldiers in the third rank to more effective use, and at the same time to address the problem of irregular fire which tended to occur in sustained volley fire, after the Seven Years' War the French military developed a new method of delivering fire. This was the *feu de rang* or 'fire by two ranks', known throughout the English-speaking world as 'firing by files', 'file firing' or 'running fire'. In this new system, although the three ranks were to remain standing, only the first and second ranks were actually to fire. The responsibility of the third rank was to reload muskets and pass these to the second rank.

After the command to fire *by independent files* was given and the men assumed their proper positions, the first and second ranks presented their muskets and fired together. The men in the first rank now reloaded their weapons, delivered and fired again. This process was repeated so that the men in the first rank fired as quickly as possible. The men in the second rank, however, did not reload their weapons but passed their weapon with their right hand to the man directly behind them in the third rank. The man in the third rank gripped the musket with his left hand while handing the soldier in front a loaded musket with his right hand. The latter was now able to present and fire the musket he was just handed. However, after firing the musket he now reloaded his weapon himself and fired it a second time. Only after this second fire did he once again exchange muskets with the man behind him. This routine allowed the man in the second rank to fire twice with the same weapon before passing it back. This ensured that the man in the rear had finished reloading his musket so that as little time as possible was lost between fires. It was always dangerous to have a front rank stand idle and unarmed as it awaited the efforts of those behind. This type of inaction tended to unnerve the men and sowed the seeds of panic.

While the men in the second and third ranks followed this routine, the first rank concentrated on firing and reloading their own muskets. There was no attempt to coordinate their efforts with those behind them.[13] Clearly, one of the chief aims of this new system was to allow the men to fire as quickly as possible. One veteran French officer, whose post-war speciality was the scientific analysis of musket fire, recalled his own personal observations of wartime practice:

> The troops must in the 'fire by two ranks' fire the most shots possible, and, in all the others, fire with the greatest possible togetherness . . . It is curious to see, when the fire by two ranks commences, the alacrity with which the serre-file animates and pushes the soldier to charge and fire as briskly as possible; stunned by the gun shots which leaves them with an earache, by the exhortations of their officers, fearing the emission of the neighbor's fusil, not only thinking not to adjust, but often firing without putting the shoulder piece to the shoulder, and it is thus that one burns 8 or 10 cartridges, to execute fire by two ranks, in combat.[14]

A careful reading of the French regulations of 1791 sheds some light on some additional reasons why this new method had been developed. It had long been recognized that in the heat of the action many infantrymen lacked sufficient presence of mind to load their weapons properly. All too frequently, when the trigger was pulled only the powder in the flash pan ignited and the charge remained unignited in the barrel. The noise and the smoke from other muskets, however, made it difficult for the soldier to see that his weapon had failed to discharge. Urged on by his officers the soldier would reload his weapon, which, with its multiple charges in the barrel, would either fail once again to discharge or explode with sometimes fatal results. An experienced soldier with the presence of mind to look for certain telltale signs was usually able to avoid this problem. Officers taught their men to look at the muzzle before reloading. If there was smoke issuing from the barrel, the charge had ignited and they could proceed with reloading their weapons. If there was no smoke, the gun had not discharged, and corrective action was necessary to clear the barrel. When introducing the fire by files the men were instructed to hand their muskets back to the third rank whenever they noticed this type of misfire.[15]

Despite the obvious emphasis on speed, proponents of this new fire system felt that it also allowed greater accuracy:

for, independently of the noise, which may occasion many mistakes ... it is impossible to give soldiers, in presence of the enemy, a sufficient degree of coolness to attend to the word of command, and to observe the caution which regular firing by platoons and divisions requires. Nor am I very certain that it is any great misfortune to an army, that, after a few discharges, the fire by files takes place of itself. This fire being at will, a soldier, notwithstanding the smoke, can, in my opinion, aim much better than he is able to do when firing at the word of command given by the officer, who frequently, through excessive eagerness, hurries him, and obliges him to fire before he has had time to aim properly ... hence it follows that fire by files, which besides is very brisk, must do more real execution than a regular fire; ... this fire has the further advantage of animating the men, keeping them constantly in action, and rendering them insensible to danger: but they should be accustomed to cease firing the instant the signal is given.[16]

Charged with appraising the various French infantry practices at the Campe de Boulogne in 1804, Marshal Ney felt that firing by files was 'with the exception of a very few moments, absolutely the only kind of fire which offers much greater advantages to the infantry than those above-mentioned [referring to direct and oblique firing].'[17] Despite this enthusiastic endorsement, Ney felt himself forced to concede, however, that a number of problems were encountered on the battlefield. Since the men in the second rank did not load the musket themselves, they did not have the same confidence as they would had they always loaded the musket they were to fire themselves.

Another more serious difficulty was frequently encountered, one that could prove to be a serious liability on the battlefield. According to Ney even the most experienced officers in French service had found that it was next to impossible to stop the men from firing once they were engaged in this type of fire, especially when they were within effective musket range of the enemy. Whenever this happened, all semblance of order was lost, and the men would continue to fire at will, in spite of the officers' efforts and commands to stop the fire. This would eventually compromise the battalion finding itself in this situation. If the fire was prolonged the battalion would start to run out of ammunition, which always proved to demoralize the men in the firing line. French infantry facing well trained German soldiers 'formed from the severest discipline . . . [and who are] . . . cooler than any other' would get the worst of the exchange, if it went on for any time. Ney concluded that the solution to this problem was to order the men to charge the enemy 'boldly with the bayonet, and by an act of vigor force the enemy to retreat' as soon as the first two ranks had fired for the first time. The third rank was to 'post its arms' and patiently wait as a reserve to be used only when a critical moment presented itself. Interestingly enough, Ney made these observations in 1804 several years before the British would employ similar spurts of fire followed by a bayonet charge time and time again to repulse French attacks during the Peninsular War.[18]

Although the fire by files method of firing is generally seen as a late-eighteenth-century development, there are some grounds to believe that its origins can be traced to the fertile mind of Maurice de Saxe. Writing in 1732, de Saxe described a method he recommended to be used when firing at an enemy positioned behind hedges, a river, etc. The leader of each file was to step forward a pace and aim at individual targets among the enemy in front of him. After firing he was to hand his musket to the rear and take a loaded one in its place. Because during de Saxe's time the French army still

76

deployed along four ranks, the file leader, chosen from among the best shots, could fire four times before he had to rely on a musket loaded by one of the rear ranks. Though there are obvious differences between de Saxe's method and that used later by French Revolutionary and Napoleonic armies, such as when it was to be used, and the supervision of the fire of each group of two files by NCOs in de Saxe's version, both methods obviously share the loading of the muskets by the rear ranks and aimed fire in the sense that the individual soldier chose the exact moment when to fire rather than on the word of command.[19] If the fire by files method of firing did originate from the early fire delivery system described in *Mes rêveries*, it would not be the first tactical practice or method that French authorities had borrowed from the great French marshal.

THE DEVELOPMENT OF ACCURATE 'LEVELLING' PRACTICES

Not all military men accepted the 'quick fire' philosophy which came into ever increasing vogue from about 1750 onward. There were those who continued to maintain that accurate fire was far more valuable than a succession of quickly delivered volleys. Over the next several decades another school of thought would slowly emerge which espoused an entirely different philosophy as to how best to utilize infantry fire. Writing in the 1750s, Colonel James Wolfe, soon to gain immortality on the Plains of Abraham, cautioned younger officers that: 'There is no necessity for firing very fast; a cool and well levelled fire, with the pieces carefully loaded, is much more destructive and formidable than the quickest fire in confusion.'[20] In the era of massed volleys, it was not possible for the individual soldier to 'aim', in the truest sense of the term. In order to aim properly, the soldier had to coordinate the processing of pointing the firearm at the target with his breathing, and then pull the trigger when he felt that the musket was pointed directly at the intended target. In other words, in aimed fire the soldier must always choose the moment to discharge his weapon. In volley fire, an officer, such as the colonel or the company captain determined the exact moment to fire, and it was unlikely that the soldier would have his weapon perfectly aimed at the exact moment when required to fire. As de Saxe pointed out, this produced a fire that was usually several yards from the mark.[21]

The practical solution was to have the men along the firing line 'level' their pieces before each fire. In the case of 'levelling', all the muskets along the line pointed at the same general 'height', such as the middle of the enemies' bodies. At first, even experienced officers were unaware how important it was to have the men properly level their weapons. There was no systematic method of adjusting the weapons' level to account for changes in elevation and distance. The results of not paying attention to these factors could be, and occasionally were, catastrophic. Maurice de Saxe as a young soldier at Belgrade (1717) never forgot the complete destruction of two Imperial battalions on a hill. Though they had properly reserved their fire until extremely close range, they only managed to kill about thirty enemy horsemen and within seconds were cut to pieces by the Turkish cavalry. Scarred by this experience, for the remainder of his life de Saxe emotionally proffered this as the classic example of the ineffectiveness and unreliability of infantry fire.[22]

It is difficult for us to fathom that as great a tactical genius as Maurice de Saxe never understood something as simple as the effect of firing downhill on aiming techniques. It was simply that even the most knowledgeable military men of his time did not realize the difficulty of firing at downhill targets and how it was necessary to compensate when firing downhill at close range by further lowering the barrel. This was never intuitively obvious to the soldier, and was psychologically quite difficult to perform, since to the common soldier properly compensating for distance and firing downhill, it would appear that he was about to fire into the ground well in front of his adversaries!

Such a simple concept as *systematically* raising or lowering the musket barrel according to the enemy's distance and elevation was extremely slow to emerge in European warfare. However, by the mid-eighteenth century some officers began to understand the necessity of doing just this. The first step, however, was but a modest improvement. Some officers, especially in the British army, began to admonish their troops to fire 'at the middle of the enemy's body'. Unfortunately, this dictate was applied with little consideration given to range. Troops were made to level at the middle of the enemy's body, whether they were fifty or 120 paces distant, and more often than not the musket balls would lodge in the ground in front of the enemy formation or sail harmlessly over their heads. Before too long, it was noticed that at very close ranges, even when every effort was made to level the muskets at the prescribed height, the troops frequently fired above the enemy's heads. When this occurred during the final moments of an enemy assault, disaster almost invariably followed; the troops, unable to reload in time for another volley, would be forced to flee. Noticing the tendency for troops to fire high at a nearby enemy, some officers ordered their men to level their pieces lower. Rather than directing their muskets towards the middle of the enemy's body, the men were enjoined to point their weapons at the enemy's knees instead. However, the distance separating the firing troops from their targets still was not considered, and the men levelled their pieces at the enemy's knees, regardless of their range.

In the 1780s, however, a few military experts began to understand the relationship of range to the musket ball's trajectory, and that this had to be systematically taken into account by the levelling process. The further the distance of the target the higher the men had to level their firearms. They would start off by levelling low at the closest ranges. However, as the distance increased the point that had to be aimed at was raised higher and higher until at the limit of the musket's effective range it was necessary to aim several feet over the enemy's heads. The exact amount of elevation, of course, depended upon the distance of the target. As we will see in Chapter 12, there were a number of reasons why the practice of proper levelling was never universal. Although this advance in military science began to be documented in the professional literature from the 1790s onwards, it is clear from both theoretical writings and battle accounts that its benefits had never been appreciated fully by all officers and their men. Moreover, there continued to be those who advocated the delivery of a rapid succession of volleys, and this practice made it difficult for the men to level properly before each volley.

REASONS FOR SELECTING FIRE SYSTEM

When selecting a fire system an officer responded as much to the needs of the particular situation as he did to the doctrinal directives established by his army's military authorities. So, for example, one might find the same infantry using 'fire by ranks' when deployed in square and warding off charging cavalry, and then later in the same battle 'firing by files' when engaged in a firefight with enemy infantry. In order for a fire system to be of general use, it had to perform adequately in four or five key areas. Probably the most obvious was whether a method of delivering fire allowed a great amount of fire power to be delivered in the same instant or over a short period of time. However, there were other considerations that were equally important to officers: how well did the fire system allow men to reload after firing; were the officers able to maintain control over the men so that they continued to fire only when ordered; and especially important, if cavalry was near, did the fire system allow a reserve to be maintained? Each fire system performed with varying degrees of success in these areas and thus had advantages and disadvantages. No system was unequivocally the best in all four areas, and this led to the debates that raged in military circles throughout the entire period.

In order to comprehend fully the fire systems used during the Napoleonic period, it is necessary to understand how the various systems in use evolved during the preceding period. Each of these earlier systems encountered certain problems that were presumably overcome by the system which replaced it. The all-too-common view is that the systems in use were new. In fact, they were often nothing more than reincarnations of earlier methods or slightly modified ones. Only by comparing the full spectrum of fire systems can one determine to what extent they were really new or borrowed from the past.

PART II

GRAND TACTICS IN THE NAPOLEONIC ERA

CHAPTER 6

The Origins of the 'Impulse' System of Warfare

HISTORY HAS FREQUENTLY PORTRAYED the seemingly sudden and dramatic transformation of warfare during the Revolutionary and Napoleonic Wars as a practical response to the reduced capabilities of the largely volunteer French army and the effects of the myriad political and social convulsions then engulfing Revolutionary France. This view was especially popular among those observing events from foreign soil. The unexpected French success at holding their numerous enemies at bay, campaign after campaign, by the late 1790s had forced some of those on the opposing side to attempt to fathom the transformation of the art of war within the French army. Unaware of any relationship between the new methods of fighting and possible antecedents in established French tradition, foreigners tended to view the adoption and widespread use of these new tactical and grand tactical systems as a spontaneous and reflexive response to the harsh set of military realities which beset French military authorities as they desperately attempted to deal with the deterioration of the regular standing army and the combined forces of the anti-French alliance.

According to this view, at this moment of extreme peril, high-ranking officers in the field were faced with a dilemma. The dismemberment of the officer class caused by the defection, immigration and internment of the nobility from which it had been exclusively drawn up, resulted in a decreased capacity to command. To raise the strength of the French army quickly, on the other hand, an unprecedented number of untrained recruits had to be rapidly funnelled into the field forces, significantly lowering the proficiency of the units who received these raw levies. This analysis continued by arguing that when confronted with a mass of men incapable of performing the traditional tasks and manoeuvres, the French officers purposely devised columnar formations and methods of fighting. The use of the lengthy lines, etc. were cast aside for attack columns and swarms of skirmishers because the untrained men were incapable of doing anything else. Officers in the Revolutionary army were forced to devise simpler procedures and manoeuvres when confronted with men insufficiently trained to perform the various tasks that had been required of regular troops, such as advancing and fighting in line.

This explanation could only arise because there was little knowledge outside of France about much of what had occurred in the French army prior to the Revolution. Foreign observers, though familiar with certain seminal works, such as de Saxe's *Mes rêveries* or Guibert, were effectively denied access to the full range of argument which had seasoned French officers' daily conversation for decades, or the practical trials periodically attempted on French parade grounds. Almost all of the tactical 'innovations' so strongly associated with the Revolutionary and Napoleonic period were not only devised and experimented with during the preceding linear period, but also were well known and continued to be advocated by a substantial portion of the French officer class up to the revolution. Among these were the use of columns of attack, columns of waiting, and skirmishing in open order. These were not obscure developments that once conceived were immediately relegated to some remote repository of arcane and useless ideas. The works of Chevalier de Folard, Marshal de Saxe, Mesnil Durand and Guibert among others had their share of vocal followers right up to the storming of the Bastille. Many of the so-called 'new' practices had even seen limited battlefield application during the Seven Years' War. Rather than devising new methods and practices, it was more a case of the French military taking existing concepts and techniques 'off the shelves', as dusty or relatively untried as these might have been.

Another common explanation for the success of new French methods was that these new practices were somehow more congruous with the attitudes, feelings and values of the great masses of patriots then pouring into the army, and that these tactical innovations somehow arose spontaneously on the battlefield as a result of these underlying sociological changes. Robert Jackson, a former Inspector-general of British military hospitals, writing in 1816, noted that prior to the Revolution, the French army used training and fighting methods similar to those in most other European armies, but after the Revolution these 'did not suit with the present condition of things', and it became necessary to utilize new methods that were 'more corresponding with the existing circumstances of the people.'[1] These views echoed those of an anonymous British military analyst just as Napoleon was beginning his ascent to prominence two decades earlier:

> The new military system was well adapted to the character of the nation, because every individual soldier was more left to his own understanding, and personal valour, than Prussian tactics admit ... The restless impetuosity, which submits to no law, was rendered more prominent in the character of the French, by the influence of the revolution. A system of tactics, which opened a wide field to the activity and personal valour of every individual, and demanded an active, rather than passive obedience, could not, therefore, but be highly pleasing to the nation at large, and produce important results.[2]

This explanation for the radical transformation of the French art of war, however, is at best partial, explaining the reaction of the French soldiers to these non-traditional methods only *after* they were in use, and not the reason why they were adopted in the first place.

No matter how attractive the new tactics were to individual soldiers once they were in use, it still had to have been necessary for the higher levels of the officer class and the senior members of the military establishment to first order or otherwise cause these tactics to be adopted. Regardless of the naive point of view common among popular histories, at no point was it ever a case of the men resorting to columns and skirmisher tactics on their own in spite of the wishes of their officers. At the Battle of Jemappes, for example, one of the earliest instances where the French infantry resorted to numerous columns as they closed towards the enemy, it is clear that these formations were not only approved by the officers but also were, in fact, ordered by the highest authority present, General Dumouriez, in his instructions prior to the battle.

THE REASONS FOR CHANGE

While the out-of-control events of Revolutionary France and changing social climate explain the enthusiasm with which the 'new' French methods of fighting were embraced, they do not account for the breakdown of the linear fighting methods nor the nature of warfare which was destined to replace it. By the opening of the French Revolutionary Wars, a deeper set of forces had already been at work for many years moulding the shape, direction and scope of the transformation of warfare that was to take place on the European battlefield. Engendered neither by changing social conditions nor the decline in the average capabilities of French fighting forces, this change was instead the inevitable product of a number of newly introduced practices, each in themselves small and not overly consequential. Their collective effect, nevertheless, went wildly beyond the expectations and designs of the authors of these individual innovations.

In order to understand the nature of these forces and how they led to the creation of an entirely new approach to warfare on the European battlefield, it is necessary to examine why linear tactics had come about in the first place. Only then can one appreciate why by the late eighteenth century linear methods of warfare were moribund and their replacement inevitable.

CHARACTERISTICS OF LINEAR WARFARE

The introduction of the flintlock musket and socket bayonet at the end of the seventeenth century, in effect forced a total re-evaluation of existing military doctrine and practices during the 1689–1710 period, and ultimately transformed European warfare on every level. The most important effect of the new weaponry was a transformation of the formations henceforth to be used on the battlefield. The deep, bulky formations soon disappeared. The discontinuation of the matchlock with its dangerous lit fuse allowed the files in a formation to be brought more closely together, producing a firmer, less amorphous formation. At the same time, the ability of the bayonet to defend against enemy cavalry allowed the number of ranks to be reduced from six to five and even three, thus resulting in thinner and wider formations. These changes in the infantry formations brought about

86

the most distinctive features of linear warfare. Henceforth, the opposing armies typically would face off against each other, drawn up in two or three long parallel lines. Each army tended to act as a single body whose parts moved and operated in the same general direction. The cavalry was forced to occupy either the flanks or be positioned as a reserve in the rear, and little mutual support between cavalry and infantry elements was possible.

The grand tactical properties of the linear system originated from the need to compensate for a single weakness of the newly adopted thin formations: the necessity to protect their vulnerable flanks. The bayonet made the pike largely redundant, and the latter weapon soon disappeared. Though overall this was a positive step, simplifying the organization of each formation and increasing its overall capability to fight off cavalry, it was not without some drawbacks. The thin formations with their reduced number of ranks were much more vulnerable on their flanks than the denser six- to ten-rank formations of the seventeenth century. Moreover, there were no longer pikemen available to be placed along two or three files on either flank. To protect the thin, highly vulnerable flanks, it became necessary either to position another formation on each flank of the battalion, or *appuy*, that is 'anchor' it, on some impassable terrain, such as a large river or a morass. Responding to this need to protect each battalion's flanks, the formations were placed in line side by side so that the characteristic lengthy lines were strung across the battlefield.

Once deployed in line anywhere remotely in the vicinity of the enemy, a battalion had to remain in line for the duration of the contest. These were the days before cadenced marching was widely known in western Europe, and officers were able to retain order during an advance only with the greatest difficulty. The lack of cadence precluded any sophisticated manoeuvres to go from column to line and vice versa. As a result, changing formation amidst the din and confusion of battle era was not as common as it would later become. These lengthy lines accounted for the relatively symmetrical application of force. They also explain the difficulty of moving large bodies of troops once the combat had begun in earnest and the lack of true concentrations of force that would be a dominant feature of the Napoleonic period which followed.

Forced to maintain a lengthy line of battalions, the army formed a 'single, unified body'[3] in the sense that it functioned as a *single entity* acting along a *single axis of operations*. Once the troops were deployed into their battle formations, the commander-in-chief could have his troops do nothing and await his opponent's advance, or he could order his own general assault. If his troops were to advance they would have to do so along the length of the line, or at the very least a major portion of it. Without taking special precautions, it was difficult in open terrain to order part of a line forward while holding another part back. The very nature of a line made this impractical. If, for example, two brigades along a line had advanced beyond supporting range of a portion of the line which remained stationary, their flanks which had previously run into the remainder of the line would now be exposed, while the line which remained behind now had a large gap in it. Under the worst conditions, the entire two brigades which had advanced could be rolled up in an instant by enemy cavalry, if the latter made an unexpected appearance. Talented commanders such as Marlborough and Frederick circumvented these difficulties and devised ways of fragmenting the line into manageable parts, so that each could be assigned a different grand tactical objective. However, this was only achieved by overcoming the *intrinsic limitations of the linear system*. The most usual method was to fragment a line so that individual groups of battalions in line were separated by natural terrain, such as woods or villages, or when in a large open area deploying the groups so that significant gaps were left between each.

In this linear period, the commander-in-chief found himself in a paradoxical position during the raging of the battle. Any orders given to units within a line had to apply to the entire line, or at least a substantial portion of it. However, once the line was engaged, it became extremely difficult to continue to command an extended line as a single body. Localized activity would fragment the line, breaking it up into a series of engagements each with a life of its own, enjoying varying degrees of success or failure. Firefights would sporadically break open up and down the line, immobilizing entire battalions as their men became tied down to the task of returning the fire directed toward them. As the opponents neared one another, charges would be ordered with varying results and friendly battalions could be found running to safety, holding their ground, or even over-zealously chasing bodies of the enemy they succeeded in pushing back. In the confusion and smoke entire battalions would remain motionless and unengaged, awaiting the outcome of the battle as it raged in front of them or on some other part of the battlefield. Some enterprising officers would lead individual regiments or brigades into the thick of the fray, but the entire system worked against doing this easily or effectively. It must be remembered that at this time, once anywhere near the enemy, battalions were forced to advance in line. It was difficult to issue these troops any meaningful orders, let alone have them executed, since their advance or retreat out of the line could create a weakness that could easily be exploited by the enemy.

THE CHANGE

To sum up, linear warfare arose out of the introduction of the five-, then four- and ultimately the three-rank line, and the resulting need to protect each battalion's flanks, coupled with the difficulty of manoeuvring easily into line and then back into column. As long as these limitations remained unaddressed, a commander's grand tactics were unavoidably restricted to the symmetrical and rather inflexible repertoire of options traditionally associated with linear warfare. However, once it became possible to maintain at least some of the troops in column during an engagement, new non-linear methods gradually became possible, which offered a much broader spectrum of grand tactical options to commanders. By the end of the 1700s, these developments were to have as great an impact on how warfare was conducted as those which had produced linear warfare in the first place.

All of these changes stemmed from two sets of unrelated developments. The first was the advent of new manoeuvres that made it possible to go quickly from column to line or line to column. The other was the Prussian infantry's almost accidental discovery of a way to gently decrease a column's vulnerability to enemy cavalry, even when taken by surprise. The first of these developments, the discovery by the Prussians between 1748–1756 of non-processional or 'perpendicular' methods of manoeuvring into line, occurred shortly after the Prussians adopted cadenced marching. No longer required laterally to traverse the ground along which it was to deploy, using these new manoeuvres a battalion could approach directly from the rear, march right up to where it was to form line and then immediately deploy to the front of the column. This not only sped up the deployment process, but more importantly eliminated a set of preconditions that had to be met before line could be formed. Previously, it had been necessary for all battalions that were to be part of the same line to follow each other in a lengthy column. This column would approach the intended battle line from the rear and then traverse the entire field from the left to the right. All the battalions in the same line deployed at the same time, and then only when the entire column was straddled along where the line was to be formed.

Frederick experimented with these new methods of deploying an army during the early stages of the Seven Years' War. However, given his insistence on maintaining the rigid command structure and his unwillingness to follow these new methods to their logical conclusion, these attempts did not prove successful. However, if these new methods were abandoned as a means of deploying an entire army, more modest uses were quickly found. Officers soon discovered these new manoeuvres offered a convenient means of circumventing broken terrain and other types of obstacles. Individual battalions could form line, return to column and redeploy back into line again, without regard to what their neighbour on either side was doing. Just as important, the reduced time required to go from column to line meant that columns could be maintained closer to the enemy than had been hitherto possible. Formerly, the commander would order his infantry to form line when still between 1000 and 2000 paces from the enemy. Now, after the introduction of the new manoeuvres, battalions could change formations up to approximately 400 to 500 paces from the enemy line, although prior to the Revolution this was rarely done. This meant columns could be employed even after the battle had begun in earnest.

During the same period, the Prussians stumbled on a second innovation which further increased the feasibility of using columns during the heat of the action, but whose true significance would not be appreciated for nearly forty years. During one of Frederick's numerous tactical experiments, it was discovered that a closed order column when threatened by enemy cavalry could be made almost impregnable by having the men in the third rank of each company in the column run to a side of the column and face outward. The result was a dense formation that became known in the English-speaking world as a 'closed square', because it lacked the space in the centre characteristic of the traditional 'hollow' square. Prior to the advent of closed squares, columns were particularly vulnerable to hostile cavalry. A commander could not afford to keep his infantry in columns if there was any chance of enemy cavalry in the general area, and the front and flanks were not protected by a continuous line of friendly infantry. When attacked suddenly by a mounted force, the infantry column either had to attempt to form line or manoeuvre into a hollow square, both tedious and time-consuming operations. To be guaranteed success, these manoeuvres had to begin when the enemy cavalry was still a kilometre or more distant. Since these conditions could rarely be ensured once the battle became general, in practice this meant that during the linear age columns were eschewed on the battlefield.

The ability to form closed squares would ultimately change all this. Infantry in closed columns could quickly form an effective defensive formation without either having to go through the elaborate manoeuvres required to form line or a traditional hollow square. The result was that now infantry could remain in closed column until the opposing cavalry had approached to several hundred paces. Obviously, this afforded the commander much greater tactical flexibility. This ability to maintain columns closer to the enemy, although certainly an important accomplishment for individual formations would, in turn, lead to a development that would greatly enhance an army's fighting capabilities as a whole. This, of course, was the advent of *columns of waiting* and *mixed order* during the Seven Years' War, as well as a rejuvenated interest in the *column of attack* with which the French had periodically experimented throughout the eighteenth century with little success.

The French were the first to discover the utility of *columns of waiting*. Almost an inadvertent development, it came about from a growing tendency of some French infantry commanders to maintain a part of their forces in column slightly to the rear, even during the height of the engagement. Since very few moderns will be acquainted with the notion of a *column of waiting*, this term requires a few words of explanation. During this period there were many ways of describing a column. Columns were described by their width: a column of companies, a column of divisions, a column of squadrons, and so on. Columns also could be described by their density; for example, a column at full interval (open column), a column at half interval (half open column), and a column at quarter interval (closed column). Occasionally, however, tacticians would classify a column according to the *function* it served. From this point of view, at the beginning of the linear period there had originally been three types of columns. *Columns of route* were employed to move large masses of infantry and cavalry across the countryside; *columns of manoeuvre* were used to move the troops around the battlefield; while *columns of attack* on rare occasions, such as at Spires (1703) and Denain (1712) were hurled directly at the enemy.[4] A *column of waiting* was simply a column used to hold troops in reserve until the time they were needed for action. In other words, the men in this type of column 'waited' until they were directed into the action.

Although the French during the Seven Years' War were hardly as proficient as the Prussians in their marching and manoeuvring capabilities, their adoption of cadence in the early 1750s, coupled with the ideological influence of Folard and his disciples, prompted the occasional tactical experiment even on the field of battle. Sufficiently comforted that their infantry columns could now quickly deploy into line if required by circumstances, on a few occasions they experimented with leaving some of the infantry in the second or third lines in column until they were needed. In orders issued before Minden (1 August 1759), Marshal Contades required one battalion of each brigade to remain in column while the others were to be formed in line. At Kloster Kamp (16 October 1760) the six battalions of the Normandie Brigade were initially kept in column, and it was only after marching through the front line that they finally deployed. The most extensive use of columns of waiting, however, occurred during the Battle of Bergen (13 April 1759). Here, all eight battalions in the second line remained in column.[5]

It was this new-found ability to remain in column closer to the enemy that eventually would make possible another new formation, one destined for much notoriety: the *mixed order*. As its name implies, this was a hybrid formation consisting of two 'pure' formation types: line and column. Part of a battalion remained in line while the remainder was deployed in column on its flanks and slightly to the rear. Mixed order had originated among the Prussians in the mid-eighteenth century as a means for circumnavigating patches of broken terrain. When a portion of a battalion's frontage was obstructed by something like a small pond or morass, the unobstructed part of the battalion continued to advance in line. That part directly behind the hindering terrain would immediately ploy into column while the remainder of the line continued to advance. As soon as the battalion had cleared the encumbering terrain, the troops in the column would deploy back into line. The line never came to a halt during these manoeuvres. However, in this form mixed order was only a temporary formation, the line remained the primary man-oeuvring and fighting formation. As long as the linear grand tactics were strictly adhered to, it couldn't be used for more powerful purposes.

THE 'IMPULSE' SYSTEM OF GRAND TACTICS

The full import of these innovations would not be realized until the French Revolutionary Wars, when events would quickly demonstrate that a strict adherence to linear tactics was no longer necessary. The ability to utilize columns and mixed order formations once an engagement began would ultimately spawn an entirely new grand tactical system which posterity would somewhat myopically closely associate with Napoleon and his triumphs. The nearly universal adoption of the new Prussian-style manoeuvres meant that it was inevitable that someone would eventually discover that it was no longer imperative to deploy all of one's infantry into line prior to the battle. The order to form line could be delayed until the enemy was well within sight and the commander had time to analyse his opponent's intentions; something he had previously been unable to do with anything like the same degree of ease or safety. Infantry could now be kept in closed columns well within a kilometre from the enemy, and in extreme cases could even be maintained as close as 400 or 500 paces before being ordered into line.

This, in turn, would quickly lead to the realization that not only was the line not the best 'waiting' formation, it was a barely adequate one at that! Lines took up a lot of space, only permitting a limited number of troops along a portion of the front. Although less vulner-able to artillery fire than dense columns, lines were otherwise more difficult to keep out of harm's way since they couldn't reasonably be expected to hide behind small obstacles. Several columns, on the other hand, could be safely tucked away behind the type of villages or small promontories frequently encountered on the European battlefield. These *columns of waiting* would eventually transform the very way French commanders, and later their counterparts in other European armies, would deploy their forces before and during the battle. No longer forced to deploy their infantry along two parallel lines with cavalry on either flank, commanders could keep the troops in the second and third 'lines' in rows of columns, an arrangement

Two rows of columns quickly changing their direction of march

that would become known as a 'column of battalions'. By the height of the Napoleonic Wars, French commanders, at least at the opening of the action, would deploy even the front line in these columns as they jockeyed for position and attempted to deceive the enemy as to their true intentions. An even more significant advantage of the column of waiting, however, was the increased flexibility it afforded on the grand tactical level once the action had begun. It was difficult to move a lengthy line straight forward under the best of circumstances. It required an extraordinary effort and more time than was usually available under battle conditions to have an extended line change its direction of march. True, the Prussians under Frederick the Great had devised manoeuvres such as redeploying a line perpendicularly to the right or left to accomplish just this; but these were complex manoeuvres which could barely be performed on the parade ground, let alone the battlefield.

The same number of battalions 'ployed' in column, however, could easily be moved diagonally or even perpendicularly to the left or to the right. The series of the battalions, let's say in a 'line of columns' would simply advance forward. Each closed column turning on a pivot point would then change its direction of march to the left or to the right, whatever was demanded by the situation, and the whole force would now have succeeded in altering its facing and march. During this manoeuvre, the attention and energies of the officers within each battalion could be devoted to events affecting that particular battalion, with much less concern to what was happening in the neighbouring units. In contrast, if a change of direction was attempted while these same battalions were deployed in a lengthy line, most of the officers' attention had to be devoted to ensuring that the battalion retained its proper position in the line relative to the other units. The repercussions of these new manoeuvres and methods of deployment were certainly not limited to the infantry arm; the way cavalry would be deployed and then used was equally affected. At the height of linear warfare, cavalry had been forced to operate initially upon the flanks; partially because of the space required by the long lines of infantry, but even more because interspersing cavalry along a line heightened the vulnerability of neighbouring infantry, once it became necessary to advance the cavalry out of alignment with the infantry.

Dense bodies of infantry, drawn up in closed columns, were not nearly as vulnerable to enemy cavalry as the flank battalions along a line. The potential vulnerability of the battalion's flanks was thus minimized. Now, if any cavalry parcelled among the infantry was forced to move forward, which was what it had to do if it were ever to enter the fray, the infantry, remaining in closed columns, were able to defend themselves against enemy cavalry. Columns of waiting not only offered greater flexibility of movement, they also afforded greater grand tactical flexibility. By providing increased security against enemy cavalry, they made it possible for cavalry to be distributed along the entire width of the battlefield, and thus opened the way for increased combined arm support. As long as large blocks of cavalry were placed on either flank, they were generally forced to enter the engagement at more or less the same time as the infantry. The infantry and cavalry actions were simultaneous but separate. Only after the enemy cavalry was defeated and driven from the field could the friendly cavalry attempt to assist its infantry counterpart in the centre of the field.

The ability to maintain infantry columns changed how cavalry could support the foot soldier. Interspersing cavalry between groups of infantry battalions in column or behind the infantry in general ensured that the cavalry tended to enter the fray in the secondary stages after the infantry had gone into action and created some weaknesses in the enemy formations. Combined arms support became possible, and cavalry could be more effectively used to achieve the commanders' objectives compared to the days when the reliance upon linear formations made it necessary for the cavalry to act as a completely independent force.

MORE EFFECTIVE USE OF RESERVES

Another intrinsic weakness of the linear system was that it was much more difficult to establish or utilize an effective reserve than in the so-called 'Napoleonic' grand tactical system destined to replace it. Forced to remain in line throughout the engagement, whatever force was positioned to the rear had to be spread out along a considerable frontage. Six thousand infantrymen in ten battalions, for example, would be stretched over almost a mile. A brilliant commander such as Marlborough managed to overcome these limitations and effectively use reserves. He simply positioned a number of lines one behind the other in the area considered to be of critical importance. Nevertheless, this represented a much less effective use of manpower than was possible later during the Napoleonic period. *Columns of waiting* permitted a far greater number of men to be concentrated into a relatively small area. A sizeable force maintained in these columns could be placed anywhere behind the line. Moreover, the commander was afforded much greater flexibility in their use. He was free to throw these battalions into the fray either individually or as a group, as circumstances required. This flexibility had been largely denied during the heyday of linear warfare when the reserve was invariably deployed in line.

MULTIPLE AXIS OF OPERATIONS

About the same time that Frederick the Great was overseeing the creation of an entirely new manoeuvre system (*c.* 1748), French authorities were introducing another innovation that eventually would have as far reaching an impact: the organization of the French field army into semi-permanent groupings called 'divisions'. The original purpose of this organizational change was simply to facilitate the speedy deployment of the army. During the Wars of Austrian Succession, the French army had demonstrated a marked inability to deploy quickly. It was hoped that by assigning a fixed number of regiments to a lieutenant-general as well as predetermining their position in the line, the deployment process would be speeded up.[6] The unintended effect, however, was to unconsciously create a permanent command relationship between the lieutenant-general and the constituent regiments in his division. It must be remembered that up until this time though there were lieutenant-generals and generals of cavalry who functioned as the next rank below the commander-in-chief, the officers of this rank in practice only carried out the commander-in-chief's orders and grand tactical designs. These senior officers were rarely free even to choose how these orders were to be implemented since the troops under their command were part of a more all-encompassing line and had to conform to the movements of the whole.

This tradition of dividing the army into divisions, instituted near the end of the War of Austrian Succession, never quite died out and re-emerged in France in 1780s and 1790s. The ordonnance of 17 March 1788, for example, mandated infantry and cavalry brigades to be composed of two regiments. This proved impractical and the forces tended to be organized into the twenty-one administrative divisions authorized by the same regulation. Proving to be quite practical, this system met the requirements imposed during wartime. In 1793, a 'division' consisted of twelve battalions, two squadrons and twenty-two cannons and was divided into two brigades.[7] The following year (1794) divisions typically contained three demi-brigades.[8] By the Napoleonic period, this 'divisional' system assumed even greater significance. By 1805, Napoleon continued this hierarchical organization of the French army through the introduction of the 'corps' which for movement and operational purposes during the campaign was a small army and capable of independent action. Although the divisional organization had not been introduced specifically to influence grand tactical practices once beyond the deployment stage, nevertheless, when coupled with the increased flexibility provided by the new manoeuvre systems and columns of waiting, it provided the death blow to the *single entity, single axis of operation* quality of grand tactics, so pervasive up until that point. On one hand, the commander-in-chief was freed from distracting minutiae. The specific details of how his orders were to be implemented were left largely to corps and divisional commanders, allowing the commander-in-chief to focus on the development of the grand tactical plans and the overall co-ordination of these various forces. At the same time, the division became a much more organic entity than a lieutenant-general's command of comparable size during the linear era. Subject to conforming to the overall grand tactical dictates imposed by the army's commander, the corps or divisional commander was usually free to employ his forces as he saw fit. The divisional commander decided where the artillery was placed, the extent of the skirmishers to mask the front, and how the infantry was deployed and when its individual elements would come into play.[8]

A similar increase in flexibility was also encountered at the army level. No longer forced to deploy along lengthy extended lines, the army ceased to function as an indivisible unit. It thus became easier to split up available forces so that each of the corps- or divisional-size forces could temporarily function independently while still working towards a common overall goal or plan. The battle ceased to be a single expansive action raging from one side of the battlefield to the other. Instead, at least during the initial phases, it became a number of separate actions fought by individual corps or even divisional-level forces. Each division, if ordered, could operate along a unique axis of operations. One part of the army, for example, could fight an action along the army's front while another either held off a threat to its flank or even its rear or, if on the offensive, worked its way around the enemy's position. Not only could each division or corps now orient itself independently of the remainder of the army, it no longer had to be physically connected to its neighbours. It became possible, at least occasionally, to allow significant intervals to appear between these forces, even during the heat of an engagement. When circumstances demanded, a division, now deployed in depth along several tiers, could easily defend itself on an exposed flank.

Not only could the available forces be fragmented spatially, they could now also be distributed over time, that is 'phased', in a manner hitherto impossible. In linear warfare, it had been extremely difficult to hurl a succession of forces against any given length of enemy frontage. True, in most cases there was a second line, and usually a reserve even behind that. But, in practice, it was difficult to advance these fresh forces through the first line, or if fortune had frowned upon these first efforts, through the stream of fugitives struggling to the rear.

Probably the greatest significance of this new highly flexible system was that it reduced the 'element of chance' and maximized the role of skill, both on a tactical and grand tactical level. As long as two opposing armies were forced to meet each other straight on, the day's result depended mostly on the troops' will to fight, or the series of fortuitous events that inevitably punctuated every battle. The skill of the officers was devoted to getting their men to fight up to or beyond their normal capabilities. There was little chance for ruses or stratagems designed to bring in irresistible force to bear at the critical place at the critical time. Although posterity tends to refer to this newer method of fighting as 'Napoleonic warfare' or 'Napoleonic tactics and grand tactics', this is misleading. The original terminology that was used, the 'French School' or the 'Perpendicular Order', is more appropriate. After all, this system is rooted in developments that occurred decades before the French Revolution and was never the product of any single individual. In this work, the system replacing classic linear warfare is termed 'impulse warfare', which refers, of course, to one of the most distinguishable characteristics of the new system: the replacement of extended lines along a single axis of operations by large force blocks or 'impulses' which could operate along multiple axes and be phased over time.

It was not so much that the political and social changes in Revolutionary France forged new behavioural attitudes which demanded new military methods, but that the Revolution effectively removed from power an élite whose world view had been at odds with the grand tactical systems struggling for acceptance from the 1720s onward. The attitudes and values underlying the new grand tactics were incompatible with the social and philosophical values of the higher nobility and monarchy who traditionally made up the upper echelons of the military establishment. As long as the traditional monarchy remained, the ideological system justifying its existence effectively prevented the new art of war from ever being applied to the battlefield in any meaningful fashion. The grand tactical systems put forward by Folard, de Saxe and their successors implied a delegation of responsibility and authority never tolerated in the classical linear system. Though the commander-in-chief remained as always the final arbiter of the objectives and the broadstroke actions to be taken, once the next layer of subordinate officers were briefed with his plan, they would be given a hitherto unprecedented amount of freedom to determine the details of how this would be implemented for the troops under their command. In marked contrast, the classical linear system mirrored the monarchist world view. All action flowed mechanically from the decisions and will of the supreme power at the top of the chain of command. Each subordinate down the chain of command had to act within strictly prescribed boundaries. The need to form lengthy continuous lines meant that each brigade commander's actions had to conform to the overall structure imposed by the commander-in-chief.

One of the clearest examples of the extent to which an ideological and/or social value system could influence the selection and employment of grand tactical systems on the battlefield occurred during the Seven Years' War period. Immediately prior to this war, Frederick, through a series of experiments, had devised the very same manoeuvre system that would later serve as the foundation of the so-called 'Napoleonic' grand tactics.[9] His discovery of perpendicular 'deployment' manoeuvres allowed columns to approach the enemy much more closely than hitherto possible.[10] For the first time, the use of mixed order formations when near the enemy also became feasible. However, the tactical implications of these new formations and manoeuvres were not lost upon Frederick. Even prior to the outbreak of hostilities in 1756, Frederick had planned to use an entirely new method of deploying his infantry forces before the start of every battle. The Prussian infantry would advance in several lengthy columns directly forward towards the centre of the intended line, and when it reached the appropriate position the battalions would fan out on either side and use the 'deploy' to manoeuvre into line.[11] This new deployment system and Frederick's other major grand tactical innovation, his synthesis of the march by lines and advance by echelon manoeuvres to produce his oblique attack, both show Frederick's undying reliance on the existing linear methods of fighting. Though both these developments were highly innovative, neither changed the way the battle was resolved in the final moments. The infantry ultimately formed long continuous lines, and in the final moments resolved the conflict in the traditional manner. Frederick could never have brought himself to espouse the radical transformation of warfare on the grand tactical level envisioned by progressive

French thinkers about the same time. In fact, he was unable to follow the results of his own tactical innovations to their logical conclusion.

This unwillingness to dabble in a new grand tactical system did not arise because Frederick thought these systems were not useful. Rather, this conservatism arose out of the recognition that the linear system best suited a political power structure endorsed by all of European aristocracy. In other words, ultimately linear warfare reflected his view of kingship and the role of each person in Prussian society. In this sense, the Prussian army and how it was to conduct itself on the battlefield was a microcosm of an enlightened monarchy. The common soldier was reduced to an automaton, and a minimum of authority was delegated to even top level officers. In its purest form, the linear system was based on an authoritarian command structure. The commander-in-chief retained control, and as little authority and initiative as possible was delegated to subordinate officers. On the field, the commander-in-chief not only would specify in detail what was to be achieved, but exactly how it was to be accomplished. Subordinate parts remained at all times part of the same overall structure and had to conform to the overall objectives, movements and structure.

The impulse system of grand tactics implied a different set of political relationships. The subordinate blocks making up the army functioned as semi-independent entities. Divisional and corps commanders would be allowed a hitherto unknown degree of initiative and authority, and unless hampered by specific instructions from the commander-in-chief, were free to devise how to carry out their assigned objectives, in other words to select the tactics to be used.

The French monarchy and aristocracy at the end of the *ancien régime*, though militarily less conservative than Frederick and his successors, nevertheless instinctively understood the political ramifications of Folard and his followers' recommendations. Although never articulated in these terms, it was this rather than purely military considerations that stopped French military authorities from adopting the grand tactical systems that had been so vociferously advocated by the *ordre profond* school as long as the French monarchy existed. These obstacles were removed with the French Revolution followed by the elimination of the aristocracy from government and army. The delegation of increased command authority to subordinate officers on the battlefield did not offend the political sensibilities of French Republicans the way it had their predecessors. Thus, rather than it being a case where political events created new values and sensibilities which in turn led to the development of new approaches to the military art, it was much more a case that these newly arising sentiments eliminated prejudices and barriers that prevented previously devised reforms from being employed.

CHAPTER 7

Revolutionary and Early Napoleonic Armies
(1792–1802)

1792–1795

UNTIL RECENTLY there have been few studies willing to take a detailed look at how warfare was conducted on the European battlefield during the French Revolutionary Wars. The great majority of military historical works that have focused on this era, such as Colonel Phipps' *The Armies of the First French Republic* or Arthur Chuquet's *Les guerres de la Révolution* have adopted mostly a strategic or operational perspective. As a result, our understanding of how these armies functioned is based on a few of the more prominent battles or actions such as the Battle of Jemappes or the cannonade at Valmy. Unfortunately, in turn, this has meant that the perception that the French Revolutionary armies fought *exclusively* in either column of attack or large swarms of skirmishers was allowed to remain undisturbed until recently.

Jean Colin, the great turn-of-the-century French military historian, was one of the first to challenge this view. In his *La tactique et la discipline dans les armées de la Révolution* Colin argued that the French *armée de la Moselle* most frequently actually relied on the traditional line formation during the first campaigns. Unfortunately Colin's analysis was almost exclusively restricted to the training reports written by the Comte de Schauenbourg, and was not representative of what happened in the field in the great majority of cases. Two recent works, John Lynn's *The Bayonets of the Republic* and Steven Ross' *From Flintlock to Rifle*, have thrown much needed light on this area and show clearly that a much wider spectrum of tactical practices was used by the French armies during the first campaigns than has previously been thought. These two authors have independently concluded that although the aggressive use of columns and skirmishers was indeed employed in a majority of cases between 1792 and 1796, the use of line, squares, and even relatively complex manoeuvres was also frequently found.

Since the publication of Folard and de Saxe's works, the debate between the advocates of the *ordre profond* and the *ordre mince* had raged among the officer corps. Those of the *ordre profond* school of thought argued that combat was best settled by cold steel delivered by massive columns of attack, while their opponents, the *ordre mince* school, argued that the traditional deployment and advances in line continued to be the most effective. There is evidence that this division of informed opinion continued well after the commencement of hostilities. General Charles François Dumouriez, a friend of the influential tactician Guibert and commander of the *armée du Nord* in late 1792 and early 1793, favoured a combination of line and column. In certain respects, Guibert represented a compromise between *ordre profond* and *order mince* pundits. Guibert reasoned that the column was the most suitable formation for manoeuvring around the battlefield while the line remained the best for engaging in fire combat. This afforded a significant departure from the way armies had once acted during the first phases of the battle. In the heyday of pure linear systems, hours were spent deploying into lengthy lines, which, once formed, offered no other option than moving straight forward. In Guibert's system, all preliminary movement could be done in columns thus speeding up the process.

Judging from the conduct of his troops at Jemappes it certainly appears that Dumouriez subscribed to this view. Forced to endure a galling cannonade, the French forces remained in line during the battle's first phase to minimize casualties. When the attack was finally ordered, the French battalions in the centre of the field were instructed to assume the divisional columns prescribed by the *Réglement du 1er août* ('division' here refers to a subsection of a battalion). The French generals had anticipated that the battalions would have to redeploy into line and this form of column was the most conducive to this end. As events turned out, this proved to be a wise decision.

The advance in columns slowed down as the attackers neared the enemy. Auguste Marquis de Dampierre, who commanded a portion of this advance, recalled:

> We marched in . . . column up to one-quarter of cannon range [about 200–225 paces]. Then, since we were losing men, Generals Dumouriez and Beuronville ordered me to deploy the columns . . . The movement was made like a peacetime manoeuvre . . . As soon as the eight battalions had finished deploying, I commanded them to march forward and to beat the charge.[1]

But such clock-like precision appears to have obtained only in a minority of cases. Most battalions in the assault found themselves unable to re-deploy into line under a severe fire. Leclaire, another high-level officer at Jemappes, reports that only three of his companies managed to regain line. A 'diabolical fire' from the Hungarian grenadiers in front of them forced many of the men in his command to seek refuge at the back of the columns.

The French forces temporarily stymied, the outcome of the battle hung in doubt. As many of the French troops started to stream to the rear, Dumouriez and his officers made every effort to rally their men and resume the offensive. Gradually their collective efforts paid off and they were able to stabilize the situation and stem the flow of fugitives from the field. None would be more successful than the Duc de Chartres. Rallying the men in the woods of Flénu, he formed a massive column that he dubbed the *bataillon de Mons*. Handing these men the first flag he could find and providing them with a single cannon, he ordered the column to attack the enemy's centre, which it did with complete success. The 5th and 17th Regiments (formerly Navarre and Auvergne, respectively) also in column followed its movements and the enemy was irreversibly defeated.[2] Dumouriez was certainly not the only French general officer during these early campaigns who believed that it was imperative that in the final moments of the advance the men should be brought back into the traditional line formations. General Alexis, Comte de Schauenbourg, was in command of the training camp for the *armée de la Moselle*. Both in the various instructions he penned and the exercises he ordered his charges to carry out, Schauenbourg emphasized the importance of linear formations during the rigours of combat.

But Dumouriez and Schauenbourg were in the minority. Most

officers realized that linear formations posed tremendous difficulties for their all too often ill-trained troops, and that not only were assaults in columnar formations in this respect easier to perform but also best exploited the mood of the raw but enthusiastic conscripts.

The annals of these early campaigns are filled with scores of examples of French columns on the offensive. One of the earliest is the attack near the Croix-aux-Bois on 14 September 1792. Leclaire recalls, 'I deployed five battalions in column . . . I directed the heads of the columns there, ordering the charge to be beaten and lowering our bayonets' (Lynn, *The Bayonets of the Republic*, p. 251). French columns were successful in the open field at Hondschoote, when they were used to take villages at Wattignes and Ypres. These columns were frequently assisted by large numbers of skirmishers, who would pester the enemy in front of them. The French assault of Fort Mulgrave (11 November 1793) consisted of columns of grenadiers supported by light infantry in skirmish order. Columns supported by large groups of skirmishers are found at the Battle of Hondschoote (8 September 1793), and the actions at Nottweiler and Bersheim (14 September and 2 December 1793, respectively).

It must not be thought that a battalion was forced to maintain a single formation during a battle, or that it only changed formation solely to facilitate manoeuvres. During the early campaigns we find many examples of a battalion or regiment fighting in column, only to disperse later as skirmishers, and then possibly reform and resume the attack in line or column. At Hondschoote, Jourdan's force began its assault in closed columns. As soon as it came under fire, many of the columns broke down into skirmishers. Nevertheless, the attack continued unabated. Though additional columns were sent in as reinforcements, many of these similarly dispersed into skirmishers. Fortunately, sufficient columns remained and these eventually were able to break through the enemy's entrenchments. An example of how a battalion could be forced to make a series of formation changes during the middle action occurred on 19 September 1793. As to be expected, the French assault consisted of a number of battalions in column of attack. However, one battalion faced with enemy small arms fire deployed into line to return the fire. The firefight over, it ployed back into column, only later to be forced back into line a second time. Another instance on 5 May 1794 is described by General Jean-Louis Dessaubaz, the commander of the attacking force: 'I deployed my left column in order of battle and en tirailleurs

... My column having rallied, I advanced part of it in mass and stopped the enemy.'[3] Both Ross and Lynn in their respective studies found many examples of French infantry fighting in line even during the opening campaigns. Lynn analysed 108 engagements in his work. He established that line was used in some form or other in forty-four of these combats. Out of the fifty-five examples of line found in these engagements, twenty-two were used defensively.[4] We find an example, as early as 22 March 1793, when a French infantry battalion was ordered to seize a hill from the enemy. The attack in closed column successful, the battalion then deployed in line to hold off a counter-attack. The Battle of Wattignes provides another example. Ballard's division, though initially successful, was unable to hold the Austrian field works and was forced to fall back. One French regiment was able to repulse the pursuing Austrians by deploying into line and delivering regular volley fire.[5]

ARTILLERY IN THE OFFENSIVE

Reluctant to rely on what amounted to an inexperienced infantry and an unreliable cavalry, during the early campaigns commanders sometimes were forced to place a disproportionate amount of the burden upon the artillery arm. Several notable engagements, such as the Combat of Spires and Battle of Valmy, were, in fact, decided almost exclusively by the French artillery arm. At Spires, a small enemy force deployed in front of the town and awaited the arrival of the three French columns that were converging upon that spot. The centre column was the first to appear. General Neuvinger, who commanded this column, deployed his force and ordered his artillery, of which there was an abundance, to come into action. The enemy attempted to resist and responded with their own lively fire. The superiority in French artillery soon decided the affair; the enemy force was soon forced to retire from the field and began an orderly withdrawal into Spires.[6]

French artillery played an equally decisive role at Valmy (20 September 1792), an important action which stopped the Prussian advance on Paris in its tracks and gave the struggling young Republic a brief respite to reconstitute its fledgling forces in the field. After a vociferous but largely ineffective Prussian cannonade, Karl-Wilhelm, Duke of Brunswick ordered the Prussian infantry forward. Bands playing, standard bearers calmly moving ahead of the formations to ensure that alignment was perfectly maintained, the infantry advanced with all the precision and composure of troops at review. It was at this point that General François Kellermann ordered the French infantry forward in three large columns, each of an entire battalion frontage. The two armies closed in upon one another. However, when the forces were still separated by 1200 metres the French artillery began to reply to the Prussians. After dismounting whatever artillery pieces were observable, the artillerymen then redirected their destruction upon the advancing Prussian infantry. Brunswick was soon forced to concede that his attack was doomed to failure and he recalled his troops. The French had won the day without their infantry being drawn into the action.[7]

THE COMBAT OF KIRRWEILER

All of the above examples were instances of French success on the battlefield. Not all confrontations ended as happily for the Revolutionary forces, however. The French Revolutionary War was, in fact, a sea of seemingly endless battles, combats and skirmishes, the great majority of which have been long forgotten by posterity. Frequently during this campaigning, the Allied forces also found themselves the victor. If the French forces enjoyed the advantages of *élan* and high morale associated with a sense of national purpose, and a momentary element of surprise provided by their new fighting techniques, the Allied forces were nevertheless both more professional and more experienced. The enthusiasm and zeal of the French volunteers could at times overcome their inexperience and lack of training and yield the much needed victories, such as Valmy and Jemappes. Almost as often, these did not weigh as heavily in the scale as the experience and discipline of the Allied armies.

The political turmoil arising in the wake of the French Revolution was soon to cast its own shadow on the French capacity to command. Promotions frequently became more a reflection of political allegiance than a recognition of proven military competence. Even general officers were appointed who had little experience at command and none at handling troops under battlefield conditions.

This incompetence in the highest of ranks sometimes led to disasters. In the Vendée, for example, a Republican general was foolish enough to lead his infantry column through hostile countryside without taking any of the usual precautions. No scouts, advanced guard, flankers or even skirmishers were detached to mask the column's movements or to probe for the enemy. The entire force remained in column and made its way along a narrow road lined on either side by thick hedges. The lower ranks of officers also appear to have been negligent and little effort was made to dress the ranks which became increasingly disordered as the column advanced along the road. Charrette, a Vendean rebel commander, managed completely to surprise the Republican troops. His forces first attacked the centre of the needlessly elongated column. Taken completely off guard and threatened with encirclement the men in both halves of the column broke and fled. The skirmish soon became a total rout.[8]

Unfortunately, the records of the myriad of battles, combats and affairs making up the Revolutionary Wars are quite sketchy, and where they exist almost always describe only portions of these engagements. One of few detailed accounts of an entire engagement is an account of the combat of Kirrweiler penned by Gneisenau in his biography of Marshal Blücher. The Combat of Kirrweiler serves as interesting contrast to Jemappes and Valmy. A relatively small affair, it was in many respects typical of many of the seemingly countless engagements that were almost a matter of course during these early campaigns. The fervour of the French volunteers frequently could make up for deficiencies and yield the much needed victories, such as Jemappes. Almost as often, it did not weigh as heavily in the scale of needed qualities as the experience and discipline of the Allied armies.

As several French columns advanced through the Pfalz countryside, they encountered a smaller Prussian force, which through the cunning of one of its colonels and the discipline of the Prussian troops was nevertheless able to defeat the larger force. The action began as the French column, about 6,000 strong, advanced towards Kirrweiler and Maikammer via Fenningen and Edighofen. The French force comprised two large cavalry formations accompanied by infantry and artillery. The Prussian forces facing the French, commanded by General Wolfrath, consisted of four battalions of infantry, two companies of jaegers, about ten artillery pieces, and the Black Hussar regiment commanded by Colonel von Blücher. One infantry battalion and the two jaeger companies were positioned on some heights in the vicinity of Kirrweiler. Another infantry battalion and the horse artillery were posted on slightly elevated ground on the road leading to Neustädt and Winzengen. A third Prussian force consisting of the remaining two infantry battalions and five artillery pieces occupied the ground between Duttweiler and Kirrweiler.

At first only encountering light opposition, the French were able to push through Kirrweiler without too much difficulty. Once through the town, French skirmishers broke away from the main columns and spread themselves in the cornfields on either side of the road. Sporadic firing appears to have broken out along the two lines as the flankers and skirmishers from the two sides began to engage in the corn fields. The French, enjoying both a superiority of force and support of their own horse artillery, continued their advance unabated, intending to position themselves between the town they had just taken and the Prussians in the fields beyond. Riding ahead of his regiment to survey the situation, Colonel von Blücher quickly concluded that, given the large superiority of French numbers, he and his comrades would be unable to rely on a standard defensive posture. Realizing that the French were not always sufficiently disciplined, he decided to attempt to outwit his opponents, and ordered the withdrawal of the mounted flankers who had been contesting French progress. At the same time, a portion of his Hussar regiment went through the motions of retiring, but in actual fact was only repositioned behind some heights slightly to the rear. The French fell for Blücher's trap and their skirmishers quickened their advance without taking any precautions such as being accompanied by nearby 'supports'. As the Prussian hussars waited silently in hiding, the main French column continued its advance unaware of the threat.

As the column neared, Blücher seized the opportunity and ordered his hussars to attack the flank of the French column at a point near the gates of Kirrweiler. The French skirmishers were taken by surprise and attempted to flee. They could not outrun their pursuers and were ridden down, killed or scattered. Moments before, the French artillery had unlimbered to cannonade General Wolfrath and his forces, so that when faced with this unexpected threat they were not able to fly quickly out of harm's way. Making the best of the situation, the artillerymen prepared to fire canister at the enemy cavalry. Unfortunately for the French, a Lieutenant von Armin managed to capture the guns before they were able to fire. The Prussian hussars rode on toward their main objective, the French column. These latter proved to be as unprepared as their skirmishers, and the column broke, its men attempting to regain the safety of the town. Many of the French soldiers were cut down. The men in the front of the column were more fortunate and made it to the town's gates. Unfortunately, their progress was unexpectedly checked by their own brothers in arms. The French troops in the town seeing their comrades' plight attempted to enter the field to render assistance. The bottleneck at the gate stopped both groups from achieving their designs. The hussars caught up at this point and all resistance in Kirrweiler quickly came to an end. Two artillery pieces were captured.

The other French column, still intact, beat a hasty retreat, and escaped unscathed. The French dragoon regiments, meanwhile, had maintained their position around Edesheim. Those Prussian hussars not consigned to conveying the French prisoners to the rear were ordered forward once again towards Fischlingen. Once there, Blücher espied the French cavalry in the countryside beyond and decided that they too might be approached without being noticed. For a second time that day, the Black Hussars managed to surprise a French force by taking advantage of the terrain to approach unnoticed. The French dragoons managed to form line in the last seconds, but, discomfited by the Prussian mounted skirmishers, they attempted to withdraw. Blücher had retained a portion of his hussars for just this contingency. As the French dragoons rashly wheeled into column, they were charged. In the middle of the manoeuvre they were unprepared to meet the onrush and were soon broken. They attempted to flee but many were cut down or taken prisoner. The French losses for the day in this area of the field totalled two hundred dragoons killed and one hundred made prisoners; elsewhere von Goltz's hussars were even more successful, killing and wounding 600 Frenchmen and taking another fifteen officers and 500 men prisoner.[9]

This battle is interesting because it provides a necessary counterweight to the proposition that the French forces, fuelled by patriotic fury, always managed to overcome their more experienced and more professional adversaries.

1796–1800

Given the voluminous experience afforded by the continuum of hostilities making up the French Revolutionary Wars, it can hardly be surprising that the always struggling, sometimes inept French military was finally able to transform itself into a truly professional military entity. As the immediate threat of foreign invasion gradually diminished, the French military authorities were able to turn increasing attention to discipline and training of the troops. Moreau, for example, was able to run his army close to traditional lines, and was even able to gain a begrudging respect from his enemies. A British officer would observe in 1802:

> In Germany, Moreau, drew nearer to the ancient method of warfare. Trained and instructed by Pichegru, one of the greatest captains in France, Moreau imitated his master, in giving more order and regularity to his plans. The military character of Moreau is different from that of the other French generals; there is less boldness and fire, but more talent, method, and science in it.[10]

This return to basic discipline and training was not limited just to Moreau. With the rigours of the 1797 campaign over, Bonaparte turned to the task of laying a solid foundation for his army. Officers were ordered to study the regulations. The troops were required to perform the prescribed platoon level drills in the morning and the battalion drills in the evening. Regimental exercises were conducted twice a week.[11]

These trends spilled over on to a grand tactical level, and from 1796 we find occasional examples of more sophisticated grand tactical operations on the battlefield. During the Battle of Biberach, fought in southern Baden between the French and Austrians under Archduke Charles in October 1796, we see the French army using combined arms techniques where the artillery, cavalry and infantry operated to support each other or to achieve one pre-ordained objective. About a month earlier a French force under Jourdan had been defeated at Würzburg, while a second French force led by General Jean Moreau was forced to retire through the Black Forest, closely pursued by an Austrian force commanded by the Archduke Charles.

Lieutenant-General Duhèsme, well known for his light infantry service, provides the following account of the battle. The Austrian force, though inferior in numbers, were positioned in a strong position on a round wooded hillock, and supported by Austrian artillery which with expert placement was able to dominate the plain separating the two armies. However, on a strategic level the French were abetted by a second force under the command of Desaix which was in the process of making its way around Lake Buchau which lay to the side of Biberach. General Saint-Cyr, who commanded the central French force directly in front of the Austrians' strong position, ordered his command forward. The two divisions of infantry participating in the assault were deployed 'in mass by battalions', that is, in closed order columns, possibly columns of attack. These were arranged *en échiquier* (in a checker board pattern). The light infantry was dispersed as tirailleurs along the front of the 'line' of battalions. The cavalry made up the rear and were prepared to pass through the intervals between the infantry battalions if the enemy infantry started to be pushed back by the French infantry. The French artillery, meanwhile, had been carefully but silently moved on to the various hillocks on and around the position occupied by the French force.

The assault began with the French artillery firing so furiously, according to Duhèsme, that the Austrian artillery had difficulty returning the fire. At the same time, the infantry moved quickly forward at the *pas de charge*. The light infantry kept pace and so intimidated the Austrian infantry that the latter began to withdraw without ordered volleys being given. A general pursuit now began. The retiring Austrians were closely followed by the light infantry but these were soon overtaken by the French cavalry which had been released to pursue the Austrian fugitives. The Austrian command attempted to put a stop to the pursuit by ordering a number of cavalry countercharges against the French light infantry still in the plain. The officers commanding the French light infantry were now sufficiently experienced to deal with such contingencies and simply ordered their skirmishers to retire on to platoons slightly to their rear, which had been maintained in closed order precisely for this purpose. These bodies slowly and in an orderly fashion made their way back to the infantry battalions in mass and the initiative of the pursuit was now left to the French cavalry which pushed the Austrians back to Biberach. In the meantime, the force under Desaix had itself reached Biberach and the retiring Austrians were taken in flank and 5,000 prisoners and twenty artillery pieces taken.[12]

Although the Battle of Biberach hardly ranks among the most decisive battles of the era, it nevertheless is worthy of close scrutiny by anyone attempting to piece together a picture of how the French army fought by the late Revolutionary Wars and for anyone chronicling the step-by-step evolution of 'Napoleonic' warfare. The initial disposition of the French forces and how they were used during this battle is highly informative, showing the degree of tactical sophistication that was starting to manifest itself. This was in stark contrast to the grand tactically impoverished volunteer armies of the early years of the Revolution. By looking at this battle and extracting the general principles that governed the positioning and use of the various arms during the conflict, we derive what is very nearly a model for many of the decisive battles of the true Napoleonic period, such as Austerlitz. The tirailleurs (skirmishers) precede the main infantry body to pester the enemy. These are supported by small local reserves which remain in a close order formation, a short distance to the rear. The main body of infantry is kept in dense formations further back still, and is followed, in turn, by the cavalry which is spread out along the width of the battlefield behind it. The regular infantry assumes these columns as much to allow the cavalry at the critical moment free passage to the front as to employ columns of attack.

This is one of the salient characteristics of the new system of warfare then starting to emerge: the hitherto unprecedented degree of combined arms cooperation. In classical linear warfare, cavalry and infantry were generally assigned different areas of the battlefield in which to fight. Almost invariably, the infantry was positioned in the centre and the cavalry was relegated to one or both flanks. It is true that during the thick of the fighting, cavalry might eventually find itself fighting amidst friendly infantry forces, but this was only after much manoeuvring and the defeat of the enemy cavalry. It was never a preconceived objective built into the deployment doctrine. In this new combined arms approach, the first phase of the assault was delivered by skirmishers and artillery. After the enemy was sufficiently softened up, the next thrust was delivered by the main body of the infantry, still in formation. Finally, as opportunities offered themselves, the cavalry poured through the gaps between the battalions of regular infantry, rushed to the front, either to deliver the *coup de grâce* of a weakened enemy, or pursue an already defeated enemy. On the other hand, if events went the other way and the French forces were stymied or even repulsed, the cavalry was in position to counter attack before the enemy could effectively pursue the French infantry.

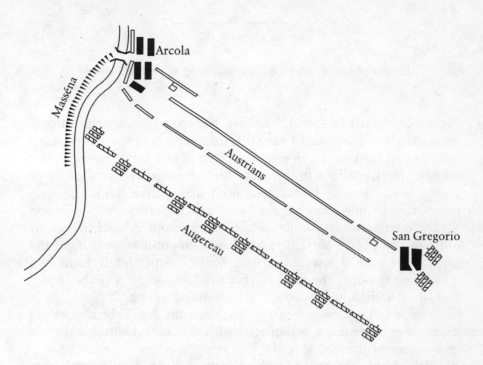

Augereau's division in mixed order at Arcola

Mixed Order

There appears to be an increased use of mixed order during the Italian campaigns under Bonaparte. During the third day of fighting at Arcola, for example, Augereau's division was drawn up in mixed order in front of the Austrian position between Arcola and San Grégorio. Small battalion-sized closed columns were positioned periodically along a single line. Typically, one or two battalions were deployed in line between a column on each flank.[13]

The use of mixed order may have been at least partially responsible for the French victory that day. The Austrians went on the offensive and attacked the French in front of them, and started to push back the

Variety of mixed order used at the crossing of the Tagliamento

French centre led by General Robert. Bonaparte, seeing the danger, immediately commanded General Cardane to take the 52nd Demi-brigade and turn on the victorious Austrians in flank.[14] It is not clear whether the battalions in this demi-brigade were in mixed order or completely in line. If French battalions making the flanking movement were in line, they would have had to perform a conversion (i.e., a quarter-wheel) while in line. On the other hand, if one or more of the 52nd's battalions were in open column, to achieve the same effect each tier would quarter-wheel independently forming a line facing towards the enemy. This would have been both simpler and quicker than any comparable movement in line.

Again, at the crossing of the Tagliamento (14 February 1796) many demi-brigades were deployed with the central battalion in line and a supporting battalion in half open column on each flank.[15] A thick skirmisher screen formed from a light demi-brigade was positioned in front of each infantry division. Each of these light demi-brigades was supported by a grenadier battalion on either flank in half open column. During the actual assault the demi-brigades in this mixed order formation moved forward in echelon, supported by some cavalry squadrons on either flank. The reserve cavalry was positioned a little to the rear on either flank of the advancing force.[16]

However, probably the most notable use of mixed order during this period occurred during the critical point of the Battle of Marengo, when General Desaix, attempting to thwart the advancing column of victorious Austrian infantry, deployed three French infantry demi-brigades in echelon refused towards the right. As discussed, the 9th *légère* in the front most echelon had only its central battalion in line, the 30th *de ligne* slightly behind had its two battalions in line, while the 59th *de ligne* was deployed exactly like the 9th *légère* in front.[17]

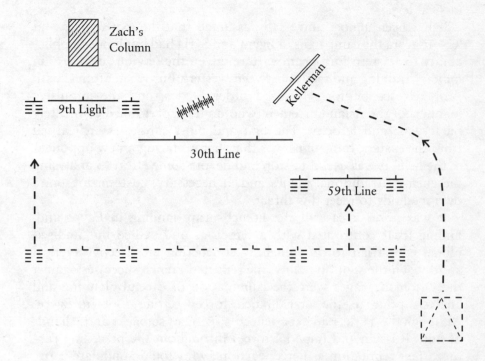

Desaix's use of mixed order at Marengo

Oriental Interlude

The French army's campaign in Egypt and Syria is usually viewed as an interesting but a relatively inconsequential sideshow compared to the real crucible of conflict in Europe. David Chandler, in his epic *The Campaigns of Napoleon*, has referred to this eastern venture as an 'Oriental Interlude'; a poetic but apt description, provided we accept this assessment of the fleeting importance of the eastern theatre of operations. Its seemingly most important lasting result was on a grand strategic level. The Far East remained inaccessible to the French, given continued British hegemony of the Mediterranean and both the North and South Atlantic. Nevertheless, it is possible that the real significance of these experiences in the Middle East was that they forced a change in the very manner that the French infantrymen would later meet their Austrian and Prussian opponents on a purely tactical level.

It has been almost universally assumed that the experiences and lessons from the campaigns in Egypt and Syria had but limited applicability to western European warfare, given the obvious disparity in military training and tactics between western European armies, with their reliance on formal closed order tactics, and the impulsive manners of the Asian horsemen, who on their part relied completely on fervour and ferocity. The first and most subtle lesson learned from the eastern campaigns was that, before facing a new opponent in the field, it was useful to stop and devote some effort to analysing the enemy's traditional tactics and, if necessary, customizing one's own methods to meet this threat.

It was never a case of the French army landing in Egypt and, finding itself confronted with a ferocious and skilled but undisciplined equestrian force, somehow concocting an effective tactical antidote on the spot. In reality, the repeated French successes against the Ottoman armies were the culmination of careful planning and analysis prior to the first French forces setting foot in Egypt. Although the Turks had experienced a string of setbacks at the hands of both Russian and Imperial forces throughout the preceding century, their reputation as fierce warriors, who could annihilate entire battalions in a moment if given the slightest opportunity, remained essentially untarnished. French senior officers were aware of the potential peril afforded especially by the Turkish and Mameluke horsemen, and took steps to counter this threat. Even by 1798, the French had taken notice of the large rectangular squares that had been used with success by the Prince of Cobourg, General Suvarov and the Comte de Clerfayte, as well as other Austrian and Russian generals who had fought against a Turkish horde.

The French Revolutionary armies had occasionally used small battalion-sized closed columns. These had a fair chance of survival when assaulted by European cavalry. However, Turkish and Mameluke horsemen, in addition to being better individual horsemen, were much more ferocious than their European counterpart. Had the French deployed their infantry in a large number of these small closed columns, it would have been inevitable that at least a few would have been broken. The sight of even several battalions being slaughtered down to the last man would have been demoralizing to the helpless remainder.

The solution that was settled upon was to adopt the large-sized squares already tried and tested by the Austrians and Russians in their own wars against the Turks. These squares consisted of a continuous line of men, six ranks deep, made to face in all four directions. At the Battle of Chebr-Keis (or Chebreisse) on 13 July 1798 (25 messidor an VI) Bonaparte deployed his infantry into four or five large divisional squares. These were actually large rectangular formations, and were placed in echelon with respect to one another. The small cavalry force that was present, and the equipage along with any noncombatants, was placed in the hollow space in the centre of each square. The interval between each battalion in the square was protected by either artillery[18] or carabiniers taken from the regiment.[19] When Bonaparte confronted Mourad-Bey's main force eight days later at the Battle of the Pyramids (Battle of Embabe; 21 July 1798), the army was deployed into similar formations.[20] At the Battle of Sedyman, a subsequent engagement involving a smaller French force, Desaix's division utilized smaller battalion-sized squares. Reliance upon these smaller square formations was probably just as much a reflection of increasing French confidence and a corresponding decrease in their fear of the Mameluke and Turkish horseman, as it was the result of less available infantrymen.

The results in all these confrontations were virtually identical. The Ottoman forces were driven off with sizeable casualties with relatively few losses to the French. Probably Desaix's struggle with Mourad-Bey's forces at Sedyman is the most illustrative in this regard. Desaix's division was pitted against five to six thousand cavalry plus an infantry garrison tending the entrenchments of Sedyman. Here, Desaix eschewed the larger divisional-sized square and ordered his infantry into battalion squares. His *éclaireurs*, that is, scouts, were forced into smaller 200-man squares. Once again, the French suffered relatively minor casualties while inflicting a major defeat on their enemy.[21] (See Chapter 1, pp. 17–20.)

These highly successful experiences against the Turks, Mamelukes and Arabs were not completely 'neutral' events, that were discarded or forgotten the instant the troops returned to their native France. Like the sundry Mameluke and other Asiatic corps that were later integrated into the French establishment upon return to French soil, vestiges of these eastern battles would remain in the collective French psyche, subtly transforming future conflict on the European battle-field. Writing in the 1820s when there was a general post mortem among the French military, General Foy would observe that these squares used in Egypt would become a 'fundamental formation' used when needed in later campaigns.[22] The French infantry's use of a series of large multi-regiment squares specifically designed to meet the threat posed by the Turkish and Mameluke horsemen, had proved to be a wise and entirely successful precaution. However, a more enduring lesson, one with near universal application, was not lost upon the French military planners. This was the need to cus-tomize tactics to meet those of the enemy in an upcoming campaign. As we will see, similar considerations led in 1805 to the creation of a more sophisticated form of the mixed order formation when the French were faced with the prospect of facing Russian Cossacks. The next year they adopted the 'squares oblique to the line of battle', a formation developed in 1801 when opposed by the highly regarded Prussian cavalry in 1806.

At the heart of these innovations was a transformation among the French military of some of the most basic attitudes regarding battle-field warfare. The French, long regarded as the most impetuous of all European armies, had faced and conquered an adversary whose ferocity and daring was on an even higher order of magnitude. They succeeded in doing this by reversing what had lately become their almost inevitable role. Rather than assuming the offence from the very beginning, the French in Egypt systematically assumed the best position and set of formations available, waited until the enemy assault eventually played itself out, and then once the enemy's strength was depleted finally assumed the offence, crushed the enemy and thus secured victory. This is not to say or even imply that the French penchant for aggressive first assaults was completely dis-placed. It was not. However, this new philosophy was an important recurring theme which would help mould the French army's approach at Austerlitz, and serve as the cornerstone of the new-found French stoicism at Marengo, Jena and Auerstädt.

One of the immediate consequences of these attitudes was a newly reawakened willingness to experiment with 'waiting' formations. A 'waiting formation' is any formation whose function is purely to hold a body of men in a given position as a reserve until events would warrant these to be thrown into the fray. The French first started to explore the uses of waiting formations to a limited degree during the Seven Years' War; however, these invariably were either columns of waiting or mixed order.

It must be remembered that many writers throughout the eighteenth century had characterized the French army as dynamic and aggressive in the first assault, but quickly demoralized once it had suffered the first setback. Marengo, more than any other battle, shows the French army's newly acquired capability of putting in a second, third, fourth and even fifth effort, despite suffering a series of setbacks in succession. Until the very last moments of the battle, the French army was placed almost exclusively on the defensive. Faced with initially overpowering odds, though forced to retire a number of times, they nevertheless tenaciously held on, forcing the Austrians into a long, gruelling affair. Of course, late in the afternoon the French were able to capitalize on Austrian carelessness and the arrival of fresh reinforcements, and win the day. Future events would show that the French army was capable of the same stubbornness and elasticity at Austerlitz and Auerstädt, where in each case the enemy had assumed the first offence.

The willingness to assume a defensive posture, if only briefly for the first phase of the battle, presupposed two sets of newly acquired abilities that had been beyond the grasp of most in the French army during the Revolutionary period. The first was a demonstrable increase in the average discipline exhibited by the troops of the line. It takes considerably more discipline to stand and await a cavalry charge than to advance precipitously during the first stages of an assault or to stand off at a distance and fire wildly. On a tactical level, this increase in discipline manifested itself, in turn, in such things as the willingness to use controlled volley fire in defensive situations. Of even greater importance, officers began to be sufficiently confident in their men to order them into larger, more complex formations and to be able reasonably to expect them to manoeuvre into other formations under battle conditions, if needed. We see the largest of these formations during the Egyptian Campaign, such as the divisional-sized squares at the Battle of the Pyramids (21 July 1798) and the combat at Chebr-Keis (13 July 1798). During the linear era a square was considered a formation of last resort. Infantry only assumed a square when it was forced to by opposing cavalry. In this sense, the act of adopting the square was in effect an admission of the temporary superiority of enemy forces in the area. As soon as the imbalance in power had been rectified, the friendly infantry had to be manoeuvred out of the square and back into line, before any other objectives could be pursued, and this was necessarily a time-consuming process. Thus during this earlier period, to form a square was to place one's grand tactical plans into abeyance and assume a completely passive position.

One of the powerful concepts that emerged from the eastern campaigns was the idea of forming a series of infantry squares more or less at the same time, positioned so as to provide mutual support for one another. The squares were so formed that they were no longer passive nor forced to be purely reactive to the opponent's movements. There were two reasons. Firstly, the skilful placement of the large squares relative to one another allowed a damaging cross fire by both small arms and artillery. Just as importantly, the infantry in the large squares could be thrown back on the offensive much more quickly than in the days when combat took place along lengthy lines. Now, the battalions in a large divisional square could quickly ploy into column and the division was ready to advance or manoeuvre. This required only a fraction of the time that it took to place the same number of troops along two parallel lines. Thus, in the eyes of the French military, the idea of placing the entire army in a number of infantry squares was no longer viewed as a type of unavoidable temporary capitulation to the enemy's actions and capabilities, but as a type of large waiting formation that would wear out any enemy foolish enough to throw itself against these bulwarks.

Obviously, it was certainly not a case of simply transporting a tactical system tailored to meet and defeat the Asiatic horsemen into a universe peopled by Austrian, Prussian, British and Russian adversaries. These large and relatively clumsy formations would not have been feasible against a European army equipped with well-served artillery. The six-rank depth of each side would result in a large number of casualties. The enemy would simply stand off and systematically begin to destroy each square until enough damage had been inflicted to ensure the success of the very first cavalry assault. The Turks and Mamelukes, however, not only possessed much less artillery than their European counterparts; of even greater importance, they lacked competent artillerymen.

The Egyptian campaign and then the events on the French right at Marengo had demonstrated the utility of being able to deploy all of the battalions along a line into battalion squares when faced with vastly superior numbers of enemy cavalry. However, a potentially

Final position

Initial position

The *carré oblique* (Oblique Square); g – grenadiers; v – *voltigeurs*

significant problem arose if all these battalions simply formed square using the methods prescribed by the 1791 infantry regulations. All of the squares thus formed, by definition, were deployed along the same axis. This meant that the left and right sides of each square were directly facing the neighbouring square on that side. Unfortunately, this also meant that, whenever they delivered fire this other square was in harm's way, while they, in turn, would be on the receiving end of fire from the other square.

In the years immediately following Marengo, the 33rd *demi-brigade de ligne* enjoyed the reputation of being probably the most proficient at performing the officially sanctioned manoeuvres over any other in the French army. Stationed as a garrison unit in Paris, it spent its time not only perfecting all of the manoeuvres prescribed by the 1791 regulations but also experimenting with innovative procedures as well. This was somewhat atypical, since almost all of the other demi-brigades relied almost exclusively on the prescribed manoeuvres.[23] In 1801, the 33rd experimented with a new method of forming square: the *carré oblique à la ligne de bataille* (square oblique to the line of battle). This should not be confused with the Prussian Oblong square of the Seven Years' War period which was nothing more than a rectangular regimental square. Some clever fellow soon realized the easiest and most effective solution was simply to rotate all the squares forty-five degrees. Then, each of the sides of the squares no longer faced its neighbour, but looked out into the plain. When firing straight ahead there was no longer any chance of 'friendly fire', to use a modern term for an age-old problem.

CHAPTER 8

The Zenith of French Practices (1805–1807)

THE WORKINGS OF THE HUMAN MIND, like water cascading down a mountainside, tend to seek the path of least resistance. When it comes to the task of intellectually creating order out of chaos, there has been, and always will be, an irresistible urge to reduce the complex, multi-tiered fabric of reality into at most two or three readily understandable 'high concepts'.[1] Military history is no different from all other intellectual activity in this regard. So, not surprisingly, there has always been a temptation to try to distil the wealth of principles and techniques that made up the Napoleonic 'Art of War' into a few easily digestible sentences. Even some highly talented military historians have succumbed to this temptation and, for example, have been content to attribute the differences between British and French infantry fighting techniques and performance simply to the differences between the intrinsic characteristics of massed columns versus line. This is a tremendous over simplification, which, though suggested by a cursory look at the Peninsular War, is applicable but to a narrow spectrum of the entire range of tactical phenomena encountered during the entirety of the Napoleonic Wars.

The notion that the French army fought exclusively in closed columns is so far removed from the events that occurred on the battlefield during the 1805, 1806 and 1807 campaigns one wonders how much of an effort, if any, did those subscribing to this 'column only' theory of French grand tactics make to understand the French army's performance during these, the most notable of Napoleon's campaigns! When forced into battle, the French armies repeatedly exhibited a much greater flexibility on both the tactical and grand tactical levels than that acknowledged by such simplistic representations.

The destruction of the Allied armies in succession at Austerlitz (1805), Jena and Auerstädt (both 1806) represents the high water mark of French capabilities and accomplishments during the entire Napoleonic period. Rather than simply the product of Napoleon's personal genius, these seemingly 'easy' victories were just as much the result of the new French method of combat, at that point just reaching its zenith after about thirteen years of sporadic development. Much has been written about how Napoleon was able to deceive the Allies about his true intentions prior to the battle of Austerlitz and how by hiding much of his army behind the Zuran Hill he was able to lure the Austrian and Russian forces into a trap in the Goldbach valley. However, when we look at the details of this battle and the other major actions highlighting the 1805 and 1806 campaigns, the superiority of French grand tactical capabilities during the period becomes evident. True, Napoleon's capabilities as commander-in-chief were vastly superior to those of any of those he opposed at this point, but it is equally true that the instrument at his disposal, the French army, was also superior to those available to Allied commanders during these campaigns.

The theoretical basis for the new French methods, that is, the impulse system of warfare, had been laid by Folard and de Saxe well before the Seven Years' War. Though the French Revolutionary armies made the first stumbling efforts to put many of these precepts into practice on a large scale soon after the commencement of hostilities, it required a number of campaigns before even the more talented French commanders were able to employ consistently its many but disparate elements with sufficient command as to render distinct advantages over those continuing to rely on traditional methods. The culmination of this evolutionary process came in 1805. It was during this campaign against the Austrians and Russians and then again the next year against the Prussians that we see the new grand tactical system employed at its full potential. Probably the most accurate index of just how much the impulse system had totally eclipsed the once traditional linear methods of the French army is the degree to which the army ceased to act as a single unified body on the battlefield. Broken down into a number of component units, each, if necessary, capable of acting upon its own axis of operations, all of these blocks nevertheless were effectively orchestrated to accomplish a common overall plan.

The Battle of Austerlitz provides an excellent illustration of the use of multiple axes of operations, and its efficacy. Soult's corps on the French right flank was given two objectives: to hold the southern portion of battlefield, the area between Tellnitz and Sokolnitz, and simultaneously to advance up to the Pratzen Heights and attack the Allied columns in the flank and the rear. This corps thus operated along two separate axes: the southern facing towards three o'clock, and Saint-Hilaire's and Vandamme's divisions moving roughly in a five o'clock direction. Meanwhile, Lannes' corps, Murat's cavalry, Bernadotte's corps and the guards behind them operated towards the east, that is, towards three o'clock. Thus, not only did these groups operate independently of their immediate neighbours, but most of these moved and operated along a different axis of operation. True, as the battle unfolded the Austrians and Russians were forced to follow suit, but this was an action dictated by circumstances and not an intentional part of the Allies' mode of grand tactics.

The success of these operations is usually attributed to the genius of Napoleon's battle plan, seen as some abstract idea that was somehow purely the brainchild of that great French commander. In other words, once the elements of the plan had been thought out and communicated to the subordinate commands, given the intrinsic virtues of the plan, success was virtually guaranteed. Rarely, if ever, is the French army accredited for its ability to carry out this very sophisticated series of operations, which it must be pointed out was a capability which far surpassed that of any of its opponents at that point. There are other yardsticks which allow us to gauge just how much the impulse system had matured, from the first tentative steps taken in 1792 until Napoleon's middle campaigns. For example, another very important feature of the impulse system was its increased capacity to support combined arms operations: in other words, more effective support of infantry by cavalry and artillery, etc.

Once freed from the strict constraints intrinsic to the linear system, the French cavalry arm was no longer forced to fight segregated actions against its enemy counterpart. Parcelled out behind individual bodies of friendly infantry, it was now in position to provide efficacious and timely combined arms support. Interspersed along the entire length of the fighting line initially sheltered behind less ephemeral infantry formations, it was in position to wait until circumstances provided an opportunity to inflict a grievous wound on the enemy. If unsuccessful and repulsed, the proximity of these friendly infantry formations provided the needed succour and allowed the cavalry to rally quickly and return to the action.

Once again, Austerlitz provides revealing examples of these capabilities.

Fate was to pit Bagration's command against Lannes' V Corps which Napoleon had expected to be able to circle to the rear of the Allied army's right flank unopposed. Observing the danger in the northern quarter of the field, Liechtenstein, who had originally been ordered to move to the south west into the Goldbach valley, directed his cavalry back across the Pratzen Heights. Soon 4,000 Russian horsemen began their assault on Lannes' advancing corps. These numbers, however, were quickly repulsed by canister combined with small arms fire delivered by both French infantry and horse.

After much effort, Generals Uvarov and Essen were able to restore order among the shaken Russian cavalry. Unfortunately, before the Russians were able to rally completely, the Grand Duke Constantine's Uhlan Regiment became overzealous and charged the French light cavalry in front of them. Disordered, the French light cavalry quickly retired through the intervals between the French infantry formations. Either to pursue the fleeing French cavalry or to attempt to ride down the infantry behind them, the Uhlans continued to advance. As they charged forward, Caffarelli's division on their right and Suchet's on their left formed line, and a rolling fire erupted when the Russian cavalry had advanced to close range. The Uhlans rode the length of the two divisions. The resulting cross-fire greatly disordered the Russian horsemen, who after suffering over 400 casualties were forced to retire.[2] The interspersal of cavalry and infantry elements meant that sizeable bodies of French infantry were always within supporting range of the cavalry. The Uhlans, though initially victorious, came face to face with determined infantry upon whom they broke and were pushed back.

ARTICULATED NATURE OF DIVISIONS

Probably the greatest advantage conferred by the impulse system, the so-called 'French school', was not how it provided a more powerful and flexible tool for the commander-in-chief; rather, it was the way it altered the way divisional-sized units were able to conduct themselves in the face of the enemy, especially during the crises of a hard fought combat. By the beginning of the War of the Third Coalition, a French division was much more 'articulate' than a similarly sized force in any of the armies it faced. Each of its units were able to carry out individuated tasks, so that the whole could perform complex series of operations. This factor more than any other allowed French mid-sized formations to fight more effectively than opponents still encumbered with the traditional linear methods and accounts for much of the French success over their Austrian and Prussian foes.

In classical linear warfare even mid-sized formations tended to be surprisingly *unarticulated*, that is, all of its component elements were forced to act as a single block. The regiments and brigades making up a lieutenant-general's command during the Seven Years' War, roughly comparable in size to a French division, rarely, if ever, functioned individually during a set piece battle. In all but a few chance occasions, the parts continuously conformed to the movement and actions of the whole. As long as an army espoused *purely* linear methods, this monolithic quality was unavoidable. Once deployed, a force, regardless of its size, tended to remain in line for the duration of the contest. Its battalions only begrudgingly reverted to column when this was the only practical means of circumventing some obstacle, and then only for the shortest time possible. The ineluctable result of the fragile formations then in use, there was no alternative. As a result, grand tactical assignments tended to be given to the overall force, and its component parts carried out these objectives as a unit. However, once columns acquired the ability to deploy much closer to the enemy and to repel any unexpected cavalry assault, the relationship between the component unit within a command and the overall force was profoundly and inexorably altered.

The same forces that allowed for a French army to operate along multiple axes of operations, employ more sophisticated combined arms operations, the effective use of reserves, etc. were just as dramatically felt at the corps, divisional and even brigade level of organization. In the new French system it was quickly recognized that in order to utilize a division's full fighting potential, its component parts had to respond individually to battlefield exigencies as they arose. This is not to say that these units were acting on their own accord – most assuredly not! It meant that the divisional or corps commander, however, could assign a battalion, regiment or brigade a separate task, that is, to do something different from what its neighbour was doing. No longer forced constantly to maintain a single division-sized formation, the component battalions, regiments and brigades more often than not mutated into a wide assortment of different configurations. During a full-scale engagement, a brigade, for example, might start off in several columns, deploy a part of its force into line during an engagement, and then form several squares when challenged by enemy cavalry. The threat over, the brigade might ploy back into the original columns to resume its advance.

The ability for units to act *differentially*, in turn, meant that at any given time the division was in all likelihood itself in a hybrid formation, with its component units in an assortment of different types of formations, in marked contrast to the symmetrical stance previously required by linear grand tactics. In the 1805–1806 campaigns, it would not have been unusual, for example, to find a French infantry division of four regiments (let's say twelve battalions), with four battalions attacking a position in column supported by skirmishers thrown out of a fifth battalion, while another regiment, let's say three battalions, had deployed in line to support an open flank. All the while, the remaining three battalions might be held in reserve in columns of waiting. This ability for individual units to act either in unison with or independently of its parent division meant that the divisional commander was afforded both greater tactical and grand tactical flexibility. When on the defensive, the ability to divide the command into subgroups, each reacting to a different local threat, afforded many more tactical options. The advantages were probably even greater when the division was ordered on the offensive! This ability to assign individual goals to component elements within a division had a number of benefits. It facilitated both combined arms operations and multi-tiered concentrations of force. As we will see, it also, albeit inadvertently, confused the enemy who was used to both operating within and conceptualizing simpler troop configurations. So many permutations were available that it became much more difficult, sometimes impossible, for the enemy to predict what the divisional, corps or army commander would do.

Even a cursory examination of the battles during the 1805 and 1806 campaigns affords many examples of how French divisional and corps commanders articulated the elements within their command. We have already seen how Soult's corps at Austerlitz pursued

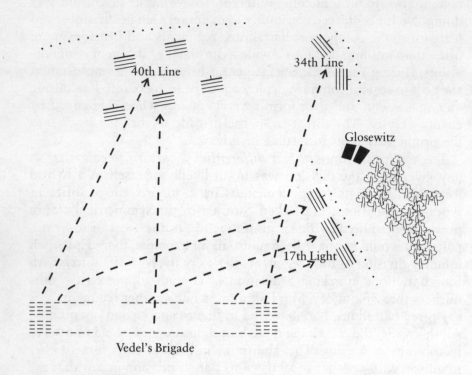

Suchet's division using multiple *axes of operations* at Jena

two grand tactical goals from the very outset of the French offensive; part was to advance up the Pratzen Heights, the other to protect the French right in the south.

At Jena, Napoleon's battle orders required Suchet's division to execute a similar two-pronged orientation. Initially, deployed along two lines with columns positioned 'interline' on either flank, Videl's brigade ployed into columns and advanced straight ahead. The 34th regiment *de ligne* in column on the right advanced with Videl's brigade and then once clear of the village of Closewitz veered to the right to protect that flank. Meanwhile, the 17th *légère* ployed into column, marched across the division's front and attacked Closewitz Woods while its élite battalion threw itself at the village. Thus, almost each regiment was assigned not only a different tactical objective, but each had to fight as a separate unit, often physically separated from their nearest neighbours, and sometimes even facing a different direction.

The same type of observations apply to Gudin's and Friant's divisions at Auerstädt. As General Friant's command advanced to support Gudin's beleaguered division, the 111th Regiment, directed to fall in beside Gudin's right, was battered by a Prussian battery. The second battalion of the 108th was immediately ordered to capture the battery which it did in short order. General Kister's brigade, the 48th and 33rd Regiments, moved towards the right to swing past Spielberg, Zecknar and Benndorf in order to threaten the Prussian flank in that area. Pestered by an annoying group of Prussian skirmishers, Friant ordered four voltigeur companies into action as a countermeasure. During the action, the division's artillery was broken into three demi-batteries. These advanced from one advantageous position to the next as the division gradually beat back their opponents. The 33rd was ordered to deploy and face the enemy in line, which it did successfully, then the 108th was ordered to take the village of Poppel with the bayonet, which it also succeeded in doing. Meanwhile, a portion of the 48th fought as skirmishers while the majority of the regiment remained in closed column as support. Finally, when the Prussians were finally thrown back in disorder the 48th, 108th and 111th were ordered to attack the woods to the rear of Eckartsberg and two Prussian batteries respectively. Although in seeking to portray this action in the broadest strokes we could simply represent the division as endeavouring to conduct one simple action – overpower the enemy in front of it – in reality many of the battalions and regiments once again were given unique tasks. As important, it is clear from Friant's report to Davout on 16 October that this general considered his command as a collection of different tools which he was willing to use – and in the heat of the battle *did* use – differentially.

VARIETY OF FIGHTING FORMATIONS

Continued Development of Mixed Order Formations

The period of relative peace between 1801 and 1805, and the opportunity to digest the lessons of the previous nine years of continual fighting, was to effect a significant change in the way the French conducted themselves on the battlefield. Nowhere was this change more noticeable than in the transformation of the concept of *mixed order*. Up to this point, mixed order formations usually applied to individual demi-brigades, and occasionally to an entire brigade. Typically, a mixed order formation had consisted of the middle battalion in line with a battalion in column on either flank. It is not clear exactly at what precise point French military thinkers began to experiment with much larger, divisional-sized mixed order formations. However, it is clear that by 26 November 1805 Napoleon attempted to prescribe this type of formation for use among his marshals.

French infantry divisions of this period often contained two brigades, that is, four or five regiments plus divisional artillery. In a letter to Marshals Soult and Bernadotte, Napoleon ordered that both battalions in the first regiment in each brigade be deployed into line. The divisional artillery was to be placed on either flank of this line as well as in the intervals separating each battalion. The second regiment in each brigade was to be maintained in closed columns by division, i.e. two platoons wide, directly behind each flank of the brigade's first regiment in closed column by division. Some divisions contained a fifth regiment. In these cases, this regiment was positioned in two columns by division, 100 paces behind the second regiment in each of the two brigades.[3] In all cases, however, a cavalry squadron or division was placed behind each infantry brigade.

This larger version of mixed order differed from its predecessor in several important ways. The formation was able to bring a much greater amount of firepower to bear. The line portion of the formation was now four battalions wide, instead of only one, thus permitting the division to bring a much greater amount of small arms fire at any one time. More importantly, the formation was now supported by the divisional artillery carefully placed along the line. The new configuration also increased the formation's defensive capabilities. The presence of one or two tiers of infantry columns in the rear increased its ability to defend against enemy cavalry attempting to attack its flank or rear. This represented a marked improvement over the older demi-brigade-sized mixed order formations with but a battalion in closed order on either flank. These larger varieties of mixed order allowed one, or even two tiers of entire regiments to be set in motion once the enemy's actions were detected. If needed, regimental-sized lines could be formed *en potence*, i.e. facing either

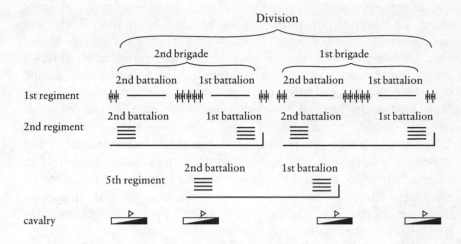

Division of attack formation prescribed by Napoleon (26 November 1805)

flank, or the front line extended to its full divisional frontage. The presence of friendly cavalry at the rear further reduced any potential cavalry threat. If the enemy cavalry attacking the formation did not exceed a regiment or so, the friendly cavalry could countercharge once the enemy's motion was momentarily checked by infantry.

The presence of cavalry at the rear also greatly increased the formation's ability to exploit any success by vigorously pursuing a defeated enemy. Invariably the greatest number of casualties were inflicted on an enemy not during the actual struggle, but after the issue was settled and the victors pursued the defeated and cut down everything that was not fast enough to remove itself from harm's way. It was extremely difficult for any type of ordered formation to effectively pursue the vanquished, since to remain effective it had to retain its formation while the defeated would disperse in all directions. The usual practice was to detach individual companies to effect the pursuit, but these were of insufficient strength to inflict much damage. Friendly cavalry available for local support, however, meant that the pursuing force was not only capable of much quicker movement but also able to inflict more grievous losses whenever it managed to catch up with those attempting to flee the victorious division. Future events would demonstrate that most often this large mixed order formation would be supported by numerous skirmishers thrown out in front of it. This skirmisher screen could be used both offensively and defensively.

It is certainly interesting to speculate what prompted the French command to adopt the larger versions of the mixed order during the 1805 campaign. However, a possible clue appears in the letter Napoleon drafted on 26 November which ordered a cavalry squadron or division at the rear of the formation to protect against 'Cossacks'. Clearly, the prospect of once again facing irregular, but expert light horsemen was at the minimum an incentive for adopting such a formation. It will be recalled that the French had encountered a similar tactical challenge when they faced Turkish and Mameluke horsemen in the Egyptian campaign. In this previous instance, they had also resorted to large formations with significant depth, supported by cavalry to the rear of the formation and artillery interspersed in the intervals between infantry formations. Significantly, however, there were several marked differences between the tactical demands faced in Egypt and Syria and those anticipated for the current campaign. In the earlier case, the Turkish horsemen, though generally regarded to be more skilled and ferocious than their Russian counterpart, were rarely, if ever, accompanied by regular infantry or, for that matter, any artillery capable of delivering anything like effective firepower. In the Middle East, the potential effectiveness of the enemy cavalry had necessitated large hollow squares to be adopted, while the absence of infantry and effective artillery made these cumbersome formations feasible.

This certainly would not be the case when the French met a combined Austrian/Russian army, or even one consisting exclusively of Russian elements. Russian small arms fire and artillery could not be ignored and the large divisional squares would be too vulnerable and unwieldy. On the other hand, positioning additional closed columns to the side and rear of the formation would achieve a similar result. When attacked by light cavalry, battalions in closed columns would simply form 'closed square'. The small detachment of cavalry in the rear would countercharge, while the infantry inflicted casualties on the enemy horsemen as they passed by at relatively short range. The need to counter the Cossack presence was not the only consideration leading to the adoption of larger mixed order formations. Napoleon also expected the Russians to follow the example of Suvarov and

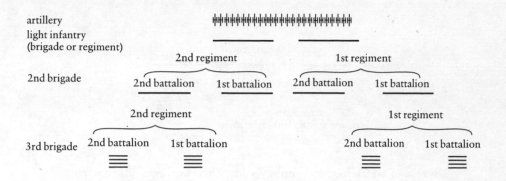

Division of attack formation prescribed by Soult for Vandamme's command
(1 December)

employ dense columnar formations. In his letter to Marshals Soult and Bernadotte which prescribed the large mixed order formation, Napoleon explained: 'In this order of battle, you will find yourself when opposed to the enemy [with] the fire of the line and closed columns all formed to oppose his [the enemy also in line and columns].'[4]

Interestingly enough, as events turned out, despite Napoleon's efforts to dictate the exact position of each of elements making up a division, it did not prove to be entirely successful. Though the divisional mixed order formation was indeed used on the battlefield, it always in some unique form differed slightly from the model proposed by Napoleon. Marshal Soult, for example, did not hesitate to alter quickly the official model, and several days later on 1 December issued his own set of instructions for Vandamme's division. The infantry formation was to be protected by artillery and light infantry positioned to its front. The divisional artillery was positioned as the lead element, while the light infantry, a regiment or even a brigade in strength, stood 100 paces in front of the two brigades of regular infantry behind it. In this proposal, the first brigade of regular infantry was deployed in line while the four battalions in the second brigade remained in column behind the flanks of the battalion in line.

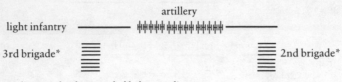

Division of attack formation prescribed by Soult for Legrand's command
(2 December)

For his other division, commanded by General Legrand, on 2 December Soult devised yet another version of divisional level mixed order. This time, the artillery was guarded with light infantry on either flank rather than slightly to the rear. The infantry of the two brigades or regular infantry remained in a divisional column at half interval, i.e. the column was a division of a battalion wide with space between each tier in the column equalling the frontage of a platoon. Neither of these plans was actually employed during the Battle of Austerlitz. Michiels in his work, *Au soleil d'Austerlitz*, distilled Marshal Soult's after-battle report and compared it with Colonel Poitevin's journal and a ledger drawn up for the 4th *de ligne* and the 24th *légère*. He concluded that the artillery and the light infantry regiment were in columns by division stationed along the division's front. Each battalion within the two line regiments was formed in column by divisions separated at platoon distance. This yielded four columns in two tiers.[5]

It is on these three lines of columns that Saint-Hilaire's division, in front of Puntowitz, and those of Vandamme in front of Girzikowitz, were formed.

It is interesting to look at the initial deployment of French forces

Division of attack formation actually used by Saint-Hilaire's division at Austerlitz

at the beginning of Austerlitz. In the area between Girzikowitz and Santon almost all of Caffarelli and Suchet's divisions were in columns of attack. Caffarelli's ten battalions were deployed in three waves of columns, each separated from its neighbour by an 'entire distance', that is, the space needed to deploy that battalion in line. The exception was the 17th *légère* which was positioned on the Santon. Suchet's division, on the other hand, was in two waves of columns of attack. The units in Bernadotte's corps were similarly configured. Both Drouet and Rivaud's divisions were placed in three waves of columns of attack, all at 'entire distance'. The guard was similarly deployed in closed columns at full distance between battalions in the same wave, and the cavalry of the guard were in regimental closed columns by squadron. The artillery in each of these divisions was placed in the intervals between the battalions, as instructed by Napoleon's letter of 26 November.

Just prior to the French assault on the Pratzen Heights the French infantry in this area were ordered to deploy from the ordinary closed columns into 'attack columns on the centre'.[6] Saint-Hilaire's division, though not strictly in mixed order, adopted a division formation loosely similar to that given to Soult's corps on 2 December. The difference was in Saint-Hilaire's version the brigades in the rear were

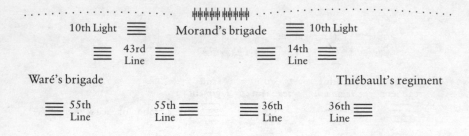

Saint-Hilaire's division on the Pratzen Heights (Austerlitz)

deployed in a number of battalion-sized closed columns, rather than the single brigade columns advocated by Soult, and a screen of skirmishers was thrown out front with the divisional artillery at their centre.[7]

The French infantry continued to resort to mixed order frequently throughout the remainder of the Napoleonic Wars. At Jena, for example, Claparede, concerned about the potential threat posed by the Prussian cavalry, deployed his brigade into mixed order before advancing. The 17th *légère* and an élite battalion deployed in line along its front, while the 34th and 40th *regiments de ligne* were kept in closed column, one on either flank. The entire formation resembled a square since Videl's brigade deployed into line immediately behind Claparede's troops.[8] Similarly, at Eylau, Augereau's corps advanced into the action in line, with each of its division's flanks supported by columns 'at a distance of a platoon', that is, each tier in the column was separated by a distance equivalent to a platoon's frontage.

Mixed order would be resorted to again at Friedland and at Montmirail. At Fuentes-de-Onoro (5 May 1811) five battalions attacked the village Pozo-Bello. The centre battalions remained deployed in line while those on the flanks were in column. The same technique was used at the Battle of Borodino (7 September 1812) during the attack on the Great Redoubt.[9]

The Oblique Square

Troubled by the ferociousness of eastern horsemen during the Egyptian campaign, the French army had met this threat by adopting large divisional squares. As we have seen, when the French troops returned back to France, the 33rd *regiment de ligne* drilled with these *carrés oblique*, oblique squares. It appears that these lessons were not lost and in fact influenced the behaviour of French troops when at last they were called upon to combat Prussian troops.

Although the Prussian army had seen only some limited combat during the early Revolutionary Wars, its reputation up to the start of the 1806 campaign was based largely on its exploits during Frederick the Great's time. Not surprisingly, it was with some trepidation that the French set off to do battle with the highly vaunted Prussian cavalry, which still enjoyed the reputation based on a string of notable successes under Seydlitz during the previous era. During the previous year's campaign, the French military authorities had responded to the expected Russian cavalry threat by placing local cavalry reserves at the rear of the divisional mixed order formations, whose flanks were protected by closed columns. Though sufficient against the irregular Cossack cavalry, this would not guarantee complete safety against the quality of cavalry expected from the Prussians. There is some evidence that the French military remembered its Egyptian campaigns. The dense formations of the latter would be impractical against the Prussians, who unlike the Mamelukes and Turks could be counted on to use their artillery with deadly effect.

The French came up with a number of solutions to this dilemma. At Jena, Suchet's division was initially deployed as a large divisional square. The 17th *légère* formed the front face, and Videl's brigade the rear. Both were deployed in line. The two flank sides were formed by the 34th and 40th Regiments, both in closed columns. Thirteen miles away at Auerstädt, Gudin and Morand's divisions had to endure large-scale attacks delivered by the Prussian cavalry. On the right, Gudin's force met a series of impetuous charges delivered by the veteran Blücher. The 25th and 12th Regiments, as well as a battalion of the 21st, bore the brunt of these assaults in battalion and regimental squares. The other battalion from the 21st remained in line to connect this flank with the French forces in Hassenhausen. Interestingly, the three squares were placed obliquely to one another to maximize the effect of the cross-fire.

Morand's response to another cavalry threat later that morning is even more illustrative. His division, initially advancing in closed columns, deployed in battalion lines and then, when faced with the enemy cavalry, manoeuvred into two rows of battalion squares. These were positioned to form the *carrés oblique*, rehearsed so frequently by the 33rd Regiment in 1801.[10] Lest it be thought this arrangement was fortuitous, Gneisenau's observations on the effect of these precautions on Blücher's efforts should be considered. Writing his biography of the Marshal, Gneisenau attributed the failure of the Prussian cavalry on Gudin's right to the potency of the new French formations more than any other factor:

His [Blücher's] old manoeuvres, of indirect charges following each other in succession, and skirmishing on all sides, first throwing the files into disorder, and then, by a heavy unexpected charge, to break through, were here found of no avail. The new tactics of Napoleon, of drawing up his infantry in alternate squares, flanked by light artillery, and connected by troops in line, frustrated all Blücher's desperate attempts to make an impression. He felt himself foiled. On making his last charge he had his horse killed under him. He then drew back his cavalry in good order towards Eckärtsburg, and passed through Auerstädt.[11]

The Line Formation

The French rarely deployed in line along the entire battle front. This only occurred when the army was forced grand tactically to fall back completely on the defensive, such as at Marengo. Linear formations in the French army tended to be utilized more on a local level, that is, occasionally by a division or more commonly by a brigade. This could be useful if the unit had to remain in the presence of the enemy or became engaged in an extensive firefight. Occasionally during the heat of the action, French units deployed into line 'involuntarily', that is, without the prior intention or consent of the divisional commander. Moreover, in certain rare situations, such as the Battle of Maida (1806) French infantry were even drawn up in the battle lines of old as they assumed the offence.

Though both French doctrine and the collective desire of the troops mandated an offensive posture whenever possible, necessity sometimes forced the French to fall back on the defensive. In these cases, the infantry, finding itself on the defensive on open terrain,was forced to give up its columnar formations and deploy into line. The line continued to be the most suitable formation for the defence, allowing the maximum number of muskets to be brought to bear against an approaching enemy. In terms of its effect on the defender's morale, the line was also superior to a column in this application. Any psychological boost given to the troops in column in the first stages of an assault was lost as soon as a column stopped and the men were condemned to continued inaction. Unable even to see the approaching enemy, let alone deliver any type of meaningful fire, the troops in the middle and rear of the column were at a disadvantage compared to any of their comrades who awaited the enemy in line.

Probably the most notable instance of the French adopting line on the defensive occurred during the Battle of Marengo. Victor and then Lannes, unexpectedly finding themselves confronted by the entire Austrian army and greatly outnumbered, deployed whatever forces were at hand in the traditional linear formation: the infantry deployed along two multi-battalion lines in the centre with the available cavalry positioned on either flank.With each successive setback, the French attempted to reform these lines until the overall cohesiveness had been destroyed by the overwhelming Austrian forces. It was only after four or five hours when the French were forced to fall back in disorder that isolated units were forced into defensive columns, that is, 'closed squares', and squares. French infantry, however, certainly never limited the traditional line to purely defensive applications, but used it frequently as a brigade, regimental or battalion-level formation in most of the major contests between 1800 and 1809.

There were several reasons why English-speaking observers tended to overlook whatever use of line among the French did occur. Firstly, in the British army of around 1800, deploying into line in practice meant to deploy one's entire force into one or two parallel lines; each battalion was in line beside its neighbour. It is not surprising therefore that the same criteria were used to assess the practices and formation of the enemy, in this case the French. It was certainly a rare day indeed that the French, when not on the defensive, deployed more than a few battalions into a continuous line. However, if the French rarely deployed divisional-sized units completely into line, they very frequently threw entire brigades and smaller organizations into line even during offensive operations. French infantry would often form line when it was necessary to bring small arms fire to bear, or when they were compelled to stop and wait for further orders or developments. They also appear to have formed battalion and regimental-sized lines occasionally to perform local offensives.

During the struggle for the Pratzen Heights at the battle of Austerlitz, portions of the French infantry are found deploying into line for both these reasons. It fell to Thiébault's brigade to attack and take the village of Pratzen. The actual assault was initially conducted by Colonel Mazas who led the second battalion of the 14th *de ligne* deployed in line. When this first assault failed, the 36th *demi-brigade* and the first battalion of the 14th were next thrown in. Here once again, at least part of the attacking forces were in line: the first battalion of the 14th deploying as it ran forward.[12] This second assault succeeded in carrying the village, and in the next action that quickly ensued on the plain beyond Thiébault ordered part of his brigade into line for a third time that morning. Thiébault ordered his forces forward to catch up with Morand's forces, which at that moment were being attacked by Kamenski's brigade of about 4,000–5,000 men. Saint-Hilaire, who commanded Thiébault's brigade, ordered the first battalion of the 14th *de ligne* to move up and deploy to the right of the 10th. This apparently had the effect of restoring the unequal struggle. By this point, the main body of Thiébault's brigade made its way to the front. However, four new regiments were observed marching in close towards the front of the French line. Suspecting a ruse, Thiébault deployed his 36th Regiment into line on the right flank of Morand's 10th. The 2nd battalion of the 14th remained in column at the left flank to be able to meet any threat that might be directed against this flank or the rear. Because Thiébault has provided a particularly detailed account of this action which sheds light on a variety of issues pertinent to both tactics and the combat experience in general, a more detailed treatment of this action is provided in Chapter 22.

We do not have to even leave the struggle on the Pratzen Heights to find other examples of the French infantry using lines. After throwing Russian infantry under Grand Duke Constantine's command out of the village of Blasowitz, Bernadotte's corps in a number of columns continued its advance beyond Blasowitz. His infantry originally deployed in line on the commanding Pratzen Heights, the Grand

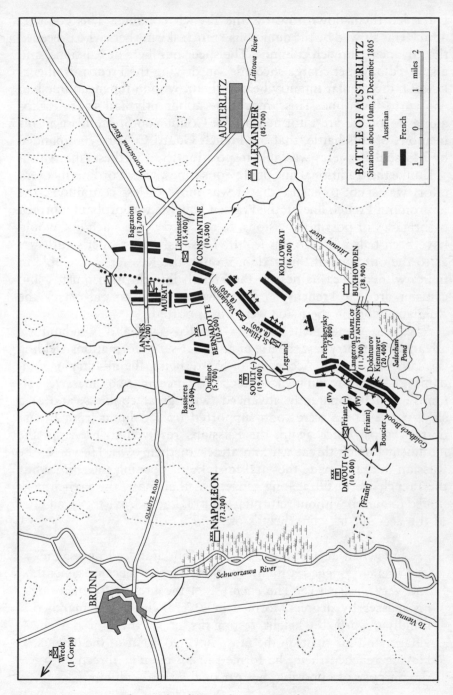

The Battle of Austerlitz, 2 December 1805

143

Duke led them down towards the French columns. This counter-attack was slowed by the numerous French skirmishers who preceded the advancing French columns. The sheer numbers of Russians, and a spirited bayonet charge succeeded in driving the French tirailleurs in upon the regular infantry behind them, who in the meantime had chosen to form line. This French line apparently had sizeable gaps along it, for we are informed by the Count von Stutterheim in his memoirs of this battle, that the French Guard Cavalry commanded by Marshal Bessières was able to position itself in these 'intervals'.

Unlike the traditional line of previous times, where ordinarily every effort was spent to ensure that it was more or less continuous, the impromptu French line on the Pratzen Heights was probably formed by brigades or possibly divisions. In this latter case, each line would have been half a division in width. To satisfy the reader's curiosity as to the outcome of this action, though the Russians were able to inflict withering casualties on the French line through musket and canister fire, the French guard cavalry was able to push back the Russians, who on their side were unsupported.[13]

A second engagement between the Russians and Vandamme's advancing infantry saw the use of a similar set of formations yielding the same net results. According to Stutterheim, the infantry in Vandamme's corps recommenced their advance in two 'massive columns', which apparently advanced 'with great coolness, and at a slow pace'. These were soon supported by a column from Bernadotte's corps. Once again, the Russians resolved to pre-empt the imminent French threat with an attack of their own. However, the Russian infantry made the fatal mistake of opening their fire while the French were still at long range. On their part, the French continued to march without returning the fire. Let us leave the remainder of the account in Stutterheim's original words:

> . . . but when at a distance of about one hundred paces, they [the French] opened a fire of musketry which became general, and very destructive. The enemy [i.e. the French] opened out his masses by degrees, formed in several lines, and marched rapidly towards the height, resting his left on the church of the village, and his right on the most elevated point of the heights. Having reached them, he formed in an angular direction, for the purpose of opposing the rear of the third column.[14]

French infantry also occasionally formed line during an assault despite the express wishes of the officers commanding the overall situation. Whether these impromptu lines were formed as an act of desperation on the part of the men or were sanctioned by battalion or regimental commanders is usually impossible to determine. However, from the point of view of the commander, in either case the result was the same and these could be classified as 'involuntary formations'. The following example recounted by Gouvion Saint-Cyr is highly illustrative in this regard. The Seventh Corps on its way to relieve the besieged forces inside Barcelona found itself in an extremely difficult situation in the last days of their journey. Having fought an ongoing series of skirmishes with Spanish forces attempting to block their progress, they finally had run completely out of food and nearly out of powder and ball for the infantry's muskets (there was only enough left for one hour of combat). The corps had no artillery to speak of. To make matters worse, when they bivouacked one night they were nearly surrounded by the enemy. Given this situation, Saint-Cyr, the commander of the French force, felt there was no alternative but to position his men in a single column and charge straight forward and break through the Spanish forces standing between them and Barcelona. At daylight the French troops were formed up into a single column, and it was in this formation they were to fight. The French had advanced 100 paces when a fusillade broke out on either flank of the formation, who contrary to orders had begun to deploy. Fifteen minutes later the Spanish directed their cannons at the head of the French column.

Pino who was commanding the division at the front of the French column sent an aide-de-camp back to the commander of the French forces, asking for orders. Time was recognized to be of the essence and Pino was told that his troops 'must fight in the order they found themselves'. The commander understood there was no time to change formations and any such change would have been slowed down by the broken nature of the ground. It was so wooded that it would have required three hours for a formal reconnaisance of the Spanish position. Moreover, lack of ammunition meant it was not possible to sustain the firefight for more than a few moments. To rectify the problem, Saint-Cyr ordered Pino to ensure that his second brigade stayed in column. At the same time, he ordered Souham's division to move to the left and to the right of General Reding's command. The Italians, who had deployed and started to fire, were hard pressed and pushed back before finally rallying slightly to the rear. Finally the troops which remained in column were sent towards the Spanish line in front of them. Realizing that their only salvation lay in quickly overthrowing the Spanish in front of them, they attacked with determination. They managed to break through at all points and the Spanish were beaten back in great confusion.[15]

Another example of these 'involuntary' deployments into line is provided by Lieutenant-General G.P. Duhèsme in his *Essai sur l'infanterie légère*. In one of the myriad of minor actions taking place during the 1805 campaign, the Austrians under Archduke Charles were able to push back six French infantry battalions to the village of Caldiéro. Here, the French battalions rallied and returned to the offensive. Duhèsme in this counter attack personally led three battalions of the 20th *regiment de ligne* which were deployed 'en masse', that is in closed order columns arrayed in echelon. However, the lead battalion as it neared the enemy 'deployed mechanically, and in spite of my orders'.[16]

Maida

One of the best examples of the French attacking in an extended line formation occurred at the Combat of Maida (4 July 1806) where a French force under General Reynier encountered a small British expeditionary force led by Major-General John Stuart near Calabria, Italy.[17] The French forces consisted of the 1st and 23rd regiments *légère*, a battalion of the 42nd *de ligne*, the 1st Swiss Regiment, the 1st Polish Regiment and a squadron from the 9th Regiment of *chasseurs à cheval*. There were also four cannons from the 1st Regiment of light artillery for a total of about four thousand men.

During the night of the 3rd, the French reconnoitred the various roads in the surrounding area to determine which would most readily allow the artillery to move towards the British camp. General Reynier, commanding the French force, advised his men that they would attack the British at daybreak, and that this assault was to be conducted without musket fire, and resolved solely with the bayonet. The French troops appeared to be enthusiastic and eagerly awaited the opportunity to come to grips with the British force. Unfortunately, the French plans had to be delayed. It was necessary to wait until the arrival of the 42nd *de ligne* which was on its way from Reggio. It only arrived at six o'clock in the morning. Meanwhile, as the

French forces idled the British worked their way inland. General Reynier finally gave the order for his troops to ready themselves for the attack. His instructions were to form in battle on the regiment furthest to the right as soon as it had crossed the Amato. In response the French regiments left a defensible position, crossed the Amato and began to manoeuvre to form a line in the plain.

At about this time the British army neared and formed its line by what the commander of the French artillery looking on described as 'a simple half turn to the left'. This tells us the British had traversed their intended line of battle, moving from left to right, and once the British army had positioned itself along the battle position in an open order column (right in front), they formed line by quarter-wheeling each of the platoons or divisions in the column. Line would have formed in moments, with each platoon in battalion in its normal order. The British did not hesitate. Immediately after line was formed, the order to attack on the double was issued in an attempt to attack the French as the latter manoeuvred to place its regiments into line.

The French regiments meanwhile scrambled to place themselves in line. The three battalions in the 1st *légère* were originally on the right side of the French forces but crossed over to the left flank in front of the other regiments. As a consequence, it ended up in line slightly in front of the others. To its right and slightly to the rear came the 1st Polish Regiment followed by the French artillery. The 1st Swiss and the 23rd regiment *légère* were still further back on the French right. The squadron of the 9th *chasseurs à cheval* on the French right moved further outward presumably to make way for the infantry behind it. As often happened, the horses threw up a considerable amount of dust, temporarily obscuring the main French force from the British view. However, as the dust settled, the French were seen to be advancing.[18]

General Compère, who commanded the brigade on the French left flank, rigorously started to apply General Reynier's orders without taking into account all of the events that were beginning to unfold. Seeing the advancing British line, Compère was anxious to deliver a stroke before the British could close. There was no time to wait for the French line to be fully formed, and the order to advance with lowered bayonets at the *pas de charge* was given. When offering an opinion of Compère's actions many years later, the officer commanding the French artillery argued that the French infantry, facing an enemy themselves hell-bent on closing, should have delivered a well-levelled volley before setting off. What followed was an inadvertent French advance in echelons, with each of the regiments to the right of the 1st *légère* attempting to catch up. As fate would have it, the British encountered a similar problem so that their right, made of a composite brigade of 800 light infantry,[19] was also slightly in front of the others. This meant that both forces on this side of the field were advanced, while those on the other side were mutually refused.

At Maida, both sides can claim to have been on the offensive. The two armies neared each other in what to the participants appeared to be a matter of moments. Although Reynier had been emphatic in his instructions to deliver the assault *à prest*, that is, without firing, Dyneley has commented on the highly inaccurate, and thus ineffective, French fire experienced in the final moments of the attack. The roots of this inaccurate fire certainly cannot be attributed to any disorder in the advancing ranks. According to Dyneley, who was positioned with his artillery about ten yards in front of the light infantry, the French advance was conducted in the 'finest order it is possible to conceive'. To describe what happened next is probably best left to Dyneley's own words:

> We halted, formed into line to oppose them, and then advanced. It would be impossible to describe with what steadiness we came on. I was at this time on the right and about 10 yards in front of the light infantry. The French advanced firmly towards us, keeping up a tremendous fire of musketry which either fell short or went over our heads. When we were about 100 yards apart, Colonel Kempt, who commanded the light infantry, with incredible coolness gave the order 'Halt!' 'Throw down your blankets, shoes,' etc.; then the order 'Forward!' and in a few seconds after 'Charge!' Our men reserved their fire until within a few yards of the enemy and then fired into their faces. The French turned tail and those who could run fast enough escaped the bayonet, the whole of the rest were either killed, wounded or taken prisoners; in short, Bonaparte's first regiment of infantry was cut to pieces.[20]

From two other eye witnesses we learn of several other details. The British light infantry apparently delivered but two volleys. These however, proved to be murderous and were sufficient to drive back the French infantry which until then eagerly sought to come to grips with their British counterpart. The first discharge left half the men and 27 officers *hors de combat*. Despite these losses, the 1st *légère* managed to regroup. It was at this moment that the 1st Polish Regiment pulled up to the leading French elements and joined the front line just as it set off once again at the *pas de charge*. The French experienced a second volley which seemed to destroy the right half of the French line. The determination of the French to reach and overthrow the British infantry was such that French had continued their advance almost to the very last moment before contact. This can be deduced from the nature of many of the French casualties that were suffered at this point. James FitzGibbon noted that the French though they finally turned and ran, had waited too long before doing so. The British were sufficiently close that they were able to bayonet more than 300 of the French before the latter were able to build up speed as they ran. It must be borne in mind that in a pursuit, after the first one or two seconds, the fleeing force, no longer encumbered by their weapons, is able to move more quickly than the pursuer.

The day after the battle Lieutenant Sandham visited the sick bay of the ship to which he had been assigned. He described his observations many years later in a conversation with Captain Dyneley who himself had been present at the affair as an officer with the British artillery:

> It was curious to see the wounded in the 'sick bay' the following morning – all the French on their faces, being stabbed in the back; while all the British lay on their backs being shot in front by the volley which the French fired as they advanced to the charge.[21]

Undoubtedly, the effectiveness of the British infantry fire was one of the decisive factors in determining the victor in this contest. Although the French managed to get off at least one volley, it proved to be ragged and ineffective.

To summarize, when greater detail is considered the French are found to utilize a full array of different formations on the battlefield. Although columns certainly were the predominant formation of waiting, during the initial phases of the contest battalion-, regiment- and brigade-sized lines were also occasionally used in most contests, along with the occasional mixed order formation. Once again, French infantry assaults were conducted both in line and in column. At Auerstädt, for example, the actual infantry conflict took place with both sides in lines, as did much of the fighting on the Pratzen Heights at Austerlitz. One of the French concerns during both the 1805 and 1806 campaigns was how best to meet the cavalry threat. In 1805 large divisional mixed order formations were prescribed to counter irregular Russian horsemen. The next year, hollow squares and oblique squares were utilized to resist the feared Prussian cavalry.

CHAPTER 9

The Allied Response to French Fighting Methods

INITIAL RESPONSE

THOUGH VARIOUS ALLIED ARMIES found themselves pitted against French antagonists throughout most of the 1792 to 1805 period, these conservative establishments were slow to react to the new French methods. All stubbornly clung to the traditional methods of fighting. Serious, comprehensive reform challenging the most basic elements of linear warfare had to await the humiliations of the 1805 and 1806 campaigns, over thirteen years after the commencement of hostilities. The main thrust of Austrian reforms forged under the Archduke Charles' tutelage, for example, only took hold during the 1806–1809 period, while the Prussian response was only completed with the new infantry and cavalry regulations in 1812.

The overwhelming reaction among the Allied military was initially to deny the importance of the early French achievements. French victories, it was opined, were merely an accident of circumstances or the short-term result of the effusion of passion let loose by social upheaval. Foreign observers were quick to conclude that the tremendously powerful social forces unleashed by the revolution had effectively undermined the capabilities of the French army, now but a shadow of the professional armies that had been available to the Bourbon kings. French generals and senior officers were considered 'but little acquainted with the scientific branches of the art of war',[1] while the ordinary officers were 'ignorant, inexpert, and inferior to all others', and the army was 'composed of troops of the line without order, and of raw and inexperienced volunteers'.[2] It was the ignorance of the officers and ineptitude of the men that compelled the Republican commanders to throw large unwieldy masses against the enemy along the entire battle front, rather than any thoughtful design or intent. The troops' indiscipline and lack of training had made more precise attacks or coordinated activity impossible. Surely, there was nothing in these chaotic methods that professional troops ought to emulate!

The tenacious ability of the French to stymie the combined Allied efforts during the wars of the First and Second Coalitions, however, gradually forced the less doctrinaire among the Allied military to reassess French capabilities and take a more objective look at their methods. The relatively rough terrain in Flanders favoured the French armies' use of large numbers of skirmishers, a radical departure from the methods that had been used in earlier wars. Not surprisingly, this was one of the new practices that attracted the most notice among the Allies. The same could be said of the newly raised French horse artillery and the relatively new practice of utilizing ricochet fire against troops under normal battle conditions, instead of limiting its use to formal sieges. Unfortunately for the Allies, limiting their attention to French *tactical* practices actually hindered their understanding of the true nature of the French innovations. By limiting the analysis of the French methods of such things as skirmishing methods, columns of attack and horse artillery, even the most progressive Allied military thinkers ignored the structural elements that were the main source of strength of the new impulse system. The effectiveness of the new French system arose not from the tactical innovations introduced or popularized by the Republican armies, but from the intrinsic superiority of the new grand tactical impulse system over its linear antecedent. Completely overlooked was the ability of major elements within a French army to act independently along multiple axes of operations, more effective cooperation between the French infantry, cavalry and artillery arms, and most importantly the ability to concentrate an overwhelming force at the critical point.

The Allied inability to penetrate the heart of the new system was neither a fortuitous oversight nor the consequence of collective folly or intellectual mediocrity. Intellectual forces were systematically at work which hampered the Allied military intelligentsia's ability to grasp the nature of warfare unfolding around them and its importance. Part of the reason lay in the very nature of human intellectuality and spirit itself. Like so many before and since, the Allied military establishment unconsciously sacrificed veracity for the comfort of the intellectually familiar.

The Revolutionary period had begun with unquestioning endorsement of the linear system by the entire non-French military establishment. The product of constant training and inurement into tradition, four or five generations of officers had been thoroughly indoctrinated into linear warfare. And, prior to several seminal tactical innovations around the mid-eighteenth century, it was indeed the most practical solution to the challenges then posed on the European battlefield. However, the system of warfare so convenient when the musket had first been introduced in the 1680s, by the 1790s clearly had started to fail. What had once been the only viable grand tactical apparatus became less and less effective as the consequences of the new tactical developments manifested themselves on the battlefield. The linear system, dignified by a lengthy rule, at some point had been elevated unconsciously from a purely conceptual tool to the military equivalent of a world view. Its propensity to symmetry and the geometric conveniently melded with the philosophical beliefs and attitudes of the Age of Enlightenment. Just as importantly, it was also in accord with the prevailing political order.

The real threat of the new French methods was that they challenged the philosophical, political and social attitudes upon which the linear system was based. To contemporaries it must have appeared that the new French actions were chaotic. To emulate them was to purposely reject the rational and orderly and espouse pandemonium.

If Allied revulsion to the unorthodoxy of French revolutionary armies was nothing more than a natural human response to unexpected radical change, the unavoidable result of psychological inertia, their inability even to understand accurately what the French were doing on the battlefield stemmed not from a set of attitudes but from the complex, multi-faceted nature of impulse warfare itself. The new French methods had the appearance of randomness and thus proved totally impenetrable even to those thoroughly vanquished as a result of their effectiveness. Those on the receiving end of a French attack could not but help notice the clouds of skirmishers pestering them, nor did it require any unusual perspicacity to perceive the threat of dense columns as these neared. Independent bodies of cavalry would inevitably follow, but their arrangement and actions appeared to be as haphazard as the light troops that preceded them. The Allied commanders and officers were hard pressed to isolate anything that could be construed as 'systematic', and what eluded them almost to the end of the Napoleonic Wars was an understanding of French *purpose*.

This apparent confusion did not simply lie in the eye of the beholder. In the days of Marlborough and Frederick a commander had a relatively limited number of options at his disposal. Unlike the method of warfare that would replace it, the linear system consisted of a small number of easily recognizable building blocks. Moreover, in a great majority of cases, a commander deployed his forces so that they conformed closely to these idealized structures. Armies, for example, were almost always drawn up in two or three lines with the infantry in the centre and the cavalry on the flank. True, there was variation in the detail, such as where to put the hussars when faced with enemy cavalry or the distance to be maintained between the lines, etc. However, despite differences arising from predilections of individual commanders or regional differences, the overall army formation was modelled on a handful of extremely well defined, hence easily recognizable, paradigms. Moreover, there were a limited number of ways of handling these structures. In this sense, the linear system was made up of a *discrete repertoire of rigid structures and formally accepted patterns of movement*.

This is precisely what baffled Allied observers, who quite naturally sought to find comparable structures in the French system. There appeared to be near infinite variation in the patterns of French deployment, etc. The impulse or 'French School' as it was sometimes called, was not a predefined set of formations or structures that had to be applied in the prescribed way. There was no longer a fixed way of doing things, no longer a limited repertoire of formations or way of manipulating these. In its stead, the impulse system offered its followers a set of *powerful grand tactical principles*. True, there remained a body of formally accepted formations and manoeuvres, and some of these, such as columns of waiting, columns of attack and mixed order, served as the most common means of implementing these principles. Nevertheless, the new art of war was not defined by one or even several ways of arranging the army in battle. French commanders were much more free to manipulate these building blocks in whatever manner was required by circumstances to implement the overall principle, such as to bring the reserve to bear at a critical time and place or to ensure successful cooperation between cavalry and infantry.

The result was that there was a seemingly infinite number of ways of achieving a grand tactical end. No two commanders, though both might hold troops in reserve in columns of waiting, would use exactly the same method of achieving the objective. To guarantee a reserve, one divisional commander might maintain his battalions in close order along three 'lines'; another might deploy the first line and have several brigades to the flank and rear in mixed order, etc. Consequently, we find seemingly endless variation in the formations that were used and the manner that these were manoeuvred around the battlefield. In the later part of the 1790s, a new-found professionalism slowly worked its way into the French military, as officers and men became seasoned. However, many of the Allies interpreted this trend as a backing off from the practices utilized by the Revolutionary armies, and a return to the traditional style of warfare. An anonymous British military commentator in 1799 wrote that the most convincing proof that the French method of warfare was not worthy of emulation was that the 'French Generals themselves began to relinquish it at the end of the campaign of 1796 . . .'³ Having the benefit of the rear view mirror of history, it is obvious that the Allies' growing realization that the French fighting methods of 1792 were no longer those of 1796–97 was quite accurate. Rather than being an admission of the inferiority of deficiency of the Republican fighting methods, however, this subtle transformation was in actuality a progression to a higher, more effective form of fighting, the effectiveness of which would only truly be appreciated by the Allies after the disastrous 1805 campaign.

TACTICAL DEVELOPMENTS

Almost from the very start of hostilities, the Allies had viewed the frequent reliance on clouds of skirmishers and heavy columns of attack as the two most salient characteristics of the new French method of fighting. So, not surprisingly it was from this point that Allied military analysts began their investigation into what worked for the Republican armies and what lessons could be applied to their own armies. There was much resistance to both of these innovations and contemporary military periodicals frequently carried diatribes about the new French methods. In practice, prior to 1809 there was no systematic effort among either the Austrians or the Prussians to employ columns of attack or waiting on a battlefield. There are actually a handful of examples of the Austrians using columns of attack. Frederick the Great had used columns of attack as a secret weapon at several times during the Seven Years' War. These closely guarded techniques were unveiled to the military world upon the publication of General Warnery's *Remarks on Cavalry* in German in the 1780s and then in English in 1805. The Austrian cavalry on at least one occasion mimicked the Prussian cavalry's column of attack. At the battle of Neerwinden on 18 March 1793, they used an identical formation when they came within a hair's breadth of destroying the French infantry in front of them.[4] During the battle of Marengo, the first Austrian infantry assault against this village was delivered by a massive infantry column.[5]

However, these were isolated incidents and in no way indicate any trend in formal doctrine among the higher Austrian military authorities. Experimentation with skirmishers among both the Austrians and the Prussians, though still very limited, was actually more common than that with columns of waiting and attack. In 1794, the Austrians in the Low Countries started the practice of occasionally throwing out the third rank as skirmishers.[6] In Prussia, though the authorities might resist the use of skirmishers on the battlefield, they slowly and begrudgingly began to acknowledge their usefulness in the *petite guerre*. At first glance, we would have expected skirmisher tactics to be even more odious to a conservative clinging to linear warfare than columns of attack. Infantry fighting as skirmishers, after all, were called upon to leave the line and to adopt at best a highly fluid formation. No longer guided by their officers and NCOs for each and every motion, to a much greater degree they acted according to their own judgement. In contrast, troops in columns were tightly constrained and maintained in highly ordered formations, still moving and firing at the officer's control.

However, skirmisher tactics could more readily be adapted to traditional linear tactics; the offensive use of heavy columns of attack could not. The act of throwing out skirmishers, even large numbers of these, did not prevent the officer from arranging the main body of his army the same way as he always did. The overall plan, that is of where he would position the artillery and cavalry, as well as how and when they would be used remained essentially unchanged.

But this certainly was not the case when a commander started to utilize columns of attack or even columns of waiting. He could only utilize these formations by departing from the familiar territory of linear warfare. To form a number of columns meant that the army's overall configuration necessarily departed from a two-line symmetrical formation, where all the troops in an area generally advanced in unison. A more sophisticated orchestration of troops movements was required and concomitantly a more complex set of grand tactical procedures and goals. This accounts, for example, for why the Allied armies gradually were able to accept the usefulness of fighting in skirmish order while they were never able to find a place for columnar tactics until they became willing to explore alternatives to the linear systems after the disastrous 1805–1806 campaigns. It also goes a long way to explaining why such a conservative military establishment as the British ultimately were able to adopt skirmishing tactics in the Peninsula, even though they stridently ridiculed and rejected all other essentials of the impulse system introduced by the French.

OTHER TRENDS

Compared to the unruly masses of the French whom they opposed, it is easy to regard the Allies as stodgy traditionalists. However, prior to the outbreak of the Revolutionary Wars the European military tended to think of themselves as a progressive force that through parade ground experimentation and resulting analysis had succeeded in pushing Frederick the Great's art of war to its logical conclusion. The period of almost undisturbed peace during the 1770s and 1780s gave military establishments much time for reflection and parade ground training. The result was the Prussian battlefield philosophy which spread throughout most of western Europe. Military leaders were entranced with the idea of orchestrating the flawless manipulation of forces and drill manuals of the period, and even the French *réglements* of 1791 devoted much attention to complications such as changes of faces and countermarches.

Armed with these new manoeuvres which seemed to imbue their troops with clockwork precision, commanders toyed with methods of perpendicular deployment, as opposed to the parallel methods that had been used under real battle conditions. The Prussians had deployed their army three times using perpendicular methods during

the Seven Years' War (Lobositz, Reichenberg and Gross-Jägersdorff)
but had to abandon their experiments because of the slowness of the
procedure and the increased vulnerability of the lengthy columns
to enemy artillery at close range.[7] However, Frederick the Great's
repudiation of perpendicular deployment did little to check this concept and the possibilities that it seemed to promise to a great many
tacticians from the 1770s onward. In its original form, the perpendicular method of deployment invented by Frederick and his generals
in the late 1740s, was still a cumbersome affair and required a large
number of battalions to manoeuvre in unison. But as the new
Prussian-style manoeuvres were popularized throughout western
Europe, a simpler form of perpendicular deployment eventually suggested itself. This was the 'adjutant's walk', an extremely useful
manoeuvre that would be used on countless occasions later during
the Napoleonic period.

In a sense, it grew out of the traditional methods of parallel deployment. It was common practice for one officer from a battalion,
usually the adjutant, to ride ahead and go to where the battalion
would finally deploy into line. This practice had arisen for several
reasons. The adjutant functioned as a guidepost, allowing the battalion to see its final destination. He also sought to ensure that there
was enough room for his battalion to fully deploy. Previously, a
battalion, part of a lengthy column, would be forced to move to this
position by 'square movements' that is, it had to advance straight
up along one side of the battlefield and then turn ninety degrees
and traverse the battlefield until it reached its allotted position. The
adjutant moving alone was not subject to these restrictions. A short
cut was found whereby he simply travelled directly along the hypot-
enuse to the desired location. However, with the introduction of the
various new-style manoeuvres perfected by the Prussians in the late
1740s, the traditional perpendicular methods of deployment were
no longer completely binding, and a battalion, at least in theory,
could follow its adjutant and take its own unique route to its final
place in line.[8]

Although prior to 1809 there is little to suggest that the Allies had
deciphered the main principles of the French grand tactical system,
by 1805 the Austrians and the Russians had clearly appreciated the
potential advantages of perpendicular deployment. Weyrother's plan
had called for the Allied army to move to their left into the Goldbach
valley in four lengthy columns. For this to succeed, the Allied

columns would be forced to advance in these columns well within 1,500 paces of the French army, itself already in position. This was only feasible if the Allied battalions deployed into line quickly, and was not possible if the entire column was forced to traverse the entire field of battle.

AUSTRIAN REFORMS

The failure of the Austrian army to stand up to Bonaparte during the 1800 campaign finally convinced the Emperor Francis and his advisers of the need for some sort of military reform. The Emperor's brother, the Archduke Charles, was one of the few among the upper military echelons to emerge from the recent débâcles with his reputation intact. Even before the war was concluded with the Treaty of Lunéville, Charles was appointed field marshal and president of the *Hofkriegsrat*, a civilian and military body charged with many administrative routines, such as lower-level promotions, issuance of routine orders and even many strategic and operational planning functions. Faced with a declining economy and an administration which taxed whatever resources were available, Charles decided to tackle the problems imposed by the overly burdensome bureaucracy before focusing on purely military matters. Though a conservative by nature who never envisioned challenging the existing system, Charles nevertheless alienated the reactionaries at court. As war clouds once again started to gather, the court regained the ascendant and the Archduke lost favour with his brother. The modest efforts at reforms were placed in abeyance, and the Austrian army went to war in 1805 using virtually the same methods as it had in 1796 and 1800.

Events, however, would soon force the Emperor to restore Charles to grace and influence. The even greater humiliation suffered during the 1805 campaign forced everyone but the most myopic reactionary to concede that immediate military reform was essential if further embarrassments were to be avoided. Renewed efforts at reform began in early 1806. Together with Carl Friedrich von Lindenau, Charles authored *The Fundamentals of the Higher Art of War for the Generals of the Austrian Army*, which was intended to provide Austrian commanders with the comprehensive strategic vision that had been so noticeably absent throughout recent wars. Tactics was not to be ignored, and a new cavalry regulation appeared in January 1806, followed by its infantry counterpart in March of the next year.

The new regulations did not represent a significant departure from existing practices. Much of their content treated similar, if not identical formations, manoeuvres and procedures to those already in place since the 1780s. Austrian infantry, for example, was still offered a myriad of ways of forming battalion and regimental square, and the fundamental methods of forming line and column were unaltered. Nevertheless, there were several noticeable changes in approach to grand tactics. The occasional need to form skirmishers on the battlefield was at last formally conceded and the procedures to be used in these situations detailed. The skirmishers were to be drawn from the third ranks and were to be the 'brightest, most cunning, and reliable' soldiers within the battalion. The front two ranks were always to remain in closed order formations and thus up to one third of the battalion could fight in extended order. The authorities envisioned that skirmishers would usually be used when on the defensive; their primary role to defend friendly infantry in closed formations from clouds of enemy skirmishers. Austrian skirmisher tactics followed what was now classical theory: the front chain could be positioned up to 300 yards from the remainder of the battalion in the rear. Supports in the form of two additional platoons would be positioned at the 100 and 200 yard mark, respectively.[9]

Even more significantly, the infantry regulations sanctioned the judicious use of closed columns of waiting and attack, up to then regarded by tradition-oriented tacticians as some sort of French devilry. These came in several varieties: the *division masse* and the *bataillon en masse*. The division masse consisted of six companies positioned in two closed order 'columns'. The battalion's first, third and fifth companies were stationed behind one another in the right column, fifty-six to sixty paces to the left. Charles introduced this formation as a counter to the French column of divisions. This did not prove popular among Austrian infantry officers and was in practice only used when Charles was present on the field.[10] The 'battalion mass' was a column one company wide by six deep, in other words roughly fifty-five to sixty men and eighteen ranks deep. Normally, this formation manoeuvred in 'open order', that is, with the normal space between each rank in a closed column; however, either when threatened by enemy cavalry or intended to drive home an assault on enemy infantry, it assumed 'closed order' where this distance between ranks was roughly halved.[11] The battalion mass was used to manoeuvre around the battlefield within relatively close range of the enemy, since it was less vulnerable to enemy cavalry.

The introduction of these two new formations did not mean that Charles had completely accepted the new French methods. When on the offensive Charles still emphasized the use of the traditional line. The musket was to be used at longer ranges, while the men had to trust to their bayonets at close in. An advance was to be preceded by skirmishers from detached companies, or if available from nearby *jäger* units. The bulk of the infantry in line behind the skirmisher screen was to advance at the slow pace until 150 paces from the enemy, at which point they were to quicken their pace. The officers were to order the charge when their troops had closed to sixty paces. When this happened, the skirmishers retired through the intervals between the formations and the men in the line rushed in with lowered bayonets. So great was Charles' confidence in the line that, provided the formation's flanks were well secured, he insisted that the line could withstand a cavalry charge, no matter how vigorously ridden home. Musket fire was withheld until fifty paces. Then, a devastating volley would shatter the horsemen. In this moment the infantrymen were to lower their bayonets and deliver a determined charge of their own.[12] There has been a tendency among late-nineteenth and twentieth-century military historians to think that many of the decisive actions on the Napoleonic battlefield were resolved through brisk and well-aimed small arms fire. One result is to view Charles' advocacy of bayonet charges as archaic. Closer inspection of actual doctrine called for and used by each of the major European armies shows that this was pretty much in line with that used by the Russian, French and even British infantry.[13]

The only possible criticism of Austrian charge doctrine is not that it demanded a slow and steady advance and relied upon cold steel as the final arbiter. Quite the contrary, if there was indeed a weakness, it was that it called for the charge to start when still sixty paces from the enemy. Other armies officially called for the bayonet charge to commence when only twenty to forty paces from the enemy, and the Austrians having a longer distance to traverse would be much more likely to be disordered and thus vulnerable to a pre-emptive counter charge. When war with France once again erupted in 1809, Charles quickly introduced some additional changes. Following the lead of the French and the Russians, Charles sought to establish artillery concentrations. Older less useful artillery pieces were removed and battalion guns withdrawn and placed in reserve. A corps organization used with such good effect by the French was established soon after commencement of hostilities. The nine corps thus formed were smaller than their French counterparts, however, and consisted of between twenty to thirty battalions, sixteen to twenty-four squadrons and seventy to ninety artillery pieces. Unfortunately, as it turned out these were never to be used to their full potential. Despite the recent tactical innovations, no effort had been made to conduct large-scale manoeuvres. As a result, senior officers had little experience in handling these large formations and were unfamiliar with combined arms techniques. Used to the traditional system where even senior commanders meticulously followed orders, corps commanders tended to lack initiative and relied on orders from the commander, thus losing the ability to respond effectively to the enemy's actions or exploit opportunities as they arose.[14]

Unfortunately, little effort has been made in the English-speaking world to chronicle the attempts at reform within the Austrian army between 1805 to 1809. As a result, Austrian efforts tend to be portrayed as either an inept and poorly executed attempt to copy the newer French methods of combat wholesale, or, quite the opposite, as distinctive, homegrown responses to these outside developments. Most of what we are able to learn about the efforts of Archduke Charles and his staff, and the reasons for their decisions is limited to what can be gleaned from a few isolated comments by several prominent contemporaries. Nevertheless, as we piece together these tiny fragments of information, a more detailed picture emerges, one that shows the efforts at reform to have been a more elaborate process, involving a greater number of factors and more contributors than previously suspected. Some Austrian innovations, such as the 'battalion mass', were indeed local adaptations of practices commonly used elsewhere for over a decade. Historians have frequently viewed the 'battalion mass' as a truly Austrian formation, somehow unique among those available to the other western Europe armies. The battalion mass, however, was neither new, nor particularly 'Austrian', but simply a local version of the 'closed column' which existed, at least informally, in the repertoire of formations available to almost every European army prior to the outbreak of the Revolutionary Wars. If there is anyone who should be singled out for the distinction of 'inventing' this formation it would be Frederick the Great, whose infantry were the first to form closed columns simply by reducing the spacing between the tiers in the column so that they were roughly at 'quarter distance'.

In the French regulations of 1791, the 'closed order' column is sometimes referred to as a *colonne serrée* but more often as a *colonne en masse*, that is, a 'column in mass'. And, even more illuminating, it is occasionally referred to as a *bataillon en masse*, i.e. 'battalion mass',[15] showing conclusively that as early as 1791, in the French tradition a closed order column was sometimes thought of as a 'battalion in mass' or 'massed battalion'. That this concept worked its way eventually into Austrian military circles becomes even more convincing when we remember that the term for 'battalion mass' in Austrian was literally *bataillon en masse*, the exact same term as the French formation with almost identical geometrical configuration and set of uses. So the term itself, 'battalion mass' was not new, being taken from then current French usage. Some may argue that the use of this closed column to ward off cavalry made it a distinctive formation. A glance at the British infantry regulations of 1797 describes how a closed order column is to form a closed square in a manner very similar to that later adopted by the Austrians. Clearly, the use of the Austrian 'battalion' was also not new.[16]

Of course, much that had to be learned about the new fighting methods was more conceptual in nature. Rather than simply adopting a new manoeuvre or formation, it was the use of a number of principles governing how these formations and manoeuvres would be used that had to be grasped. The Baron de Jomini serving in the French army during the early Napoleonic Wars wrote a number of pamphlets on tactical and grand tactic issues during the brief respite from hostilities between 1807 and 1809. These appear to have had a greater impact on the development of Austrian thought than on the French readership for whom they presumably were originally intended. At the Congress of Vienna in 1814 the Baron had an opportunity to closet himself with the Archduke Charles to discuss events of the late wars. During the conversation the Archduke thanked de Jomini for his recommendations contained in a small pamphlet entitled *Résumé des principes de l'art de la guerre*, published in 1807 at Glogau (Silesia). This somewhat obscure work would probably have escaped the archduke's attention had it not been for the efforts of General Walmdem to acquaint the Austrian commander-in-chief with its contents while the two were sequestered at the baths of Warmbrun in 1808. In this work, de Jomini advocated the abandonment of linear warfare where both lines stretched themselves across the battlefield. During the 1805 and 1806 campaigns de Jomini became convinced that the traditional linear system had fallen irreversibly behind French methods:

> What I had seen in the celebrated campaigns of Ulm, Austerlitz, Jena and Eylau had proved to me the difficulty, if not the impossibility, of hurling an army against an enemy in position, and causing it to march in lines deployed in two or three ranks. By that intimate conviction I was induced to publish the *Résumé* which was intended as a last chapter of my *Traité des grandes opérations militaires.*[17]

In the place of a linear system, de Jomini recommended that when on the offensive the troops along the first and second lines be positioned in rows of battalion columns instead.

When war once again erupted in 1809 between the French and their now perennial foes the Austrians, initially Charles believed that de Jomini's views would be of little use during the upcoming campaign. Events, however, were soon to force Charles to change his opinion. At Essling, the Austrians found themselves occupying a limited frontage, given the troops at their disposal. Almost as an afterthought, the Archduke Charles ordered part of his army, especially the *Landwehr*, to remain in columns. Later charged by the '*cuirassiers d'Espagne*' the Austrian infantry repulsed the French cavalry, a feat that Charles conceded would have been impossible had they remained in the traditional line. Encouraged by this success, Charles employed a similar approach at Wagram, and with near identical results. For two days Charles was able to withstand the French fury. Finally, the Austrian commander was forced to retreat not because his army had been destroyed or rendered ineffective, but because his left wing had been outflanked. Once again, the Austrians' noticeably increased ability to withstand the French fury was at least partially due to the use of these battalion-sized columns. Impressed with these 'successes', the Austrians started to keep their rear, less-trained troops in columns until they were needed.

Given the scope of French successes during this period, it is natural to assume the new French system of warfare was the sole external influence on the development of Austrian military doctrine. An almost off-hand comment by de Jomini suggests that the Austrians

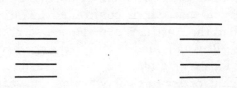

Mixed order formation used by General Benningsen at Eylau

may have been simultaneously influenced by a second body of thought and battlefield practice. In discussing the ideas he had set down in his *Résumé des principes de l'art de la guerre*, de Jomini admitted that he had been impressed with the 'mixed' formation that the Russian general Benningsen had employed at Eylau. In Russian infantry regiments of three battalions, the 'centre' battalion was deployed in line while the 1st and 3rd battalions were placed on either flank in closed columns.[18]

This formation, of course, is remarkably similar to the simple mixed order formations used occasionally by the French in the late 1790s in Italy. More interesting, however, Benningsen's formation was also almost identical to that Suvarov used against the French during the same period and against the Turks and Poles during the several decades prior to this. Like Benningsen, Suvarov had part of an infantry regiment deploy in line with the remainder in columns behind.[19] So successful had this formation proved against the irregular troops during Russia's Turkish campaigns, that upon arriving in Italy Suvarov immediately sought to convince his Austrian allies that they too should adopt this formation.

Unfortunately, this advice given neither at an opportune time nor in a diplomatic manner caused the Austrian commanders to resent Suvarov's arrogance to presume to teach them how to fight an enemy that at that point he knew by name only. The result was that the

Austrians completely ignored the Russian commander's advice and continued with their methods of waging war unaltered. When the Russians and Beningsen arrived in central Europe in 1807, it was a different setting from that which confronted Suvarov in the late 1790s. Not only had the Austrians experienced several unsuccessful campaigns but the Prussians had been nearly crushed at Jena and Auerstädt the previous year. Given the recent disasters, the Austrians were not as arrogant or set in their ways as ten years previously. Whether it was due to Benningsen's greater tact or the humility or the sobriety produced by this string of reverses, the military establishments in the various Allied armies were much more willing to take a look at what the Russians could contribute.

In an article in the *Spectateur militaire* in the 1820s, a French officer recollected that by the later campaigns the Austrians had significantly departed from a strict adherence to linear practices. According to this officer, from 1809 onwards the Austrians almost always kept inexperienced troops such as the *landwehr* (militia-type units) in a row of closed columns behind the experienced troops deployed along the first line.

PRUSSIAN REFORMS

After the fateful events of 1806, the Prussian military found itself in a similar situation to their Austrian counterparts, for much the same reason. The defeats at Jena and Auerstädt and the scattering of the remainder of the Prussian army during Bernadotte's, Lannes' and Murat's pursuit of Prince Hohenlohe to Stettin, forcefully demonstrated even to the most myopic reactionaries that traditional linear systems could no longer be exclusively relied upon. The debate was no longer whether French methods should be examined and adopted, but which procedures and practices ought to be emulated.

The first step at Prussian reform was the appointment of Graf Lottum and Major General von Scharnhorst to head a newly created Military Reorganization Commission. This body quickly issued a number of far-reaching proposals. In September 1807 the commission recommended that the nobility's monopoly of the officer class be ended. It also pressed for universal military service, as well as a more humane system of military discipline. Much of this was eventually accomplished over the next several years. Regulations issued in August and November 1808 put an end to advancement exclusively by seniority, and finally allowed all citizens with the required education requirements to hold commissions. Other regulations abolished corporal punishment. Efforts were also made to rationalize the army's organization. The only organizational distinction to be tolerated was between cavalry and infantry. On 20 November 1807 a new organization structure was issued. Henceforth, each infantry was to consist of two musketeer battalions, one light infantry battalion, two grenadier companies, and a depot or garrison company. The whole of the third rank was also to be trained to fight in skirmish order.[20] Of even greater importance was the reform in army administration. In 1810 the military School for Officers was opened in Berlin, while staff officers were first assigned to army commanders in 1813.

Although this process of military reform arguably went through even more fits and starts than those which occurred in the Austrian army, and during the early stages probably had encountered even greater opposition, by 1812 a much greater degree of progress was achieved. In many respects, the reform process culminated in the infantry and cavalry regulations issued on 15 January 1812 and drafted by a commission headed by Scharnhorst, Clausewitz and Yorck. The Prussian 1812 infantry and cavalry regulations demonstrate at least among their authors a greater understanding of the principles underlying the new impulse system of grand tactics, than any other document or instructions issued by any of the Allies during the entire period. Like the Austrians, the Prussian authorities recognized henceforth infantry would have to rely on column as well as the traditional line. Columns were recommended for movement and offensive operations, while the line continued to be considered the most suitable formation when an assault by enemy forces was expected. Mounted troops likewise were no longer to rely exclusively on linear formations, but were to learn how to attack in column, echelon and line.[21] However, what most differentiated the cavalry and infantry regulations from any existing set of instructions or regulations, regardless of arm, was its emphasis on combined arms support, and the degree to which this was spelled out in any highly articulated set of formations and procedures.

The brigade became a self-sufficient unit, made up of infantry, cavalry and artillery elements whose doctrine now required close cooperation and support. In 1812, the Prussian brigade in the field

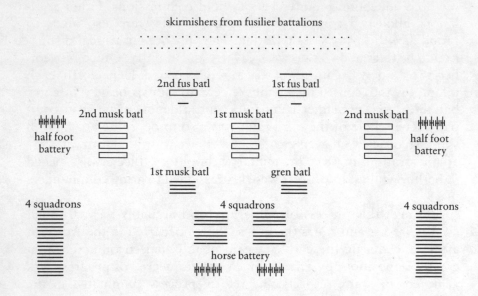

Brigade formation for an attack (1812)

consisted of two infantry regiments, ten to fourteen squadrons of cavalry, one battery of foot artillery and a second of horse artillery. Each infantry regiment, in turn, contained two musketeer battalions and a lighter fusilier battalion. The grenadier companies were taken from their parent battalions and permanently assigned to a grenadier battalion that remained under brigade command.[22] The authors of the 1812 regulations took great pains to spell out exactly how this combined arm formation was to position its elements and how it was to typically conduct itself in combat.

In a dramatic departure from the traditional two thin lines, the Prussian military authorities now advocated a multi-tiered columnar approach, structurally akin to the large French division-sized mixed order formations prescribed by Napoleon during the 1805 campaign.

Whenever the brigade had to stand in readiness, or assume a defensive posture, a skirmish line was to be thrown out along its front. The brigade's two fusilier battalions deployed in line some distance to the rear. Supports for the skirmishers were positioned between the chain of skirmishers in front and the fusiliers in line behind. The main body of infantry, three musketeer battalions, remained in column in the third tier, placed 100 paces behind fusiliers in line. To be able to easily deploy into line, should circumstances require this, each of these battalions was separated from its neighbours by a full interval. One half battery of foot artillery was placed on either side of these three columns.

The infantry reserve, an additional 150 paces to the rear, formed the formation's fourth tier and consisted of the grenadiers and the remaining musketeer battalion. In closed order column, these were positioned behind the intervals of the three columns in front of it. The cavalry was positioned 150 paces behind the infantry reserve and was also retained in column in a fifth tier, four squadrons roughly behind the foot artillery on either side of the third tier and four squadrons in a double column behind the interval of the musketeer and grenadiers in the fourth tier in front of it. The battery of horse artillery was positioned in the rear behind the middle of the formation.[23]

If called upon to assume the offensive, Prussian doctrine called for a quick aggressive advance that would culminate in the final moments with the threat of *cold steel*. The infantry regulations mandated that the troops be tightly constrained until they were a mere twelve paces from their foe, when a spirited bayonet charge would be unleashed.[24] Confidence in the bayonet as the ultimate arbiter of the contest continued among the Prussian military until the close of the Napoleonic wars. In his instructions in 1813, Blücher observed that the French army had proved, like many of its own adversaries before it, to be noticeably vulnerable to bayonet attacks delivered by massed formations. He instructed his troops to exploit this tendency; officers, however, were cautioned against allowing these assaults to degenerate into an indecisive fusillade.[25] This aspect of Prussian infantry doctrine of attack fits in with that espoused by virtually every other major military power. As we will see in Chapters 11 and 13, the French, and even the British, placed the greatest importance on spirited bayonet charges when delivered at the right moment.

To facilitate the bayonet charge, the Prussian 1812 regulations required the brigade to modify its formation before assuming the offensive that was to be pressed home. As the brigade neared the enemy, in order not to disrupt the troops in closed order, the skirmishers would fall back through the intervals between the columns. Meanwhile, the three tiers of infantry columns were reduced to two. To accomplish this, the two fusilier battalions, initially deployed in line, would ploy into column and work their way on either side of the musketeer battalion and the grenadiers which until then had formed the reserve. Thus, the two musketeer and fusilier battalions formerly constituting the third tier (counting the skirmishers) now were at the front of the formation and prepared for the upcoming confrontation by closing the ranks to quarter interval. The second 'line', that is, the two fusilier, the musketeer and the grenadier battalions – all in closed columns – remained 150 paces to the rear. If the enemy to be attacked was a prepared infantry in ordered formations, the cavalry and horse artillery would remain at the rear until an opportunity presented itself.

CHAPTER TEN

The Decline of French Tactical Capabilities

LOSS OF MEN

A KEY CONCEPT TO ALL GRAND TACTICS generally, and to the French impulse system especially, is the concept of applying at the appropriate moment an irresistible force at the critical point on the battlefield. Prior to 1807, this irresistible force, rather than being a single body or formation, was most often the product of several forces working together to achieve the desired effect. As we have seen, Austerlitz, Jena and Auerstädt all provide excellent examples of the French infantry exhibiting this type of tactical finesse. So many times during these middle campaigns as soon as a forward French force encountered and engaged the enemy, the reserves were sent in as needed and gradually exploited weak points as these were revealed. This required a sophisticated orchestration of all available tactical elements: skirmishers, artillery, cavalry, as well as infantry in line, columns of attack and columns of waiting. In the commander's mind, 'preponderance of force' was not simply gathering more infantry or artillery than that available to the enemy and overwhelming the opponent by simply throwing these forward.

After 1807, there was a movement towards adopting single-step solutions. 'Irresistible force' increasingly started to be seen as a single formation whose intrinsic strength or imposing size would force the issue. Rather than achieving a breakthrough by a sophisticated and articulated interplay of moveable parts, greater and greater importance was attached to the notion of 'mass'. Instead of hitting the enemy with a series of smaller forces in succession, commanders began to succumb to the temptation of throwing what appeared to be an irresistible force against a critical enemy position. Moreover, there was a tendency naïvely to associate size with strength: the bigger, the more imposing the formation, the stronger it was supposed to be. Thus, the tactical sophistication notable in the 1805 and 1806 campaigns became less common. This was as much a trend in artillery and cavalry tactics as it was in infantry practice. In the case of artillery, for example, this heavy handed tactics took the form of large batteries, such as the hundred guns at Wagram. After 1812, French cavalry began to rely more and more on mass formations on the attack.

However, it was in the infantry arm where this new emerging preoccupation with 'mass' took the most extreme forms. Multi-battalion, even multi-regiment columns now were occasionally used to achieve a critical offensive operation on the battlefield. The first instance of the French resorting to large multi-battalion columns is observed at Wagram. Receiving several urgent orders from Napoleon to attack, Macdonald ordered his command forward. The enemy, themselves advancing, stopped and began to fire at the advancing French. Seeing the presence of a large body of enemy cavalry forming up for the charge, Macdonald prepared his infantry for the imminent cavalry onslaught and drew the various elements in his command more closely together. The result was a large 'square'. Its front consisted of eight battalions deployed in line, two rows of four battalions apiece, the left face was formed by seven battalions in closed column, while on the right there were six battalions in a similar formation. The rear was unintentionally left open, Macdonald believing this to be covered by elements from Nansouty's cavalry.[1] The Austrian cavalry as it approached was exposed to combined artillery and infantry fire, and was then finally repulsed by lowered bayonets. The large French formation then resumed the offensive, and though suffering heavy losses from Austrian firepower, nevertheless succeeded in barging through the Austrian position.

Arguably Macdonald's column was an expedient forced upon him in desperate circumstances. However, this would not be the last time a French army had recourse to these extra large formations. Massive infantry columns would appear at Waterloo, though this time they were anything but successful. Bugeaud saw the results of these monstrosities with his own eyes. Describing what unfolded, this observer records:

> A *corps d'armée* moved to the enemy in three columns, the fraction of which was a battalion deployed in line of columns. It paid dearly for that folly. A brigade of English cavalry rode through it, trod it under feet, and would have carried it off as prisoners of war, but for the brilliant charge of two regiments of lancers, one of which was commanded by Colonel Zocqueninot.[2]

The exact size and composition of these large columns is still an ongoing debate, and frequently the point of discussion in a number of military historical journals. Perusing contemporary Prussian sources, de Jomini concluded that there were four columns, each of two brigades. The battalions were deployed in line one behind the other, six paces apart.[3] Paret in his work on Yorck and Prussian military reform, concluded that these four columns consisted of six, seven, eight and nine battalions, respectively, and had a frontage varying between 150 to 200 metres and a depth between twenty-five to thirty-five metres.[4] Regardless of the exact composition and dimensions of these columns, all observers and historians agree that they were large multi-battalion affairs and not the single battalion columns so commonly in use.

Wagram and Waterloo were not the only instances when the French resorted to these large, monstrous formations. On another occasion in one of the later campaigns, Bugeaud personally observed an entire division advance to the enemy in 'column by regiment'. These had advanced to within musket range of the enemy before starting to deploy. The result was predictable: before the deployment could be completed, the entire massive formation was put into disorder and all the men started to flee.[5] Bugeaud penned these accounts in the early 1830s when many of the officers responsible for these fiascos were still in office, and so he constructed his critique of French military science with the greatest discretion. To protect a reputation, he sometimes withheld the name of an engagement or battle, since to provide even this was enough to implicate the person responsible. It can be argued that Macdonald's large column at Wagram, and Senarmont's adroit use of heavy concentrations of artillery at Eylau and Friedland were *ad hoc* affairs, solutions driven by the particular circumstances encountered during these engagements. There is mounting evidence, however, that this reliance upon 'mass' was part of a larger trend, one which placed ever increasing importance on obvious strength and initial benefits, as opposed to subtler, but ultimately more decisive benefits.

Events at Waterloo showed that the strength of these large formations was largely illusory. Although these multi-battalion columns might appear intimidating, they were a waste of resources. True, the men in these formations initially might feel more confident, and the enemy force would feel more intimidated than if assaulted by a smaller force. So there was indeed a temporary benefit at the beginning. The problem was that in reality it was just about as easy or as hard, depending upon how you choose to look at it, to stop a single battalion column as it was these massive affairs. Success or failure hinged upon the behaviour of the troops at the front of the column. If they lost confidence and stopped, the progress of the entire column behind them was blocked. At the same time, because so many battalions had been placed in the formation, this meant that there were few other troops available as a reserve to come to their rescue if they were stopped.

To sum up, these massive columns might afford some relatively small psychological advantage, but the cost in resources was many times that which was gained, and the gain was far less than that which could be achieved using other means. However, as the quality of men, officers and NCOs started to decline in the later campaigns, their simplicity and initial benefits started to make these formations appear attractive.

There are a number of other tactical developments that show how these considerations were at work, especially after 1809. The reintroduction of regimental artillery, the proliferation of cuirassier regiments, and the introduction of lancer units are all excellent examples. Although a detailed treatment of both artillery and cavalry tactics has been deferred to Chapters 15 and 20, it is necessary to discuss briefly one or two aspects of these tactics to show how they fit into these trends.

French regimental artillery, though originally abolished in 1798, was re-introduced in Davout's, Oudinot's and Masséna's corps in June 1809, and then on a broader scale in March 1811. This was not a result of some new analysis which showed conclusively that divvying up a sizeable fraction of the artillery and allocating it among individual regiments was a more efficacious use of artillery than concentrating these in field batteries. Quite the contrary. Artillery experts knew that from a purely theoretical point of view this was a retrogressive step; artillery was always more effective when concentrated. However, this was no longer the guiding consideration. The quality of troops had declined, and something was needed to boost their morale during the type of hard-fought engagements that had become almost standard fare. Although regimental artillery never inflicted much damage, the noise was found to encourage raw troops who were more influenced by nearby sights and sounds than by what was actually being done to the enemy some distance away.

In many respects the introduction of cuirassier and lancer regiments is very similar in this regard. In 1802, Napoleon authorized the distribution of cuirasses to the most senior cavalry regiments, who were to be henceforth known as 'cuirassier regiments'. Although the benefit of wearing heavy chest armour is obvious, not all cavalry experts believed that this was a positive step. The additional weight meant that it required more time for the horses to reach a gallop and their maximum speed would be reduced. However, what could not be denied was that the riders themselves felt a little more confident, since they were a little less susceptible to enemy small arms fire than they would have been without the cuirasse.

It would appear that the introduction of lancer regiments was at least in part due to similar considerations. With the exception of de Brack and one or two others, almost all military tacticians writing on the subject agreed that the lance was not a particularly effective weapon against a skilled enemy cavalry determined to resolve the issue with cold steel, at least when held by someone who had not been trained in its use since early adolescence. However, regardless of the pro's and con's of the lance, it was found to buoy the troopers' morale, as if they really did enjoy some advantage over their enemy. This would be an important consideration after 1812, when larger numbers of poorly trained cavalry recruits on poor mounts entered the ranks.

Although at first glance the re-emergence of regimental artillery, the popularization of cuirassiers and the introduction of lancers into the French army does not appear to be even remotely related to the use of large multi-battalion columns of attack, there is a connection. In all three cases there is an attempt to provide an immediate advantage of morale, through what is functionally a 'quick fix': specifically, providing thick chest armour, a longer weapon, or one or two cannons placed beside the infantrymen. At first glance this seems to be an appropriate trade off. For example, the much needed bonus in morale appears to be worth more than whatever speed is lost in the case of providing a heavy cavalryman with a cuirasse. But these seemingly simple solutions to low troop morale and lack of training give up a lot more than what is at first apparent. The basis of morale was, in essence, transferred away from the soldier and now predicated to some feature of his armour or armament.

The poverty of this approach did not escape detection, and was noticed by a number of the more discerning officers in French service. To many of these, nothing proved the tactical and grand tactical bankruptcy more clearly than the unthinking over-reliance on heavy columns during the Empire's final years. With the return of permanent peace by the end of 1815, there began the type of *post mortem* analysis among professional military men that inevitably follows each major war. Aided by all the advantages of hindsight, the more reflective quickly realized that the tendency towards the concentration of mass in large formations overall was a deadend. Bugeaud, now a colonel, for example, would observe that these massive formations 'seemed to have . . . announced amongst us the decline of the [tactical] art.' Quite naturally, there were those who placed the blame with Napoleon, as the commander-in-chief, and as the individual ultimately for the content of all higher level orders. General Lamarque, for example, claimed that he had been ordered to form the massive column at Wagram.

Others faulted individual general officers. In a work published in the first years of the Restoration, *Napoleon au tribunal de Cesar et d'Alexandre*, the author attributed these formations to a 'false interpretation of orders'. Bugeaud was a leading participant in this debate. In his *Quelques manoeuvres d'infanterie (Some Infantry Manoeuvres)* which appeared in the *Spectateur militaire* in the 1820s, the always insightful Bugeaud proffered a slightly different, but far more illuminating explanation. As opposed to the author of *Napoleon au tribunal . . .* who suggested that the misinterpretation of the orders arose out of the inadequacy or inexperience of the officer responding to the instructions, Bugeaud placed at least some of the blame on the language used to transmit the orders and advanced the theory that fatuous reliance upon these large columns, in fact, was due to a nomenclature problem.

By the late Napoleonic Wars, orders routinely contained a wide variety of technical jargon. Much of this arose out of terms and language codified in the 1791 regulations, and these tended to be the source of little ambiguity. However, there were a great many other terms which had worked their way into French military parlance with no such formal recognition or consensus. Onc such term was the *colonne par bataillon*. In the official 1791 regulations, a closed column is referred to generally as a *colonne serrée* or more infrequently as a *bataillon en masse*.

Although this might appear to be a trivial distinction, significant purely on a terminological level, it is possible that this was actually the occasional source of confusion in the field. It will be recalled there were three systems of classifying columns: by depth (e.g. closed order column), by width (e.g. column by companies) and by usage (e.g. column of manoeuvre). The single most common method was to refer to a column by the width it occupied. For example, if the column occupied the width of a squadron, it was referred to as a 'column by squadrons'. A column by companies was a company wide, while a column by divisions was a division wide. (Division here refers to a fraction of a battalion.) It would be natural for someone encountering the term *colonne par bataillon* to interpret this as a column with the width of a battalion's frontage, in other words several battalions deployed into line one behind the other. Incidentally, this mistake is frequently made by modern historians and military history buffs when they first start reading military scientific works from this period.

However, gradually the context within which this term is used suggests another, quite different meaning. French officers often referred to a battalion in column as a *colonne par bataillon*, especially in those cases where there was a series of battalions on the horizontal row, separated at full deployment distance. In this case, *colonne par bataillon* refers to a single battalion column whose frontage was either one or two companies wide. Bugeaud's point is that if a commander's instructions called for the formation of *colonne par bataillon*, an officer could believe that the intention was to form a large column out of a series of battalions deployed in line, one behind the other, even if the commander had simply intended to have these smaller, single battalion columns formed. In retrospect, it is unlikely that Bugeaud's argument explains every instance of these large columns that occurred in the field, although it might account for a few. What is interesting about his argument from our perspective, however, is that it shows the level of inexperience that had crept into the French officer ranks by the late Napoleonic period and the type of problems that this caused.

Writing during a later period, Ardant du Picq would come closer to the real source of the problem during Napoleon's last campaigns:

> Infantry and cavalry masses showed, toward the end of the Empire, a tactical degeneracy resulting from the wearing down of the elements and the consequent lowering of standards of morale and training. But since the allies had reorganized and adopted our methods, Napoleon really had a reason for trying something so old that it was new to secure the surprise which will give victory once.[6]

The key words in this passage are 'lowering of standards of morale and training'.

The relationship between the virtual destruction of the *grande armée* during the retreat from Russia in 1812 and the ultimate failures of Napoleon's last three campaigns has long been recognized. David Chandler has estimated that out of the 655,000 troops that crossed the Vistula in 1812 only 93,000 men remained by January the next year. Much of the field artillery was also lost as the French armies precipitously made their way back across eastern Europe. The French were only able to retain 250 pieces of the 1300 taken into Russia. But probably the most irretrievable loss was in horseflesh. When one includes the artillery arm and transport services, over 200,000 horses were lost.[7] Although Napoleon and his staff, through Herculean efforts, would find substitutes for much of the lost artillery, and fill the infantry ranks with the young and the aged, it would be the cavalry arm where these losses would prove irreplaceable. The quality of both cavalrymen and their mounts would never again equal that which existed during the 1806, 1807 and 1809 campaigns. The infantry that was rapidly raised fought bravely and often performed better than could have been reasonably expected. Nevertheless, just as often signs of their lack of training and inexperience appeared. At Hanau, Colonel Dolfs led twenty squadrons against General Maison's division. The latter, though formed in eight squares and protected by eighteen guns, was swept away after a mere fifteen minutes.[8]

However, rather than purely the result of a single nightmarish campaign, the decline in French fighting capabilities was just as much the result of an ongoing process of decline noticeable as far back as Aspern-Essling and Wagram, and which had begun two, possibly even three years earlier. Beginning with the campaign against the Russians in central Europe in 1807, Napoleon and his armies encountered much greater resistance in the field than anything previously experienced. The Russian soldiers proved to be a more determined foe, unwilling to break and flee even when faced with certain defeat and death. Thiébault describes the Russians' bravery at Austerlitz:

> In those terrible shocks whole battalions of them were killed without one man leaving his rank, and their corpses lay in lines in which the battalions had stood ... It is true we had been warned that the Russians, even when too severely wounded to march, would take up their arms again after their enemy had gone forward, reload them, and put their conquerors between two fires ... I saw some stand alone defending themselves as they might have done in the middle of their battalions. I saw some shot through and through and ready to drop, loading as calmly as at drill; so we suffered heavily, and the capture of that house ... proved to me the truth of the saying that it is easier to kill six Russian soldiers than to conquer one.[9]

Thus, the contests against the Russians were bloodier, inflicting high casualties even on the victor. When France once again marched against the Austrians two years later, a similar increase in the casualty rate was encountered, if for different reasons. Charles' second effort at military reforms started to make themselves felt. For the first time, the French found themselves pitted against opponents who were beginning to use methods similar to those which had previously yielded so many victories to the French. As a result, not only were the battles now more hotly contested, with the French just barely managing victory, but the rate of casualties started to soar. The decisive defeats of 1805 and 1806, though inflicting substantial casualties on the enemy, had not been the slugging matches of Eylau, Wagram or Borodino.

While reviewing a military work in 1802, Scharnhorst had observed that the Revolutionary Wars had been noticeably less bloody than the Seven Years' War. The well-respected German military historian Hans Delbrück not only agreed with this assessment but went further, asserting that more soldiers were killed during a single campaign during the Seven Years' War than all those who were lost during the Revolutionary Wars.[10] We do not have to go far for the explanation. During the classical linear period, the great majority of confrontations took place between two forces deployed in line. By the mid-eighteenth century, quick unopposed assaults succeeded much less frequently than they had fifty years previously, and an action was usually only decided after a firefight. All other factors being equal, two sides with an equal frontage would inflict more or less the same number of casualties on each other, so the affair was necessarily bloody for everyone involved.

During the Revolutionary Wars and Bonaparte's campaigns which followed them, frequently a major portion of a battle, or even the entire contest, would be resolved by a sudden change of *morale*, such as would occur if one body of troops perceived it was suddenly threatened by the unexpected arrival of enemy troops in its flank or rear, or if it was attacked by what appeared to be an irresistible number of massed columns quickly bearing down upon it. Individual regiments and brigades, such as the 85th Regiment at Auerstädt, might suffer tremendous casualties, but decisive victory was achieved without a greater majority of the units being roughly handled. The same could not be said from the 1809 campaign onward. When opposing armies resolutely contested the issue, massive casualties were inflicted on both sides, as with what happened at the Battles of Eylau and Borodino. In the short run, an army could sustain the loss of a sizeable amount of ordinary foot soldiers which could soon be replaced. Raw recruits could be forged into experienced troops after a season, or at the most two. However, both officers and NCOs required considerably more time and practical experience to master their craft. When considered as a body, these required four or more years in the field during the era of which we speak. To a large extent, this explains why the French army started to display a new-found professionalism from about 1796 onwards. It was not simply that French armies enhanced their fighting capabilities as a number of new practices and concepts were discovered and employed. It was also that the average competence of the officer and NCO classes increased as these accrued several years of 'on-the-job-training'. This trend of increasing average capabilities of officers and NCOs was reversed after 1807. Henceforth, officers and NCOs were lost at a greater rate than they could be replaced, and the army's overall capabilities slowly diminished. It was this need to compensate for this lower average capability of officers and NCOs that forced a gradual change in the focus of French tactics.

In order to explain how two opposing armies, each armed with similar weapons but each espousing a different grand tactical system, will interact with one another during battle, it is necessary once again to return to the sports arena. On one level, the interaction between grand tactical systems is very similar to the dynamics of play that arise in table tennis where two players or teams with different 'styles of play' are opposed to one another. If a 'speed' player meets a 'spin' player and both are as adept in their own style of play as the opponent, the game quickly devolves into a struggle to see which player is able to impose their style of play on the other. In other words, each player attempts to dictate the pace, flow and direction of play. The speed player makes every effort to hit the ball so that it flies as quickly as possible while the other player constantly is 'slicing' so that the ball slows down markedly and its spin dominates play. To a very large extent, the victor will be the player who is able to ensure that most of the game is played within the boundaries imposed by their style, rather than that of their opponent.

Exactly the same can be said when two armies which employ different grand tactical systems became locked in combat. Obviously, the ultimate goal is to defeat the enemy, if not to completely crush the other's forces, then at least to drive his army from the field. However, in order to carry out our designs it is first necessary to guarantee that the 'game', that is the battle, will be played according to our own rules rather than the enemy's. In the case where a truly Napoleonic army met a purely linear army the interplay between the two grand tactical systems was very much a struggle of 'styles'. The army using the linear system would attempt to overthrow his opponent with 'broad sweeps', usually, in the form of a determined advance conducted over a vast expanse, or massive cavalry attacks generally on the flanks. His opponent, on the other hand, would seek a concentration of force at specific points, and would orchestrate these over time to achieve phased assaults or impulses.

However, a commander's grand tactical goals never unfolded in a vacuum but were invariably affected by the enemy's activity. A truly Napoleonic army would not willingly provide the linear army with the time needed to perform the latter's expansive movements.

Skirmishers would be sent out to pester and annoy the enemy. Smaller packets of forces here and there would attempt to draw the linear army prematurely into combat at points of its own choosing. Meanwhile, the Napoleonic army would begin its operations against critical points, and then when the appropriate time came would begin its own offensive against critical points along the opponent's line. In other words, the army using the traditional grand tactical system would not be given the opportunity to unfold its plans as initially designed.

This is a fairly accurate description of what happened during a majority of Napoleon's battles during the early period. From 1800 until 1807 the French pretty much succeeded in dominating the 'style of play' on the European battlefield. The French commanders were constantly able to impose their grand tactical methods over those of their adversaries. In 1806, for example, the Prussians entered the campaign expecting that their renowned and much feared cavalry would quickly ride over the French infantry, whom they thought incapable of resisting a well-led and adroitly executed cavalry charge. The French came prepared and by being able to manoeuvre quickly through a series of formations, such as column to line to square, back to column again, etc., were able at Auerstädt to withstand repeated assaults and thus frustrated the Prussian 'game plan'. Much of the French success should be attributed to the ability of the higher French military authorities to accurately assess the characteristics and capabilities of their prospective opponents and then prepare an effective tactical and grand tactical countermeasure. We have already seen how in 1805, Napoleon prescribed large mixed order formations at least in part to meet the supposed threat of Russian irregular horsemen. Again, there is some evidence that next year, the oblique square was revived to counter the even more feared Prussian cavalry. Possibly, this is the first example in history of an army modifying its tactical doctrine almost yearly in order to account for its enemy's capabilities as these changed campaign by campaign.

Although after 1806 the French command continued trying to prepare to meet their opponents, increasingly they were forced to modify and revise their plans and goals on the battlefield to meet their opponents' actions, just as in earlier campaigns their enemies had been forced into the unenviable role of playing catch up. We can say that from 1809 onwards, the French did not dominate the 'style of play' as they did previously. Except in the peninsula where they were routinely defeated by the dogged British, they would still manage to win a majority of set piece battles. However, there were to be no more glorious, almost painless victories, such as Austerlitz or Jena. Eylau, Wagram and Borodino were successes, but not in the old style. They were costly slugging matches, where even the victor stopped to lick his wounds. We do not have to search far for the reasons. The French no longer had a monopoly on the new methods.

Like Frederick the Great, Napoleon profited from what he was able to learn from unexpected occurrences on the battlefield. What had started as an ad hoc response to the Russian attempt to create a localized artillery superiority was amalgamated into permanent French doctrine. Probably one of the best summations of Napoleon's late tactical and grand tactical 'style' was proffered by Lieutenant Colonel Frederick Maude, a late-nineteenth-century military historian.

> His battles began by a preliminary development of the struggle, the opposing infantry were led to a premature consumption and movement of their reserves, and a development of their artillery. Then when the enemy had sufficiently shown his hand, an overpowering force of artillery was brought up to case-shot range, which poured in force considerably heavier than any repeaters of to-day could develop, before which no columns or lines could stand; and when their work of preparation was sufficiently completed, a mass of cavalry was, to use an expression of Hohenlohe's, induced to run away in the direction of the enemy, and behind them the massive columns of the infantry marched up to occupy the conquered position, and frequently reached and held it without firing a single shot . . . but if they failed, there was left in his hand his final reserve – the Guard; and the strength of these lay almost entirely in their extraordinary capacity for enduring heavy losses.[11]

Although Maude paints this picture in relatively attractive terms, this model represents the ossification of French military thought and practice during the Napoleonic era. The objective of each phase and each arm is now achieved through the amassing of brute strength and superiority, rather than the sophisticated articulation of diverse tactics. The problem with the simplistic approach is that it invites the enemy to respond in kind. Thus, an army can only continue to win by having larger grand batteries, a greater concentration of cavalry in a critical area, etc. Forced into these bankrupt practices by the continual and irreplaceable drain of officers, NCOs and men, the battles become blood baths where victory goes to who has the most men, or who throws in the last fresh reserve, rather than who devises the best strategic or grand tactical plan. Gone are the days of complete victory at relatively inexpensive costs in human life.

And, after the catastrophe in Russia and the disaffection of his German allies, complete victory is what Napoleon so desperately needed and what proved to be unobtainable. Conversely, given the deteriorating strategic situation these costly victories were just what Napoleon and the French army could least afford.

PART III

INFANTRY TACTICS

CHAPTER 11

French Firepower in Practice

WHEN WE STOP TO IMAGINE how the French infantry conducted itself during an actual attack, it is probably only natural to conjure up images of large numbers of men compacted into dense columns marching quickly toward their foes with shouldered muskets. The underlying philosophy remained unchanged during the entire Revolutionary and Napoleonic period. As we have already seen throughout the period, French doctrine continued to demand a quick advance without stopping to fire until the last possible moment.

This was the theory. In practice French infantry were often found to resort to quite a different approach. Although some instances can be found of French infantry quickly advancing without firing, thus forcing the enemy to turn and flee before both sides came to grips, on many if not a majority of occasions, French infantry when on the offensive relied on small arms fire much more heavily than suggested by official doctrine. In his treatise on light infantry tactics written between 1812–1814, General Duhèsme provides a most illuminating example of what tended to occur in a battle. At the Battle of Caldiéro the French infantry on the left wing attempted a series of advances. Their progress checked, a lengthy but indecisive firefight broke out along the length of the line. Duhèsme provides the following description of his experiences upon reaching the front to restore order and recommence the attack:

> I saw some battalions, which I had rallied, halted and using an individual fire which they could not keep up for long. I went

there, I saw through the smoke cloud nothing but flashes, the glint of bayonets and the tops of the grenadiers' caps. We were not far from the enemy however, perhaps sixty paces. A ravine separated us, but it could not be seen. I went into the ranks, which were neither closed nor aligned, throwing up with my hand the soldiers' rifles to get them to cease firing and to advance. I was mounted, followed by a dozen orderlies. None of us were wounded, nor did I see an infantryman fall. Well then! Hardly had our line started when the Austrians, heedless of the obstacle that separated us, retreated.[1]

It must not be thought that this deviation from the prescribed practice was attributable simply to the inexperience of the troops or their officers. As Colonel du Picq has pointed out, the French troops here demonstrating such a noticeable lack of coolness in this example were veterans of the Empire. The Austrians, however, were just as 'reliable', and had they moved first it was highly probable that the French would have given way instead.[2]

A close examination of other engagements of the period shows that the departure from tactical doctrine described in the above passage was a far from isolated occurrence. As we are about to see, official Prussian after-battle reports for both Jena and Auerstädt show that many actions devolved into extended firefights, before the French were able to rally and overthrow their opposition with a final offensive effort. The French infantry's propensity to begin to fire during the assault frequently was the cause of their discomfiture. This was especially true whenever they faced off against British infantry. The frequency with which these attacks devolved into firefights is at variance with the way most modern readers envision how the French infantry acted on the offensive: always attacking at the quick pace, reserving their fire and attempting to intimidate their opponents in the final moments with the threat of the lowered bayonet.

One fact seems to have long ago been forgotten! During the Napoleonic Wars, it was the French infantry and not the British infantry, which enjoyed the higher reputation for the efficacious use of firepower. The lofty reputation now so closely associated with British infantry, though based on this body's performance during the Peninsular Wars and the Hundred Days campaign (1815), came about only as a result of the British memoirs and accounts that proliferated in the years *following* the conclusion of these conflicts.

According to the authors of the *Instruction sur le tir, à l'usage de MM. les Elèves des Ecoles de Saint-Cyr et de Saint-Germain*, a French instructional work written in 1813, '. . . French firearms are, without contradiction, much superior to those of other nations, and one knows that the natural address is one of the distinctive qualities of the French.' Written by an officer in French service, these remarks might strike someone in the English-speaking world as chauvinistic and an overly optimistic assessment of the French infantry's small arms capabilities.[3] Interestingly enough, however, an English observer during the period confirms this evaluation. According to Robert Jackson, at one point the Inspector-General of British Army Hospitals, on a purely mechanical level the French excelled not only in their ability to deliver ordered volleys but in their performance of all aspects of the manual of arms: 'the explosions from the [French] firelock astonish by the close repetition.'[4] The one caveat frequently noted by contemporary British observers was that the French infantry tended to open their fire at too long a range. According to Jackson:

> The sharp-shooters, and even the regular battalions, commence their fire at too great a distance, often fire at an elevation; and, as they are said to fire on many occasions without ramming, they fire with great celerity, so as to give the idea that they calculate to make an impression on the enemy by noise, rather than by the actual destruction by bullets.[5]

Jackson's description, penned in the 1810s could just as well have described the Prussian infantry under Frederick the Great almost fifty years before. Such was the influence of the proliferation of cartridges and the attendant 'quick fire' philosophy. Hennel, in his account of the British infantry storming the heights at Vera, substantiates Jackson's observations: 'The French who delight in a long shot (the Spaniards & they are well matched at this – famous ammunition wasters).'[6] This predilection to firing during the attack was never limited to the French, but appears to have equally infected all of the other continental armies.

In the early years of the flintlock era, the attacking infantry had often been able to advance relatively close to the defenders before any musket fire broke out on either side. The phenomenon of the attacking infantry advancing until forty, thirty or even only twenty paces from the enemy before halting and delivering a single fire and then attempting to run in with lowered bayonets, occurred much more frequently than later during the Revolutionary and Napoleonic Wars. The Battles of Calciato (War of Spanish Succession) and Fontenoy (1745) are but two of the instances of these close range murderous volleys during the earlier period. In marked contrast, throughout the Revolutionary Wars and the early Napoleonic Wars, almost all infantry versus infantry assaults either resulted in one side turning and fleeing as the combatants neared one another, or the action devolved into an extended firefight which lasted until one side or the other eventually decided to try to end the struggle with a bayonet charge. It was not unheard of during this later period for these desultory firefights to last as much as one, and in at least one case, three hours, before being finally resolved with a renewed advance or the intrusion of other, nearby events.[7]

What is noticeably different from the earlier period, however, is that there are few or no examples during the Revolutionary War, of the French, or any of their continental opponents, advancing up to ten to thirty paces, stopping, and wilfully delivering an organized volley. This change, from the withholding of fire until the most propitious moment when a single but devastating volley was unleashed, to the frequent use of a continuous but indiscriminate fire at a relatively longer range, can be largely attributed to the new-found abundance of gunpowder and prepared cartridges and the nearly universal endorsement by continental armies of the 'quick fire' philosophy of firepower popularized by Frederick the Great's Prussian infantry during the Seven Years' War. It will be recalled that from the 1750s onward it had become fashionable among the infantry in virtually all continental armies to emulate the Prussian infantry's alleged ability to loose off mechanically 'five rounds per minute'.

The first application of the quick firing method probably occurred within defensive tactics. No longer limited to a single volley, it now became increasingly viable for the defender to unloose a number of rapidly delivered shots (volley or individual fire) once the attacker had advanced within the musket's effective range. A defender now might opt to begin firing at 150 or even 200 paces and hope eventually to cause sufficient casualties to thwart the assault. There were also advocates of 'quick fire' while on the offensive. Repeated fire was seen as a means of softening up the defender. Moreover, even those who still advocated the quick assault with shouldered muskets, where fire was reserved only for the final moments, found it impossible to ignore the repeated volleys of the defending forces. Often, their troops were involuntarily drawn into a firefight by the defender's repeated fire. The attacking force was now frequently faced with a defensive fire which not only commenced at a longer range but was also of increased rapidity and duration. This very much increased the pressure on the attacking force to stop and return the fire. And when the attacker stopped either to return fire or initiate it, a lengthy firefight usually resulted. We need not go any further than the Prussian after-battle reports drawn up after Auerstädt to find several examples of general infantry advances breaking down in long drawn out firefights.

At the Battle of Auerstädt, for example, the Infantry Regiment Count Wartensleben (IR 59), during its attack on the French infantry in front of it, halted, delivered several volleys and then engaged in a three-hour exchange of 'battle fire' (the men fired individually) before being ordered to resume the advance once again.

> The battalion halted, fired three volleys, which were returned and we now engaged in a 'battle fire' lasting nearly three hours in which the battalion line continually advanced while the enemy was pulled back gradually ... After the passing of the mentioned three hours during which the 1st Battalion had dwindled down to half-strength through, dead, wounded, and stragglers from this vigorously maintained and murderous small arms fire in which even enemy batteries fired at us, but most of the balls bounced over us, we noticed a reduction in the enemy fire and a wavering of the enemy line, which may have been around 2 p.m., Major von Ebra, although already wounded, on foot at the head of the battalion with a colour in the hand, ordered the advance with the bayonet ... and we thus threw back the wavering enemy in front of us ... We now had just thrown back this enemy line ...[8]

During the same battle, the Krafft Grenadier Battalion also found itself eventually drawn into a prolonged firefight. A thick fog covering the field hampered its initial attempts to close to the French infantry. Two battalions of the French 85th *de ligne* were deployed along a sunken road. Unobserved, the latter waited until the Prussian grenadier battalion had advanced to within fifty paces before unleashing several volleys. Though surprised, the grenadiers managed to return two volleys. The suddenness of the enemy fire and the loss of several dead and wounded succeeded in breaking the Prussian battalion, which apparently contained mostly recruits.

Now, according to Major von Krafft's report:

> Through the greatest efforts of all the battalion, it was brought back to order in a small hollow about 60 paces back and led against the enemy again. Although the battalion was shot at with cannister in this second attack, it was nevertheless more successful and the two enemy battalions were after a mutual, hefty musket fire lasting a long time, thrown back in disorder, and in this, 1 captain, 2 subalterns and 30 men of the 85th Line Regiment were taken prisoner.[9]

As illustrated by the first example, although an exchange of musketry could result in a meaningful number of casualties, many of these lengthy firefights devolved into nothing more than a 'timid exchange of shots' fired by two opposing bodies separated by a relatively long distance. This was especially the case when both sides consisted of untrained or already demoralized troops. Experienced and well-led infantry knew that its fire must be used sparingly and were more likely to reserve it for when it was truly needed.

Where these long-range firefights occurred, both groups of combatants hoped that the sheer volume of musket balls fired would frighten the enemy away from his current position. This, however, was the least efficacious way of fighting. In these situations, both sides tended to remain in their position until some other factor, such as the arrival of reinforcements on one side, tipped the balance to the side of the one receiving the additional troops. The continuous firing would result in dense clouds of smoke, which on a windless day would remain over and around the men doing the firing. This smoke obscured the enemy and made anything resembling accurate fire absolutely impossible, and made the fire of even the best placed troops 'uncertain and practically without effect'.[10] Decisive action often had to await the influence of some outside event, the men exhausted from the repeated firing and discouraged by their casualties. And, if it was the other side which received some unexpected benefit, they were inclined to break more readily than fresh troops still as yet undemoralized.[11]

This type of prolonged firefight was something outside of the general British experience, and when encountered at Waterloo it struck

English and Scottish observers as somewhat curious. However, the examples just provided demonstrate clearly that, among continental opponents at least, this type of firefight occurred more frequently than we have been led to believe.

FIRE BY FILES

One of the reasons why French assaults so frequently devolved into indecisive firefights lay in the nature of French doctrine. French infantry often relied on the *fire by files* method of delivering fire. Even advocates of this system, such as Marshal Ney and the American tactician Duane, realized that every effort had to be made to train the men to cease firing when commanded to do so. Unfortunately, conditions on the battlefield made this one of the most difficult types of fires to stop once begun.

Although the *fire by files* method of firing called for the third rank to abstain from fire while it loaded muskets for the second rank, *feu de billebaude* or 'battle fire', where everyone in the battalion blazed according to their own individual whims and capabilities, was the most common occurrence. In his memoirs published in 1822, General Friant questioned the wisdom of assigning such a passive role for those in the third rank to any true Frenchman. In his experience, the noise, smoke and confusion occasioned by casualties was sufficient inducement for most in the rear rank to begin firing as rapidly as those in the first two ranks. However, unless the soldier was willing to risk the wellbeing of his comrades in front of him, most of the shots were directed harmlessly into the air.[12]

Unfortunately for those in the front two ranks, not everyone in the rear rank possessed sufficient social conscience or marksmanship. The chaotic conduct of the French infantry while employing fire by files and the risk of being shot from behind was considered by many French military authorities a major problem. Marshal Saint-Cyr attributed no less than one-quarter of all French infantry casualties to being hit by friendly fire from the rear rank. And, as raw recruits formed an increasing percentage of the troops in the later campaigns this problem grew in enormity. So many of these types of injuries were experienced at Bautzen and Lutzen, that initially Napoleon believed many recruits were trying to inflict these wounds upon themselves to escape further service. Gradually, the cause of the problem began to be understood, and, in fact, was one of the considerations that induced Napoleon to experiment occasionally with the two rank line in his later campaigns.[13]

Held captive at Saint Helena after his final downfall, Napoleon set his rationale down on paper:

> The fire of the third rank is recognized as very imperfect, and dangerous to those in the first two; one prescribed the first rank to place its knee on the ground in fire by battalion, and in voluntary fire, the third rank loaded the muskets of the second: this order is bad; the infantry must be ranged only on two ranks, because the musket only permits this order.[14]

Napoleon was certainly not alone in this opinion. Such luminaries as de Jomini, Jacquinot de Presle and Gouvion Saint-Cyr were in complete agreement.

FRENCH FIRING HIGH

We have already considered Robert Jackson's observation that even veteran French troops fell into the error of opening their fire at 'too great a distance, [and] often fire at an elevation'.[15] A quick perusal of personal accounts of various British actions against the French appears to add credence to this claim. Wheeler tells us how at Vitoria one British infantry charge was conducted with such celerity that 'altho they sent us a shower of balls and bullets very few done any harm'.[16] The 73rd British Regiment of Foot encountered a similar experience in 'Germany' during the 1813 campaign. Recounting the critical portion of the action in Morris' own words: 'As we began to ascend, the enemy fired one volley, which being ill-directed passed over us harmless, or nearly so; and then they abandoned their position.'[17] Hennel provides yet another example at Salamanca:

> By this time it was quite dark [and] our skirmishers (3rd Caca-dores) opened upon them upon the brow of the hill and immedi-ately the French returned it which passed mostly over our heads. We had express orders not to fire until ordered. Our regiment was well prepared to give them an excellent charge but they received another lesson that afternoon that they will not forget

in a twelve-month. Had they stayed til we came up twenty yards further they might have given us a most destructive volley but they rapidly fired a volley or two that passed mostly over our heads and they ran away.[18]

To these examples, we must add the experience at Maida, where once again a French volley delivered from close to medium distance did little damage, being fired over the British infantrymen's heads.[19]

There is little evidence to suggest that British infantry suffered from this propensity to fire high anywhere to the same degree as their French counterparts. Both French and British observers, in contrast, are found to consistently comment on the devastating effect of British volleys. This difference in the accuracy of musket fire between the two arch rivals is attributable to the British infantry's heightened awareness of the importance of properly levelling their muskets and their increased ability to successfully implement these practices under fire.

Although an increasing number of infantry officers throughout western Europe had begun to advocate adjusting the level of the muskets according to the range of the target, there was never complete agreement on how high the musket should be raised for each distance. Firearms experts in the British and French armies, for example, devised slightly different range versus levelling algorithms. Although the French infantry in the 1790s, like their British counterpart, were advised to level at the enemy's feet at extremely close range, at longer ranges they were required to level their weapons higher than the British infantry at the same range.

The chart below shows where the infantry should aim when firing at a target at various ranges. It presents the views of two tactical experts of this period: the American William Duane (1808) and *Guide de l'officier particular en campagne.*[20]

	Duane (1808) (yards)	Guide officier (toises)	
600	'above enemy battalion'		
400	1½ feet above head		
300	hat	100–120	head
200	middle of body	90–100	neck
		80–90	chest
100–120	knees	60–80	belt
		30–40	feet

When we consider that a 'toise' is just a little more than two yards (this old French term denotes precisely 6 French feet, or 1.949 m), we see that, firing at similar ranges, the French infantry was instructed to level higher than their British counterparts. According to Duane's levelling recommendations, for example, infantry firing at 100 yards were to level their muskets at the enemy's knees, while at the same range the French authority had the men levelling at the waist.

The tendency became even more pronounced in the works of several French authors written just after the Napoleonic Wars. Although in the chart below de Brack, Lallemand and the *Instruction* of 1822 each used a different unit of measurement, all three are in agreement as to where to level the musket when firing at a given range.

De Brack (1830s) (paces)	Lallemand (1820) (yards)	Instruction (1822) (toises)
	320 5′ above	
195 hat plume	200–250 1–3′ above	90–100 upper head dress
170 head	140–200 head	70–90 head
130 shoulders	100–140 shoulders	50–70 shoulders
100 chest	0–100 middle body to 90 middle of body	0–50 chest

However, all three French experts no longer recommended levelling at the enemy's feet at close range; French infantry now was never to level lower than the enemy's waist.

The fact that the French, at least officially, recommended levelling higher than their British counterpart at the same range implies that a higher trajectory was required to hit the target for the French weapon. This, in fact, fits in with the prevailing expectation that the British musket, the famed Brown Bess, was superior to the Charleville musket used by the French during this period.

Soon after the conclusion of the Napoleonic Wars both British and French writers, awestruck with the long string of British successes, eagerly concluded that at least a part of the reason for this success lay in the superiority of the Brown Bess over the French Charleville. In his much-lauded history of the Peninsular War, Colonel Napier opined: 'It is well known, whether from the peculiarity of our muskets, physical strength and coolness of the men, or both combined, that the fire of an English line is, at all times, the most destructive known.'[21] Monsieur Dupin, a French military analyst writing about the same time, further expanded upon the supposed attributes of the Brown Bess:

> the British musket is remarkable on many accounts; ... The calibre of the English musket is larger than that of the French; and, as the piece itself is shorter, it is not much more weighty. The calibre of this arm being thus superior, and equal to ours in other respects, it carries further, notwithstanding that its length is less than the French fire-lock.[22]

The fact that former adversaries joined together in bestowing accolades on the Brown Bess was sufficient to ensure the longevity of the belief in its superiority, regardless of its real capabilities. It cannot be denied that the Brown Bess did possess some qualities that endeared it to the British infantryman. Having a shorter barrel, it weighed less, and therefore was less fatiguing when loading or charging bayonets. There was also substantially more windage than was tolerated in the French military musket. It was much easier to drop the ball down the barrel and ensure it reached the bottom by banging the piece's butt several times on the ground. Though the British infantry certainly was not alone in utilizing this 'quick fire' tactic, the Brown Bess' greater windage made it easier to use than muskets with less windage.

Unfortunately, it was these very qualities which made the Brown Bess easier to use that produced an inferior ballistic performance. Firing a fourteen-bore ball, the British Brown Bess appeared to carry much more of a punch than the French twenty-bore musket in use throughout the Napoleonic Wars. However, even British gun makers were quick to point out the Brown Bess' liabilities. Its maximum range was inferior to the French musket. There were three reasons: length of barrel, explosive force compared to weight of ball, and the amount of windage that was tolerated. The Short Land model of Brown Bess had a shorter barrel (42 inches) than the French musket (44.76 inches) which meant that its explosive gases propelled the ball for less time. Firing a ball .69 inch in diameter compared to that of .75 for the Brown Bess, but using roughly the same amount of powder in the charge, the French weapon was able to achieve a significantly higher explosive force to projectile weight ratio. Moreover, whatever explosive effect was acting on the projectile within the Brown Bess tended to dissipate faster because of the weapon's greater 'windage', referring to the difference in the diameter of the ball compared to the inside diameter of the barrel. The net effect of these various factors was to impart less of an initial velocity to the ball.[23] This meant, given the same elevation of the barrel, the ball would travel lower and over less distance. So judging the matter purely from the performance capabilities of the two weapons, we would expect the British to be levelling higher than the French, rather than the other way around.

The effectiveness of British musket fire lay elsewhere than in the physical nature of the weaponry used. Although the formal properties of ballistics were certainly not common knowledge even among veteran officers during this period, many experienced officers and infantrymen acquired an intuitive sense about the trajectory of a ball after it left the musket. Gradually, it was recognized that, in a great many cases, for a very short period of time the ball was actually thrown above the barrel's line of sight. This phenomenon probably needs a little explanation. The American tactician Duane observed:

> At its delivery from the cylinder, the bullet or ball describes a curve ... this curve line ... immediately cuts a line of level, and passes it upward, from thence at a given distance drawn to the earth by gravitation, to which all bodies are subjected, it again inclines to the former line, cuts it and finishes its parabolic course to the end of its fall.[24]

Anyone even vaguely familiar with physics in general or ballistics in particular knows that as soon as any projectile is fired it immediately is affected by the force of gravity. So, Duane's observations about the ball going above the 'line of level' at first glance appear to be erroneous. Yet despite this apparent violation of the laws of gravitation, Duane's observation nevertheless accurately described the trajectory for a great many musket balls fired on the battlefield. The reason lay in what now is called 'human error'. There were two distinct errors that when committed tended to cause the projectile to be thrown higher than expected.

Modern 're-enactors' have frequently encountered a phenomenon sometimes referred to as 'flintlock flinch'.[25] When an untrained person fires a smoothbore musket, there is a decided tendency to flinch, either while pulling the trigger or as the powder flashes up in the musket's flashpan. In a modern handgun or rifle any motion of the hand after the trigger is pulled does not meaningfully affect the bullet's trajectory. The bullet simply clears the barrel too quickly for any secondary motion of the gun to have much influence. Flintlocks were much more susceptible to hand motion, however. The reason did not arise because of the speed of the ball hurled out of the flintlock, but rather because of the nature of the apparatus used to ignite the powder in the barrel. A musket ball actually had a higher initial velocity than a modern standard issue .38 calibre handgun. Travelling about 1,000 feet per second, a musket ball would clear a 42″ barrel in less than 3/1000 of a second. This meant that *once the charge in the barrel had exploded*, just like modern weapons, secondary motions of the hands did not influence the ball's trajectory. However, there was a much greater interval between the time the trigger was pulled, the flash ignited, and the main charge in the barrel exploded. William Greener, a prominent London gunmaker in the 1820s and 1830s estimated that there was approximately a half-second delay.[26] During this delay, it was common for the forward hand to be raised a small amount. It must be remembered that the soldier's forward hand would act like a fulcrum so that whatever amount it was raised would elevate the mouth of the barrel several times this amount. An experienced marksman such as a hunter could avoid this problem by looking down the barrel, learning to pull the trigger without jerking the gun, and keeping their eyes open during the flash. This same talent could have been inculcated into new troops by allowing them to 'shoot' the gun a few times with only powder in the flash pan, and then a few more times firing a 'blank' charge. However, given the doctrine of volley fire and the realities of military economy during this period, this was rarely done. It was possible for even veteran soldiers who had survived a number of campaigns, never to learn to fire their firearms accurately.

This problem of an undesirable flinch tended to affect raw, inexperienced troops. However, another common error probably was responsible for many more shots going astray since it plagued even the most seasoned of soldiers. A subtle problem, rarely commented upon in period literature, it might have gone unnoticed had it not been for the close scrutiny of all theory, methods and practices which characterized French military efforts of the 1820s. One French officer, preoccupied with the analysis of the new types of muskets and rifles then being considered for use, recollected that during his wartime experience during combat few men actually followed the proper procedure when firing their muskets under battle conditions. The prescribed procedure required the infantrymen to lower their heads on the shoulder piece to adjust their sighting. The left eye was to be closed, while the right eye looked down the barrel so that the shot could be fired accurately and without the 'least movement'.[27] However, the 'insufferable' recoil of the musket caused the musket to jump up violently and frequently strike the infantryman's nose or cheek, not to mention inflicting painful bruises in the shoulder area. According to the French officer, a day never went by during the campaign when he did not see a bloody nose as a result of the musket's kick. Part of the problem was the wood used in the musket's stock. Most were walnut, which though handsome, conducted vibrations more readily than did most other alternatives, and absorbed little of the recoil. Bird's-eye maple, for example, was much less of a conductor and would have been more suitable in this regard. However, many gunmakers considered maple too gaudy and brittle for the rigours of war, and, except for a brief period during the Napoleonic Wars when walnut became scarce, it saw little application.[28]

The discomforts of the recoil, an intrinsic part of the firing experience, soon forced many soldiers to take a number of short cuts, which, though resulting in fewer minor cuts and abrasions, greatly lessened the accuracy of the fire. If the soldier's shoulder was already tender, he could hold the musket so that the end of its stock was away from his shoulder, though of course, his head would tend to remain upright. Many other soldiers recognized that they had to lower their head down near the breech, but to avoid a bruised lip, positioned their head on the stock so that a minimum of discomfort would occur. Unfortunately, this usually also meant sacrificing the ability to look down the musket barrel. Another common trick was to hold the musket's stock firmly against the shoulder without lowering the head anywhere near the breech. The result was that all too often the men:

> . . . stunned by the gun shots which leaves them with an earache, by the exhortations of their officers, fearing the emission of the neighbor's fusil, not only thinking not to adjust, but often firing without putting the shoulder piece to the shoulder, and it (sic) thus that one burns 8 or 10 cartridges, to execute fire by two ranks [i.e. fire by files], in combat.[29]

Of course, the end result in all these cases was highly inaccurate fire, since the men were unable or unwilling to look down the musket barrel to see roughly where it was pointed. In those cases where the men fired their weapons keeping their heads upright, the tendency to fire high was much worse than if they simply closed their eyes. For the most part conscientious, a great many of the men would still attempt to level their pieces while holding their heads erect. Keeping the eyes six to ten inches above their musket, they would continue to look through the sight at the end of the barrel and at the enemy beyond, raising or lowering the barrel accordingly.

Trying properly to level the pieces while holding the head upright to avoid minor injuries necessarily caused the barrel to elevate slightly more than if the infantryman had been looking along the barrel through the sights. More than anything else it was this pernicious practice that caused many volleys to be fired above the enemy's heads, even at relatively close ranges between twenty to fifty paces.[30]

The answer to the question of the superiority of British musket fire over French, is that it appears that the French designed their levelling scheme according to the theoretical characteristics of their muskets, while the British, on the other hand, designed a method of levelling that took into account not only the weapon's theoretical performance but accounted for the performance of the average soldier using the weapon.

CHAPTER 12

Small Arms Fire

THEORETICAL VERSUS PRACTICAL EFFECTIVENESS OF MUSKET

Anyone familiar with modern day small arms undoubtedly would probably expect a horrific casualty rate as a result of the prolonged firefights that frequently occurred on the Napoleonic battlefield. Although very high casualties were indeed inflicted by musket fire in certain situations, when considering all of the firefights that occurred in any sizeable conflict, the overall losses were very much less than what we would anticipate. This was not due to any intrinsic inaccuracy of the flintlock musket. Hunters and marksmen armed with the musket were able to achieve remarkable accuracy up to between 100 and 150 yards, and many modern day musket enthusiasts are able to duplicate this result with this weapon.

By the late eighteenth century military authorities became increasingly interested in trying to determine the effectiveness of the musket, both under ideal conditions on the fighting range and during the rigours of the battlefield. At first lacking hard data, tacticians were able only to guess the accuracy of infantrymen firing at targets during peacetime practice. The English physician Robert Jackson, the British Inspector-General of Army Hospitals in 1803, for example, estimated that at 100 to 120 paces 'one in three [shots] at least will strike within the volume of a man's body'.[1] William Duane writing in America at about the same time placed the theoretical accuracy at about 20%: 'not 1 out of 5 shots hit an object at the height of a horse's head at 300 feet away.'[2]

However, by the turn of the nineteenth century, tacticians began to try to accurately determine the 'theoretical' effectiveness of the musket under ideal conditions. In France, for example, a musket was fixed to a permanent rest and then fired at a target 150 metres away. The resulting 'mean error' for the Charleville at this distance was determined to be 1.75 metres by 3.00 metres.

About this time several experiments were conducted in Britain and France to try to determine the percentage of shots that hit a target. Both experiments came to almost the same conclusion, as shown by the chart below.[3]

Picard	Müller	Percentage Hits
75m (82 yds)		60%
	100 yds	53%/40%
150m (164 yds)		40%
	200 yds	30%/18%
225m (246 yds)		25%
	300 yds	23%/15%
300m (328 yds)		20%

Müller's experiment differentiated between raw and veteran troops. The value to the left of the slash ('/') in the 'Percentage Hits' column indicates the results for veteran troops; the value after the slash gives results for the less experienced counterpart. Most military experts agreed that musket fire was most effective when delivered at targets less than 150 metres distant.[4]

The tests described by Picard and Müller relied on the standard smoothbore musket. But how did contemporary rifles fare? During the reform era after 1807, the Prussians tested the accuracy of a number of muskets and rifles. Scharnhorst published the results in 1813:

	120 yds	160 yds	240 yds
Prussian rifle (plaster bullets)	68%	48%	31%
Prussian rifle (cartridges)	51%	26%	
Prussian musket, 1809		21%	

In other words, at 160 yards the Prussian rifle firing plaster bullets was roughly two and a half times more accurate than an

1809 model of the Prussian musket. Scharnhorst pointed out that a rifle required twice as long to reload and therefore the number of casualties produced by each per unit time was about the same, but a musket expended about three to four times as many rounds.[5]

If one relied exclusively on these experiments to determine the casualties that would be inflicted within this range one would expect extremely high casualty rates, where a 500-man battalion firing even at 150 metres would inflict 200 casualties. Of course, nothing of the sort happened on the battlefield. However, the inefficacy of musket fire under battlefield conditions was generally recognized by contemporary military authorities, who not only attempted to account for this seeming anomaly but also to discover some way of making small arms fire more effective.

Although there was no consensus about the exact 'coefficient of effectiveness' of musket fire, if we may use this term, just about everyone who attempted to evaluate the effectiveness of musket fire admitted the percentage of shots fired in anger that succeeded in hitting a target were extremely low. This, however, was the theoretical performance of musketry conducted under the most favourable of circumstances. Military men knew that the actual performance under battlefield conditions was much lower, and many tacticians attempted to calculate the percentages of casualties inflicted during previous battles. One contemporary historian noted that the Prussians at the Battle of Czaslau had to expend 650,000 cartridges to inflict about 6,500 Austrian casualties – dead and wounded (i.e. a 1% casualty rate).[6] This turns out to be a high estimate of the flintlock's effectiveness. Guibert felt, for example, that only 2,000 out of 1,000,000 (0.2%) of all shots resulted in some casualty, while Piobert thought it was necessary to fire between 3,000 and 10,000 (0.01% to 0.03%) shots to effect a single hit.[7] Colonel Napier, like his compatriot Jackson, appears to have had a high estimation of the effectiveness of musketry in action. Based on his experience fighting the French throughout the Peninsular War, Napier concluded: 'not one out of 300 balls expended, took effect.'[8] This appears to be an overly optimistic assessment. At Vitoria, for example, the British infantry were able to inflict only one casualty for every 800 rounds fired.[9] Hughes, a modern writer specializing in the statistical analysis of firepower concluded that well-trained infantry were able to inflict a 3 to 5% casualty rate.[10]

The chart below shows estimates from a number of military writers of what percentage of shots fired hit a target.[11]

Guibert	Gassendi	Piobert	Anony-mous	Jackson	Napier	Hughes	Decker
2/1000	1/3000	3/10000	1/1000	5/1000	1/300	2/100	1/10000
.2%	.03%	.03%	.1%	.5%	.3%	3–5%	.01%

To help visualize the implications of these figures in practical terms, the rates of effectiveness quoted by these analysts meant that if a single infantryman was able to fire three rounds per minute continuously, something that would not be possible for any length of time, between twenty-three minutes and 82.25 hours would elapse before the enemy suffered a single casualty. Or, if we consider a 500-man battalion firing continuously, between .005 and ten casualties would be suffered every volley. It must be remembered that these estimates counted all firefights, including those conducted at long and even ineffective ranges. The rate of casualties inflicted by the musket at point blank and close range obviously were on a different order of magnitude.

REASONS FOR INEFFECTIVENESS OF MUSKET

Depending upon whose figures are used, the theoretical coefficient of accuracy of the military flintlock at about 100 paces ranged between 50% to 20%, while the percentage of shots that produced casualties during a large-scale battle was found empirically to be somewhere between .01% and .5%. In other words, the best case musket fire during battle conditions was at least 40 times less effective than that which one would expect after witnessing the various accuracy trials conducted during this general period.

This sizeable discrepancy between the *theoretical* and *practical* accuracy of the musket has been attributed to a wide spectrum of causes. Obviously, the fact that almost all small fire, except that employed by skirmishers, tirailleurs or jägers was *unaimed* fire contributed more than any other factor to the surprisingly low rate of casualties that were inflicted. However, making this observation is not without its own dangers, since, unless accompanied by the necessary qualifiers it implies that the military authorities of this time could have avoided this problem by somehow employing *aimed* fire in all cases on the battlefield.

Many twentieth-century historians like to speculate on how much the effectiveness of musket fire could have been increased if only the infantry had been regularly allowed to indulge in target practice. The example that is usually cited is how much the effectiveness of the British infantry's musket fire improved after General Moore's reforms in infantry training in the early 1800s.

Although appealing to the modern reader who models his views on aimed rifle fire in the post-First World War combat environment, this argument ignores how warfare was actually conducted on the battlefield during the Napoleonic era. If few resources generally were devoted to peacetime target practice, rather than indicating either near universal dereliction of duty or profound imbecility among the higher levels of the officer corps, this demonstrated a pragmatic understanding of the necessities of the battlefield as they then existed. Quite early it had been realized that the ordinary soldier confined to closed formations would rarely, if ever, be able to use aimed fire during an engagement. As long as the infantrymen had to be grouped together tightly in closed order formations, aimed fire could never be feasible, except on a few isolated occasions. Aimed fire and volley fire were by their very nature mutually exclusive practices. Most situations demanded regularly delivered and strictly controlled volleys. For example, a body of infantry attacked by cavalry usually had to withhold their fire until the critical moment, and then part of the formation had to fire in unison.

If in most cases aimed fire was not feasible on the field of battle, adjusting the 'level' of the musket according to the range of the target, however, was possible. And, as we have already seen, articulated levelling systems had been adopted by many European armies in the closing years of the eighteenth century. Unfortunately, most infantry failed to take advantage of levelling techniques under the heat of the battle. This appears to have been a near universal observation, applicable to the infantry in all armies. Writing in the late 1790s, the German reformer Bülow remarked:

Sometimes the soldier fires too low, and the reason of this inaccuracy, in either case, is that the soldier, accustomed, ... to a mechanical manner of handling his firelock, most frequently levels it at the same height, without attending sufficiently to the differences of the distances at which he stands from the enemy, or to that of the positions he occupies with regard to him.[12]

An almost identical observation would be made about ten years later by a French officer: 'It is this false idea . . . which is in nearly all the soldiers, that at whatever distance they find the enemy, they must aim at the middle of the corps . . .'[13] Lest it be thought that the British infantry were immune from this tendency, the following remarks of a prominent English gunmaker must be considered: 'When they [British infantrymen] come to fire ball, they, as directed, fire as good a line as they can. The meaning of elevation is unknown to them, and in nine cases out of ten, the ball never reaches the distance the target is placed at.'[14] These remarks, though only penned in the 1830s, were intended to describe the performance of the British infantry during the Peninsular War and the Hundred Days Campaign.

Although this advance in military science began to be documented in various professional literature from the 1790s onwards, this practice of proper levelling was never put into universal practice. There were a number of reasons. It is clear from both theoretical writings and battle accounts that its benefits had never been fully appreciated by all officers and their men. Moreover, the continued advocacy of a rapid succession of volleys in some armies, made it difficult for the men to level properly before each volley. Another problem was simply inadequate training. Even if an infantry unit was fortunate enough to receive target practice, this training was of a surprisingly limited value on an actual battlefield. Unlike modern armies, which make every effort to train their troops in conditions as close as possible to those likely to be encountered, eighteenth-century and Napoleonic troops trained under the most idealized of conditions. Whatever target practice did occur was always conducted on as level ground as could be found. However, even the least obstructed of European battlefields was rarely, if ever, totally flat. There were always at least slight differences in elevation between the positions occupied by friendly and hostile troops when separated even by fifty or sixty paces. Unfortunately, if troops were trained exclusively on flat terrain, which was invariably the case, the tendency was to apply the exact same practice and habits to all firing situations, regardless of circumstances.[15] This meant that there was a decided tendency for most infantrymen to elevate their pieces the same amount for a given distance, whether the enemy was at the same height or over five or ten metres above or below. The resulting aberrancy, though slight, was enough to mean that most of the shots would often be hurled just slightly over the enemy's heads or, conversely, at their feet.

The differences between firing and target elevations also caused other problems. Unlike modern weaponry, the flintlock was very much more limited as to how much it could be fired upwards or downwards. It was not a weapon that could be fired effectively when the barrel was raised at too high an angle or significantly lowered. The nature of the difficulty encountered in each case was different, however. On the one hand, it was discovered that raising the barrel more than 15° had no effect on the range of the weapon, and so was pointless.[16] On the other, the problem with lowering the barrel was that under battlefield conditions it proved very difficult for the men to accurately 'level' (to aim in a general sense) their weapons at a target below them. The problem with lowering a weapon to hit a target downhill stemmed from the fact that the soldier had to additionally lower the barrel when firing at a target at close range to take into account the initial rise in the trajectory at very close range. It appears that soldiers instinctively recoiled from making this second adjustment since it appeared to throw the ball into the ground before reaching the enemy.

In addition to factors leading to inaccuracy which stemmed from the nature of the weaponry and training then in use, there was a large assortment of others which arose out of the nature of actual combat. Probably the single most significant factor was the confusion and disorder inevitably occasioned whenever a large body of men attempted to fire their muskets for any extended time under battle conditions. As many contemporary observers pointed out, the attempts to get the men to execute quickly a series of volleys almost always devolved into disorganized voluntary fire or 'running fire'. According to *chef de bataillon* Hulot, it was because of this 'so very detrimental practice of multiplying the number of discharges, and [making] these with rapidity, instead of executing these with accuracy and precision' that 'infantry fire does not generally produce a very great effect'.[17]

Once the fire became general, that is, once it devolved into each man firing at will, it became relatively ineffective. In addition to the profuse smoke given off by the muskets, there were a variety of other factors that tended to reduce the effectiveness of both volley and individual fire. Although the infantryman, no longer bound by his officers' commands, could pick his own target and moment to fire, and thus, in theory, could aim, a number of other factors worked against any sort of accuracy. As we have already seen, Duhèsme was surprised to find that his battalion, firing at any enemy battalion one hundred paces away, was only able to inflict three or four casualties as the result of a lengthy firefight.

The high level of excitement which always accompanied these actions, the smoke that enveloped the men after a few shots as well as a myriad of 'annoying incidents' quickly produced pandemonium. An officer was fortunate if his men produced a 'horizontal' fire, that is, more or less levelled against the oncoming enemy, as opposed to the all too frequent 'haphazard' fire, where many if not most of the muskets were pointed too close to the ground or up in the air.[18] General Mitchell provides a gripping account of the breakdown of order and thus aiming ability during a firefight:

What precision of aim can be expected from soldiers when firing in line? One man is priming; another coming to the present; a third taking, what is called aim; a fourth ramming down his cartridge. After a few shots, the whole body are closely enveloped in smoke, and the enemy is totally invisible; some of the soldiers step out a pace or two, in order to get a better shot; others kneel down; and some have no objection to retire a step or two. The doomed begin to fall, dreadfully mutilated perhaps, and even bold men shrink from the sight; others are wounded, and assisted to the rear by their comrades; so that the whole becomes a line of utter confusion, in which the mass only think of getting their shot fired, they hardly care how in what direction.[19]

The recoil of the musket would sometimes further this chaos, causing a soldier to brush his neighbour and possibly derange the latter's aim. Matters were far worse if the infantry formation had been forced to begin the action before they were able to take off their knapsacks. The rear ranks then had even less space for firing between the ranks in front of them, and more than ever were forced to fire up in the air, wasting ammunition and adding to the general confusion.[20]

SMOKE, DUST AND FOG

Before the introduction of smokeless powder in the waning decades of the nineteenth century, a considerable amount of thick smoke was produced whenever a small arm was discharged. The gases thus produced are heavier than air, and so this smoke often would stagnate directly over the spot where the pistol or musket was fired. This was only a minor inconvenience for the hunter or marksman who usually fired his weapon individually. A single musket did not produce a tremendous amount of smoke, and if the smoke did block his vision, he could simply move a few feet. However, smoke often proved to be a significant irritant when a number of persons fired their weapons in the same general area, as was the case, obviously, whenever infantry fired a volley in line. In this situation, a vast amount of dense smoke was always produced. Unless there was a noticeable breeze, the smoke would float above and around the men who fired their weapons and would totally obliterate their view. If the men were attacking and had only stopped to deliver a fire, the clouds of smoke would be left behind as soon as the troops recommenced their advance.

We have already seen how at the Battle of Caldiéro, General Duhèsme approached a battalion on the French left wing where the smoke was so thick that when he arrived he saw 'nothing but flashes, the glint of bayonets and the tops of the grenadiers' caps'. Though the enemy was only sixty paces distant behind a ravine, neither the enemy nor the ravine could be seen.[21] This was a common situation, and we find references to difficulties caused by smoke in many of the accounts of battles of the period. At Austerlitz, for example, both sides afterwards commented on the lack of wind and the resulting billows of smoke that covered the battlefield. A newspaper correspondent for the *London Times* claimed it was so thick at points that 'men were unable to see each other, at the distance of twenty paces'.[22] Similarly at Borodino, the smoke was so thick that the men in the dense French formations could hardly see their enemy who were in equally concentrated masses.[23]

Fog could create similar problems. At the Battle of Jena, the Saxon battalions of Frederick Augustus and Rechten, hampered by a dense fog, were able to make out only indistinct masses moving in the distance upon which they immediately began to fire. The French 11th *légère*, finding itself fired upon, returned fire, judging distance and direction of the enemy by the flashes in the mist and the sound of the reports. Both sides continued the engagement for several minutes without either being able to make out clearly their intended victims because of the mist.[24]

Dust clouds occasionally posed the same type of problem. One very noticeable example occurred during the Battle of Prague (6 May 1757). Although this lies outside the primary period covered in this work, it has been included because it shows the extreme degree of confusion that could be caused whenever the troop's vision was completely obscured by either smoke, fog or dust. Leading his hussars against the Austrian hussars, Colonel Warnery, after defeating the enemy horse, found himself in a sudden but extremely violent dust storm caused by the horses.

A very extraordinary circumstance happened to me in this battle; in the second charge, our cavalry fell off to the left . . . and threw me into disorder; there then rose the greatest cloud of dust that I ever beheld; it was impossible to see the head of the horse I rode. I called out to my people to incline to the left; I then ordered the assembly to be sounded; a trumpeter obeyed within four yards of me. My hussars came in, and when the dust cleared off, I found that the trumpeter who had obeyed my order in sounding belonged to the enemy. It may be judged by this what confusion we were all in.[25]

Although dust storms obviously covered a much greater area, the billows of smoke caused by volleys of musketry could be just as blinding.

FIRES

If the general mayhem caused by the din of the artillery, musketry and the screams of the dying and the wounded, as well as the large clouds of smoke hanging over portions of the battlefield was not enough, occasionally another even more fearful danger presented itself. This was the possibility of part of the battlefield catching fire.

In our mind's eye we tend to picture European battlefields as mostly flat terrain topped with short grass cultivated with the same meticulousness as that found in front of the average city hall. If the land being fought over was used for pasture this indeed might be the case; however, if it was farmland the crops could be quite high. During the summer months, especially if the rain had been stingy during the preceding period, this could be potentially as dangerous a fire hazard as forested areas in the American south west. And the events and occurrences on the battlefields offered a vastly greater temptation to fires than that provided by the most careless of campers. Dozens if not hundreds of cannons spat out burning wadding and the battlefield could be littered with hundreds of thousands of partially ignited spent cartridges. Even the infantryman's spent cartridges could pose a similar threat, if the grass and vegetation was dry enough. This danger was most pronounced in the Mediterranean areas where during the summer months the dry weather and very hot temperatures dried out whatever vegetation was to be found. Once again, Coignet proves to be an invaluable witness to this type of event:

> We could not see one another in the smoke. The guns set the wheat fields on fire, and this caused a general commotion in the ranks. Some cartridge-boxes exploded; we were obliged to fall back and form again as quickly as possible. This weakened our position, but the situation was restored by the intrepidity of our chiefs, who looked out for everything.[26]

This danger, although frightening to anyone who was close at hand rarely proved fatal or even harmful to those who were as yet unhurt, and still capable of moving to safer ground. On the other hand, it could prove fatal to those who were unfortunate enough to have already been wounded. A British subaltern officer offers this account of those that were not lucky enough to be still able to move out of harm's way:

> On passing the ravine where the contest had been more severe, I perceived that a high sere grass which grew there had taken fire from the wadding of the guns; and the poor fellows who had fallen there, wounded and deprived of the power of escape, were literally burnt to death; which gave them all the appearance of pigs that had been roasted . . . these dead Frenchmen, who could now be distinguished only by their ear-rings, as the

English and French lay there in mixed numbers, with their clothes entirely consumed.[27]

Another example occurred at Salamanca where the men in two British divisions were threatened by fire caused by the numerous cartridges strewn over the battlefield. The smoke that was generated rolled over the men in huge clouds and some of the men thought they were about to be suffocated.[28]

RAIN

Unlike the breechloading rifle which replaced it, the musket with its external firing mechanism was very susceptible to the elements. Heavy or continuous rain, for example, would mean that it would be virtually impossible to use. The Napoleonic Wars provide many examples of this sort. At the battle of Katzbach neither side was able to use its firepower and had to rely on the bayonet to decide the issue.[29] A heavy rain during the Battle of Dresden also stripped much of the infantry of their firepower and Latour-Maubourg's personal escort, a half-squadron of lancers, were able to walk up and impale two groups of Austrian infantry in battalion square.[30]

FIRING ON OWN MEN

Throughout the age of the musket, the phenomenon of troops firing on friendly forces was all too common. In fact, this has remained a problem down to the present day as the recent events in the Gulf War have so tragically demonstrated. Two factors tended to exacerbate this problem: the all-too-often similarity of dress for friend and foe, and the reduction of vision caused by the smoke resulting from musket fire.

Just how difficult it was sometimes to recognize the national origin, and thus allegiance, of a body of men while still at a distance is demonstrated by the experience of Captain von Reuter's artillery battery during the Battle of Ligny (15 June 1815). Captain Reuter had watched the 14th Prussian Infantry Regiment advance ahead of him to try and take possession of the village of St Amand. So, when several hours later he saw lengthy lines of skirmishers coming towards him he initially thought they were friendly Prussian troops, and allowed the two lines to continue to approach unchallenged. It was only when the two lines had approached to within 300 paces that his surgeon noticed the red tufts on the shakos, a sure sign that the skirmishers were not Prussian but French! Reuter then ordered his gunners to begin firing, and a struggle ensued.

The difficulty here stemmed from the fact that the infantry on both sides were wearing dark blue 'habits', or great coats, which though of a different hue and tone, were not truly distinguishable at a distance. In this instance, the confusion led to not firing when the circumstances required it; however, just as often it led to infantry and artillery firing on friendly forces.[31] During the entire series of Napoleonic Wars there were probably innumerable examples of this type of unfortunate occurrence. However, we need to only consider two examples to demonstrate its occurrence.

At the Battle of Austerlitz the 26th French *légère* assigned to Legrand's Division attempted to come to the assistance of the 3rd *de ligne*. Perceiving indistinctly troops positioned on the other side of the Goldbach, it began to fire even though the colour of the troops being fired upon was indistinguishable. As it turned out, the other troops were from the 108th *de ligne*.[32]

A similar event occurred at the Battle of Wagram. Two columns of infantry from the Army of Italy having crossed the Russbach were in the process of ascending the Plateau to join Dupas' command. The Saxon infantry attached to Dupas were in the rear and were the first of his command that the two columns encountered. The Saxons were wearing white uniforms and in the distance appeared similar to the Austrian infantry. The two columns began firing on the Saxons who, surprised at being fired upon from their rear, quickly returned the fire. Unfortunately, the confusion spread, since the troops under MacDonald and Grenier both began to waver, thinking themselves suddenly attacked from both the front and the rear.[33]

Unfortunately, on rare occasions infantry found it imperative to fire on purpose on friendly troops as happened at the Battle of Pultusk (26 December 1806). Charged unexpectedly in the left flank by cavalry, the first two battalions broke and fled. The battalion of which Bugeaud was a sous-lieutenant was able to form square. The refugees from the other two battalions found themselves between the enemy cavalry and the resolute infantry in the brigade's one remaining battalion. Many of the refugees ran towards that battalion and tried to enter its ranks, but were kept at bay by the continuous rows of bayonets. When the enemy cavalry had approached to twenty paces, the battalion began to deliver ordered fire, which cut down scores of friend and foe alike. Fortunately, the cavalry was repulsed, and those of the fleeing French infantry who still survived were now able to make their way to safety.[34]

RUNNING OUT OF AMMUNITION

It was during these extended firefights where the most ammunition was expended. A single battalion might expend upwards of 15,000 cartridges. And, although there might be casualties on both sides, this tactic almost always led to a temporary stalemate.

This type of continued fire often led to a number of problems. The most obvious was running out of ammunition. One extremely experienced officer observed that on the battlefield it was common to see battalions run out of ammunition after a half hour of firing, long before the firefight was decided one way or another. When this happened, one would hear the infantrymen yelling for more cartridges, followed quickly by men streaming to the rear ostensibly to go and look for more cartridges. After a short while the firing line was sufficiently thinned that retreat or even defeat became inevitable.[35] When this happened the firing line was usually forced to retreat, although history records some interesting alternatives. One of the British regiments advancing into the Pyrenees in the Pampeluna area ran out of ammunition while defending a prominent hill against French infantry which was advancing up the hill, after just having pushed back the 50th and 71st Regiments of Foot. There being a plethora of loose rocks and stones in the immediate area, the British soldiers started to throw rocks at the enemy which they kept at bay until reinforcements arrived and the position was maintained.[36]

One of the best examples of how a unit should have conducted itself was provided by the 14th regiment *de ligne* while fighting in the Alps during the Hundred Days. Forced to fight an Austrian regiment for eight hours, it reserved its fire for only the critical moments. The Austrians, who on this occasion were on the offensive, fired continuously. The 14th withheld its fire until the Austrians neared their position, then at the appropriate moment they conducted battalion fire followed by a bayonet charge at close distance. This they repeatedly performed successfully. At the end of each assault both sides returned to their positions. The result was that the 14th managed to keep the superior Austrian force at bay for eight hours while still managing to conserve one-third of its cartridges at the end of this time.[37]

Another problem associated with continual firing was that musket barrels could heat up. When this happened there was a real danger of the cartridges exploding while the charge was being loaded. This, of course, was a serious danger which could result in the maiming and even death of the infantryman. When this happened, firing was discontinued until the barrels cooled down sufficiently. We have already seen how in the early 1800s William Duane determined, for example, that the musket barrel became too hot for the infantryman to fire after twenty-five rounds were fired in a little over four minutes. After this, the infantrymen had to hold the musket by its sling while reloading and ramming home the ball.[38]

Interestingly enough, there is at least one record of a very novel solution to the problem which occasionally occurred under battle conditions. Captain Coignet in his memoirs recounts how at the Battle of Marengo his battalion ran out of ammunition, firing at the enemy who enjoyed vastly superior numbers:

> Our muskets were so hot it became impossible to load for fear of igniting the cartridges. There was nothing for it but to piss into the barrels to cool them, and then to dry them by pouring loose powder and setting it alight unrammed. Then as soon as we could fire again, we retired in good order.[39]

Unfortunately for Coignet and his fellow soldiers their trials were still not over, and they started to run out of ammunition and were very hard pressed. However, at that point the Consular Guard arrived with eight hundred men. Each of these men had their linen overalls filled with spare cartridges. These reinforcements processed to the rear of the fighting line where they handed out the ammunition.

Although the above factors would impair the troops from conducting themselves exactly as rehearsed during peacetime practice, it should not be thought that formal systems were always discarded in the heat of the battle, and firefights automatically broke down into 'voluntary' fire, where each soldier fired at will.

In an eye witness account there is a tendency to describe the unusual, whatever makes that particular occurrence distinctive or unique. By the Napoleonic time, all the methods of delivering fire had been established for quite some time prior to the outbreak of hostilities. As a result, it is rare that observers comment one way or the other on how fire was delivered in a specific situation. However, several notable observations have come down to us, and they demonstrate that formal methods of delivering fire were used on the battlefield, at least occasionally.

One of the best examples is provided by the 55th de ligne at the battle of Austerlitz. Assigned to Marshal Soult, the regiment was in the front line part of the force to deliver the decisive attack on the Pratzen Heights. However, a thick fog covered the marshy land where the regiment was initially positioned, and it was ambushed by a battalion of Russian chasseurs ordered to defend that edge of the plateau. It appeared that the Russians, however, were equally surprised, giving the 55th Regiment time enough for it to 'fire by battalion'. In this context, this term referred to a situation where the whole battalion was ordered to fire at once, a technique used when one heavy volley was desired or there were only a few moments available. This was enough, however, to make the Russians retire back up to the plateau behind them. The 55th Regiment quickly followed the retiring Russians up the slope, but on reaching the top they found additional Russian infantry facing them. At this point, they started to deploy into line, and for the remainder of the action fired by platoons and by divisions. Once the battalion was deployed, it was immediately ordered forward to attack. For the remainder of the battle 'one only acted by fire of two ranks'.[40]

What struck contemporary military authorities as being so notable was not that the 55th Regiment delivered ordered volleys in the manner prescribed by the regulations, but that during the same general action it used several different types of fire systems, and all while under significant duress.

Saint-Cyr tells of a time during a Peninsular campaign when men in his seventh corps were surprised to find the Spanish troops opposed to them using a wide assortment of fire systems. As the French attack columns (here this refers not to the usual battalion-sized 'column of attack' but to lengthier columns consisting of several battalions, each in closed order column, one behind the other) approached the Spaniards they were met with a mixture of 'fire by files', platoon firing, and battalion fire from the various units along the defending line. We are told that all of these fire systems were performed with 'precision', and were followed by a well executed 'passage of lines,' to allow the second line to come to the front. This indicated a degree of instruction amongst the Spanish that the French had not expected. Unfortunately for the Spanish, their officers appeared to have been inexperienced, and these volleys were begun while the French still were outside the effective range of the musket, so little harm was done to the attackers.

The French responded to the fire by doubling their pace and charging with their lowered bayonets as they neared the Spanish lines. At the last moment the Spanish turned and fled.[41]

CHAPTER 13

British Tactics in Practice (1809–1815)

COMMON PERCEPTION ABOUT BRITISH INFANTRY

Temporarily excepting the notable Hundred Days, a majority of British/French confrontations during the Napoleonic Wars occurred during the struggle for control of the Iberian peninsula. Glancing through the standard references of this campaign, known as the Peninsular War, we are immediately struck with the number of occasions where the British infantry defeated its French counterpart. Many of these were relatively minor skirmishes, standard fare during the *petite guerre*, as the day-to-day contests during the campaign were known; others were large scale, set piece battles with the most serious of repercussions, such as Albuera, Talavera or Salamanca.

Common wisdom over the last hundred years or so has had the British consistently defeating the French because of the stolidness of the British soldier and use of effective firepower. 'Effective Firepower' here refers to the presumed ability to fire 'five rounds per minute' achieved by continuous peacetime training and encouraged by the likes of Sir John Moore's reforms. What this means is that when the attacking French were at a certain distance, let's say between 100 and 150 paces, the British were thought to deliver a series of volleys as the French continued their assault or stopped to return fire. Presumably, after a number of volleys the enemy, sufficiently discouraged by cumulative casualties, would lose its resolve and discontinue the offensive.

In his *Forward into Battle* Paddy Griffith has already provided the following passage from Jac Wellar's *Wellington in the Peninsula, 1808–1814* to demonstrate the tendency to attribute the practice of repeated fire to British infantry of the period. However, this passage so typifies attitudes found throughout many other modern works that perhaps it is not out of place to repeat this quotation in the present work:

> The first volley from the First Battalion of the Fiftieth was fired at a range slightly over 100 yards; others followed it regularly at 15 second intervals as the range gradually shortened. Slowly, the flanks of the 50th wrapped around the column. The British line was using every one of its muskets; the French could reply with no more than 200 of their 1,200 firearms. General Thomières, who commanded the French brigade, endeavored to deploy the column to line under fire, but found this impossible. The French recoiled at each volley; they finally broke and fled to the rear with the riflemen in hot pursuit.[1]

Perusing the numerous British memoirs and battle accounts that are commonly available, however, we quickly discover that there is little or no basis for this notion that British troops somehow defeated the French utilizing a continuum of well-orchestrated volleys. Only rarely do we find the British infantryman engaged in any type of continuous fire in the manner associated with Frederick's Prussian infantry which, as we have already seen, was sometimes imitated by even French infantry during the Napoleonic era. In fact, the overwhelming body of evidence suggests most convincingly that the recurring British success was due to something other than crushing their opponents by the weight of fire derived from mechanically unleashing 'five rounds per minute'.

If anything, the British were characterized by their niggardly attitude regarding the delivery of fire. During the Peninsular campaign, it was the French and the Spanish infantry who were notorious for delighting in the 'long shot', where they commenced firing while their enemy [the British] were still well over 100 paces distant.[2] The British, in comparison, almost always withheld their fire until close, if not extremely, close range. Usually, a single volley was resorted to before the final rush upon the enemy with lowered bayonets.

Going beyond the types of secondary sources that have unfortunately characterized much of modern historiography, we do not have to wade far through period memoirs and battle accounts to find numerous detailed accounts of exactly what the British infantry did do on the battlefield. Paddy Griffith in *Forward in Battle* is one of the first to note the discrepancy between first-hand accounts and the previously accepted theory.

Private Wheeler, for example, describes an instance at the Battle of Nivelle. After driving the enemy from behind a hedge, the 51st Regiment was soon counter-attacked by a reinforced enemy. In this instance, the men in Wheeler's regiment:

> allowed them to come within a very short distance of us, and then we poured a volley into their faces and before they had well got over their surprise we were upon them with our bayonets.[3]

Time and time again the British infantry tactic of waiting until the enemy had advanced to close range, delivering a murderous volley and then charging the enemy was adopted. We will look at a number of other examples when we take a detailed look at the mechanics underlying the British tactic.

Possibly because the innumerable combats and frays during the Revolutionary and Peninsular Wars are so completely overshadowed by the events of a single day in 1815, there is a tendency to assume that the natural posture of the British infantry was on the defensive. Though it is true that on many notable occasions the British assumed a defensive mode, such as at Bussaco, Vimero and Talavera, on a day-to-day basis during the continual campaigning they vigorously pursued offensive operations as a matter of course. Upon occasion, the British assumed the offensive during a set piece battle, such as at Salamanca and Vitoria.

An examination of eye witness accounts reveals that the British infantry utilized these tactics of a sparse fire followed by a determined bayonet charge even while on the offensive. Hennel provides us with an example of a British attack in the storming of the heights of Vera:

> A company of the 95th opened up the business. About 20 men with 20 supporting them marched coolly up the hill . . . The French who delight in a long shot (the Spaniards & they are well matched at this — famous ammunition wasters), began directly they, our men, showed their heads. However, the 95th

moved regularly (I do not mean in line) up the hill to within
30 yards of the top without firing and then, by way of breathing,
gave a volley, loaded & advanced to the top, the support close
behind them. The French did not attempt to defend it but moved
to their left, not without music, in quick time.[4]

There are other examples of contemporary accounts showing British
infantry using one or two quick volleys or even avoiding firing
altogether and the launching into an aggressive bayonet charge. For
example:

On the 3rd of May, at daybreak, all of the cavalry and sixteen
light companies occupied the town. We stood under arms until
three o'clock, when a staff-officer rode up to our Colonel and
gave orders for our advance. Colonel Cadogan put himself at
our head, saying, 'My lads, you have had no provision these
two days; there is plenty in the hollow in front, let us down
and divide it.' We advanced as quick as we could run and met
the light companies retreating as fast as they could. We continued to advance, at double quick time, our firelocks at the
trail, our bonnets in our hands . . . The Colonel cries, 'Here is
food, my lads, cut away.' Thrice we waved our bonnets, and
thrice we cheered; brought our firelocks to the charge, and
forced them back through the town.[5]

DIVERSITY OF BRITISH INFANTRY SYSTEMS

The chronic failure to correctly identify the British infantry's methods
of attack and defence is partially attributable to the fragmentary
nature of the accounts that have come down to us. Whatever descriptions of British tactical practices in the field have come our way via
memoirs are brief, and were primarily intended to portray some
larger event, such as the events of a notable engagement, or provide
'colour' or background detail. Rarely do these first-hand accounts
make a self-conscious and concerted effort to describe an entire tactical system or even an individual tactical practice. Moreover, whenever these first-hand accounts are assembled, at first glance they
appear to suggest that the British infantry, rather than limiting itself

to any one body of doctrine, in fact utilized a wide range of differing systems, techniques and practices.

The diversity of infantry tactical practices during the Napoleonic Wars is in noticeable contrast to that up to the Seven Years' War period, where much greater consistency is found. Theoretical treatises by tacticians in the early period such as Kane and Bland, as well as Parker's account of the Royal Regiment of Ireland's actual conduct at Malplaquet, all describe the same type of infantry attack. The British infantry advances slowly at a deliberate gait, periodically stops, and conducts platoon fire by individual 'firings', before resuming its advance. The main offensive element is a series of well delivered volleys unleashed at successively decreasing distances. There is a greater emphasis on the role of preliminary small arms fire and correspondingly less on the use of a spirited attack with lowered bayonets once within point blank range.

Scanning the various personal accounts of actions in the Peninsula and during the 1815 campaign, however, the British infantry are found to employ a number of different tactics, none of which conform exactly to the earlier practices. Rather than the methodical delivery of a series of well orchestrated volleys at decreasing ranges, the British attacks are characterized by increased aggressiveness and a corresponding reluctance to fire. Whatever musket fire does occur either appears to be a response to the enemy's fire or is a preparatory action before the charge with bayonets is initiated.

A few examples should suffice to demonstrate these trends. George Gleig's memoirs provide an example of an assault delivered by the 85th Regiment during the crossing of the Bidassoa on 7 October 1813. This action began with the battalion wheeling into line from column and then immediately advancing upon the enemy:

Not a word was spoken, nor a shot fired, till our troops had reached nearly half way across the little hollow, when the French . . . fired a volley. It was well directed, and did considerable execution; but it checked not our approach for a moment. Our men replied to it with a hearty British cheer, and giving them back to their fire, rushed on to the charge . . . and after having exchanged several discharges of musketry, that we succeeded in getting within charging distance. Then, indeed, another cheer was given, and the French, without waiting for the rush, once more broke their ranks and fled.[6]

Costello, recounting his experiences at the Battle of Vitoria, tells how he observed the 88th Regiment of Foot performing a slightly different variation on this type of tactic. After deploying into line, the 88th continued its advance towards the enemy until it was three or four hundred yards distant. While still at this distance the French began a 'running fire' which Costello tells us was executed from the right to left of its line. Continuing the account in Costello's own words:

> As soon as the British regiment had recovered the first shock, and closed their files on the gap it had made, they commenced advancing at double time until within fifty yards nearer to the enemy, when they [i.e. the British] halted and in turn gave a running fire from their whole line, and without a moment's pause cheered and charged up the hill against them. The French meanwhile were attempting to reload. But being pressed by the British, who allowed them no time to give a second volley, came immediately to the right about, making the best of their way to the village.[7]

Once again the British infantry, when fired upon, soon stopped and returned the fire. If Costello's estimate of the distances are indeed correct, the final British charge was initiated while the two forces were still separated by 250 to 350 paces!

Both of the above accounts describe the British stopping to fire before finally launching into a devil-may-care charge. The actions of the British infantry in both cases differ from earlier British doctrine not only in the increased aggressiveness, but also it would appear that the musket fire had been relegated from the primary means of destroying the enemy's will to resist to simply giving back whatever the enemy attempted to inflict.

Examples of the British entirely eschewing the use of small arms fire can also be found. In his memoirs entitled *The Letters of Private Wheeler*, Wheeler provides the following account of an assault delivered by the 51st Regiment of Foot in the peninsula:

> As we advanced the shot whistled brisker, Sir Thomas was in front, he wheeled around his horse, and order us to deploy on the first Division. Sir Thomas sat with his back to the enemy shading his eyes with his cocked hat, watching the companys

deploy. He expressed his satisfaction at the manner we had performed the movement. We was soon within point blank distance of their line. Sir Thomas then gave the word double quick, in a moment thirty buglars was sounding the charge and off we dashed in double quick time with three cheers, and away went the enemy to the right about. We had now gained the ridge without discharging a single musket, our bugles sounded the 'halt' and 'fire'.[8]

The conduct of this regiment in this particular case appears to be most 'un-British'. The British infantry is seen advancing at a normal pace until within about seventy to 110 paces then it began its charge at the double quick time without resorting to musket fire. Except for the apparent deployment of the battalion into line on its first division while on the march, this is essentially the French *à prest* attack used during the Nine Years' War and War of the Spanish Succession. The only other difference in this case was that once the enemy began its precipitous retreat, a rallying was sounded and the men ordered to deliver a volley at the fleeing enemy. This final touch reflects a tactic developed in the mid-eighteenth century. Frederick the Great during the Seven Years' War had ordered his infantry to extend these 'fare-wells' whenever broken enemy infantry began its rout.

This example of the British infantry utilizing an aggressive assault without firing was not some freakish occurrence, functioning as the exception that proved the rule. Sifting through the available memoirs affords other instances where this type of tactic was employed. Kincaid, for example, provides the following account of the regiment at Vera:

We immediately marched down to the foot of the enemy's position, shook off our knapsacks before their faces, and went at them.

The action commenced by five companies of our third battalion advancing, under Colonel Ross, to dislodge the enemy from a hill which they occupied in front of their intrenchments' and there never was a movement more beautifully executed for they walked quietly and steadily up, and swept them regularly off without firing a single shot until the enemy had turned their backs, when they served them out with a most destructive discharge.[9]

This example is almost identical to the efforts of the 51st Regiment of British Foot just discussed, except for the absence of the advance at the double once within point range.

Although there are many variations in the details, these examples demonstrate some general principles that permeated British infantry tactics, specifically, the quick advance usually only stopping to return fire. Then even when this fire occurred, only one or two volleys were exchanged, before a quick charge with lowered bayonets was launched at the enemy still reeling from the volleys at close range.

THE ROOTS OF THE BRITISH TACTIC

When considered collectively, these and the numerous other examples that can readily be extracted from commonly available memoirs and accounts, demonstrate that the tactic of delivering a spirited bayonet charge at the final moment represented a doctrinal departure for the British infantry compared to the doctrine it had employed in the earlier period. This fact was not completely lost upon contemporary observers. Writing in the early 1830s General Mitchell, for example, observed:

> . . . a charge of bayonets, – a thing that hurt nobody, but was out of the conventional rules of European warfare, – invariably put the whole to flight, though generally with what might be deemed a trifling loss. This was the constant tale from Vimiera to Waterloo, whenever the French were the assailants; and when the British were the attacking party . . .[10]

Clearly General Mitchell saw British reliance on the bayonet as distinctive, for he mentions that it 'was out of the conventional rules of European warfare'. Mitchell, obviously, saw the use of the bayonet charge as not only something new for the British but also a tactic not employed by the other European armies. Though this may have been the perception among the British military of the time, it certainly was not completely accurate. Looking back at how infantry conducted itself during the early eighteenth century, clearly the practice of a quick bayonet charge while on the offensive or defensive certainly was not new to European warfare.

French doctrine throughout the entire musket era had demanded a spirited attack with shouldered firelocks, concluded by a charge with lowered bayonets in the final moments. In the 1690s, for example, Colonel de Greder would order his men to extinguish their fuses (the infantry carried matchlocks in his time), and when his infantry had advanced to sufficiently close to the enemy he urged them to attack with their bayonets and swords. Later during the 1730s while writing his influential *Mes rêveries*, de Saxe would urge the infantry to withhold its fire and then settle the affair at very close range with either a destructive volley or an impetuous charge with the bayonet.[11] This type of spirited attack with its threat of cold steel, however, had never been strictly limited to the French infantry. During the Great Northern War, Charles XII of Sweden would lead his men, now armed with flintlocks, on equally aggressive charges with sword and bayonet. Inspired by Charles' example, a young Frederick the Great, during the War of Austrian Succession and the first campaigns of the Seven Years' War, would require his infantry to attempt similar attacks.

Thus, when the entire spectrum of infantry doctrine developed since the introduction of the socket bayonet is considered, it becomes apparent that the British reliance upon bayonet charges was not, strictly speaking, new in itself. However, this does not mean that British military during the Napoleonic era consciously emulated existing doctrine. The new aggressiveness of the British infantry should not be viewed simply as some sort of mechanical and whole-sale duplication of pre-existing continental systems. The average British officer had little or no awareness of these tactical antecedents. Unlike the modern world, where governments allocate vast human and monetary resources to monitor the accomplishments and actions of potential opponents, no comparable surveillance mechanisms or level of interest existed up to well into the Napoleonic Wars. And some military communities were more isolated than others. The result was that throughout the eighteenth century a sizeable intellectual chasm existed between French and British military ideology.

Moreover, even in continental Europe the older methods of the direct assault were no longer held in high esteem. A significant change in sentiment had come over the military establishment. By the early 1790s the spirited bayonet charge had long been out of vogue in most European military circles. The popularity of this type of attack had reached its zenith during the 1740s when Frederick the Great, following the lead set by the French and Swedish infantry, ordered his foot soldiers to march with shouldered firelocks when attacking the enemy. The increased availability of gunpowder with the concomitant increase in defensive fire, however, soon forced Frederick, even when his infantry forces were on the offensive, to return to quickly delivered volleys, the hallmark of his father's infantry drill in the 1720s and 30s. It was this last Prussian development that was to capture the imagination of several generations of future European officers. Frederick's continued victories and his ability to hold off numerically superior forces during the Seven Years' War so impressed most military intellectuals that Prussian methods held sway over military establishments from the 1760s until well into the 1790s.

Well into the French Revolutionary Wars almost every army continued to have its share of 'five rounds per minute' pundits. Taking Santa Cruz' logic to its extreme, advocates from this school argued that the mechanistic delivery of repeated volleys, while either on the attack or defence, would necessarily lead to the destruction of an enemy lacking in these fire delivery capabilities. This 'quick fire' approach was still, if only informally, the most popular philosophy underlying infantry tactics throughout the early 1790s. By its very nature, this philosophy was inimical to any sort of advance without firing, and attached only greatly reduced importance to the bayonet.

In this sense, the British tactic of reserving fire until a critical moment, followed by the quick advance with lowered bayonets, represented a break with the accepted views held after the conclusion of the Seven Years' War, especially those current among the Austrian and Prussian infantry.

HOW THIS TACTIC WORKED

Despite any similarity with earlier continental tactics, British bayonet charges during the Napoleonic era were nevertheless distinctive in the frequency with which they occurred and their astonishingly high rate of success. It is no exaggeration to say the majority of battles during the Peninsular campaign can boast at least one attempted British bayonet charge. Several battles were graced with a number of these energetic attempts to resolve the local confrontation with a rather determined application of cold steel. Durban, for example, tells how on 16 May 1811 what appeared to be a continuous fire of British artillery and musketry was periodically punctuated by 'partial charges of the bayonet'. The same writer goes on to claim that British and Portuguese infantry made no less than eleven bayonet charges during the First Battle of the Pyrenees.[12] Judging from the accounts that have come down to us, a great majority of these spirited charges were successful – a much higher rate than that enjoyed by any other contemporary army. This naturally leads to the question why did the British enjoy a disproportionately high rate of success?

There has been a tendency in many historical works, especially those written by English-speaking historians from the mid-nineteenth century onward, to view the British infantry accomplishments during the Peninsular campaign and the Hundred Days as arising simply from a fortunate collection of national qualities. Terms such as 'stolid', 'doggedly determined' and 'British courage' pepper these descriptions. Works written prior to the twentieth century often refer directly to, or imply, some sort of intrinsic 'national character' as the basis of these capabilities. These views are echoed as much in serious military treatises as they are in the more popularly oriented memoirs.

In his work on training methods, Doctor Robert Jackson noted that the British soldier, though much less prone to the species of enthusiasm often displayed by the soldiers of some other nations, was 'as courageous and determined as any' and particularly good at retaining self-control, and when defeated tended to retreat in an organized fashion rather than being easily routed.[13] Later in the same work, Jackson also noted that British troops:

> independently of physical power and the confidence connected with it, unite more readily to form impressive charges, or repel formidable attacks with a firmness and resolution superior to the common soldiers of France.[14]

Thomas Dyneley, a British artillery officer, who saw service throughout the Peninsular War, also commented upon the eagerness with which the British infantry participated in the final charges: 'The British soldier rejoices in his bayonet.'[15] Later works often clothed similar views in quasi-sociological concepts and terms: rather than a result of innate qualities, the British infantry possessed their legendary steadiness because of socially engendered and transmitted attitudes and values.

The fact that soldiers from different regions and ethnic and social backgrounds did exhibit distinctive attitudes and habits, and that these attitudes, values and beliefs affected their performance in action in a variety of ways cannot be denied. Although a comprehensive catalogue and analysis of these socially transmitted values and behavioural patterns is, unfortunately, beyond the scope of the present study, one related question cannot be ignored. Was the recurring British infantry's performance simply based on the quality of the material i.e. the collective 'character' of its troops as manifested under battle conditions, or was this success due to the ability of the British military to develop and utilize a tactical system that best exploited these socially transmitted traits?

The question has been largely dismissed. In the absence of obvious evidence suggesting a set of distinctive British infantry tactics, many historians have concluded these never existed, and, instead, attributed the repeated ability of British infantry to seize the initiative and pre-empt their enemy with an aggressive charge to the quality of the fighting men and their officers. The fighting capabilities of the British infantryman during the Napoleonic period were such that their exploits and accomplishments resist disparagement by even the most thorough and rigorous of analysis. Nevertheless, detailed tactical investigation demonstrates that the chronic success of the British infantry was less the product of its material than the fortunate confluence of the effects of a large number of tactical practices, some obviously purposive and significant, others seemingly trivial and accidental!

The overall psychological and physical dynamics underlying the British infantry tactic were pre-eminently simple: wait until the distance separating the two forces has been reduced to where, when the fire was finally delivered, it could not help but be effective, if not overpowering. Then, while the enemy is still recoiling from the shock caused by the devastating volley, rush in with lowered bayonets. The enemy staggering from their casualties and totally overawed by a ferocious charge delivered in a moment of vulnerability, almost inevitably turns and flees.

The intuitive mastery of the inner psychological dynamics of combat demonstrated by British infantry during this period was comparable to that displayed as a matter of course by successful modern street fighters. Nevertheless, though the tactic and its effects only took seconds to unfold, and for the most part was performed by the rank and file and lower echelon of officers almost unconsciously, as though performing some long-rehearsed communal ritual, a complex set of intertwining dynamics were at work bringing about a profound and consistent result. The British tactic relied upon two disparate elements: an effective fire followed by a forward movement conducted with such alacrity and determination that it invariably convinced the opposition that the British soldiers had every intention of resolving the affair with cold steel. Once the enemy was convinced of this, a complete rout was only a fraction of a second away.

Reviewing various primary sources, there can be little question that British firepower, when it was finally delivered, was, shot for shot, at least if not more effective than that of any of their adversaries. Marshal Augereau, for example, had been quick to attribute no mean portion of the British success to effective firepower.[16] Moreover, French sources, describing the battlefield experience were not reluctant to cede the devastation commonly experienced as a result of these British volleys. Unfortunately, Augereau's comments, and others like it, succeeded in side tracking many generations of future English-speaking historians who naïvely attributed to the British soldier the ability to deliver repeated fire quickly, mechanically and accurately. In other words, the notion that somehow British infantry crushed its opposition by delivering 'five rounds per minute' unfortunately took root.

The true roots of British effective fire, however, lay neither in Frederick the Great's belief in 'quick fire' nor the modern conception of 'accurate' fire. The British were able to produce consistently a withering fire, because they succeeded in making their men withhold fire until the final moments and because they demonstrated a greater determination to make their men 'level' their volleys. The first fire delivered at fifty paces, or even as little as thirty or twenty paces, would be significantly more effective than that delivered at 100 or 150. The result of a single volley at close range, steadily levelled and delivered could be equal or greater to the sum of numerous volleys delivered during a prolonged but disorganized firefight at longer ranges.

Writing at the turn of the century, Sir Charles Oman mistakenly assumed that the British infantry had engaged in a number of repeated volleys during the course of a single engagement. Based on this assumption, he then attempted to demonstrate that British fire superiority arose because of the intrinsic differences between the British reliance upon the two-rank line and the French use of deep closed columns. Oman argued that virtually all the infantrymen could bring their muskets to bear in a British battalion deployed along two ranks, while only those at the very front of the French column could fire. In statistical terms, 100% of the British infantry along the line could fire, compared to somewhere between 12% to 23% of the French troops. This assumes only the first two ranks of the French column could fire effectively and that the column was either by company or division. Oman argued that this discrepancy in fire-power capabilities inevitably caused the French to suffer horrendous casualties which inevitably destroyed their will to continue the con-test. In recent years, Oman's analyses have been largely discredited because it has been convincingly shown that the British almost with-out exception engaged only in controlled volley fire or short bouts of file fire, rather than the continuous sort that had been assumed by most British military historians from the late nineteenth century onwards.[17] It must be pointed out, however, that though some of Oman's overall conclusions can no longer be accepted, his observa-tions about the intrinsic fire capabilities of the two different forma-tions remain valid, even if their opportunity for application has been greatly reduced. A 500-man British battalion deployed along two ranks would certainly be able to bring many more muskets to bear than its French counterpart, when the latter had remained in a deep column with a frontage varying between 40 and 80 files. Of course, such an advantage would only apply during the one or two volleys the British infantry did, in fact, fire, and not the five to ten that has been traditionally ascribed to them.

A much more important factor which led to the relative effective-ness of British firepower was the more consistent use of levelling techniques while delivering fire. It will be remembered 'levelling' was the practice of having all the muskets in a unit point at the same general 'height', such as the middle of the enemies' bodies. In the 1750s, this problem was partially ameliorated when many officers began to admonish their troops to fire 'at the middle of the enemy's body'. Though this practice recognized the need to point the barrel, it still failed to account for variation in 'distance'. Despite these modest gains, the subtleties of adjusting aim to compensate for the distance of the enemy by firing uphill or downhill, though known to marksmen and hunters for centuries, were largely unapplied in a military setting prior to the Napoleonic Wars.

In the late 1790s, a number of British military writers began to point out the various pitfalls when firing from or at different heights and how to overcome this problem. These developments apparently were of the highest importance to British forces who would spend most of their campaigning in the mountainous and rough Spanish countryside. At the outbreak of the Revolutionary Wars, however, the understanding of the need to level the muskets was certainly not limited to the British infantry. The French infantry regulations of 1791, for example, prescribe approximate heights to level to several key ranges.[18]

However, witnessing the effects of enemy musket fire first hand, Doctor Robert Jackson assures us that, other than the British infantry, it remained a near-universal practice for continental infantry to fire at the 'middle of the enemy's body'. This rather crude form of levelling really did not account for the effects of range and differences in terrain elevations. If the enemy was within ninety paces, for example, and the muskets were pointed at the middle of the body, given the rise of the musket balls within point blank range, a majority of the projectiles would be flung safely over the enemies' heads. This lack of adequate levelling might account for the frequency with which we find accounts of the French firing above the heads of the British infantry, such as at Maida or what we know occurred to the 73rd British Regiment of Foot in 'Germany' in 1813.[19] The French fire, although delivered at a relatively close range, wizzed above the advancing British infantrymen's heads. The British continued the advance with even greater resolve and the final result was now predictable. The British infantry appear to have been more willing to use levelling in practice as well as showing a greater appreciation of the need to modify levelling practices according to the terrain. The increased fire effectiveness of these new practices cannot be over-emphasized.

The overall efficacy of the British infantry tactic, however, did not stem solely from the one or two volleys that were typically delivered in the final moments of the attack or defence, regardless of their destructiveness. We encounter over and over again first-hand accounts describing how the British infantry, whether attacking or awaiting the enemy, charged in with lowered bayonets, immediately after a volley before the enemy was given time to regain its balance. With surprising frequency, British officers and NCOs were able to restrain the rank and file up until the very last moments, so that their men's aggression had been reserved up to the exact moment when its release would achieve maximum impact. Their ability to maintain control in part stemmed from the sparing use of orderly volleys.

> All firing beyond one volley in a case where you must charge, seems only to cause a useless interchange of casualties, besides endangering the steadiness of a charge to be undertaken in the midst of a sustained file fire, when a word of command is hard to hear.[20]

By eschewing prolonged fires British officers were able to minimize the loss of command control. The ability to issue the command to charge, still possible after a single organized volley, would have become impossible the instant the firing became general. Troops engaged in general firefights were condemned to remain stationary. Yet the confusion, the noise, the flurry of activity all conspired against being aware of, let alone following their officer's pleas. By using musket fire judiciously, and then only in one or two quick spurts, the ability to return instantly to the offensive was immeasurably greater than among those who allowed their troops to engage in lengthy firefights.

We could say that the British infantry had invariably managed to 'put in the last word'. Situations where infantry advanced against infantry on open terrain were metaphorically akin to the two drivers recklessly playing 'chicken' in a barren stretch of midwestern country road. In both cases, human nature demanded that the participants, regardless of how close they would approach one another, had to attempt to avoid a collision in the final moments. One side or the other would break before the two forces met. The real feat of the British infantry is that it was consistently able to make its final bid in the 'penultimate moment'. In other words, from the enemy's vantage point, when the British bayonet charge was finally unleashed, so little distance separated the two forces that even the faintest attempt to counter-charge necessarily would have resulted in the two sides actually crossing bayonets. And since flesh and blood seeks to avoid mêlées in open terrain about as vigorously as 'nature abhors a vacuum', this meant that, in effect, there was no other practical option for the other side than to hastily vacate their position. It must be borne in mind that the soldiers did not consciously think of these things, the whole affair transpiring far more quickly than even to read this paragraph.

DISTINCTIVE FEATURES OF THE BRITISH CHARGE

Although providing an explanation on one level, the above analysis raises a more fundamental question: why were the British infantry consistently able to demonstrate greater determination during the last moments of the confrontation which, in turn, seemed to lead inevitably to the destruction of their opponent's will to fight?

Other than the difference in formations typically used to implement the attack and the tendency for the British soldiers to better level their firearms, there is little in the French and the British tactical systems of attack and defence to explain the wide differential in performance encountered throughout the Peninsular War. The structural similarity between the British bayonet charges and the traditional French à *prest* attack have already been noted. Both tactics relied on a quick, aggressive assault capped with a bayonet charge. The only apparent difference was that French doctrine called for the advancing infantry to completely abstain from firing, even if fired upon, while the British tended to stop and deliver one or two quick volleys.

The British soldiers of the day, like their counterparts in all other armies, more often than not accepted a chauvinistic explanation for their accomplishments. The British infantry's stubbornness or dependability during these crucial moments was simply a result of the virtues of 'British character'. They saw themselves as simply more determined, better led or perhaps somehow 'braver' than the enemy they faced. Describing an engagement, General Mitchell provides an example: 'when the British were the attacking party, they had, from the natural hardihood of the men, still greater advantages.'[21] Another example is found in Dyneley's memoirs:

> I know that the French soldier advances to meet the British bayonet with more hesitation, I will not say trepidation, than he would meet any other enemy. The British soldier rejoices in his bayonet.'[22]

This bluster is natural enough and is found sprinkled throughout the writings of every other nation fortunate enough to be successful in arms.

Sir Charles Oman attempted to re-direct the analysis from the supposed quality of the combatant troops to the structural aspects of the tactics employed by the two armies. Unfortuantely, the usefulness of Oman's explanations have been minimized as it has become increasingly clear that the British rarely went in for extended firefights. The British infantry's more reliable performance during the crucial moments of an engagement instead is attributable to one or two seemingly trivial details of French and British tactical practices. The differential in effectiveness between the two systems lay neither in their respective objectives nor overall structure, which was much more similar than has been previously recognized. The real difference arose because of the manner the men were allowed or even encouraged to act in the final moments of the attack.

The French assault was proverbial for its initial ferocity, not only during the Napoleonic wars but as far back as the introduction of the flintlock and socket bayonet. Marshal Puységur writing in the 1730s and 1740s commented on the initial French aggressiveness. This disposition certainly had not changed by the advent of the Napoleonic wars and Gleig when describing the action at Bayonne, attests: 'Nothing can be more spirited or impetuous then the first attack of French troops.'[23] The French rank and file during the advance were allowed a greater degree of individual freedom and action than in those armies that clung religiously to the notion of mechanistic force. True, as in every other western European army, French soldiers were required to maintain their position in the line throughout action. However, once the advance at the double had begun, when within 200 to 100 paces of the enemy, the men usually had the freedom to yell and gesticulate individually. This had been the case especially during the early campaigns of the Revolutionary Wars where the volunteer portions of the French infantry frequently advanced in looser columnar and line formations than had been the practice. Rather surprisingly, the same freedoms were all too often allowed even when the French were on the defensive. Describing the action around him at Salamanca, Gratten was struck by the rowdy behaviour of the French defenders. He noted: 'the calm but stern advance of Wallace's brigade was received with the beating of drums and loud cheers from the French.'[24] Gratten provides another example in the same action when moments later the main body of Thomières' division launched a local counter offensive:

They [the British] speedily got footing upon the brow of the hill, but before they had time to take their breath, the entire French division, with drums beating and uttering loud shouts, ran forward to meet them, and belching forth a torrent of bullets from five thousand muskets, brought down almost all of the entire of Wallace's first rank, and more than half of his officers.[25]

Returning to the action around Bayonne, Gleig was struck by the noticeable difference between the French and British infantrymen's demeanour. Gleig was able to uncover several important differences between the way the men in the two armies tended to act:

They come on, for a while slowly, and in silence; til, having reached within a hundred yards or two of the point to be assailed, they raise a loud but discordant yell, and rush forward ... The ardour of the French is, however, admirably opposed by the coolness and undaunted deportment of Britons. On the present occasion, for instance, our people met their assailants exactly as if the whole affair had been a piece of acting, no man quitting his ground, but each deliberately waiting till the word of command was given, and then discharging his piece.[26]

The anonymous Scot who penned *A Soldier of the Seventy-First* similarly contrasted typical British and French behaviour:

We gave them one volley and three cheers – three distinct cheers. Then all was still as death. They came upon us, crying and shouting, to the very point of our bayonets. Our awful silence and determined advance they could not stand. They put about and fled without much resistance.[27]

This coolness of the British infantry was noted time and time again by both French and British observers. This silence which so impressed observers and the enemy alike was no accident and was the result of the determined efforts of the battalion's officers and NCOs. Several sources record how the officers would go about calming their men: 'After the first huzza the British officers, restraining their men, still as death. "Steady, lads, steady" is all you hear, and that in an undertone.'[28] And again, 'No one that day could have observed our Colonel during the heat of the action, and not admired his cool and soldier-like bearing. "Steady, lads – show no hurry," was his cheering exhortation . . .'[29]

The actions of the British officers were in stark contrast to the French officers who sought to achieve a diametrically opposite goal. Making every effort to create a spirited first offensive, they would do everything possible to stir up their men. 'How different the duty of the French officers from ours. They, stimulating the men by their example, the men vociferating, each chaffing each until they appear in a fury, shouting to the points of our bayonets.'[30]

If the morale of their officers was good, they advanced in front of their battalion to lead the men on by their example. The French officers would often become very animated, and struck many of their British opponents as though they were 'dancing'. 'They [the French infantry] wavered, and hung behind a little; but, cheered and encouraged by the gallantry of their officers, who were dancing and flourishing their swords in front, they at last boldly advanced to the opposite side of our hedge, and began to deploy.'[31] They only positioned themselves behind the line if the men's reticence forced the officers to prod their charges by threatening the latter's buttocks with the points of their swords.

In contrast, the British officers following the Prussian example typically kept most of their officers behind the advancing line. The rationale behind this technique was that it reduced officers' casualties and better prevented anyone from escaping the ranks and squirming their way to the rear. In those rare instances where the British officers remained in front of their men it was usually because the men were advancing too quickly or displaying premature enthusiasm. In these cases, they would attempt to hold the men back so a more orderly advance was re-established.

These differences were not merely cosmetic. They represented two entirely different philosophies on not only how best to manage the men's morale, but also when and how the men's energy should be released. The two tactical systems, despite more superficial similarities, such as when to fire and lower bayonets at the last moment, on this lowest level were actually in opposition.

In the French system, all the stakes were placed on the determination, energy and ferocity of the first assault. All the microdynamics underlying this set of tactics worked towards working the men up as soon as the attack had begun in earnest. From a purely psychological perspective, this type of assault was the European equivalent of Turkish offensive philosophy where absolutely all of the emphasis was placed on the first phase, and no plans or systematic steps were taken among the *attacking elements* to ensure an even distribution of effort over any extended period of time. Whipping soldiers into a frenzy not only guaranteed they would exert themselves to their absolute physical limit, it also created an awesome first impression which naturally tended to demoralize the enemy. The problem with this approach, however, was that it made impossible any emotional reserve and actually lowered potential resistance to any subsequent counterattack. The more enthusiastic the soldier was during the first phases of the assault, the more he was liable to break if the first efforts proved unsuccessful and a serious check or reverse was encountered. A person who 'gives it his best shot' – when this appears to achieve no perceptible effect – is much more easily intimidated than if he just stood there and did his best to absorb the punishment.

The British at least intuitively recognized these issues and espoused a completely different set of priorities. Everything was done to control the men's emotions, that is, to hold them back both physically and psychologically. All of the emphasis was placed on maintaining an emotional reserve which was to be unleashed only at the critical moment. Although this is obvious from the occasional references to British officers running in front of their line and then physically trying to hold their men back during an advance, it was also the real reason for maintaining the silence. The impressions of the anonymous Scot have already been cited. However, the Scot went on to provide an illuminating description of just how much this silence could bolster of the morale of the men up and down the line:

> In our first charge I felt my mind waiver; a breathless sensation came over me. The silence was appalling. I looked alongst the line. It was enough to assure me. The steady, determined scowl of my companions assured my heart and gave me determination. How unlike the noisy advance of the French![32]

Of course such control could not be maintained indefinitely, and the British devised an effective means of dissipating their emotions in carefully controlled quantum amounts. This was the purpose of the 'British cheer', which was issued occasionally at critical points during the initial advance and almost invariably before the final charge.

Sometimes, it was a single cheer, but usually it was three cheers.[33] 'We formed front across the road, and charged – the French officers in the rear urged their troops forward ... we were then joined by a brigade of Brunswickers, gave them three cheers and charged the French along the heights.'[34] Blakeney would observe:

This sudden movement on the part of the enemy was met by a corresponding formation of ours; we wheeled into line and advanced. Not a word was spoken, nor a shot fired, till our troops had reached nearly half way across the little hollow, when the French, raising one of their discordant yells, – a sort of shout, in which every man halloos for himself, without regard to the tone or time of those about him, – fired a volley. It was well directed, and did considerable execution; but it checked not our approach for a moment. Our men replied to it with a hearty British cheer, and giving them back to their fire, rushed on to the charge ... and after having exchanged several discharges of musketry, that we succeeded in getting within charging distance. Then, indeed, another cheer was given, and the French, without waiting for the rush, once more broke their ranks and fled.

So predictable was this final charge that in his memoirs of the Peninsular Wars he concluded that the 'well-known thundering British cheer [was the] sure precursor of the rush of British bayonets.'[35] The cheers before the charge in part served as a signal that the attack was to enter the next and final phase. It also helped the men make the transition from struggling to maintain complete control to rushing in on the enemy with unbridled passion. By retaining a reservoir of emotion and unleashing this in the final moments long after the enemy's emotional outlets had crested, the British had almost guaranteed the success of their attack or defence. The charge, when it finally came, completely transformed the infantrymen from inconsequent cogs in a large formation passively following orders, to a collectivity of furious warriors monomaniacally trying to kill the enemy in front of them.

James Anton who had served with the 42nd Royal Highlanders during the Peninsular War and in France in 1814 and 1815 noted the profound psychological change on the soldiers during the charge:

No movement in the field is made with greater confidence of success than that of the charge; it affords little time for thinking, while it creates a fearless excitement, and tends to give a fresh impulse to the blood of the advancing soldier, rouses his courage, strengthens every nerve, and drowns every fear of danger or of death; thus emboldened amidst shouts that anticipate victory, he rushes on and mingles with the fleeing foe.[36]

Thus the British were statistically more successful than the French because they had created a tactical system which better managed the men's emotions and fears. The causal elements in this system existed on the lowest possible level, such as when to cheer and when to keep silent, the proper use of martial music, and so on. In this regard, this accomplishment was analogous to the Prussian cavalry attack at speed, or the French Napoleonic cavalry trick of only unsheathing their swords at the very last moment. All three of these are examples of tactical systems which garnered available psychological forces until the critical moment when they were let loose to establish a local superiority of emotional force and determination.

Was this tactical system self-consciously created in the way Frederick and his generals purposely developed the cavalry charge at speed during the 1740s? Almost certainly not. It is much more probable that these various elements originated at a grass roots level, the product of years of pragmatic observations. Never part of the official curriculum of the troops' training, it was disseminated through the army during conversations in the barracks and by peer imitation. Regardless of its origins, it proved to be one of the most powerful tools in the British military arsenal.

REASONS FOR FRENCH SUCCESS

So far, we have attempted to explain only why British infantry was so consistently successful over their French counterparts during the Napoleonic Wars. This same French infantry, however, had managed to dominate their continental opponents for most of the Napoleonic Wars. Why they were able to do so is just as worthy of consideration.

Much of the French success from 1796 to 1809 must be attributed to Napoleon's operational genius and the French military's decided grand tactical superiority. So frequently, Napoleon, benefiting from the newly invented system of independent corps movement, was able to orchestrate these large bodies of troops so that the enemy found itself unexpectedly facing greatly superior forces either at the start of the battle or at the critical point during the conflagration. Many times the outcome of the battle was decided before it began. And, once the battle was underway, these advantages were compounded by the French use of the impulse system of grand tactics. This, of course is looking at things from a grand scale perspective, but what about the events taking place on the localized or tactical level?

When one examines the performance of the French armies from 1796 to 1809, how many times does one read of opposing brigade or divisional-sized forces coming into contact, and the French infantry finally emerging victorious after a tenacious struggle? So many times, the French infantry on part of the battlefield effected a local success because it was finally able to renew an offensive because it was willing and able to effect a last Herculean effort. French success on this tactical level has usually been attributed to the reliance upon columns of attack preceded by swarms of skirmishers. This view portrays tradition-bound opponents, deployed along thin lines, becoming panic-stricken as they observed the numerous dense French formations quickly advancing against them. Forced to remain in line and unable to counter the French skirmishers, whatever will to resist was soon extinguished as the defenders were provoked into a premature, uncontrolled fire.

This by itself is but a partial explanation. If these were the only forces which determined the victor, then the French, not the British, would have been successful in a majority of their assaults during the Peninsular War. However, the British infantry usually managed to hold off and drive back the French assaults, despite their reliance on linear formations and the presence of numerous French skirmishers. Were these localized French successes purely the result of superior French grand tactics, or was there a set of micro-tactical forces at work which allowed the French infantry so frequently to defeat Austrian, Prussian and Russian infantry similar to that which allowed the British infantry to overthrow its French opponents?

A clue is provided in General Duhèsme's writings. This officer tells us he was frequently able to defeat larger Austrian forces deployed in line by charging in with three or four battalions in closed columns, arranged either in echelons or *en échiquier*. Duhèsme freely admitted that such a feat certainly was not restricted to French troops. The

Austrians were able to rush in their columns and overthrow the French infantry almost as easily. Faced with onrushing Austrian columns, the French infantry would begin to deploy and quickly commence a 'lively fire'. On a number of these occasions, Duhèsme was sent forward to restore the situation. Now, it was the turn of the Austrian battalions, just moments before on the attack and still in column, to form line. However, the Austrian battalions were unable to adjust to the sudden turn of events and would soon turn tail and flee.

At first glance, General Duhèsme's account appears to substantiate the traditional 'column overthrowing line' explanation for French successes. However, in his description Duhèsme went on to note that, once on the defensive, the Austrians, like the French defenders before them, would begin a spirited 'file fire', that is fire by files, but with the same lack of success. In spite of their recent success, the Austrians in their turn became dispirited and fled upon the approach of the rapidly advancing French columns.[37]

To understand why this tended to happen we must return to the nature of British/French infantry confrontations in the Peninsula. Though French methods facilitated a furious initial attack, toleration of heightened individualism at the very same time increased the chances of the advance devolving into a protracted firefight. As we have seen, against the British during the closing years of the Napoleonic period, the French commitment to the spirited attack with abandon was doomed to failure. Both British culture with its ubiquitous and unrelenting demand for reserve, and the harangues and vigilance of the officers forced the men into abstinence of fire. Caught amid an unfolding frenzy, the French infantrymen would be overturned by the inevitable bayonet charge so artfully delivered at the moment of greatest vulnerability.

One of the great ironies of the Napoleonic Wars was that the very adoption of the quickly delivered multiple firing approach for the defence was the single most important factor empowering the French column of attack which utilized the quick advance without firing – what had once been called the à prest attack. When opposed to the Austrians, Prussians or Russians, the French met with no such stoicism encountered later in the Iberian Peninsula. Subscribing to Frederick the Great's 'quick fire' philosophy, the Austrians, Prussians and Russians, threatened by an imminent attack invariably attempted to defend themselves with a succession of quickly delivered volleys.

Usually, fire was ordered when the French were still somewhat distant, more than seventy-five paces away. Rarely, if ever, was there any attempt to withhold fire until the last moment and settle matters with the *arme blanche*. However, once the men in the ranks were allowed to fire more than once or twice, generally volley fire broke down into an uncontrolled fire. As soon as this happened, officers were deprived of the options that British officers would later use with so much effect. In other words, once the fire became general officers lost control and the battalion or regiment was reduced to a continuous and disorganized firefight.

This type of defensive stagnation actually benefited the French who typically adopted the offensive role. True, their own assault just as frequently came to a standstill as the French infantrymen sought to return fire. But the mutual standoff more often than not worked to their advantage. Strung out along tenuous lines, the defenders were less apt to receive timely reinforcements. Moreover, the Allied commanders had less articulated control of their troop's action and movement. The French benefited from more articulated abilities. This meant they had more reserves to throw into the fray than opponents constrained by linear tactics.

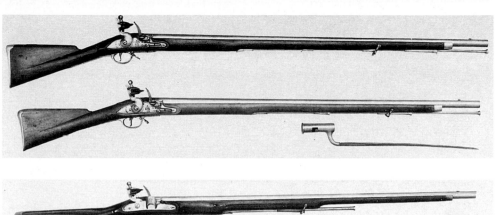

British 'Napoleonic' muskets. From top to bottom:
Short Land Musket, India Pattern Musket, Duke of
Richmond's Musket (c.1790), and the New Land
Pattern Musket (c.1802), the lock used on the India
Pattern and (bottom) the 'ring-necked' cock
introduced in 1809

The Baker Rifle and bayonet used by the 95th Regiment (Rifle Brigade)

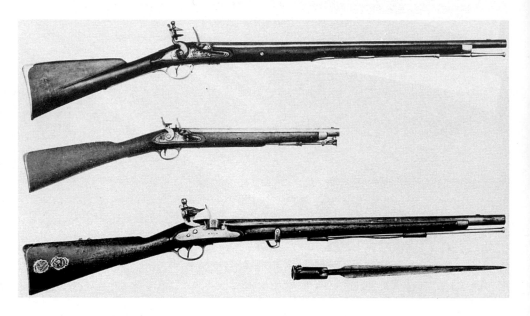

British cavalry small arms: The Eliott, Paget and Pattern 1796 carbines

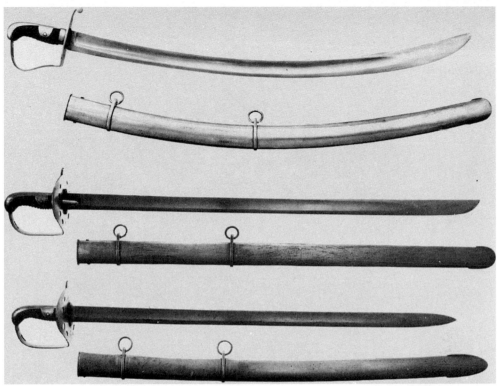

British cavalry swords. From top to bottom: Light
Cavalry – Pattern 1796, Heavy Cavalry – Pattern
1796, Heavy Cavalry – Pattern 1796 with
modified spear point, and a Pattern 1796 officer's
sword

The 6-pdr. gun and the $5\frac{1}{2}''$ howitzer, the most common British artillery pieces of the Napoleonic period

A French field artillery piece captured at Waterloo

From top to bottom: side views of 3-pdr., 9-pdr. and 12-pdr. guns

A brass 4⅖″ howitzer of 1811

Round shot, common shell, and spherical case.
Also shown are cut-away views of common shell
and spherical case

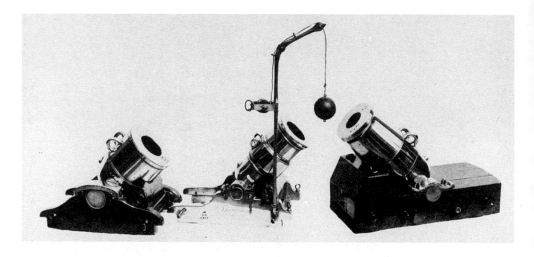

Models of several types of British mortars. The
derrick is used to load projectiles into the muzzle

CHAPTER 14

Light Infantry and Skirmishing

THE WIDESPREAD USE OF SKIRMISHING TACTICS was one
of the most distinguishing characteristics of the new art of warfare
during the French Revolutionary and Napoleonic Wars. In simple
terms, skirmishers did not assume the highly formalized close order
formations, but fought in loose extended lines. Unlike his comrades'
line or column, a skirmisher chose both his target and exactly when
he wanted to fire, thus making possible *aimed* fire.

On the Napoleonic battlefield, skirmishers served several different
purposes. In an offensive situation, they advanced in front of the
ordered formations and reconnoitred all the ins and outs of the terrain which the commander could not view from some commanding
position to the rear. At the same time, their presence partially or
even wholly masked the movement of the main body of the army
behind them, helping the commander to conceal his true intentions
and preventing his opponents from determining the true point of the
principal attack.

When the battle was fought on rough or diverse terrain, skirmishers, rather than regular formations, would be sent in to take or
hold this type of terrain, if sufficient numbers were available. It was
only with the greatest difficulty that troops could be made to fight
effectively in dense woods while in closed formations. Skirmishers
were much more suitable for this type of fighting. Once within firing
range, skirmishers would pester the enemy forces with a galling
aimed fire, denying the enemy the luxury of firing and reloading in
a more controlled manner. When on the defensive, skirmish fire was

used to disrupt and disorder the enemy infantry as it advanced against the friendly forces in regular formations. If the skirmishers' annoying fire could goad the troops in an ordered formation to stop and return the fire, much of the impetus of the attack would be lost as control of the troops slipped away from the leaders and the engagement broke down into scattered firefights. Skirmishers also frequently provided an effective means of covering a retreat. Their fire could slow down the pursuers, and when finally forced to flee themselves, they were able to travel much more quickly than the foot soldier in line or even column.

Skirmishing and light infantry tactics in general first came to the attention of military men in the English-speaking world as a result of the French and Indian War and the American War of Independence. It is hardly surprising, therefore, that contemporary British military writers believed that these practices were 'invented' during these conflicts. English-speaking historians later would accept these observations at face value. Since the French Revolutionary Wars began only nine years after the conclusion of hostilities in North America, naturally it was concluded that the widespread use of French skirmishers was simply a popularization of light infantry tactics that had been used so effectively in the colonies. It was reasoned that these practices were brought back to France by returning volunteers who then proselytized these new methods in the years before and after the storming of the Bastille. This explanation was substantiated by Lafayette's claim that he introduced the concept of employing skirmishers in mass on the European battlefield.

Unfortunately, this view ignores a number of tactical experiments that took place during the first half of the eighteenth century. While it cannot be denied that the return to France of veterans inured to skirmishing tactics must have helped popularize light infantry tactics in the French army, the veterans did not introduce light infantry tactics in Europe. Skirmisher tactics did not originate in North America; formalized light infantry tactics had been experimented with, systemized and even to a limited extent tested on the European battlefield prior to the outbreak of the French and Indian War in 1754.

The first irregular infantry companies, the so-called 'free companies' or *compagnies franches*, were introduced into the French infantry at the siege of Luxembourg in 1684. These were transient units intended to perform the various duties associated with siege operations, such as outpost duties, sallies, etc. The first permanent free companies came into existence in 1689. However, the demands of the campaigns in Catalonia and eastern and northern France forced these free companies to assume a different role; they functioned as what would later be known as *infanterie légère*, light infantry, that is they performed the wide miscellanea of tasks that arc always a part of the day-to-day campaigning, including patrolling and, if necessary, fighting in broken terrain. Found to be of great use, their numbers were gradually expanded during the Nine Years' War and the War of Spanish Succession. Although almost all the free companies were disbanded in 1715, their utility in the *petite guerre* was not forgotten, and a new batch of these independent companies was created during the late 1720s.[1]

It was at this point that French military authorities began investigating how troops fighting independently as skirmishers could best support and be supported by troops in close order formations. During one of the camps of instruction in 1727, three related exercises were conducted where a portion of a battalion was deployed as skirmishers. In the first experiment, the grenadiers were detached and spread out in a skirmish line in front of the battalion in line. After discharging their muskets, they filed to the rear, to the left and right of the battalion and then began to reload. In the next exercise, the grenadiers and the battalion behind them were ordered to advance. Once the grenadiers fired and fell back, the *picquet* (pickets) advanced up to the skirmish line and then fired in their turn. The last exercise experimented with the use of skirmishers to protect the battalion during a retreat. The picquet and the grenadiers were thrown out as skirmishers while the battalion fell back in an orderly withdrawal.[2]

These exercises, though involving many concepts and practices that would become standard fare during the Revolutionary and Napoleonic Wars, were highly unusual for the time. There is no indication that any of these were adopted after the field camp of instructions, and they would have amounted to little more than a footnote in some weighty tome of the history of tactics had it not been for Maurice de Saxe. In 1732, bed ridden with a persistent fever de Saxe decided to take advantage of the hallucinations he was experiencing and write a small volume which could be described as a sort of military scientific fantasy. In it, among many other things de Saxe wrote what he thought was the best method for infantry to deliver fire. Traumatized by his experiences at the Battle of Belgrade, de Saxe had little confidence in volley fire. Instead, he advocated that when defending against enemy infantry, a skirmish line was to be thrown out between ten to 200 paces from the battalion. These would begin firing individually when the enemy had approached to within 300 paces. This fire, deliberate and carefully aimed, would continue until their adversaries had closed to fifty paces. Then they would retire, passing through the intervals in the line on either side of the battalion. Undisturbed by their neighbours, de Saxe believed this type of aimed fire was ten times more effective per musket than any volley.[3] Although *Mes rêveries* was actually written in 1732, it was published only in 1756 when it had a tremendous impact. Copies even found their way into the American colonies and influenced the officers stationed there.

The original *compagnies franches* were relatively small units, usually about seventy to eighty men. However, starting with the War of Polish Succession and continuing up to the end of the Seven Years' War a large number of battalion-sized units were raised, such as the *Chasseurs de Fischer*, *Volontaires royaux*, *Volontaires bretons*, etc. These were not intended as front line battle troops, but functioned as 'light infantry' during the campaign. Prior to the war of Austrian Succession, these irregular troops were used exclusively as light infantry during the day-to-day rigours of the campaign, and were not employed during a set piece battle. However, during the Battle of Fontenoy (11 May 1745) the *Arquebussiers de Grassin* of about 900 foot and 300 cavalrymen were thrown into the Wood of Barry to hold off a larger Anglo-Hanoverian force. During the Seven Years' War, little more than a decade later, French skirmishers were to see even more service on the battlefield. At Sunderhausen (23 July 1758) seven companies of grenadiers were dispersed in front of twelve French battalions deployed in line. Three other grenadier companies were placed in a small wood on the French right, while a light infantry volunteer force in another small wood secured the opposite flank. The French regular force in line was similarly preceded by a line of skirmish at Lutternberg (10 October 1758). Even greater diversity of skirmisher tactics is found at the skirmish at Lippstadt (2 July 1759). Faced with Hanoverian jaegers in skirmisher order, the French commander ordered a body of dragoons to dismount and skirmish. Meanwhile, a 500-metre skirmish line was thrown out on front of the main force in line while a 'picquet' was placed behind a hedge on the right flank. Finally, during the Battle of Bergen (13 April 1759) volunteer units fought as light infantry in the woods while some of the regular units around Bergen fought alternately in line as skirmishers and then in column.

The success of these tactics prompted Marshal de Broglie to try to form permanent chasseur companies in every battalion to perform any skirmishing that became necessary. In a letter from Marshal de Broglie to the minister of war dated 30 March 1760 we learn that a number of regiments during the winter of 1759–1760 trained fifty men per battalion to use aimed fire and formalized skirmishing tactics. After the war, de Broglie continued to lobby for permanent skirmisher companies in the French army, and the 1764 ordonnance sanctioned a section of tirailleurs for each column of attack.[4]

The role that skirmishers were to play on the European battlefield and their value would be debated almost continuously up until the French Revolution and the next round of general hostilities. However, it is accurate to say that as long as peace lasted their value was downplayed and they were largely ignored in the official documents issued over the next thirty years. The infantry ordonnance of 1776 alone provided any description of how the skirmishers were to conduct themselves. Officers were enjoined to use skirmishers while deploying the remainder of the troops in the traditional line. The chasseur companies were to be sent forward and occupy whatever cover or broken terrain was available. Here, they were to pester the enemy artillerymen with their aimed fire. They were to operate strictly in open order, but were always to be ready to fall back and reform as soon as signalled to do so by their officers.[5]

SKIRMISHERS DURING THE REVOLUTIONARY WARS

During the summer of 1792, even before the war had begun in earnest, General Dumouriez ordered that a small number of troops from each line regiment in the *armée du Nord* be trained in light infantry techniques. The desire to fully exploit skirmishing tactics certainly was not peculiar to Dumouriez. One of his successors, as well as commanders of some of the other armies would issue similar sets of orders. The next summer, General Jean-Nicolas Houchard upon taking over the command of the *armée du Nord* prescribed similar groups of skirmishers be formed in each battalion. According to his

23 August 1793 *Instructions*: 'From now on there will be sixty-four men per battalion . . . selected as *tirailleurs*, these men to be chosen among the most valorous soldiers and the best shots . . .'[6] A few months later, in October, General Jourdan would order his divisional generals to utilize light infantry tactics, arguing that these instructions were well fitted to inexperienced conscripts then entering the ranks.

Events on the battlefield would soon demonstrate the usefulness of skirmishers. However, instead of these small numbers prescribed by the standing orders of generals' instructions, during the first few campaigns in practice large numbers of skirmishers were frequently thrown out. During the Battle of Hondschoote (8 September 1793), for example, the attacking force in a line of columns, once under enemy fire, largely dispersed and then continued the advance as skirmishers. Similarly, at the combat of Nottweiler (14 September 1793) entire battalions broke down into skirmishers.[7] These are only two of many examples that can be found of entire battalions acting *en débandade*, that is, completely in skirmish order, without any closed order formation being retained.

General Duhèsme, who managed to survive both the Revolutionary and Napoleonic Wars, commented that during these early campaigns the skirmishers were invariably thrown out *en débandade*. This term refers to the practice of throwing out large number of skirmishers, usually without reserve, such as when an entire formation broke down and fought in this manner. According to Duhèsme, the value of holding a local reserve to support the front skirmisher line only came to be appreciated by French commanders in 1794.[8] We have already seen the fate of French skirmishers at Kirrweiler who recklessly advanced across unexplored ground without a nearby formation to find shelter when unexpected enemy cavalry made their appearance.

SKIRMISHER TACTICS

French skirmisher tactics during the Napoleonic era are generally thought of as large clouds of skirmishers thrown along the entire width of the friendly forces. Another popular misconception is that the skirmishers would be most numerous in front of the focal point of the French attack, and that once in range of the enemy they would automatically commence a continual fire until the friendly regular forces had advanced beyond them in the last stage of the assault.

In reality the use of skirmishers, at least when led by experienced and competent officers, was governed by a set of more sophisticated principles. Just as regular infantry was only to deliver fire in certain situations, skirmishers were constantly admonished to refrain from firing until their firepower could be effective:

> Nothing is so stupid or injurious as those [wrongdoings] and skirmishing that lead to nothing. You waste your men and your ammunition without advancing the affairs, and the means will often be wanting at the decisive moment.[9]

The best time for skirmishers to deliver their fire was usually just prior to the final moments when the friendly formations were to engage the hostile infantry. Skirmisher fire was even more effective when the enemy had already been disordered by other events, such as artillery fire.

Like that of regular infantry, the skirmishers' fire was to be controlled as much as possible, it 'must not be lavish any more than that of the lines'. The practice of throwing out skirmishers to exchange fire with the enemy was to be strictly avoided. The officers' duty was to control the skirmishers and just prior to the commencement of the main attack point out what portions of the enemy's line or position they were to fire upon. The officers were also to indicate the positions the skirmishers were to advance to before beginning to fire. The regular troops behind the skirmishers meanwhile were ordered to halt, and were only to recommence their advance after the skirmishers began their fire. These controls were necessary in order to minimize the enemy's opportunity to respond appropriately to a skirmisher threat. Whenever a body of skirmishers was thrown against the enemy and left there, the enemy would react by detaching their own skirmishers. Given the proximity of their main force the enemy almost always could throw out more men than the French skirmishers available. This would force the skirmishers to retire or be ordered back, and in either case would stall or even abort the upcoming attack. The other alternative was to reinforce the French skirmishers with more troops in extended order. This was hardly more convenient since only with great difficulty could the enemy skirmishers be pushed back to their own lines, and the attack was significantly delayed. For this reason, the experienced officer leading the skirmishers held them back until the 'instant of attack'. Contrary to modern expectations, the skirmishers were not to be thrown on the intended point, instead they were to, 'as much as possible, be thrown on the point that is not the thickest of the fight.'

When the critical moment finally arrived and the ordered formations were in the last stages of attempting to close with the enemy, the skirmishers were to retire. This was done by running through the intervals, or spaces, between the advancing battalions. If this was not easily accomplished, they could throw themselves on the ground and lie flat in order to let the ordered troops pass over them. Those near the extremities of the enemy's lines were to run outward, right or left, to gain the enemy's flank. There, they were to demoralize the enemy with abrasive fire or start to take prisoners.[10]

In the French army, there was no uniform policy defining the positioning of the skirmishers relative to their parent organizations, and the tactical arrangements varied from commander to commander. Fortunately, the instructions Lieutenant-General Duhèsme issued to his division during the 1805 campaign have survived and these provide an insight into how skirmishers were handled on a brigade and divisional level.

During the march across the countryside, the voltigeurs were responsible for the regiment's security. In a three-battalion regiment advancing in columns of route, the voltigeur companies of the right and left regiments marched by files 100 to 150 paces on either flank. The voltigeur company of the middle battalion was positioned 100 to 150 paces in front of the regiment. Marching in a column of platoons, each on two ranks, the voltigeurs provided the sentinels who would scout the regiment's line of march. A third of these voltigeur companies were detached as skirmishers. Their responsibility was to secure whatever heights, clusters of trees, houses, etc. lay along the line of march. As soon as the regiment started to manoeuvre out of column of route and into 'battle order', the voltigeurs on the left of the column positioned themselves to the left of the battalion at the run, those to the right of the column guarded the right of the formation. It must be remembered that 'battle order' was frequently battalions formed in either company or divisional columns in closed order. If the battalion commander deemed fire combat necessary, the battalion would deploy into line, and the skirmishers from the centre company would be placed on the flank most likely to be threatened. Here, the skirmishers could either be placed as an extension to the line or *en potence* to prevent the battalion from being outflanked. In either case they had standing orders to take advantage of whatever terrain was available.[11] If the regiment was ordered to attack the enemy, frequently its three battalions would be ordered to form columns of attack. The captains of the voltigeur companies would immediately order two-thirds to three-quarters of their men into skirmish order. The remainder remained in close order to provide a rallying point should the skirmish line be repulsed.

Although the foregoing is primarily a discussion of Duhèsme's 1805 instructions, it is probably not out of place to include some advice proffered by Blücher, Bugeaud and Marmont, contemporaries who were every bit as knowledgeable and experienced as Duhèsme. The skirmishers supporting the advancing columns had to remain in the intervals between the columns and must not mask the latter's forward movement. Marmont felt that this would ensure that the enemy's fire would be divided between the formations and the skirmishers pestering the enemy.[12] Blücher disagreed, asserting that the skirmishers beside the columns would be able to fire in confidence, knowing that the enemy could not resist firing at the dense columns.[13]

In any case, assuming that the enemy deployed in line with few skirmishers, the skirmishers in front of Duhèsme's division were to pull back in the final moments of the attack and re-enter the intervals between the advancing columns. Here, they would continue to harass the enemy with well-directed fire, which Duhèsme anticipated would still inflict more casualties than the enemy in line would be able to inflict on the French attackers. Meanwhile, all the division's guns were to be placed in one or two batteries, supported by grenadier companies. The French skirmishers were directed to aim especially at the enemy gunners, who, harassed by this withering fire, would be unable to dish out as much as they received.[14]

The number of skirmishers that would be thrown out varied according to circumstances and the number of enemy skirmishers encountered. Duhèsme believed that occasionally it was necessary to have a battalion or even an entire regiment fight *en débandade* ('helter-skelter'). Although a regiment would take up a large lateral space when fighting in this mode, it was imperative that the overall direction of the skirmishers remain under the control of a single officer, such as a *chef de bataillon* or the colonel. It was also necessary to maintain a part of the battalion or regiment in closed order as 'supports' in case it became necessary to quickly rally the skirmishers and reform a formation.[15] In this approach, Duhèsme appears to be at variance with someone like Bugeaud, who subscribed to a more controlled approach to firepower. Instead of replying with 'parallel fire', that is reciprocal fire, Bugeaud prescribed pushing the enemy skirmishers back with a quick series of thrusts by troops in a column of attack.[16]

If, on the other hand, the regiment was attacked by a superior force and it became necessary to withdraw the skirmishers, the captain would blow a whistle and the skirmishers would reform in a convex line and then slowly retire through the intervals between the battalions until they regained the rear of their own battalion. However, this usually wasn't possible if the regiment was unexpectedly attacked by cavalry. Here, the skirmishers would fall back on to their supports and position themselves back to back to form a rallying square. If they were able they would then retire at the run to the battalion formation, which they would enter through the column or square angles. Once back with the main formation their main responsibility was to protect the battalion guns. Should the battalions themselves be forced to retire, they would do so *en échiquier* (checkerboard pattern). The skirmishers would be once more sent out to cover the retreat. As the regiment continued to retreat, the first line of skirmishers would fire, and then, as they were reloading their arms, pass through the second line behind them. The latter would fire only when the new second line of skirmishers had been established behind them.[17]

Of course, French doctrine called for offensive action whenever possible, and skirmishers would usually be employed during a general advance against the enemy. As soon as a defending force was ready it was to switch modes. Every second battalion would advance, thus forming a large echelon (staggered) pattern. The voltigeurs from the first line of battalions marched in front in open order. The captains of the companies would throw out more and more skirmishers as they neared the enemy. However, under all circumstances they were cautioned to keep at least ten to fifteen men in reserve. These were to serve as a rallying point if those in front were surprised by enemy cavalry or superior numbers of the enemy. The voltigeur companies from the second line of battalions were to advance as soon as those from the first were pushed back.[18]

HOW SKIRMISHERS WERE TO FIGHT

An individual skirmisher, even when menaced by a lancer, still had a chance, not only of survival but overthrowing his feared opponent provided he kept his head and displayed sufficient courage. The trick was to continue to face the approaching horseman, thus providing no clues about the intended movement. At the last minute, the infantry was to spring to his right, that is place himself on the horseman's blind side, i.e. the latter's left, and thrust his bayonet at the horse. If he was able to strike or block the enemy's lance, he was to close in at once.

Skirmishers were much less vulnerable in broken terrain. If attacked by cavalry, the light infantryman could hide behind a tree, fence or hedge. During a skirmish near San Milan (13 June 1813), near Vitoria, an officer in the 1st Battalion, Rifle Brigade found himself attacked by a French hussar. Springing behind a tree the British officer circled around always keeping the tree trunk between him and his mounted adversary. The officer spotted a rifle lying on the ground nearby which he was eventually able to run out and grab. He then allowed the Frenchman to approach again and calmly shot him through the body.[19]

In extremely dire circumstances, such as when assaulted by more than two horsemen, the skirmisher was advised to pretend to be struck by an enemy musket ball. He was to fall down and then thrash about for a few seconds, and then lie still. Since a horse will not willingly step on a man, and, unless armed with a lance, the rider could not hit anything on the ground, the prostrated infantrymen would live to endure future engagements.

If the skirmishers were unable to return to their supporting formations or take advantage of broken terrain, they were to form a 'rallying square'. All the men within distance would run towards the officer or NCO who gave the order to rally. The first men to arrive would stand back to back, and then the successive groups would be made to face a different direction so that the square would gradually grow layer by layer. Rallying squares could be as small as the men from three or four files or up to about eighty infantrymen. The man in the front rank would lower their bayonets as if to charge, but a little higher so that the bayonet would point to the left eye of an imaginary opponent directly in front. Under no circumstances were the men to fire, for if they were caught denuded of fire, the enemy cavalry could rush in and attack with sabre or lance. One of the most notable examples of infantry forced into this type of desperate struggle occurred at the Battle of Alexandria (21 March 1800). The 42nd Regiment was caught off guard when the French cavalry managed to enter the formation before daylight. However, the Highlanders fought back to back and shoulder to shoulder and rudely repulsed the enemy horsemen.[20]

However, if caught in skirmish order in open terrain, skirmishers were much more likely to be cut down, such as the unfortunate light troops under Colonel Hill's command at the Battle of Fuentes-de-Onoro. When first assaulted by Montbrun's cavalry, Hill rallied his men in time. Apparently flushed with his recent success and holding the enemy horse in too little regard, he unfortunately ordered his men to return to skirmishing prematurely, before the French cavalry had retired to a safe distance. The latter, realizing that they could make no impression on the main body of the British infantry, redoubled their attack on the skirmishers. The order to rally was issued too late, and the men attempted to rally by forming a line on the right when there was only enough time to rally upon the centre. As a result, the French cavalry mixed with the skirmishers whom they slaughtered.[21]

PRUSSIAN LIGHT INFANTRY

Although large-scale adoption of skirmisher tactics had to wait until after 1806, the Prussian infantry had dabbled in this new form of warfare at least fifteen years prior to the French Revolutionary Wars. Despite Frederick the Great's predeliction towards closed order formations and a strict reliance upon linear methods, the value of light infantry could not be denied indefinitely, even in the increasingly conservative Prussian army. A number of measures were taken to establish not only light infantry but also introduce riflemen into Prussian service. Recognizing the need to have skirmishers in each company to serve in the patrols, on 3 March 1777 the cabinet authorized ten men in each infantry company to be exercised as skirmishers.[22] Exactly ten years later to the day, ten *schützen*, that is riflemen or sharpshooters, were added to each company. Armed with their *schützengewehr* M 1787, which had an accuracy between a musket and a standard rifle, these were to pester the enemy at a longer range than possible with the traditional musket.

These first steps were only intended to allow greater independence for isolated battalions and regiments during the day-to-day activities of the campaign, and not to modify the infantry tactics on the conventional battlefield. The specialty troops in each company were to provide security while marching through the countryside and fill the advance posts when bivouacked, so that men would not have to be siphoned off the fusilier battalions. However, after 1787 several other innovations were introduced that certainly would have modified Prussian infantry tactics had they been fully implemented. Twenty fusilier battalions whose main responsibility was to fight in wooded and mountainous terrain were established between February and June 1787. Clothed in green, these new fusilier battalions were equipped with a *füsiliergewehr*, a lighter and more precisely manufactured version of the standard musket. The first Prussian manual for light infantry was issued on 24 February 1788. Overall, the practices and tactics prescribed by this regulation were similar to those for the regular infantry, the major difference being that the light battalions were to form along two ranks and there were some instructions for skirmishing in open order.[23] When the regulations were issued for the regular infantry on 26 February the next year, the importance of skirmishing and aimed fire was once again noted. All of those assigned to skirmisher duty were always to fight in this mode, and for the first time some provision was made for skirmishers fighting in relationship to the remainder of the battalion in closed order. For example, when a regiment or battalion attacked an enemy outpost, the skirmishers were to advance 100 paces in front of the line. The skirmishers, through their aimed fire, were to damage and disorder the enemy, thus preparing the way for the regular troops behind.[24]

Unfortunately, as later events would demonstrate all too conclusively, this string of innovations proved to be mere paper reforms and did not reflect the way Prussian infantry actually conducted itself in anger. The conservative attitudes of both Frederick William and the Prussian nobility prevented these reforms from ever really being put into practice. Originally destined for specialist functions, the fusiliers in practice followed a training regimen that was identical to that for the regular infantry. None of the troops was given the opportunity to practise fighting in skirmisher order and virtually no attention was paid to developing any proficiency in aimed fire. Troops armed with muskets fired only dummy bullets during the few allotted target practices each year, and although riflemen fired live cartridges, they were allocated only nine rounds per session and they had to provide the lead bullets themselves.[25]

Prior to 1807–1808, the distinction between light infantry and skirmishers apparently was little understood in the Prussian service. Ironically, although *schützen* had been added to each company in order that each company could fulfil the battalion's light infantry tasks without having to draw men from the fusilier battalions, in practice quite the opposite occurred. Typically, in crisis situations, commanders grouped together the companies' *schützen* and assigned these to the advance or rear guards, usually some distance from the parent battalion.

In a letter written to Frederick William from a French prison after the Jena–Auerstädt disasters, Prince Auguste of Prussia would attribute a considerable measure of the Prussian army's lacklustre performance to the battalions' lack of skirmishers. What happened at Jena and Auerstädt was part of a wider problem. Colonel von Raumer in his report on 14 October explained:

> at daybreak, all the Schuetzen of the regiment, joined by a squadron of dragoons from the Queen's Regiment, were assigned to the command of Adjutant-General von Pfuhl to form a patrol . . . and unfortunately the regiment had to fight the entire battle without Schuetzen . . . and due to lack of Schuetzen, the left flank company of the battalion was used for that purpose.

A Lieutenant-Colonel von Hallmann recollects a similar deficiency. Denuded of their riflemen who had been ordered to perform security and reconnaissance duties and hard pressed by the French, they had to throw out one of the regular companies as skirmishers.[26]

Post-1806 Reforms

The ignominious defeats of 1806 proved to Frederick William the need for immediate military reform. The value of skirmisher tactics on the battlefield was recognized as one of several important issues that needed to be addressed. Gneisenau, who had served as a light infantry officer at Saalfeld and Jena, sent the King proposals for reform on 27 February 1807. He urged that a large body of light infantry be raised immediately and that men be thoroughly trained in skirmishing tactics and aimed fire. He also suggested that even the regular infantry receive some practice in skirmishing in order that they become more self-reliant during battle.

Five months later, on 25 July a Military Reorganization Commission was set up to investigate the causes of the poor Prussian performance during the late campaign and to recommend solutions to the problems thus uncovered. The five man panel originally was made up of Count Friedrich Karl von Lottum, Karl von Bronikowski, Karl von Massenbach, and Gneisenau and chaired by Scharnhorst. King Frederick William provided a nineteen-paragraph outline which enumerated what he considered to be the important areas that needed redressing. Paragraph six discussed the need for a higher proportion of light infantry to regular infantry, while paragraph seven considered the formation of a free corps to be used in a light infantry capacity. The abolition of the *schützen* company was mentioned in the appendix. Their role could henceforth be performed by the third rank of infantry which could be trained in skirmishing tactics.

The Military Reorganization Commission ultimately concurred with most of these views. The battalion's *schützen* company was formally abolished on 20 November 1807, its place taken by the third rank who were when necessary to operate as skirmishers. Twenty or thirty infantry in the first two ranks were also required to be trained in skirmisher tactics, so that they could serve as replacements for the third rank as these were required because of sickness or casualties. Henceforth, over one-third of the entire Prussian infantry were to be able to function as skirmishers, at least in theory. The 'Provisional Instruction for the Training of Troops' issued on 3 June 1808 went several steps further. In addition to the third rank as skirmishers, it prescribed that all infantry, regardless of where they were positioned in the battalion should practise aimed fire periodically. Twenty-five rounds were to be distributed to each man for this purpose at target practice. All skirmish fire was to be conducted 'at will', that is, left to the discretion of the shooters and not by the command of the officers.[27]

As we have seen in an earlier chapter, the Austrian infantry was adopting the third rank as skirmishers roughly at about the same time. This was predicated upon the feasibility in certain situations of relying upon a two-rank line so that the men in the third rank could be employed for some other purpose. This idea that the two-rank line could be relied upon started to gain acceptability among a number of German military writers from the early 1790s onward. In the various regulations and instructions issued during this period we find several tactics based on the two-rank line, and one case at least where it was actually put into practice. The Duke of Brunswick, for example, in his *Instruction for my Regiment* which was issued in 1791, had several additional platoons formed from men taken from the third rank.

In 1794, the Austrians used a slightly different variant of this in the Army of Cobourg in the Low Countries. A reserve stationed to the rear of the battalion and formed from men in the third rank could be moved to either flank as needed. This prevented the battalion from being easily outflanked and allowed the formation to oppose a larger force on an equal footing.[28]

Two years later Heinrich von Porbeck and Adam von Ochs, authors of the Hesse infantry regulations of 1796, produced the first German infantry manual which provided detailed instructions for the use of skirmishers. The battalion's skirmishers were to be taken from the men in the third rank.[29] Several other instances of the two-ranked line with the third rank detached for special purposes are found in the literature during this period. In his 'Instruction for the Inspection of Lower-Silesia' (July 1798) Prince Hohenlohe called for a reserve to be formed from these men, while Field Marshal von Möllendorf in his 'Instruction on the Formation', a document intended for the Berlin regiments, advocated forming an entire second line by this means.[30]

Considering these facts, it becomes obvious that the Prussian and Austrian approach, drawing upon the third rank for the battalion's skirmishers, was part of a larger trend that had been emerging in the Germanies at least as far back as the early 1790s.

PART IV

CAVALRY AND ARTILLERY TACTICS

CHAPTER 15

Cavalry Combat

THERE IS A TENDENCY to think that cavalry employed a single set of tactics once on the battlefield for all occasions. For example, heavy or medium cavalry would always form line and then advance quickly towards the enemy starting at a walk, then proceeding to a trot before ending up closing at a gallop. In actual fact, by Napoleonic times much of the cavalry had been trained in a variety of tactics whose use depended upon the type of situation encountered and the objective to be accomplished. When considering heavy, medium and light cavalry together, there were three basic methods of combat then in practice. The cavalry could charge in a closed (ordered) formation or fight as either skirmishers or foragers.

Regular Formations

Although cavalry would frequently fight as skirmishers or foragers during the day-to-day struggles of the campaign, on the battlefield they were usually pitted against the enemy in an ordered formation, such as a line or echelon. Line was most frequently employed. A line allowed the greatest number of sabres to be brought to bear against the enemy, and gave the regiment a wider front, which helped to outflank the enemy.[1]

There were, in fact, several types of cavalry line formations. The squadrons in the line could be packed together so that a continuous line or 'curtain' was formed, with no spaces left between each squadron. Known as *en muraille*, this practice had both its advocates and its detractors. It originally had been developed while fighting the Turks during the late 1600s; the compact formations prevented the ferocious eastern horsemen from penetrating the ranks or going between individual squadrons in the formation. Unfortunately, it was difficult to maintain a line *en muraille* at speed. As the line charged forward, the width of the formation would expand, horses would be literally squeezed out of the line, and line would be irreparably disordered.

The earliest form of 'line' was not a real line at all, but more a series of dashes. Before the Prussian introduction of sophisticated manoeuvres, it allowed a squadron, if necessary, to manoeuvre out of its position in the 'line'. In those days, even the most fundamental manoeuvre, such as turning towards the rear, required these large 'intervals'. The use of full intervals, as it was termed, became much less frequent by the mid-eighteenth century. After this point, it was used mostly by cavalry positioned in the second line or the reserve, or when cavalry was threatened by a larger equestrian force and it was necessary to occupy a certain stretch of front. It was generally held that it was better to stretch a line out so as not to be outflanked on either side than it was to simply stop the enemy from penetrating the gaps between the squadrons. In this latter case, the incoming enemy could be quickly met by the cavalry in the second line, positioned several seconds behind from the first.[2] However, once the enemy started to roll up the flank, no amount of reserves or reinforcements could reverse the situation.

From the 1740s onwards, however, it became usual to place the squadrons within each cavalry regiment close together with ten to thirty paces between one another. This distance was small enough that the cavalry were functionally a continuous line: there were no gaps for the enemy to enter easily. On the other hand, there was enough space between squadrons to allow the frontage of each to expand during the advance, thus avoiding the overcrowding of the horses which led to the disordering of the line. This configuration was by far the most commonly used type of line by Napoleonic times, and *en muraille* had been basically discarded.

A line was useful when attacking enemy cavalry acting as skirmishers: the dense formation would psychologically overpower the enemy in loose and scattered disposition, and was certain to resolve the issue without actual combat. The line was also useful when attacking a critical enemy position in clear terrain only a short distance away. Each horse in the line was locked into place by its neighbours, making it more difficult for horse and rider to get out of harm's way by gradually arcing to one side and returning to the 'previous night's grazing'. The most significant drawback of a lengthy line was that of all formations it was the most susceptible to disorder through movement or slight variations in terrain. Except in the best trained squadrons, the formation would soon be disordered if either a lengthy distance had to be traversed or even slightly rough terrain encountered.[3]

Echelon

The echelon formation had been accidentally discovered by the Prussian cavalry during the Second Silesian War. The potential advantages of this formation were not lost on military authorities, and this new formation continued to be used throughout the Napoleonic Wars, especially when cavalry attempted to assault infantry.

Many military authorities believed that the echelon offered a number of advantages over the traditional line. It allowed cavalry to deliver an assault in two different directions: either straight ahead or diagonally to one side. For example, if the echelon sloped backwards on its left side, by eighth-wheeling each echelon 45° towards the left, a line could quickly be formed which could then advance in that new direction (9 o'clock to the original facing). This ability to deflect the attack to one side could prove very useful when facing either an inexperienced enemy or one which had started to advance uncontrollably straight ahead. When Frederick discovered this formation, he applied this innovation to the 'oblique attack' concept that he had been developing roughly at the same time. The echelon allowed the cavalry to quickly turn to one of the sides, so that the commander could direct this mass to attempt to outflank the enemy. By Napoleonic times, this grand tactical use of echelons had been discarded in practice, if not in theory, and this formation was recognized as offering tactical benefits which, though more localized, were none the less significant. Many cavalry men felt this was the best formation to deliver an attack against enemy infantry.

In an echeloned attack the various echelons would reach the enemy line at different times; with obviously the echelon furthest in front being the first. In fact, the echelons behind could be held up to await the result of the first echelon's assault. If it was successful, they could alter their advance straight ahead and exploit any gap in the line which now appeared. If the enemy withstood the first echelon's assault but were visibly shaken, the second would throw itself upon the enemy line with even greater chance of success. This process could be repeated until the line broke. Since each wave could also be timed to reach the enemy only moments apart, the enemy infantry would not have time to reload after firing at the first echelon, thus improving the chances of those behind. On the other hand, if it was obvious that the infantry were determined and unsubdued, the assault could be called off before all the echelons were engaged. Those that were not used in the attack could now cover the retreat and allow the others to rally and reform.[4] It was also much easier to manoeuvre troops in an echelon; for example, squadrons in this formation could pass through friendly infantry with relative ease. Not only did it require less effort to deploy into echelons than form a regiment-sized line, but it was also simpler to ploy back into column from echelon, since each echelon could quickly form a column of troops.[5]

Although echelon was often used to attack enemy infantry formations, many did not consider it a good method of engaging enemy cavalry. More traditionally oriented cavalrymen felt that an enemy deployed in a near continuous line would enjoy a decided advantage. Because of the frequently occurring large gaps between each echelon, about half the men in the line would have no one in front of them when they met the enemy, and they would be free to try to work their way around the flank of the nearest echelon. The defeat of the first echelon could result in its being thrown back upon those in the rear, thus impeding the progress of the assault.[6]

Those who favoured using the echelon against enemy cavalry cited the same advantages as the formation was known to enjoy when attacking infantry. They also argued that though the enemy line could outflank the lead echelon, this very action made the outflanking enemy vulnerable. Those elements in the line that now started to curl inward would be almost instantly taken in flank and overthrown by the second and third echelons that were only a few seconds behind the first.[7]

En échiquier

Cavalry also could be ordered to assume the checker or *en échiquier* formation. In terms of its geometry this was identical to the infantry counterpart of the same name: it consisted of two rows of troops, each unit separated from its neighbour on that row by a complete 'interval'. It was formed by having every second block of cavalry (often two squadrons) either advance or retreat a short distance. As with infantry, it was used to protect a retreating army. The front row protected the rear as it retreated and then the front began its own retreat.[8]

Closed Columns

The primary function of closed cavalry columns was to allow the cavalry to enter and deploy on to the battlefield as expeditiously as possible. It was much easier to control the movement and direction of cavalry in this formation than in line or even in a more extended type of column. It was difficult to keep cavalry in line properly aligned, and delays were necessary to straighten out the line. Lengthy columns tended either to bunch up or stretch out into uncontrollably long monstrosities. A closed column, on the other hand, could be kept in hand to be used when favourable circumstances presented themselves. Only those portions that were necessary were deployed, the remainder were kept in column as a reserve. More than any other formation a closed column hid much of the friendly force from the enemy's view. Dense columns from afar tended to look exactly like a line of the same width, whereas lengthy columns gave away their numbers by the tail which was visible from a distance. This deceived the enemy, and helped prevent him from making the appropriate response.

Most authorities agreed that under ordinary circumstances cavalry was not to attack while still in column. There were several serious drawbacks. Its depth made the formation extremely vulnerable to artillery firing round shot, while the density of the formation greatly increased the confusion and made maintaining order at the gallop almost impossible. The rear ranks, though possibly bolstering the morale of those in front, were unable to bring their sabres to bear, unless both formations came to a halt and a lengthy mêlée occurred. And this very rarely happened.[9] However, the greatest weakness of a closed column were its flanks. The long flanks of a deep formation were weak and vulnerable to a countercharge by an opposing line, which, given its greater width, could envelop the column. Unlike infantry in a closed column, cavalry in this formation could not form line facing the flank. Infantry when attacked on the flank simply turned 90° to face that direction, and a line was instantly formed. Not so with cavalry. In order for the cavalry in each rank to form line towards the flank, a relatively large interval had to exist between each of the troops or squadrons in the column in order for the cavalrymen to be able to quarter-wheel or turn by threes or fours into the new line facing the flank.[10]

There were two exceptions, however, when charging in column was considered, if not desirable, at least acceptable. If an enemy cavalry or infantry formation was taken by surprise and there was no time to deploy into line, the friendly cavalry was to attack immediately regardless of its current formation. The same was true if an advantageous situation presented itself, but the ground did not permit a general advance in line, or the enemy was too close for the friendly troops to risk performing a manoeuvre in the face of the enemy.[11] These same principles applied when attacking infantry, and one of the most successful uses of cavalry columns in the attack was, in fact, effected against this arm. During the Battle of Leipzig (17 October 1813), Blücher encountered the remnants of Marmont's corps, which had already been forced to retreat by Yorck, and realized that he had to attack the retreating French quickly. His cavalry, two thousand strong and led by General Wittgenstein, appuyed its right flank on the Parthe. Formed in closed columns, the Russian cavalry began a massive charge, pushing back the French infantry to the Halles gate in the walls around Leipzig.[12]

The other situation where a cavalry charge in column was considered acceptable was the reverse of the first; in other words, when the friendly cavalry was surprised by a superior force of enemy cavalry and cut off from its support. In this case, the surprised cavalry was to quickly group itself into a compact mass and cut its way through the enemy line.

General de Brack informs us that light cavalry also used this technique occasionally when confronted with a large force of enemy heavy cavalry. The goal was to avoid receiving the enemy charge in line since the sight of the approaching heavy cavalry was usually enough to tip the psychological scales and make the light cavalry retire. Instead, the mêlée was to be localized so that the light cavalry would have a better chance of reducing the affair to a series of personal combats where the light horsemen would have an advantage. As the heavy cavalry advanced towards them in line, the light cavalry would form closed column at the gallop upon the centre of the line. This meant that most of the enemy cavalry now without an enemy in front of them rode past. The light cavalrymen, on the other hand, were able to fight those heavy cavalry men they encountered, exploit the gap and spread outward to attack the flanks and rear of other enemy troops still present.[13]

At the beginning of the Revolutionary Wars, the Austrians at least on one occasion used a similar set of cavalry tactics to defeat the French cavalry facing them. Monsieur Montjoy, the adjutant for General Dumouriez, tells us that at the Battle of Neerwinden (18 March 1793) the Austrians charged the French horse with several squadrons of cavalry in closed column. Directly behind this dense column followed additional cavalry in line. However, the Austrian formation was only partially successful. Though at first it defeated every opposing cavalry formation it encountered, ultimately it was defeated by a French hussar regiment which succeeded in taking it in flank.[14] Contemporaries apparently thought this tactic to be quite innovative, which shows they were unaware of the latest military works being published in the Germanies. With the advantage of hindsight, we now know that the Austrians were simply employing Frederick the Great's 'secret' cavalry column of attack. Given the publication of General Warnery's original German version of Remarks on Cavalry in the 1780s, which provided a comprehensive description of Frederick's secret column, it is hardly coincidental that the Austrians experimented with this much recommended formation.

In the original Prussian version, successfully employed several times during the Seven Years' War, the column of attack consisted of five squadrons of dragoons in closed column and ten squadrons of hussars in line directly behind the dragoons in column. As this hybrid formation neared the enemy, the dragoons in column would launch an all-out charge at the gallop. The hussars in line continued to advance at the trot. The purpose of the hussar line was to offer a more extended target to enemy artillery to draw it away from the dragoons in column. At the same time, the hussars now some distance behind the dragoons would provide a second charge, if needed, or they could continue to advance in line and support the dragoons from additional cavalry once the dragoons overthrew the first line.[15]

THE ACTION

Among the many other tactical innovations, Frederick the Great was responsible for developing the charge tactics that would be employed, at least in theory, by the cavalry in most armies until the late 1800s. Frederick had inherited a particularly poor specimen of cavalry from his father, one which wallowed in ignominy for the first several campaigns during the Wars of Austrian Succession. The Austrian cavalry, used to attacking their Turkish opponents, emphasized the importance of maintaining an ordered formation at all times and charged only at a fast trot. Frederick found that by having his cavalry advance slowly at first and then in the final moments rush in at greater speed, he was not only able to compensate for his troopers' poor horsemanship but actually gain a decided advantage of morale over the Austrians who continued to advance at a slower gait. The distance the Prussian cavalry was to charge at a gallop was gradually increased from a modest thirty paces in 1741 to 200 paces in 1744, and thence to a quite unreasonable 1,800 yards in 1755.[16]

In its final form, the Prussian charge doctrine divided a cavalry attack into five distinct phases. The cavalry would begin its advance at a walk and then after a distance began to trot. The cavalry would only start to gallop when within 150 to 200 paces from the enemy. When the distance between cavalry forces closed to seventy or eighty paces, the trooper applied his spurs and the horse moved at full speed. The charge *à la sauvage*, what Frederick termed the grand *coup de collier*, was reserved for the last twenty paces.[17] Frederick reasoned that a charge at a trot gave the troopers too much time to think and allowed them to give in too easily to their instinct for survival. A charge at speed, on the other hand, caused the cowards to be forced along with the courageous.

This method of attack, ignoring minor regional variations, was the theoretical model used by virtually all western European cavalry throughout the Revolutionary and Napoleonic eras. Although the charge at full speed in the final moments would quickly disorder the attacking cavalry, by Napoleonic times, its psychological effect on the enemy was almost universally recognized:

Only the necessity for carrying along the man and the horse at the supreme moment, for distracting them, necessitates the full gallop before attacking the enemy, before having him put to flight.[18]

The Westphalian cavalry, for example, would trot forward towards the enemy cavalry until they were about 100 paces distant, then rush forward at the gallop.[19] The British Cavalry regulations of 1799 required a much longer charge at full speed: the gallop was to replace the trot when at 250 yards and to finally break out to *à la sauvage* at eighty yards. At this point the horses were made to gallop as fast as possible without breaking up the order of the formation.[20] The version of charge advocated by the Prussian tactician Marwitz was similar: the gallop was to be sounded at 300 paces, while the final charge commenced at sixty paces.[21]

CONTACT VERSUS NO-CONTACT (CAVALRY)

The Prussian charge doctrine which served as the official doctrine throughout the entire Napoleonic period was designed to buoy the troopers' morale so that they would run headlong into the enemy cavalry. Of course, in practice this rarely, if ever occurred. Ardant du Picq, the brilliant French tactical analyst writing prior to the Franco-Prussian War, estimated that 'forty-nine times out of fifty' one side hesitated, became disordered then fled before any actual contact was made.[22] There were two reasons for this potential check, each originating independently of the other, but which inevitably combined to prevent two forces from colliding. These were the psychological dynamics operating simultaneously within the psyche of both the rider and his horse. As much as the various riding methods, manoeuvres and offensive doctrine were designed to over-ride the cavalrymen's personal feelings, they couldn't completely cir-cumnavigate the rider and horse's most basic instincts for self preservation. Efficacious use of doctrine could delay reaction to these instincts for a time, but ultimately a force's will to fight was no greater than that of the individuals out of which it was made.

The Frederician charge ideally was to be conducted 'knee to knee' so that there was no space between the individual horses within a squadron. This practice, when properly executed created a truly imposing spectacle. Though it increased the chances that the other side's will to continue would be broken first, at the very same time it ultimately guaranteed that no contact at speed would be made. At some point, the horse, who probably never really bought into the honour system and the regiment's *esprit de corps* as much as his rider, would try to avoid running into the enemy horses coming towards him. Obviously, if two opposing forces in close order formation actually met at the gallop both sets of horses would run into each other causing death among human and equine participants alike. If it were possible, the horse would attempt to swing towards the flank. However, the whole point of the ordered charge at speed was to prevent just this type of occurrence. Riding knee to knee effectively prevented the horses within a squadron from moving in any direction but straight ahead. If the horse was unable to veer off to either side, ultimately it would simply pull up at the last second.

Meanwhile, very similar considerations were at work within the rider's psyche, and as the opposing walls of horses and men neared to closing, the rider, if only unconsciously, would begin what the horse had already started to do: look for a way of avoiding the collision. Almost always one side possessed greater elan and/or a greater will to fight than the other. The side which possessed the lesser of these prerequisites would become disordered first and then break off the charge. According to du Picq, 'three quarters of the time this will happen at a distance, before they can see each other's eyes'.[23] When this happened, the breaking up of the charge would start while the advancing line was still fairly ordered.

In order for a cavalry force to be willing to close to combat with an enemy cavalry force a number of conditions had to exist. The men had to have confidence in their riding and fighting ability, as well as having complete confidence in their horses and their weapons.[24] For the two forces to close, both sides had to be 'pre-eminently brave troops, equally seasoned in morale, alike well led and swept along'. However, du Picq conceded that 'all these conditions are never found united on either side, so the thing is never seen'. This meant that in practice when two groups of veteran and brave troops faced off in the last few seconds the horses would start to pull back, the cavalrymen reining in, and the two lines of cavalry would end up staring at each other 'face to face'. At this point, the two forces then would advance into a mêlée at a walk, or alternatively one side would flee. An excellent example of this type of occurrence was provided in the Peninsular War during the retreat of the British army from Burgos in 1812. A French force of three squadrons of French *chasseurs à cheval* encountered several squadrons of the British rear guard somewhere between Villadrigo and Villaropegue. Each side deployed along the traditional two lines and then advanced at the charge, but at the last moment the two forces pulled up so that they stood facing one another. For a few moments both groups were motionless, until a French cavalryman made a swipe at the English rider opposite him. Immediately everyone else plunged forward and a general mêlée ensued. The British finally beat off the French who suffered heavy casualties, including the death of their colonel.[25]

The same occurred at the Battle of Friedland (14 June 1807) but on a much larger scale. In a letter to the Honourable George Canning from Memel dated 22 June 1807, Sir Robert Wilson, then attached to the Russian army in an official capacity, provides this description:

> about noon. The Russian cavalry, one hundred squadrons, had endeavoured to gain the left of the enemy. Having succeeded, a part charged the French cuirassiers: who ran away, but being met by some officer they rallied and returned to their pursuers who checked their career. Although both parties mutually declined the shock they advanced until they met sword to sword, when the Russians were overpowered after a few minutes . . .[26]

As opposed to the theoretical model employing a charge at speed, in actual practice many heavy and medium cavalry regiments during the Napoleonic Wars only charged at the trot, or even a fast walk. When both sides employed a slower gait during the charge, such as a trot or walk, the likelihood of actual contact was greatly increased. The Battle of Heilsberg, on 18 June 1806 illustrates this. The French Cuirassiers d'Espagne, armed with lances and in closed order, advanced at a walk against the Zeiten Dragoons. Both sides met and a fierce and prolonged hand-to-hand struggle ensued. The confusion was general along both lines with each trooper seeking individual opponents. Seemingly, the contest was prolonged with successful troopers seeking new opponents after they dispatched their first. Purportedly, one French officer received a total of fifty-two wounds during this affair while Captain Gebhardt, a Prussian dragoon officer, received twenty. Gebhardt managed to grab a broken French lance which he used as a club to disable a number of French horsemen, before being killed by a kicking horse.[27]

There were several other possible endings for a charge, other than one side fleeing outright or both sides reining up and then fighting. Occasionally, when one horse would swerve to a flank to avoid collision, it was immediately followed by most of the remaining horses. Horses were known to sometimes 'follow the leader' even when their masters were taking every step to prevent this from happening. This problem was more acute when either inexperienced or improperly trained horses were involved. It is probable that this type of occurrence was all too common in the French cavalry during the Revolutionary Wars, and again after 1812 when there was a dearth of well-trained horsemen left in service.

Another possible outcome was when the cavalry in the opposing lines 'threaded' one another. In this case, the horses rode right through the other line in the spaces separating the enemy horses. Of course, this wasn't a possibility if the enemy was able to maintain a 'boot-to-boot' formation. It was only possible if the other formation had opened up sufficiently during the latter stages of the charge, or had conducted a charge *en fourrageur* where the cavalry intentionally opened up so that there was one or more paces separating each horse. This had been more commonly used in the French army in the late seventeenth century, and threading was more frequent when this charge doctrine was more commonly found on the battlefield.

THE PURSUIT

Another phenomenon associated with charges conducted at speed was a full-scale but highly disorganized pursuit of the broken force by the victorious side. The British cavalry action at Campo Mayor is most illuminating in this regard. After defeating their French counterpart, the British cavalry continued their charge for several miles before being swept back by French cavalry reserves.[28] The official doctrine employed by most cavalry called for the victorious force not to pursue a mounted enemy in full retreat for any extended distance. Instead, the regiment was to quickly rally a slight distance in front of where the two forces would have met if the other side had not fled first. To rally quickly was of critical importance. As long as the body of victorious cavalry was disorganized, which would be invariably the case in the moments that followed a successful charge, it would be vulnerable to a counterattack by any enemy cavalry in the area who were not involved in the original charge. The other disadvantage was that as long as the cavalry regiment remained disordered it was no longer under the control of its officers and could not be employed to exploit any opportunities that might arise during the ebb and flow of the battle. On the actual battlefield it was not always possible for the officers to rally their men after a successful charge. And the cavalry of certain nations, such as the British cavalry, proved more intractable than others in this respect.

It was naturally a great temptation to follow the fleeing enemy cavalry. The riders on the losing side would have slowed down their horses and turned them around before flying 'hell for leather' in the opposite direction.[29] There was no such need to slow down on the victorious side, so often the successful cavalry would find itself amidst those forced to flee. And it was in this situation that most casualties were inflicted. At Eckmühl, for example, the defeated Austrians suffered fourteen times as many casualties as did the victorious French cuirassiers. Unfortunately, the Austrian cuirassiers were not provided with back plates and most of the casualties they suffered were taken in the back.[30]

There were other inducements to pursue the enemy, even if this meant ignoring the officers attempting to get the men in the formation to rally. One was *fear*. As long as the enemy was heading in the opposite direction they could not reform and renew the attack. One tendency at work was the desire of cavalrymen to chase the fleeing enemy as far as possible to ensure that they did not return on the battlefield that day. Then, of course, there was simple blood-lust. Once the frenzy of killing began and the men were caught up in the chase, there was a tendency among many to go beyond the bounds of reason and even self-interest.

Close pursuits often led to numerous casualties among those fleeing, and were always lop-sided affairs. There was no way the losers could redress the situation unless they were first able to break away from their pursuers and gain an opportunity to rally themselves. But a close pursuit always prevented this. With the enemy close behind, the fleeing cavalry could not even attempt to fight back. This would have required the individual horsemen to first stop and turn around. The fleeing horsemen, in addition to being demoralized were unable to see the state of affairs behind them. An individual horseman might be pursued by a single adversary, or he might be followed by a group. The victorious cavalry to the rear on the other hand could see everything that transpired in front of them. If the horseman in front attempted to stop and turn, the followers would see these motions and adjust their movement so as to be atop of their opponents before the latter were ready to defend themselves. These dynamics would often make the pursuit a long one, and the fleeing cavalry would continue until they were able to rally, aided by rough terrain or the presence of friendly troops, or if they were less fortunate, until their horses would go on no further.[31]

In the case of cavalry fleeing pell mell, chased by their victors, it is natural to assume that the cavalry being chased would open up and disperse. In practice, the reverse tendency was true. The retiring troops would tend to seek protection in numbers and crowd together. It was this trait that allowed the victors to inflict the greatest number of casualties. By crowding together tightly the fleeing men encountered one more obstacle hindering them from using their weapons effectively. At the same time, the rush away from the victorious enemy was slowed down. Any fast horses that had originally been in the first rank would find themselves behind any slower and/or poorly mounted horses that had been positioned in the rear of the formation. This meant these were forced to remain 'at the tail of the column, to be sabred and captured while serving as shields to their guilty companions'.[32]

This tendency to crowd together though common to regular cavalry in western Europe had never been a characteristic of the irregular cavalry in eastern Europe, such as the Hungarian hussars, or any of the Asiatic horsemen of Russia and the Middle East. Horsemen thoroughly trained in the art of individual mounted combat knew that the best chance of survival in a rout was for each horseman to spread out from the pack and go his own way. Obviously, this had the advantage of obviating the problems caused by herding together. If attacked, the horseman was free to use his weapons without being encumbered by friendly troops around him. Similarly, whether the rider's horse was slow or fast, it was completely free to rush forward as quickly as possible, without having to make its way around slower horses or jump over those fallen to the ground. A less obvious, but certainly not less important, advantage was the effect it had on any pursuer trailing the lone horseman. Victorious troopers pursuing a rag tag group of fleeing horsemen could rush up and begin to sabre the hapless fugitives one at a time almost with impunity. All of the foe were within sight directly to the front. To the sides and the rear were a number of friendly cavalrymen partaking in the pursuit.[33] This was not the case when a trooper chose to follow a lone horseman. As the pursuit continued, the pursuer increasingly became separated from his own forces, and at some point the chase could devolve into a lone horseman following one other. When this happened, there was no longer immediate succour to be had from the flanks and rear. Quite the contrary. At any moment other enemy horsemen could pop out from behind whatever terrain presented itself. This tended to make the pursuer more wary and the pursued increasingly desirous at some point of turning around and making a stand.[34]

WEIGHT OF HORSE

In medieval times, the heavily armoured and armed horsemen out of necessity were mounted on the strongest, most sturdy horses available. As most of the rider's armour gradually disappeared during the course of the seventeenth century, the main battle cavalry continued to be mounted on large, strong horses. At the same time, the tradition of dividing the mounted troops into several categories according to purpose and equipment had also slowly arisen. There were dragoons, who, armed with long infantry muskets, were originally envisioned as 'mobile' infantry, to use a modern term. Hussars, who originated in Hungary, were introduced into western Europe as a quick but irregular force that could be unleashed against the enemy's countryside to cause as much consternation and inconvenience as possible.

The majority of the cavalry, however, continued to be that destined to fight their enemy counterpart on the battlefield. Whereas irregular cavalry, such as hussars, were always mounted on small fast horses, dragoons were mounted on larger horses, while the main battle cavalry were seated on the largest available. Throughout the early eighteenth century, cavalry versus cavalry tactics was dominated by the concept of 'weight of horse'. It was believed that if two bodies met in equally good order, the side with the larger men and horses would ultimately be victorious, especially when the difference in weight was significant.

As a result, 'heavy' and 'light' cavalry were each endowed with a different set of fighting tactics. Largely the result of the Turkish Wars which punctuated the late seventeenth century, it became the common wisdom for heavy cavalry to charge enemy cavalry at a trot to ensure that a boot to boot formation was maintained throughout. Light cavalry, on the other hand, fought the enemy in a much looser order, coming quickly in at a full gallop, firing their pistols at the enemy, and then pulling back before the enemy could retaliate or come to grips. The occasion for this type of warfare presented itself most frequently in the countryside during the day-to-day operations of the campaign, rather than during formal set piece battles.

De Grandmaison provides an excellent description of hussar tactics so typical of light cavalry up to the end of the Seven Years' War.

> A squadron of cuirassiers or heavy horse, that makes close and steady, does not apprehend the shock of the light horse; but if by a false movement, in a manoeuvre too slowly executed, it opens or exposes its rear, it is in the instant briskly charged . . . [the light cavalry] has nothing else to do, but scatter themselves all about the latter, and harass them by firing their muskets and pistols, and when it has forced it to wheel about, the light horse throws itself on the flanks, always skirmishing and avoiding the fire of the rear, as soon as it begins its march. If the retreat of this heavy squadron is long, it becomes troublesome and dangerous, on account of greater numbers being killed and wounded in a compact body, thus skirmishing with one dispersed and scattered, which has also the advantage of firing with more certainty.[35]

Light cavalry up to the mid-eighteenth century invariably fought in a loose order, that is, close order tactics were eschewed. This was primarily because it was almost universally held that light cavalry, which consisted of small men on diminutive horses, could never successfully compete against heavier forms of cavalry using the latter's terms and doctrine. Only by avoidance, quickly striking when an opportunity fleetingly presented itself, and then immediately withdrawing, could light cavalry ever cause any mischief to their heavier counterparts.

The gradual charge at speed doctrine of the Prussian cavalry was destined to change this, however. It was recognized that an orderly formation moving at speed would overthrow an enemy either more disorganized or moving more slowly. The concept of 'weight', though still held to be important, was now only one of three factors in the equation. Zieten was the first to understand this. Completely running against the common wisdom of the time, he frequently led his hussars to success against more heavily mounted foes. By the mid-nineteenth century, Nolan would observe: 'The success of a cavalry attack depends not so much on the description of the cavalry or horse employed, as on the determination of the men.'[36] Or, in the words of a near contemporary:

It is from the impulse derived from the speed of the horse, that the rider derives the advantage which, from a confusion of ideas, we sometimes ascribe to the weight of the horse; and it is the power and strength of speed, which we must therefore cherish, instead of imaginary power derived from weight.[37]

During the Napoleonic Wars there are repeated instances of light cavalry overthrowing more heavily mounted cavalry. At Jena, for example, when a Prussian cuirassier unit charged the until then victorious French, Ney sent in the 3rd Hussar Regiment. The hussars during their preliminary manoeuvres were able to momentarily hide their presence from the oncoming cuirassiers. They waited until the enemy was within striking range and then charged the cuirassiers in flank, thus totally disordering the latter.[38]

During the campaign of 1811 near Campo Mayor (25 March), two squadrons of the British 13th Light Dragoons with some hussars under the direction of Colonel Head charged and routed the French 26th Regiment of dragoons, and while chasing them to the Gates of Badajoz killed and captured a great number of the French cavalrymen.[39] In this case the French dragoons represented a slightly heavier form of cavalry. More dramatic success, despite an even greater inequality of weight between opposing sides, was displayed at Waterloo. Here, the 10th and 18th British Hussars succeeded in overthrowing a number of French cavalry units, many of which were cuirassiers. Similarly, during the retreat from Villa-Franca, in Catalonia, the 13th Regiment of French cuirassiers were completely routed by the Brunswick Hussars.[40]

However, probably the most dramatic victory of light cavalry over heavy occurred at Leipzig. The carabinier brigade was advancing in column with the 1st Carabiniers in the lead. Suddenly, a force, mostly of Hungarian hussars, bore down upon the French column. General Sebastini, the commander, openly laughed contemptuously at the thought of hussars attacking carabiniers and an observer by the name of Rilliet thought that the hussars would flee as the French drew their swords and showed a willingness to fight. The overconfidence of the French, however, prevented them from taking sufficient precautions, i.e. countercharging. As a result, the 1st Carabiniers broke and fled when the hussars were still 100 paces away. They ran into the 2nd Carabiniers which routed, in turn, and together they dragged away the 1st Cuirassier regiment in the column's rear.[41]

Skirmishers

It appears that the French, for example, used mounted skirmishers extensively prior to the start of a battle while each army sought to gain the desired initial positions. Pressing forward, the amorphous ranks of skirmishers would annoy the ordered formations in front of them with unrelenting fire. As with infantry skirmishers their goal was to provoke the officers and/or their men into a premature fire, or, if the enemy was still in column, to force deployment before the latter could carry out its own plans and stratagems.[42] The mounted skirmishers' contribution was not limited to its ability to harass. Mounted skirmishers were an effective means of scouting either the enemy's position or the ground to be passed. The skirmishers advanced in front of the main body to prevent the enemy from hiding behind broken ground and observed the army's motions and intent. Cavalry regiments were also advised to use small groups of skirmishers prior to a regular cavalry charge during a set piece affair. It was extremely important for the commander and his officers to know the exact lie of the land in order to prevent a formation from running into some hidden rough terrain, such as a ditch, march or sunken road during the charge. If necessary, skirmishers could signal the advancing formation to stop, and prevent the horrible casualties that would necessarily arise from the formation running into this terrain at breakneck speed as they closed at the gallop during the final moments of the charge.[43] Such a precaution was not taken by the 23rd Light Dragoons of Anson's brigade at the Battle of Talavera, when it ran precipitously into a hidden ditch and was effectively removed from that day's action.

Mounted skirmishers were also used as a rear guard when it was necessary to retire from an enemy body of cavalry. Just prior to the action at Villars-en-Cauchies, four Austrian cavalry squadrons unexpectedly found themselves facing a large French force made up of all three arms. After initially retiring in a rather precipitous fashion, they stopped, reformed after 400 yards and threw out skirmishers to effect a more orderly retreat.[44] Conversely, it was also useful to deploy skirmishers when the enemy cavalry failed to stand up to a charge delivered by an ordered formation. As the enemy cavalry line turned and retired, rather than pursuing with the entire squadron or regiment it was more efficient to detach a smaller body. The individual skirmishers, no longer restricted by the need to maintain formation, would ride directly towards an individual enemy at the fastest gallop.[45] This also had the advantage of allowing the remainder of the squadron to maintain order, to protect the skirmishers or to enter the fray as needed.

By the late Napoleonic Wars, skirmish tactics had evolved to the point where there was cooperation between mounted and infantry skirmishers when necessary. In the open countryside, the cavalry was to support its infantry counterpart. When operating in rough, broken terrain, the roles were switched and the infantry moving and defending itself with greater facility had always to look out for the cavalry.[46]

Mounted skirmishers were also occasionally used to attack heavier cavalry which for some reason was stationary or only able to move slowly. This was used with great effect by the then Colonel von Blücher (later of Waterloo renown) against French dragoons in the combat of Kirrweiler in Pfalz on 28 May 1794. Deceiving the French advance guard with a clever false retreat, Blücher's hussars managed to scatter quickly several French infantry columns that had been lured into open ground. Continuing on, the hussars almost caught two French dragoon regiments off guard. The Prussian hussars had approached to within thirty yards before one of the dragoon regiments had managed to form line facing the unexpected threat on its flank. Forced to rein up, the Prussian light cavalry was initially embarrassed and its men started to waver. The French cavalry facing them were in a perfectly ordered formation. Moreover, both French horses and their riders were noticeably larger than their Prussian counterparts which would be a factor if both sides attempted to charge one another. Undaunted, Blücher immediately ordered his men to halt and dispatched a number of small parties of hussars who were ordered to ride up and down the French line and fire into the stationary French dragoons. True, the Prussian hussars were armed only with pistols but they had spread out in extended order and acted individually, two of the most essential characteristics of skirmishing. The French dragoon commander's error was that he believed he could simply intimidate the smaller hussars and his command remained motionless as a result. The Prussians, however, had been ordered to fire upon the French mounts, who in closed order, afforded excellent targets. Despite the intrinsic inaccuracy of the pistols, quickly a number of horses fell victim to Prussian firearms and confusion began to creep through the French ranks.

Realizing that his positioning was becoming increasingly untenable, the French commander ordered his regiment to abandon its position. However, still contemptuous of the enemy light cavalry in front of him he failed to take the precautions mandated when retiring or changing positions in the face of the enemy. He simply ordered his command to form column by quarter-wheels (presumably simultaneously to the right). Blücher had retained a strong reserve just for this eventuality. The reserve was immediately ordered to charge the French troopers who as they quarter-wheeled into column unwisely presented an exposed flank to the Prussians. The Prussian hussars succeeded in riding through the French dragoons in short order. The action resulted in two hundred French casualties and 100 men taken prisoner, including the colonel-commander.[47]

When cavalry fought as skirmishers, it adopted 'extended order', where each cavalryman positioned himself several or more paces from his neighbour. The individual horses were kept far enough apart from one another to reduce the collective casualties from enemy small arms fire. Deploying as skirmishers was useful when a cavalry screen was needed, for example, when it was necessary to hide the preparatory actions of troops in formation to the rear. An effective screen, however, required that numerous cavalry be thrown out in skirmish order. The screen was to be nearly continuous with only small spaces allowed between each squadron in the screen. However, it was universally considered good practice to always maintain a portion of the squadron in ordered formation in the rear as a 'support'. The Saxon cavalry regulations of 1810 prescribed that no more than 25% of the men should ever be engaged as skirmishers at any one time, that is never more than one platoon per squadron.[48]

The distance between the screen and the support varied according to the mission. In a true screen, the skirmishing line would advance ahead and conduct individual fire, making as much noise and smoke as possible. However, if the cavalry was simply scouring the country-side either to reconnoitre the terrain or look for scattered enemy soldiers, the skirmish line could be maintained at as little as forty or fifty paces in front of the supports. The intervals between the skir-mishers from each squadron were also widened to the same distance, i.e. forty or fifty paces. In either case, when the charge was sounded, it was necessary to 'rally' (reform) the skirmishers directly back into the formation. They were to halt and let the ordered formation advance in front of them. They were not to make a wide circuit around the formations in the rear. To do so, would have been much more time consuming and would have left the formations exposed during the process.[49] There was great variation from army to army, and in the Saxon cavalry mounted skirmishers were allowed to advance up to 150 to 300 paces from the main body of the squadron, with the second line of skirmishers trailing fifty or so paces beyond the first.[50]

In the official drill booklets and regulations, cavalry skirmisher tactics tended to be ignored, or only cursorily treated. Fortunately, the Saxon cavalry regulations of 1810 provided a detailed description of how mounted cavalry was expected to fight. Before actual fighting erupted, the cavalryman was required to hold the carbine in his right hand, its butt resting upon his thigh. When ordered to fire, the horseman had been trained to aim over the horse's head and slightly towards his left, roughly around the 'eleven o'clock' position. Turn-ing his horse to the right to make aiming easier was strictly forbidden, since this would have offered the horse's profile as a target, greatly increasing the chances of being hit. As soon as the carbine was fired, if circumstances permitted, the horseman was to let go of the carbine and immediately draw his sabre, rush at the enemy, and seek to gain the latter's left (and vulnerable) side. At the same time, every effort had to be made to deny his own left side to the enemy. As the mounted skirmisher rushed the enemy, his 'no. 2', stationed about fifty paces behind, was to draw his carbine and advance to his initial position to cover the front skirmisher should he be forced to retire. As he fell back, the Saxon mounted skirmisher was to let go of his sabre, and then fire his pistol in order to keep any prospective pursuers at bay.

Of course, it was not always possible to rush in, sabre in hand and attack the enemy. In these cases, a prolonged fire erupted. The skirmishers in the front rank would fall back, after firing to where their 'no. 2s' were positioned and reload their carbines. The no. 2, meanwhile, would advance and the fire and the whole cyclical process was repeated.[51]

If measured simply in terms of the number of enemy casualties produced, skirmishing while on horseback was usually ineffective. Nolan records hearing from old veterans that during the Peninsular War, cavalry were known to skirmish for the entire day without a single casualty being inflicted on either side.

Foragers

The second method of attack was to fight *en fourrageur*, or as the Germans sometimes called it, the 'swarm attack'. This style of attack was very similar to the standard French cavalry attack during the 1670s and 1680s. By Napoleonic times it was no longer the chosen method when confronting enemy cavalry in ordered formation. However, it could be profitably used when speed was of the essence, and the enemy being attacked was not in an ordered formation, nor capable of a determined resistance.

The cavalry advanced ultimately at the gallop; not in the close order style developed by Frederick the Great, but in a much looser order. There was no attempt to keep the horses along the same rank 'knee to knee', and all the files in the formation, except those carrying the colours, would open up so that there might be one or two paces between individual horses by the time the enemy position had been reached. The files carrying the colours and those adjacent would remain in close order so as to protect the flag. The frontage of the formation would thus increase approximately 50%. This meant that the concentration of horsemen along the front was about half way between the ordered formations, such as line, and the extended order used by skirmishers.

In the last moments when charging as foragers, each cavalryman would then seek an individual opponent, whom he would try to fell with either cut or thrust.[52] The reason for opening up the files, was that the increased space per horse allowed greater manoeuvrability for the horses, as well as giving a chance to the riders to wield their weapons. Fighting *en fourrageur* had enjoyed greater popularity before Frederick introduced the attack of the tight formation at speed to decide the contest by purely psychological means. In the earlier part of the eighteenth century, looser and/or slower attacks meant that the opposing forces did occasionally come to grips and decided the affair with 'cold steel'. The basic rationale underlying the attack *en fourrageur* was to attempt to frighten the opponent with the attack at speed, but if necessary to settle the issue by manoeuvring in place to kill or disable the opponent.

By the turn of the eighteenth century, the attack *en fourrageur* was no longer used to attack enemy cavalry in an ordered formation. However, it survived as long as did cavalry as a special purpose technique. Fighting as foragers was useful when attacking enemy infantry deployed as skirmishers, charging an already defeated enemy to prevent it from rallying, or, when necessary, attacking an artillery position. It was also used to create diversions, that is, to create quickly an engagement so as to confuse the enemy and hide the arrangement of the main attack which would be delivered elsewhere.

In the case of attacking artillery, the cavalry were to begin the attack when 500 or 600 yards from the enemy. Unlike those cases when attacking hostile cavalry, the friendly cavalry would immediately set off at the gallop and would fan out from the centre of the formation. This was done to draw the fire of the artillery being attacked and at the same time threaten its flanks. As the front line cavalry attacked furiously in this loose order, additional cavalry in columns of squadrons advanced rapidly to either attack the infantry supporting the enemy artillery or fall on the rear of the battery.

Regardless of what use cavalry was put to when fighting as foragers, it was extremely important to supply 'supports', that is, a small body in formation, in the rear nearby. This allowed the foragers to rally more readily, reducing their vulnerability to being taken easily by enemy cavalry still in formation.[53]

CHAPTER 16

Cavalry Weapons

Dᴜʀɪɴɢ ᴛʜᴇ Nᴀᴘᴏʟᴇᴏɴɪᴄ ᴇʀᴀ western European cavalry was armed with a small range of potential weapons. This repertoire was essentially limited to the sword, pistol, carbine and the lance. Obviously, there was a tremendous amount of minor variation in each of these weapon categories, these differences being generated by local traditions and the preferences of each military establishment. Numerous works exist cataloguing and describing these differences. However, probably the reader is less interested in the minute differences in appearances, sizes and weights of cavalry weapons than in knowing how these various weapons were actually used in combat.

SWORDS/SABRES

In theory, there are two general methods of striking an enemy with any sword: the 'thrust', a stabbing motion which attempts to impale the intended victim, and the 'cut' which is a slashing motion. Since the sword was always held in the right hand, in a cutting motion the sword was swung from right to left, while a 'backhand' cut moved from left to right. The debate as to which was most effective during actual combat had raged among experienced cavalrymen throughout the century leading up to the Napoleonic Wars. This was particularly the case in Frederick the Great's Prussian cavalry where opinion appears to have been evenly divided. General Warnery, a distinguished hussar officer, for example, preferred the

286

thrust, while Frederick the Great was indifferent to the means used to vanquish the enemy, as long as the end was accomplished.[1]

The proponents of the thrust argued that it allowed greater reach. The thrust was delivered while approaching the enemy from the front and the trooper would lean forward with the sword extended in front. They also argued that the wounds caused by a thrust were much more serious than those caused by a slash. In fact, often a single thrust could prove to be fatal while cavalrymen frequently survived many slash wounds. According to General de Grandmaison, a lieutenant-colonel of *Volontaires des Flandres* during the Wars of Austrian Succession:

> One stab in the body is frequently mortal, which is not often the case with 20 cuts. Since the use of lances and helmets has been abolished in France, and foreign countries, it must be observed that in all engagements of cavalry, the greatest number of wounds have been cuts not stabs.[2]

This debate was a significant one, since the method of delivering the blow against an opponent affected not only the offensive tactics but even the shape of the weapon to be used. If cavalry was expected to thrust at its opponents, it had to be equipped with a straight sword, while if it was to slash it was given a curved or slightly curved weapon, such as a 'sabre'.

By Napoleonic times, it appears that most officers assigned to medium and heavy cavalry favoured the thrust, if only because it fitted with the spirited attacks then in favour. 'Mademoiselle' de Brack,[3] certainly an extremely experienced officer, offered this view after the conclusion of the Napoleonic Wars:

> It is the points alone that kill; the others serve only to wound. Thrust! Thrust! as often as you can: you will overthrow all whom you touch, and demoralize those who escape your attack, and you will add to those advantages that of always being able to parry and never uncovered.[4]

Nevertheless, even in the highest of circles in the British army, there were some who advocated the use of the cut when fighting. The *Rules and Regulations for the Sword Exercise of Cavalry* issued in 1796 advised against thrusting at a mounted enemy. According to this manual, the difficulty with the thrust was that there was but a single way of administering it, with the point held straight ahead. This allowed the opponent to anticipate where the blow was to be delivered and devise a parry. Should the defender be able to parry and bring his own sword inside that of the attacker, the tables were instantly turned. Now, the original attacker with his sword on the outside would be unable to block and most likely suffer an incapacitating, if not fatal blow. For this reason, the *Sword Exercise of Cavalry* manual recommended only thrusting at a fleeing enemy, since the latter was obviously in no position to block the strike. The authors also felt that the thrust suffered from a further disadvantage when used against enemy cavalry. A thrust was delivered by holding the sabre or sword in *terce*, that is, gripping the hilt so that the trooper's thumb and the curved sabre were facing down. On the positive side, this meant the sword was held slightly above the shoulder. The trooper held the sword in this position because the thumb was protected and because it was much less fatiguing to the trooper, an important consideration in a lengthy charge. However, the sword held above the shoulder was not very manoeuvrable.

The British sword manual did concede that thrusts could be made effectively against enemy infantrymen. Given their lower level, *vis-à-vis* the mounted cavalrymen, the sword did not have to be held above the shoulder and the manoeuvrability problems were thus avoided or reduced.[5] Despite the British manual's claims for the efficacy of the cut, there appears to be a preponderance of evidence that, in terms of the types of wounds inflicted, the thrust was far and away more effective. A Captain Bragge of the 3rd (British) Dragoons provides us with the following observations regarding the casualties suffered at the engagement at Bienvenida in April 1812:

> Scarcely one Frenchman died of his wounds although dreadfully chopped, whereas 12 English Dragoons were killed on the spot and others dangerously wounded by thrusts. If our men had used their swords so, three times the number of French would have been killed.[6]

In practice, both the thrust and slash were employed on the Napoleonic battlefield, often with the same troops employing both methods during different phases of the same engagement.

The use of the charge at the gallop or even the fast trot would tend to promote the use of the thrust, at least in the first instant of contact. As long as formation remained compact, the thrust was the only offensive motion possible. If the two sides 'threaded', that is, passed through each other, slashing was possible, for the trooper would first thrust at his opponent just at the latter came into range for a split second before riding past. It was for this reason that medium and heavy cavalry on the continent were generally issued straight swords.

If the mêlée became general, however, the formations on both sides fragmented into a series of numerous individual combats. Each contest would inevitably be reduced to each man slashing at his opponent while attempting to block the latter's blows. Only occasional thrusts were likely to be attempted. The horses would be less under the control of the rider as he focused his attention on the enemy. There would be incessant movement as the horses circled one another and even turned on a fixed position. The opponent's position was constantly and quickly changing relative to the cavalry-man's front. This would make thrusting movements more difficult, and tempted a less adept cavalryman to slash at his enemy as the latter moved to his side or rear.

Light cavalry, such as hussars, *chasseurs à cheval* and *chevaux légers* were often called to fight an enemy force in the countryside during the day-to-day actions of the campaign. These were spon-taneous actions that could occur on any type of terrain and under many different circumstances. Here, actions were much more the result of unexpected encounters and involved smaller parties, and so they were more frequently settled by individual efforts as opposed to the massed charges so typical of the battlefield. Slashing techniques were more likely, and to accommodate this, light cavalry was almost universally given sabres, which had a slightly curved blade suitable for slashing.

The French cavalry authorities, at least when it came to the relationship between weapon design and combat techniques, appear to have had clearer understanding of the ebb and flow of individual combat than others. Unlike their British counterparts, French light cavalry were equipped with a sabre that could be used both to thrust and cut effectively.

Regardless of whether they were armed with a sabre or a sword, experienced cavalrymen followed a number of precepts when fighting in individual combat. One of the most effective slashing techniques was the 'backhand' blow. Its purpose was to strike at an enemy passing by one's flank. It was also useful when fighting a cuirassier who had armoured protection only on his front, as was the case with the Austrian cuirassiers. The best place to swipe at an enemy was at neck level. When threatened with a blow most cavalrymen would instinctively lower their heads, so a strike levelled at the neck would strike the face instead, whereas a blow aimed at the head might go over the cowering trooper. On the other hand, if the blow proved to be low, when aimed at the neck it could hit the shoulder or arms, still disabling the enemy horseman.

Expert swordsmen knew just how to handle the weapon so that the maximum damage was inflicted on the opponent whenever a blow did land. The trick was not to swing the sword so that the edge hit the enemy straight on. Rather, when swinging the weapon, the blade was brought to bear so as to 'tend to touch with the flat side instead of the edge'. It is probable that the author of these remarks meant that the sword was to describe a downward arc so that it sliced the victim at an oblique angle rather than hitting the body surface at a right angle. This caused a sawing motion which allowed the weapon to penetrate more deeply.

There were also some tricks used when thrusting the sword. When the blow was aimed at the rib area the sword was held so that the blade was 'sideways', i.e. it was parallel with the ground. This allowed the blade to enter cleanly between the ribs, instead of becoming stuck in the bones in the rib cage. It was equally important that the trooper draw back the sword the instant it started to penetrate, otherwise the shock of contact could injure the now victorious swordsman. Many inexperienced cavalrymen were disabled with a sprained wrist for an entire season because of a clumsy thrust. By quickly extracting the sword from the enemy's body, another blow could be administered in very quick succession, if one was still needed. Many adversaries would surrender after being 'stuck'. However, if the enemy failed to surrender, it was recommended that a backhand swipe be delivered immediately. It was just such a one—two combination of thrust/backhand blow that the French cavalryman Guindet used to dispatch the Prince of Prussia during the combat of Saalfeld.

To achieve maximum effect, another technique had to be applied as soon as the sword hit the other person. The swordsman would draw his hand backwards at the instant of contact to amplify this sawing effect. This last technique was apparently not known among western Europeans prior to the outbreak of the French Revolutionary Wars, but experienced French cavalrymen acquired it from their Mameluke confrères from about 1798 onwards.[7]

EASTERN STYLES OF SWORD HANDLING

Very few military authorities in western Europe appear to have fully understood the reasons why Asiatic horsemen, such as the Turks or Mamelukes, were so effective at hand-to-hand combat. The latter's success in individual hand-to-hand fighting was usually attributed to their remarkable horsemanship developed by years of training in the saddle, their legendary ferociousness, and their skill with their weapons. Captain Coignet, having served alongside Mamelukes in French service in numerous campaigns, eagerly attested to the skill displayed by the Mamelukes in the handling both of their horses and weapons in his 'notebooks': 'They could do anything they chose with their horses. With their curved sabres, they could take a man's head off with one blow, and their sharp stirrups tore the loins of the men they encountered.'[8] Though writing in a later era (1853), the British General Charles Shaw provides a vivid description of the Circassian horsemen and their prowess with both swords and firearms while atop a fast moving horse:

> The skill with which the Circassians use their weapons is really beyond belief. I have seen them repeatedly fire at a piece of card lying on the ground, at full speed, without ever missing.
>
> They will pick up a piece of money from the ground while executing a charge, by holding themselves round below the horse's belly, and, after seizing the piece, suddenly throw themselves back into the saddle. They form the choicest body of cavalry in the Turkish service, and I have watched them, when charging, attack their opponents with a sabre in each hand, managing their reins with their mouths; they will spring out of their saddles, take aim and fire from behind their horses, then jump into their saddles again, wheel around, and reload their guns as they retreat in full career. They are perfect madmen in the attack, and few would withstand the utter recklessness of danger they evince.[9]

In 1852, Captain Nolan, whom posterity recognizes as both a skilled cavalry tactician and perspicacious military historian, attended the Russian Imperial cavalry reviews. Here, he witnessed the exploits of the élite of the irregular troops in Russian service, both Cossacks and Circassians. His observations were very similar to those that would be noted a year later by General Shaw:

> I saw a few sheets of paper placed on the ground opposite the Emperor: he gave a signal to some of the Cossacks and Circassians formed in line a few hundred yards off. Down they all came at speed racing with one another: the first up fired at the marks either with pistol or carbine; the sheets of paper flew up in pieces: those who followed fired into the fragments that were at hand, blowing them into atoms.[10]

Though taken from a later period, these exploits show the capabilities of the better-trained horsemen in many of the eastern armies during the eighteenth and nineteenth centuries.

Captain Nolan in his classic work on European cavalry ascribed much of the success of eastern horsemen and the terror they invariably struck into the hearts of their western opponents not only to their fighting techniques but also to the sharpness of their blades. To illustrate his point, Nolan tells of his own experiences during the Second Sikh War (1848–1849) in India. A small force of Nizam's irregular horsemen fighting on the side of the British were able to defeat a much larger force of Sikhs. Nolan was nowhere near the actual engagement, but his attention was drawn to the affair when he came across a doctor's report of the wounds suffered by the enemy who were captured. Entries in the report read: 'Both hands cut off', 'leg cut off above the knee', and so on. These types of wounds were outside the experience of those whose service had been limited exclusively to European warfare. Ruling out that the horsemen of the Nizam were literally giants, Nolan speculated that they were able to inflict such ferocious wounds either through the use of some novel type of sword he had never before encountered or by employing some mysterious but effective striking technique. Uncertain, he was highly curious and wanted an opportunity to meet such distinguished warriors.

Later events were to show that neither was indeed the case. His curiosity was soon satisfied when the force to which he was assigned was ordered to Hyderabad where a squadron of the very warriors in question joined the escort to which he was attached. In short order, Nolan went to see these men and their weapons. To his utter amazement they were armed with discarded British Dragoon swords! These blades were 'mounted after their own fashion', that is, given new guards and grips. However, there was one obvious difference. The edges resembled a razor 'from heel to point' and were encased in a wooden scabbard and not the metal one ubiquitously used by Europeans. Nolan finally connived an opportunity to interview a veteran warrior in the group. The latter quickly informed him that the discarded British weapons were in great demand among his people and were highly useful when the necessary modifications were made. They were useless, though, when kept in their original European form. The remainder of the conversation should be recounted in Nolan's own words:

> Nolan enquired: 'How do you strike with your swords to cut off men's limbs?'
> 'Strike hard, sir!' said the old trooper.
> 'Yes, of course; but how do you teach the men to use their swords in that particular way?'
> 'We never teach them any way, sir; a sharp sword will cut in any one's hand.'

This apparently untrained group of irregular horsemen were able to inflict the most deadly wounds on their enemy simply because of the sharpness of their weapons.

During the Napoleonic Wars western European cavalrymen occasionally had to deal with eastern enemies who brandished these razor-sharp swords. When this happened, horrendous wounds were experienced like those Nolan would later encounter in India. In addition to the various exotic eastern units in French service, such as the Mamelukes, the Cossacks were also known to carry these deadly weapons. A pamphlet circulating among cavalry officers in Berlin in 1812 noted that the Prussian cavalry were struck with such terror of the Russian horsemen (presumably the Cossacks) that only their sense of honour and the *espirit de corps* of the regiments to which they belonged induced them into close combat with foes so armed.[11]

However, before dismissing the European sword as a completely useless encumbrance, de Brack's observations about the casualties taken at Essling should be considered: 'At Essling, I saw some cuirassier helmuts cut entirely through by sabre blows; and how many troopers have I seen killed because of having lost their headdresses!'[12] The effectiveness of Asiatic horsemen in individual combat may not have been the result simply of their extreme skill in horsemanship and the sharpness of their weapons. A clue about an additional factor is almost inadvertently provided by General Mitchell of the British army:

> Go into any sword-cutler's shop in London, and the chances are that you will not find a single well poised, and well mounted sword, unless accident throws a Turkish scimitar or an old Highland claymore in your way . . . Of all modern swords the Turkish scimitar is by far the best mounted: – not the overbent scimitar, *for we do not understand the use of these weapons* [italics mine], – but those, which, like the best of them, are only slightly curved towards the point.[13]

Mitchell was quick to point out that western cavalrymen had never understood the secrets of the effective use of the 'overly bent' scimitar. Mitchell was very much the denizen of nineteenth-century England, and had little understanding of other cultures, especially those beyond the pale of European 'civilization'.

However, today those with some experience in eastern martial arts can provide some insight into the nature and use of this weaponry. A highly curved sword has a different set of properties than a straight sword. It not only has a different effect on what it strikes, but it is handled in an entirely different manner. As we have seen, western military authorities who wanted their cavalrymen to strike at the enemy with *thrust* equipped their men with straight swords; those who favoured the *cut* or slash equipped theirs with sabres, with slightly curved blades. However, light cavalry whose responsibility was to perform reconnaissance and housekeeping duties, had to be as prepared for the type of individual combat that frequently occurred during the vagaries of the *petite guerre*. Unlike the battlefield, the opposing horsemen would approach each other at the walk or the trot, and there would be a lot of circling and movement as the two horsemen fought. Here, the slash was considered, if not the most desirable method, the most 'do-able' for the average trooper, given the levels of equestrian skills that could reasonably be expected from troopers in any of the western European armies. It was for this reason that light cavalry was invariably armed with the slightly curved sabre.

However, starting some time in the Middle Ages (or possibly earlier) eastern horsemen took these types of considerations further. For these eastern warriors, mounted combat was *always* individual combat; there was no such thing as the use of rigid formations and the charge at speed to break the enemy's will prior to contact. Unlike the situation faced by western cavalry where it was relatively uncommon for men in open terrain to fight hand to hand collectively, eastern horsemen frequently had to fight groups of enemy horsemen in fast moving, highly congested frays. The true advantage of the highly curved sword was that in addition to inflicting more severe wounds it required less space to be used effectively. Thus, it was extremely useful in tight situations where the horsemen were pressed together. Any swordsman knows that a straight sword, though effective in the thrust, does not cut well. The slightly curved sword cuts more effectively, but less than a very curved sword. Western soldiers always feared the Turks, knowing that in an individual fight the Turk could lop off a limb in a single blow. This was as much due to the *shape* of the blade as it was to the *sharpness* of the weapon.

The slightly curved sword must be swung in a relatively wide arc to achieve a cutting effect. A horseman carrying this type of weapon must swing with his arm fairly extended. In other words, when he swings, the pommel (the end nearest him) must follow an arc so that at the end of the stroke the pommel is always two or so feet away from his torso. A highly curved sword, such as a scimitar, can achieve the same or greater cutting force even though it transcribes a much smaller swing radius. Western European swords and sabres designed for cutting strokes were intended to strike the enemy by a motion towards the centre of the target, much like hitting a branch or thin sapling with a modern machete. However, the design of the oriental scimitar was intended to allow its owner to strike the intended object so that the blade was drawn along the surface, rather than directed towards its centre. Skin and clothing would offer little resistance to the sharp blade and would allow the sword to slice through the object it hit, much like the action of a saw. Simply striking the side of the target head on would bring the sword to a stop and result in a dramatic reduction in the cutting effect.

In addition to allowing a blow that would lop off a limb or a head, the use of a highly curved weapon like the eastern scimitar offered another very significant advantage. The movement required for this blow required less extension of the sword arm. In a close press, a mounted swordsman could achieve very deadly results by striking a circular blow without the pommel ever moving further than twelve to fourteen inches from his chest. A western European cavalryman armed with either a straight sword or a slightly curved sabre thus was in a highly disadvantaged situation, having insufficient room either to thrust or slash or even counter effectively.

THE RE-INTRODUCTION OF THE LANCE

By the beginning of the nineteenth century, the lance had come back into fashion after having been discarded in western Europe for approximately two centuries. Although the Napoleonic lancer could trace his lineage back to the heavily armoured medieval knights, these 'modern' lancers were the offspring of a lighter version that officially appeared after the reorganization of the Polish cavalry in 1717. No longer fully clad in plate mail atop horses themselves protected by armour, the front rank of the Polish 'heavy cavalry', drawn exclusively from among the ranks of the Polish nobility, was armed with a fourteen or fifteen foot lance. This heavy cavalry was of two types: the *husarz* and the *pancerny*. The heavy, full body armour of their forefathers had disappeared and these warriors were now only protected by a cuirasse on their front and back. In the case of the *husarz* this armour was plate, while the *pancerny* donned only chain mail.

Entrance into the light cavalry was less restrictive, this body admitting both Polish nobility and Tartars descended from those who had first entered Lithuania after the conquests of Tamerlane. Though they carried the same offensive weapons (lance, pistol and sword) as their heavier counterparts, the light cavalry wore no defensive armour.

The prowess of the Polish cavalry soon became legendary, and the wild irregular Russian and Ukrainian horsemen sought to copy their methods. The heavily clad cavalry in both eastern and western Europe gradually succumbed to the tendency to discard all armour, and it was the Polish light cavalry that served as the model, rather than the noble, and more prestigious heavy cavalry. One of the first leaders of this Polish light cavalry was a certain Lithuanian nobleman by the name of 'Hulan'. At this time it was a common practice to refer to a corps by the name of its commander, and in the German states the term 'Hulan' or 'Uhlan' soon became synonymous with any cavalry armed with lances. The influence of the Polish lancers was certainly not restricted to the wild regions east of Poland. Strongly believing in shock tactics, in 1734 Maurice de Saxe raised a *pulk* of uhlans for use in the short-lived War of Polish Succession (1733–1738). In 1745, Frederick the Great followed suit and formed a regiment of lancers of highly questionable skill that he referred to as 'Bosniacks'.[14] Whether because of the dismal failure of Frederick's Bosniacks or because of some other factor long lost to history, the Polish lancers ceased to inspire western cavalry for more than fifty years. However, renewed contact occasioned by the Second and Third Partitions of Poland once again sparked westerners' interest in this unique cavalry form.

Hoping for the re-creation of their native state, a great many Polish troops fought under the French during the Napoleonic Wars. One of the subsequent effects was to re-introduce the lance into western Europe. Several Polish lancer regiments were added to the French establishment, and these were followed by six French regiments. Other armies soon followed suit. A 'Uhlan' regiment of six squadrons was added to the Bavarian cavalry establishment by an order dated 19 August 1813.[15] In the same year, the Prussians adopted the lance for the Landwehr.[16] In 1815 the Westphalian cavalry established a Leib-Uhlanen-Corps, taking its men from the Leibjäger-Garde Squadron in the Garderegiment.[17]

With the re-introduction of the lance into western Europe, once again popular opinion regarded it as a formidable weapon able to intimidate an enemy during the final moments when the two opposing sides approached each other. Its obviously longer reach was perceived as bestowing a decided advantage over the opposing swordsman. Possibly one of the most ardent advocates was 'Mademoiselle' de Brack, who even after the return of peace continued to boast: '[the lance's] morale effect is the greatest, and its thrusts the most murderous of all the *armes blanches*.'[18] If we judge by the number of newly raised lancer regiments or existing regiments who adopted the lance during this and the succeeding period, the view appears to have some credibility. However, after several years of experimentation with the weapon, the majority opinion among veteran cavalrymen was that the lance never afforded the insurmountable advantage originally expected of it. It was generally ceded that the lance was an intimidating weapon against untrained troops and a real threat when handled by cavalrymen trained in the use of the lance since their early youth. However, since this latter condition rarely, if ever, existed in western European cavalry regiments, in practice it was less effective than has been commonly understood.

For example, both General Marmont and the Baron de Marbot, neither of whom could be classified as inexperienced or impractical, concluded that all other things being equal, well-trained troopers armed only with swords would ultimately best well-trained lancers. Both agreed that the real advantage of the lance was its effectiveness against infantry. Interestingly enough, these analyses were made by two officers who had served in the French army during the Napoleonic era, the very army which had re-introduced the use of the lancer to western Europe. The passage below is provided by Marmont's *The Spirit of Military Institutions or Essential Principles of War*, written in the post-Waterloo period, and used to train new officers:

> The lance is the weapon for cavalry of the line, and principally for those destined to fight against infantry. The sabre cannot supply its place: armed with sabres, what use can cavalry make of them, if the infantry remain firm, and are not struck with fright? The horseman cannot sabre the foot-soldier; the bayonets keep the horses at too great a distance. On the other hand, let the horse – which remains the only offensive arm of the cavalry soldier – be killed; he falls and opens a breach, and that breach gives to those nearest to him the means of penetrating the ranks. The strife is then entirely to the advantage of the infantry. On the contrary, suppose the same line of cavalry, furnished with a row of pikes which stand out four feet in front of the horses; and the chances are very different.[19]

The potential effectiveness of the lance against infantry was substantiated by British infantrymen who faced French lancers. Sergeant James Anton, present at Waterloo, offers this assessment of the lancers' prowess against infantry:

Of all descriptions of cavalry, certainly the lancers seem the most formidable to infantry, as the lance can be projected with considerable precision, and with deadly effect, without bringing the horse to the point of the bayonet; and it was only by the rapid and well-directed fire of musketry that these formidable assailants were repulsed.[20]

And just how devastating an effect lancers could have upon infantry unlucky enough to be unable to ward off these assailants with continuous or well-directed fire was dreadfully demonstrated at the Battle of Dresden (17 August 1813). A heavy rain had fallen from the previous night and made it impossible for the infantry to use their muskets or the cavalry to charge at anything faster than a quick walk. During the height of the action, one of Latour-Maubourg's brigades encountered two large Austrian squares supported by a battery positioned in the intervening ground. Although the battery was quickly driven off by the mere threat of a charge, the Austrian infantry stood firm. Two assaults, which could only be delivered at a walk, failed. Latour-Maubourg then sent for his personal escort which comprised half a squadron of lancers. As soon as these were now stationed at the front of the column a third charge was ordered. The defenders were unable to fire, and the lancers advanced unhindered within a few feet of the infantrymen whom they started to methodically spear. Gaps soon appeared, which were immediately exploited by the remainder of the column, and the squares were destroyed.[21]

The lancers were also useful when operating in the general countryside, such as when attacking a convoy. The retreating infantry would invariably take cover behind carts, trees, rocks, fences, artillery pieces or whatever other obstacle they found. They could even shield themselves for a few moments behind ponies, horses or oxen while they presented their arms and attempted to fire at their attackers. Horsemen armed only with swords were unable to harm the infantry in these situations. These were not always proof against cavalry armed with lances, whose extended weapons could reach beyond such obstacles.[22] But when it came to the lance's capabilities against light cavalry, Marmont had less respect:

But the sabre is more befitting than the lance for light troops. In hand to hand conflicts, a short weapon is handled more easily, and is more advantageous than a long one. All other things being equal; it is certain that a huzzar or chasseur will beat a lancer; they have time to parry, and return the blow (riposter) before the lancer, who has thrown himself upon them, can recover himself for defence.[23]

Events during the Seven Years' War lent credibility to Marmont's seemingly contentious claim that a hussar or *chasseur à cheval* would best a lancer in hand-to-hand combat. The Prussian cavalry, especially the hussars, were intimidated when they first encountered Cossacks armed with the lance and shied away from any attempt to close to contact. A small group of officers devised a simple, but effective remedy. They rode in front of the lines about to be engaged and challenged some Cossacks to hand-to-hand combat. In the resulting series of fights, the officers cut down several of their opponents, showing their men how they could best these opponents armed with what appeared at first to be an unbeatable weapon. The hussars, no longer afraid of this new weapon, 'soon mastered their opponents'.[24]

General Marmont's observations regarding the ultimate superiority of cavalry armed with swords against lancers is substantiated by the recollections of a fellow French cavalry officer, the Baron de Marbot. Marbot, previously an aide-de-camp, served with the 23rd *chasseurs à cheval* in Russia and the later campaigns in France. In his two-volume memoir, *The Memoirs of Baron de Marbot*, this officer provides an account of how the 23rd Chasseurs armed with sabres met and defeated Russian Cossacks of the Guard, equipped with fourteen-feet lances during the Battle of Polotsk (26 August 1812):

The meadow being large enough to hold two regiments in line, the 23rd and 24th formed the first line, General Corbineau's brigade, consisting of three regiments, forming the second, and the cuirassiers following as reserve. The 24th, which was on the left, had in front of it a regiment of Russian dragoons; my regiment was facing Cossacks of the Guard, known by their red coats and the beauty of their horses. These, though they had arrived only a few hours before seemed in no way fatigued. We advanced at a gallop, and soon as we were within striking distance General Castex gave the word to charge. His brigade fell upon the Russians, and at the first shock the 24th broke the dragoons opposed to them. My regiment met with more resistance from the Cossacks, picked men of large stature, and armed with lances fourteen feet long, which they held very straight. I had some men killed, a good many wounded; but when, at length, my troopers had pierced the bristling line of steel, all the advantage was on our side. In a cavalry fight the length of lances is a drawback when their bearers have lost their order and are pressed closely by adversaries armed with swords which they can handle easily, while the lancers find it difficult to present the points of their poles. So the Cossacks were constrained to show their backs, and then my troopers did great execution and took many excellent horses.[25]

Marbot concluded that the length of the lance was actually a severe drawback in the close press of the mêlée. The swordsmen had enough room to wield their weapon while the lancers only with the greatest difficulty were able to present their points to their personal opponent.[26] General de Brack recommended that whenever French cavalry encountered enemy lancers in a mêlée the best tactic was to move in upon the lancers in order to crowd them together. According to de Brack:

The lancers, jammed together, can neither point nor parry, and one of two things must happen: they will either throw down their lances, in order to get to their swords, or they will retain their lances, and in this case you will have the best of the bargain.[27]

The Cossacks, known to be truly adept with the lance, had developed a technique to counter this problem. They awaited their enemy holding their lance a little towards the right. When the adversary was close enough, the Cossack parried the lance by making a 'left parry', a circular motion from right to left. This forced the onrushing cavalrymen to swerve slightly to their right. As his enemy passed by, the Cossack turned quickly around and could now assume the offensive, being on the attacker's flank or rear. The Cossacks relied on this technique when facing French lancers, who were equipped with a slightly longer weapon. If the Cossacks attempted to go on the offensive first, the French having the advantage of a longer reach could parry the Cossacks' thrust. The Cossack held the lance pointing a little to the right, because in this position there was little the enemy lancer could do to hit the Cossack's lance or in any way prevent the block he intended to use.[28]

The Cossacks were also known to use these same blocking movements as offensive techniques. When de Brack's regiment charged a group of Cossacks near Eylau, a certain Captain Brou managed to catch up with one of these usually elusive adversaries. Positioning himself and his horse to the left of the Cossack, the latter's capture or demise appeared imminent since his lance was positioned to the 'right front'. However, before Brou could strike the Cossack, his intended victim stood up in his stirrups and using an 'around parry', a circular movement normally reserved for blocking a lance thrust, knocked the Captain off his horse and captured the officer's horse. The Captain was about to be made prisoner, but was saved by the timely charge of the 7th French Hussars led here by Major Hulot.[29]

The lancers themselves appear to have been aware of the lance's drawbacks against cavalry and often attacked with the drawn sword against an equestrian enemy. French General de Brack, who commanded some lancers of the Imperial Guard, provides two such examples in 1814: against Russian lancers at Hoagstraten, near Breda; and against Prussian lancers at Pont-à-Tecir below Lille. In both cases, the action occurred along a narrow road with a ditch on both sides. De Brack ordered that carabiniers precede his column. The lancers following behind placed their lances in the carrying bucket and drew their swords. The carabiniers fired when near the enemy and the remainder rushed into the gaps thus created. The enemy was cut down without any appreciable loss to the French lancers.

Some experienced Cossacks shared this reticence about relying on the lance against an expert foe. Though the Cossacks of the Don, the Ural, and Tschernomor retained the lance, the Line Cossacks, who were in near continuous conflict with the highly skilled Circassians abandoned their traditional weapon, declaring that though it was a good weapon against bad horsemen, it was only an encumbrance against Circassian horsemen.[30]

Colonel Ardant du Picq, writing prior to the 1850s, felt that one of the intrinsic limitations of the lance was supplied by the horse, rather than the weapon itself. Given its length, even small movements by the lancer could result in a significant alteration in where the point was headed. The horse, which often made small movements not part of the rider's design, could cause the point to miss its intended target at the very last moment before the lancer could compensate. A related problem was the sheer force of the blow and how this could be transmitted back to the lancer, sometimes with disastrous effect. A lancer who succeeded in sticking his lance into an enemy while at the gallop was subject to being knocked off his horse. Unlike a sabre, which rarely remained in the body of a victim, a lance which had struck home would pierce through the body and because of the shock of the contact was passed back to the person holding the weapon.[31] Among Europeans, it was always considered a great ignominy for a lancer to abandon his weapon. Asiatic spearmen had no such compunctions, and would leave their weapons in the first horsemen they were able to run through or simply throw them away before closing to hand-to-hand combat. De Brack cautioned against the European view, which he felt was based on a misplaced sense of honour. A lance lost because it rested in an enemy's bosom was always a lance well spent!

The attempt to regain a lance that had struck home needlessly endangered the lancer. De Brack recounts how several times he saw the lance so adroitly used by French troops that the weapon penetrated the victim's shoulder blades. More often than not, the dying man's feet would become entangled in the stirrups. The victim dragged along by his horse often would, in turn, drag the lancer who, of course, would make every effort to regain possession of his weapon. Sometimes, this would lead to unfortunate results for the lancer who was unwilling to abandon his weapon, already used with great effect, or who was no longer paying sufficient attention to his own personal safety.

> At Reichenbach, the bravest lancer of my regiment was killed, under similar circumstances, in disobedience of my orders, through a misunderstood, stubborn defence of honor. In vain I called out to him, 'Your lance is well lost'; he did not believe me, and being cut off from his comrades, was overwhelmed by numbers and killed.

Even when the enemy fell immediately to the ground the lance usually was lost, unless the lancer had the luxury of painstakingly removing the lance from the now deceased victim.

> Near Lille, a young soldier of the same regiment found himself

in a similar condition; I made him abandon his lance. The Prussian whom he had run through fell about fifty paces from the spot where he was wounded; we retook the ground which we had been obliged to yield for a few minutes, and my lancer having dismounted to recover his lance, succeeded in doing so only by carefully pushing it through in the same direction in which it entered.[32]

Captain Dyneley, a British artillery officer serving in the Peninsular campaign, however, noticed one subtle advantage enjoyed by the lancers over other types of cavalry:

They [Polish Lancers] are armed with a long lance, at the end of which is a flag fixed so that, when our dragoons make a stance to receive them, the flags frighten their horses, and they go about and the lancers have them through the body in the 'twinkling of an eye.'[33]

In other words, although the mounted swordsman might have an ultimate advantage over the lancer, all was in vain if his horse started to bolt to the rear, which, of course, exposed the rider's back to his opponent.

Captain Nolan of the British cavalry disagreed with Dyneley, feeling the lance's pennant possessed a number of disadvantages.[34] Although it tended to frighten the opponent's horse, the latter would bolt so unexpectedly and sufficiently far that the opponent was carried beyond the lancer's reach. The pennant also inadvertently helped the opponent parry the threat. The pennant was very noticeable, and even during the frenzy of the mêlée, its size and colour helped the adversary to sense the position of the point and the direction it was heading. Another, more strategic, disadvantage was that the pennant was quite noticeable even at long distances, and provided enemy artillerymen with a convenient target.[35]

Although we have quoted a number of experts who opposed arming cavalrymen with lances, this opinion was by no means unanimous. Not all knowledgeable cavalrymen disparaged the usefulness of the lance in cavalry versus cavalry action, and a number of military writers championed its cause. This was especially the case in the late nineteenth century. In the years just before the First World War, a British cavalry officer named Wilkinson noted the success lancers had enjoyed against mounted swordsmen in numerous peacetime competitions that had been held among the British cavalry:

> I have watched, recorded, and judged hundreds of competitions between men equally expert in the use of their weapons, and not withstanding the enormous disadvantages under which the lance had to compete, it always won the majority of contests, and frequently a very large majority of them.[36]

The Prussian cavalry authority Roemer was another advocate of the lance. In his classic work *Cavalry: its History, Management and Uses*, to support the confidence he placed in this weapon Roemer listed a number of instances during the Napoleonic Wars where lancers achieved notable success.

At a critical moment during the battle of Eylau, Platoff and six hundred Cossacks of the Don were temporarily able to restore the battle. Five years later at Albuera, French lancers taking advantage of a mist were able to gain the rear of a British division and soon able to wreak havoc among the latter's ranks. Again, at Leipzig in 1813 the Cossack guard led by Orloff Denizoff was able to severely punish a body of French cuirassiers. Finally, at the fateful battle of Waterloo, a French lancer regiment under Colonel Bro almost entirely destroyed the Household and Union brigades.[37]

RENAISSANCE OF CUIRASSIERS

The practice of equipping heavy cavalry with armoured chest pieces, called cuirasses, had almost died out by the time of the Seven Years' War. However, under Napoleon's rule the French army gave new life to this practice. Many of the campaigns, hitherto, had taken place on relatively uneven and broken countryside. Future fighting augured to be on terrain more favourable to cavalry. Probably in recognition of the need to develop a cavalry force capable of meeting heavy cavalry such as the Austrian cuirassiers equally, both Ney and Kellermann had urged Napoleon to equip some of the French cavalry with steel helmets and chain mail epaulettes. Napoleon responded by ordering six cavalry regiments to don a full cuirass, in addition to the 8th Regiment which had retained its cuirass from the monarchical times. Over several years additional cuirassier regiments were formed so that by 1810 there were fourteen of these heavily clad regiments.[38]

Although a regiment of cuirassiers manoeuvring on parade was indeed a majestic sight and must have been frightening to an enemy about to receive their charge, not all military experts favoured the re-introduction of body armour for cavalrymen. One opponent to the cuirass was the British general John Mitchell. Writing in the 1830s, Mitchell conceded that the cuirass offered frontal protection against musket fire. However, this 'slight, precarious and accidental protection', was not worth the relatively minor protection it offered, since it was gained only by burdening the horsemen with a 'continual annoyance', which interfered with the trooper's motions. He argued that such protection was unnecessary anyhow, since the enemy infantry 'must have time to give the cavalry one fire only; it must be their first and last, and will not, at the best, be very destructive'.[39]

General von Pappenheim, later a general in the Bavarian army but who fought on the French side during the Napoleonic Wars, remembers how the French cuirassiers were able to charge only at the trot. Encumbered with their heavy appointments, they were unable to move at a faster pace:

> I was a witness . . . of the dreadful price which the French had to pay for their slow advance on Aspern. They attacked in column – at a trot, being incapable of any quicker movement: the rearmost men driving on the foremost, who were thus forced to advance indeed: but at what a loss.[40]

We'll see later that von Pappenheim felt this reflected an overall problem with French tactics and was not just a result of wearing a *cuirass*. Some cavalrymen such as Captain Nolan, a cavalry tactician writing in the mid-nineteenth century, felt that the cuirass actually made the trooper more vulnerable in other areas of his body. Although it could protect a cuirassier from a slash or thrust in the chest area, its weight decreased the horseman's manoeuvrability and gave him a decided disadvantage when fighting with a man not so encumbered. And, of course, once the cuirassier's bridle or sword-arm were injured he was at the mercy of his opponent. The same was true if the more agile enemy chose to disable or kill the horse, instead.[41] Sergeant-Major Cotton relates such an occurrence at Waterloo:

A hussar and a cuirassier had got entangled in the mêlée, and met in the plain in full view of our line; the hussar was without a cap and bleeding from a wound in the head, but that did not hinder him from attacking his steel-clad adversary. He soon proved that the strength of cavalry consists in good horsemanship and the skilled use of the sword, and not in being clad in heavy defensive armor. The superiority of the hussar was visible the moment the swords crossed; and after a few wheels a tremendous fencer made the Frenchman reel in the saddle, and all his attempts to escape his more active foe became unavailing; a second blow stretched him on the ground, amidst the cheers of the light horseman's comrades, the 3rd German Hussars, who were ardent spectators of the combat.[42]

Nolan went on to quote an Imperialist officer who had served in the struggle against the Hungarians during the latter's quest for independence in 1848. In the officer's experience, the cuirass provided no practical advantage, other than the 'morale' effect on those wearing the defensive armour.

From what the cuirassiers say, their cuirass saved them from many a bullet, and many a thrust, in the mêlée. This *may* be true, and the advantage of armor probably is, that those who wear it fancy themselves safer, and are, therefore morally stronger, and more ready to look danger in the face.[43]

However, it was just this 'morale' effect that so endeared the cuirass to its proponents. One such advocate of the cuirass was Ardant du Picq, who wrote his famous *Battle Studies* some time during the 1850s and 1860s. Du Picq argued that when it was necessary to hurl cavalry against enemy infantry ensconced in an important position, the attack should always be made with cuirassiers. According to this military analyst, this type of cavalry could be counted on to conduct the charge with the most vigour and resolution, and would be the most likely to be able to come to grips with the enemy infantry. He reasoned that protected by this body armour the cuirassiers: 'need only half the courage of the dragoons, as their armor raises their morale one half. But since cuirassiers have as much natural courage as the dragoons, they are all the same men, it is proper to count the more on their action.'[44] At about the same time as du Picq was eulogizing the cuirass, the Prussian cavalry tactician, Roemer, was championing the same cause. Roemer was particularly irked that its foes cited difficulties posed by weight and restrictions in dexterity. The weight of a cuirass was roughly the same as the many petticoats women wore during the period, and like this female garment the weight rested not on the shoulders nor chest but the waist. Surely if *petite* women could move about carrying this weight, it couldn't be much of an encumbrance to a large, powerful man! To drive home his argument, Roemer pointed out that the Circassian horseman, possibly the most accomplished of all Middle Eastern horsemen, performed their fabled feats of unparalleled horsemanship fully clad in chain mail.[45]

The cuirass was not the only defensive measure taken by cavalrymen to protect themselves against thrusts and slashes which were all too likely to be received during a mêlée. It was common practice for men in heavy and medium cavalry regiments who were not equipped with bullet-proof iron cuirasses to take their own measures to protect their chest from potential injury. Frequently, the men would roll up their outer coat and tie it across their chest. Many experienced officers favoured this practice, since in addition to providing some protection to the trooper from enemy sword action, it increased his access to his pistol holster while allowing his bridle hand to be kept closer to the horse's neck which, in turn, facilitated greater control over the horse. However, cavalrymen always had to make certain that the rolled coat did not constrict their movements, and, whenever engaged in hand-to-hand combat, had to avoid allowing the enemy to grab the coat and thus unhorse them.[46] A Lieutenant Roth von Schreckenstein, who served with Saxon Zastrow Cuirassiers assigned to Latour-Maubourg's 4th Cavalry Corps during the 1812 campaign at Borodino, informs us the Saxon Life Guard Regiment regularly used this practice.[47]

CHAPTER 17

Cavalry versus Infantry

F ROM TIME IMMEMORIAL cavalry has been called upon to attack and overthrow its pedestrian counterpart. In certain respects, these demands only increased during the Napoleonic Wars. During the linear period cavalry had most often been placed on the flanks of the army and usually had to take on its enemy counterpart before it could be turned against the opposing infantry. By Napoleonic times, with ever increasing frequency, cavalry was removed from the flanks and interspersed along the second or third lines to support the infantry in front. Preliminary cavalry-versus-cavalry engagements were no longer inevitable and the cavalry became free to attack enemy infantry formations as soon as the opportunity presented itself.

Cavalry-versus-infantry engagements tended to be of two kinds. Whenever a body of cavalry suddenly came upon infantry and found the latter unprepared, a clash was almost certain. Unless the infantry was protected by broken terrain, the cavalry held a decided advantage. There was little need for formal tactics, and the fray quickly turned into a collection of individual contests, as the troopers sought to run down and sabre their prey. This frequently occurred during the *petite guerre*, at the start of a general engagement, if one side was surprised, or at the end of a hotly disputed contest as the enemy infantry fell back, disorganized and demoralized in defeat.

The opposite type of situation tended to occur during the heat of the battle when cavalry was called upon to overthrow enemy infantry in an ordered formation and a critical position had to be taken.

Cavalry was especially useful during the latter stages of an engagement when the enemy infantry started to weaken, and the cavalry was sent in to deliver a *coup de grâce* or crush isolated elements which continued to offer organized resistance.

Whenever cavalry and infantry met in these set-piece actions where both elements were prepared, each followed their own set of tactics. There were a few notable instances where infantry 'charged' enemy cavalry in formation, such as at Fuentes de Onoro in 1811, when a body of Brunswick infantry led by Colonel Herzberg chased away a small force of French cavalry with lowered bayonets.[1] However, almost always the cavalry assumed the offensive role as the infantry fell on the defensive.

Even by the beginning of the eighteenth century there existed an extensive body of experience regarding how cavalry and infantry tended to behave whenever they encountered each other. To fully understand how cavalry handled itself against infantry, it is necessary to treat these tactics as they existed on two separate levels. The first, and more basic level of tactics, dealt with the psychology of both horse and horseman during the advance, and how the average infantryman would respond to the sight of the enemy cavalry approaching him. This level of tactics recognized that both the cavalryman and his infantry counterpart tended to act and respond in a definite and predictable fashion, in a way that was in accordance with 'human nature'. The second level consisted of what is normally associated with the term: the set of instructions or 'doctrine' used by either side, as they struggled to overthrow the defending infantry or stand fast and repel the oncoming horsemen. Obviously, it is necessary to understand the first level before any meaningful examination of the second can be made.

Experienced cavalry officers knew that, if well-motivated infantry were in formation and determined to maintain their position, they would need to do more than simply ride over the defending infantry. In order for cavalry to be successful, it had first to undermine the infantryman's resolution and courage, if this was not already achieved by other means such as by prolonged artillery fire or nearby events on the battlefield. Only when the defending ranks started to question their safety or, better yet, began to waver as individual men recoiled backwards, did the cavalry have a reasonable chance of creating and entering a breach and then destroying the infantry formation. Fortunately for the cavalry, the very act of approaching the defending infantry, even when in the tightest formation, was enough to severely test the determination of the average infantryman.

It is an awful thing for infantry to see a body of cavalry riding at them at full gallop. The men in the square frequently begin to shuffle, and so create some unsteadiness. This causes them to neglect their fire. The cavalry seeing them waver, have an inducement for riding close up, and in all probability succeed in getting into the square, when it is all over.[2]

Another writer of the period pointed out that the very approach of a large body of cavalry would shake the defender in the literal sense of the term. The force of the horses' hooves striking the ground would make the earth shake for a considerable distance around. And, this would only amplify any trembling caused purely by nervousness.[3] It was not uncommon to see the defenders in the final moments rocking from foot to foot, as drunken men: 'and as they stood to receive the shock they were about to be assailed with, they reeled to and fro like men intoxicated.'[4]

As the level of agitation among the ranks rose, the control of the officers accordingly declined. If the defending unit was inexperienced or contained numbers of recruits, some of the men might start to fire on their own, before receiving orders from their officers. This not only produced a ragged and ineffective fire, but further intensified the confusion among the ranks. The infantrymen used the process of loading and firing their weapons to cope with their anxieties, and unless they were veteran troops trained to withhold their fire, they would attempt to fire as fast as they could. The resulting fire was much more inaccurate than an aimed and deliberate fire. It also increased the chances that the infantry would be denuded of fire when it was critically needed: in the final moments when the cavalry was twenty to thirty paces away. Moreover, premature fire could lower the men's morale, since afterwards the men would tend to feel powerless, and the line would often start to waver.

Though premature fire was also experienced when defending against enemy infantry, it was a more pronounced problem when defending against cavalry. Inexperienced troops were often duped into firing because they simply misjudged the distance separating them and the oncoming horsemen. Apparently, the combined height of rider and horse misled many of the defenders who rather naïvely thought that they must be at the same distance as a man who appeared just as large as horse and rider.[5]

Contrary to the expectations of many modern readers, cavalry was usually not exposed to repeated firing once it started its attack in earnest. Many authorities felt, in fact, that the infantry were able only to deliver *one* effective fire. Given the speed of the horses, the cavalry could cover the effective range of the musket in about a minute.[6] Fortunately, a number of cavalrymen attempted to calculate the speed of the horses, and some of these observations have been handed down to us. An estimate of a horse's speed and the average length of each stride for each of the more well known sources is provided in the accompanying charts:

	Speed[7]				
	Decker	Rittenberg	Vergnaud	Gassendi	Lallemand
Walk	120p	100p	100m		
Trot	240p	180–200p		200m	200m
Gallop			400m	400m	400y
(long strides)		480p	250p		
(at the charge)		600p	300p		

m = metres/minute   p = paces/minute   y = yards/minute

Length of Stride for Gait Used[8]

Speed	Length of Stride	Stride/ Minute
Walk	25cm	113–124
Trot	120cm	164–180
Gallop	390cm	390

The infantry could, in theory, deliver fire several times during the time it took for the enemy cavalry to close. However, to do so meant that the first, and most effective fire, had to be delivered while the cavalry was still at long range. This first fire would produce few casualties, as would any subsequent fire at shorter ranges, being hurried and less well aimed. Ironically, premature fire also helped buoy the morale of the oncoming cavalry. As long as the infantry withheld its fire, the cavalryman stood in fear of the moment when this fire was unleashed. Once this fire was delivered, the troopers, believing that the greatest danger had passed, would usually resume the attack with even more impetuosity than before.[9]

Premature fire was not the only problem the defenders faced. Even when the men in the ranks mastered their fears and fire was effectively reserved for commanded volleys, a similar dynamic was operating on the officers' psyche. Inexperienced officers were more likely to succumb to the same impulses that affected their men and order the volleys before the enemy had arrived within truly effective range. When this occurred, once again the defensive fire proved to be relatively ineffective.[10]

Experienced cavalry officers realized another psychological dynamic could be exploited, as soon as the charging cavalry had advanced to close range. Most foot soldiers were more afraid of the horse than the man it carried. This was recognized as far back as 1755 when Count Turpin de Crispé wrote in his influential *An Essay on the Art of War*:

> the soldier, incapable of reasoning like an officer, is often more frightened at the horse than the man; and being too much confused to present his piece, and fire properly, will fall back, and consequently make an opening in the battalion, through which resolute cavalry will not fail to enter.[11]

Even if the defenders did not immediately pull back out of the line, the cavalry still had a chance at success. Many soldiers, especially those less experienced ones, would freeze up and fail to reload their weapons. This tendency was one of the reasons which prompted cavalrymen to often circle an enemy formation. No longer threatened by powerful volleys, they hoped that the resolve of many of the defenders would ultimately fail, creating the much sought after gaps in the formation.[12]

Advancing close to the defending line proffered another benefit. Though it was commonly recognized that no horse would willingly impale itself on the infantryman's bayonet, horses were known to run into the protective row of bayonets after being wounded. A horse's response to being wounded to a certain extent depended upon whether the wound was caused by an edged weapon or a firearm. When the injury was inflicted by a hand-held weapon, the horse, unless it received a mortal wound, would attempt to stop in its tracks and the rider could do nothing to 'urge him forward'. However, a horse wounded by an unseen object, such as a musket or cannonball, was unable to identify the source of the injury and tended to become 'untractable and wild'.[13] This was especially true if the horse was hit in the breast area.[14] Horses tended to fall forward or push onward in the direction which the blow was received. General de Grandmaison who commanded the *Volontaires des Flandres* during the Wars of Austrian Succession, had observed that about fifty per cent of the horses hit by musket fire at close range:

> animated by the fire and the blood, falls with fury and impetuosity on the infantry, whose breastworks of bayonets is not able to sustain the weight of the horses in fury. The riders cannot any longer command them, they rush headlong, and make an opening for the rest of the squadron, to penetrate and break the battalion, which it cannot oppose this shock, a manoeuvre sufficiently quick and exact.[15]

Good cavalry would attempt to take advantage of this phenomenon by advancing quickly up to the enemy line or square. It was hoped that a horse made wild by injury would throw itself on the opposing line. Infantrymen seeing the oncoming horse would be forced to move out of the way or be trampled by the uncontrolled beast, and a breach would be created that the remainder of the squadron could immediately exploit.[16] During the era of the musket there were two notable examples of a wounded horse bursting into an otherwise solid formation. The first occurred in Bavaria during the War of the Austrian Succession, when a hussar's horse, after being shot, wildly sprang forward and impaled itself on a *chevaux de frise* that had been placed in front of the defending line. The momentum of the horse overturned the *chevaux de frise* thus exposing the infantry taking refuge behind it.[17] The second occasion took place at Garcia Hernandez on 23 July 1812 when the leading squadron of von Bock's Brigade of Dragoons of the King's German Legion destroyed a battalion of the French 6th *légère* regiment after a mortally wounded horse and its rider fell on to several files along one face of the square.[18] A more detailed account of this illustrative engagement is left to Chapter 22.

Although experienced officers were aware of the tactical possibilities offered by a horse being killed or wounded near enemy infantry, there was no attempt to incorporate this knowledge into formal doctrine. It was left to the Turks to develop a pre-defined tactic which attempted to systematically exploit a horse stumbling into an enemy line or square. While serving with the Duc de Richelieu's

Russian troops in the 1807 campaign against the Turks, the young French émigré, the Comte de Rouchechouart, frequently witnessed the following technique:

> Five or six hundred horse tried to break our infantry, which was formed in two squares. Vigorously repulsed by a fire at close range, they turned around, but reformed a short distance away, to attack another face of the square. Receiving another volley, and exasperated at being unable to breach in this human wall, ten of the most intrepid rushed forward as far as the bayonets of the first line; turning their horses round, they made them back, rearing so as to throw men and horses upon our soldiers, thus hoping to make a way for their comrades; but fell victims to their heroism without being followed ...[19]

It appears, however, that as a campaign wore on it became increasingly difficult to get veteran horses to even approach the enemy line. Seasoned horses, having experienced the horrors of fighting at close quarters, became more reluctant to move to the closest range. General Mitchell, referring to the beginning of the Revolutionary Wars, remarked:

> There was no appearance then of the fresh light that has since dawned upon the horses, and rendered them so conscious of the danger to be apprehended from the fire of the infantry as to make them bear their reluctant riders far away from the bayonets of the infantry.[20]

The incessant wars of the eighteenth century gave the infantry an opportunity to devise an effective antidote to cavalry coming in close and hoping that the horses would impale themselves or fall mortally wounded on the multi-layered rows of bayonets. This tactic was simply to deliver a volley fire while the cavalry was still at thirty paces or so, rather than waiting until the final moment.[21]

By the Napoleonic era, it was generally recognized that if the defending infantry consisted of veteran troops, well-led and determined to hold their position, they would be difficult or even impossible to overthrow. Infantry could be overpowered, however, if they were caught unprepared, the troopers lacked the necessary resolution, or their officers committed some blunder. Therefore, it didn't

make much sense to throw a regiment against every infantry formation encountered during the ebb and flow of battle. This would have
resulted in needless losses, and it must be remembered that each
cavalryman and horse was a precious commodity that could effectively take years to replace. Moreover, even ignoring possible casualties, regimental commanders sought to avoid needless failures,
knowing that these adversely affected the men's morale for the
remainder of the day and perhaps even the entire campaign. Except
for the most critical situations, it was far more practical to first
launch smaller detachments against the infantry to test its 'solidity' or
gradually fatigue the defenders. During the first half of the eighteenth
century, a common practice had been to precede the main cavalry
attack with that made by a small party of fifteen to twenty 'commanded men'. These were to draw the fire of the enemy infantry and
pave the way for the main body just slightly behind. Though it lessened the casualties in the first wave, it also was too small a force to
cause much effect.[22]

Frederick the Great had devised a more effective means of achieving the same ends. This was the attack of echelons. The cavalry was
deployed in echelon, that is, the squadron furthest to the right was in
front, with each of the remaining squadrons deployed an increasing
distance to the rear. Typically, the second squadron was to the left
and one 'interval' to the rear of the first, and so on. The echelon
could be performed easily even if the cavalry regiment happened to
be in line. The right squadron simply advanced straight forward to
begin its attack on the enemy infantry. As soon as it had advanced
150 paces, the next squadron on its left started forward, and the
third began its advance when the second had travelled 150 paces.
This process was continued with each successive squadron in the
regiment.

The defending line was threatened with a series of waves, rather
than one large-scale assault. Each successive squadron could be
brought to bear against the same section of the enemy line, and not
simply that portion that was immediately to its front when the charge
began. This could be achieved either by having that squadron slowly
drift towards the intended target, or make a quarter-wheel any time
before it was brought to the gallop. The first squadron would bear
the brunt of the defending line's fire, and probably be repulsed. Its
men would simply retire to the rear and reform. The next squadron,
however, might reach the defenders before they were able to reload,

or at worst would be exposed to a much more irregular fire. Each successive squadron would have an increasing chance of success. As soon as one squadron succeeded in breaking through the defending line, the others would attempt to exploit this breakthrough.

Another advantage offered by the attack in echelons was that it was much easier for each squadron to move forward. The frontage of each squadron was only a fraction of that of an entire regiment attacking in line, and the problem of the horses crowding together, which would disrupt a line, was correspondingly less.[23]

Others advocated that cavalry attack infantry in a column formation: the cavalry attacking in a dense formation would have a greater effect on morale than a similar attack made in line. The infantry driving off the first and second squadrons of the column, but seeing the remaining echelons still coming up, would begin to wonder if the attack was ever going to end, and start to waver.[24] Secondly, the attacking cavalry would be forced forward by the last squadron in the column which, taking no losses, would remain determined to close with the enemy. The old proverb 'one wedge drives another' was commonly cited to justify this tactic. However, even by Napoleonic times, the ability of infantry to produce repeated volley fire as well as the increased presence and effectiveness of artillery, usually made an attack in deep formations too expensive to be practical under normal circumstances. However, regardless of their individual tactical preferences, experienced cavalry officers agreed that when the defenders were caught off guard, the only important concern was to attack quickly, regardless of what formation the cavalry happened to be in at that moment.[25]

For this reason, the best time to attack an infantry line was as it was moving or when it had been shaken by artillery fire. It was especially desirable to attack an infantry column deployed in open order (at full interval) or any type of column that started to lengthen out beyond its allotted proportions. In this case, if the ground permitted, the cavalry was to attack quickly in flank and cut the column into two. If cavalry had to attack a line that was as yet unshaken, it was best to attack one of its wings (flanks). The line could only manage to send off a few shots against the attackers and it would often be disordered by the threat on its flank. If an attack on a flank was not possible, and the line was lengthy, the cavalry should then attack its centre.

In any case, experienced cavalrymen always recommended a vigorous charge, if not throughout the entire advance, at least in the final moments as they neared the enemy line. If gaps appeared in the infantry formation, the trooper was to take advantage of this good fortune and immediately enter the ranks. A good stratagem was to yell 'prisoner' while doing this, hoping that the infantrymen would lose their courage and determination and throw down their arms. When this happened, the cavalry was to make certain that the infantrymen laid down their arms and then were separated from their weapons as quickly as possible. It was advisable to position a few squadrons between the prisoners and the remaining enemy to prevent an easy rescue. Meanwhile, the main body of the cavalry regiment reformed. On the other hand, if the cavalry entered the enemy formation and the infantrymen continued to resist, they were to be sabred mercilessly.[26]

Probably de Brack's observations about the tendencies of the infantry of various nationalities to react differently in this situation is not out of place:

The Austrian infantry throw down their arms, and every soldier claims to be a Pole; they will faithfully follow you as prisoners. The Prussian infantry throw down their arms, but take them again promptly if they perceive help coming. The Russian infantry lie down, allow the charge to pass, rise and make renewed use of their arms. The Austrian skirmishers, clothed in grey, and armed with carbines using forced balls, are lost if you press them in the open; do not hesitate to charge them; they are yours, for they will not have time to reload their carbines.[27]

For infantry to be able successfully to ward off cavalry, it was critically important to be aware of the threat at the earliest moment and to start the necessary preparations in a timely manner. A good cavalry officer was adept at exploiting any irregularities of the ground that might exist to reduce the time available to the defender to begin to react. The undulation of ground found on many battlefields was often severe enough to create periodic dead spots in the infantry's line of sight. Cavalry positioned in these 'dead spots' would remain unobserved by the defending infantry. An experienced cavalry officer would take advantage of these 'hollow spots' to approach the infantry as close as possible without being observed. This could significantly reduce the amount of time an infantry unit had to prepare itself for a cavalry attack once it finally spotted the attacking cavalry. In extreme cases, if the cavalry had managed to advance sufficiently close before being observed, the defenders would not have enough time to form square and could be forced to surrender without the attacking cavalry having to strike a blow.

The anonymous author of *Maxims* provides a stratagem that presumably was used by some knowledgeable French cavalry leaders when the enemy infantry was positioned on hilly terrain with some adjacent dead spots. The cavalry was to advance towards the defenders as though to attack. The infantry, if in line, would begin its preparations to form square. The cavalry, meanwhile, would start to retreat, preferably in an open column of divisions, as though intimidated by the square and trying to move back out of the reach of musket fire. In reality, it would head for a 'dead spot' caused by the unevenness of the ground where it was out of sight, but still within musket range. However, as soon as this ground was reached, the command 'left wheel into line, gallop, march forward' was given. Line was immediately formed, and the charge begun. The cavalry would re-enter the infantry's view so suddenly and sufficiently close that a 'murderous fire' often was avoided. When this happened, the infantry's morale tended to collapse while the attacker's morale was buoyed in an equal proportion, and the assault was almost certain to be successful.[28]

That these tactics were not simply theoretical 'stratagems', practical only on the training field or the theoretician's notepad, was demonstrated during the Waterloo campaign. During the Battle of Quatre Bras, Kellermann, taking advantage of undulating terrain, was able to lead the 8th Cuirassiers to within 100 yards of the right flank of the 69th Regiment of Foot before the latter was aware of the danger. Lacking sufficient time to prepare, the British infantry was ridden down within moments.[29]

Other cavalry techniques were also frequently used to exploit the terrain when attacking enemy infantry. For example, an experienced cavalry commander would spot when the defenders were positioned on rather too steep slopes. If these slopes were such that horses could still manage the ascent, they could actually work to the defenders' detriment rather than live up to the defensive benefits that were anticipated. The reason was simple; infantry on steep slopes almost invariably fired too high against anyone rushing them from a slightly lower position. It must be remembered that it was necessary to 'aim' a musket at the enemy's knees when he was within sixty paces, and conversely to fire about five feet over his head when at the maximum effective range (about 400 paces). It was difficult for these adjustments to be made while lowering the barrel to aim at the target further down the slope. As a result, in these circumstances the fire usually went over the heads of the attacks unless it was withheld at the very last second. Gentle slopes which could act as an impediment to the onrushing cavalry, but which did not interfere with the proper levelling of the muskets were therefore far preferable. Just how much a slope could interfere with the infantryman's aim was demonstrated at the Battle of Belgrade. Two battalions of imperial infantry were literally wiped out in moments after a volley withheld until the enemy was at thirty paces failed to kill more than thirty-two Turks.[30]

Good cavalry officers also knew when to break off the attack and order the retreat. If after advancing close, they detected that the enemy infantry were protected by some hidden obstacle, or the defenders retained enough presence of mind to calmly reload their weapons, they were to order their men to withdraw at full speed. The riders were to bend low into the saddles to minimize the chances of being hit by enemy fire, and rally back into their formation once outside of musket range. They would then watch their quarry for the first available opportunity to renew the attack.[31]

Before closing this study of the principles upon which all feasible cavalry tactics were based, it is necessary to consider an observation made by the French Marshal Marmont regarding the training of the front line cavalry horses. Marmont observed that although continual practice at charging simulated enemy troops on the practice field greatly aided the understanding and ability of the cavalrymen, it actually had a deleterious effect on the horses' performance when faced with the situation on the battlefield. During peacetime training, the cavalry was often made to charge a line of friendly infantrymen. Of course, the horses were made to pull up in the final seconds, or were directed to pass through the intervals in the defending line, before the infantry broke or the horses began to pull up or swerve. Unfortunately, it was noticed that this also taught the horses to stop at the final moments. The horses 'being thus accustomed to avoid the point of attack as an obstacle, they can never be made to come to close quarters, for their habits accord with their instinct, and perhaps with that of their riders'.[32] These observations were not limited to Marmont; other officers in other armies had come to similar conclusions about this practice. An officer serving in the British army wrote in 1809 that it was the 'most dangerous exercise ever pursued, and to which foot officers are much attached', since it steadied the infantry man 'at the expense of the mounted man'. The same author attributed the failure of the Prussian cavalry at Auerstädt to the Prussians using this practice technique during their annual spring and autumnal reviews. During this battle, the Prussian cavalry was ordered to charge the French infantry on three occasions. Each time the horses wheeled about the moment the first volley was delivered, this in spite of effort by the officers and men to have the horses 'obey the spur'.[33]

Writing after the Napoleonic Wars, Marshal Marmont suggested a different method of allowing cavalry to practise charging friendly infantry on the parade ground. As in the established method, friendly infantry were deployed in a line facing the cavalry participating in the exercise. However, the infantry assumed a much looser order than on the battlefield, so as to allow the cavalry to pass between the individual files. The first time the cavalry 'charged', the simulated assault was delivered at a slow pace, even a walk. Though even at this gait some of the horses would attempt to turn away, the rider would be able to have the horse pass through the ranks, eventually. The same drill was repeated over and over, so that the horses became used to approaching the infantry in front of them, and gradually the speed of the advance was quickened. Each time the drill was performed some of the infantry were allowed to fire, though of course, no ball had been loaded. The number of men firing was also gradually increased, so that, if the infantry was deployed along six ranks the noise and smoke during the practice was approximately equal to a battalion firing under actual battlefield conditions. Marmont concluded that cavalry trained in this manner would charge home much more effectively than cavalry units trained using the traditional method, or not trained at all. In his view the horses 'well set up and accustomed to precipitate themselves upon a fire they have learned to face, will of their own accord carry the riders along, if the latter should be tempted to moderate their ardor'.[34] What is not clear, however, is whether in proffering these ideas Marmont was drawing upon actual experience during his fighting career, that is, what was actually attempted during the Napoleonic Wars, or whether this method of training was only devised after the peace that followed these wars.

INFANTRY DEFENDING AGAINST CAVALRY

Although there were minor variations from army to army and period to period, the basic tactics infantry used to ward off enemy cavalry remained fairly much the same throughout the entire era of the flint-lock musket. The most notable development, once these tactics had been established at the beginning of the eighteenth century, was the increased reliance on the square by the time of the height of the Napoleonic Wars.

It has already been noted that the sight of a body of cavalry approaching in closed order and at speed tended to unnerve many of the infantrymen who were to bear the brunt of the assault, especially if they were as yet unseasoned by the horrors of several large-scale actions. For any set of tactics to be successful, these psychological dynamics had to be taken in account, and had to offer officers a means of controlling their men, and being able to withhold fire until almost the last moment. When a cavalry charge appeared imminent, the officers took steps to make certain the distance separating the lateral files were closed to a minimum, about fifteen inches from the left of one man to the next. This was a slightly tighter arrangement than if the infantry were engaging enemy infantry in a firefight. In this latter case, the added 'elbow room' would be useful when reloading and delivering their pieces. However, when faced with cavalry, the compactness of the formation and an increased number of bayonets per metre was more important than any convenience in reloading.

During the War of Spanish Succession, when Allied horsemen encountered French infantry at bayonet point, each rider faced approximately ten foot soldiers. By 1800, the near universal reliance on the thinner three-rank line meant there were only six or seven infantrymen to each cavalryman. In other words, the defending line threw out about six or seven bayonets for each thirty-six inches of its length. This assumes each infantryman along a rank occupied fifteen to eighteen inches, and each cavalryman thirty-six inches. This was still more than enough to intimidate any horses and guarantee that, since horses, like men, will never willingly impale themselves on a row of bayonets, the oncoming cavalry would pull up or swerve prior to making any actual contact.

Even in those rare cases when enemy cavalry made it right up to the defending infantry line, the infantry enjoyed a preponderance of steel. The foot soldier standing in the first rank always enjoyed approximately a one-foot advantage of reach over his adversary on horseback. The average musket extended about four feet beyond the soldier's reach, compared to about three feet for the average sword or sabre. However, the men in the rear ranks, being positioned further back, were unable to project their bayonets as far as those in the front. It must be remembered that the first rank was often made to kneel and reserve its fire to be able to fire just in these very cases where the cavalry was at point blank range. Even when the first rank was kneeling, their bayonets, though unable to easily reach the riders high atop the horses, still served as a deterrent as they could reach the breasts of the horses.[35]

As the cavalry neared, the next and most crucial task facing the officers in the defending line was to ensure that the infantry remained steady and the men withheld their fire until ordered. The officers were to see that the men observed a 'profound silence', so that the men could more readily hear the officers' commands, and someone starting to do something on their own would be much more notice-able. This helped the officers control the men and reduced the risk of the latter starting to fire on their own initiative.[36] It must be borne in mind that in the days before the breech-loading rifle, the defending infantry could only count on the delivery of a single well-aimed and delivered volley. The oncoming cavalry would cross the last 200 paces in twenty to thirty seconds.[37] Although well-trained infantry might be able to deliver two or three rounds during these final moments, experienced officers rarely risked this. According to one British general: 'More than one volley is, of course, entirely out of the question, because the hurry and anxiety of loading a second fire, would lead to unsteadiness, certain of producing defeat.'[38] The remaining question was at what point to deliver this volley. It was important that this first fire, the only volley which could be relied upon, was not thrown away before the cavalry was sufficiently close. Berenhorst, for example, felt that even when a volley was withheld until only sixty paces separated the two forces, it was all too common for the fire to miss its mark.

To minimize this possibility, in the early eighteenth century the common wisdom had been to save the fire until the very last moment when the enemy cavalry was just about on top of the line being assaulted. The purpose of this tactic was to create a 'rampart' of fallen men and horses. The horses in the following ranks would turn away rather than step on the fallen, and their progress thus would be effectively checked. The soldiers were advised to 'fire in the nose' of any horse that still wanted to advance into the line of infantry-men.[39] It was discovered that this tactic, though producing the most murderous fire, had one very serious potential drawback. When firing at this extremely short range wounded horses could fall directly on to the defending line. A horse killed or completely debilitated by a musket wound required ten to fifteen paces to fall down; anything in its path would be knocked over.

The solution was to fire at twenty to forty paces. This was a close enough range to guarantee frightful casualties, while still distant enough to allow the wounded animals to stop or crash into an empty plot of earth. It meant that the infantrymen started to fire before the horses had advanced close enough to intimidate the men into moving reflexively backwards. Yet, the infantrymen were still close enough to be able to charge with lowered bayonets, if ordered to do so, after delivering a volley.[40] A determined bayonet charge could be most effective if executed immediately after a volley, while the enemy cavalry was in confusion. At Crefeld during the Seven Years' War, three Hanoverian battalions were able to completely repulse oncoming French cavalry, though they were in line with unprotected flanks by charging with cold steel after an effective volley at close range.

Several methods of delivering fire were recommended for either a line or square attempting to ward off cavalry. One school of thought advocated volley fire, since it maximized the casualties that could be inflicted in a single moment. Those of this view felt that 'Cavalry will only be beaten when so many of them fall on a sudden, [and] that disorder ensues', and thus avoided individual fire or even fire by individual ranks.[41] Obviously, the single most powerful volley could be delivered using 'battalion fire', where men along the whole length of the battalion fired at once. However, this practice was definitely frowned upon. This denuded the whole battalion of fire until everyone reloaded, and in this twenty to thirty seconds the enemy cavalry would have traversed the last 200 paces. Moreover, the oncoming cavalry, aware that all of the infantry had fired, would have little else to fear and would rush in all the more precipitously to test the defending line of bayonets.[42] These deficiencies with bat-talion fire against cavalry became even more pronounced if the cavalry attacked in a series of echelons.[43] In this case, it was often recommended that only those platoons being directly attacked begin to fire, all others reserving their fire for the echelons still to come.[44]

However, other authorities felt 'divisional firings', where one-third or one-quarter of a battalion fired at the same time, had their own set of limitations. If an entire division fired, and the cavalry in front of them continued its charge, this section of the battalion which just fired was vulnerable until its men reloaded.[45] This was not much of a danger if the cavalry had attacked in line, but was a real concern if they had attacked in echelon instead. Here, the cavalry could charge the same part of the line approximately every ten to twenty seconds. Nevertheless, some tacticians, such as Müller, felt if the infantry was on fairly rough terrain where the cavalry slowed down and became slightly disordered, a divisional fire was very useful. In this case, two adjoining platoons fired simultaneously. The part of the line that just fired would not be vulnerable to a new assault while they loaded, since attack by echelons was not possible, and even a charge in a line had to be conducted more slowly.

Those favouring volley fire recognized that it was critical to ensure that at least a portion of the defenders always reserved their fire along the length of the line or side of a square. For this reason, the first rank often was ordered to keep back its fire for a critical moment. Or, if only a portion of the line was attacked, such as when charged by enemy cavalry *en echelon* or *en échiquier*, only the part of the line directly threatened was to fire; the remainder were to continue to hold back.[46]

Some officers felt that the infantry's goal, when threatened with cavalry, was to produce continuous fire. Those with this view often advocated 'fire by files', while those who wanted a local reserve advised using either platoon firing or fire by ranks. Platoon firing could be used if only a portion of the line was threatened. Fire by ranks was useful if the enemy attacked in a lengthy line, since the noise caused by the discharge of numerous muskets was more likely to frighten the horses.[47] However, if the cavalry attacked *en fourrageur*, in a loose formation, it was advisable to have the rear rank retain its fire since the cavalry could renew its attack more quickly and unpredictably. In any case, if a substantial fire was kept up after the one truly trustworthy first volley, it was universally believed that the enemy cavalry would eventually be driven back.[48]

Experienced infantry officers recognized that the first cavalry attack was the most critical. Cavalry that was repulsed during the first attempt was easier to frustrate in the second. According to Turpin de Crispé:

> If the enemy can be prevented from breaking into the column at the first charge, it is very certain his ardour will be greatly abated in the second, and still more in the third, till at length he shall be repulsed with great loss, and the detachments perhaps escape without losing a man.[49]

An excellent example of a battalion employing exactly these tactics was provided in the 1806 campaign during the combat of Prenzlow. Remnants of the Prince Auguste of Prussia's grenadier battalion and the grenadiers of Rheinbabe, about 400 strong, were attacked by a much superior force of the 8th, 16th, and 21st French Dragoon Regiments, which totalled somewhere between 1,000 and 1,200 troopers. The French cavalry was eventually reinforced by the 5th and 12th Dragoons, yielding a total of about 2,000 men. The Prussian battalion determinedly met the onslaught deployed along three ranks. According to Prince Auguste, who personally commanded his battalion on this occasion:

> My battalion was formed on three ranks: the first rank with knee on the ground, with charged bayonets, and as much as I can recall it did not fire a shot; the two others only fired at 20 to 30 paces. The French cavalry repeated seven times, and vainly, the lively attacks.

Karl Decker, a respected German tactician in the period immediately following the Napoleonic Wars, tells us that during each of these charges the French cavalry lost between ten to fifteen horses. It is interesting to note that this four or five per cent loss proved sufficient to thwart the assault. To provide the epilogue, the Prussian force was finally dispersed while attempted to cross a morass about two German miles from Prenzlow when artillery firing grapeshot was successfully brought to bear. In the end Prince Auguste, nine officers and an undisclosed number of men were taken prisoners by the French.[50]

The complete success of a small number of lancers to practically totally annihilate two large Austrian squares has been described in

Chapter 16. However, their success was due to the defending infantry's inability to fire due to continuous rain. It must not be thought that lancers were able to close with the same impunity against infantry which still possessed its ability to deliver a regular fire. De Brack recounted the frustration of his lancers at Waterloo who were unable to break an English square. One of his men then resorted to an interesting expedient:

> not being able to break down the rampart of bayonets which opposed us, [one of the lancers] stood up in his stirrups and hurled his lance like a dart; it passed through an infantry soldier, whose death would have opened a passage for us, if the gap had not been quickly closed.[51]

Any discussion about how infantry defended itself from massed cavalry attacks, should also include a brief description of a technique that was periodically used by Russian infantry. When attacked by cavalry, a line of infantry would remain stationary until the cavalry were almost upon them. Then, the troops would quickly fall flat on the ground. Horses never intentionally step on prostrate men and so the riders, armed only with swords, would be unable to inflict any wounds. So the horses would jump over the infantry on the ground and be forced to advance a distance in order to rally. In the mean time, the infantry would be able to pick itself up, turn around and fire upon the cavalry that had just passed. This was the technique used by Saxon troops under Marshal Schulembourg against Swedish cavalry led by Charles XII, and again by Russian troops when attacked by Seydlitz at Gross-Jägersdorff.[52] The technique is of interest to this present work, since the Russians occasionally used it during the Napoleonic period, for example, at the Battle of Trebia against the French in 1799.[53]

WHO WOULD WIN?

The debate as to whether infantry or cavalry held the intrinsic advantage in an encounter raged throughout the Napoleonic period and several decades beyond. One side felt that well-led, experienced infantry who were fully prepared held an unsurmountable advantage over any cavalry force that might be pitted against them. The opposite view was, of course, that if properly trained and led correctly cavalry would be certain to destroy an infantry formation in front of them. The partisans of these conflicting viewpoints were more or less divided along with the arm they served: infantrymen naturally thought they possessed the intrinsic advantage, while most cavalry officers adhered to the opposite belief. This debate about who held the intrinsic advantage was as old as the very division of soldiers into the foot and mounted arms itself. However, in its current form the controversy arose anew as soon as the infantry were equipped with socket bayonets, abandoned the pike, and were deployed along thinner formations, that is, during the 1689–1715 period.

Marshal Puységur writing in the 1740s probably summed up the pro-infantry position most succinctly: 'If infantry understands its force, the cavalry can never break it.'[54] The well-known English tactician, Humphrey Bland, writing during the same general period, seconded this opinion, and further explained that infantry would necessarily repulse attacking cavalry, since the destructive fire of a single platoon was sufficient to 'break any squadron'. The whole trick, opined Bland, was to get the infantry to 'know its own strength' and to retain its fire until the last moment, instead of throwing it away when the enemy was still at a distance.[55]

Almost a hundred years later, the Russian general Okounef, relying on his experience during the Napoleonic Wars, echoed these convictions:

> The superiority of the infantry over the cavalry is so great, whether this arm is formed in squares or column to resist them that one can say hardily that an infantry which succumbs to the shock of cavalry is bad infantry, or at the least, an infantry which badly behaves.[56]

Lieutenant-Colonel William Thomkinson, a British cavalry officer who had seen the success of the British squares at Waterloo and the damage they inflicted upon the French cavalry, noted in his memoirs that it was 'almost impossible [for cavalry] to succeed against infantry'. Nevertheless, he enjoined infantry officers always to take the greatest precaution when threatened by enemy cavalry, for not all infantry possessed the first and most important prerequisite to withstand a cavalry charge: that is, to know its own strength. He observed that he had 'seen the best of troops more afraid of cavalry than any other force'.[57]

> Indeed it has been pretended by experienced officers, who had themselves frequently directed charges, that a complete line of infantry without spaces or intervals is impregnable, even though it never fires a shot.[58]

However, before anyone concludes unequivocally that all other factors being equal, infantry could always ward off a cavalry force, regardless of how determined and well-led its men, consideration should be given to Marbot's account of an action near the post-house of Kliastitsi on 23 July 1812.

> The Marshal gave orders to Mons A . . . (acting colonel of the 23 chasseurs à cheval regiment) to attack them [the Russian battalions], and he gave word for the second line to pass to the front, which I duly executed. As soon as the 23rd were reformed in line we marched upon the Russian infantry which halted and steadily awaited us; it was Tamboff regiment. When we were within striking distance I gave the word to charge. This was carried out all the more efficiently for the stimulus which the fact that their comrades of the 24th were watching gave to my troopers. The enemy committed the serious blunder, as I think it, of spending all its fire at once, by giving us a volley, which badly aimed as it was emptied a few saddles. A file fire would have been far more destructive. Before the Russians could reload we were upon them at the full speed of our excellent horses, *and the shock was so violent that they were overthrown in heaps* [my italics]. Many rose again and tried to defend themselves with the bayonet against the trooper's points; but after losing heavily they fell back, and at last broke, many being killed or captured as they fled towards a cavalry regiment [the Grodno Hussars] which was coming up to their aid.[59]

This is not to suggest that the horses literally bowled over the infantrymen while still proffered six or seven bayonets per yard of frontage. However, the general confusion and one or two weak-willed men fleeing to the rear could provide the space needed for the single cavalrymen to enter the ranks and begin the rapid process of dismembering the defending formation.

One school of cavalry officers felt that success would be achieved whenever the officers managed to have the troopers under their command actually close upon the defending faces of the square. These officers attributed whatever failures that did occur to the unwillingness of the men and horses to continue the advance in the final moments. Proponents of this view were not limited to any one army, and were found in the cavalry arm of each nation. The British General Mitchell writing in the 1830s attributed most cavalry failures to insufficiently trained horses.[60]

Von Bülow writing in the late 1790s had expressed similar sentiments. This author observed that ironically whenever cavalry was successfully repulsed, invariably its forward motion had been checked after the first volley, in those cases where the infantry had managed to reserve its fire until twenty or thirty paces. The irony was that now the greatest danger was past, and a determined cavalry continuing the attack would be most likely to penetrate the defending infantry, now largely confused and vulnerable.

> I know I shall be told of many instances of deployed infantry repulsing cavalry, but surely the latter have wanted courage in those instances. All the officers of cavalry, who have been in service, declare unanimously, that, in general, their troops do not retreat, till after they have received the fire of the infantry, that is to say, when there is almost nothing too fear. This conduct is unaccountable: it is doing too much or too little. If the troops, after receiving the fire, were to clap spurs to their horses, and give them the bridle, they would penetrate the ranks. In general the fault is thrown on the horses, which, it is said, will not advance when once they are seized with fear. Certainly . . . but the fact is, that these animals are very warlike, and, when their spirit is roused; rush undauntedly upon the bayonet, as we have often seen.[61]

Before von Bülow's views are dismissed as overly optimistic, the achievement of the Mecklenburg-Strelitzer Hussars at the battle of Möckern, on 16 October 1813 must be considered. Noticing the 1st *regiment d'Artillerie de Marine* engaged in a firefight with a Prussian infantry battalion, this hussar regiment, while advancing in column at the trot, fanned out into line and then enthusiastically charged the French infantry at the gallop. The latter seeing the advancing cavalry quickly formed square. The French withheld their fire until the first Prussian squadron, on the right and slightly in the lead, was only twenty paces distant. NCO Saeskow, who was positioned on the right of the second squadron, described the effects of this fire and the events that followed:

> The muskets cracked out; I felt a jerk under my chin; my shako, struck by a bullet, fell to the ground. Wrapped in powder smoke, I saw through it the enemy bayonets, for we were on them in a few bounds, almost immediately after their volley; and this I remember yet, as if it happened today; a bayonet thrust in the nose made my horse rear right up in the air; whether I then spurred him or kicked his ribs, I don't know anymore, but I went into action, I cut right and left about me, they gave me room, and I found myself, I don't know how, in the midst of the square, followed by the Hussars, who now also broke through . . . Things now dissolved into individual struggles. I cut a man diagonally across the face, who had thrust through my clock without wounding me; another I cut through the shako to the skull, so that he fell . . . The square had been scattered completely, and a mass of prisoners gathered up.[62]

This was the debate as it then existed. However, this debate has never totally subsided, and with the demise of cavalry, military historians have replaced military scientists among the ranks of those holding conflicting viewpoints.

It is probably fair to say, though, that in the last several decades a majority of historians and enthusiasts studying this question have begun to side with the infantry officers' point of view, that is, if infantry 'understands its force', it cannot be broken. Keegan, in his classic *The Face of Battle*, offers one of the strongest expressions of this view. Basing his judgement on the repeated failures of the French cavalry to break the British infantry at Waterloo, he concludes that '"Here comes those d—d fools again" seems to be an appropriate judgement on this type of conflict [i.e. between infantry and cavalry].'[63] Keegan thus suggests this outcome was inevitable, not just at Waterloo, but whenever cavalry encountered determined infantry, properly prepared. He continues by citing Jac Weller's observation that each cavalryman, occupying a thirty-six inch front, faced at least four infantrymen, and the effects of each relatively ineffective fire would almost always be sufficient to break the attacking cavalrymen's will to continue the offensive. The problem with this point of view, at least in this very opinionated form, is that it tends to reduce the entire cavalry versus infantry issue to a one-sentence formula: experienced infantry if well led and not caught off guard will always be able to hold off attacking cavalry, regardless of the latter's tactics, quality and leadership.

There were some experienced cavalry officers, who though they did not share the bravado of some of their more outspoken colleagues, nevertheless felt that during the typical battle the cavalry arm would almost always be given an opportunity to overthrow some infantry formations, regardless of the latter's experience or preparedness. These officers did not think it was merely a matter of getting their horses to continue to close against the enemy infantry in the last seconds of the attack. They knew full well the limitations of both their men and the mounts under them, and realized that just rushing in against determined infantry prepared to meet the assault was just throwing away the lives of good men and valuable mounts. These officers realized that cavalry's success lay in being able to take advantage of errors committed by the infantry. This view, again, was not limited to any one army, and an excellent example is found in the writings of a British cavalryman around 1799: 'A commander of cavalry, who does not know to make his dispositions to profit by the faults of the enemy's foot, will never do great things if the infantry behave well.' The same officer goes on to point out that the Prussian cavalry's greatest successes at Hohenfriedberg, Zorndorf, Kesseldorf and Rossbach during the Seven Years' War came about, not because they had to charge infantry 'which was yet in perfect order, and had sustained no loss; they [the Prussian cavalry] availed themselves of a lucky moment, and this defeated the enemy's foot, already partly broken and in disorder.'[64]

These faults just alluded to not only referred to gross errors, such as catching infantry in flank, or in the process of manoeuvring, but included a whole host of minor improprieties. And a competent and highly experienced officer knew how eventually to translate a number of minor errors into the same result as one egregious blunder. All this meant that during a lengthy battle, where there may have been a number of cavalry versus infantry engagements, though most tended to result in the infantry holding their own, the cavalry could gain occasional but important victories. Often, the results of an engagement were reduced to the influence of unforeseen events, such as the reaction of a neighbouring unit, and so on. This is all the more significant, since the quality of not only the men and officers, but also the mounts during the 1815 campaign, was well below that found at the zenith of the French cavalry's capabilities between 1805–1812.

To conclude, veteran infantry, well led and prepared for a cavalry assault, was likely to withstand even the most determined series of charges. This, however, does not mean that cavalry was useless against infantry. Experienced cavalrymen realized that during any large-scale engagement, opportunities would arise, allowing an astute cavalry officer to surprise an infantry battalion or in some other way exploit a fortuitous weakness. The trick was to spot these occasions, without falling victim to impetuosity which would lead to futile and self-destructive attacks against well-prepared infantry.

CHAPTER 18

French Cavalry Tactics

GENERAL TACTICS

W HEN WE THINK OF HOW FRENCH CAVALRY conducted itself
we tend to think of one or two most notable tactics, such as the
classical Napoleonic Era charge at the walk, trot, gallop charge
against enemy cavalry, or cavalry circling round an infantry square
that stood its ground. In fact, the tactical system actually employed
by the French cavalry was very much more diverse. French cavalry,
like those of all other nations, fought in a variety of different ways
depending upon the situation they found themselves in. One French
general observed that French cavalry used three different sets of
offensive tactics: as skirmishers, foragers (*en fourrageur*) and regular
formations. This last category was, in turn, broken down into fighting in lines and in columns.

USE OF MIXED ORDER

The French adherence to the 'impulse' or perpendicular school of
grand tactics also influenced the way cavalry was handled on a tactical level. French cavalry was frequently placed as a second line to
support the infantry in the first, rather than being always placed on
the army's wings as had been the usual practice until the start of the
Seven Years' War. However, when acting on its own, a body of

cavalry continued to be deployed along two lines with an additional reserve.

It was recognized that in a cavalry engagement, the victor was usually he who was able to throw in the last fresh reserves. As a consequence, the French concentrated on using formations that protected the flanks and allowed a local reserve. These supports had to be moveable, since to be effective the first line had to move forward whenever it was required to go on the offensive, or even defend its current position. This use of local supports for each unit represented a significant tactical development. Prior to this, cavalry always sought to support its flanks, but used impassable terrain instead of a formation or additional troops. Using terrain possessed intrinsic grand tactical limitations since, if it prevented the enemy from turning the cavalry's flank, in the same way it stopped the friendly cavalry from outflanking the enemy. Moreover, if the cavalry had been 'appuyed' (anchored) on a morass or town and was called upon to advance, the protective flank was left behind and its flanks became vulnerable.

Prior to forming line, the French cavalry would manoeuvre in a series of columns. The flanks of these columns were protected by positioning several additional columns to their rear. Typically, these were two columns of troops, which were in open order to be able to face any direction quickly. If the cavalry was threatened on a flank, the rear column on that side would turn in that direction and then deploy into line. The other rear column would also face the direction of the threat, but would work its way to the latter's flank if the first column was not able to defeat it by a frontal attack. Meanwhile, the main body of the cavalry was given time to reposition itself and if necessary join in the engagement on its flank.

Even when the brigade was to operate in line, it frequently adopted a type of mixed order. As in the case of infantry which often resorted to a similar formation, this was to provide a local reserve and support each flank. Most of the brigade was deployed along a conventional line. However, supporting columns were placed on each flank running to the rear. Also, if the front line was extensive, an additional column ran backwards from the centre. If possible a reserve was added in the form of a third 'line', which actually took the form of a closed order column positioned behind the centre of the formation. Its purpose was quickly to move to any point threatened along the first line or on the flanks of the columns forming the second 'line'.[1]

CAVALRY VERSUS INFANTRY

French cavalry, like its corresponding arm in other armies, was not expected to attack an enemy infantry formation that showed signs of determination and remained in good order. In these situations it was to wait until the hostile infantry was first shaken by either artillery or musket fire. However, this caution was not warranted when enemy infantry was caught in the middle of a manoeuvre or demonstrated any type of equivocation. In this case, unless the infantry was protected by insurmountable natural terrain, the French cavalry was to attack immediately and with all possible force.[2]

A very good example of what cavalry could do against raw troops occurred during the retreat of Blücher's Silesian army from Vauchamps in February 1814. Here, a body of French cuirassiers managed to block the Russian line of retreat:

> A hostile regiment of cuirassiers formed to make an attack on three Russian battalions at our head. These happened to be newly formed battalions just arrived. Their commanding officers halted and made ready; they allowed the enemy to advance to sixty paces before they gave the word 'Fire'. Instead of the 1st and 2nd ranks of the leading columns only giving fire, the whole three battalions fired at once, and exhibited the spectacle of three 'pôte â feu'. Nothing hindered the cuirassiers from breaking into the battalions (not squares), for not a horse or a man had fallen, but they had turned about.[3]

Obviously, no cavalry could expect to obtain such results automatically, especially when opposed to veteran or trained troops. Though shaken or inexperienced troops could be quickly attacked with few preliminary precautions, resolute infantry had to be attacked very methodically or even entirely avoided. This difference in approach meant that the French cavalry first had to determine the quality of the infantry it had encountered and its willingness to stand and resist.

One method of 'testing' the enemy infantry was for the French cavalry to pause within 400 or 500 yards of it. A small body of horsemen were detached and sent against the infantry at the gallop. In dry weather this would raise a lot of dust, and could agitate inexperienced troops, who might start to fire despite their officers' efforts to prevent this. If this happened, the French cavalry were to attack immediately whether in line or column. The disorganization in the infantry ranks caused by the premature fire and the resulting lack of firepower when it was truly needed gave the cavalry every chance of success.[4] Experienced troops would not be intimidated by the cavalry feint and would maintain a 'bold face'. Fire would be withheld and only a few skirmishers detached and sent out to meet the small body of attacking cavalry. If this happened, the French cavalry was not to attack immediately but either to wait for friendly artillery or attempt to discover or create a weakness by stratagem.[5]

It was sometimes necessary for the cavalry regiment to attempt to overthrow an infantry formation, regardless of the casualties that might be suffered. This would be most difficult if the defending infantry had formed a series of squares *à crémaillère* and was accompanied by some artillery. A *crémaillère* refers to a group of squares that were essentially placed *en echelon*. The advantage of this formation was that each square in the chain supported its neighbour with its infantry fire, but was positioned so that this fire would not hit the men in the next square. When French cavalry confronted infantry prepared in this fashion, doctrine called for it not to enter the space separating the individual squares. To do so would only subject the cavalry men to a cross-fire which would cause significant casualties without guaranteeing a positive result. Rather, the cavalry was to position itself at one corner of the infantry formation and then attack one square after another in succession.

According to the anonymous author of *Maxims* two squadrons were sufficient to break the first square. Initially, these were positioned in closed column forty-five degrees from one of the square's sides and out of musket range. So positioned, it would see one side of the first square slightly to its right and another slightly to its left. A dozen skirmishers rode out to the left and right to about medium range in order to mask the actions of the squadron behind them. The first squadron was divided in two, one half advancing at the trot on the side of the square slightly to the right, the other attacking the side to the left. This first squadron was a feint designed to draw the square's fire.

The second squadron waited until the first squadron neared the square, and then began its advance also at the trot. If either of the two sides threatened by the first squadron began firing, the second squadron immediately began to charge at the gallop. The first squadron would soon be overtaken by the second. It would continue its advance to support the second squadron which was now in front of it. Meanwhile, the skirmishers would fall in with the second squadron and lead the charge. The entire attack proceeded along the 'capital' of the square (forty-five degrees to two sides, heading towards the point where two sides meet). This meant that each side fired at the oncoming horsemen at a very oblique angle and the cavalry casualties were reduced to a minimum. Once the cavalry reached the first ranks of the square, it had to 'at all costs cut an opening'. As soon as an opening was formed, the troopers were to order the enemy infantry to throw down their weapons and start to gather together prisoners and immediately have them march in the direction of the regiment's reserves, which would not actually have engaged the enemy. Any resistance, however, was to be met with instant and violent reaction: those who did not immediately surrender were to be sabred 'mercilessly'. No time was to be lost trying to overpower the enemy, or coax them into submission.

This was one method of attacking an infantry square. However, as history has repeatedly demonstrated, cavalry charging square was never certain of success. Good officers and commanders were also trained to be prepared for failure and disappointment. The first potential problem was unexpected resistance or problems offered by the ground to be traversed during the charge. This could be soft earth causing the horses to slip and fall, or obstacles might not be perceived from a distance. These types of dangers were potentially serious and sometimes resulted in the effective destruction of the entire attacking formation. Therefore experience dictated that as soon as they were noticed or encountered the mounted skirmishers would signal the main formation behind them and the charge would be aborted immediately. Whenever the cavalry was forced either to abort the charge or retire after an unsuccessful charge, it was to pull back at full speed, and rally once out of musket range. If fired at, the men would ride low in the saddles, attempting to decrease their target profile. Should it be decided to renew the attack against the square, it was considered ill advised to attack the same two sides of the square; the approach of these would be obstructed by the dead and wounded men and horses which would inevitably litter the ground in front of that side of the square.[6]

Colonel du Picq writing in the 1860s tells us of how through a conversation with an experienced officer who had fought during the

Napoleonic Wars he learned of another, apparently very effective, method of cavalry attack against infantry. In this case, the attacking cavalry would first position itself to the right of the enemy infantry along the same axis of deployment. The cavalry would then expeditiously pass along the enemy's front in an extended column, 'horse following horse'. At the proper moment, the cavalry would quickly turn to the right and attack the enemy infantry who were only a short distance away. This technique could only be performed while the cavalry was moving from the right to the left. The cavalrymen were trained to hold their swords in their right hand. If the cavalry rode directly in front of the enemy infantry, each trooper was in a position to strike an opponent as soon as he turned to the right, and possibly even before turning, as he continued to ride along the front. This was not possible if the cavalry was travelling in from left to right, since his sword arm was no longer on the same side as the enemy.

This tactic when properly and courageously applied had several advantages. By approaching from the flank, the cavalry avoided most of their exposure to enemy fire. The whole process would require only several moments, always less than ten seconds from the moment the cavalry first started to traverse the enemy front. For most, if not all this time, the enemy would be startled, then confused. The cavalry riding along its front after all might be friendly, considering the direction it was riding and its apparent origin. Individual soldiers not forewarned by the cavalry's approach from a distance would await instructions from their officers. This would take at least several moments, and by this time the cavalry could very well be in the process of attacking. When the cavalry did strike, it was in position relative to the trooper's weapon, something that was not true in any straight-on charge.

Du Picq tells us his source claimed this method was 'infallible', and du Picq himself felt this was the only method of cavalry attack against infantry capable of producing 'deadly results'. He admitted, however, this tactic required 'officers who inspire absolute confidence in their men and dependable and experienced soldiers . . . in short, an excellent cavalry, seasoned in long wars, and officers and men of very firm resolution'. Du Picq concluded his analysis with the realization that these stringent prerequisites meant that it was rarely possible to employ this tactic on the battlefield.[7]

This tactic might strike the modern reader as far fetched, and impossible to implement under battlefield conditions. What is interesting, however, is the similarity between this manoeuvre and another tactic practised by the Prussian cavalry prior to the beginning of the Seven Years' War. The tactic apparently was designed to facilitate the attack and destruction of an isolated enemy infantry battalion, unsupported by neighbouring infantry. The Prussians would take five or six squadrons and form them up into two 'columns by half squadrons', i.e. each a half squadron wide. One column would advance on the right side of the infantry to be attacked, the other on the left. Each column would take care to not to move in front of the infantry to be attacked, but to remain on its left or right flank, depending upon the side they were approaching. When 150 paces from the enemy infantry, the Prussian cavalry quickened the pace to the gallop. The first squadron (sometimes the first two) in each column advanced straight forward 200 paces, fifty paces beyond the enemy's position, and then come to a halt. The purpose of this was to guard the other squadrons which would assault the infantry from being attacked in turn.

The remaining squadrons in each column advanced until they were even with the enemy infantry and then quarter-wheeled towards the infantry. The squadron on the right attacked first, advancing (from right to left) across the entire front of the enemy infantry. Then a squadron from the left column advanced across the front (from left to right). This alternating pattern continued until all the squadrons had attacked the enemy.

THE CHARGE

Like other European armies of the period, the French cavalry officially modelled its charge doctrine on the system developed by Frederick the Great. When attacking either enemy infantry or cavalry, the cavalry were to start off at a walk, proceed to a trot, before finally breaking into a gallop as they neared the enemy. The official charge procedure as dictated by the French cavalry regulations of 1813 was as follows. The troopers were ordered to draw their sabres and then proceed forward at the trot. After 150 paces they were to start to gallop. When the cavalry had covered an additional 100 paces, the colonel was to order the trumpets to sound the charge and the horses' pace was to quicken and their stride lengthen. The cavalrymen were to stand up in their stirrups and lower their hands without letting go of the reins. Those in the front rank were to hold their sabres outstretched, while those in the rear were to hold theirs above their head. All the while, of course, the cohesion of the formation was to be strictly maintained without.[8]

Writing in 1815, the anonymous French general we have repeatedly cited recommended a similar routine.[9] The cavalry were to walk thirty or forty yards, trot about 200 yards, and then break out into the gallop. At this point the enemy cavalry was still about 150 yards distant, and depending upon the speed of their adversaries, they would gallop sixty to eighty yards until contact was made. The general's guidelines were not as far from the regulations as might first seem, since the above recommended distances assumed the enemy was standing still. If the enemy was moving, these distances were to be halved. For example, if the enemy trotted while the friendly cavalry was trotting, the latter would only trot 100 yards.

Both of the routines just described, allowing for minor differences in distances, are identical to General Warnery's description of the classical charge as developed by the Prussian cavalry 1741–1744.[10] In practice, however, during Napoleonic times the French rarely charged at the prolonged gallop required by the official regulations. Occasionally, examples are found of the French attacking at a fast pace, but this gait appears to have been acquired only in the final moments. At Marengo, for example, when charging Austrian squadrons under Pilatti, General Kellermann broke into the gallop at only fifty paces.[11] French cavalry often utilized an even more controlled gait, charging at only a fast trot. There were even instances where they awaited the enemy's advance at the halt with presented carbines. This so surprised the enemy cavalrymen, who relied on a much more vigorous charge, that a number of accounts of French practices have fortunately come down to us.

The 1809 campaign provides a memorable example. Von Bismarck, best remembered for his several treatises on cavalry tactics, was serving with the Württemburg Cavalry, and provides a description of the French assault in his influential *Cavalry Tactics* which gives a very close look at how the French heavy cavalry fought:

> Meanwhile the cuirassier divisions had followed at a trot, and met the attack of the Austrian Reserve (i.e. Heavy) Cavalry in so brilliant a fashion that the Infantry of Lannes' corps halted

to cheer them ... The cuirassiers laid special stress on riding boot to boot, and never moved at a faster pace than a trot. One heard constantly from their ranks their officers speaking to their men 'Serrez, cuirassiers, serrez'. Just before closing with the enemy the generals and the colonels again repeated the command 'En avant, marche, Marche!' which was repeated by all the men; but the pace was never increased. This 'en avant' was only the French equivalent of the Russian 'hurrah'.[12]

Another German officer, von Pappenheim, confirms this observation. As we have seen, von Pappenheim witnessed the cuirassiers's slow advance at Aspern. The large men laden with heavy 'cuirasses' and unable to move quickly because of their weight only charged at a trot. Von Pappenheim went on to conclude that this had a greater impact than simply reducing the speed of the cavalry charge. He felt it had structural impact on French cavalry tactics. Combat was reduced to throwing heavy masses at the enemy. No longer was there any attempt at finesse and victory was now to be won by he who threw in the most men or the last reserve. Von Pappenheim sensed the cost: 'Only Napoleon, with his genius and vast resources, could afford to purchase victories at such a price'.[13]

This practice was certainly not limited only to the 1809 campaign. For example, at the Battle of Heilsberg (18 June 1806), several squadrons of the *Cuirassiers d'Espagne*, a French lancer regiment, and two regiments of Prussian horse engaged one another, the cuirassiers only advancing at a walk. Given the slow speed of the approach, it is not surprising that the opposing bodies were able to close and a real mêlée followed.[14] Yet another example was provided at Hanau when the third regiment of the *Gardes d'honneur* moved to support the *Grenadiers à cheval* which had just been pushed back. Though only able to advance at the trot by maintaining a 'fierce disposition' they were able to turn to defeat the newly victorious enemy cavalry.[15]

Certainly the charge at the trot was, in part, a response to practical necessities. The French cavalry declined sharply during the Revolutionary period with the removal of most of the nobility in this arm, the inability to provide sufficient quantities of suitable mounts, and the continual drain of human resources caused by years of continual conflict. One cavalryman writing of the period also attributed this slow method of advance to the French tendency, in the case of heavy cavalry, to place heavy men on their mounts. It was always difficult to get horses carrying heavy men to move at speed for any extended period: it became even harder if these heavy men were also wearing body armour, such as a cuirass.[16]

The military analysis that followed the Napoleonic Wars shows that most non-French military authorities felt the French use of the charge at the trot was simply the pragmatic response to the reality of bad mounts, heavy cuirasses, and poor horsemanship. The Crown Prince Hohenzollern, in his very informative *Conversations On Cavalry*, offered this comment about the 'typical' horsemanship found among Murat's cavalry: 'Not one of his [Murat's] horsemen of these masses would have been able to give horse another direction, had he meant to do so.'[17] He went on to recount the following incident which his uncle had personally observed:

My own uncle, who brought up a brigade against Murat's great attack at Liebertwolkwitz, told me that his horse ran away from him (he had just mounted a troop horse, his own having been killed). It galloped with him towards Murat's masses and passed them within ten paces. The hostile horsemen cursed at him and struck at him, but not a single one had sufficient control over his horse to approach him, and all rushed on in the direction once taken, in one wild, deep mass, without order and without stop. Hence it would seem that, although Murat started the cavalry at a trot, it became voluntarily or involuntarily a runaway at full speed. Nor did they remain closed up, as least they did not preserve order, for my uncle describes them as a wild, runaway mob.[18]

Here, this lack of control deprived the French cavalry of the fruits of victory on this occasion. Though able to ride through some runaway Russian batteries, they were soon swept away by an allied counter-charge which, despite the disadvantage of inferior numbers, succeeded because it was conducted in closed order.

This view that the French attacked exclusively at the trot, which was the accepted view for much of the nineteenth century, was not completely accurate. The following incident, provided by Captain Ganzuage, an officer in the Prussian Lancer Guard who served with Russian forces during the 1813 campaign, shows that both the charge at the gallop, as called for by official doctrine, and the charge at the trot co-existed even on the same battlefield.

On 11 October 1813, Colonel Bichalow's brigade of Cossacks, serving as the advance-guard for General Bülow's corps, had halted at Debitch. The picquets standing guard for the brigade soon became involved in a skirmish with the French positioned on the road to Eilenburg. Captain Ganzuage continues:

> As we approached some hillocks, and while very carelessly driving the French before us, a regiment of Chasseurs that had been concealed by the ground, suddenly made their appearance. Fortunately for us, they attacked us only at a trot, and in a column of squadrons, so that we easily evaded their onset of these superior numbers. The officer commanding the Cossacks had, at the beginning of the affair, left one-half of his men behind, to act as a reserve, – an arrangement that, in a little time, again brought the action to a stand; for as soon as this second line joined us, the French halted, threw out skirmishers, and, going to the right-about, retired at a trot, followed by the whole swarm of Cossacks, who, every moment expected to see their enemies get into confusion; every Cossack being firmly convinced that, as individual horsemen, he had nothing to dread from such unskillful riders. We had thus followed the French column back to the very hill where they attacked us, when we perceived another body of their cavalry advancing, at a round [sharp] trot, against our left flank; they appeared to be two squadrons, and proved, as I afterwards learned, to be the Hussars of Alsace. To meet them our commanding officer wheeled up a division and remained with the right and centre facing the Chasseurs, which had again halted and reformed. The Hussars then sounded the gallop, and two squadrons, hitherto concealed by the leading squadrons, darted out at either flank, wheeled into line, and the whole threw themselves at full gallop, without firing a single shot, in two minutes not a Cossack remained on the field.[19]

In addition to showing that the two methods of charging enemy cavalry existed side by side, this also demonstrates how effective the charge at speed could be against irregular horsemen.

The phenomenon of having an official charge doctrine and another seemingly more widely used practice would have remained an enigma to posterity had Fortuné de Brack not written his wonderful book of advice to French cavalry officers. Returning to active duty in 1830, after a fifteen-year absence from duty, de Brack found French cavalry to be in decline. Most of the troopers had never experienced real warfare and were naïvely performing their tasks according to the regulations. De Brack set out to explain the actual practices used during the recent wars.[20] In this work de Brack provides a myriad of interesting notes, ranging from a detailed description of how to interrogate prisoners to what to do with captured muskets. Nevertheless, one of the most significant passages is his extraordinarily detailed account of a French cavalry charge. This passage helps reconcile the differences of the official charge at the gallop versus the charge at the trot just examined.

Once the order to charge was given, the commanding officer was to bring the cavalry as close as possible to the enemy while preserving a 'moderate' gait, that is, the trot. This was to maintain proper alignment and order within the formation. The platoon and squadron commanders, meanwhile, coaxed back into the formation anyone who attempted to hang back by calling out their names. The *serre-files*, the NCOs and officers positioned at the rear of the second rank of troopers, on the other hand, were less subtle. They helped retain order by vigorously pushing anyone who attempted to slow down. The order to charge at speed was only to be given at the last moment, when opposing forces were approximately fifty paces apart. Now, the emphasis previously placed on order and cohesion, was suddenly and completely focused on the quickest possible 'impulsion' (the weight of the advance, i.e. weight × velocity). As the horse started its fastest gallop, the trooper bent forward in the saddle so that his head was protected by the horse's head and neck. This helped to protect him from the musket shots that by now would be coming 'thick and fast', and apparently also allowed the horse more 'spring' in its stride. A less obvious advantage was that this protected position obscured the trooper's sight, making him less aware of the dangers immediately in front of him, and presumably more willing to continue on.

The official regulations called for the sabre to be drawn before the start of the charge, even when the cavalry began from a stationary position. Experienced officers, however, knew this was a mistake. In terms of its effect on morale, the best time to order the men to draw their sabres was while the formation was moving rapidly, a few seconds prior to the expected contact.

Drawing the sabre prematurely had several disadvantages. The chance of surprise was eliminated: it instantly revealed the regiment's intent to charge and gave the enemy the longest time possible to prepare for the coming charge. The defenders no longer had any doubts about the importance of the movement about to be executed. If, on the other hand, the attacking cavalry kept their swords sheathed, the defenders had to second guess all of the preliminary movements marking the start of any advance. An even more serious defect, however, was that it denied the advancing cavalry a significant psychological edge that otherwise could be gained over the defenders. The very process of drawing the sabre, if performed at the critical moment, could intimidate the defenders and help undermine their resolve to stand and fight. The gleam of the exposed blades, all drawn in unison, as the attackers bore down in the final moments was an awesome sight, one that could affect even very brave men. Drawing the sabre also helped to buoy the attackers' morale, creating a type of temporary intoxication. According to de Brack, the trooper who drew his sabre just before using it grasped it with greater strength, more spirit, and struck the enemy with livelier force.

If there was a positive effect on morale in drawing the sabre during the last moments, there was a negative one in drawing it prior to the charge. Whatever feelings were created by pulling out the sabre was necessarily short-lived. As the moments passed, the trooper's sense of his sabre would gradually diminish, and any advantage thereby gained would be lost. Unsheathing their weapons, giving the spur to their horses, and heading into the oncoming enemy were all to be parts of a single act.

Until the charge was sounded by the trumpets, the men were to remain silent. This was absolutely necessary if the men hoped to have any chance of hearing their commanders' orders.[21] In this regard the French were merely following what had become standard cavalry practice since Frederick's time. However, as soon as the actual charge began, the men were to yell 'Avancez!' (Forward), as loudly and as much in unison as possible.

When the trumpets sounded the charge, and the transition was made from the controlled gallop to the *charge à la sauvage*, any officers previously in front of the formation allowed the first rank to catch up so that a portion of the horse became buried in the ranks.

This was identical to infantry practice throughout the entire epoch and used to achieve the same goal: an officer that continued in front of the following infantry or cavalry would strike out and be an obvious target as the opposing forces came to close range.[22] All of the officers and NCOs who had previously concentrated on maintaining order within the formation, now focused exclusively on the mêlée. The platoon and squadron commanders strove to be the first to reach the enemy's line. The *serre-files* were to work their way to the front and use their swords. A moment before the cavalry reached the enemy, the troopers were now to stand up in their stirrups, shout vigorously and then bring down the sabre that was poised above their head. This sudden movement, elevating the rider's position, once again was contrived to help confuse and intimidate the opponents.[23]

According to de Brack, this was the actual charge technique used by the light French cavalry during the Napoleonic Wars. It differs from the foreign observers' impressions in that the French attempted to charge in the final moments as they closed with the enemy.

Although the reasons for the French use of the charge at the trot may have originated out of necessity, there were at least a few notable French cavalry leaders who felt this method was actually superior to the charge at the gallop. General Lasalle, for example, when seeing the enemy approaching at the gallop, would often exclaim, 'There are lost men.' At first glance, this is a surprising view, especially coming from such a distinguished and successful cavalry leader as Lasalle. Frederick's method of the gradual charge ending in the *charge à la sauvage* appears on a psychological level the best means of bolstering the morale of the attacker while simultaneously intimidating the opponent.

However, those who advocated the charge at the trot felt that this method offered other psychological advantages. De Jomini provides us with a portion of this rationale. Firstly, the advance at the trot allowed the retention of a more cohesive formation, something of critical value in the last moments of the charge. The enemy approaching at a gallop would necessarily start to spread out and the originally tight formation start to loosen up. When this happened, the advantage would swing to the slower moving units, provided they were still in a tight formation. The second rationale offered by de Jomini was felt to be even more decisive. The men at the gallop, though initially feeling the advantage of speed and vigour, would ultimately be discomfited by their opponents moving at the trot, if these latter remained resolute to the very end.[24]

This appears to be contradictory and so needs some explanation. Lasalle and de Jomini both acknowledged that the charge at a gallop provided an initial psychological edge. The speed of the advance would make victory appear inevitable to the galloping horsemen, especially when they viewed the slower moving enemy. This is exactly what Frederick the Great counted on when he urged his cavalry to close on the enemy first with the controlled gallop, then in the very last moments with uncontrolled abandon. And usually, seeing their opponents closing in at a gallop in a relatively tight and cohesive formation, the enemy would feel themselves disadvantaged, lose their confidence, and in the final moments, turn and attempt to flee.

However, though offering this initial advantage, the charge at the gallop also contained the seeds of its own destruction. Those favouring the charge at the trot felt that if the cavalry were able to resist the initial fear of the oncoming enemy, and continue the advance, the advantage would swing away from the enemy moving at the gallop. The fast moving troopers would ultimately need somewhere to go as they neared the enemy in those final moments. One line of horses and men would never literally ride into or over the opposing line. So the galloping cavalry had three options. If the enemy were in a loose enough formation, the cavalry at the gallop could 'thread' the enemy, that is, pass through it by riding between the enemy files. This was common enough at the beginning of the eighteenth century when less emphasis was placed on close formations. However, this option ceased to be available if the enemy continued in a tight formation, the exact benefit offered by charging at the trot. There would be no gaps between the men and no intervals between the platoons or squadrons to penetrate, since the riders at the trot would be much more likely still to be moving 'knee to knee.' So, the galloping cavalry now could either pull up to avoid collision or swerve around the oncoming cavalry continuing at the trot. Du Picq provides an excellent description of this unconscious process that would occur in an instant:

A troop at the gallop sees a massed squadron coming towards it at a trot. It is surprised at first at such coolness . . . Galloping men do not reason these things out, but they know them instinctively. They understand that they have before them a moral impulse superior to theirs. They became uneasy, hesitate. Their hands instinctively turn their horses aside. There is no longer freedom in the attack at the gallop. Some go on to the end, but three fourths have already tried to avoid the shock. There is complete disorder, demoralization, flight. Then begins the pursuit at a gallop by the men who attacked at the trot.[25]

The very fact that the charge at the gallop offered a momentary boost to the morale was seen by some as a disadvantage in the long run. They argued that this did not really affect the cavalryman's willingness to fight, and thus it was artifice which could backfire. These advocates felt that if the men were really willing to fight the trot was sufficient. They did not have to divert themselves with the unchecked speed of the unrestrained gallop.[26] Lasalle would reassure his men by ordering them to: 'Go resolutely and be sure that you will never find a daredevil determined enough to come to grips with you.'[27]

Interestingly enough, after the conclusion of the Napoleonic Wars, the Baron de Jomini repudiated Frederick the Great's charge-at-speed doctrine and supported the French charge doctrine:

> The fast trot seems to me the best gait for charges in line, because everything depends in such cases upon the ensemble and good order of the movement – things which cannot be obtained in charges at a fast gallop.

Once successful however, the French heavy cavalry would immediately pursue the defeated at a flat out gallop. As du Picq later attested: 'The cuirassiers charge at a trot. This calm steadiness frightens the enemy into an about face. Then they charge at his back, at a gallop.'[28]

Regardless of whatever gait was actually used during the charge, French officers – like their compeers everywhere – had learned a few tricks through the vast experience afforded by the period's seemingly endless wars that could be used with advantage against unsuspecting enemy cavalry. If threatened by an enemy cavalry charge that was for various reasons likely to be successful, a smart commander would attempt immediately to position his command behind some not-so-easily detected obstacles, such as a ditch or sudden undulation. If the enemy cavalry force did not take the appropriate precautionary measures, such as sending out scouts or mounted skirmishers to investigate the lie of the land, his force would become disorganized as it encountered the hitherto invisible obstacles suddenly appearing. The commander was instantly to seize the moment and charge in turn. The disorganized enemy would most likely be easily over-whelmed.[29]

Another effective measure was correctly to judge if the enemy horse had begun its charge at too great a distance. If it had, it would inevitably arrive with its horses 'blown', that is, completely winded. This would force the horse to begin to slow down, and it would be less controllable. A commander who noticed that the enemy started its charge too far away was to hold back his own cavalry 'without stirring' until he noticed the telltale signs of the horses being 'blown'. At this point, he was immediately to begin his own counter-charge. If he had timed it right, his regiment would threaten contact just when the other was in a breathless condition and success was almost certain. De Brack informs us his regiment was able successfully to pull this trick off against Ponsonby's brigade at Waterloo.[30]

Even if the enemy started its charge at an appropriate distance, a similar ploy could still be used. The commander could wait till the enemy had traversed one quarter of the distance separating the two forces, before starting his counter-charge. At this distance the force counter-charging was still able to arrive at the projected point of collision at full speed, a trot or the gallop depending upon doctrine and practice. However, because this force covered three-quarters of the distance, the chances were that it was subject to slightly less disorder and arrived in a more cohesive state.[31]

During the Seven Years' War, the Prussian cavalry had mastered numerous methods of deceiving the enemy during a charge in order to derive some advantage at the critical moment. However, typically the Prussians achieved this through superior manoeuvrability and/or the use of some innovative formation, such as the echelon. They were able to outflank their opponents by swinging a squadron or two around the end of the opposing cavalry's line from behind their charging line. The French, on the other hand, appear to have relied more heavily on timing: when to start a charge versus when to hold back. This difference in tactical approach and methods was likely to be based on the equestrian capabilities typically available to each. The Prussians trained continuously in peacetime and were master horsemen. The full gamut of known tactical options was available to them. The French were mediocre horsemen, and had to rely on techniques that were based on the skill of the officers and the quality of their judgement rather than on pure horsemanship *per se*.

FRENCH CAVALRY USE OF CARBINES

During the Napoleonic Wars, French cavalry occasionally resorted to firearms when fighting a mounted opponent, rather than always attempting to defeat them with cold steel. When this did happen, the cavalry about to fire would generally come to a complete halt. The men would pull out their carbines, wait till the opposing horse was almost completely upon them, and then fire in the enemy's face. Immediately after the volley, if the enemy continued to advance and there was still an opportunity, the French cavalry would then attempt to move again to meet the enemy at the trot.

Probably the most notable instance of this tactic being successfully employed was at the Battle of Eckmühl (22 April 1809) where carabiniers in the centre of Nansouty's command halted to fire at the Austrian cavalry less than 100 yards distant. They immediately recommenced their movement after the general discharge, whereupon they and the cuirassiers next to them in the same line met the Austrians at the trot. After several minutes the Austrians, who were greatly outnumbered and threatened on both flanks, were defeated and fled precipitously back to Köfering.[32] This was not an isolated incident, occurring because of the vagaries of a particular situation or commander. The use of firearms by French cavalry to engage enemy cavalry on the battlefield can be found in most campaigns of the period. It was not limited to carabiniers, but was used by most other types of French cavalry.

At the Battle of Friedland, the cavalry attached to the Ninth Corps found itself facing a superior force after it had force marched at a 'fast trot' four leagues just to reach the battlefield. A large body of enemy cavalry started to face its direction and intended to initiate a charge as soon as it was fully deployed. Baron de la Ferrière, who commanded the Ninth Corps' cavalry, realized this force was too fatigued to attempt to struggle with the enemy in a full-scale charge. Instead, he placed his cavalry behind some slightly irregular terrain. There, his cavalry awaited the enemy with carbines presented and their swords dangling from their wrists. The resulting volley proved to be sufficiently devastating that the enemy cavalry retired before completing its charge.[33]

The use of the carbine to defeat enemy cavalry certainly was not new. It can be traced at least as far back as to the last decades of the seventeenth century when the Imperial cavalry (Hapsburgs) fought the Turks. Because of the Imperialist successes and the importance of these wars to Christendom generally, it gained momentary acceptance at the French court in the mid-1690s. However, it was largely repudiated by the defeat of the eight squadrons of the *gendarmerie* by five British squadrons at the Battle of Blenheim (13 August 1704). However, despite its seemingly complete loss of credibility after Blenheim, the use of the carbine from the saddle appears never to have been totally abandoned in French service and reappears in the time of the French Empire.

In its earliest form, the French trooper allowed his sword to hang from his right wrist while he aimed his carbine. Once the trooper fired, he would let go of the carbine, which itself was attached to his saddle, bandolier or other part of his equipage, and he would then grasp his sword while he either awaited the enemy at the halt or started off at a trot. The goal of this tactic was to inflict as many possible casualties among the first rank of the attackers. It was hoped that those in the following ranks would be checked by the falling horses and men who were hit by the small arms fire. Those advocating this technique at the turn of the eighteenth century felt this tactic maximized the chances of individual combat, something the French cavalry of the period apparently enjoyed. What is not clear is to what degree the carbine tactics of French Napoleonic cavalry differed from their eighteenth century antecedents.[34]

A very detailed and thus highly illustrative example of the French cavalry successfully using carbines against their enemy counterpart is provided by Captain Parquin in his colourful memoirs. At the battle of Eylau (8 February 1807), Parquin's regiment, the 20th *chasseur à cheval*, was deployed in line on the left of the 27th *légère* and in front of the 7th *chasseur* regiment. The rest of the story is probably best left in Parquin's own words:

About two o'clock in the afternoon an immense force of cavalry moved forward against us, but only at a walk, as the snow and the mossy soil admitted of no quicker pace. The troopers were filling the air with hussahs [hurrahs], to which some of our chasseurs responded by shouting 'au chat!' which means 'to the cat'; since *hussah* sounds to a Frenchman as if one said 'to the rat!' The joke quickly spread along the whole length of the regiment.

Colonel Castex now inquired if our carbines were loaded. On receiving an affirmative answer he gave the order 'Carbines ready!' – as in campaigning we had the practice of carrying those weapons at the hooks. He next ordered the officers to fall into place in the column and then he did so himself.

Meanwhile the huge mass of dragoons was steadily approaching us, still at a walk, Colonel Castex regarding them perfectly unmoved. Only when the Russians had approached within six paces of us did his voice ring out sharply: 'Fire!'

The command was carried out by our regiment as steadily as if on parade. The effect of this one volley was terrific – almost the entire front rank of the Russian dragoons were mowed down. But scarcely a moment did the enemy waver, for almost immediately the second line took the place of the dead and wounded and the conflict became general. Were it not for Captain Kermann's presence of mind our regiment would now be in the greatest peril, for a swarm of Cossacks rushed against our left flank so as to place us between two fires. To his own command the Captain promptly ordered: 'Squadron, to the left, wheel!' and this defeated the enemy's plan. At length the Russian cavalry column, although double ours in number, realized its total failure to cut into our ranks and was forced to turn bridle without inflicting serious damage. Nevertheless more than 100 men of the 20th Chasseurs were either killed or wounded. The Russians suffered a loss of at least 300 men for the square of the 27th infantry poured in on them a damaging fire as they were slowly falling back.[35]

This tactic of awaiting the enemy was not limited to the use of the carbine. French cavalry sometimes elected to receive a charge with pistol in hand, or the sword outstretched.[36] However, more often than not, these tactics ended in defeat. Even skilled cavalry lost the advantage of 'momentum' so that the enemy mounted on smaller horses could attack with advantage, as illustrated by the following incidents. At Sahagun, the French 7th Dragoon Regiment awaited the British 15th Hussars' attack at the halt and was overthrown. A squadron of French *chasseurs* in front of Castello Branco awaited the charge pistol in hand and were defeated by Captain White's troop of the 13th Hussars. The Prussian Brunswick Hussars were able successfully to attack a French cuirassier regiment though they had just overthrown a body of French light cavalry. Another such incident occurred in front of Napoleon on 20 April 1809.[37]

For a highly detailed description of French cavalry being defeated while waiting at the halt, we are once again indebted to General Mitchell for his translation of Captain Ganzuage's memoirs of the 1813 campaign:[38]

While we (the Don Cossacks) were yet engaged in driving back the advanced parties, a mass of cavalry, greatly exceeding us in number, advanced in haste from the town, and drew up in our front; they were found in 'column of squadrons', and as the skirmishers fell back, we soon had nothing but this heavy mass in front of us. Though the Cossacks could gain little in a contest with so large a force, it was equally evident that still less was to be risked in assailing them; so that, urged on, partly by their natural instinct, and partly by command, they pushed forward to the attack. The French advanced at a slow trot a short distance to meet us, and under the apprehension, probably, that the Russians would attempt to dash into the intervals between the squadrons, they were closed up to quarter distance. Thus formed, they bore directly to the centre of our line, which instantly spread out, the Cossacks throwing themselves on the flank and the rear of the hostile columns; and the French, finding no enemy to contend with in front, soon halted, whilst the warriors of the Don kept firing into the mass or spearing the flank files.

The French had by this time got into such complete confusion that they could undertake no evolution of any kind, and the Cossacks, on their side unable to move in compact order, never thought of dispersing by a bold onset the helpless mob they were assailing. The flank files of the French having faced outwards, and their rear files having gone to the right about, the whole party sprung their carbines, and a regular, if not very destructive, fusillade ensued, which lasted for half an hour. At the end of that time the heads of some infantry columns, accompanied by artillery, were seen advancing, and the first shots from the latter released the French from their unpleasant pre-dicament; the whole swarm of Cossacks vanishing. It was per-fectly evident that a want of skill in manoeuvring, and a total ignorance of the real value of cavalry action, had induced the French to crowd together in column. One third of their number, well and bravely led, would have driven the three regiments of Cossacks from the field with perfect ease. This action also gave proof of the utter unfitness of the Cossacks for anything like a home charge, as well as of the little that can be effected by their loose and irregular mode of fighting.[39]

Though the hope was that the carbine or pistol fire would cause sufficient casualties to corrode the other side's will to fight, the prac-tice of firing while atop a horse was fraught with many difficulties and limitations.

Like all smoothbore hand-held weapons that found their way into military applications, both pistol and carbine were relatively inaccur-ate weapons under the best of circumstances. Whatever accuracy they did possess was dramatically reduced even further by their user being on horseback, in motion or not. This meant that cavalry relying on its firearms had to advance close to the enemy cavalry at a slow pace, thus largely depriving itself of its offensive capabilities if it then chose to close to the mêlée and attempt to resolve the issue with swords.[40] The problem of accuracy was further exacerbated by the necessity of attaching the butt end of the carbine to the trooper's bandolier or part of his saddle. Frequently, the strap was fairly short and even when it was sufficiently long it was sometimes in the way, further complicating the trooper's ability to aim the weapon.[41]

Potentially there were further problems. Only the front rank of the cavalry line could ever fire its firearms, unlike infantry which could fire two and three ranks at once. This resulted in a thin fire, and once this was delivered, there could be no further firing until the engagement was decided one way or the other. The horseman could not reload until he came to a halt or a very slow walk, and this would not happen as long as the enemy continued to advance. Firing on horseback could also have an adverse effect on the squad-ron or regiment as a whole. The smoke produced from the carbine sometimes settled over the cavalry that had just fired its carbines. If the carbines were fired when the enemy was still a way off, the opposing cavalry might attempt to outmanoeuvre them while their vision was obstructed by the smoke.[42]

The horses themselves were another potential source of difficulties. Firing from the saddle demanded discipline on the part of the mounts. Unfortunately, it was not unusual for a squadron to have several skittish horses. Often, these could become unsettled as the trooper cocked his carbine. This made it more difficult to present the firelock and any sort of aiming impossible.[43] This problem tended to become increasingly serious during the course of a campaign. Horses lost through injuries, death and disease had to be replaced by 'remounts'. Very often, circumstances demanded these remounts be rushed to a regiment before the horses could be brought to the normal peacetime level of obedience and training. As a result, these remounts were often more 'gun-shy'.

Even those who advocated using carbines while mounted admitted it had its weaknesses. To be effective, the defending ranks had to maintain their order throughout. Any confusion among the ranks, and the line would break. This could be extremely difficult to achieve when the enemy was bearing down at a gallop. In this latter situation, there was a tendency for the end files to break to the rear, and these would be quickly followed by the remainder of the formation.[44]

MAMELUKES

During the Egyptian campaign (1798–1801), a number of corps were formed in French service from men from the various near eastern regions, such as *légion cophte*, *légion syrienne*, *légion maltaise*, etc. Many of these men accompanied the French army on its return to France in 1800–1802. The cavalry units thus formed were made up of excellent eastern-style riders. Ferocious fighters, on an individual basis they had control over their horses and complete mastery of their weapons. According to one observer in the French infantry, they 'could take a man's head off with one blow'. He also noted that they were able to strike down enemy infantrymen by kicking them in the groin. Since they wore very sharp stirrups, this could cause serious injuries.[45]

Captain Parquin, who served throughout much of the Napoleonic Wars with the 20th Chasseurs, recounts the impression the Mamelukes made in a military review in January 1805:

The Mamelukes dashed forward at a full gallop, making no pretense of order or alignment and halting their steeds abruptly whenever they took the impulse; it was exactly like a flight of pigeons changing from one ground to alight to another some distance away.[46]

Parquin also witnessed these same horsemen in combat later that year after the French crossed the Vistula, near Warsaw. On 24 December the Mamelukes charged a Russian battery of twelve pieces which had been bothersome to the French infantry columns as they attempted to deploy. The Russians, seeing the bright colours of the Mameluke horsemen, thought they were being attacked by Turkish horsemen and were quite chagrined. The Mamelukes pressed their attack and carried off all twelve pieces in the battery.[47]

Over the years, these various foreign cavalry units began to be formally drilled in the same way as the regular French cavalry.

CHAPTER 19

The Artillery Arm

TYPES OF SMOOTHBORE ARTILLERY

As with the other major types of weaponry in use, artillery remained relatively unchanged until the very end of the era of the smoothbore musket. Despite a series of iterative developments, artillery pieces during the Napoleonic Wars displayed the same general ballistic properties as their predecessors had during Marlborough's time. True, lighter carriages had been designed, calibres became increasingly standardized, elevation screws were adopted and several new types of projectiles were introduced. Collectively, these resulted in greater mobility, slightly more accurate firing and a modest improvement in rate of fire. Nevertheless, with the exception of the British shrapnel shell, overall the same type of projectile delivery systems remained in use, and in 1815 the performance of an individual 12-pounder firing round shot was only fractionally better than its counterpart using the same type of ammunition in 1703. Despite this fact, artillery during the Napoleonic Wars proved to be considerably more deadly than a hundred years before. However, this was attributable more to a gradual adoption of more effective doctrine and practices as well as the introduction of several new types of projectiles, than it was simply to the improvement in the ordnance.

In the early days of firearms, the great preponderance of artillery were 'guns'. These hurled a stone or iron projectile directly at the intended target. Damage was caused by the impact of the projectile against the target, and was proportional to the weight of the projectile and its velocity at impact. By the Napoleonic era, between seventy and eighty per cent of all the ammunition fired by guns in the field consisted of 'round shot', which was simply a solid iron ball. Round shot could be used against heavy targets, such as masonry, or lighter objects, such as men, horses, wagons or gun carriages, not to mention the occasional wall or gate. The heavier the round shot, the greater its striking power at long distance. Müller, for example, estimated that at 1,000 yards round shot fired from an 18-pdr. (pounder) had a velocity of 840 fps (feet per second), that from a 9-pdr., 690 fps, while a 6-pdr. ball, only 450 fps.[1]

Guns were rarely elevated more than three or four degrees and thus had a flat trajectory. Higher elevations resulted in more curved trajectories and round shot hitting the ground at a greater angle was apt to bury itself harmlessly in the ground.[2]

To achieve both a long range and maximum damage at impact, it was necessary to impart the highest possible initial muzzle velocity. This meant prolonging the time the gases acted upon the projectile within the bore. To achieve this, guns were endowed with long barrels. Guns typically had barrels that were twelve to twenty-four times the diameter of the bore.[3]

The various types of guns were differentiated by the weight of the projectile they fired. So, for example, a '4-pounder' fired a four-pound ball (round shot). Guns came in a wide variety of sizes ranging from the small and relatively ineffective one-pounder, used by the Danish horse artillery during Napoleonic times, to large 68-pounders used on ships or coastal defence.

Although a gun was able to project its charge considerably further than other types of artillery, such as a mortar or howitzer, the general consensus was that 1,200 yards was the extreme effective range for any type of ordnance in the field. Beyond this range an artilleryman could not make out the target within the naked eye, so aimed fire was impossible. There were other considerations that could reduce this range, however. During the Napoleonic Wars, the standard reference work for French artillerists was Jean-Jacques Gassendi's *Aide-mémoire à l'usage des officers d'artillerie*. While Gassendi believed that it could be productive to fire at an enemy as far as 1,000 to 1,200 metres,[4] Vergnaud felt this range could only be obtained using heavy (siege) 12-pounders and argued that the intrinsic inaccuracy of the 8- and 12-pdrs. employed in the field made it impractical to fire at further than 900 metres.[5] The effective range of the smaller calibres was even less. According to the *Manuel de l'artillerie* published in France in 1805, the effective range of a 4-pounder was only about 800 yards.[6]

The barrels of artillery pieces had traditionally been cast in either brass or iron. (Although the actual metal that was used was brass, these were invariably referred to as 'bronze' pieces, and so this practice is continued here.) Initially, brass was the metal of choice because it was easy to cast and the pieces were lighter, an important consideration for 'field pieces', as artillery destined for battlefield use was known. Iron is actually lighter than brass. However, since brass is more elastic, there was less risk of the barrel bursting and the barrel walls could be thinner than the same calibre cast in iron; thus the overall weight of the piece was significantly lightened. Iron pieces of ordnance, however, gradually were discovered to have their own, equally important advantages. In addition to being less costly, iron barrels were considerably less susceptible to wear. They were much more suitable for situations demanding either heavy charges, prolonged firing or a high rate of fire for any period of time.[7]

MORTARS

Soon after the introduction of artillery, the utility of a second type of ordnance was discovered. Sometimes, the best method of destruction was simply to lob heavy stones or pieces of metal onto the intended target. This worked best when the target was large, such as a town or castle. This application required the artillery piece to throw very heavy weights in an extremely arced trajectory. Emphasis, therefore, was on the weight of projectile and not on muzzle velocity.

This resulted in the creation of an artillery piece known as a 'mortar' which was quite different from a gun in design. Mortars tended to have large-bore calibres with extremely short barrel lengths. Since they were intended to have high parabolic trajectories, the barrel tended to be permanently elevated in a fixed position, usually around forty-five degrees. The range was adjusted by changing the amount of charge used in each case. Given its trajectory, the mortar was useful when it was necessary to fire over intervening obstacles, such as small hills, woods and houses. Mortars were used primarily in siege operations and only rarely in the open field.[8]

The effective range of most mortars was approximately 800 yards, even though medium and heavy mortars were physically able to hurl their balls much further. The maximum range of a twelve-inch mortar when elevated between forty-two to forty-five degrees was about 1,200 yards, for example. Louis de Tousard, a widely recognized artillery expert of the time, warned against the use of mortars for 'random fire', that is, firing beyond the effective range, unless the goal was simply the wanton destruction of property in a large town.[9] In contrast, mortars could achieve accurate fire within their effective range.

HOWITZERS

For several centuries, the gun and the mortar were the only types of artillery in use. However, by the early 1700s a third type of ordnance gradually gained acceptance among European armies. Occasionally, it had been found desirable to fire an explosive charge near the intended target, rather than attempt to destroy it through direct impact, such as when the line of sight to the target was blocked by a parapet or some other small obstacle. Destruction was accomplished through the force of an explosion rather than the impact of the projectile itself and a premium was placed on the amount of explosive the projectile contained, rather than its velocity. However, because the damage was inflicted through explosive force, rather than by weight, the projectile was considerably lighter than that fired from the early mortars.

A type of artillery piece known as a howitzer was designed to accomplish this method of destruction. Since a high projectile velocity at impact was no longer relevant, shorter barrels were acceptable, and typically the length of a howitzer's barrel was only four to six times its bore calibre. However, in order to throw as large an explosive shell as possible, howitzers had larger bore diameters than a gun. Quickly, it was discovered that howitzers worked most effectively when a higher, slightly curved trajectory was employed.[10]

Howitzers were slow to gain acceptance. They were only adopted by the French army in 1747–1748, for example, and then only by 'happenstance'. Victors at the Battle of Fontenoy in 1745, the French seized several howitzers from the allies and were extremely satisfied with their performance at the sieges of Bergen-op-Zoom (July to September 1747) and Maastricht (May 1748).[11]

Howitzers could fire round shot when forced by circumstances; however, they were mostly used to fire explosive shells. They enjoyed an advantage of both accuracy and range over mortars. The typical howitzer, elevated about twenty-one degrees, could accurately project common shells containing an explosive charge more than 1,400 yards, compared to about 800 for a mortar.

Unlike guns, both mortars and howitzers were referred to by the inside diameter of their barrel, such as a 'ten-inch' howitzer.

TYPES OF PROJECTILES

Although the properties and uses of round shot have already been discussed, the various other types of ammunition used by guns, howitzers and mortars require additional explanation.

Common Shells

A second type of projectile, used primarily by howitzers and mortars, consisted of a round shell filled with gunpowder, and was referred to as a 'common shell'. A lit fuse would burn down until it reached the main charge and explode. It was possible to adjust the time the shell would take to explode, and hence the range, by fitting the shell with the appropriate length of fuse. During the eighteenth century it had been discovered that it was not necessary to light the fuse before the shell was rammed down the mortar or howitzer barrel. The flash from the propellant charge would automatically light the fuse. Because of the higher stresses that operated within the barrel, this technique was found to work less effectively with guns, and this explains why common shells were limited to mortars and howitzers.[12]

Although common shells filled with a relatively small amount of gunpowder possessed only a tiny fraction of the explosive power of a modern 'high explosive' shell, they were nevertheless capable of inflicting severe casualties among those unfortunate enough to be standing where they landed.

Some artillery experts, such as the Austrian von Tielke, believed that common shells were often more useful than round shot.[13] Unlike round shot, which was harmless once it came to a standstill, the common shell continued to pose both a psychological and physical threat even after it lost all of its kinetic energy. As with cannon balls fired *à ricochet*, in the final moments the men would be terrorized as the common shell bounced around near their ranks. Even once it came to a complete stop, the sparkling fuse signified the continued presence of the danger.

Karl Röhrig, who served with the French allies at the Battle of Leipzig (16–19 October 1813), willingly attested to the effectiveness of the common shell. Within fifteen minutes, his battalion, drawn up in square, had sustained over a hundred casualties from a pounding administered by enemy guns and howitzers. Landing in the hollow space in the middle of the formation, a shell dug a crater in the ground. There was a moment of suspense as the horrified onlookers stared at the shell, its fuse still burning. Suddenly, there was a loud explosion, and though no one in Röhrig's company was injured, the battalion's second and third companies suffered heavily.[14]

Common shells could be extremely effective against cavalry. According to the Russian General Okounef, the trick, however, was to prepare the fuses and aim the common shells so that they exploded at just about the moment they entered the ranks of the cavalry troopers:

> If a shell falls into a column and bursts there, not only the losses of men are great, but the negative moral effect rendered is still more sensible. Against cavalry, the shell has the highest effect. Leaving aside the losses which it occasions, it so startles the horses that if the shock can be made to coincide with the moment when the shells hit the squadrons, the success can never be doubted.[15]

Canister

Although it was discovered early in the development of artillery that a number of projectiles could be fired at once from a single artillery piece, it remained until the eighteenth century for this capability to be utilized in a systematic fashion. The advantage was that the numerous projectiles would spread out, theoretically increasing the number of casualties that could be inflicted, while simultaneously decreasing the need for accuracy. Unfortunately, there were two practical problems. Firstly, the collection of projectiles placed pell-mell in the barrel greatly increased the wear on the inside of the barrel. Equally important, each discharge produced few casualties since the projectiles would start to spread out as soon as they left the muzzle, and would be flung over too wide an area to cause much damage to any target more than forty to fifty paces distant.

By the mid-eighteenth century, it had been discovered that these problems could be reduced by placing the collection of cast iron balls in a container of some sort. For example, two different approaches were used in the French army prior to the Seven Years' War. Thirty-six balls were secured to two pieces of wood and covered with a cloth. The whole was wrapped together using a wire or a cord. The result reminded artillerymen of a bunch of grapes and became known as a 'grapeshot'. In French service of the time this was almost exclusively used by 6- and 12-pounder guns.

French 4- and 8-pounders firing multiple projectiles during this period used a different technique. A number of musket balls were placed haphazardly into a tin canister or container. The number of the balls in the container and their arrangement was not important. The resulting projectile was known as 'case' or 'canister shot'. The advantage offered by the external casing was that damage to the barrel was reduced to normal proportions, while the durability of the casing was intended to ensure that it survived until a distance outside the gun, thus reducing the scatter of the small projectiles to manageable proportions.

At first, in many armies canister met with less success than expected. During the Seven Years' War, the French discovered to their chagrin that they consistently received more casualties at the hands of Austrian guns firing canister than they were able to inflict using the same methods. After the conclusion of the Seven Years' War a series of experiments was conducted at Strasbourg to measure scientifically the effectiveness of various types of artillery projectiles. A target having the same frontage as a squadron of cavalry, that is, about thirty-six yards wide with a height of eight feet, was set up in front of some artillery. Its distance from the firing artillery was gradually increased to determine the effects of fire at each range.

In the first experiment, a heavy artillery piece fired grapeshot at the target. This proved to be almost completely ineffective. Not only did the grapeshot scatter too widely, but the individual balls were rendered nearly harmless. They were smashed as they bounced off the inside of the barrel or as they collided with each other at the great speeds achieved in the first moments after the charge exploded. The result was that the majority of the balls in the grapeshot harmlessly 'fell to pieces' as soon as they hit the ground in the field in front of the artillery. The version of canister then in use in French service fared even worse in these trials, having an even shorter effective range. The problem was that the balls in the canister tended to fuse together. They either fell short or, if they did manage to reach the target, they possessed such diminished velocity that they lacked the penetrative power of a single ball uninfluenced by the others in the canister.

There is some evidence that the French artillery were not the only ones to suffer from the defects of this early canister design. In his instructions to his artillery officers issued in 1782, Frederick the Great emphatically cautioned against using canister against the enemy that was more than 100 paces distant. Never one to create tactical guidelines on a whim or without a great deal of thought Frederick came up with this admonition because of his perception of the efficacy of canister at various ranges based on the experience of Prussian artillery.[16] As a result of these experiments the French introduced two new canisters of wrought iron. Differing only in size, the new cartridges prevented the balls enclosed therein from being flattened or knocked to pieces.[17]

By Napoleonic times, the artillery in most armies fired canister at much longer ranges than possible during the Seven Years' War, suggesting that the original range limitations had been overcome. The British artillery manual, published in 1808, declared the canister's maximum range to be 300 yards.[18] French experts were even more optimistic. The absolute range of canister varied between 500 and 700 paces, depending upon the calibre of the artillery piece, although the effective range could be considerably less. The fifth edition of the *Manuel de l'artillerie*, published in the year XIII, for example, prescribed the following ranges for canister:[19]

Large balls		
12-pounder	400 toises	800 paces (approximately)
8-pounder	350	
4-pounder	300	
Small balls		
12-pounder	350 toises	700 paces (approximately)
8-pounder	300	
4-pounder	200	

Experienced artillerymen, however, never recommended that canister be used at these extreme ranges. Gassendi, for example, enjoined artillery officers to use canister only up to a range of 400 metres; Vergnaud, another French artillery authority of the period, believed canister could be used with effect up to 500 metres.[20]

There were two possible reasons for the discrepancy between the British and French estimates for the maximum effect range of canister. The first is a possible difference in the casing housing the bullets. In other words, did the British canister suffer from the same deficiency which had so adversely affected the performance of French canister during the Seven Years' War? The second explanation could arise out of a possible difference between British and French doctrine. Several French sources called for canister to be fired *à ricochet*. In other words, unless it had rained or the terrain was broken, the artillerymen would aim their pieces so that the contents of the canister hit the ground in front of the intended victims. Like regular round shot, these smaller bullets would skip at a high velocity and still cause grievous wounds among the unfortunates along their path. Just as the use of ricochet fire for round shot extended its effective range, so did this practice for canister. If French artillery did fire canister *à ricochet* and the British did not, this would account for the difference in the ranges that were advocated in their manuals.

One last note should be made. Although by the early 1800s the original grapeshot had long disappeared, artillerymen in the British army tended to use the terms 'canister' and 'grapeshot' synonymously. In British service, the only true 'grapeshot' was employed by the navy on its warships, and so strictly speaking the use of the term by land forces was incorrect. The same cannot be said of the French army. Here, by the outbreak of the Napoleonic Wars, the term grapeshot, at least when used by artillerymen serving with ground forces, had taken on a sightly different meaning. Grapeshot referred to any *ad hoc* collection of objects that were placed in the barrel, such as musket balls, nails, etc. This would be resorted to when the artillery was threatened and regular canister no longer was available.[21]

Cartridges

The first cartridges began to be used by artillery during the War of the Austrian Succession. Previously, artillerymen had used loose powder to charge their pieces. In the hours preceding the engagement, mounds of balls and tons of gunpowder were placed near the artillery position. Using a *lanterne* (ladle), artillerymen scooped the powder as needed and poured it down the mouth of the barrel. This was both a more time consuming and a dangerous arrangement than the cartridge system by which it would be replaced.

A controversy among artillerymen had delayed the introduction of cartridges for artillery for several decades. At the beginning of the eighteenth century, it had been commonly believed that the range of the projectile was in direct proportion to the amount of charge used. This belief effectively blocked the adoption of cartridges because artillerymen demanded loose powder, thinking that the flexibility of the charge size offered by loose powder was critical to complete control over range. In France, this controversy took the form of an ongoing debate between the master artillerists, de la Vallière and Belidor. A series of experiments was eventually conducted which demonstrated that this theory was erroneous. Beyond an optimum charge, range was purely a function of the elevation of the barrel.

The way was now cleared for the elimination of loose powder, and General de Brodarc introduced the use of *gargousses* or cartridges to the French army. This was the same officer who was responsible for the French adoption of the small but ultra-mobile 'Swedish pieces' which were assigned to individual infantry regiments.[22]

EFFECTIVENESS OF ARTILLERY

One question that was continuously debated throughout the entire period between artillery and infantry officers was which was the more effective: artillery or small arms fire. Opinion appears to have been nearly equally divided, and a consensus was never reached.

Some commentators, like Doctor Robert Jackson, to whom we are already indebted for a number of other observations, felt that artillery was typically not as effective as it was believed:

The effect of artillery is chiefly destructive where it sweeps the level surface of the plain, or where it is directed through a hollow way. In broken and irregular grounds, the noise occasions panic among the inexperienced, the actual destruction is comparatively small.[23]

Doctor Jackson's observations were based simply on his personal experience and he made no effort to substantiate this claim through any type of analytical argument. There were others, professionally involved with this issue, who did make a concerted effort through rigorous analysis to demonstrate the superiority of one arm or the other.

Von Clausewitz, writing after the conclusion of the Wars of the Empire, as the Napoleonic Wars were then known in France, maintained that artillery was a superior engine of human destruction to infantry firepower. He observed that a Prussian battery of eight 6-pounders occupied less frontage than one-third of an infantry battalion and required the use of only one-eighth the number of men. His experience was that the battery 'certainly does twice, if not three times, as much execution with its fire'.[24]

Writing roughly about the same time and using the same type of yardstick, that is, how many casualties were inflicted per unit of frontage along the battle line, General Allix came to quite a different conclusion. Like von Clausewitz, Allix began his argument by estimating the number of infantrymen which occupied the same frontage as an artillery piece. Allix observed that thirty-six infantrymen deployed along three ranks took up the same stretch of ground as a single cannon. First, he considered the case where artillery fired round shot at an enemy within musket range. He argued that each time an artillery piece fired a single shot, the infantry 'can fire at the same time 36 balls well directed'. General Allix concluded that thirty-six 'well directed' shots inflicted a great many more casualties than one well-placed cannon ball.

Allix's assessment of canister fared little better. French heavy canister at the time contained forty-one balls. However, these spread out throughout a wide cone. Mathematically, it could be demonstrated that most of the forty-one balls either hit the earth in front of the line of men or, worse yet, went harmlessly over their heads. The French general estimated that, even when the artillerist aimed low to allow richochet fire, about three-quarters of the balls were 'lost in the ground'.[25]

This type of analysis of the effectiveness of artillery fire certainly was not new. In the 1770s and 1780s von Tielke, an Austrian artillery officer, attempted to quantify the casualties that could be expected to be suffered through artillery fire. Von Tielke observed that six rounds per minute was the upper limit in practice. Although it was certainly possible for the artillerymen to fire their pieces more quickly, they rarely did so since they were unable to aim their shots, which as a result would be largely ineffective. Von Tielke's experience was that the infantry, on the other hand, could advance between 100 to 120 paces per minute without being forced to break into a run. This meant that, as the battalion advanced 200 to 250 paces, it would be exposed to between twelve to fifteen rounds for each gun in the enemy battery in front of it. Unfortunately, since the target infantry formation was in constant motion, for the fire to be effective the artillerymen would have to realign the gun after every shot, something that was impossible when firing five or six rounds per minute. This meant most of the shots would completely miss the target at a high rate of fire.[26] If the artillery was placed in front of the enemy formation, each round could not be expected to kill more than three men; in practice, its average was about one man killed for each round fired.

Unfortunately, von Tielke's analysis stopped short of estimating an average number of casualties inflicted per gun during an infantry assault. But if we accept von Tielke's analysis, then it would be safe to estimate one casualty per fire, where each gun in the battery fires two to four times per minute. A six-gun battery could be expected to inflict about twenty-four to forty-eight casualties, firing at an enemy infantry battalion as it traversed about 250 paces of ground. A greater number of casualties could be expected when the artillery succeeded in firing upon the target formation at an oblique angle. In this case, it was not uncommon for a single ball to kill or severely injure more than four or five men, depending upon the angle it entered the formation. Greater numbers of casualties could also be expected when artillery fired upon stationary targets, such as when an enemy battalion had to cross a bridge or individual companies broke off to form column. Not only would it be reasonable to expect to fire twice as many shots under these circumstances, but the accuracy would be increased because it would be unnecessary to realign the guns. Furthermore, if the battalion was ploying into column, each shot striking a deep column would inflict many more casualties than that striking a line.[27]

However, before we accept von Tielke's calculations unthinkingly, the experience of the American Civil War should be considered. After the hotly contested battle of Murfreesborough, General Rosencrans, the Union commander, declared that out of 20,000 rounds fired by Union artillery it had been estimated that this resulted in only 728 casualties.[28]

We have not yet answered the question raised by Doctor Johnson, von Clausewitz or General Allix. Which was more effective – a battery of artillery or a body of infantry occupying the same stretch of ground? The answer is anything but conclusive. As we have seen, if experienced infantry was led by competent officers it could withhold its fire until the enemy was extremely close and then fire a single volley before rushing in with lowered bayonets. A 500-man battalion delivering a volley by battalion at thirty paces might inflict 200 casualties or more upon the enemy. During the Napoleonic Wars, however, most firefights were much less disciplined, erupted at much greater ranges, and thus caused only a fraction of the casualties. In these cases artillery fire was probably more effective.

HORSE OR 'FLYING' ARTILLERY

Although the invention of horse artillery usually has been attributed to Frederick the Great, actually the Russians merit this distinction. At first this new type of artillery was commonly referred to as 'flying artillery' for the speed with which it was able to deploy; however, the name 'horse artillery' eventually took hold and this is the term that will be used through the remainder of this book.

During the early campaigns of the Seven Years' War, the Prussian cavalry, in the first stages of repulsing Russian cavalry, frequently would find itself suddenly confronted by enemy artillery seemingly appearing out of nowhere. After a number of such surprises, Frederick concluded that some elements of Russian artillery had been assigned to the Russian cavalry and were equipped so that it was able to effectively follow the latter's movements. The Prussians followed suit and an experimental body of Prussian horse artillery was created at Reichennerfdorff, near Landshut, in 1759.[29]

The Prussian horse artillery at first deceived their Austrian opponents, just as the Prussians had been deceived by the Russians, as we learn from von Tielke's account:

More than once, when we wished to be beforehand in taking of a height or a post, we have found it already occupied by Prussian troops and cannon; nor could we but suppose, that these consisted in part of infantry, as they fired at us out of 12 or 18 pounders. Afterwards, when it was too late, we have, by means of deserters, found out our mistake, and that we had been deceived by a few light cavalry.[30]

The newly introduced Prussian artillery was instantly as successful as the Russians had been, and it was almost immediately accepted as a permanent feature of the Prussian army.

To achieve the speed and manoeuvrability needed to allow the artillery to keep up with the cavalry they were to accompany, the carriages were of lighter construction than their traditional counterpart. In the case of large guns, the horse artillery would fire hollow round shot, thus reducing the weight of the caissons so that they could move faster. The artillerymen rode on their own horses, or, in the worst case, on the artillery pieces so that they could keep up with the faster movement. The horses were always harnessed to the pieces during movement. So, for example, crossing rough terrain or during inclement weather, the artillerymen would dismount and assist the beasts to draw the artillery across the countryside.[31]

Try as he might, Frederick was unable to keep the Prussian 'innovation' a total secret. After the conclusion of the Seven Years' War, the Austrians gradually managed to decode many of the Prussian 'secret' tactics, such as the cavalry column of attack. In 1783, they also experimented with horse artillery during some manoeuvres near Prague. Unfortunately, the Austrians never really appreciated horse artillery's need for extreme mobility and so they settled for a compromise between foot artillery and what was actually required. Instead of mounting the artillerymen each on their own horses, as the Russians and Prussians before them, their artillerymen rode on converted hunting carriages that were known as *wurst* wagons. The artillerymen sat on the stuffed covers, their legs dangling on either side, much like a child on a 'hobby horse'.

The French were more or less aware of these developments and during the decade before the French Revolution a protracted debate regarding the pros and cons of adopting horse artillery continued unabated. Its advocates were unsuccessful in introducing the new type of artillery into French service until 1791, when Duportail, the minister of war, directed the commanding officer of the Metz Division to form two companies of horse artillery. The National Assembly gave its stamp of approval on 11 January 1792. Every effort was made to choose suitable men and officers for this venture. As a result, the newly formed corps within a few weeks demonstrated that it was more than able to keep up with the light troops it was designed to support, thus silencing the sceptics who had long opposed the adoption of horse artillery.[32]

This modest experiment proved extremely successful and, in April 1792, Duportail's successor, de Narbonne, further increased the French horse artillery establishment to nine companies.[33] Intrigued by the possibilities offered by this innovation, de Narbonne approached the whole affair systematically and with the greatest determination. A committee with representatives from the infantry, cavalry and artillery arms, as well as some of the more distinguished field officers and engineers, was convened. The committee was charged with formulating the best method of raising and training the newly raised horse artillery, and settling the details of their equipment and armament.

The committee attacked the issues conscientiously and displayed rare far-sightedness. Its policies laid the basis for the superiority that the French would enjoy in this area throughout the entire period. Fortunately for the French army, the committee quickly recognized that there was a desperate need for fast moving artillery to rapidly take its place at critical positions in order to provide the needed support for the masses of inexperienced troops then making up most of the French army. The true advantage of horse artillery was in its ability to manoeuvre unencumbered. To this end, every artilleryman was to be mounted on his own horse. This not only allowed the battery to move more quickly and over rougher terrain, but also minimized the inconveniences experienced whenever individual horses were killed or disabled. It was also essential that the horses supplied to the horse artillery were of a better quality than those which had been supplied to the foot artillery.

When it came to the size and power of the ordnance to be used, the committee had to balance the mobility of the smaller pieces against the striking power permitted by the medium and heavies. Given these choices, it was decided to lean towards striking power. Each battery was to have six artillery pieces. Wherever possible the horse artillery was to have 8- and 12-pounder guns with one or two six-inch howitzers, while the ammunition was carried on light caissons.

One of the toughest questions was how to raise these new horse artillery batteries without proportionally weakening the regular artillery, which at this time faced its own set of difficulties. The solution that was settled upon was that only two experienced artillerymen would be assigned to each gun. The remainder of the men would be taken from the infantry forces, especially from the light troops. There was some discussion about training the artillerymen in cavalry manoeuvres so they could more effectively interact with elements of that arm. This motion was defeated, and it was decided only to train the artilleryman in how to mount and dismount his horse quickly. It was left to the artillerymen's own judgement as to how to best follow cavalry.[34]

The French horse artillery was quick to cover itself in glory. The victory at Luçon, where French forces commanded by General Tuncq inflicted 6,000 to 7,000 casualties on the Royalist army under General Charette, was largely attributable to this fast moving artillery.[35] Because of these successes, the French horse artillery was increased to twenty companies in February 1793 and again to thirty later in the summer. Finally, on 7 February 1794, horse artillery obtained its own separate organization. This expansionist trend continued in the Napoleonic era and by the height of the Napoleonic Wars this arm had been expanded to a full nine regiments, each of six companies.[36]

SPHERICAL CASE OR 'SHRAPNEL'

Spherical case had been invented by Henry Shrapnel in 1784. It differed from common shell in two important ways. It had a thinner iron shell and the hollow centre was filled with musket balls mixed with gunpowder. Like common shell, a fuse ran between the outside of the shell to the gunpowder. It was designed to explode over the heads of the enemy troops sending a lethal dose of musket balls among their ranks. Artillerists could predetermine range by adjusting the size of the fuse.

Unfortunately for the British artillery, Shrapnel's original design was flawed. Friction between the bullets and the gunpowder frequently caused the shells to explode prematurely, resulting in gross inaccuracy and sometimes even casualties among the artillerymen. Undaunted, Shrapnel redesigned his invention, and an improved version was finally adopted by British artillery in the field in 1804.[37] The new form of ammunition was immediately popular among British artillerymen and was used with success through the Peninsular War and the Hundred Days campaign.[38]

Overall, shrapnel proved to be much more effective than canister.[39] The author of the *Madras Gunner* claimed that the

> comparative destruction with that of a round shot will be, generally, as the number of shot within the shells to one; that is to say, a 3-pounder, twenty-two to one in its favor, a 6-pounder, fifty to one, etc, etc. in which calculation I have not enumerated any effect from the splinters of the shell.

This was certainly an overestimation of the effectiveness of shrapnel. The difference in performance was at least partially attributable to the differences in ballistic properties of the two types of projectiles.

In the instance of case shot (canister), the contents of the canister would start to disperse at an early stage during its trajectory. How soon this would begin to occur depended upon the durability of the external casing. Typically, the disintegration of the canister occurred at about 100 yards beyond the muzzle. Once this outer shell fell apart, the individual smaller balls with their reduced mass started to slow down rapidly because of wind resistance. It was impossible to fire the canister's bullets more than 700–800 yards with any effect, while round shot in most cases could be fired effectively to at least 1,200 paces and could still cause injury at 2,000. These performance characteristics had several practical ramifications. Given these restrictions on range, it was much easier to use canister on defence, than while on the offence. Moreover, the most effective use of canister occurred once the enemy had advanced to within the range of small arms fire, thus increasing the artillery's vulnerability.

The use of shrapnel obviated many of these problems. The bullets within the shrapnel shell were enclosed within heavy casing. This shell, with its collective mass, was much less affected by wind resistance than the individual canister bullets. Consequently, shrapnel had roughly the same range as ordinary round shot. The author of the *Madras Gunner* pointed out that if the shell exploded in mid-air, the bullets and the shell fragments, even though they were blown away from the shell's position, at the same time continued their forward motion with the same velocity as the shell prior to exploding. The fragments 'completed the shell's tract or curve'. This same authority tells us he had observed the fragments and bullets travel as much as 400 yards beyond where the shell exploded.

It was these considerations which caused British advocates of shrapnel to liken the use of shrapnel to canister which could be fired 'to any distance within the range of the piece'. The casualties inflicted by shrapnel, even at the most extreme range, tended to be comparable to canister at medium range. This meant that shrapnel could be used offensively, and not just as a response to enemy activity. A concomitant advantage was that it was no longer as necessary to thrust the artillery into the thick of the action, exposing it to musket fire and opportunistic cavalry charges.

There were also a number of other advantages. Like canister, shrapnel did not require the same type of accuracy as round shot. As a result, it could be fired more quickly. Round shot caused damage through impact, so it had to hit its victim directly, and intervening irregular terrain, houses, fallow fields, etc. acted as obstacles, minimizing or even negating its effect. Shrapnel inflicted its damage through the explosion: it could be fired over these obstacles so that it exploded in mid-air or as it bounded along the ground beyond.[40]

NATIONAL VARIATIONS

At the beginning of the eighteenth century, there had been a tremendous variety in the size of guns used in the field. De Vallière and Gribeauval, though differing in details, began the arduous task of standardizing the types of ordnance used in their respective armies. De Vallière's system essentially emphasized power and range, while Gribeauval prioritised mobility. De Vallière's guns were longer and possessed thicker barrels. The result was that Gribeauval's version of the 4-pounder weighing only 290 kilograms was forty per cent lighter than its equivalent in de Vallière's system. French authorities oscillated between the virtues of the two artillery systems, but finally went with the Gribeauval system in 1774.[41]

Despite the fact that there was considerably less variation in artillery by the start of the French Revolutionary Wars, this certainly did not mean the ordnance or the approach was identical in all cases.

For example, in an attempt to gain greater mobility, the Austrian guns were endowed with slightly shorter barrel lengths than their French equivalents. In Austrian service, the length of the barrel was sixteen times the calibre of the bore, rather than the eighteen found among French ordnance. The Austrian gunners, as a consequence, were required to use slightly less explosive powder for each charge – about a quarter the weight of a bullet, instead of the one-third rule followed by French artillerists.

Calibre	Weight of Piece	Weight of Powder
Austrian		
6-pounder	700 lbs.	1½lb.
12-pounder	1500 lbs.	3 lbs.
French		
6-pounder	850–900 lbs.	2¼lbs.
12-pounder	1750–1800 lbs.	4 lbs.

Writing after the conclusion of the Napoleonic Wars, a French ordnance officer pointed out that this difference in the propulsion charge was anything but trivial. A series of trials comparing the accuracy of differing calibres of ordnance with varying charges, demonstrated that the larger pieces using optimal-sized charges (equivalent to about one-third of the weight of the projectile) were more accurate at longer ranges. This French officer's analysis provides the scientific basis for Scharnhorst's empirical observation, made during the height of these wars, that two French 8-pounders were as effective as three Austrian pieces of the same calibre, two French 12-pounders were equivalent to three Austrian 12-pounders or five Austrian 6-pounders.[42] Many artillery officers, both British and French, felt the French artillery also possessed a similar advantage over their British counterpart.

The British army entered the Revolutionary Wars equipped with an assortment of 3-, 6-, 9-, and 12-pounder guns as well as a miscellany of howitzers. Of these the light 6 pdr. was the most highly regarded. Not only did the British suffer from inferior numbers of artillery pieces, but initially these were inferior to their French equivalents in performance.[43] In siege operations at the beginning of the Peninsular War, for example, British artillery had difficulty keeping up a prolonged fire against a well fortified target. At this point, British guns and howitzers were 'bronze'. If they fired more than 120 rounds during a twenty-four-hour period, the brass would soften and the barrels begin to droop. On the other hand, not only could iron guns be fired three times as much during the same period without any deleterious effect on the barrels, but they were also able to accommodate larger charges. By 1811, however, the British had been able to rectify the problem, by completely switching over to iron guns.[44]

A more pressing problem was encountered during hard fought engagements in the field. The British more often than not found themselves out-gunned: much of their artillery consisted of 6-pounder guns. Generally placing greater emphasis on 'weight of shot', the French tended to equip their artillery with heavier ordnance, such as 8- and 12-pounders. There were two ramifications. Not only did heavier artillery possess greater striking power, more readily punching its way through obstacles such as earthworks, stone walls, etc., but also it had greater range. Müller estimated that a 12-pounder was twice as effective as a 6-pounder, which, in turn, was 50% more effective than a 3-pounder.[45]

Not all artillery officers felt that smaller ordnance was hopelessly out-classed by their larger brethren. Though larger pieces could fire further and provide greater punch, other factors were also relevant when the critical action occurred, that is, when the opposing forces were within 500 toises (roughly 1,000 paces) of one another. At this distance, the enemy was within effective range of most ordnance found on the field. Moreover, in these cases the target was almost always cavalry and infantry. Most of the projectile's kinetic energy was superfluous for the task at hand: the destruction of horseflesh and human matter. These officers argued that in the typical combat zone, defined as the distance within which most of the decisive manoeuvring occurred, a higher rate of accurate fire was much more important than weight of shot or absolute range. Here, smaller pieces could enjoy an approximately 3 to 2 advantage in the effect they would have on enemy troops. Considering all these factors, experienced artillerymen felt that five 6-pounders, four 8-pounders and three 12-pounders were able to produce the same effect when firing within 1,000 paces.

The exception to this was when artillery was forced to fire canister. Maximum effective range was as important a factor as rate of fire and heavier artillery thus had a distinct advantage.[46] In any case, determined to address any shortcomings, Wellington saw to it that the British artillery was equipped with heavier ordnance for the start of the 1815 campaign.[47]

CHAPTER 20

Artillery Tactics

Despite the technological and tactical advances in the use of artillery, and the increasing use of large massed batteries capable of unprecedented destruction, most military authorities during the period under consideration still considered artillery, like cavalry, to be a supplemental arm to the infantry which was to bear the main brunt of the battle. Cavalry could not be counted upon to break well-led infantry in a defensible position. Artillery, although able to break enemy infantry when sufficiently massed or carefully orchestrated to achieve converging fire, was unable to exploit its own success. Echoing the informed sentiment of the time, General Allix would write in *Spectateur Militaire* during the 1820s: 'the infantry is the real force of the army and decides the success of battles.'

However, when handled adeptly, artillery was recognized as an invaluable tool, capable of serving in a number of vital roles during a set-piece engagement. At close range, artillery was generally unable to inflict a greater number of casualties than competent and well-led infantry occupying the same frontage. Efficient use of this arm, therefore, demanded that it be directed at targets beyond the range of musket fire, or if at close range, against targets that were proof against small arms fire. The most obvious example of the latter was when the enemy ensconced himself in some small but well-defended position, such as a town, redoubt, flèche, château, etc.[1] Artillery could also be extremely effective whenever the enemy was forced to concentrate its forces into a tiny area, as was usually necessary before crossing a river at a bridge or a ford, or when troops were forced to pass through a defile, that is, a narrow passage through hills or woods.[2] Artillery was, of course, also useful on the open field, where once again dense columns were especially vulnerable. Prior to the start of the battle, artillery could be used against enemy 'columns of route' (i.e., columns used to manoeuvre through the countryside) to force them to deploy while still at great range. In addition to forcing the enemy to show the extent of its forces, it deprived the enemy of its initiative and gave friendly forces additional time for last minute manoeuvring. Similarly, once the action began, artillery could be used to thwart the enemy from indiscriminately attacking in closed columns. The enemy commander would be disinclined to throw masses of troops against a large body of concentrated artillery and would be forced to resort to thin linear formations instead.

Given its extended range, artillery was also extremely useful as a preliminary measure, softening up the enemy formations while the two opposing forces were still some distance apart. The enemy, forced to wait in the open, would gradually sustain casualties and be weakened, making it more vulnerable to the true attack delivered later either by the infantry or cavalry arm. Infantry in closed columns or hollow or closed squares were particularly vulnerable to this type of preliminary measure. If properly positioned and led, artillery could continue to lend its assistance during the actual assault. Placed on a hill above or on a flank, it would continue firing until the final moments, thereby increasing the chances of a successful conclusion to the assault. And, should the attack prove successful, given its range, artillery could continue to inflict casualties and disorder the enemy formations long after the latter escaped beyond musket range. This was useful when attempting to unsettle any rear guard which might still remain. Finally, artillery could be used to eliminate or at least neutralize the enemy's artillery. This role became increasingly widespread during Napoleonic times.[3]

Armies of the period tended to utilize a wide variety of artillery. Not only were they equipped with a mixture of guns, howitzers and mortars, but each of these came in an assortment of sizes. The gun especially was subject to variation. Experience had taught that different sized guns, that is, different calibres, were best suited for particular situations. At some point during the campaign an army would find its operations blocked by a fortress, a walled town or some other variety of permanent fortification. The quick and efficient destruction of this type of obstacle required large calibre guns, such as the 24-pounder. Although 12-pounders possessed the required range and were capable of dismounting the defending guns along the ramparts, they did not have sufficient striking power easily to punch their way through the thick walls and embankments. Prior to the Napoleonic Wars, armies frequently had been equipped with 16-pounders to accomplish this task, but these had proved inadequate. Napoleonic armies, as a result, often had one or two batteries of twenty-four pounders to accommodate any exigency that might arise. These field versions of the 24-pounders had shorter barrels than those used in regular siege warfare, and fired reduced charges, typically less than one-third the weight of the round shot being fired.

However, the great majority of an army's artillery pieces were true 'field pieces', whose smaller weight allowed them more readily to follow all of the army's movements. Here, light material and construction and ease of movement were the important factors. By Napoleonic times, field pieces were typically 6-, 8-, and 12-pound calibre guns, although there were still some 3-, 4- and 9-pounders in use. The 12-pounders though less mobile, were very useful in destroying bridges or breaking down field fortifications encountered on the battlefield from time to time, such as redoubts and flèches. This was no mean contribution, since the failure to destroy such obstacles could delay an army's progress by one or two days and determine the success or failure of an operation or, under extraordinary circumstances, an entire campaign. These 12-pounders, which were lighter and had shorter barrel lengths than the 12-pounders mounted on permanent fortifications, were equally suited to the defence of field works. The smaller calibres such as the 3-, 4-, 6-, 8- and 9-pounders though lacking in this type of brute force, were enough for the purpose at hand: the destruction of soft targets, such as the men and horses in the opponents' army in front of them.[4]

Not everyone approved of the heavier calibres in the field. A number of senior French artillery officers, for example, felt that even 12-pounders needlessly encumbered the army as it struggled to traverse almost every conceivable variety of terrain in daily operations. In the mid-1790s, Generals Kléber, Desaix and Moreau sought to eliminate this calibre from their respective artillery parks. General Allix, the chief of staff of the artillery during Years II and III in fact had proscribed the use of the 12-pounder in the field.

General Lespinasse, commander-in-chief of artillery under Napoleon during the latter's first campaigns, espoused the opposite point of view. In his *Essai sur l'organisation de l'artillerie*, Lespinasse noted that, in order for artillery to achieve decisive results, not only was it necessary to amass large batteries, but it was also vital to include at least a few of the larger calibres because:

> the soldier who hearing the boom of these thunderbolts on the flanks of the army, is truly reassured, and who, confident in his bayonet, as in the general in command, he burns to melt on the enemy, [the latter] . . . embarrassed by the small cannons, can only oppose him the fire of exercise.

Even General Allix, who originally opposed the inclusion of these heavier artillery pieces in the field, later had to admit that they occasionally came in handy. Looking back after the conclusion of the Napoleonic Wars, Allix admitted that at least on one occasion five 16-pounders, judiciously placed on either flank of the army of the Pyrénées-Occidentales, crushed the Spanish columns opposite them and were responsible for a French victory.[5]

Reliance upon such heavy guns proved to be a momentary aberration, and until 1813 the French continued to use normal-sized field pieces. The disaster of the Russian campaign combined with the defeats at Katzbach, Dennewitz and Culm in the following year (1813) resulted in the loss of over 1,600 artillery pieces. Hard pressed to replace these, Napoleon authorized the introduction of 16-pounders as an unavoidable expedient.[6]

THE USE OF DIFFERENT TYPES OF AMMUNITION

Each type of ordnance and ammunition tended to be used in a unique application. The general practice for the guns in an artillery battery was to fire round shot (that is 'cannon balls') as long as the enemy remained at the long or medium ranges, and then, if required by circumstances, to switch over to canister at closer range. Because round shot required a flat trajectory, it could not be fired over obstacles of any height, including friendly troops. By placing a battery on some sort of elevation, such as a hill, it was physically possible to fire over friendly troops; however, this was rarely done, since the troops were generally found to react adversely to the shot and shells flying over them. Artillery officers of the day distinguished between four different methods of firing round shot: point blank, direct (*à plein fouet*), ricochet (*à ricochet*), and at random.

Both point blank and direct fire were intended as accurate fire where the round shot was aimed directly at the intended target. In modern parlance, point blank fire tends to mean simply firing at extremely short range, for example, when the enemy had approached to within twenty to eighty paces of the artillery. In fact, point blank fire had a very precise technical meaning keyed to the projectile's trajectory. The limit of point blank fire extended considerably beyond what is now usually associated with the term, its limit being about 300–400 paces for many calibres of artillery.

Like a musket ball, the trajectory of the round shot was a parabola. After leaving the barrel, the round shot was forced above the line of sight, this latter being a straight line connecting the artillery piece and the target. The point where the round shot cut above the line of fire was known as the 'first point blank primitive'. Typically, this was immediately in front of the artillery piece. Pulled down by gravity, the cannon ball would soon cross back under the line of sight. This point was referred to as the 'second point blank primitive'. The term 'point blank' had a very different meaning among the British. According to General Lallemand:

> they suppose the piece to be mounted on its wheels and placed upon a horizontal plane, the bore of the piece is also horizontal; if it is fired in this position, the point blank distance is that between the muzzle of the gun and point where the trajectory of the projectile crosses the horizontal place on which the wheels rest.[7]

For a 8-pounder Gribeauval gun with a 2¼ lb. charge, the second point blank primitive was at 384 yards, while for a 4-pounder with a 1½ lb. charge, this distance was 342 yards.[8] Of course, in calculating the ranges of these two 'primitives', it was assumed that the artillery piece's barrel was perfectly horizontal. The formal definition of point blank fire, the one used daily by every artilleryman, was all fire directed at targets between the first and second point blank primitives.

Direct fire referred to any aimed fire where the target was beyond the second point blank primitive but still within the effective range of the piece. However since the target was beyond the second point blank primitive (where it came down across the line of sight), it became necessary to elevate the artillery piece's barrel several degrees to obtain the needed range. This was the functional difference between point blank fire and direct fire. In point blank fire there was no need to calculate the required elevations; the barrel could simply be kept horizontal. In direct fire, however, the artillery officers had first to estimate the ranges of the target and then calculate the elevations of the barrel needed to send the ball the required distance.

Ricochet fire, that is, firing à ricochet, referred to the practice of aiming short so that the round shot would skip once or more along the ground in front of the target. Occasionally, accuracy was not an issue when the artillery was required to fire at extreme ranges, as would occur when bombarding a large area such as a town or fortification. This was known as 'random fire', and was rarely employed on the battlefield.[9]

Up to the French Revolutionary Wars, almost all round shot was fired using either point blank or direct fire. However, by the Napoleonic Wars the effectiveness of ricochet firing, especially at longer ranges, had become widely known. Nevertheless, direct fire continued to be used at intermediate ranges and whenever accuracy was paramount, such as in counter-battery fire or where individual targets such as a house or some other obstacle had to be destroyed.[10]

Regardless of the technique used, officers were cautioned against firing prematurely. All too often, as soon as the enemy became visible, long before they had entered within effective range, officers from nearby infantry would rush over and implore the artillery officers to begin firing as quickly as possible. To succumb to these pleas invariably led to a waste of ammunition and a lack of ammunition when it was truly needed. Von Tielke assures us that: 'Out of a great number of shots you may perhaps happen to kill a horse; but that will but ill repay for waste of powder and ball.'[11] Despite this general injunction, there were two cases where it was permissible to fire beyond the effective range of their pieces. Occasionally, a commander would purposely order a premature artillery fire when there were many inexperienced or 'ill disciplined' troops within his command. The sound of the salvoes of the friendly artillery generally buoyed the troops' morale. This was a 'double-edged sword', however, since firing artillery without visible effect invariably had the unfortunate effect of rendering the enemy 'more audacious'.[12] It was also permissible to fire at these long ranges when it was necessary to deceive the enemy of one's overall strategy.

When facing an enemy attack, the general consensus was that artillery officers were to avoid salvoes, where all the artillery pieces in the battery fired in unison. Two reasons were cited. It was important to ensure continuity of fire so that the battery was never denuded of its fire. It was also important to give no opportunity to the enemy soldiers to relax between firing, such as invariably occurred when firing salvoes (a minimum of about fifteen seconds). However, there were two schools of thought among artillery officers as to what to do in lieu of salvoes. Gassendi, who was effectively the official voice of the French artillery, insisted that guns within the battery should fire individually, that is, in no particular order or orchestrated rhythm. Frederick the Great, who had also devoted much attention to the development of more effective artillery practices, in his instructions to artillery officers (10 May 1782) opined that independent fire was unable sufficiently to disorder or psychologically threaten the men being fired upon, and should be avoided. In its stead, he recommended 'odd and even' firing, where every second gun along the battery fired at the same time, in a sense creating twice as many demi-salvoes.[13]

As long as the enemy remained at long range, the artillerymen were to fire with deliberation, but were to increase their speed as the enemy approached. It was always important for the artillery fire to be accurate, however. Badly placed round shot which sailed harmlessly over the enemy heads seemed to add to the latter's confidence.[14] Frequently, infantry assaults against artillery were preceded by clouds of skirmishers. In these cases, the artillery was to ignore the skirmishers and let their own infantry supports handle the latter.[15]

Unlike the common foot soldier, artillerymen generally were readily able to retain their composure while firing. According to Ardant du Picq:

Even at close range, in battle, the cannon can fire well. The gunner, protected in part by his piece, has an instant of coolness, in which to lay accurately. That his pulse is racing does not derange his line of sight, if he has will power. The eye trembles little, and once the piece is laid, remains so until fired.[16]

By the Napoleonic period, it was recognized that, when faced with an enemy attack, the best method was to aim just a little in front of the advancing troops. Firing at the centre or the rear of the column only made the attackers quicken their march, lessening the number of rounds that could be let off before the firing had to be interrupted while the gunners realigned their pieces to adjust for the diminishing range. Firing in front of the advancing troops, on the other hand, was just as effective as firing directly into the formation, since the round shot would bound into the formation anyway. Seeing the balls landing in front of them, the troops became intimidated and reflexively began to slow down, increasing the amount of time the artillery had to fire uninterrupted. These same considerations applied when firing canister at close range. Like round shot, if the ground was dry and hard, canister balls also ricocheted and it was useful to fire in front of the enemy formation as it advanced.[17]

When firing at retreating infantry, the artillery were to fire *over* the fleeing enemy. The rationale for this has been provided by the Austrian artillery authority von Tielke:

Their terror and confusion will increase, their flight will be slower, they will disperse more, and you will have an opportunity to take a greater number of more prisoners.[18]

If the enemy persisted in advancing the artillery would eventually switch to canister. The transition from round shot to canister was not simply a function of the range, but also the type of target being fired upon. We learn from General Okounef that experienced artillerymen were more likely to continue longer to fire round shot at dense infantry columns than they would for infantry in line or cavalry.

Round shot was most effective when directed at dense formations. Human flesh and blood had little impact on the course of a 4 to 12 pound iron spheroid travelling at little more than 2,000 feet per second. A cannon ball possessed sufficient kinetic energy to pass through dozens of men, if they were all unfortunate enough to find themselves along the same path of destruction. This meant that the greater the depth of the attacking formation, the more casualties were caused by the round shot. There were many instances of entire files of men being destroyed by a single cannon ball. Canister, on the other hand, lacked this penetrating capability, and rarely inflicted casualties beyond the first rank it struck. The men in the rear ranks did not fear canister the same way as they did round shot, and they would continue to urge the column forward, despite the punishment taken by the front ranks. This was another reason why the bravest and most experienced men were grouped together in senior companies. The battalion commander determined to take an enemy position would usually form the column so that the senior companies were in the first tier. This was partially so that they would have the best chances of braving the canister that frequently punctuated the closing moments of the assault.

Another consideration was that canister was not the most appropriate weapon against narrow formations. The numerous balls in the canister were enclosed in a tin cartridge, to ensure that they did not start to disperse into an ever-enlarging cone until beyond the artillery piece's barrel. Despite this precaution, the projectiles spread out over a wide area even at a range of 100 paces. This meant that most of the thirty-six bullets or so in the case would go off above, below, or on either side of the target formation. Obviously, the wider the formation or the greater the height of the target, the more bullets would be likely to score a hit. An extended line was a much better target for canister than a narrow column. Cavalry were more vulnerable to canister on both accounts. Cavalrymen atop their steeds provided a target almost twice as high as an infantryman and thus likely to take almost twice as many hits. Furthermore, cavalry, especially that of the Allies, tended to attack in line formation.[19]

When artillery was used to support infantry it was placed either on the flanks of the infantry or along the line in intervals between individual formations. The traditional practice had been to place artillery on either side of an infantry body to produce a cross fire; however, this ceased to be practicable if the infantry was sufficiently wide. Unlike earlier times where the artillery was placed relatively near the line, by Napoleonic times batteries were often pushed to more advanced positions, between 60 to 150 metres in front of their supporting formations. These more advanced positions minimized or eliminated casualties among the supporting formations should a caisson explode. This trend was also, however, partly a response to the ever-increasing presence of friendly skirmishers. Artillery along an infantry line would have to be silenced as soon as the friendly skirmishers were sent out or risk firing on their own troops. Artillery in an advanced position had a much easier time supporting the skirmishers by continuing to fire on their common enemy. Of course, the artillery could not be placed too far in front. It always had to be close enough that the infantry could come to their timely support if attacked.[20]

Regardless of where the batteries were placed relative to the neighbouring infantry, the artillery officers were enjoined to avoid needlessly dispensing their guns. Any good artillery officer recognized that the true effect of artillery was in its ability to demoralize the enemy at a critical moment, rather than physically to eliminate the opposing force. This was aptly put by a military writer in the 1790s:

> The more artillery is dispersed, the more scattered becomes its fire, and the less terrifying and decisive its effect. It is not the number of slain, which decides the victory, or dispirits the combatants. The troops know full well, that some must fall, and they have neither time nor inclination to count them. In order to strike terror into the enemy, and put him to flight, something uncommon must be effected; whole platoons and ranks must be swept at once. This terrifies the troops; which ever way they look, death stares them full in the face, and it becomes a very arduous task for the officers to keep the men steady and in order.

The same writer observed that 3,000 losses to artillery dispersed along the entire length of the enemy army would cause far less demoralization than the same number of casualties inflicted on two or three brigades. If the artillery fire was dispersed, the casualties on any portion of the line were minimized; the officers were able to redress the line and fill vacant files with men from the rear ranks. On the other hand, when the artillery fire was sufficiently concentrated, the sheer number of casualties made this task extremely difficult, if not impossible. The casualties would occasion openings in the ranks which could be exploited by a sudden and determined counter-attack. Sensing the mounting disorder and becoming terrified, the men would become disordered and the advance would slow down or come to a halt.[21]

RICOCHET FIRING

In ricochet firing, or to use the technical term of the time, firing *à ricochet*, the projectile is purposely made to hit some intermediary object, such as the ground or a parapet, before continuing on towards the intended target. The first known reference to ricochet firing appeared in 1672 in a treatise authored by the Venetian engineer, Thomas Meretti. The great French fortification engineer Vauban appears to have first experimented with ricochet fire at the siege of Ath in 1697. However, at this early stage the practice was used exclusively against enemy artillery behind defensive fortifications. Up to this point, the besieger's batteries had no choice but to engage in the laborious process of trying to destroy the defender's guns by aiming through the embrasures along the enemy fortifications or through those openings that would inevitably appear as the merlins became increasingly damaged. Vauban instead decided to devise a way of destroying the enemy's artillery *en rouage*, that is, through the destruction of the wheels and carriage. To accomplish this the artillery battery was positioned perpendicularly to the pieces to be eliminated. The friendly artillery was given small charges and sited so that the round shot would graze over the enemy parapet. Travelling at a relatively low velocity, the balls would bound, i.e. ricochet into the *terrepleine* (space) immediately beyond the parapet. Since the enemy artillery was facing sideways, they offered an excellent target and almost every ball would count, as it bounced off the walls and earthen ramparts in this confined space.[22]

As Vauban's success at Ath became widely known, ricochet firing was quickly adopted by military engineers throughout western Europe. However, a considerable time would elapse before this technique would be used on the open field. Faced with the task of issuing guidelines for his artillery officers in the 1780s, Frederick the Great enjoined his subordinates to rely only upon direct fire (*à plein fouet*). The artillerists were cautioned against trying to hit the enemy after the round shot had hit the ground. So foreign was this practice to Frederick and the Prussians that he referred to it as 'curved' fire, not recognizing it to be a variant of the by now traditional use of ricochet fire to disable the defenders' guns during a siege.[23] Writing at about the same time, von Tielke, for example, admitted that despite his extensive battlefield experience, he had never witnessed ricochet fire *purposely* used against enemy troops in the field.

The reason for this seventy-year delay was that the version of ricochet fire effective against artillery within fortifications differed considerably from that which would be used later on the battlefield. Ricochet fire used in a siege required that the projectile strike the parapet or the ground beyond at a relatively obtuse angle. To achieve this, the barrels of the guns were elevated between eight to fifteen degrees and loaded with reduced charges to achieve the needed trajectory. However, this same type of trajectory was not very useful on the battlefield. If the ground was soft, the balls would bury themselves harmlessly in the earth; if it was hard, the round shot would bounce high above the enemy troops.

Up to the end of the Seven Years' War, artillerists were content to rely on direct fire when aiming at enemy formations. It was unavoidable, however, that many of the balls aimed at one formation, whether they hit or not, would strike the ground beyond and ricochet towards other troops further to the rear. Observant officers noticed that these balls were more effective once they began ricocheting than before they had first struck the ground. Ordinary round shot could only be expected to kill at most two or three men in a formation. The cannon ball, 'only observed in its effect', created relatively little fear and hence disorder. The smoke, the noise, the act of moving forward meant that only those right next to the victims were aware of the results of round shot. Ricochet fire, on the other hand, was perceptible *prior* to impact and thus succeeded in spreading much more terror among the troops. Since it was perceived while still a distance in front of the formation, everyone looking in that direction would observe it. Von Tielke explained:

> . . . balls which the troops perceive striking the ground about 100 or more paces in front of them, and approaching them with short bounds, cause much unsteadiness, waving, pressing, and confusion in the ranks, as everyone endeavours to get out of their way.[24]

Von Tielke proved to be a far-sighted military analyst and was able to predict another benefit of ricochet fire. It could be used against troops beyond the effective range of direct fire. Like Frederick the Great, von Tielke observed that artillery officers were habitually cajoled or even ordered into firing before the enemy had advanced to within effective range. Of course, not only was this a waste of valuable ammunition, but also it had the disastrous effect of buoying the enemy's spirits while demoralizing friendly troops who all too clearly perceived its ineffectiveness. In this case, the artillery officer was in a no-win situation. As von Tielke observed, 'if he does not fire, he is accused of irresolution; and if he fires without striking the object (which must be the case at such a distance) he is accused of want of skill.'[25] One solution to this dilemma was to use ricochet fire. With an effective range almost twice that of direct fire it could inflict casualties even at 1,500 paces.

During the Napoleonic period, the Prussian reformer Scharnhorst performed an intriguing experiment to ascertain the effectiveness of ricochet fire and direct fire. Four 12-pounders and four 6-pounders took turns firing at a target which consisted of a long strip of continuous boards, 200 feet wide and six feet high. In the first trial, the target was placed 900 toises away for 12-pounders and 675 toises for 6-pounders. In the second trial, both types were placed between 450 to 500 toises. It was observed that the 12-pounders fired approximately three rounds every two minutes, while the 6-pounders fired on the average four rounds during that same time. The chart below shows the number of hits that were scored after thirty minutes.[26]

Calibre	Type of fire	No. of shots	Hits
at approximately 1,800 yards (900 toises)			
12	direct	180	0
	ricochet	180	36
at approximately 1,350 yards (675 toises)			
6	direct	240	0
	ricochet	240	60
12	direct	180	16
	ricochet	180	45
at approximately 900–1,000 yards (450–500 toises)			
6	direct	240	20–30
	ricochet	240	60 (approximately)
12	direct	180	20–30
	ricochet	180	60 (approximately)

Events during the Napoleonic Wars would prove the accuracy of von Tielke's observations. In his *Instruction of Field-Marshal Blücher For the Chief of Brigades* penned at the start of the 1815 campaign, Field-Marshal Blücher claimed that round shot fired *à ricochet* was more effective at long range than it was at a shorter distance. This was because at the shorter range, obstacles such as minor undulations of the ground had a much greater effect on the trajectory of the round shot as it bounded. Blücher, for example, recommended placing infantry behind a temporary escarpment, something as simple as a one- or two-foot mound of earth, which, because it altered the trajectory of the round shot while it ricocheted, greatly reduced casualties. Troops positioned further away at extreme range, however, could not seek the protection of small terrain obstacles. So convinced of this was he that he ordered troops finding themselves fired upon by artillery 2,000 paces distant to advance to between 800 and 1,500 paces to minimize the effect of ricochet fire.[27]

The ball fired by a gun would speed along a relatively flat trajectory and, if the ground was dry, upon hitting it the ball would bound up and continue along its way. Periodically it would hit the ground at ever-decreasing intervals until, having spent most of its energy, it rolled along the ground before coming to a complete stop.

In his seminal work, *An Account of Some of the Most Remarkable Events of the War*, von Tielke concluded that to promote the use of ricochet fire, ammunition wagons should be equipped with a few dozen cartridges especially designed for ricochet fire.[28] In the years between the publication of von Tielke's book and the outbreak of the French Revolutionary Wars, artillery officers throughout Europe became aware of the potential of ricochet fire. The result was that it was frequently and effectively utilized throughout the general conflagration that embroiled Europe at the turn of the nineteenth century.

CASE SHOT

Case shot or canister was used by either guns or howitzers against enemy troops that had advanced to within close range. As we have seen, by Napoleonic times the external casings were more durable, and as a result canister could be used effectively at much longer ranges than had been possible previously. Canister possessed several other advantages at close and medium ranges. An artillery team firing round shot, out of necessity, had to lay the gun each time it was fired, since an advancing enemy was no longer at the same range the next time the piece fired, approximately fifteen seconds later. When they fired canister, however, this type of accuracy was no longer necessary, and they could fire as quickly as was humanly possible.[29]

Obviously, the chief value of this type of ammunition was that many projectiles could be hurled against the enemy simultaneously, which, it was hoped, would cause many more casualties than a single larger ball travelling a further distance. Tousard calculated that canister caused twice as many casualties as round shot fired at the same range, and cited the results of an experiment conducted by the French army after the Seven Years' War to substantiate his position.[30]

Gun type	Distance (yds)	No. of hits	Size of ball
12-pounders	800	7–8	large
	700	10–11	large
	600	25	small
	500	35	small
	400	40	small
8-pounders	700	8–9	large
	600	10–11	large
	600	25	small
	500	40	small
4-pounders	600	8–9	large
	500	16–18	small
	400	21	small

By Napoleonic times, the value of ricochet fire had come to be recognized, and artillery officers were advised if the weather was dry and the ground sufficiently firm to aim low even when firing canister. Under these conditions the smaller balls would hit the hard ground and continue in an erratic course wounding and even killing those unfortunate enough to be standing along their path. As with the larger round shot, the use of ricochet fire significantly increased the effective range of fire.[31]

Artillery was capable of firing round shot and canister simultaneously. However, the situation had to be extremely critical indeed to induce an artillery officer to succumb to this temptation, since the combined wear of round shot and loose odds and ends would have thoroughly ruined an artillery piece's barrel in a little more than ten minutes. In an extremely critical situation, where the destruction of the guns was less important than the position, a commander might order this practice. This was exactly the situation in which General Thiébault found himself when confronted by a superior force on the Pratzen Heights.[32]

HOWITZER TACTICS

Prior to the Napoleonic Wars, howitzers had seen rather limited use on the open battlefield, usually being reserved for formal siege operations and special situations during campaign operations when it became necessary to destroy hard-to-hit targets, such as dwellings and bridges covered by the terrain, or field works like redoubts, entrenchments, etc. Mounted on carriages designed to allow high trajectories, howitzers, for example, were better suited to deliver the eighteen to fifteen degree trajectory required by ricochet fire to hit the artillery behind the parapets, walls, and other types of fortifications or field works.[33]

An expanded role for howitzers had to wait for the post-Seven Years' War period with its increased focus on the formal analysis of available weaponry and proliferation of published works dealing with every aspect of military art and science. Experienced artillerymen, such as von Tielke, now were able to explain to their less imaginative brethren how a howitzer had a great many applications even on a battlefield devoid of field works, villages or towns. For one thing, an explosive shell following a high trajectory was extremely useful in 'hilly situations' or even on markedly undulating terrain. Shells could be fired into the 'hollows' between high ground or on to the tops of promontories – something that was impossible for a gun. Von Tielke went further, arguing that the utility of the howitzer was not merely in its ability to hit difficult-to-reach positions but in its more devastating effect on its victims.

> The shells occasion more confusion, and strike more terror into the troops, than the cannon-balls, for not only their bounding, but also their bursting is formidable.[34]

Another potential advantage of howitzers would gradually become apparent during the next round of major wars that would interrupt European serenity. Because of their significantly larger bore calibre, case shot was appreciably more effective when delivered from howitzers than fired from guns.

In the late 1700s howitzers represented only about seven per cent of the ordnance in the field. The Austrians and the Prussians were the first to increase the number of howitzers. During the early 1790s, the French quickly followed suit and by 1793 roughly one-third of all French artillery in the field were howitzers. The realization that howitzers possessed an all-purpose utility led not only to greater numbers finding their way to the field, but a change in the way artillery pieces were organized in the field. Instead of organizing the howitzers into separate batteries as had been the custom, howitzers and guns were grouped together to form integrated batteries capable of performing a more diverse set of functions than the homogeneous batteries they replaced.[35]

Just how useful howitzers and explosive shells could be was amply demonstrated at the Battle of Dennewitz (6 September 1813). Even after the Prussians managed to carry the villages of Dennewitz and Goelsdorff the French line continued to *appuy* its right on the village of Rohrbeck. Determined to undermine the French by seizing this position, Count Tauentzien formed his infantry into four columns. A battery of 12-pounders commanded by a Colonel Diedrichs was ordered to advance in front of this attacking force. The battery fired several rounds of explosive shells and in less than two minutes the entire village was in flames. The enemy was forced to precipitately flee the protection of the village and the Prussian infantry advancing at the *pas de charge* succeeded in capturing the village, taking insignificant casualties.[36]

COUNTER-BATTERY FIRE

One of many debates that continued throughout the Napoleonic period was whether artillery should be exclusively used against cavalry or infantry, or whether it was best directed against its enemy counterpart when the opportunity presented itself.

Those who favoured 'counter-battery fire', as the practice of directing artillery piece against artillery piece was termed, reasoned that it was more advantageous to direct one's artillery fire against enemy batteries than against his troops. A British author writing in the 1790s argued that it was more important to destroy a single enemy cannon than it was to disable 100 or even 200 infantrymen. The author reasoned that an army having sustained significant cavalry and infantry losses could still keep in the field and maintain its effectiveness. At a pinch, infantry replacements could be rushed to the field using garrison troops with four or five weeks of training.

However, artillerymen once removed were not so easily replaced, and an army lacking their services would suffer in its overall effectiveness.[37]

General Lallemand had served with the Imperial Guard and was one of those who advised against the use of counter-battery fire under normal conditions. Nevertheless, Lallemand was forced to concede that sometimes it was necessary to engage in counter-battery fire, if the enemy's artillery was inflicting greater damage than one's own artillery, or if it was exposed and there were no other available targets. Many artillery officers, when engaging an enemy artillery, ordered their battery's fire to be directed along the entire front of the enemy battery. Each artillery piece within their command, in effect, had a different target. General Lallemand decried this practice as useless. Although each of the enemy's pieces were inconvenienced, losing several men or horses, it was rare that any were put completely out of service. Unintimidated, the enemy fire continued unabated. Instead, Lallemand advised the officer commanding the battery to ensure that all the guns within the battery concentrated their fire upon a single target. Then, as soon as the enemy gun was dismounted or destroyed they were to turn their attention to a new target. Thus enemy guns would be destroyed one at a time, until none remained operative.[38]

The memoirs of General Vionnet Viscomte de Maringoné provide us with an account of the French artillery doing precisely this. Vionnet was the *major-commandant* of the 1st and 2nd *régiments de tirailleurs* young guard. At the combat of Gross-Garten (27 August 1813), Maringoné's brigade was ordered to advance against a village where the enemy had positioned fifteen artillery pieces. The enemy battery fired relentlessly, and Maringoné was forced to ploy his troops into column and hide them behind some undulating terrain. The general commanding the French division sent twelve artillery pieces to ameliorate the brigade's situation. These were positioned on either side of the column. Maringoné ordered the guns to aim at one of the enemy guns which was soon destroyed. This process was continued and after two hours nearly all of the enemy's guns were silenced. Unfortunately for the French, all of this was to little avail, for as soon as the enemy battery was rendered ineffective another battery, this time twenty cannons of larger calibre, took its place and succeeded in causing more damage than its predecessors.[39]

Occasionally, the officer commanding a battery of light artillery would come under fire from enemy artillery of a heavier calibre. When this happened, the textbook approach was to advance the guns as close as possible to the enemy fire, without advancing to within canister range. This would minimize the difference in calibres.[40] Colonel Serruzier found himself in just such a situation at Jena. His battery of 4-pounders came under the fire of Prussian 12-pounders, six hundred metres distant. This unfortunately was within the enemy battery's canister range, and unless something was done immediately the French battery faced certain extinction. Serruzier ordered half of his pieces (the even ones) to double their fire. Under the cover of the clouds of smoke thus created, the odd pieces advanced to within the enemy's point blank range. The enemy was unaware of this movement and continued to fire at the original range. The odd pieces now began to fire quickly as the even pieces were moved up in turn. The Prussian battery lost all of its advantages and, further, found itself firing at the wrong range. The French guns, on the other hand, were able to fire extremely accurately and, one by one, the Prussian guns were destroyed and the battery soon destroyed.[41]

To be effective, counter-battery fire demanded the greatest possible accuracy. Not only did this mean pointing the gun in the right direction, but it meant establishing the correct range of the target. To estimate the approximate range of an enemy battery, some artillery officers used the following method. The officer would look at the enemy battery and wait for the latter to fire. As soon as he saw a flash, he would count the seconds until he heard the report. He would take this number and multiply it by 173 toises (369 yards), giving him the range of the enemy battery.[42]

BATTALION GUNS

Gustavus Adolphus introduced a super-light gun with a tough leather barrel reinforced with iron hoops during the Thirty Years' War. Gradually, these were adopted by other western European powers, and, for example, various light guns, known as *canon à la suédois* were in use in the French army by 1740. These guns, too long and heavy for their infantry support role, proved a total failure at Fontenoy. Despite this, another version of *canon à la suèdois* was reintroduced into the French army by an ordinance of 20 January

1757.[43] The Prussian army also experimented with regimental guns during this period. 3-pounders were distributed to each regiment by a decree of 11 August 1741; however, by the beginning of the Seven Years' War these had been replaced by 6-pounders, and the old 3-pounders were relegated to the second line.[44]

Most armies adopting these light guns encountered similar experiences. They were typically distributed among infantry regiments, for whom they were to provide local artillery support. On the positive side, the noise of the discharges was found to boost the troops' morale, an especially important consideration if the troops were inexperienced. Otherwise, the light guns were a disappointment. The very lightness which allowed the cannons to accompany the infantry precluded any real striking power; moreover, one or two artillery pieces could never produce the results of an entire battery or even half battery.

Despite these limitations, battalion guns continued to be employed in some armies well into the Revolutionary and Napoleonic Wars. Battalion guns, for example, were only withdrawn from the British army in 1802, when they were replaced by five-gun field batteries, containing four 6- or 12-pounders and one light 5.5 inch howitzer.[45] The French army had withdrawn its battalion guns after the Seven Years' War. However, the tremendous expansion of the French army and influx of green troops forced French military authorities once again to resort to this expedient. Battalions in the National Guard were authorized to add two light artillery pieces on 29 September 1791. Volunteer battalions began receiving artillery pieces in July, October and December 1792, while the general reorganization in 1793 authorized all infantry battalions to have these guns. Each demi-brigade now included six 4-pounders served by seventy-four artillerymen.[46] Of course, these light guns fared no better or worse than their predecessors. With the increasing professionalism in the French army from 1796 onward, the need for these stop-gap measures was largely reduced and the battalion guns were discontinued in 1798. However, the seemingly endless series of wars, the mounting casualties, the new influx of raw levies all induced Napoleon to reintroduce battalion guns 1809–1812.[47]

Given their *raison d'être*, battalion and regimental guns always had to act in strict coordination with their parent unit. *The Bombardier and Pocket Gunner*, authored by a Captain Ralph Willet Adye of the Royal Regiment of Artillery in 1802, provides a description of the duties of and procedures to be followed by battalion guns in British service. Nevertheless, these are fairly representative for this entire class of artillery of this period.

Although in a review the battalion's two guns were to be positioned to the right of the line, ten yards apart and ten yards to the right of the grenadiers, in battle they were not so constrained and the officers were enjoined to position their artillery in the most convenient position to 'annoy' the enemy. Once positioned and unlimbered, they were to be advanced a little further by hand, so as not to obstruct the view of the pivots and thus interfere with the deployment of the battalion. To ensure that the guns could quickly be brought into play, in the field the battalion guns were to be placed in front of the battalion when advancing and at the rear while retiring. In the case of lengthy multi-battalion columns in closed order, the guns were placed on the outward flank.

The battalion's guns were to be used to cover its movement, or protect its weakest point. Thus, the artillerymen should continue firing, if the battalion was required to perform any complex manoeuvre, such as a change of front. If the battalion manoeuvred into square, the guns were to be placed in the weakest angles, with the limbers in the centre of the square. In a case where the battalion was to retire by alternate wings, the guns had to be manoeuvred so as to be in the half of the battalion that was closest to the enemy. They were only to fire when absolutely necessary.[48]

TERRAIN

It did not take artillerists long to discover that hills and promontories often allowed them to work their pieces with great effect. In an elevated position they were able to see and fire over the minor variations in the ground that characterized most of the European countryside. This is not to say, however, that the artillery could be placed on elevated terrain indiscriminately. Thinking that all heights could be used to advantage, inexperienced artillery officers often found their pieces unable to fire upon the enemy below them. And, if fortune did not smile on their cause that day, they might discover too late that they were unable to defend themselves from attack.

The potential hazards of placing artillery on elevations were recognized at least by the mid-eighteenth century. Frederick the Great, for example, in one of his frequent admonitions to his officers, had cautioned against placing artillery on too high an elevation. In the decades following the Seven Years' War, artillery officers devised more rigorous guidelines to be used whenever positioning artillery on hills or any other type of elevated terrain. Artillery could be used efficaciously on the top of straight, gentle slopes. It had been discovered that when firing down hill, the artillery ordnance could not be depressed as much as the barrel of a musket.[49] And, even in those cases where the artillery managed sufficiently to lower its barrels to fire in the depths below it:

> the effect of the fire of your lines or your artillery is almost lost, the shots being too plunging, whilst the aim of the skirmishers that precede the hostile column is very sure.[50]

Convex slopes were especially to be avoided. An enemy advancing up this type of incline was screened by the curvature of the hill, and could not be fired upon until the last moment. Contrary to logical expectations, concave slopes were hardly less accommodating to defending artillery.[51] Frequently, the shots hitting the ground near the base of the incline would go over the heads of the enemy troops at various points on the slope. Commanders defending concave slopes with artillery were advised to station other batteries on neighbouring slopes which could rake the intermediate positions on the slope.

A perfect position was atop a hill with relatively straight and gentle slopes. Ideally, the height of this hill was equal to between $1/20$ and $1/16$ the distance of the target being fired at with an overall gradient of two to four degrees to the horizon.[52] If indeed it proved necessary to defend a steep hill or embankment, this was far more effectively done with infantry. As von Tielke pointed out, 'A great part . . . of the declivity of a height will remain totally untouched by the cannonshot, though it may be well defended by the fire of the musketry.'[53] According to at least one expert opinion, '. . . there is no height, which cannot be defended with musketry.' Unlike artillery, which could not easily or safely be brought to the edge of a steep gradient or drop, infantry could be positioned right along a cliff or even along the slope itself, allowing them to get a better shot at the enemy. When called upon to defend these steep hills, if artillery support was still deemed necessary, the batteries were to be placed on appropriate terrain on either side of the slope so that the enemy would be raked with a crossfire as it attempted to work its way up the hill.[54]

Artillery was considered to be relatively ineffective against enemy troops on an elevated position. All the latter had to do was retire a few paces and the round shot would bound harmlessly over their heads.[55]

CHAPTER 21

Cavalry and Infantry Attacking Artillery

ONCE A GENERAL ACTION BEGAN, infantry, even more than its cavalry counterpart, was frequently subjected to artillery fire. The effect of this fire depended on the type of projectile being fired, as well as the range of the target and the intervening terrain. The hollow shell which would explode soon after hitting the ground was intimidating to the foot soldier. However, unless these shells were fired by volleys and landed within the formation, they had little effect. As a result, the infantrymen had little to fear from artillery pieces firing hollow shot individually.

Of course, an infantryman unfortunate enough to be standing anywhere along a ball's path would suffer extremely serious wounds, if not instant death. However, the most dangerous position for both infantry or cavalry was to find itself at the artillery's 'second point blank primitive', that is, where the ball grazed the ground at the 'first bound'. At this point, the height of the trajectory was low enough that it did not bound over the troops. Moreover, troops in front of the bounding ball had insufficient response time to get out of harm's way.

Infantry could always reduce artillery's effectiveness by slight movements. If the infantry moved, the artillerymen were forced to relay their pieces, which could take some time if they had to fire test shots. However, eventually after these first trial rounds their fire would soon regain its accuracy.

If exposed to murderous point blank fire, a commander would frequently order the infantry to move slightly forward or backward.

This was especially expeditious when the infantry discovered it was positioned at 'second point blank primitive'. If the ground was undulating or there were slight changes in elevation or the ground was wet, usually moving fifty paces to the front or back was sufficient. Infantry exposed to ricochet fire, however, could only lessen the effect through lateral movements to the left and right. In this case, the distance they had to move varied with the situation.

General Okounef tells how, at the Battle of Polotsk, he was specifically instructed by Count Wittgenstein to hold a position along the road leading from Polotsk to Witepsk. Once in position, he was almost immediately beset by three pieces of French artillery which fired upon his battalion in a lively fashion for several hours. While under fire he conducted a series of small movements to the left and to the right in order to minimize casualties. Using this method, at the end of the cannonade Okounef discovered his battalion had suffered only one officer wounded, two soldiers killed and one musket destroyed.[1] This was a well-known technique, one which experienced officers were expected to take advantage of, circumstances permitting. At the Battle of Leipzig (16–19 October 1813), the commander of Karl Röhrig's battalion, which was positioned directly in front of an enemy battery, was severely criticized by the brigade commander for not taking these precautions, after his battalion suffered over a hundred casualties.[2]

There were several factors which limited the use of this solution on the battlefield. For example, this tactic was not possible when the formation was ordered to protect a specific position, such as a bridge or crossroads, and thus had to remain absolutely stationary. Even when not so restricted, officers were cautioned against moving their troops too often. These types of movement tended to undermine the troops' courage, making them feel like 'small game' trying to avoid the hunter's aim.

Officers were also advised to take advantage of the terrain. Even small irregularities, such as ditches with elevated sides, minor undulations in the ground or even furrows running obliquely or crosswise to the troops' position, could lessen the artillery's effectiveness. Cannon balls hitting these obstacles might be deflected slightly to one side or assume a higher trajectory and bounce over the troops' heads. At the same time, these obstacles also made it more difficult for the artillerymen to evaluate correctly the distance of the infantry targets. This meant they would often fire short or too far and, obviously, this also lessened casualties.

The commander had recourse to one last tactic when his troops had to endure continued artillery fire. He could order his men to lie on the ground. However, this was not without its potential negative effects. Experience had repeatedly shown that it was extremely difficult to get the troops to stand up again after they had been ordered on the ground.[3]

Often, circumstances on the battlefield would require an infantry or cavalry force to attack an enemy battery. If we imagine a row of cannons side by side belching nearly continuous sheets of flame and shot, it is natural to assume that, except under the most exceptional of circumstances, the artillery was able to resist any cavalry or infantry assault that might be hurled at it. It seems logical that the artillery could only be overthrown if crushed by a preponderance of force (and then only after inflicting truly gargantuan losses on the attacker), or if the artillery was the victim of some chance circumstance, such as a caisson exploding, or if the artillery mistakenly fired over the heads of the attackers because they had just been firing at some other, more distant target and failed to resight their pieces. Reality was much less conclusive than this simplistic view suggests. Like the debate as to whether infantry was intrinsically stronger than cavalry or vice versa, informed opinion appears to have been divided according to the arm in which the officers served.

Quite naturally, most artillery officers felt that well led, strongly positioned artillery would always succeed in fending off the opposition, while both infantry and cavalry officers felt that properly executed attacks would succeed in taking the enemy artillery's position. Napoleon, for example, even at the end of his military career, never lost his respect for the arm in which he had originally been trained:

> As to pretending to rush upon the guns and carry them by the bayonet, or picking off the gunners by musketry, these are chimerical ideas . . . In a general system, there is no infantry, however intrepid, that can, without artillery, march with impunity the length of five or six hundred toises [about 3,600 feet], against sixteen well placed pieces of cannon, served by good gunners.

He went as far as declaring there had not been a single instance during the just-concluded hostilities where '...twenty pieces of cannon, judiciously placed, and in battery, was ever carried by the bayonet'.[4]

Many informed officers were of the opposite opinion. Among these latter could be found de Jomini and the Count von Bismarck, a German cavalry officer and grandfather of the famous Prussian chancellor destined to reunite Germany. Both adamantly denied the so-called lethalness of artillery. Von Bismarck scoffed: 'Artillery is not so formidable as it is generally believed, and deserves not the respect which troops often show for it,'[5] while waxing more poetically de Jomini opined, 'cannonades are salutations to which one replies with little loss'.[6]

When all the French Revolutionary and Napoleonic Wars are considered, we see that even artillery which was securely positioned and supported by infantry was destroyed or captured seemingly a countless number of times. At Jena/Auerstädt alone, the French infantry captured four Prussian batteries through frontal assaults while the French cavalry took a fifth battery. Although it would certainly be grossly inaccurate to say that artillery was easily taken, it certainly was overthrown far more frequently than an infantry square by cavalry.

Although the simplest way of attacking an artillery battery was to launch a straightforward assault, circumstances often demanded a much more subtle, planned approach. A sophisticated body of infantry and cavalry doctrine emerged which had been designed to counter the artillery's effectiveness and increased the attacking party's chances of success. The methods used were slightly different for infantry and cavalry.

INFANTRY ATTACKING ARTILLERY

Well into the French Revolutionary and Napoleonic Wars, most infantry attempts to capture or destroy enemy artillery necessarily devolved into straightforward assaults by troops in a close order formation. Forced into lengthy lines, the only expedient was a precipitate advance on the enemy's battery. The use of skirmishers to attack artillery, or the sophisticated coordination of several different formations had yet to be devised.

Writing in the late 1790s, the Russian Marshal Suvarov describes the tactics he wanted his infantry to employ in this type of situation. The infantry would advance in the usual manner until the enemy guns began to employ canister. As soon as the advancing infantry reached eighty *sazhens* (i.e. 560 feet or about 200 paces), assuming they were still subject to canister, the officers were to order the men to run forward ten to fifteen paces. This quick movement was intended to remove the advancing formation from the centre of the artillery target zone. Having advanced, the attacking infantry would be momentarily outside the canister's killing zone and the defending artillery would have to re-sight their pieces. Meanwhile, the attackers would continue their advance. Once within sixty *sazhens* (420 feet), the infantry would charge their bayonets, meaning that the musket was taken from the shoulder and placed at the horizontal. The final bayonet charge was only to be delivered when the attacking infantry had closed to within thirty paces.

From our comfortable perspective almost two hundred years later, it is natural for us to assume that the defending artillery had the uncontestable advantage. We tend to conjure up images of the foot soldier doggedly but hopelessly advancing into the mouths of the blazing guns, and thus into inevitable oblivion. The actual results of infantry attacks against artillery suggest a far different picture. As frequently as not, the infantry gained the upper hand and succeeded in carrying the artillery position.

On a single day in 1806 (14 October), in four separate assaults on Prussian artillery positions French infantry captured or destroyed no less than thirty-two artillery pieces. At the onset of the conflict around Auerstädt, leading elements of Gudin's division under General Gauthier managed to capture a six-gun battery in front of Hassenhausen. Friant's division was even more successful. The 111th Regiment advanced at the *pas de course* against an enemy battery, despite the fact that the latter was able to fire six volleys of canister. Responding to Davout's direct orders, the second battalion of the 108th Regiment then captured another six-gun Prussian battery. This same regiment overran another three artillery pieces when it captured the village of Poppel.[7] Meanwhile at Jena, the first and second battalion of the 16th *légère* stoically withstood repeated volleys of canister and managed to capture eleven guns from a twenty-gun battery.[8]

General Thiébault's account of his actions at Austerlitz provides an example of just such an action. Having just taken the Pratzen village, Thiébault started to rally the men in his command so that he could catch up with Morand and le Vasseur. To his right, he noticed 120 French skirmishers engaged in what was apparently a desultory fire with Russian artillery, who on their side, were directing their fire against the captured château. Thiébault, considering this fire 'ridiculous', immediately put a stop to it. His own force had now managed to regroup into columns, and thus would be quite vulnerable to artillery fire if the Russian gunners chose to change their targets. Thiébault decided that the hostile artillery should be assaulted using a number of small columns by 'squads' and looked for a low-ranking officer, such as a sub-lieutenant or even a captain, to lead the assault. Unfortunately, at this point there were few officers to be found, let alone to be spared, and the French general, calculating that three or four minutes' march at the double would suffice to bring his dense columns to bear against the Russian guns, decided to lead the attack himself. The enemy artillery turned its attention to the advancing French and opened up with grapeshot, i.e. canister. Though Thiébault himself was wounded, his men managed to cross the last fifty paces before the enemy was able to reload. The Russian infantry acting as supports panicked and fled, and the French columns succeeded in slaughtering the Russian gunners and capturing their pieces.[9]

Unlike peacetime reviews where batteries worked in isolation, artillery on the battlefield was usually supported by some nearby infantry. In these cases, experience had all too often demonstrated that a simple frontal assault was almost always extremely bloody and frequently ineffective. A more effective way of defeating enemy artillery was first to attack the enemy infantry serving as supports. If these were defeated, the enemy artillery would either have to retreat or be captured or destroyed by an assault which now could be launched from either its flank or rear.

By Napoleonic times, several distinct formal methods of attacking artillery supports had evolved. One tactic was to divide the attacking infantry into two parts: the first and larger portion was directed against the supports, while the other portion advanced towards the artillery pieces in skirmish order. The skirmishers would stop about 250 paces in front of the battery and take cover behind whatever irregular terrain was available. A firefight would now almost certainly erupt. The artillery would invariably fire canister, which, given the distance and the extended order of the skirmishers, would be less than devastating. On their side, the skirmishers would attempt to take good aim and shoot the individual gunners and battery's horses.[10] Many artillery officers felt that once the horses were killed or disabled the guns would inevitably be taken since without mobility they would be more susceptible to the vicissitudes of the battle.[11] However, if at any point during the fusillade the enemy artillerymen showed any disorder or hesitancy, the skirmishers were immediately to rush in and attack them with the bayonet. Meanwhile, as the skirmishers threatened the artillery pieces the main body of the attacking troops was to advance on the supports. The attackers would advance either in line or column, depending upon the situation at hand or the specific tactics of that army.

It should be pointed out that some French generals did not think skirmishers to be particularly effective against enemy artillery. General Thiébault, for example, considered, 'This sort of shooting [i.e. skirmishers at artillerymen] could only be ridiculous', and, as we have seen, when he caught sight of his skirmishers firing at Russian artillery near the Pratzen Heights, he immediately ordered them to desist.[12]

Irregular troops of various nations, such as the Jacobite Scots, eastern infantry and the soldiers of the Vendée used much cruder tactics, though if the men were sufficiently brave, no less effective. The irregular infantry would quickly advance against the enemy artillery. As soon as they saw the flash of the guns being fired, they would immediately throw themselves on the ground. Since the projectiles of these days were relatively slow moving, one or two seconds might elapse between when a gun was fired and when the cannon balls would pass over their heads. They would now quickly get up and resume the advance. They would repeat the process of throwing themselves on the ground and getting up until they reached the battery, which they were certain to capture unless they had been checked during the advance.[13] It should be noted that even regular troops were tempted to periodically fall down on the ground to preserve their lives when faced with imminent artillery fire. This was especially the case for skirmishers, who, not being part of a closed order formation and being spread out, were less under an officer's control.

An account has been given of Captain Reuter who, during the Battle of Ligny, was misled into believing that two lines of skirmishers approaching him were the Prussian 14th Infantry Regiment with whom his battery was temporarily attached (see page 213). Finally, undeceived by the sharp eye of his surgeon, he ordered a slow but continuous firing of canister upon the French skirmishers. The French skirmishers, now 300 paces distant, responded by delivering a volley and then threw themselves on the ground to escape the effects of the grapeshot that continued to be fired at them. Captain Reuter tells us that the canister fire kept the French skirmishers 'glued to the ground'. The same incident also illustrates how a battery was often put out of service. A few moments later, Captain Reuter noticed about fifty French horsemen led by a staff officer approaching rapidly from his left and rear. Stiff hand-to-hand fighting began moments later and the capture of the battery was only avoided by one of the French horses panicking after its rider was dismounted and the beast running off. The other horses in the attacking party followed, despite all the objections of their riders.[14]

A slightly different tactic, referred to as the *en herse* order, was used when attacking artillery supported by cavalry. Here, it was necessary to provide protection to the advancing skirmishers against any possible cavalry counter-attack. A body of skirmishers still advanced towards the guns. However, two precautions were taken. Small bodies of men in ordered formation, usually closed columns, were positioned behind the skirmisher line. These functioned as an ordered nucleus that the skirmishers could run into, should they be closely pressed. However, just as importantly columns of infantry in closed order advanced on either flank of the skirmishers. These were positioned to repel any cavalry attack coming from either flank, the most probable direction of an enemy cavalry action.

Sometimes artillery defended itself by advancing its infantry supports in front of it. Of course, once this action was taken the guns could no longer fire. Infantry could attack the supporting infantry and the guns behind using an *en tenaille* attack. In this case, the skirmishers and some other troops in closed order in the centre were held back, in other words the centre was 'refused'. The main assault was delivered by two pincer-like movements on either flank, presumably by infantry in column. This type of movement was known as an advance *en conversant*.

Writing just after the conclusion of the Napoleonic Wars, Karl Decker, a prominent military analyst, observed that an infantry attack against enemy artillery which was supported by infantry often was successful if for no other reason than the ineptness of the supports. Even up to the 1830s, infantry received no formal training in how to act in concert with the artillery it was often called upon to defend.[15]

The discussion so far has been confined to cases where it was necessary to attack artillery which on its side was supported by either infantry or cavalry. Occasionally, however, the enemy artillery was caught in a more isolated position, or such a strong sense of urgency was dictated by the overall situation that the officer commanding the infantry would be forced to choose a more direct method of attack. In either of these cases, it could be necessary to make a quick frontal assault, even if it meant maintaining the attacking force in closed order, that is, in regular formations.

CAVALRY ATTACKING ARTILLERY

The chance of a cavalry force successfully taking an enemy artillery position was appreciably better than that for infantry. The reason lay simply in rapidity of movement. Artillery would typically open up on the assaulting force when it was still 800 to 1,000 paces distant. Infantry covering this ground was probably subjected to four times as many firings as its cavalry counterpart and could be expected to take correspondingly more casualties. Cavalry, on the other hand, could cross this distance in about three minutes.[16] The artillerymen would have to resight their guns with each firing. This led the British officer Wilson to claim that cavalry were able to close this distance without the artillery being able to fire more than twice, and so their 'execution is seldom of any consequence'.[17] This opinion appears to be substantiated by events at the combat of El Bodon. On the British side, Arenschildt's battery was positioned near the edge of a ravine. Ten squadrons of Montbrun's cavalry charged this battery at a 'sweeping pace'. The battery began firing canister with demonstrable alacrity at 'point blank' range. Though the guns had an effect on the attacking cavalry, the French horse managed to cross the ravine and mounted the steep banks unchecked. The British gunners were massacred at their guns and the artillery taken.[18]

In many respects, this was the ideal cavalry assault on artillery. Most ventures were rarely as successful. Suffering a great many more casualties, the attacking force was either forced to fall back or to modify its original plan of attack. Captain Parquin recounts just such an occurrence in an action near Valcourt on 20 March 1814. Riding at the head of his squadron, the brigadier general ordered Parquin and his squadron to charge three Russian batteries (eighteen pieces) 'at the full gallop' in the open ground in front of them. Completing the story in Parquin's own words:

> Instantly I complied with that order, but by the time we were a hundred paces from the cannon their showers of grape-shot had so mercilessly thinned the squadron that I commanded a deploy of 2 platoons to the right and two to the left, in skirmishing order, thus leaving the middle plain unoccupied. The Red Lancers of the Guard immediately swept into the opening and also charged the enemy's cannon; we captured every one of them.[19]

No competent cavalry officer ever seriously contemplated attacking an enemy battery with his troops in closed order, if other alternatives were available. Cavalry advancing in line were likely to incur horrendous losses as it attempted to move through canister range. If the enemy battery was on flat terrain, a more reasonable tactic and one prescribed by contemporary doctrine, was to attack in skirmish order so as to engage the battery's attention. At the same time, other mounted forces would charge the artillery's adjoining infantry supports and then, if successful, work their way to the battery's flank or rear.[20]

Whenever time was of the essence or there was insufficient mounted force at hand, the cavalry had directly to attack the guns without first attacking and defeating the supports. In this case, the entire success or failure of the operation rested upon the mounted skirmishers attacking the guns. The attacking cavalry, in skirmish formation, advanced directly towards the guns. The experienced cavalry commander, however, would attempt to approach from a direction so that the enemy guns lay between the attackers and infantry supporting the enemy battery. This would prevent the enemy infantry firing upon the cavalry out of fear of killing their own artillerymen.[21] The cavalry continued to advance against the enemy guns until they entered canister range. Here, the skirmishers spread out from the centre and, at the gallop in a pincer movement, worked their way to the flanks of the battery. Cavalry, like infantry, could adopt *en herse* order, with the flanks advanced and the centre refused.

The cavalrymen sometimes were allowed to conduct a desultory fire until they arrived 'under the fire of the guns.' This mounted fire, 'apparently without design', did not tip off the artillery as to the cavalry's true intentions.

As the cavalry turned outward, the artillery would have to change its aim or become totally ineffective. This gave additional time to the cavalry as it advanced. If there was enough smoke or dust thrown up by the battery, the cavalry could work its way to the flank without even being observed and the battery would continue to fire straight ahead now without effect.[22] Finally, once within range, the cavalry was to charge in with the rapidity of lightning, cut down the artillerymen, and make the drivers bring the guns to their side. Using just such tactics, Württemberg cavalry succeeded in capturing five guns at the battle of Strasbourg, 28 June 1815.[23]

In actual practice, batteries were often placed upon whatever hillocks or promontories presented themselves. Artillerists were known for their habit of selecting terrain to help point their guns towards the most opportunistic targets or the probable direction of attack. At the same time, batteries were as likely as not placed behind sunken roads, ravines, hollow ground etc. for purely defensive reasons. A competent cavalry commander knew how to take advantage of these accidents of ground. If the battery was positioned in front of undulating ground, another, simpler, method of taking guns was often used. Dividing his force into two, the cavalry commander could order a feint from one direction, while the main attack was delivered from another.[24] If this was timed properly, the cavalry stood a good chance of success. The gunners who aimed and fired at the feint would have little time to fire at the real danger thus allowing the attackers to close in and take few casualties.

The Battle of Jena provides an example of cavalry successfully charging and capturing a battery of enemy artillery. A battery of horse artillery in Prince Hohenlohe's command had succeeded in positioning itself in front of the Prussian infantry line. Unfortunately for this Prussian artillery there were clumps of trees in front of some of its line of sight. Ney ordered the 10th *chasseur* regiment to attack the enemy battery. The cavalry regiment was able to take advantage of a clump of trees to form and then dashed forward at the gallop and captured all seven guns, despite the presence of the infantry behind it.[25]

Before attempting to attack enemy guns, however, it was important that the cavalry commander first ordered a quick reconnaissance of the ground to be traversed. This task was to be performed by some bold and well-mounted men. This force had to be small enough and scattered so as not to tempt the enemy gunners to fire upon them. Their purpose was to discover the lie of the land and uncover any hidden features which could force the cavalry to pull up or, worse, cause the horses to stumble and fall, injuring or killing their riders. General Colbert did not forget this most fundamental precaution even under the pressures of battle at Wagram. Ordered by Napoleon to charge the centre of the Austrian line, his preliminary reconnaissance revealed impractical terrain which prohibited a charge from being conducted. He thus saved his brigade from needless losses and was able to participate to take a prominent role in the final phase of the victory.[26]

There was mixed opinion as to what to do with the guns, should the cavalry charge prove successful. Some felt that the cavalry should kill the artillerymen and team horses and attempt to bring the guns back, while others believed this only caused a delay which often proved fatal. Whenever the guns were to be left behind, it then became essential to destroy the ammunition, cut the traces and, if possible, also to spike the guns (see page 413).[27] Other cavalry officers felt that though the gunners should be cut down, the drivers should be spared to help turn the guns around and drive the captured guns back to their own lines. Of course, the drivers were not always willing to cooperate and attempted to hang back in the hope that friendly forces would rescue them. De Brack offered this advice in this situation:

> Threaten to run them through with your sabre. Should this produce no fear? Throw them to the ground. Let two of the troopers take the bridles of the two lead horses to lead them; other troopers will beat the horses' sides with the flat of their sabres, and thus force them along.[28]

If, on the other hand, events were such that it proved impossible to retain control of the captured pieces, they were to be destroyed or rendered useless. In theory, this was done by driving spikes down the vents which would make any subsequent firing impossible. This, of course, required that spikes and hammers be issued to the cavalry prior to the charge. More often than not, this was not done, either for the lack of tools on the scene or the opportunity to distribute them. However, even when the spikes and hammers were unavailable, experienced cavalrymen, given a few moments, could render the guns inoperable. They shot the horses so as to make any further manoeuvring of the pieces more difficult. The sponge staffs used to sponge the inside of the barrels between firings and ram down the charges were broken. If there were ravines or cliffs nearby the pieces were thrown over and thus damaged.

An experienced artillery officer would have his command retreat only a short distance back towards his lines when pushed from captured guns and have his men rally (reform) there. This was in order to be able, if an opportunity presented itself, to return to the charge and recapture the guns a second time and try to bring them back to safety.[29]

SPIKING THE GUNS

Given the lengthy and expensive manufacturing processes and difficulty of transport, artillery was a valuable resource not easily replaced during the rigours of a lengthy campaign. Every precaution had to be taken to protect the artillery from accidental damage and, of course, the malicious intent of one's opponent. If a sudden retreat was called for during regular campaigning, it was important to prevent these assets from falling into enemy hands. This meant destroying or otherwise disabling whatever artillery could not be withdrawn. Similarly, during a battle, captured enemy artillery would have to be destroyed, if there was any chance of the enemy regaining the newly captured position.

If the artillerymen had a few hours, there were a number of methods available to disable an artillery piece. If it was a brass cannon, the barrel could be stripped from its carriage. A large fire was lit under its centre while its weight was supported on either end of the barrel. The tin, one of the component metals in brass, would eventually start to melt and the piece would sag in the middle. Some artillerymen would attempt to saw off the trunnions; others would fire a round shot into the artillery piece to be destroyed. Neither of these methods was very effective.

One of the quickest ways of disabling an artillery piece, and the most common method on the battlefield, was to 'spike the gun'.

Using a mallet or hammer, the soldier would simply drive a specially designed steel spike down the vent near the rear of the barrel. Ideally, the spike was thicker at the head and tapered off slowly towards the point. The French version was six-sided, and each of these splays had upward facing teeth. These did not interfere with the spike being driven into the vent, but once in prevented the spike from being easily extracted.

It was common practice to equip infantry and cavalry destined to be launched against enemy artillery with spikes. These took moments to insert. Although it could often be removed, a spike required hours of intensive effort, something that was not available during a hotly contested battle. To remove a spike from a vent, the artillerymen would insert a charge of powder of about one-third of the weight of the ball used by that piece. This was mixed with powder and quick match (i.e. the powder used in fuses) and then carefully rammed down the barrel. Next two balls or wood cut into a cylindrical shape were rammed down even harder and then ignited from the muzzle. Frequently the spike would be blown out after several attempts.

There was another method of disabling a gun, which, though requiring slightly more time, was more effective. A cylinder of hard wood was driven down the bore, followed by round shot wrapped in felt. This was then forcibly driven in. The whole became extremely difficult to remove. Typically the enemy would raise the barrel and then attempt to burn out the felt by shoving in burning charcoal coals. Felt does not easily burn and the lack of oxygen down the barrel guaranteed that the fire was extinguished before much of the felt was burnt.[30]

DEFENDING THE GUNS

Artillery pieces were expensive to produce and, of more consequence, difficult to transport to the field in a timely fashion once the campaigning had begun in earnest. It is not surprising that in most armies, the artillerymen were enjoined to make every effort to protect their pieces and prevent their capture or destruction.

> As a gun is attached to the dragoons ... The commanding officer is confident that the cavalry will never abandon the gun without orders from him. Till that moment they should regard

it as committed to their charge of their courage; and therefore consider its loss incompatible with their honour.

If the enemy should endeavour to cut off any of our parties the same judgement must be exercised. But above all things the safety of the gun attached to us must interest all, and no effort must be withheld that can avert the disgrace of its loss.[31]

Although official French artillery doctrine also called for the artillerymen to 'hold on to the last extremity',[32] the French were frequently observed to display a different attitude towards the defence of their guns.

Though the French gunners were renowned for the manner in which they boldly brought their guns into play, when hard pressed they frequently abandoned their pieces with seeming unconcern. Firing canister until the last moments, they would defend the guns until it was no longer prudent to do so and usually succeeded in making certain that the enemy paid as dearly as possible for their guns. So often, the enemy was only able to take the French guns by advancing over the bodies of their comrades and, once in possession of the French artillery, they discovered it had been acquired at too high a human cost.[33]

This willingness to abandon the guns and not fight to the last was, in part, based on the realization that generally it was unwise to attempt to withdraw artillery pieces under extreme circumstances. For even if the cannons could be saved, the disruptive effect on the friendly infantry made such efforts counter-productive overall. Unable to quickly pass over rough terrain, the retiring artillery would sooner or later make its way on to the roads and obstruct the movement of the other two arms. A greater problem, however, was the effect on the army's morale: 'the act of withdrawing [artillery] marks discomfiture, and more than almost any other thing communicates panic to young troops.'[34] The wisdom of this approach was lost on many of their opponents. There were some among the British military that lauded such pragmatism. An anonymous British officer writing in 1809 observed:

There is a failing in the artillery bordering on romantic tenacity; they would have a whole brigade cut up, to preserve a single gun. To a loss of a single piece of ordonnance, they attach as much disgrace as we do to the capture of our standards. It is commendable to save them, if prudent; but deliberate murder to defend them to excess.

The same officer opined that at Corunna it would have been better had the British abandoned their guns, and thus many British lives would have been spared.[35]

CHAPTER 22

The Reality of the Battlefield: Utility of Manoeuvres

THAT A SIZEABLE GAP EXISTED between accepted theory and the realities of battlefield practice was well known by the time Napoleon ascended his imperial throne. Throughout the musket era one school of thought maintained that manoeuvres or other fancy practices rehearsed on the parade ground had little or no use on the day of battle. Officers belonging to this camp felt that their primary function was to set up their men in as favourable a position as possible and then motivate them during the contest through their efforts and example. However, even in the heyday of linear tactics, which were notoriously less manoeuvre-oriented than the tactical systems that ultimately replaced them, astute commanders recognized this to be a gross over-simplification. Marshal de Saxe, for example, retorted that indeed if there was no utility to manoeuvring on the battlefield, after the initial deployment of the troops there would be little to do but simply advance straight forward and resolve the issue with cold steel. The battle would belong to the side which had the greatest élan or at the very least who possessed the most endurance.[1]

History, however, has demonstrated in almost every battle punctuating the eighteenth century that an infantry battalion or a cavalry regiment often was forced to assume a number of different formations during a single action. If nothing else, the irregularities of the ground required many battalions temporarily to ploy into column to work their way around impassable terrain before redeploying back into line. More importantly, troops were often ordered to move around the battlefield as commanders used chess-like moves in a bid to bring an insuperable force to bear to gain a critical position. The Battles of Blenheim, Ramilles, Leuthen and Prague are good examples of the use of manoeuvres in the linear period to achieve grand tactical objectives.

Of course, these types of manoeuvres became very much more frequent during the Revolutionary and Napoleonic Wars. No longer restricted to compensating for circumstances and terrain accidentally encountered, manoeuvres increasingly reflected an attempt to implement premeditated designs to outwit the opposing forces.

EXAMPLES OF MANOEUVRES ON THE BATTLEFIELD

By looking at more detailed battle accounts and personal remembrances we can gradually assemble a lengthy list of occasions when troops performed sophisticated manoeuvres on the battlefield, even when near sizeable enemy forces. This appears to be as true for the armies which scrupulously attempted to adhere to the by then classical linear conception of warfare as it was for the French, who enthusiastically experimented with a wide array of new tactical methods. Often, these manoeuvres were as simple as wheeling a portion of a battalion in line inward to bring additional firepower to bear on an outflanked enemy. The commander of the Swiss forces recounted how this type of manoeuvre was used against the French during the Battle of Neueneck (near Berne) on 5 March 1798:

> I instantly formed an oblique order of battle, attacked their left wing with my right, outflanked it, put it to rout, ordered the enemy to be pursued by our own riflemen, and two companies of foot, wheeled to the left about with the remainder of the right wing, and placed the French by this maneuvre between two fires.[2]

British infantry, never known for either fancy manoeuvring or enthusiastically experimenting with new techniques, as a matter of course performed the standard manoeuvres as they formed up in line prior to the start of the battle. And individual British battalions upon occasion were found performing more sophisticated manoeuvres. At Waterloo, for example, the 42nd Highlanders and the remainder of

Dennis Pack's brigade advanced in echelon prior to forming line.[3] Captain George Wood in his memoirs recounts how during the Peninsular Wars, when his regiment was forced to retire after a hot contest with a French force, it fell back to the rear by 'alternate wings'. This was essentially a retreat *en échiquier* performed by a single battalion: one wing (half) of the battalion retired while the other continued to face the enemy and protected the retreat. After a distance, the wing that retired faced about, while the other half now fell back. This process of alternate halves retiring was repeated, until they succeeded in getting out of the enemy's reach.[4]

The British 71st Regiment of Foot at Waterloo provides an example of an infantry formation forced to make a similar sequence of transformations. Ordered to occupy some heights, the battalion first stood in square for a short time, then moved a 'considerable distance' in column, before forming line and delivering several volleys before breaking the enemy with a bayonet charge. This transformation from column to square to column then finally to line could have been performed by the various wheeling manoeuvres then in universal use. However, the 71st was also known to have employed some march-by-files manoeuvres earlier that same day. Forced to retire from one of its original positions, each company file marched by the right towards the rear.[5]

Even the Spanish infantry occasionally surprised their French adversaries by demonstrating a command of some formal manoeuvres on the field of battle. Gouvion Saint-Cyr tells us how in one of the many combats that occurred during the 1808 campaign, the Spanish infantry in a perfect line, upon the approach of French columns, began to deliver fire by files, platoons and battalion exactly as prescribed in the regulations. Even more surprisingly, after one or two volleys, the battalions in the second line performed the complicated 'passage of lines' manoeuvre, once again in perfect line. There was only one slight problem, however. Both the fire and the subsequent manoeuvre were completed before the French had advanced to within effective musket range, so it was all for naught.[6]

Cavalry even more than infantry was required to change position frequently as events unfolded on the battlefield. If the cavalry regiment already had deployed in line, this meant forming column, moving to the new location and then deploying into line once again. When considering all of the engagements of the entire period, this scenario was repeated a countless number of times. So commonplace was it, that the specifics are rarely described in battle reports or memoirs; mention is only made of a regiment moving from position A to position B. But always implicit in this movement is a sequence of manoeuvres so vital that without them no repositioning could take place. Occasionally, however, in reports, memoirs and descriptions of battles, enough description is provided to show that these transformations were indeed taking place. During an action near the post-house of Kliastitsi on 23 July 1812, for example, it is known that the 23rd *chasseurs à cheval* Regiment, standing in the 'second line', was ordered to attack some Russian battalions in the Tamboff regiment. To do this, it had to pass through the intervals between the friendly regiments in the front line, and then redeploy into line.[7] Obviously, to pass through the first line it had to assume column and before attacking it had to first redeploy into line.

Cavalry regiments had to be able quickly to form line while on the move to take advantage of any transient opportunities that presented themselves during the heat of battle. At the Battle of Möckern, 16 October 1813, the Mecklenburg-Strelitzer Hussars, seeing the 1st Regiment *d'Artillerie de Marine* forming square, were forced to form line while advancing at the trot while apparently in a column of squadrons.[8] As the hussar regiment rushed to the attack, the first squadron inclined to the right while the fourth fanned out obliquely to the left. The actual manoeuvre was conducted at the gallop.[9]

Bock's brigade of the 1st and 2nd Dragoons Regiments of the King's German Legion attempted an even more ambitious manoeuvre when personally ordered by Wellington to charge several French squadrons at Garcia Hernandez on 23 July 1813. Forced to gallop through a narrow valley, Bock's brigade assumed a column of 'section of threes'. Bock realized that to catch the French squadrons in flank he could not stop to form line, and gave the order 'On the move – Line to the front.' Though line was never truly formed – the rear ranks could never catch up to the leading elements since everyone was still advancing at the gallop – the French squadrons, unexpectedly threatened on their right flank, quickly retired.[10]

These examples are probably sufficient to demonstrate the frequency with which both cavalry and infantry manoeuvred on the Napoleonic battlefield. However, one further example is provided, not only because it is a wonderful illustration of how cavalry regiments were often forced to manoeuvre before being able to charge their enemy, but it clearly shows the degree to which manoeuvres in the field were limited to the officially approved manoeuvres provided by the regulations. More importantly, it shows how seemingly mundane considerations, such as whether it was easier to form line from column to the right or left, could influence grand tactical issues, such as where to direct the assault against the enemy's position. The following account was originally provided by Colonel Marbot in the *Spectateur militaire* in 1827 when offering a number of improvements to the cavalry regulations of Year XIII.

While retreating towards Eylau on 6 February 1807, the Russian army left a rear guard made up of much of its best infantry to defend the defile of Landesberg. The general commanding this force positioned eight battalions near the village of Hof. Both terrain and weather conditions favoured a defensive action. The Russian infantry was deployed in line atop some undulating terrain which formed a gentle hill near the centre of the line. The position was protected by two stretches of swampy land about 900 feet in front of the Russian line. The only avenue of approach was along a narrow tract of land between the two morasses. A covering of glazed snow would make any frontal assault of the defensive position even more difficult.

Intimidated by this strong position, the French light cavalry which had been pursuing the Russian forces were forced to pull up. Arriving soon after, Napoleon realized that there was little time to be lost if the pursuit of the main body of the Russian army was to continue. Unfortunately, the French infantry was still a distance away, and so one of the light cavalry brigades was ordered to attack the Russian right, which appeared to be the weaker of the two flanks. The brigade formed a column by platoons in normal order (i.e. the right platoons took their normal positions in front of the column) and made its way quickly through the defile. Passing into the open field beyond the defile, the column headed towards the Russian right flank at the gallop. Notwithstanding the large number of French squadrons participating in the assault, the Russian infantry remained in line.

In his account of events, Marbot contends that as soon as the French cavalry reached the Russian line it should have faced inward, simultaneously quarter-wheeling the platoons to the right, thus forming line in 'inverse order'. It is not certain whether the command for this manoeuvre was ever issued or whether, if issued, it was muddled by the subaltern officers in its execution. It appears that one *chef de peleton* wanted to form line in inverse order, while the others began to manoeuvre their platoons so as to end up in normal order along

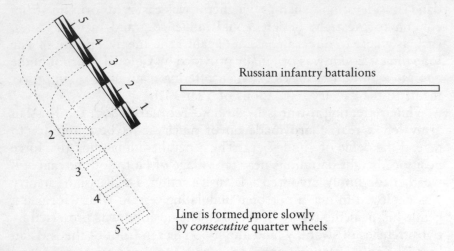

Russian infantry battalions

Line is formed more slowly
by *consecutive* quarter wheels

Light cavalry attacking the Russian right flank

the line. This momentary confusion, plus the fact that it was finally decided to form line using the lengthier but much more familiar method, gave the Russian infantry sufficient time to wheel two of their battalions *en potence*.[11] After some delays, the French finally began their charge forward. Unfortunately, the attacking cavalry were within musket range from the moment they advanced. Subjected to a murderous fire, they were easily driven off, with many of the horses being lost in the surrounding swamp. A brigade of dragoons was next to be ordered forward. These repeated the exact same movements as the light cavalry before them and, not surprisingly, achieved the same results.

About this time General d'Haupoult arrived with his cuirassiers. Napoleon promptly ordered him to attack the Russian right flank. Apparently, General d'Haupoult had always harboured a dislike for attacking an enemy's right flank, believing that this inevitably led to the confusion and delays so keenly experienced on this occasion. Conferring with the Emperor privately, d'Haupoult asked to be allowed to direct his attack against the Russian left. Though it was more strongly guarded, D'Haupoult argued this would be more than

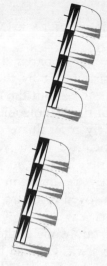

Russian infantry battalions

Line is formed more quickly
by *simultaneous* quarter wheels

D'Hautpoul's cuirassiers attack on the Russian left

compensated for by the increased speed with which the attack could be delivered on this side. Like the light cavalry and dragoons before them, the cuirassiers formed in a column by platoons and proceeded through the defile. In this case, however, two of the frontmost platoons immediately feigned a charge against the centre of the Russian line. While this was occurring, the remainder of the column advanced at the gallop slightly beyond the right of the Russian line. All the platoons were ordered to wheel into line facing their original left. This could now be performed much more quickly. After a simple quarter-wheel, all the platoons found themselves in their natural order along the line, something that had not been possible as long as the attack had been directed on the Russian right.

Line was formed in a matter of seconds and the charge then executed at the gallop. The Russians, convinced they were attacked in earnest by the two squadrons in front, did not respond quickly enough to the real threat on their left flank. Before they could recover, they were taken from the flank and the rear, and in moments the entire eight Russian battalions were ridden down. D'Haupoult was able to present Napoleon with eight standards while on his part the Emperor exclaimed this was the most 'beautiful' cavalry charge he had ever witnessed.[12]

CHANGE IN EMPHASIS

Given the apparent frequency of small-level manoeuvres, it is not surprising that by the Napoleonic period we encounter increasing discussion about the utility of manoeuvres on the battlefield. By the end of the Napoleonic wars, a number of military writers had begun publicly to evaluate officially mandated practices in terms of their practicality, that is, whether they could be meaningfully applied on a battlefield. And, for the first time, military analysts started to tackle directly the question of which manoeuvres were useful and which had proved to be impractical, as well as analysing the reasons why in each case.

Certainly one of the most experienced and most articulate of these writers was Colonel Bugeaud, an experienced French veteran of the Peninsular Wars, well known among French officers of the period for both his tactical acumen and personal bravery. Though admitting that there was much that was superfluous and even harmful in the manoeuvres sanctioned and codified in the regulations of 1791, Bugeaud was even more staunchly opposed to a blanket rejection of all small-level tactics and manoeuvres. In fact, when looking back at the wars in which he had played such an active role, Bugeaud attributed some of the causes of the French military decline and subsequent reverses to these simplistic views:

> Many military men repeat that in war there is no manoeuvring. Hence, perhaps, the contempt for the art of manoeuvring which is too often perceivable with men invested with very high ranks. That disdain has prevented due reflection on that very important part of the art of war, and accordingly dangerous habits were introduced in the army and after contributed to cause the loss of battles or their indecision.[13]

To Bugeaud, nothing proved the tactical and grand tactical bankruptcy more clearly than the unthinking over-reliance on heavy columns that became an increasingly common occurrence during the Empire's final years after 1812. Though this excessive and ill-conceived reliance on heavy columns was more the product of a decline in the officer class, rather than any self-conscious intent or adherence to a theory, Bugeaud felt it demonstrated what would inevitably occur if an army was denuded of its capability of man-oeuvring. Bugeaud's views were not that of an isolated thinker pursuing some pet hobby-horse, but reflected the opinion of many talented high-ranking officers in the French army during this period. In 1803–1804, for example, while a significant portion of the French army bivouacked at the campe de Boulogne, General Ney wrote his *Military Studies*, a treatise dedicated exclusively to infantry tactics. One of Ney's conclusions was that many of the officially prescribed manoeuvres were of little practical use on the battlefield. However, like Bugeaud twenty-five years later, Ney immediately qualified this judgement by concluding it was therefore all the more important to recognize which manoeuvres were truly useful and to limit the soldiers' instruction to these. This same conclusion was reached by General Duhèsme in his treatise on light infantry tactics, *Essai sur l'infanterie légère*, published in 1814. The consensus among these military authorities was that a good officer had to recognize which manoeuvres were to be avoided so that his troops could be instructed exclusively in those that were useful.[14]

In terms of their practicality, not all manoeuvres were created equal. Some manoeuvres, such as going from closed to open column, deploying from column into line or ploying back into column were the mainstays of any practical tactical system, and were used many times during a single day during a campaign and, of course, on the battlefield. Other manoeuvres used on the parade ground or described in the regulations, however, were useless or even dangerous, if ever attempted on the battlefield. Complicated manoeuvres, especially those involving numerous battalions, were to be avoided during an actual engagement. In this category were manoeuvres such as a multi-battalion change of face, where typically a lengthy line would face ninety degrees to either the left or the right.

Such considerations became increasingly important as the distance separating the friendly troops and the enemy decreased. Only the simplest manoeuvre could be performed in the face of the enemy and experienced officers only performed those that were absolutely necessary, such as moving towards a flank, retreating, or ploying into small parallel columns to bypass difficult terrain. A complicated manoeuvre such as a change of front could prove fatal when close to the enemy. For example, in many armies official theory called for a change of front when the enemy was victorious along a portion of the line. As they pursued friendly forces to the rear, those that stood,

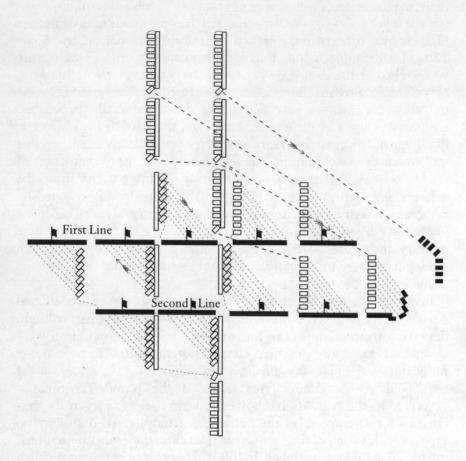

First Line

Second Line

Multi-battalion change of face manoeuvre

in theory, were to redeploy the line ninety degrees to be perpendicular to both the pursuers and the pursued. In this new position the enemy could be taken in flank, and the situation salvaged. This was the theory; experience, however, dictated otherwise. Rather than attempt this, French officers who found themselves in the situation where the friendly forces to their immediate left or right were defeated, were advised instead to have their men face the rear and quickly retreat. It then became the duty of the columns that so typically formed the second line to attack the flanks of the victorious enemy troops.[15]

On the parade ground, there was no enemy to distract the soldier's concentration, no smoke to obscure his view and no musket and cannon fire to prevent hearing the officers' orders. The soldier was able to perform his actions with much greater confidence, aware that a delay would never result in the destruction of his formation. Obviously, this calmness and precision, so absolutely essential when performing any large-scale manoeuvre, totally disappeared on the battlefield. A loss of cohesion or even a delay during a manoeuvre could result in a soldier and his companions being cut to pieces, if attacked before being able to complete the manoeuvre. This and the continual apprehension of being struck down at any moment by a musket or cannon ball contributed greatly to a high state of nervous tension.

There was another, more subtle difference between the parade ground and the battlefield. Formations, and hence manoeuvres, required less space on the parade ground than their equivalent conducted under battle conditions. During the review, it was desirable to place the men in as tight a formation as possible, not only for the sake of appearance but also to fit as many battalions as possible in the assigned area. During an engagement, on the other hand, the men required elbow room in order to bring their weapons to bear and reload after firing.[16] The theoretical limit of about twenty-two inches per file would expand to around twenty-seven to thirty inches in actual combat. The frontage of a battalion in line thus could expand twenty-five per cent or more and the mathematical limits assigned to a formation in peace would quickly disappear. This could wreak havoc on the plans of inexperienced officers who would initially continue to position their formations relative to one another as though they were still on the parade ground.

Fortunately for us, Ney and Bugeaud and other experienced and highly competent officers have listed those manoeuvres they believed to be the most valuable. According to Ney, the basis of all tactics was the ability to march in good order when changing position and to deliver fire effectively when called upon to do so. Consequently, it was imperative for the troops to master both the ordinary and the quick paces when marching, as well as to be able to march obliquely. However, for these marching skills to be effective, the troops had to be able to march well in line, closed column and column of route. It was also vital to master completely the various fire systems then in use in the French army. For this reason practising the manual of arms – the sequence of steps used to present, fire and reload the musket – was extremely important.

Based on his experience, Ney also felt that the troops should practise 'running' instead of relying on the 'quick' step when going from line to column or column back into line. Veteran troops on the battlefield, well-versed in a particular manoeuvre, would perform the necessary manoeuvres at the *pas de course* to save time. An excellent example occurred during the Battle of Austerlitz. When General Thiébault's brigade attacked the village of Pratzen, its battalions were formed in a 'line of battalions', that is in a series of closed columns, each separated by the width of a battalion. Colonel Mazas' battalion, 1st of the 14th *de ligne*, was defeated and forced to retire. In his memoirs, Thiébault recounted how the second battalion of this regiment deployed into line *at the run* as soon as it was ordered into action. After the eventual capture of the village and the Château of Sokolnitz, Thiébault had to hurry to align the battalions in his brigade with those of Morand and le Vasseur on either flank, so that the entire force would reach the next Russian line together. To do this, he rallied and reformed his battalions by sections while the whole was *on the march*.[17] The French sometimes applied the same pragmatic approach when reloading after firing. Coignet informs us that during the Battle of Montebello his battalion reloaded their muskets while they continued to march in columns of platoons.[18]

Ney believed that by sanctioning the *pas de course* officially and including it into the regular training, its use would be even further promoted.[19] General Duhèsme, expert in French light infantry tactics, had observed a similar practice. Experienced troops when ordered to quarter-wheel would often simply run into the intended position instead of methodically performing a quarter-wheel.[20]

As far as the range of manoeuvres that should be taught was concerned, Ney felt these should be limited only to the handful that were constantly used. The most obvious were those manoeuvres used to form the most common formations: forming the regiment into order of battle (line), ploying from line into closed order column, deploying back into line, forming squares. It was important that the men and officers became familiarized with their proper positions in each formation. Moreover, the troops had to be conversant with

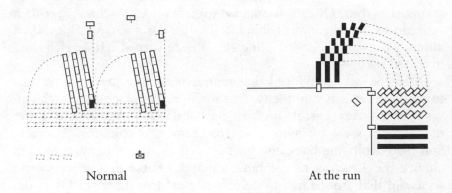

Normal   At the run

Running when performing a quarter wheel (conversion)

deploying into line and then back into column in all possible permutations: files, sections, platoons and divisions.

The next class of manoeuvres, less frequently used but still necessary because they were used in crisis situations, were those used to bypass difficult terrain or masses of friendly troops or simply to withdraw a force from an overwhelming situation. These manoeuvres consisted of change of front and change of direction, passage of defile by wings or centre (either in front, or in rear of the line), use of echelons, retreat *en échiquier* or by alternate divisions, and passage of lines.[21]

General Duhèsme in his treatise on light infantry tactics, practices and training also dealt with the practicality of various manoeuvres. Duhèsme felt that many of the official manoeuvres had little value for light infantry which spent much of its time moving in extended order. Facetiously, the general observed that the true value of formal manoeuvres to light infantry regiments was to ensure that they were allowed their share of the parade ground. Among his examples of never-used manoeuvres were changing the facing of the line, passage of lines, and facing to the rear. General Duhèsme did mention, however, that there was one situation where a change of front was useful. This was when it was necessary to retire through a defile while being threatened by the enemy from the front and on one flank. The side which was threatened would change the direction it was facing perpendicularly. It was now *en potence* and faced the direction of the enemy attack on the flank, the other half of the original line still facing the front. Once this angular formation was achieved, it then retired towards the defile behind it. The men in the front line did an about face; those along the line *en potence* turned left or right and marched by files.

Duhèsme was convinced that manoeuvres like marching in line towards the enemy and the various manoeuvres associated with columns were very useful, even to light infantry. Among the latter manoeuvres were forming closed columns and columns of attack, and then deploying back into line, as well as all manoeuvres used to change the direction of a column's march. These manoeuvres were so useful that troops had to be able to perform these readily under any circumstances – at night, in broken terrain, and under stressful battle conditions where they would be performed hurriedly – and like Ney he felt they had to also be performed at the run. General Duhèsme also felt that the men had to be able to perform these important manoeuvres while in 'inverted order'. Duhèsme recounted how one of his battalion commanders, who was ordered to act as a rear-guard during a retreat through a gorge in the Alps, utilized the *feu de chaussée* (street firing) method of delivering fire when closely pressed by an enemy column in a night-time action. This fire system had been included in almost all eighteenth-century regulations, but was finally discarded by the French regulations of 1791.[22]

USEFUL CAVALRY MANOEUVRES

Ney, Duhèsme, Bugeaud and Morand were all infantry commanders and they limited their comments to infantry manoeuvres. Fortunately, however, Captain de Brack (later General) has left a similar evaluation of cavalry manoeuvres employed during the Napoleonic period. De Brack noted that for cavalry, like infantry, it was essential that anything complicated always had to be avoided. In the presence of the enemy this was even more critical: cavalry could be cut to pieces just as easily as infantry, if caught off guard. It was equally important to avoid doing anything that would needlessly fatigue the horses.

In his work *Cavalry Outpost Duties*, published in the original

French version in 1834, de Brack probed even more deeply into what makes a manoeuvre simple or complicated than Marshal Ney or General Duhèsme before him. He linked the simplicity or complexity of an operation to the nature and number of the commands used to order in that manoeuvre. Manoeuvres that could be ordered by a single command, such as 'March', 'Platoons Wheel' were conceptually simple and had a much better chance of being successfully implemented under battle conditions. The command provided both the objective of the manoeuvre and the steps used to perform it. There was no need to extrapolate, or remember what were its component parts. Manoeuvres that required two or more commands, such as 'Changing Front on the Centre', 'Facing to the Rear in Line', were conceptually much more complicated and required the officers, NCOs and common soldiers to remember what the component steps were as well as the order in which they were to be performed. These were 'dangerous' on the battlefield since the soldiers could not be counted on to possess the needed presence of mind once they were even remotely close to the enemy, especially if they had recently been under fire.

A pragmatist with years of battlefield experience, de Brack explained to inexperienced officers how to achieve these complicated manoeuvres. The officers were to divide the manoeuvres into recognizable phases, each actuated by a single command. For example, a battalion might be in column and required to deploy into line facing the rear. The commander would first order 'Platoons Right About' and the column would instantly be facing towards the rear. Now the commander was able to order the column into line towards the (new) front with a single command. Officers also had to limit their commands to movements or manoeuvres with which the men in their command were already familiar, and there was to be no experimentation when the men were under fire:

> Execute only those which your men know, so to speak, too well, and which it is impossible for your officers or soldiers to make any mistakes; for it is necessary, I repeat, that your foresight should always make allowance for excitement, which harmonizes very poorly with difficulty. I shall go further and say that, as a man is more accustomed to using his right hand than his left, so a regiment will manoeuvre better by the right than by the left; profit then by this observation for use in

emergencies which demand the exercise of undisturbed coolness and self-confidence.[23]

Manoeuvres, that were made up of 'uniform movements' tended to be conceptually easier and thus easier to perform in the heat of battle. Among this class were manoeuvres that began at one end of the regiment and worked their way to the other or, when in column, those that started in the front and worked their way to the rear.

When close to the enemy, it was also very important to avoid manoeuvres that exposed, even temporarily, a fragment of the regiment to an attack on its flank. For this reason wheeling manoeuvres were not recommended when in the face of the enemy. For example, if the regiment was deployed in line and the commanding officer wanted to withdraw it a short distance, the most common method of breaking into column by quarter-wheeling to the right was not recommended. Unfortunately, as soon as the wheeling began, each tier in the column now formed offered its left flank to the enemy and was vulnerable to attack if the enemy was sufficiently close. A French dragoon regiment was destroyed at Kirrweiler when it attempted to form column using this method in the presence of the enemy. Though most of Blücher's Black Hussars were in skirmisher order to harass the dragoons, Blücher sent in his small reserve which were able to disperse the French cavalry by attacking the French column's flank.

A method de Brack used to form column when near the enemy was simply to have the troopers face to the right. A long narrow column was thus formed and it moved off in the intended direction by having the front of the column wheel by files and the rest following its lead. Despite the length of this column, it was still practical because line could be quickly reformed if circumstances required it. If attacked on the flank, the trooper merely faced to the left and line was instantly reformed, and the formation was ready to begin the advance towards the oncoming enemy.

Fortunately for posterity, de Brack also went on to enumerate those manoeuvres he felt were cumbersome or difficult to perform on the battlefield and thus should be studiously avoided. At the top of this list were counter-marches, that is, manoeuvres used to reverse the facing of the formation without changing the internal organization within that unit. Counter-marches, in terms of the number

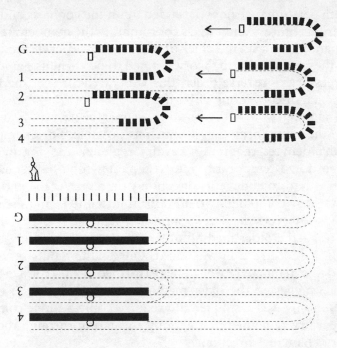

Example of a counter-march

and type of component movements, were complex and could not be performed in the face of the enemy. Movement into and out of line 'by fours' was also to be avoided, since any temporary columns formed would have very lengthy files. A direct hit by round shot would cause numerous casualties and force 'them out of all recognizable shape'.

Like his infantry counterparts, de Brack cautioned against complicated change of fronts, such as changing the facing of a regiment on its centre. This was to be avoided for several reasons. Its execution actually consisted of four sub-manoeuvres, and this violated de Brack's observation that when under fire or in the immediate vicinity of the enemy, troops should never be asked to do anything that required more than a single set of orders. One of these sub-manoeuvres was the formation of several temporary columns to manoeuvre into the new position or facing and this in itself was complex. Moreover, half of these columns had to be in inverted order. This was a departure from the most practised method of movement, when the formation was in normal sequence. This meant that

433

its smooth performance now depended upon the coolness and ability of the various officers and NCOs coordinating the manoeuvre within the formation, such as the chief of a platoon and even file leaders. Though the cavalry was, in theory, trained to perform its manoeuvres when necessary in reverse order, this was rarely, if ever, performed under the harsh conditions of battle.

When moving to another position, it was also very desirable to maintain the same formation as much as possible. For example, the official manoeuvres required a cavalry regiment moving in line to be broken down temporarily into companies (one half squadrons) whenever it had to change its direction of march. At the end of this manoeuvre, the companies would reform into line facing the desired direction. However, de Brack cautioned against this practice and advised using the older method of simply quarter-wheeling the line until the desired direction was faced. One of the flanks served as a pivot and this manoeuvre was to be performed at the trot. De Brack's experience suggested the older method was every bit as fast as the newer. Not only was it simpler and required only a single command, but the cavalry remained in a fighting formation through the entire process of changing direction.

Once the cavalry regiment had deployed into a useful formation, if enemy forces were sufficiently close, common sense demanded that the commanding officer maintain the formation and only assume another when forced to do so because of cogent circumstances. For similar reasons, the regiment was to be subdivided as little as possible and whenever circumstances permitted maintained as a single 'command'. This was so that if attacked suddenly it was able to present a meaningful force and offer sufficient resistance.[24]

AD HOC MANOEUVRES

So far, we have limited the discussion to which formal practices and manoeuvres were used on the actual battlefield and which were ignored. Despite the experienced tacticians' admonition scrupulously to avoid the complex or unfamiliar, the exigencies of combat sometimes spawned totally new methods, envisioned neither by formal regulations nor peace-time practice. This was particularly the case in a desperate situation where the regiment's officers recognized that following the established drill or procedure would not work, and unless an alternative method was found the formation was doomed to destruction.

Once again, we are indebted to Colonel Marbot for providing two detailed examples. The first occurred during the battle of Essling. Wanting to stop the advance of an Austrian infantry column near the village of Essling, Marshal Lannes ordered a *chasseurs à cheval* regiment forward to attack the enemy column's left flank. The French cavalry taken from Bruyère's brigade quickly advanced in a closed column at the 'grand trot', and soon succeeded in making its way through a gap in the enemy forces between Essling and the Danube. Unfortunately, the French mounted column's progress was suddenly and completely arrested when the column's scouts sank up to their chests into an unexpected mire. This placed the main column, only a short distance behind, in an embarrassing predicament. They had advanced up to the very edge of the mire which extended along the entire front of the column. There was no easy way to either circumnavigate the obstacle or even retire. The enemy soon noticed the *chasseur à chevals'* plight and some mounted Landwehr, the only Austrian cavalry locally available, were ordered to attack the left of the French light cavalry.

The squadrons at the front of the French column were effectively immobilized and unable to respond. The French officer commanding the column was resourceful and promptly ordered the four platoons at the rear of the column to quickly proceed by files to the left and, once clear of the column, immediately to form line facing the direction of the approaching Hungarian Landwehr. This they did, while the remainder of the regiment somehow turned itself around, moving to the rear a distance, and formed line to meet the approaching threat. All of this was performed 'in the nick of time', since at this moment a second body of enemy horsemen, a dragoon regiment, made its appearance.[25]

The second example, provided by the Battle of Katzbach in 1813, is all the more spectacular since the unrehearsed manoeuvre the French cavalry succeeded in performing was an *ad hoc* version of the infamous 'changing face' manoeuvre. This in its text-book form was rarely if ever performed on the battlefield even in the manifestation practised repeatedly on the parade ground. By the end of the day the French cavalry found itself facing vastly superior numbers of enemy cavalry. The latter was busily trying to work their way between the various groups of French cavalry spread along the front.

A light cavalry brigade from Excelmans' division in Sebastini's corps suddenly discovered it was threatened by a Prussian cavalry column whose circuitous movement had been masked by a woods on the right flank. This flank, defended by a number of French voltigeurs, had been thought to be secure. Unfortunately, the skirmishers were unable to impede the Prussian cavalry's motions. There had been a downpour and the infantrymen were unable to use their muskets.

The brigade consisted of three regiments, each deployed in line, one behind the other. By the time the French cavalry became aware of the enemy, the Prussian horse was immediately behind the brigade's right flank and the regiment in the third line, given virtually no time to respond, was instantly routed. The 23rd *chasseurs à cheval* in the second line found itself in an extremely precarious position. Though still some distance away, the enemy was charging in from the regiment's right and rear. To be able to resist, the colonel realized that the regiment had to change its front to face the right and to the rear. The textbook approach had two drawbacks. The French version of the change of face manoeuvre was notoriously tedious. However, even worse, it required the right half of the regiment to turn around and then ride diagonally towards the left rear. This meant, in effect, half of the regiment would be riding with their backs facing the enemy as the latter closed in during the final moments. The left half of the regiment would not have this problem since each of its platoons quarter-wheeled independently into the new line. The commander of the 23rd *chasseurs à cheval* solved the problem by ordering a change of front towards the right wing in inverse order. This was accomplished with no time to spare. The completed line was formed when the Prussians were only fifty paces away![26]

These are two examples of cavalry forced to utilize an *ad hoc* manoeuvre in the face of the enemy. However, probably the most extreme example of departing from the prescribed practice was provided by Marshal Ney himself during his retreat from Portugal during the Peninsular War. In command of the rear guard, Ney had been ordered to check the progress of the British following the army. The army had to pass through a relatively narrow defile and extra time was needed for the baggage to pass through. He was able to offer a rigorous rear-guard action, thus delaying the enemy's advance. However, the British received constant reinforcements so that his position first became untenable and then perilous. The French rear

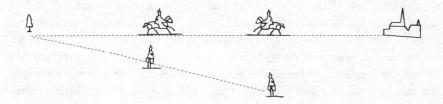

Guides providing proper alignment for the intended line

guard was atop a hill and had a narrow valley to their backs which separated them from a plateau to the rear. Ney realized that the position could no longer be held. However, an organized retreat back to the next available defensive position was equally impossible. Given the steep hill immediately behind them and the British pursuit that was sure to follow, the French would have been exposed to excessive losses. Ney coolly ordered the colours and 'guides' (men whose purpose was to serve as markers for alignment) in each battalion, as well as the senior officers and his staff, to rush down the valley and up the hill behind them. Once atop the plateau, they quickly traced out where the new line was to be formed, the guides from each battalion positioning themselves to the left and right of their battalion's intended position.

Moments later, he ordered the defending line to retire at a full run. Almost miraculously, the new line 'was reformed in no time, as if by enchantment'. Had the guides and colour bearers not been in position it would have been impossible for the infantry to reform and many men would have been lost in the rout that surely would have occurred. The incident is doubly illuminating, showing not only how quickly determined infantry could reform when certain precautions were taken, but also how competent and ingenious officers could improvise manoeuvres and movements when required to do so by extreme circumstances. Of course, it should be pointed out that this bold manoeuvre would not have been possible if attempted in open terrain in front of a large body of enemy cavalry.[27]

Marshal Ney, in fact, did not invent this practice of placing some staff officers and the colours behind the lines to serve as a rallying point upon which a new line could be reformed. British observers had noticed this technique employed about ten years earlier at Bergen, 19 September 1799. In a pamphlet arguing that British infantry should adopt certain French innovations, a Captain Haly recounts how the French battalions used a similar ploy to facilitate a battalion's rallying whenever it was repulsed:

> I observed ... that the French used these rallying points to great advantage, in the Sand Hills; where independent of reserves, they had positions behind these again, marked with white staffs having branches of straw at the top, to make it visible to the flying soldiers our people drove before them. I saw one of their corps we had thrown into confusion, fall in and form between these staffs with as much regularity as if they had been on their parade ground.[28]

General Duhèsme also alluded to a similar tactic, albeit without supplying any of the details. He enjoined battalion commanders to instruct their men when forced quickly to retreat to retire *en fourrageur* and then quickly rally one hundred yards to the rear.[29]

RUSES

If commanders were conservative about which formations and manoeuvres they used on the battlefield and usually restricted their choices to the most basic, occasionally the more imaginative among them displayed noticeable creativity in devising 'stratagems' to outwit their opponents and gain some sort of local advantage. These were personal efforts usually devised extemporaneously by an officer or commander as he responded to a situation still in the process of unfolding. Sometimes, however, they were the product of previous forethought as a conscientious officer sought an effective response to an anticipated contingency. These *ad hoc* stratagems will be referred to as 'ruses' to differentiate them from the formal pre-arranged drills and manoeuvres practised methodically on the parade ground. The word 'stratagem' is avoided since it is easily confused with 'strategy', which implies a grand scale, whereas most ruses were quite tactical in their nature and scope.

Napoleonic literature is replete with examples of clever ruses leading to the discomfiture of the opponent. These varied tremendously both in their purpose and their degree of sophistication. Many were simple one-step operations designed to accrue small advantages; others involved a number of operations and were aimed at the destruction of the enemy.

One simple trick, if threatened by an unwelcome attack, was to create the impression that one had more troops than were actually available. The following example, although taken from the earlier period, is nevertheless illustrative. During the Seven Years' War, General Warnery, threatened by a greatly superior enemy force at Reichenberg, in Bohemia, placed the 600 dragoons and hussars in his command along a single rank. From afar, General Macquire, the enemy commander, thought this long line of cavalrymen was in fact two or three ranks deep, and wrongly concluded he faced 1,200 to 2,000 horsemen. Not wanting to initiate a full-scale engagement, Macquire withdrew, even though he had managed to surround the small Prussian force who found themselves cut off from the main body marching from Zittau.[30]

Sometimes, a commander wished to create the opposite impression, that is, to make the enemy believe there were fewer troops than there really were. By quickly pulling back his flankers (scouts) and retiring part of his main body of hussars behind some heights, Blücher at Kirrweiler (1794) succeeded in deceiving the French force as to his intentions. When they most unwisely continued to advance into his vacated position without taking any precautions, the French infantry were surprised and scattered.[31]

In 1807 at the siege of Danzig, it was the French turn to employ a similar ruse, this time against the Russians. A Russian force which landed unexpectedly, surprised a portion of the French lines of circumvallation who were preoccupied with cooking their soup. General Schramm, who commanded the French forces under attack, ordered his regiment to withdraw quickly. When the Russians had driven off the French, they foolishly stopped to collect the cooking utensils. Meanwhile the French reversed their direction and attacked the Russians, who became the victims of surprise in turn. Nearly 2,000 Russians were killed, captured or wounded as a result.[32]

The most notable instance of this type of deception, however, was Napoleon's ability effectively to hide Lannes' and the Guard corps, behind the Zuran hill at Austerlitz.

To deceive the enemy as to the true number of men available in an area, it was not always necessary to withdraw them any distance or even hide them behind some large obstacle. A battalion commander could often achieve the same result simply by ordering his men to get down on the ground and lie in wait for the enemy. Though this ploy is usually associated with the British infantry during the Peninsular War, it appears that versions of it had been used occasionally by most armies throughout the Napoleonic Wars.

The Russians were observed using this trick while struggling to retain control of Pratzen village during the Battle of Austerlitz. Thiébault's brigade was ordered to gain possession of the village. Unfortunately for the French, however, the advance guard of the Russian fourth column not only had time to enter the village, but was able to pass through it and take some initial defensive precautions. The Russian infantry lay flat on the ground and awaited the French approach. Thiébault sent Colonel Mazas to take the village with his 1st battalion of the 14th *de ligne*. Though Mazas was an experienced battalion commander, he failed to send out any scouts as his men approached the village in a single line. When the French infantry reached the wide ravine on the outskirts, the Russians sprang up and pumped a murderous fire into the French ranks. Taken completely by surprise and stung by the point blank fire, the French battalion quickly fled. As an epilogue, Thiébault had taken the precaution of following with the other three battalions in closed columns in a 'line of battalions'. While Mazas was rallying his battalion, Thiébault led the 36th Regiment and the 2nd battalion of the 14th which deployed into line as it ran forward. These succeeded in overpowering the Russian infantry and took the village.[33]

The French were also known to have used this same technique. At Friedland, for example, as both sides engaged in a lengthy cannonade, the French infantry supports behind their tirailleurs lay down in the tall grass to avoid casualties, while their Russian counterparts continued standing contemptuously ignoring the effects of the French infantry fire. The main French force, maintained in dense columns, was also kept inside the woods to be out of harm's way.[34]

One very commonly occurring ruse was to mask artillery behind friendly troops until the enemy advanced to close range. Then the cavalry or infantry in front of it would move out of the way and the artillery would belch out deadly canister, much to the attacker's chagrin. This would be all the more effective, since it would be unexpected. Cavalry was the most suitable for these purposes, since it could be moved out of the way more quickly. However, infantry would serve, if needed. It was even possible to hide a battery behind hedges, garden walls, bushes, etc. At the right moment these could be pulled down or simply blown away.[35]

The encounter on the Pratzen Heights between Morand and Saint-Hilaire's division on the French side and Kollowrath's command on the Allies' side provides a wonderfully interesting illustration, since it is an example of both sides resorting to a ruse to gain an advantage over their opponents. Advancing in front of Saint-Hilaire's force, Morand bumped into Kamenski's brigade. Initially, the 4,000-man Russian force enjoyed the advantage and started to outflank the 10th *légère* opposed to them. Before the Russians could make headway, however, Morand was joined by Saint-Hilaire who deployed his men on the right of the 10th *légère*. A little later further reinforcements arrived in the form of Thiébault's brigade, which was held in columns slightly to the rear. The scales had now turned in favour of the French. However, before the French could repulse Kamenski, the three French generals noticed four regiments advancing in closed order columns on their left rear, apparently having come out of Krenowitz. Morand, Saint-Hilaire and Thiébault with the greatest of interest followed the movement of these columns with their field-glasses. There was nothing, however, that positively identified the approaching force as the enemy. Presently, an officer rode out of the approaching masses and stopped when within shouting distance. The officer entreated the French not to fire and explained that they were Bavarians. Now, the very night before a Bavarian corps had indeed joined the French army and so the situation was tricky. According to Thiébault's account, when the three generals conferred he emphatically expressed the opinion that the so-called Bavarians were suspicious and that the French must on no account be caught off guard. They could see neither Bavarian colours nor distinctively Bavarian uniforms. Thus, they agreed to make arrangements as though the 'Bavarians' were the enemy. Thiébault positioned his brigade *en crochet* to Morand's regiment. The two battalions of the 36th *de ligne* quickly deployed into line and were appuyed on Morand's left. The 2nd battalion of the 14th *de ligne* remained in column directly behind the left side of the 36th and was to serve as a reserve in case of any unexpected exigencies. Thiébault placed his remaining three guns between the two battalions of the 36th (he had earlier sent three guns to Morand). However, just at this moment Major Fontenay arrived with six 12-pounders. These had been sent by Napoleon who, from his position in the rear, was able to discern that Saint-Hilaire's situation was critical. They were placed on either wing of the 36th. Thiébault took the precaution, however, of masking each of the three demi-batteries with a squad of infantrymen, as did Morand for his guns.

Any uncertainty about the so-called 'Bavarians' was dispelled by what happened next. The officer who had called out was now joined by another who had ridden out from Kamenski's brigade. A short conference ensued, after which the four regiments resumed their advance toward the rear of the French position. Of course, now they were faced by Thiébault's line. Thiébault ordered Major Fontenay to load the guns with both round shot and canister, to be laid for a distance of thirty to forty paces. Fontenay momentarily remonstrated, observing that this would ruin the guns. Thiébault overruled him, saying that this was acceptable as long as the guns were able to fire for ten minutes. When the enemy had approached to the appointed distance, the masking infantry were removed. The surprised enemy found themselves staring down the barrels of nine large calibre guns, which immediately started to wreak havoc. The results are best left to Thiébault's words:

> My satisfaction may be imagined when I saw every round tear large square holes through these regiments till they retired a flying mass from the attack on my three battalions. I had not lost a single man, and had I a brigade of cavalry at my disposal not one of my assailants would have escaped.[36]

This discussion about various ruses would not be complete without examining at least one ruse that, proving to be unsuccessful, occasioned as disastrous results for the friendly force as had been planned for the enemy.

On 24 April 1794 at Villiers-en-Cauchies three advancing French columns encountered a small Allied advance guard made up of four squadrons of Austrian hussars and two squadrons from the British 15th Light Dragoons. The French commander positioned his cavalry to form the first 'line'. A small distance to the rear an artillery battery unlimbered, facing the friendly cavalry in front of it. To its rear, six battalions of infantry were made to form a single large square. It is obvious from this disposition along with the commander's action during the subsequent engagement that his intention was to allow the Allied cavalry to charge, and then at the last minute the French cavalry was to break to either flank exposing the enemy cavalry to a murderous point blank artillery fire.

Unfortunately, this ruse was not thought through thoroughly and was ineptly executed. The English cavalry leading the charge began to gallop when it was 150 paces from the French line of cavalry, which remained at a standstill. The French cavalry commander waited until the onrushing enemy was only sixty paces distant before ordering his troopers to unmask the artillery in position behind them. This meant that the French cavalry had about six seconds to clear the frontage of the artillery. Of course, this was not enough time and the French artillery was forced to fire before all the French cavalry had cleared the target area. The result was doubly disastrous. The French cavalry sustained greater losses due to the artillery fire than did the Allies. Moreover, the French cavalry being ordered to precipitate retreat with the enemy at its heels never regained the presence of mind to offer any determined resistance in a second encounter that soon followed.[37]

The Russian Cossacks were a perennial nuisance to regular French cavalry, whenever the latter had the misfortune of having to fight against them. Parquin tells us of an interesting ruse a French cavalry officer managed to pull off against these irregular Russian horsemen at the combat of Guttstadt. Parquin's regiment, as indeed all of General Lasalles's division, had been ordered to screen an infantry division moving through a wood to its rear in order to take the enemy in flank. As a result, it had to bear enemy artillery fire for what seemed an eternity. As if the enemy artillery was not bothersome enough, a group of Cossacks periodically would approach to harass the French formation. Each time, the French chasseurs would charge and drive off the Cossacks. This was fruitless, however, since the French light cavalry could never catch up to the Cossack force, charge as it might. The Cossacks were able to take cover behind the Russian artillery who then inflicted heavy casualties on the French chasseurs close on the Cossack's heels. Then, after an all-too-brief hiatus, the Russian horsemen returned to continue their task of unsettling the

French troopers. The colonel of Parquin's regiment, having become quite concerned, decided upon a stratagem that might eliminate this Cossack nuisance once and for all.

To the right of the French cavalry lay a clump of woods. Fortunately, at this point it was in the hands of French infantry. The colonel ordered a Captain Bertin and his squadron to circle around this wood and hide behind it until he heard musket fire. This would be Bertin's signal to charge at full speed across the plateau back toward the French cavalry regiment. Next, the colonel rode over to Lieutenant Capitan. Capitan and his squad were to ride in front of the same clump of woods. They were to station themselves 300 or 400 feet from its edge. There, they were to await the return of the Cossacks with their carbines readied. When the enemy Cossacks charged this small group of French horsemen, Capitan was to give the order to fire when the Cossacks were only six feet away. The colonel explained that although this could be expected to drive off the Cossacks temporarily, he and his men were to stand their ground until the last man if necessary, all the while continuing to fire their carbines.

The Cossacks soon made their appearance and events unfolded just as the colonel had counted on. Capitan's small force was attacked but managed to hold the Cossacks at bay. Bertin's squadron, hearing the commotion, charged around the wood and headed towards the Cossacks from their rear. Meanwhile, the main body of the regiment charged the Cossacks from the front. These latter, whose retreat now was cut off by Bertin and his men, were completely cut down or taken prisoner.[38]

With the exception of Villiers-en-Cauchies the previous anecdotes have described successful ruses. Of course, reality is structured to satisfy the natural bent of both optimists and pessimists. So, in the interest of accuracy a few failed ruses should be included. Ever since Russian infantry first made their appearance in western Europe they have been notorious for the manner in which they often defended against cavalry charges. Rather than standing firm, shoulder to shoulder, offering a veritable hedgehog of bayonets, they frequently would fall down on the ground and pretend to be dead. The oncoming horses, always loath to step on anything but firm ground would tend to jump over them. Once past, the Russian infantry would jump back up and attack the enemy from the rear. When in dire straits the Russian infantry would employ a vaguely similar ploy. They would surrender and lay down their arms. Very often, however, as soon as any chance offered itself, the Russian soldiers would seize their arms and kill their captors.

Unfortunately, this reputation worked against the Russian infantry at Austerlitz. Fully cognizant of this tendency, the French made it policy to take absolutely no prisoners until the affair was definitely settled. Defeated Russian soldiers who otherwise would have been given quarter were systematically bayoneted to death, because the French could not afford to post enough guards to prevent this threat from rising in their rear. General Thiébault recounted his experience at Austerlitz:

Up till the last hour we took no prisoners, except those who contrived to constitute themselves as such. It is true we had been warned that the Russians, even when too severely wounded to march, would take up their arms again after their enemy had gone forward, reload them, and put their conquerors between two fires. Now, in a struggle of such obstinacy, when we had to do with three or four times our own number, it would not do to run any risk; one could stick at nothing, and thus not a single living enemy remained in our rear.[39]

CHAPTER 23

Conclusion: A Blueprint for Tomorrow's Military History

ALTHOUGH THE GOAL OF THIS WORK has been to answer questions about how troops fought during the Napoleonic Wars and the reasons why these practices were adopted in the first place, it is also hoped that at the same time many other questions have been raised about the nature of tactics, combat experience and how military history should be studied at this lower level of detail. To comprehend fully the scope of these questions and their potential significance, it is necessary to review several recent trends that have affected how military history is currently approached.

When John Keegan's now highly acclaimed and influential *The Face of Battle* was first published in 1976, it heralded a new era that challenged several cornerstones of the then traditional military methodology. Up to this point, to a great many writers military history was little more than the 'study of generals and generalship'.[1] The actions of individual soldiers were treated as mere dots on the wide canvas depicting a European battlefield. The common soldier's experience, feelings and point of view, if not totally ignored, were only cursorily treated and ultimately reduced to an aside or footnote. By taking the opposite approach and eschewing the well-travelled high-level approach which had limited mainstream military history to the study of a chronology of major events or the view from the commander's tent, that is, his objectives, strategies and actions, etc., Keegan succeeded in redirecting the focus to the experiential and psychological arena. One could say Keegan democratized

446

the scope of what should be considered relevant and thus worthy of study.

Paradoxically, however, *The Face of Battle* poses a curious dilemma to anyone seriously studying either the nature of battlefield dynamics or combat experience during the Napoleonic era. Artfully written, this little volume in many respects is the very embodiment of a workable synthesis between scholarly research and analysis and the cogency and simplicity needed for mass appeal. Quite deservedly, this work will probably always remain in the pantheon of truly great military writings. Nevertheless, as the years go by the very success of this classic has begun increasingly to impede our further understanding of warfare during the Napoleonic period. The problem arises not so much in Keegan's book but in the expectations and attitudes of its numerous readers. In the minds of many military historians and probably most casual readers, *The Face of Battle* all too often has been elevated to the 'final statement' on combat experience. Like every other genuinely iconoclastic work which has rightly gained its place in our intellectual heritage, *The Face of Battle* has slowly but inevitably migrated from the truly radical which has shaken up conservative thinking and tradition to the realm of intellectual orthodoxy. This, of course, is unavoidable, and is simply a reflection of how new ideas are and always will be propagated.

Any writer of non-fiction has a number of stock literary vehicles at his disposal. Frequently, historians have relied, perhaps over-relied, on the simplicity and the power of the narrative. Facts, events and personalities are presented in chronological order. This is particularly the case for campaign studies, the chronicles of a particular war, and so on. Psychological studies have also been utilized with varying degrees of success. Keegan's work is a refreshing blend of the narrative with the experiential, and hence, at least indirectly, the psychological. The subject matter, analysis and method of presentation flow from the in-depth analysis of three major battles from widely separated points in time. Keegan's Waterloo vignette, the one we are most concerned with, is organized into five or six logical groupings, which Keegan has termed 'categories of combat'. These are simply the different practices and experiences of each of the various arms of service, cavalry versus cavalry, infantry versus infantry, cavalry versus artillery, etc. Grouping the material and treatment into these major archetypes, however, has implied that the dynamics and forces described in this particular battle somehow have a broad

447

application and are, indeed, 'universals' which describe the nature of warfare throughout the entire Napoleonic period.

In terms of the relationship between the events that took place during the engagement and contextual information needed for any deeper understanding, there are two ways of examining a battle. We can look at these events and bring what is known about warfare of the time, etc. in order to elaborate upon them. In other words, we can draw from what is known about the military science or the art of war of the period and interpret and comment upon the various phenomena encountered during the battle. The opposite approach is to first examine the actions, events and phenomena making up the battle and then theorize how warfare was conducted more generally. The first method can be thought of as taking information from the more general context and applying it to a specific application. The second is to work from the particular to gain an insight into the universal.

Many studies use a combination of both methods; however, Keegan's *Face of Battle* is noticeably more interested in the second approach than the first. This is not to say that Keegan never provides background information about tactical practices, etc. but that these represent a small fraction of the information presented, and this information often is provided to distinguish theoretical doctrine from 'what really happened under fire'. At first glance, Keegan's approach appears more attractive. What reader with any sense of intellectual self-worth would submit to the military historical equivalent of applications analyses, a pedestrian search for examples of the already known and well-catalogued, when offered the alternative of following along on a promising treasure hunt for military historical universals? It is a much more meaningful venture to look at something if it is thought to provide an insight into a much larger whole, than it is to take existing concepts and facts and apply them to a particular situation or event. But this approach, regardless of how much more emotionally fulfilling for the author to create and for the audience to read, is at the same time much more subject to error. It is easy enough for someone to isolate an action or phenomenon in a particular battle and then conclude this was the norm. But what if there were regional variations or differences in the way a technique was practised a mere few years earlier? What if the observed event was simply an anomaly, some sort of battlefield aberration from what was more commonly found over a broader sampling?

It is this problem of confusing the aberrant with the norm that one bumps into so frequently in Keegan's work. Two examples should be sufficient to illustrate. During his discussion of cavalry combat, Keegan quite correctly dismisses the idea that opposing cavalry actually met each other at speed:

> Both popular impressions and copy-book drill – and the initial charges in the two great series, British and French, were launched copy-book style – supposed cavalry versus cavalry charges to mean the meeting of dense formations at high speed.[2]

Of course, opposing cavalry formations never did literally run into one another; one side or the other would break before contact actually occurred. In this passage, however, Keegan appears to suggest that those who had first developed the prevalent cavalry charge doctrine (cavalry begins the advance at the walk, proceeds to the trot and finally accelerates to the gallop) as well as those who throughout the Napoleonic period advocated its employment shared this unrealistic expectation. Although during the final moments of each charge both French and British cavalry at Waterloo either pulled up short or loosened their ranks and passed harmlessly through one another's formations, such eventualities hardly came as a revelation to experienced cavalry officers. The tendency for opposing forces to somehow avoid running into one another had been commented upon at least as far back as the days of de la Colonie during the War of Spanish Succession. It was, in fact, this very realization that had forced Frederick and his generals to devise the walk/trot/charge tactic in the first place. Frederick realized that no cavalry on earth would voluntarily run full tilt into their opponents charging in the opposite direction. One side or the other would back down and flee or both sides would take evasive action to ameliorate the shock. However, if one side was able to retain its cohesion and continued to move at speed, the other side would always be forced to back down.

It is also important to realize that the two cavalry forces involved at Waterloo could hardly be said to be representative of so-called 'Napoleonic cavalry'. During the Seven Years' War, the Prussian cavalry under Zieten and Seidlyz performed charges modelled on the theoretical system with tremendous results. The British cavalry, however, never known for being highly disciplined, were notorious even among their own officers for their proclivity to over-zealous actions. Wellington himself was forced to concede that the British cavalry was noticeably more undisciplined than its continental peers. True, the French cavalry under Murat never matched the capabilities or spectacular achievements of those led by Seydlitz. This notwithstanding, Lasalles and Kellerman time and time again led controlled charges at a fast trot. However, the French cavalry at Waterloo lacked the experience, training, or quality of horses enjoyed by the French troopers prior to the 1812 débâcle.

Thus, when examining the conduct of the French and British cavalry at Waterloo, before we can make generalizations about whether or not the prevalent official doctrine was unrealistic, we must be aware of why it was developed, if it had been utilized by other cavalries successfully, and to what extent the French and British cavalry at Waterloo differed from other armies of that and the immediately preceding period. The answer, of course, is that both the French and British cavalry at Waterloo are relatively poor representatives of this arm for the period and it is unfortunate that anyone would attempt to generalize on the cavalry's capabilities based on their performance during this battle.

The relationship between theoretical developments in the Prussian cavalry 1742–1748 and practical events during the late Napoleonic Wars is not at all obvious and a historian can hardly be faulted for failing to unravel the convoluted threads connecting the two. However, in the second example of methodological problems intrinsic in Keegan's approach the interval separating Waterloo and other events providing a cross check can be measured in days rather than years. Summing up the relative capabilities of cavalry versus infantry when the two arms faced each other in a fair fight, at the end of his 'Cavalry versus Infantry' section Keegan rather contemptuously concluded, 'Here come "those d—d fools again" seems an appropriate judgement on the character of the conflict.' In other words, well led, steady infantry would invariably best cavalry, regardless of the latter's élan, leadership or tactics, and the British infantry realized that henceforth all cavalry assaults would be doomed to failure.

Once again this observation about the infantry's strength was anything but novel. Writing in the 1740s, Puységur noted that well-led infantry which recognized its strength would always be able to resist a cavalry assault, provided it was sufficiently prepared. However, this did not mean that infantry was invulnerable to cavalry. As we have seen, experienced cavalry officers realized that during the course of any extended engagement fortuitous events would here and there afford the cavalry with the opportunity it needed to catch an infantry formation insufficiently unprepared to receive a charge. Reeling back our examination a mere two days before Waterloo, French cavalry adroitly led by General Kellermann was able to destroy one British and one Hanoverian infantry formation at Quatre Bras.[3]

In both of these examples, Keegan has looked at some aspect of the events or phenomena observed at Waterloo and elevated these to universals which are to be applied throughout the entire era. However, when we broaden our examination to look at events during the Hundred Days and previous continental Napoleonic campaigns, as well as the body of military art and science during the era, it becomes obvious that much more of Keegan's descriptions of 'categories of combat' pertain to idiosyncratic conditions during the battle being described (Waterloo) than has been first thought.

These remarks have not been provided to malign Keegan's efforts or in any way belittle this author's contribution to the study of military history. Rather, they are intended to show that these methodological problems are symptomatic of broad-based limitations and prejudices pervading the whole of the English speaking community, rather than a want of ability or conscientiousness on the part of individual authors.

As Keegan has noted in his opening discussion of the major influences in military historiography, when Sir Edward Creasy set out to write his immensely popular *Fifteen Decisive Battles of the World*, the author selected only those highly notable events across history's long panorama that 'have helped to make us what we are'.[4] Keegan's intent was to produce a work that would head in the opposite direction: to redirect the focus from particular events and famous personalities and explore the commonality of human nature under combat conditions. But if Keegan was driven by an entirely different set of goals, ironically he chose a vehicle remarkably similar to that used by Creasy – that is, confining his analysis to several major military historical events to gain an understanding of a larger whole, in this case an understanding of human nature and the battlefield experience. The intrinsic problem with this approach is that too small a sampling has been considered to establish whether the phenomena, events, etc. being studied are indeed representative of some more general dynamic or principle.

However, there is another, much more subtle tendency at work, one which has affected the work of most English-speaking military historians. This is the belief that lower level tactics did not play a significant role in determining how a battle unfolded and its eventual outcome, hence the study of formal doctrine and training provides little insight into what actually happened during the heat of combat. The belief has enjoyed continued popularity for several reasons. One is the recognition that during the musket era complex drill systems were rarely, if ever, applied on the battlefield exactly as described in the official doctrine and practised on the parade grounds. Even simpler procedures, such as the various firing systems, could only be conducted for a few moments before invariably breaking down into a ragged and uncontrollable individual fire.

This initial impression that official doctrine was not useful seems to be confirmed whenever we glance through the various infantry and cavalry drill booklets of the time. Although we can easily spot numerous minor differences of detail, such as how many companies in a battalion, or the number of steps per minute during a march, we are hard pressed to isolate distinctive formations, manoeuvres or fire systems that would account for the French successes up to 1809 or the subsequent British victories in the Peninsula or the Hundred Days. This should not be surprising since by 1791 all armies purposely had based their official doctrine on the formation and manoeuvring system first formulated by Frederick the Great between 1747 and 1756.

A large portion of the reading public is intrigued with some aspect of history. Unfortunately, most of this interest is limited to notable events and famous personalities. Few have the stomach or patience for a lengthy and complicated discussion of seemingly obscure technology. How many will endure a detailed step-by-step examination of the evolution of the spinning wheel compared to those who enthusiastically read about the British labour riots in the early 1800s? Very few indeed. This differential between what most find interesting and what is ultimately relevant, unfortunately has infected even the most conscientious of military historians, the great majority of whom have felt that antiquated military technology is best left undisturbed on library shelves or forgotten boxes in dusty warehouses.

Unfamiliar with the full spectrum of the period's military science and its many attendant nuances, many historians have prematurely concluded that all formal practices and doctrine are of little practical use and have permanently dismissed these as purely theoretical systems. Someone of this bent looking at the French infantry regulations of 1791, for example, then tends to place a single battalion changing its direction of march on a movable pivot (an extremely common manoeuvre performed even within canister range) on the same level of impracticality as a multi-battalion change of face (which was highly impractical). The result is that all too frequently, the entire drill booklet and its contents is permanently relegated to the dusty bin of 'useless facts'.

But the failure to recognize the true significance of tactical-level events and dynamics has had a much more profound effect on our understanding of the nature of battle and the combat experience than simply the neglect of formal doctrine and arcane drills and manoeuvres. Ultimately, it has restricted the entire intellectual system we use to conceptualize how the various forces on the battlefield interact to produce the results they did.

IMPORTANCE OF TACTICS

Hopefully, this present work has adequately demonstrated that although all but the simplest and most fundamental of tactical practices were infrequently applied in their pure textbook form, *ad hoc* variants born out of necessity thickly populated every crucible of battle. At Jena, for example, we see the men of the 3rd battalion of the 16th *légère* marching up to the opposing Prussian battery and then dispersing as skirmishers. At Austerlitz, the 55th *de ligne* meeting the enemy employed, in succession, fire by battalion, by platoon and finally fire by ranks. The use of text book practices certainly was not limited to the French army. The present work abounds with similar examples provided by Austrian, Prussian, Russian, Spanish and even British troops. Thus, the more closely we examine lower level events occurring during any battle, the more we are forced to recognize the ubiquitousness of tactical practices on the Napoleonic battlefield.

There remains one fundamental question. Conceding that tactical practices occurred repeatedly during every engagement, how important were these? Did these tactical-level events ever determine the outcome of a battle? Were there ever sufficient differentials between the opponents' tactical capabilities to make the outcome a foregone conclusion? In other words, were there ever cases where the tactical systems employed by one army were so superior to those of their adversaries that victory was guaranteed, regardless of the quality of leadership, the determination of the troops or the overall strategic situation?

When we look at the various contests that punctuated the Revolutionary and Napoleonic Wars, we must concede that in a majority of cases the opposing forces enjoyed what amounted to tactical equality. If we ignore minor regional variations, most often the opposing forces employed the same types of tactical practices. And, even where opponents did not use exactly the same methods, each was able to employ sufficient tactical antidotes that most major contests were long drawn-out affairs decided by so-called 'higher-level' factors, such as who had the more competent commander, whose troops were in a higher state of preparedness or more highly motivated, etc. However, occasionally an isolated tactical-level event, which normally would have had but a localized effect, was transformed by extraordinary circumstances into the deciding factor, determining who would emerge the victor and who would be forced to flee the field. The Battle of Lodi Bridge, for example, was decided by a *faux pas* on the part of the Austrian artillery and the French infantry's ability to exploit this error. Trained to fire canister at close range, the Austrian gunners failed to modify the usual tactic to account for the lengthy French infantry columns on the bridge before them. Once near the shore, large numbers of the French infantry jumped into the water and spread out as skirmishers as they climbed ashore, where they were eventually able to overpower the Austrian batteries.

An even more spectacular result was achieved by Kellerman's cavalry at Marengo. Once again, the contest was decided by a tactical error on one side and a brilliant tactical counter-stroke on the other. The Austrians, flush with impending victory, advanced in monstrous columns unprotected by an advance guard or the flankers demanded by standard practice and common sense. Observing the Austrians' lack of preparedness, Kellerman ordered his cavalry to deploy quickly and charge. Caught off guard the massive Austrian column was completely scattered.

Occasionally, an army did find itself possessed of a significant tactical advantage over the enemy. When this occurred, the army with the significant tactical or grand-tactical superiority almost always easily won the contest. Such was the case with the French when they encountered their middle-eastern foes during the Egyptian campaigns and then against the continental Allies during the 1805 and 1806 campaigns in central Europe. In 1798 and 1799 both the French and the Turks and Mamelukes possessed the same basic set of weapons, though both sides certainly had a different proportion of infantry, cavalry and artillery. What doomed the Turks and Mamelukes to continual and certain defeat was the failure of a tactical system which relied upon individual valour and fighting capability to make any impact on the European method of fighting in highly regulated and orderly formations. The extreme unevenness of casualties suffered by the two sides demonstrates clearly that, in retrospect, the eastern forces had no chance of victory. At Austerlitz, Auerstädt and Jena, the French also enjoyed a decided advantage over their opponents, one that would ensure victory, though in this case the advantage arose from the superiority of their grand-tactical systems.

Almost by definition, however, this type of tactical or grand-tactical domination tended to survive for only a relatively brief period of time, often only a year or two, though sometimes for as much as a decade. It is probably no exaggeration to say that warfare is the most competitive of all human activities. When one side develops a temporary advantage in doctrine or training, the other side, unless fettered by deep social and cultural constraints, invariably will catch up or develop its own tactical antidotes to negate its enemy's advantages. In this regard, one can say that tactics, like water, 'always seeks its own level'.

The recognition of the increased importance of both tactics and tactical-level events during combat is not a neutral development, simply adding to the number of 'facts' at our disposal. Rather, it must force a number of *qualitative* changes in how we approach this aspect of military history. The first of these changes lies in the psychological realm. We must expand the repertoire of forces understood significantly to affect human consciousness and behaviour during combat. In recent years, interest in the experience of combat and the psychology of the individual soldier has increased in importance both among historians and readers alike. However, in its incipient form this new experiential approach has tended to have an unmistakable monolithic quality. Seeking to identify archetypal situations, historians have assumed that in each situation there is a single overriding psychological dynamic that determines the soldier's response and on a statistical level reduces their reaction to a predictable result.

For example, in the case of the two cavalry forces charging one another, it has been observed, and corrcctly so, that neither side would ride directly into their opponents at speed. The instinct of self-preservation meant that ultimately one or both sides would alter their course in some way, either by pulling up short, turning and both sides riding parallel to one another for a distance, or by the formation opening up so that both sides could 'thread' one another.

The role of tactics in these situations has been largely ignored because of the conviction that they were not applied in practice. The belief is that the impulses arising from human nature are so strong in these critical situations that they overpower prior training and make implementation of formal doctrine impossible. In our example, the subtle phases of the charge are ultimately considered to be irrelevant, because the psychological forces affecting both man and horse would result in some entirely different action. Although this view is popular among twentieth-century historians, it certainly would not have sat well with eighteenth- or nineteenth-century officers or tacticians who, because of their profession, had to delve into detail and determine which methods were the most effective in practice. These latter recognized, if we are permitted to use a neologism, that physical activity was never psychologically neutral but influenced how a typical soldier felt and acted in each situation. Frederick gradually realized that he could embolden the pathetic cavalry inherited from his father and at the same time make them appear invincible by carefully orchestrating their actions. More than half a century later, British infantry officers, otherwise employing a similar method of attack to their French counterpart, realized that subduing the men in order to create an emotional reserve and then purposely unleashing this force at the critical moment guaranteed success against their less psychologically aware opponents. Artillerymen gradually came to realize that by bouncing the round shot in front of their enemy they could rattle a formation much more than if they fired directly into it, even though they did not necessarily inflict a greater number of casualties.

These observations must force us to expand our definition of tactics. In Chapter 2, tactics was defined as 'the development of formal systems of troop movement and the use of available weaponry to derive a localized advantage over the enemy during combat'. This is more or less the standard definition as conceived since Napoleon's time. However, in light of the recognition that the nature of what the rank and file were called upon to do influenced their feelings and their continued will to fight, to our basic definition we must add: 'those tactics which proved the most successful on the battlefield were those that tended to impart a positive psychological effect on those employing them, and a negative impact on those against whom they were being directed.' Physical activity on the battlefield is never psychologically neutral but has a psychotropic effect, either positively or negatively affecting the morale of the troops, depending upon how appropriate the action is to human nature and the circumstances where it is employed.

The way military historians must set out to analyse and explain the dynamics within each commonly occurring situation must therefore change. It is necessary in any situation to see what tactics were prescribed and how these would influence human feeling and behaviour. To return to our example of cavalry charging cavalry, the analysis can no longer end with the observation that one or both sides will give way before contact. Each cavalry charge tactic to a greater or lesser extent influenced how the men responded to their fundamental instinct for survival. Cavalry travelling at speed in a tight, orderly formation benefited from positive feedback and the basic desire to avoid a mortal confrontation was delayed for a few more moments. Conversely, men in a looser formation perceived the compact mass of the enemy as possessing an almost insurmountable advantage and were a hundred times more likely to break first.

The more detailed examination of tactics and its effects on the battlefield also makes it necessary to reformulate the relationship between 'tactics' and 'grand tactics'. Rather than two truly distinctive and self-contained areas of human thought or activity, these are in reality two ends of a continuous linear scale. There has always been a temptation to view grand-tactical elements as some type of set of pure ideas, as if Frederick the Great was able to introduce the oblique attack because he was the first person to think of attacking an enemy's flank with a concentration of force quickly assembled from forces deployed along the enemy's front. The reality is that there is an intrinsic relationship between the grand-tactical options available to a commander and the movement and organizational properties allowed by the tactical systems in use. In an earlier work, *The Anatomy of Victory*, for example, we saw that Prussian oblique attack was based upon the march by lines manoeuvre.[5] This, in turn, only was possible because the Prussian infantry had adopted cadenced marching. Others had thought of the concept underlying the oblique attack, but they lacked the marching and manoeuvring systems that made it possible successfully to implement this grand-tactical ploy on the field of battle. The same type of considerations apply to the grand-tactical system employed by Napoleon and his marshals. The French certainly were not the first to think of 'concentrations of force' or operating along multiple axes of operations. Marlborough and, to a lesser extent, Frederick the Great utilized both concepts during battle. However, they were only able to do so by working around the intrinsic limitations imposed by the formations and manoeuvres then in use.

'Napoleonic Warfare,' rather than the product of one person's military genius, or a collective response to the emerging values and attitudes which culminated in the French Revolution, was instead simply the extension on a grand-tactical level of the properties and capabilities of the basic tactical system which ironically had been in place since the 1750s. For example, as we have seen, columns of waiting came about only because cadenced marching and perpendicular methods of deploying into line were introduced and commanders could maintain their troops in column well within cannon range. This was convenient not only because under ideal conditions it allowed a much greater concentration of force, but also because columns could change directions and thus manoeuvre many times more readily than could troops in an extended line. In turn, this manoeuvring capability made it possible for a large body, such as a division, corps or even army, to act along multiple axes of operations.

The causal relationship between the tactics in use and the grand tactical principles and methods that are feasible, in turn, reveals something about how both tactics and grand tactics evolve in the first place.

During the first part of a weapon's era, the main focus is on discovering the best way of utilizing the weaponry. Focus on the best psychological systems comes later.

HOW TO STUDY MILITARY HISTORY

This expanded conception of tactics and the realization that tactical-level events were important will ultimately have a profound effect on the way we must pursue military history. The traditional *de facto* approach of divorcing military history from the military science of the period under study can no longer be tolerated. Only when a wider body of knowledge is available for other researchers plying the more traditional avenues can these types of errors and myths more readily be avoided than they have in the past. To avoid these pitfalls it is necessary greatly to expand the subject matter beyond what is normally taken under consideration. The full range of elements affecting the conduct of warfare on the Napoleonic battlefield must be examined. On a purely tactical level, this means looking at a broad range of issues such as methods of delivering fire, manoeuvres, methods of attack and defence, use of cavalry weapons, cavalry charge doctrine, cavalry versus infantry techniques, and use of infantry squares.

Rather than limiting this effort to British and French practices, the experiences of all the major combatants who participated in the Napoleonic Wars must be taken into account. The research must be enlarged to include the experiences and events that occurred during campaigns usually ignored in the English-speaking world. It also means a greater number of non-English sources should be used than has typically been the case.

It is also vitally important to consider the evolutionary nature of warfare throughout the entire era that the musket dominated and defined warfare on the European battlefield. In order to be able to trace the origins of various truly innovative conceptions and practices that arose during the Napoleonic Wars, it is first necessary to determine what features of warfare were simply carried over unchanged from the earlier period and which elements underwent some degree of transformation. Even knowledgeable readers will be surprised to discover how much of the practices and tactics traditionally viewed as cornerstones of the Napoleonic system were actually developed and occasionally even used forty to sixty years before Napoleon's military début.

There is, however, an even more compelling reason why a work on the Napoleonic period should not overlook material shedding light on the immediately preceding linear period. Many of the most fundamental characteristics of combat remained constant throughout the entire reign of the musket on the battlefield. The very nature of the weapons that were used ensured that many aspects of tactical systems remained constant, regardless of the development of many doctrinal innovations. Because of this constancy in certain important areas, many detailed descriptions written in the earlier period shed valuable light on some practices and events in the Napoleonic Wars. There has always been a decided tendency for observers to pay the most attention to what is new, different or out of the ordinary. Examining the various memoirs and accounts of battles during the Napoleonic period, we encounter innumerable descriptions of forming squares, fighting in column, etc. These were practices, at least in their frequency of use, that broke with tradition and thus were notable and worthy of comment.

A conscientious historian must be equally concerned with what is generally taken for granted: in this case, what it was like to fight in line, the dynamics of the ordinary assault, or the disorder in the ranks as a formation wavered, and so on. These remained much the same as in the preceding period, and though of extreme importance when attempting to reconstruct an accurate picture of the battlefield, were largely ignored in Napoleonic memoirs. Anyone wishing to reconstruct the dynamics and properties of these tactical elements is forced to go back to eighteenth-century accounts. The introduction of the flintlock and the socket bayonet and the accompanying reduction in depth of fighting lines transformed the art of warfare. Most of those elements though well tried in later times were new to those writing in the early 1700s, and were thus worthy of description and comment in earlier memoirs and accounts.

However, not only is it necessary to compare how various characteristics of Napoleonic warfare differed or remained the same as linear warfare, it is also essential to determine what transmutations occurred during the Napoleonic period itself. Each individual topic, such as cavalry charge doctrine, must be discussed as it was found throughout the Napoleonic Wars and not merely in the form in which it manifested itself in the one or two campaigns most notable in the English-speaking world. When discussing cavalry tactics, for example, it is important to show variations exhibited among the major combatants, and not simply those used during the Peninsular War. Looking at the French army, it is important first to show the tactical practices and capabilities of the French army during the Revolutionary period before moving on to its increased capabilities and performance at the height of Napoleon's ascendancy 1805–1808. Finally, the decline of French cavalry 1809–1815 must also be examined.

No work on the Napoleonic battlefield can be complete without a thorough examination of the 'grand tactical' aspect of warfare, the variations found among different armies, and how it evolved throughout this period. Grand tactics is that part of military science which is concerned with the positioning, movement and orchestration of large bodies of troops on the battlefield. Unlike 'tactics', which deals with lower level and mechanical issues, such as firing procedures, how to move or change position, etc., grand tactics is much more conceptual in nature and is made up of a series of principles, concepts and guidelines. Its purpose is to gain an advantage over the adversary, usually by bringing an insurmountable force to an important position at a critical moment.

Unfortunately, the general view is that there were two grand tactical systems in use during the Napoleonic period which were opposite in nature and mutually self-exclusive: the linear system and a new more dynamic system introduced by Napoleon which eventually replaced its less flexible predecessor. Armies are typically seen as utilizing one system, while eschewing the other. This is largely inaccurate on two counts. It does not account for the continual evolution of grand tactical systems throughout the entire period or the regional differences which emerged. Moreover, the principles underlying linear warfare and the 'impulse' system which ultimately replaced it were not mutually exclusive. Tacticians in virtually all armies accepted concepts and practices from both the traditional approach and the new methods to create hybrid systems. Even the British army, known for its determined conservatism, began to integrate some of the most basic concepts of impulse warfare from 1812 onward, albeit almost unconsciously.

Probably the best commonly available description of the new 'impulse' grand tactical system is to be found in David Chandler's *Campaigns of Napoleon*. However, Chandler's explanation of 'Napoleonic' grand tactics is only a very general description of the some of the systems used by the French during 1805–1806. This is but a single snapshot of complex and dynamic processes subject to continual mutation and does not accurately reflect even French practices either before or after this date.

Fully to understand the panoply of grand tactical systems used during the Napoleonic period, it is necessary to begin the story with the various practices employed during the French Revolution. Contrary to common belief, Napoleon did not simply enter the scene and introduce an entirely new grand tactical system wholesale. Some of the most basic concepts in this new system had evolved long before Napoleon's entrance, while others were the product of factors and influences that were beyond Napoleon's personal control.

Many works studying the tactics of this period have inadvertently limited the analysis to the formal techniques and procedures practised on the parade ground during peacetime. Their treatment often does not extend beyond the official regulations and the manoeuvres, drills and practices these prescribed. In addition to limiting its appeal to serious scholars or enthusiasts, this approach also misses a very substantial part of what actually makes up tactics in any period. Throughout history, practice has never been completely congruent with theory. What the troops were trained to do and what they actually were able to accomplish on the field of battle often varied dramatically.

Consequently, it is important to determine which techniques actually proved useful on the battlefield and which were quickly rejected as impractical. It is also necessary to see how those practices that were used were modified when applied under battlefield conditions. The study of tactics, in addition to consisting of the codified elements of doctrine and training, must also include informal elements such as the lore and practice communicated to new officers by word of mouth and example in the field.

Notes and References

CHAPTER I

1. Bonaparte's account cited in *Battle of Lodi*, p. 16.
2. Anonymous account in *Battle of Lodi*, p. 14.
3. Bonaparte's account cited in *Battle of Lodi*, pp. 16.
4. *Battle of Lodi*, pp. 14–15.
5. Grivet, *Etudes sur la tactique*, pp. 54–6.
6. *Battle of Lodi*, pp. 14–15.
7. Lippett, *A Treatise on the Tactical Use of the Three Arms*, pp. 80–81.
8. Grivet, pp. 54–6.
9. Battle of Lodi, pp. 17–18.
10. Wood, *Achievements of Cavalry*, p. 33.
11. Chandler, *The Campaigns of Napoleon*, p. 293.
12. *British Military Library*, Vol. II, p. 420.
13. *Recueil de plans de batailles*, p. 85.
14. Wood, pp. 34–5.
15. Chandler, p. 291.
16. Petit, *Marengo, or the Campaign of Italy*, p. 25–6.
17. Thiers, *History of the Consulate and Empire*, Vol. 1, p. 247; Renard, *Considérations sur la tactique de l'infanterie*, p. 68–9; *Recueil de plans de batailles*, p. 85 refers to 'two battalions en potence' probably referring to the 30th, but all sources referred to these as in line.
18. Wood, pp. 35–6; Chandler, p. 294.
19. *Recueil de plans de batailles*, p. 85.
20. Wood, p. 36.
21. Petit, pp. 27–9.
22. Bismarck, *On the Uses and Application of Cavalry in War*, p. 49 citing *Notes on Campaign of Army of Reserve in 1800*, p. 52, Note.
23. Wood, p. 36–7.
24. de la Jonquière, *L'expédition d'Egypte*, Vol. 3, p. 212, footnote citing Donzelot's report to Berthier.
25. Rouillon-Petit, *Campaigns mémorables des Français*, p. 22 says 200 men, but General Friant in a letter to Capt. Binot 19 vendémiaire VII (10 Oct. 1798) specifically mentions the smaller

number; cited in Jonquière, Vol. 3 p. 217.

26. Jonquière, vol. 3, p. 212, footnote Donzelot's report to Berthier.
27. Jonquière, Vol. 3, pp. 212–213 – letter from General Desaix to Bonaparte 18 vendémiaire VII (10 Oct. 1798).
28. Rouillon-Petit, p. 22; also Jonquière, Vol. 3, p. 212–213 quoting letter from General Desaix to Bonaparte – 18 vendémiaire VII (10 Oct. 1798).
29. Letter from General Friant to Capt. Binot 19 vendémiaire VII (10 Oct. 1798) says 22 lay on the ground, cited in Jonquière, Vol. 3, p. 217; letter from General Desaix to Bonaparte – 18 vendémiaire VII (10 Oct. 1798) says 12 dead, 30 wounded, cited in Jonquière, Vol. 3, pp. 212–213.
30. Jonquière, Vol. 3, p. 217 – letter from General Desaix to Bonaparte, 18 vendémiaire VII (10 Oct. 1798).
31. Jonquière, Vol. 3, p. 212–213 – letter from General Friant to Capt. Binot 19 vendémiaire VII (10 Oct. 1798).
32. Rouillon-Petit, p. 22.

CHAPTER 2

1. Marmont, *The Spirit of Military Institutions*, p. 49.
2. Bülow, *The Spirit of the Modern System of War*, p. 97.
3. Mitchell, *Thoughts on Tactics and Military Organization*, p. 29.
4. Nosworthy, *The Anatomy of Victory*, pp. 192–7.

CHAPTER 3

1. de Brack, *Cavalry Outpost Duties*, p. 74.

2. de la Pierre, *Simples éléments d'art militaire*, p. 30.
3. de Brack, pp. 201–202.
4. Mitchell, *Thoughts on Tactics and Military Organization*, p. 65.
5. Müller, *The Elements of the Science of War*, Vol. II, p. 191.
6. Mitchell, p. 65.
7. Bugeaud's 'Instructions to the Fifty-six Regiment of French Infantry'; cited in *The Practise of War* (anthology), p. 177.
8. Brett-James, *1812: Eye Witness Accounts of Napoleon's Defeat in Russia*, p. 125, Captain Charles François of 30th *de ligne* at Borodino.
9. Mitchell, p. 65.
10. von Ompteda, *Memoirs of Baron Ompteda, Colonel in the King's German Legion During the Napoleonic Wars*, p. 72, in a letter to his brother Louis, dated 16 Oct. 1793.
11. Wood, *The Subaltern Officer: A Narrative*, p. 57.
12. Brett-James, p. 87. Battle of Smolensk; Lt. Christian von Martens Wurtemberger.
13. Wood, p. 208.
14. Jackson, p. 263.
15. Wood, p. 15.
16. Jackson, p. 262.
17. See Bugeaud's description p. 177 and note 18.
18. Bugeaud, I, v–vi, cited in Gates, *The Spanish Ulcer: A History of the Peninsular War*, p. 23.
19. Colin, citing Bombelles' *Traité des évolutions militaires*, Paris, 1754.
20. Carlyle, *History of Frederick the Great*, Vol. 3, p. 245.
21. Carlyle, Vol. 5, p. 203, citing Prince De Ligne's diary.
22. Duane, *The American Military Library*, Vol. I, p. 95.
23. Bugeaud, 'Instructions to the

Fifty-sixth Regiment', cited in *The Practise of War*, p. 177.

24. Ardant du Picq, *Battle Studies: Ancient and Modern Battle*, p. 127.
25. Duffy, *The Army of Maria Theresa*, p. 79.
26. Coignet, *The Note-books of Captain Coignet*, p. 79.

CHAPTER 4

1. Colin, *L'infanterie au XVIIIe siècle : La tactique*; Quimby, *The Background of Napoleonic Warfare*.
2. Quincy, Vol. 7, p. 60.
3. Colin, p. 25.
4. de Saxe, *Mes rêveries*, pp. 34–5.
5. Cited in Colin, p. 25.
6. Hatton, *The History of Charles XII*, pp. 115–16.
7. Taylor, *The Wars of Marlborough 1702–1709*, Vol. 1, p. 216.
8. Roberts, *Gustavus Adolphus*, Vol. 2, pp. 258–9.
9. Bland, *A Treatise of Militry Discipline*, 1762 edition, pp. 172–3.
10. Cited in Le Blond, *Eléments de tactique*, pp. 416–17.
11. Kane, *A New System of Military Discipline*, pp. 113–20.
12. Bland, pp. 172–4.
13. Quincy, *Maxims et instructions*, Vol. VII, p. 60.
14. The Prussians adopted cadence prior to 1740, and this was one of the advantages they enjoyed throughout the Wars of Austrian Succession.
15. Stutterheim, *A Detailed Account of the Battle of Austerlitz*, p. 100.
16. Puységur, *Art de la guerre*, Vol. 1, p. 151.

17. Belhomme, *Histoire de l'infanterie*, Vol. 2, p. 306.
18. Quincy, Vol. VII, pp. 66–7.
19. Quincy, Vol. VII, pp. 66–8; Puységur, Vol. I, p. 151; Belhomme, Vol. 2, p. 308.
20. 'Essai sur L'influence de la poudre à canon', Mauvillon, Leipzig, 1788, cited in Colin, p. 35.
21. de la Colonie, *The Chronicles of an old Campaigner*, p. 307.
22. Kane, p. 115; Belhomme, p. 199.
23. Hatton, p. 116.
24. Dundas, *Principals of Military Movements*, pp. 28–9.
25. de Saxe, p. 32.
26. Le Blond, pp. 405–7.

CHAPTER 5

1. Le Blond, *Eléments de tactique*, pp. 405–6.
2. Marquis de Chambray, 'Des changements dans l'art de la guerre depuis 1700 jusqu'en 1815', p. 9.
3. de Saxe, *Mes rêveries*, p. 73.
4. Duane, *The American Military Library*, Vol. I, p. 173.
5. Nosworthy, *The Anatomy of Victory*, pp. 189–90.
6. Carlyle, *Frederick's Battles*, pp. 47–8.
7. Duane, Vol. I, p. 175.
8. Du Picq, *Battle Studies*, p. 248.
9. Kane, *A New System of Military Discipline*, pp. 119–20.
10. Müller, *The Elements of the Science of War*, Vol. II, p. 186.
11. Duane, Vol. 1, pp. 181–2.
12. Ibid.
13. France–Regulations, 1791, pp. 47–8; also in Cooper, *A Practical Guide*, pp. 22–3.
14. *Recherches*, pp. 38–9.
15. France – Regulations, 1791, p. 49.
16. Bülow, *The Spirit of the Modern*

System of War, footnote on p. 120–21.

17. Ney, *Memoirs of Marshal Ney*, Vol. II, p. 368.
18. Ney, pp. 368–9.
19. de Saxe, p. 72.
20. Wolfe, *General Wolfe's Instructions*, p. 49.
21. de Saxe, pp. 45–7.
22. de Saxe, pp. 33.

CHAPTER 6

1. Jackson, *A View of the Formation of Armies*, pp. 147, 152.
2. *British Military Library*, Vol. 1, p. 89.
3. Delbrück, *History of the Art of War*, p. 409.
4. Colin, *L'infanterie au XVIIIe siècle*: La tactique, p. 29.
5. Colin, pp. 74–7.
6. Colin, p. 81.
7. Marquis de Chambray, 'Des changements dans l'art de la guerre depuis 1700 jusqu'en 1815', pp. 20–21.
8. Ross, *From Flintlock to Rifle*, p. 64.
8. Delbrück, p. 408.
9. Nosworthy, *The Anatomy of Victory*, pp. 183–7.
10. *New Regulations for the Prussian Infantry*.
11. *British Military Library*, Vol. 1, pp. 268–9.

CHAPTER 7

1. Lynn, *The Bayonets of the Republic*, p. 250, citing La Jonquière, *L'Expédition d'Egypte*, p. 165.
2. Chuquet, *Les guerres de la Revolution*, Vol. 4, p. 95.

3. Lynn, p. 276.
4. Lynn, p. 247.
5. Ross, *From Flintlock to Rifle*, p. 68.
6. Anon., *Mémoires de Custine*, p. 11.
7. Chuquet, Vol. II, pp. 203–9.
8. Roemer, *Cavalry*, p. 88.
9. Gneisenau, *Blücher*, pp. 27–33.
10. Anon., *Essay on the Art of War*, Vol. III, p. 189.
11. Delbrück, *History of the Art of War*, p. 402.
12. Duhèsme, *Essai sur l'infanterie*, pp. 134–5.
13. Grivet, *Etude sur la tactique*, p. 60.
14. *Recueil de plans de batailles attacques*, p. 49; Plate X, no. 31.
15. Renard, *Considérations sur la tactique de l'infanterie en Europe*, p. 45.
16. Grivet, pp. 62–3.
17. Renoir, p. 69.
18. *Recueil de plans . . . p. 66.
19. Rouillon-Petit, *Campaigns mémorables*, pp. 15–16.
20. *Recueil de plans . . .*, p. 68–70.
21. Rouillon-Petit, p. 22.
22. Spectateur militaire, *Evolutions par division d'armee*, Vol 6, p. 340.
23. Le Directeur, *Spectateur militaire*, Vol. V, pp. 53–7.

CHAPTER 8

1. In modern corporate proposal writing, this term refers to an idea which can be explained in a few sentences that the reader grasps in a moment intuitively.
2. Duffy, *Austerlitz*, pp. 123–4; Stutterheim, *A Detailed Account*, p. 93.
3. Michiels and Perciaux, *Au soleil d'Austerlitz*, p. 209; Grivet, *Etudes su la tactique*, pp. 72–3.
4. Cited in Grivet, p. 73.

5. Michiels and Perciaux, pp. 210–11.
6. This refers to a battalion column formed with the centre companies in the front.
7. Grivet, pp. 71–4.
8. Thiers, *History of the Consulate*, Vol. IV, p. 278.
9. Renard, *Considérations sur la tactique*, p. 44.
10. Grivet, p. 81–7.
11. Gneisenau, *Blücher*, pp. 37–8.
12. Thiébault, *Mémoires*, Vol. II, pp. 160–61.
13. Stutterheim, pp. 109–10.
14. Stutterheim, p. 100.
15. Gouvion Saint-Cyr, *Journal des operations de l'armée de Catalogn en 1808 & 1809*, pp. 63–9.
16. Duhèsme, pp. 447–8.
17. Oman in his lectures of 1907 and 1910 and Fortescue in first edition of *A History of the British Army* cited Maida as the classic example of the British line overcoming French use of columns; however, by 1912 in his *Wellington's Army*, p. 78 he recognized his error. Fortescue in 2nd edition of Vol. 5, 1921, similarly corrected this error; *Empire Eagles and Lions*, no. 56; 'Secondary Source History', pp. 2–7, Jim Arnold and Jean Lochet.
18. Empire Eagles and Lions, no. 56; 'Secondary Source History', p. 2–7, Jim Arnold and Jean Lochet.
19. Empire, Eagles and Lions, no. 56; Secondary Source History, p. 2–7, Jim Arnold and Jean Lochet.
20. Dyneley, *Letters*, pp. 9–10; to Captain J.K. Douglas R.A. from Messina dated 14 Aug. 1806.
21. *The Life of James FitzGibbon, a veteran of 1812*, pp. 303–4, cited in Dyneley, footnote, p. 10.

CHAPTER 9

1. *British Military Library*, Vol. I, p. 89.
2. 'The Character of the Armies of the various European powers, at the Peace of Amiens, in 1802', reprinted in *Essays on the Art of War*, Vol. III, p. 186.
3. *British Military Library*, Vol. I, pp. 90–91.
4. Ibid., Vol. II, pp. 108–109.
5. *Recueil de plans de batailles*, pp. 82–3.
6. Bressonaye, pp. 375–6.
7. *British Military Library*, Vol. I, pp. 268–9.
8. *Essays on the Art of War*, Vol. I, p. 232.
9. Rothenberg, *Napoleon's Great Adversaries*, p. 110.
10. Bowden and Tarbox, *Armies on the Danube*, p. 14.
11. Bowden and Tarbox, p. 15.
12. Rothenberg, p. 110, citing KA 1809, p. 111.
13. Rothenberg, *Art of Warfare*, p. 171.
14. Rothenberg, *Napoleon's Great Adversaries*, p. 107.
15. *1791 Regulations*, Plates volume, pp. 41–2.
16. *British Regulations of 1797*, pp. 319–20.
17. de Jomini, *Practice*, p. 192.
18. de Jomini, pp. 192–8.
19. Durand, *Empire Eagles and Lions*, #98, citing *Denkwurdigkeiten aus dem leben des Kaiserl. Russ. Generals von der Infanterie Carl Friedreich Grafen von Toll*, compiled by Theodor von Bernhardi, Leipzig 1865, Vol. I, pp. 43–5.
20. Paret, *Yorck and the era of Prussian Reform*, pp. 139–40.

21. Shanahan, *Prussian Military Reforms*, pp. 182–3.
22. Hofschroer, Pt 3, *The Courier*, Vol. 4, no. 1, p. 14.
23. Hofschroer, pp. 14–15; 'Essai sur les manoeuvres d'un corps', *Spectateur militaire*, Vol. XX.
24. Nash, *The Prussian Army*, p. 99.
25. Renard, *Considérations sur la tactique*, pp. 212–14.

CHAPTER 10

1. Macdonald, *Recollections of Marshal Macdonald*, Vol. 1, pp. 337–8.
2. Bugeaud, 'Instructions to the Fifty-sixth Regiment', cited in *The Practise of War*, pp. 164–5.
3. de Jomini, *The Practise of War*, pp. 195–6.
4. Paret, *Yorck and the Era of Prussian Reform*, p. 66.
5. Bugeaud, pp. 164–5.
6. A. du Picq, *Battle Studies*, p. 133.
7. Chandler, *The Campaigns of Napoleon*, pp. 852–3.
8. Nolan, *Cavalry*, p. 32.
9. Thiébault, *Mémoires*, Vol. 2, pp. 166–7.
10. Delbrück, *History of the Art of War*, p. 402.
11. Maude, *Cavalry Versus Infantry*, Vol. 2, p. 40.

CHAPTER 11

1. Duhèsme, *Essai sur l'infanterie légère*, pp. 442–4.
2. Ardant du Picq, *Battle Studies*, p. 246.
3. *Instruction sur le tir, à l'usage de MM. les Elèves des Ecoles de Saint-Cyr et de Saint-Germain (1813), Recherches*, p. 9.

4. Jackson, *A View of the Formation . . . of Armies*, p. 146.
5. Jackson, p. 147.
6. Zuparko, *Empire, Eagle & Lions*, no. 72, pp. 4–5, quoting Hennel describing the storming of the heights of Vera, part of a larger action known as the crossing of the Bidossa, 7 October 1813.
7. Hofschroer, *The Courier*, Part II, Vol. 3, no. 6, p. 12.
8. Hofschroer, p. 12.
9. Hofschroer, p. 12, reports from Major von Krafft referring to the role of Grenadier Battalion Krafft at Auerstädt.
10. Ardant du Picq, p. 246.
11. Bugeaud, cited in *The Practise of War*, p. 147.
12. General Loverdo, citing General Friant in *Spectateur Militaire*, Vol. 8, p. 349.
13. General Loverdo, pp. 342–3.
14. Napoleon's *Memoirs*, Vol. 5, p. 120; cited in Chambray, 'Des changements dans l'art de la guerre depuis 1700 jusqu'en 1815', *Spectateur Militaire*, Vol. 6, p. 11.
15. Jackson, p. 147.
16. Zuparko, *Empire Eagles & Lions*, 15 April 1983, no. 71, pp. 38, quoting Wheeler's description of a British infantry charge at Vittoria.
17. Zuparko, p. 37.
18. Zuparko, p. 36, quoting Hennel's description of a British regiment at Salamanca.
19. Dyneley, *Letters Written . . .*, pp. 9–10; to Captain J.K. Douglas R.A. from Messina dated 14 Aug. 1806.
20. de Brack, *Cavalry Outpost Duties*, p. 37; Duane, *The American Military Library*, p. 176; 'Guide de l'officier particular en campagne', cited in *Recherches*, p. 13; extract from Chapter VIII of the 'Guide

de l'officier particular en campagne', no. 426; 'Instruction' of 1822 cited in *Recherches*, pp. 18–19 – extract from the 'Instruction pour l'infanterie', 30 March 1822, Ch. 4; Lallemand, *A Treatise on Artillery*, Vol. 1, p. 85.

21. Cited in Greener, *The Gun*, p. 216.
22. Greener, p. 216.
23. Greener, p. 216.
24. Duane, Vol. I, p. 174.
25. In recent years the practice of history and military buffs donning period military costumes and getting together in organized groups to 're-enact' many of the period's battles has become increasingly popular. These enthusiasts are known as 're-enactors'. They provide a potential source of information and validation for anyone delving into the intricacies of warfare during the musket era, since they frequently devote a great amount of attention to mastering the period's manual of arms and weaponry.
26. Greener, p. 125.
27. *Recherches*, pp. 38–9.
28. Greener, p. 144.
29. *Recherches sur le feu*, pp. 38–9.
30. *Recherches*, p. 33.

CHAPTER 12

1. Jackson, *A View of the Armies*, p. 260.
2. Duane, *The American Military Library*, Vol. I, p. 174.
3. Hughes, *Firepower*, p. 27, citing Picard, *La campagne de 1800 en Allemange*.
4. Hulot, *Instruction sur le service*, p. 38; Bülow, *The Spirit of the Modern System of War*, footnote,

pp. 121–2; Duane, *The American Military Library*, Vol. I, pp. 174–175; Lallemand, *A Treatise on Artillery*, Vol. I, p. 85.
5. Paret, *Yorck and the Era of Prussian Reform*, pp. 271–3.
6. Anon., cited in Duane, Vol. I, p. 207.
7. Ardant du Picq, *Battle Studies*, p. 245.
8. Greener, *The Gun*, p. 245.
9. *Army and Cavalry Journal*, 1863, Vol. I, no. 1, p. 11.
10. Hughes, p. 133.
11. Estimated figures for Guibert, Gassendi, Piobert cited in du Picq, p. 245; anon. cited in Duane, p. 207, Jackson, p. 262; Decker in *Army & Navy Journal*, cited above.
12. Bülow, p. 120 and footnote on pp. 121–2.
13. *Recherches*, p. 9; Hulot, p. 37.
14. Greener, pp. 224–5.
15. Jackson, p. 261.
16. de la Pierre, *Simple éléments d'art militaire*, p. 30; *Maxims*, p. 124.
17. *Recherches*, p. 9; Hulot, p. 37.
18. Ardant de Picq, pp. 246–7, 250.
19. Mitchell, *Thoughts on Tactics*, p. 160.
20. Ardant du Picq, pp. 246–7.
21. Ardant du Picq, p. 246.
22. *London Times*, 7 Feb. 1806, p. 2.
23. Brett-James, *Eye Witness Accounts*, p. 128, Lieutenant Louis Planat de la Faye one of General Lariboisière's a-d-c.
24. Thiers, *History of the Consulate*, Vol. IV, p. 278.
25. *British Military Library*, Vol. 1, pp. 178–80.
26. Coignet, *Note-books*, p. 75.
27. Wood, *The Subaltern Officer*, pp. 90–91.
28. Gratten, *Adventures with the Connaught Rangers*, p. 248.

29. Decker, *De la tactique des trois armées*, pp. 128–129.
30. Wood, *Achievements*, pp. 94–5.
31. Brett-James, *The Hundred Days*, account of Captain von Reuter, pp. 76–7.
32. Thiers, Vol. 4, p. 69.
33. Thiers, Vol. 6, p. 422.
34. d'Ideville, *Memoirs of Marshal Bugeaud*, p. 48.
35. Bugeaud, 'Instructions to the Fifty-sixth Regiment' cited in *The Practise of War*, pp. 151–2.
36. Wood, *The Subaltern Officer*, p. 198.
37. Bugeaud, p. 151–2.
38. Duane, Vol. 1, pp. 181–2.
39. Coignet, p. 76.
40. De la Pierre, p. 31; Note: In this context 'fire by two ranks' and 'fire by files' are essentially the same thing. In his *Military Dictionary*, William Duane defined firing by files as 'generally used behind a parapet, hedge, etc . . . the first two ranks can only fire, and that must be by the two men of the same file always firing together . . . , Duane, *Military Dictionary*, pp. 157, 159.
41. Saint-Cyr, Gouvion 1808, p. 85.

CHAPTER 13

1. Wellar, *Wellington in the Peninsula, 1808–1814*, p. 47; cited in Griffith, *Forward into Battle*, p. 17.
2. Zuparko, no. 72, p. 5, citing Hennel describing an action storming the heights of Vedra.
3. Ibid., p. 7, quote from Wheeler.
4. Ibid., p. 5, quote from Hennel describing the storming of the heights of Vedra which is part of a larger action known as the crossing of the Bidossa 7 October 1813.
5. Zuparko, *Empire Eagle & Lions*, no. 70, p. 13, quote from anonymous Scot describing an action at Fuentes de Onoro, 3–5 May 1811.
6. Gleig, *The Subaltern*, p. 68.
7. Zuparko, *Empire Eagles & Lions*, no. 71, pp. 39, Costello at Vittoria.
8. Ibid., pp. 37.
9. Zuparko, *Empire Eagles & Lions*, no. 72, p. 6, citing Kincaid at Vera.
10. Mitchell, *Thoughts on Tactics and Military Organisation*, p. 64–5.
11. de Saxe, *Mes rêveries*, p. 32, 34–5.
12. d'Urban, *The Peninsular Journal*, pp. 214, 308.
13. Jackson, *A View of the Formation . . . of Armies*, p. 190–191.
14. Jackson, p. 252.
15. Dyneley, *Letters*, pp. 9–10.
16. Maude, *Cavalry Versus Infantry*, pp. 125–6.
17. Paddy Griffith, *Forward into Battle*, pp. 12–42.
18. *Réglement concernant . . . manoeuvres de l'infanterie (1791)*, pp. 118–119.
19. Zuparko, *Empire Eagles & Lions*, no. 71, pp. 37 citing Morris.
20. *United Service Journal*, March 1845, p. 403, cited in Griffith, p. 27.
21. Mitchell, pp. 64–5.
22. Dyneley, pp. 9–10, footnote citing 'The life of James FitzGibbon, a veteran of 1812', pp. 303–304.
23. Zuparko, *Empire Eagles & Lions*, no. 72, p. 9, Gleig outside Bayonne, November 1813.
24. Gratten, p. 243–4.
25. Gratten, p. 245; same action as cited.

26. Zuparko, p. 9.
27. Hibbert, *A Soldier of the Seventy-First*, p. 18.
28. Zuparko, *Empire Eagles & Lions*, no. 70, pp. 13, recounting the 71st.
29. Zuparko, *Empire Eagles & Lions*, no. 71, pp. 36.
30. Zuparko, *Empire Eagles & Lions*, no. 70, pp. 13.
31. Zuparko, *Empire Eagles & Lions*, no. 73, pp. 14, Kincaid at Waterloo.
32. Hibbert, *A Soldier of the Seventy-first*, p. 18.
33. Zuparko, *Empire Eagles & Lions*, no. 72, pp. 2.
34. Ibid., pp. 4–5, quote from Gleig describing an action in the crossing of the Bidossa, 7 October 1813.
35. Zuparko, *Empire Eagles & Lions*, no. 70, pp. 12, Blakeney at Barrosa.
36. Anton, *Retrospect of a Military Life*, pp. 107–108.
37. Duhèsme, *Essai sur l'infanterie légère*, pp. 446–7.

CHAPTER 14

1. Gremillet, *Un régiment pendant deux siècles (1684–1899); histoire du 81e de ligne*, pp. 33–4.
2. Colin, *Eléments de tactique*, p. 47.
3. de Saxe, pp. 47–8, 50.
4. Colin, pp. 75–9.
5. Colin, p. 275.
6. Citing Houchard in Lynn, *The Bayonets of the Republic*, p. 267.
7. Ross, *From Flintlock to Rifle*, pp. 67–9.
8. Lynn, p. 250.
9. Bugeaud, 'Intructions for the Fifty-sixth Regiment' in *The Practise of War*, pp. 152–3.

10. Bugeaud, pp. 151–2; 176–7.
11. Duhèsme, *Essai sur l'infanterie légère*, pp. 215–217.
12. Marmont, *The Spirit of Military Institutions*, p. 56.
13. 'Instruction of Field-Marshal Blücher For the Chief of Brigades, brigade commanders and staff officers (1815)', cited in Renard, *Considérations sur la tactique*, pp. 212–14.
14. Duhèsme, pp. 438–40.
15. Duhèsme, p. 440.
16. Bugeaud, pp. 151–2.
17. Duhèsme, pp. 217–18.
18. Duhèsme, pp. 437–8.
19. Leslie, *A Treatise on the Employment of Light Troops*, pp. 82–3; citing Surtees, *Twenty-five Years Rifle Brigade*.
20. Leslie, *A Treatise on the Employment of Light Troops*, pp. 74, 83.
21. Gratten, *Adventures with the Connaught Rangers*, pp. 64–5.
22. Bressonaye, *Etudes tactiques*, pp. 371–2.
23. Paret, *Yorck and the Era of Prussian Reform*, pp. 55–7.
24. Bressonaye, p. 372.
25. Paret, p. 60.
26. Hofschroer, 'Prussian Infantry', Part II, *The Courier*, Vol. 3, no. 6, p. 10, reports from Colonel von Raumer commander of IR no. 28 at Auerstädt.
27. Paret, pp. 122–3, 139–141.
28. Bressonaye, pp. 375–6.
29. Paret, p. 83.
30. Bressonaye, pp. 375–6.

CHAPTER 15

1. *Maxims*, p. 139.
2. *Maxims*, pp. 139–140.
3. *Maxims*, p. 139.

4. *Maxims*, p. 140; de Brack, *Cavalry Outpost Duties*, p. 209.
5. Nolan, *Cavalry*, p. 134.
6. *British Military Library*, p. 148.
7. Nolan, p. 134.
8. *Maxims*, p. 140.
9. *Maxims*, pp. 141–2; Marmont, *The Spirit of Military Institutions*, p. 72.
10. Nolan, p. 124.
11. *Maxims*, p. 141–2.
12. Decker, *De la tactique des trois armes*, pp. 187–8.
13. Nolan, p. 124.
14. *British Military Library*, Vol. II, p. 109.
15. *Warnery, Remarks on Cavalry*, pp. 75–8.
16. Nosworthy, *The Anatomy of Victory*, pp. 169–71.
17. *Warnery*, pp. 75–8.
18. Ardant du Picq, *Battle Studies*, p. 191.
19. Nafziger and Gilbert, *The Bavarian and Westphalian Armies*, p. 62.
20. Great Britain, *Instructions and Regulations for the Formations and Movements of Cavalry*, p. 32.
21. Maude, *Cavalry Versus Infantry*, p. 163.
22. du Picq, p. 185.
23. du Picq, p. 185.
24. Nolan, p. 135.
25. Nolan, p. 135; Roemer, *Cavalry*, pp. 144–5.
26. Wilson, *The Life of General Robert Wilson*, Vol. II, p. 426, letter to Honorable George Canning Memel, 22 June 1807.
27. Nolan, pp. 69–70.
28. Haythornthwaite, *Weapons and Equipment*, p. 37.
29. du Picq, p. 185.
30. du Picq, p. 187.
31. du Picq, p. 193.
32. de Brack, pp. 239–40.
33. de Brack, p. 240.
34. de Brack, p. 240.
35. de Grandmaison, *On the Military Service*, pp. 92–3.
36. Nolan, p. 54.
37. Mitchell, *Thoughts on Tactics*, pp. 190–91.
38. Thiers, *History of the Consulate*, Vol. IV, p. 280.
39. D'Urban, *The Peninsular Journal*, p. 196.
40. Mitchell, p. 181.
41. Digby Green, 'Who'll Stop the Cavalry', *Empire Eagles & Lions*, no. 72, pp. 19–20, citing quote from David Johnson's *Napoleon's Cavalry* describing how some Hungarian Hussars charged the French Carabinier Brigade at Leipzig.
42. Weis, *The Courier*, Vol. 4, no. 4, p. 3, citing Saxon Cavalry Regulations, pp. 5–6.
43. *Maxims*, pp. 136–7.
44. Wood, *Achievements of Cavalry*, p. 12.
45. Nolan, p. 143.
46. Weis, pp. 190–91.
47. Gneisenau, *Life and Campaigns*, pp. 28–33.
48. Weis, pp. 188–9.
49. *Maxims*, p. 137.
50. Weis, pp. 188–9.
51. Weis, pp. 186-7.
52. Decker, p. 193.
53. *Maxims*, p. 138.

Chapter 16

1. Warnery, *Remarks on Cavalry*, p. 17.
2. de Grandmaison, *On the Military Service*, pp. 16–17.
3. Fortuné de Brack was known as 'Mademoiselle' among his friends and peers. This nickname was in recognition of his handsomeness

and his elegance, and was not intended as a slight on his bravery which was renowned. *Cavalry Journal*, Vol. XX, no. 75, 1930, p. 72.

4. de Brack, *Cavalry Outpost Duties*, p. 42.
5. Haythornthwaite, *Weapons and Equipment*, p. 42; citing Rogers, *Mounted Troops of the British Army*, p. 153.
6. Haythornthwaite, p. 45; citing Bragge, p. 49.
7. de Brack, pp. 42–3.
8. Coignet, *The Note-books of Captain Coignet*, p. 124.
9. Nolan, *Cavalry*, pp. 55–6.
10. Nolan, p. 96.
11. Nolan, pp. 64–5.
12. de Brack, p. 17.
13. Mitchell, *Thoughts on Tactics*, pp. 191–2.
14. Roemer, *Cavalry*, pp. 345–6.
15. Nafziger and Gilbert, *The Bavarian and Westphalian Armies*, p. 25.
16. Nolan, p. 77.
17. Nafziger and Gilbert, p. 35.
18. de Brack, p. 45–6.
19. Marmont, *The Spirit of Military Institutions*, p. 78.
20. Brett-James, *The Hundred Days*, p. 59.
21. Wood, *Achievements*, pp. 94–5.
22. Wilkinson, 'The Lance in War', p. 10.
23. Marmont, pp. 78–9.
24. Nolan, p. 76.
25. Marbot, *Memoirs*, Vol. II, p. 264.
26. Ibid.
27. Nolan, p. 78.
28. de Brack, p. 47; Nolan, p. 78.
29. de Brack, p. 46.
30. Nolan, pp. 76–8.
31. Ardant du Picq, *Battle Studies*, p. 203.
32. de Brack, p. 50.
33. Dyneley, *Letters*, p. 46, while advancing on Madrid, to Mrs Dyneley, from Madrid dated 21 Aug. 1812.
34. Captain Nolan was one of the two greatest writers on cavalry in the English-speaking tradition. The other was Lt. Col. Frederick N. Maude who wrote during the 1880s. Unfortunately for Nolan and later enthusiasts enthralled by his writing and analyses, he met his fate during the charge of the Light Brigade.
35. Nolan, p. 75.
36. Wilkinson, p. 10.
37. Roemer, p. 347.
38. Elting, *Swords around the Throne*, pp. 229–30; Bukhari, *French Line Infantry*, pp. 11–12.
39. Mitchell, pp. 190–91.
40. Mitchell, p. 180.
41. Nolan, p. 45.
42. Cotton, 'A Voice from Waterloo', cited in Nolan, p. 46–7.
43. Nolan, p. 54.
44. du Picq, p. 200.
45. Roemer, p. 347.
46. de Brack, p. 49.
47. Brett-James, *Eye Witness Accounts of Napoleon's Defeat in Russia*, p. 125.

CHAPTER 17

1. Decker, *Batailles et principaux combats*, pp. 164–5.
2. Thomkinson, *Diary of a Cavalry Officer*, p. 280.
3. Berenhorst's *Betrachtungen über Kriegskunst*, cited in Nolan.
4. Gratten, *Adventures with the Connaught Rangers*, pp. 245–6.
5. Bland, *A Treatise of Military Discipline*, pp. 102–103.
6. Mitchell, *Thoughts on Tactics*, p. 42; von Bismarck in his *Lectures*

On Cavalry opined (p. 194), 'Cavalry, at the trot, moves six hundred paces in two minutes.' Wilson 'Orders to detachment of cavalry going to Cape of Good Hope prior to landing 12 Dec. 1805', p. 338, Vol. 1: 'A gun can but fire twice before cavalry should reach it, and its execution is seldom of any consequence.'

7. Lallemand, p. 347. The only real discrepancy is between the estimations of the speed of the horse at the gallop: Decker claims 600 paces/minute and most others around 400 metres (about 510 paces) a minute. Colonel Maude, writing at the end of the nineteenth century, claimed cavalry could rush the last 200 yards in 20 seconds, that is, at a rate of 600 yards in a minute; Maude, *Letters on Tactics*, p. 268.

8. Vergnaud, *Nouveau manuel complet*, p. 37; Decker, p. 197.

9. Puységur, *Art de la guerre*, Vol. I, p. 152.

10. de Grandmaison, *On the Military Service*, p. 109.

11. de Crispé; cited in Cooper, *A Practical Guide*, pp. 90–92.

12. de Brack, *Cavalry Outpost Duties*, p. 207.

13. Explanation of the Entire Exercise and use of the Pike; cited in *British Military Library*, Vol. I, pp. 26–8.

14. Puységur, Vol. 1, p. 152.

15. de Grandmaison, p. 108.

16. Cooper, pp. 90–92.

17. de Grandmaison, p. 108.

18. Wood, *Achievements of Cavalry*, p. 71.

19. Rochechouart, *Memoirs*, p. 68.

20. Cited in Maude, *Cavalry Its Past and Future*, p. 127.

21. Cooper, citing Turpin de Crispé, pp. 90–92.

22. de Quincy, *Maxims et instructions*, p. 64; also de Grandmaison, p. 108.

23. *British Military Library*, Vol. I, pp. 145–6.

24. du Picq, *Battle Studies*, p. 197.

25. von Bismarck, *On the Uses and Application of Cavalry in War*, p. 65.

26. de Brack, pp. 206–207.

27. de Brack, p. 79.

28. *Maxims, Advice and Instructions on the Art of War*, p. 160.

29. Wood, *Cavalry in the Waterloo Campaign*, p. 88.

30. de Saxe, *Reveries on the Art of War*, pp. 33–4.

31. de Brack, p. 207.

32. Marmont, *The Spirit of Military Institutions*, pp. 84–5.

33. *Strictures on the Army*, p. 45.

34. Marmont, p. 85.

35. Puységur, pp. 70–72.

36. Cooper, pp. 94–5.

37. Gassendi says 30 seconds and Maude says 20. Gassendi, J.-J. B., *Aide-mémoire*, p. 386; Maude, *Letters on Tactics*, p. 268.

38. Mitchell, p. 102.

39. Puységur, p. 71.

40. Berenhorst's *Betrachtungen über Kriegkunst*, cited in Nolan, *Cavalry*, p. 310.

41. Müller, *The Elements of the Science of War*, Vol. II, p. 193.

42. Cooper, pp. 90–92.

43. Müller, Vol. II, p. 187.

44. *British Military Library*, Vol. I, pp. 145–6.

45. Cooper, pp. 90–92.

46. Müller, Vol. II, pp. 187, 193.

47. de la Pierre, *Simple élements d'art militaire*, p. 30.

48. Cooper, pp. 90–92; Müller, Vol. II, pp. 187, 193.

49. Cooper, pp. 94–5.

50. Decker, *De la tactique*, pp. 163–4.
51. de Brack, pp. 50–51.
52. Warnery, *Remarks on Cavalry*.
53. Nolan, p. 97; Duhèsme, *Essai sur l'infanterie*, p. 161.
54. Puységur, Vol. I, pp. 70–71.
55. Bland (1762), pp. 102–103.
56. Okounef, *Examen raisonné*, p. 48.
57. Thomkinson, p. 280.
58. Müller, Vol. II, p. 193.
59. Marbot, *The Memoirs of Baron de Marbot*, Vol. II, p. 236.
60. Mitchell, pp. 101–102.
61. Bülow, *The Spirit of the Modern System*, pp. 144–5.
62. Translation from *Die Mecklenburger 1813–1815*, by John Koontz in *Empire Eagles and Lions*, no. 73, 15 July 1983, p. 6.
63. Keegan, *The Face of Battle*, pp. 154–60.
64. *British Military Library*, Vol. 1, pp. 146–7.

CHAPTER 18

1. *Maxims*, pp. 143–9.
2. Ibid., p. 156.
3. 'Müffling aus meinem Leben', Part I, Section 2, p. 134; cited in Maude, *Letters on Tactics*, p. 269.
4. *Maxims*, p. 156.
5. *Maxims*, p. 159.
6. Ibid., pp. 159–60.
7. du Picq, *Battle Studies*, pp. 196–7.
8. France – Ministre de la Guerre, *Ordonnance provisoire*, pp. 405–408.
9. *Maxims*, p. 149.
10. Warnery, *Remarks on Cavalry*, p. 46.
11. Wood, *Achievements*, pp. 30–31.
12. From von Bismarck's *Cavalry Tactics*; cited in Maude, *Cavalry, Its Past and Future*, pp. 132–3.
13. Mitchell, *Thoughts on Tactics*, p. 180.
14. Nolan, *Cavalry*, pp. 69–70.
15. Masson, Frédéric, *Cavaliers de Napoléon*, p. 73.
16. Nolan, p. 39.
17. Hohenlohe Ingelfingen, *Conversations on Cavalry*, pp. 5–6.
18. Ibid., p. 6.
19. Captain Ganzuage, *Kriegswissenschäftliche Analecten*, cited in Maude, Captain Frederick N., *Cavalry Versus Infantry*, p. 18.
20. This small book, along with those written by Captain Nolan and General Warnery, are the best works on cavalry written during the entire period. See Bibliography.
21. Warnery, p. 76.
22. France – Ministre de la Guerre, Règlements 1791, p. 407.
23. de Brack, *Cavalry Outpost Duties*, pp. 204–205.
24. du Picq, *Battle Studies*, p. 187.
25. Ibid., p. 187.
26. Ibid., p. 187.
27. Ibid., p. 192.
28. Ibid., p. 187.
29. de Brack, p. 207.
30. Ibid., pp. 207–208.
31. Ibid., p. 208.
32. Petrie, *Napoleon & the Archduke Charles*, p. 182.
33. Général Thiébault, *Manuel général du service des etat-majors*, p. 410; cited in Okounef, *Examen raisonné*, pp. 197–8.
34. Nosworthy, *The Anatomy of Victory*, pp. 122–4.
35. Parquin, *Napoleon's Victories*, p. 67.
36. Mitchell, pp. 179–80.
37. Ibid., p. 80.
38. Captain Ganzuage,

Kriegswissenschäftliche Analecten;
cited in Mitchell, p. 201.

39. Maude, *Cavalry Versus Infantry*,
p. 16.
40. Nosworthy, pp. 122–4.
41. Nolan, p. 74.
42. de Grandmaison, *On the Military
Service of Light Troops*, p. 92.
43. Warnery, p. 16.
44. Nosworthy, pp. 122, 124, 152.
45. Coignet, *The Note-books of
Captain Coignet*, p. 124.
46. Parquin, p. 31.
47. Parquin, p. 63.

CHAPTER 19

1. Cited in Haythornthwaite,
Weapons and Equipment, p. 56.
2. Hughes, *British Smoothbore
Artillery*, p. 27–34.
3. Hughes, *Firepower*, p. 13.
4. Gassendi, *Aide-mémoire*, p. 386.
5. Vergnaud, *Nouveau Manuel*,
p. 53.
6. d'Urtubie, *Manuel d'artillerie*,
p. 67.
7. Hughes, *British Smoothbore
Artillery*, pp. 22, 34.
8. Ibid., p. 35.
9. de Tousard, *American Artillerist's
Companion*, Vol. I, pp. 285–6.
10. Hughes, *British Smoothbore
Artillery*, p. 35; Hughes, *Firepower*,
p. 13.
11. de Tousard, Vol. I, p. 270.
12. Hughes, *British Smoothbore
Artillery*, p. 53.
13. von Tielke, *An Account*, Vol. I,
p. 200.
14. Brett-James, *Europe Against*,
p. 124; according to Karl Röhrig
posted near Napoleon on
Saturday 16 October 1813.
15. Okounef, *Examen raisonné des
propriétés des trois armes*, p. 342.

16. Frederick II, 'Instruction du
Frédéric, pour l'artillerie',
Spectateur Militaire, Vol. IV, p. 60.
17. de Tousard, Vol. II, pp. 244–6.
18. Great Britain – The War Office,
Rules and Regulations, p. 14.
19. d'Urtubie, p. 68.
20. Gassendi, p. 386; Vergnaud, p. 53.
21. de Tousard, Vol. II, p. 242.
22. de Tousard, pp. 343–4.
23. Jackson, *A View*, p. 264.
24. Claueswitz, *On War*, p. 195.
25. Review by 'D.M.', 'Système
d'artillerie', p. 620.
26. von Tielke, Vol. I, p. 186.
27. Ibid., p. 189.
28. *Army & Navy Journal*, Vol. I,
p. 11.
29. de Tousard, Vol. II, p. 38.
30. von Tielke, Vol. I, pp. 197–8.
31. Ibid., p. 198.
32. de Tousard, Vol. II, p. 39.
33. Okounef, *Examen raisonné*,
pp. 325–6.
34. de Tousard, Vol. II, pp. 39–42.
35. Okounef, p. 325–6.
36. Lynn, *The Bayonets of the
Republic*, p. 204.
37. Haythornthwaite, p. 60.
38. Hughes, *British Smoothbore
Artillery*, p. 56.
39. *Madras Gunner*, p. 120.
40. *Madras Gunner*, pp. 119–120.
41. Lynn, p. 206.
42. Caraman, 'Du service de
l'artillerie', *Spectateur Militaire*,
p. 417.
43. Rothenberg, *The Art of Warfare*,
p. 181.
44. Hughes, *British Smoothbore
Artillery*, p. 22.
45. Haythornthwaite, p. 56.
46. Caraman, p. 144.
47. Hughes, *British Smoothbore
Artillery*, p. 34.

CHAPTER 20

1. Review by 'D.M.', 'Système d'artillerie', p. 621.
2. von Tielke, *An Account*, Vol. I, p. 186.
3. 'D.M.', p. 621.
4 Marmont, *The Spirit of Military Institutions*, p. 87.
5. 'D.M.', pp. 623–4.
6. Okounef, *Examen raisonné*, p. 314.
7. Lallemand, *A Treatise on Artillery*, Vol. I, p. 76.
8. de Tousard, *American Artillerist's Companion*, Vol. II, p. 210.
9. Lallemand, Vol. I, p. 80.
10. *Spectateur Militaire*, 'Service de l'artillerie en campagne', Vol.??, p. 423.
11. von Tielke, Vol. I, pp. 178–9.
12. Lallemand, Vol. I, p. 347.
13. Frederick II, 'Instruction du Frédéric, pour l'artillerie', *Spectateur Militaire*, Vol. 4, pp. 57–8.
14. Great Britain – War Office, *Rules and Regulations*, p. 14.
15. Gassendi, *Aide-mémoire*, p. 386.
16. du Picq, *Battle Studies*, p. 247.
17. Lallemand, Vol. I, p. 346.
18. von Tielke, Vol. I, p. 194.
19. Okounef, pp. 342–4.
20. de la Pierre, *Simples éléments d'art militaire*, pp. 86–7.
21. *British Military Library*, Vol. II, p. 367.
22. de Tousard, Vol. II, pp. 235–6.
23. Frederick II, p. 60.
24. von Tielke, vol. I, pp. 195–6.
25. Ibid.
26. Caraman, 'Service de l'artillerie', p. 416.
27. Renard, *Considérations sur la tactique*, pp. 212–4.
28. von Tielke, Vol. I, pp. 195–6.

29. Great Britain – War Office, p. 14.
30. de Tousard, Vol. II, p. 246.
31. Lallemand, Vol. I, p. 346.
32. Thiébault, *Mémoires*, Vol. II, pp. 160–161.
33. Caraman, p. 423.
34. von Tielke, Vol. I, p. 200.
35. Marquis de Chambray, 'Des changements dans l'art de la guerre depuis 1700 jusqu'en 1815', p. 23.
36. Okounef, pp. 341–2.
37. *British Military Library*, Vol. II, pp. 367–8.
38. Lallemand, Vol. I, p. 347.
39. Maringoné, *Souvenirs*, pp. 86–7.
40. Gassendi, p. 386.
41. de la Pierre, p. 78.
42. Lallemand, Vol. I, p. 84.
43. Colin, *L'infanterie*, p. 73.
44. Duffy, *Army of Frederick*, pp. 112–113.
45. Rothenberg, *The Art of Warfare*, p. 181.
46. Lynn, *The Bayonets of the Republic*, pp. 204–5.
47. Elting, *Swords around the Throne*, p. 215.
48. Adye, *Bombardier and Pocket Gunner*, pp. 21–3.
49. von Tielke, Vol. I, p. 175.
50. von Tielke, Vol. I, p. 177.
51. *Maxims*, p. 124.
52. Caraman, p. 437.
53. von Tielke, Vol. I, p. 175.
54. *British Military Library*, Vol. II, p. 366.
55. von Tielke, Vol. I, p. 175.

CHAPTER 21

1. Okounef, *Examen raisonné*, pp. 316–17.
2. Brett-James, *Europe Against Napoleon*, p. 124.
3. Decker, *De la tactique des trois armes*, p. 166.

4. Memoirs dictated to General Montholon, Vol. I, pp. 287–8; cited von Bismarck, *Lectures*, p. 194, footnote by Beamish.
5. von Bismarck, *Lectures*, p. 202.
6. Ibid., p. 194 footnote by Beamish.
7. Davout, *Opérations*, pp. 222–3, 231.
8. Derrécagaix, *Le Maréchal*, pp. 136–7.
9. Thiébault, *Mémoires*, Vol. II, pp. 167–8.
10. Decker, p. 167.
11. *Maxims*, p. 132.
12. Thiébault, Vol. III, pp. 167–8.
13. Decker, pp. 167–8.
14. Brett-James, *The Hundred Days*, pp. 76–7.
15. Decker, p. 168.
16. von Bismarck, *Lectures*, p. 194.
17. Wilson, 'Orders to detachment of cavalry to Cape of Good Hope prior to landing' in *The Life of General Robert Wilson*, Vol. I, p. 338.
18. Gratten, *Adventures with the Connaught Rangers*, p. 111.
19. Parquin, *Napoleon's Victories*, p. 290.
20. *Maxims*, p. 160.
21. de Brack, *Cavalry Outpost Duties*, p. 211.
22. Nolan, *Cavalry*, p. 143.
23. von Bismarck, *Lectures*, p. 202.
24. de Brack, p. 211.
25. Thiers, *History of the Consulate and Empire*, Vol. IV, p. 280.
26. de Brack, p. 210.
27. *Maxims*, p. 160.
28. de Brack, p. 211.
29. Ibid., pp. 211–12.
30. Lallemand, *Treatise on Artillery*, Vol. I, p. 84–6.
31. Wilson, Vol. I, pp. 335, 338.
32. Gassendi, *Aide-mémoire*, p. 386.
33. *Strictures*, p. 25.
34. Jackson, *A View*, p. 147.
35. *Strictures*, p. 25.

CHAPTER 22

1. Duane, *The American Military Library*, p. 134.
2. *British Military Library*, Vol. I, p. 56, 'Official Account of the Battle of Neuneck, near Berne ... on March 5, 1798'.
3. Brett-James, *The Hundred Days*, p. 58, quoting Sergeant James Anton, 42nd Highlanders, in Sir Dennis Pack's Brigade.
4. Wood, George, *The Subaltern Officer*, p. 198.
5. Hibbert, Christopher, *A Soldier of the Seventy-First*, p. 18.
6. Saint-Cyr Gouvion, p. 85.
7. Marbot, *The Memoirs of Baron de Marbot*, Vol. II, p. 236.
8. Often these hussars are wrongly said to have defeated the Marine Guard; however, this is impossible since this latter regiment was not at Möckern and did not carry its eagle during the 1813 campaign.
9. Translation from *Die Mecklenburger, 1813–1815*, by John Koontz in *Empire, Eagle & Lion*, no. 73, p. 6.
10. Wood, *Achievements of Cavalry*, pp. 70–71.
11. In this case, it required more time to form in normal order than in inverted order because the column had to stop and let the front squadron quarter-wheel and move into line before the next squadron began to do the same. In other words, each squadron manoeuvred in series. If they were allowed to form in inverted order all squadrons would have performed these

actions at the same time and there would have been no delays.

12. Marbot, *Spectateur Militaire*, pp. 68–70.

13. Bugeaud, p. 164.

14. Ney, p. 372; Duhèsme, *Essai sur l'infanterie légère*, pp. 207–209.

15. *Maxims*, p. 154.

16. de Brack, *Cavalry Outpost Duties*, pp. 189–91.

17. Thiébault, *Mémoires*, Vol. II, pp. 159, 167–8.

18. Coignet, *The Note-books of Captain Coignet*, p. 67.

19. Ney, *Memoirs of Marshal Ney*, pp. 372–3.

20. Duhèsme, pp. 207–209.

21. Ney, pp. 372–3.

22. Duhèsme, pp. 207–209.

23. de Brack, pp. 191–2.

24. Ibid., pp. 189–92.

25. Marbot, *Spectateur Militaire*, Vol. III, pp. 241–2.

26. Marbot, pp. 247–8.

27. Bugeaud, in *The Practise of War* (anthology), p. 156.

28. Haly, *Military Observations*, p. 10.

29. Duhèsme, pp. 207–209.

30. Warnery, *Remarks on Cavalry*, p. 18.

31. Gneisenau, *The Life and Campaigns of Field Marshal Blücher*, pp. 28–33.

32. *Maxims*, p. 154.

33. Thiébault, Vol. II, p. 159.

34. Wilson, *Life of General Robert Wilson*, Vol. II, p. 426, letter to Honorable George Canning Memel, 22 June 1807, describing battle of Friedland.

35. Tielke, *An Account*, Vol. I, p. 185.

36. Thiébault, Vol. II, p. 160–61.

37. Wood, *Achievements*, p. 13.

38. Parquin, *Napoleon's Victories*, pp. 80–81.

39. Thiébault, Vol. II, pp. 166–7.

CHAPTER 23

1. Keegan, *The Face of Battle*, pp. 61–7.

2. Ibid., p. 147.

3. Wood, *Cavalry in the Waterloo Campaign*, pp. 87–92.

4. Creasy, *Fifteen Decisive Battles of the Western World*.

5. Brent Nosworthy, *The Anatomy of Victory*.

6. David Chandler, *Campaigns of Napoleon*.

Bibliography

Anon, *Army and Navy Journal*, New York, 1861–1865, 4 vols.

Anon, *The Battle of Lodi, or an Accurate Sketch of General Buonaparte's Campaign in Italy*, London, 1803.

——, *British Military Library*, London, 2 vols, 1798–1801.

——, 'Napoleon's Cavalry and its Leaders', *Cavalry Journal*, vol. 20, 1930, no. 75, p. 72.

——, *The Cavalry Journal*, London, vol. 20.

——, 'Combat de Maida', *Spectateur Militaire*, Paris, vol. 4, Paris, 1828, pp. 480–5.

——, *Essay on the Art of War*, London, 1761.

——, *Essays on the Art of War*, 3 vols, London, 1809.

——, Lettre de le Directeur du Spectateur Militaire', *Spectateur Militaire*, Paris, vol. 5, Paris, 1828, pp. 53–7.

——, *London Times*, London, Feb 7, 1806.

——, *The Manual Exercise as Ordered by his Majesty in 1764*, New York, 1775.

——, *Mémoires posthumes du Général François Comte de Custine* (written by an aide-de-camp of his), Hamburg, 1794.

——, *The Officer's Manual in the Field, or a Series of Military Plans Representing the Principal Operations of a Campaign* (trans. from German), 2nd ed., London, 1800 (reprinted New York, 1968). Original work written in Prussia several years after Seven Years' War under auspices of General Czetteritz.

——, *New Regulations for the Prussian Infantry*, London, 1756.

——, *The Field of Mars: Being an Alphabetical Digestion of the Principal Naval and Military Engagements*, 2 vols, London, 1781.

——, *Maxims, Advice and Instructions on the Art of War* (trans. from French Captain Auguste F. Lendy), New York, 1862.

——, *Mémoires militaires du Général Baron Dellard*, Paris, n.d.

——, *A Plan for the Formation of a Corps* (by a colonel in German service, presumably Col. George Hanger), London, 1805.

——, *The Practise of War*, Richmond, Va., 1863.

——, *Précis historique des campagnes de l'armée de Rhin et Moselle pendant l'an IV et l'an V*, Paris, n.d.

——, *Recherches sur le feu de l'infanterie*, Paris, 1826.

——, *Recueil de plans de batailles attacques, et combat gagnés par Bonaparte*, Leipzig, *c*.1805.

——, *Sentimens d'un homme de guerre sur le nouveau système du chevalier de Folard*, Paris, 1733.

——, *Strictures on the Army*, Dublin, 1809.

——, *The United States Journal and Gazette of the Regular and Volonteer Forces* (later *The Infantry and Navy Journal*), New York, 1863.

Adye, Ralph Willet (Captain), *The Bombardier and Pocket Gunner*, 2nd ed., London, 1804.

Alombert, P.C. and Colin, Jean, *La campagne de 1805 en Allemagne*, 4 vols, Paris, 1902.

Anderson, Aeneas, *A Journal of the Forces Which Sailed from the Downs in April 1800*, London, 1802.

Anton, James, *Retrospect of a Military Life*, Edinburgh, 1841 (facsimile reprint, Cambridge, 1991).

Austria – Armee, *Reglement für die Kaisserlidh-Konigliche Cavellerie*, Vienna, 1806.

Austria – Armee, *Reglement für die Kaisserlidh-Konigliche Infanterie*, Vienna, 1807.

Autane (Colonel), Quelques manoeuvres d'infanterie', *Spectateur Militaire*, Paris, vol. 5, Paris, 1828.

Baer, Fred H., 'Napoleon Was Not Afraid of It', *Arms and Armor Annual*, vol. 1, ed. Robert Held, Northfield, Ill., 1973.

Barbaroux, Charles Ogé, *The Adventures of a French Sergeant During his Campaigns in Italy, Spain, Germany, Russia, etc. From 1805 to 1823*, London, 1898.

Barber (Captain), *Instructions for the Formation of Volunteer Sharp-Shooters*, London, 1804.

Bardin, E.T., *Dictionnaire de l'armée de terre*, 4 vols, Paris, 1851.

Batechelor, Joseph B. Jr, *Infantry Fire: Its Use in Battle*, Levenworth, Kansas, 1892.

Bavaria – Kriegministerium, *Geschichte des Bayerischen Heeres*, 11 vols, Munich, 1908–31.

Beca, Colonel, *A Study in the Development of Infantry Tactics*, London (trans. Capt A. Custance), 1911.

Begunova, Alla, *Iz istori Russkoy Kavalerii*, Moscow, 1992.

Belhomme, Victor L., *Histoire de l'infanterie en France*, 5 vols, Paris, 1893–1902.

Bère, Frédèric, *L'armée française*, Paris, n.d.

von Bismarck, F.W., *Lectures on the Tactics of Cavalry* (trans. Major N. Ludlow Beamish), London 1827.

von Bismarck, F.W., *On the Uses and Application of Cavalry in War* (annotated Major N. Ludlow Beamish), London, 1855.

Bland, Humphrey (Colonel), *An Abstract of Military Discipline; More Particularly with Regard to the Manual Exercise, Evolutions and Firings of Foot*, Boston, 1747.

Bland, Humphrey (Colonel), *A Treatise of Militry Discipline*, 5th ed., London, 1743; 9th ed., London, 1762.

le Blond, M. *Eléments de tactique*, Paris, 1758.

Bowden, Scotty, and Tarbox, Charlie, *Armies on the Danube: 1809*, Arlington, Texas, 1980.

de Brack, Fortuné, *Cavalry Outpost Duties*, New York, 1893.

Brécard, Charles Theodore (General), *L'armée française travers les ages*, Paris, 1931.

Bresonnaye, Pascal, *Études tactiques*, Paris, 1909.

Brett-James, Antony, *1813: Europe Against Napoleon*, London, 1970.

Brett-James, Antony, *1812: Eye Witness Accounts of Napoleon's Defeat in Russia*, London, 1966.

Brett-James, Antony, *The Hundred Days: Napoleon's Last Campaigns from Eye-witness Accounts*, New York, 1964.

de Briquet, Pierre, *Code militaire au compilation des ordonnances des rois de France concernant les gens de guerre*, 8 vols, Paris, 1761.

Bryant, Arthur, *Jackets of Green: A Study of the History, Philosophy, and Character of the Rifle Brigade*, London, 1972.

Bukhari, Emir, *French Line Infantry 1796–1815*, New Malden, 1973.

Bülow, A.H., *The Spirit of the Modern System of War by a General Prussian Officer*, London, 1806.

Calvert, Michael, and Young, Peter, *A Dictionary of Battles (1715–1815)*, New York, 1979.

Canonage, Joseph Frederick (General), *Histoire et art militaire*, 4 vols, Paris, 1900–1908.

Caraman (Marquis de), 'Du service de l'artillerie en campagne', *Spectateur Militaire*, Paris, vol. 6, 1830, pp. 409–62.

Carlyle, Thomas, *History of Frederick the Great*, 8 vols, New York, 1903.

Carlyle, Thomas, *The Battles of Frederick the Great*, New York, 1892.

Chambray (Marquis de), 'Des changements dans l'art de la guerre depuis 1700 jusqu'en 1815', *Spectateur Militaire*, vol. 6, 1830.

Chandler, David (ed.), *The Military Maxims of Napoleon*, New York, 1988.

Chandler, David, *The Campaigns of Napoleon*, New York, 1966.

Chesney, Charles, *Observations on the past and the present state of Fire-arms and on the probable effects of the new musket*, London, 1852.

Chuquet, Arthur, *Les guerres de la Révolution*, 11 vols, Paris, 1903–1933.

von Clausewitz, Carl, *On War*, London, 3 vols, 1940.

Coignet, J.R. (Captain), *The Note-books of Captain Coignet: Soldier of the Empire 1799–1816* (reprinted London, 1986).

Colin, Jean Lambert Alphonse (ed.) and Schauenbourg, Balthazzar, *La tactique et la discipline dans les armées de la revolution*, Paris, 1902.

Colin, Jean Lambert Alphonse, *L'infanterie au XVIIIe siècle: La tactique*, Paris, 1907.

de la Colonie, Jean-Martin de, *The Chronicles of an Old Campaigner: 1692–1717* (trans. from French Lt. Col. Walter C. Horley), London, 1904.

Combe (Colonel), *Mémoires du Colonel Combe sur les campagnes de Russie 1812, de Saxe 1812, de France 1814 et 1815*, Paris, 1896.

Cooper, T.H. (Captain), *A Practical Guide for the Light Infantry Officer*, London, 1806 (reprinted London, 1970).

Craufurd, Alexander H. (Rev.), *General Craufurd and His Light Division*, 1891 (reprinted London, 1987).

Creasy, Sir Edward, *Fifteen Decisive Battles of the World*, London (36th edition), 1894.

Darling, Anthony D., *Red Coat and Brown Bess*, Ottawa, 1970.

Davout, Louis Nicolas, *Opérations du 3e corps, 1806–1807*, Paris, 1896.

Decker, Karl D., *De la tactique des trois armes: infanterie, cavalerie, artillerie* (trans. F. de Brack), Paris, n.d.

Decker, Karl. D., *Batailles et principaux combats de la guerre de sept ans considérés principalement sous le rapport de l'emploi de la l'artillerie* (trans. from German Capt. Simonin), Paris, 1840.

Delbrück, Hans, *History of the Art of War*, vol. 4 (trans. Walter J. Renfroe, Jr), London, 1985.

Denison, George T. (Lt-Col), *A History of Cavalry From the Earliest Times*, London, 1873.

Derrécagaix (General), *Le maréchal de France Comte Harispe*, Paris, 1916.

Desbrière, Édouard (Lt.-Col.), *Organisation et tactique des trois armes: Cavalerie*, 4 vols, Paris, 1906–1910.

'D.M.', 'Système d'artillerie de campagne du Géneral Allix', *Spectateur Militaire*, vol. 2, 1827.

Donkin, Robert, *Military Collections and Remarks*, New York, 1777.

Duane, William, *The American Military Library or Compendium of the Modern Tactics Embracing the Discipline, Manoeuvres, & Duties of Every Species of Troops*, Philadelphia, 1809. Contains translation of 'The System of Discipline and Manoeuvres of Infantry Forming the Bases of Modern Tactics (For use by the National Guard and French Armies, 1805.'

Duane, William, *The Military Dictionary*, Philadelphia, 1810.

Duchatelet, André Victor (Lieutenant), *Historique du 106ème Regiment d'infanterie de ligne*, Châlons, 1890.

Duffy, Christopher, *The Army of Frederick the Great*, New York, 1974.

Duffy, Christopher, *The Army of Maria Theresa*, New York, 1977.

Duffy, Christopher, *Austerlitz: 1805*, London, 1977.

Duffy, Christopher, *The Military Life of Frederick the Great*, New York, 1986.

Duhèsme (Comte de, Lt. General) G.P., *Essai sur l'infanterie légère: traite des petites opérations de guerre*, Paris, 1814.

Dundas, David (Colonel), *Principals of Military Movements Chiefly Applied to Infantry*, London, 1788.

Durand, R.G., 'Suvarov's Tactics', Empire, Eagles and Lions, Issue no. 98.

Dyneley, Thomas (Lt. Gen.), *Letters Written by Lieutenant-General Thomas Dyneley While on Active Service Between the Years 1806 and 1815*, London, 1984.

Elting, John R., *Swords Around the Throne: Napoleon's Grand Armée*, New York, 1988.

Favé, Idephonse (Captain), *Histoire et tactique des trois armes et plus particulière- ment de l'artillerie de campagne*, Liège, 1850.

Fezensac (Lt.-General), *A Journal of the Russian Campaign of 1812* (trans. Colonel Knollys), London, 1852 (reprinted London, 1988).

Fortesque, Sir J.W., *A History of the British Army*, 18 vols, London, 1899.

France – Ministre de la Guerre, *Ordonnance du roi sur l'exercice de l'infanterie (May 6th 1755)*, Paris, 1755.

France – Ministre de la Guerre, *Ordonnance du roi sur l'exercice de la cavalerie (June 22nd 1755)*, Paris, 1755.

France – Ministre de la Guerre, *Règlement concernant l'exercice et les maneouvres de l'infanterie (August 1st 1791)*, Paris, 1821.

France – Ministre de la Guerre, *The System of Discipline and Manoeuvres of Infantry Forming the Bases of Modern Tactics (For use by the National Guard and French Armies, 1805)*.

France – Ministre de la Guerre, *Instruction concernant les manoeuvres de la cavalerie légère*, Paris, Year VII.

France – Ministre de la Guerre, *Manuel des sous-officiers de cavalerie*, Hamburg, 1812.

France – Ministre de la Guerre, *Ordonnance provisoire sur l'exercice et les manoeuvres de la cavalerie (1st vendemaire, Year XIII)*, Paris, 1813 (includes *Sur l'exercice et les manoeuvres de la lance* – September 24th 1811).

Frederick II (the Great), 'Instruction du Frédéric, pour l'artillerie de son armée', *Spectateur Militaire*, vol. 4, Paris, 1828, pp. 55–60.

Frederick II (the Great), *Instructions for his Generals* (trans. Brigadier-General Thomas R. Phillips), Harrisburg, Pa., 1944.

Frederick II (the Great), *Militarische Schriften* (compiled von Taysen), Berlin, 1882.

Fuller, J.F.C. (Colonel), *Sir John Moore's System of Training*, London, 1925.

Fuller, J.F.C. (Colonel), *British Light Infantry in the Eighteenth Century*, London, 1925.

Gassendi, Jean-Jacques Basilien, *Aide-mémoire a l'usage des officiers d'artillerie*, 2nd ed., Paris, 1844.

Gates, David, *The Spanish Ulcer: A History of the Peninsular War*, New York, 1986.

Gleig, George, R., *The Subaltern*, Edinburgh and London, 1848.

Glover, Michael, *Wellington's Army in the Peninsula 1808–1814*, New York, 1977.

Glover, Richard, *Peninsular Preparation: the Reform of the British Army 1795–1809*, Cambridge, 1988.

Gneisenau, Count (Quarter-Master-General), *The Life and Campaigns of Field-Marshal Blücher* (trans. J.E. Marston), London, 1815.

Gouvion Saint-Cyr, Laurent, *Journal des opérations de l'armée de Catalogn en 1808 & 1809*, Paris, 1821.

de Grandmaison (General; formerly Lt. Col. in Volontaires des Flandres), *On the Military Service of Light Troops in the Field and in Fortified Places* (trans. from French Major Lewis Nicola), Philadelphia, 1777. Originally published as '*Petit guerre; au traité du service des troupes légers en campagne*', Paris, 1756.

Gratten, William, *Adventures With the Connaught Rangers 1809–1814*, London, 1902 (reprinted London, 1989).

Great Britain – The War Office, *An Elucidation of Several Parts of his Majesty's Regulations for the Formations and Movements of Cavalry*, London, 1803.

Great Britain – The War Office, *Instructions and Regulations for the Formations and Movements of Cavalry*, 3rd ed., London, 1799.

Great Britain – The War Office, *Light Infantry Exercise*, London, 1797.

Great Britain – The War Office, *The Manual and Platoon Exercises*, Whitehall, 1804.

Great Britain – The War Office, *The Manual Exercise as ordered by His Majesty in 1764*, New York, 1775.

Great Britain – The War Office, *Regulations for the Exercise of Riflemen and Light Infantry and Instructions for their Conduct in the Field*, London, 1803.

Great Britain – The War Office, *Rules and Regulations for the Formations, Field-exercise and Movements of his Majesty's Forces*, London, 1798.

Great Britain – The War Office, *Rules and Regulations for the Guidance of Officers and Non-commissioned Officers of Artillery* (a.k.a. *The Madras Gunner*), London, 1808.

Greener, William, *The Gun or, a Treatise on the Various Descriptions of Small Fire-arms*, London, 1835.

Grémillet, Paul, *Un régiment pendant deux siècles (1684–1899): histoire du 81e de ligne*, Paris, 1899.

Griffith, Paddy, *Forward into Battle: Fighting Tactics from Waterloo to Vietnam*, Chichester, 1981.

Grivet, Lucien Charles (Captain), *Etudes sur la tactique*, Paris, 1865.

Grose, Francis, *Military Antiquities*, 2 vols, London, 1786–88.

Gross, Baron, *Duties of an Officer in the Field and Principally Light Troops*, London, 1801.

Grosser Generalstab, *Die Kriege Friedrichs des Grossen*, 20 vols, Berlin, 1890–1913.

Guibert, Jacques Antoine, *Oeuvres militaire de Guibert*, Paris, 5 vols, 1803.

Haly, Aylmer (Captain), *Military Observations*, London, 1801.

Hamilton, Edward P., *The French Army in America*, Ottawa, 1967; contains trans. of *Manual of Arms* specified by 1755 ordonnance.

Hanson, Thomas, *The Prussian Evolutions in Actual Engagements . . . Which Were Exhibited Before his Present Majesty*, 8 May 1769, Philadelphia, 1775.

Harkonen, Jim, 'French Formations at Barrosa', *Empire, Eagles and Lions*, Issue no. 111, October–November, 1990.

Hatton, R.H., *History of Charles XII*, London, 1968.

Haythornthwaite, Philip, *Weapons and Equipment of the Napoleonic Wars*, Poole, Dorset, 1979.

Held, Robert, *The Age of Firearms: A Pictorial History*, Northfield, Illinois, 1957.

Hennet, Leon, *Etat militaire de France pour l'année 1793*, Paris, 1903.

Hibbert, Christopher (ed.), *A Soldier of the Seventy-First; The Journal of a Soldier of the Highland Light Infantry 1806–1815*, Warren, Mich., 1976 (originally published Edinburgh, 1816).

Hofschroer, Peter, 'Die Katastrophe Von 1806: Was That Really Why the Prussians Lost', *The Courier*, vol. 5, no. 3, pp. 17–24.

Hofschroer, Peter, 'Prussian Infantry Tactics from 1792 to 1815', *The Courier*, vol. 3, nos. 5, pp. 17–21 and 6, pp. 9–13; vol. 4, no. 1, pp. 13–19.

Houlding, J.A., *Fit for Service: the Training of the British Army, 1715–1795*, Oxford, 1981.

Hughes, B.P. (Major-General), *Firepower: Weapons Effectiveness on the Battlefield, 1630–1850*, London, 1974.

Hughes, B.P. (Major-General), *Open Fire: Artillery Tactics from Marlborough to Wellington*, Chichester, Sussex, 1983.

Hughes, B.P. (Major-General), *British Smoothbore Artillery: The Muzzle Loading Artillery of the 18th and 19th Centuries*, London, 1969.

Hulot, *Instruction sur le service de l'artillerie* (3rd ed.), Paris, 1813.

d'Ideville, Henri, *Memoirs of Marshal Bugeaud*, London, 2 vols, 1884.

Jacquinot de Presle, C., *Cours d'art et d'histoire militaire*, Saumur, 1829.

Jarry (General), *Instruction Concerning the Duties of the Light Infantry in the Field*, 2nd ed., London, 1803.

Jackson, Robert, *A View of the Formation, Discipline and Economy of Armies*, 3rd ed., London, 1845.

Jeffries, George, *Tactics and Grand Tactics of the Napoleonic Wars* (ed. Ned Zuparko), Boston, 1982.

de Jomini, Henri Antoine, *Histoire critique et militaire de guerres de Frederic II*, Brussels, 1842.

de Jomini, Henri Antoine, *The Art of War*, London, 1862.

de la Jonquière, C., *L'expédition d'Egypte (1798–1801)*, 5 vols, Paris, n.d.

Kane, Richard (Brigadier-General; Governor of Minorca), *A New System of Military Discipline for a Battalion of Foot on Actions with the Most Essential Exercise of the Cavalry,* in *Campaigns of King William and Queen Anne from 1689 to 1712*, London, 1745.

Keegan, John, *The Face of Battle*, New York, 1976.

Kemp, Anthony, *Weapons and Equipment of the Marlborough Wars*, Poole, Dorset, 1980.

Kosciusko, General, *Manoeuvres of Horse Artillery* (trans. from French Jonathan Williams), New York, 1808.

Lallemand, H., *A Treatise on Artillery* (trans. James Renwick), 2 vols, New York, 1820.

Latrille, General, *Reflections on Modern War* (trans. Major Havilland Le Mesurier), London, 1809.

Leach, J. (Lt. Col.), *Rough Sketches of the Life of an Old Soldier*, London, 1831 (reprinted London, 1986).

Lemau de la Jaisse, *Carte générale de la monarchie françoise contenant l'histoire militaire depuis Clovis*, Paris, 1733.

Lemau de la Jaisse, *Septième abrège de la carte générale du militaire de France sur terre et sur mer*, Paris, 1741.

Leslie, Charles (Lt. Col.), *A Treatise on the Employment of Light Troops*, London, 1843.

Lippett, Francis, J., *A Treatise on the Tactical Use of the Three Arms: Infantry, Artillery, and Cavalry*, New York, 1865.

Lloyd, Earnst M., *A Review of the History of Infantry*, London, 1908.

Lochet, Jean (ed.), *Empire, Eagles and Lions*, nos. 71–116 (April 1981–1992), Metuchen, N.J.

Longueville, Thomas, *Marshal Turenne*, London, 1907.

Loverdo (General), 'Evolutions par division d'armée', *Spectateur Militaire*, vol. 8, Paris, January–March 1832, pp. 337–68.

Luvaas, Jay, *Frederick the Great on the Art of War*, New York, 1966.

Lynn, John A., *The Bayonets of the Republic: Motivation and Tactics in the Army of Revolutionary France 1791–1794*, Chicago, 1984.

Macdonald, Etienne-Jacques, *Recollections of Marshal Macdonald* (ed. Camille Rousset, trans. Stephan Louis Simeon), 2 vols, London, 1892.

Malibran, H., *Guide à l'usage des artistes et des costumiers contenant la description des uniforms de l'armée française de 1780 à 1848*, 2 vols, Paris, 1904.

Manceron, Claude, *Austerlitz: The Story of a Battle* (trans. George Unwin), New York, 1966.

Marbot, M., 'Evolution de cavalerie', *Spectateur Militaire*, vol. 3, Paris, 1827, pp. 52–72, 229–59.

Marbot (Baron, Lt-Gen), *The Memoirs of Baron de Marbot*, 2 vols, London, 1988.

Maringoné, Louis Joseph Vionnet (General, Vicomte de), *Souvenirs de Général Vionnet Vicomte de Maringoné*, Paris, 1913.

Marmont (Marshal), Auguste Frederic Louis Viesse de, *The Spirit of Military Institutions or Essential Principles of War* (trans. Henry Coppée), Philadelphia, 1862.

Marullaz, François, *Un des grands cavaliers de l'empire*, Paris, 1918.

Masson, Frédéric, *Cavaliers de Napoléon*, Paris, 1895 (quarto ed.).

Maude, Frederick N. (Captain), *Cavalry Versus Infantry*, London, 1896.

Maude, Frederick N. (Lieut.-Col.), *Cavalry Its Past and Future*, London, 1903.

Maude, Frederick, N. (Lieut.-Col.), *Letters on Tactics and Organization or English Military Institutions and the Continental Systems*, Leavenworth, Kansas, 1891.

May, E.S. (Major), *Guns and Cavalry: Their Performances in the Past and Their Prospects in the Future*, London, 1896.

Michiels, René and Perciaux, Raymond, *Au soleil d'Austerlitz: l'apogée de l'empire*, Geneva, 1974.

Miot, Jacques, *Mémoires pour servir à l'histoire des expeditions en Egypte et en Syrie*, Paris, 1804.

Mirabeau, Honoré, Gabriel Riquechi (Comte de), *Monarchie prussienne sous Frederic le grand*, 4 vols. & atlas, London, 1788.

Mitchell, John (Lt.-Col. R.A.), *Thoughts on Tactics and Military Organization*, London, 1838.

Müller, William, *The Elements of the Science of War*, 3 vols, London, 1811.

Murray, Stewart (Lieut.), *Discipline: its Reason and Battle Value*, London, 1893.

Nafziger, George. F., and Mike Gilbert, *The Bavarian and Westphalian Armies: 1799–1815*, Cambridge, Ontario, 1981.

Nafziger, George F., *The Russian Army 1800–1815*, Cambridge, Ont., Canada, 1983.

Nafziger, George F., *The Wurttembourg Army: 1793–1815*, Leeds, 1987.

Nafziger, George F., 'Historical Perspective on the Use of Napoleonic Artillery', *The Courier*, vol. VIII, no. 3.

Napoleon I, *Tableau historiques des campagnes d'Italie depuis l'an IV jusqu'à la bataille de Marengo*, Paris, 1806.

Nash, David, *The Prussian Army: 1808–1815*, London, 1972.

Ney, Michel, *Military Studies* (trans. G.H. Caunter), London, 1833.

Ney, Michel, *Memoirs of Marshal Ney*, London, 2 vols, 1833.

Niemeyer, Joachim, and George Ortenburg, *The Hanoverian Army During the Seven Years' War*, Copenhagen, 1977.

Nolan, L, *Cavalry: its History and Tactics*, Columbia, S.C., 1864.

Nosworthy, Brent, *The Anatomy of Victory: Battle Tactics 1689–1763*, New York, 1990.

Okounef, Nikolai Alexsandrovich, *Examen raisonné des propriétés des trois armes de leur emploi dans les batailles et de leur rapport entre elles*, Paris, 1832.

Okounef, Nikolai Alexsandrovich, *Considérations sur les grandes opérations de la campagne de 1812 en Russie*, Brussels, 1841.

Oman, Charles (Sir), *Wellington's Army 1809–1814*, London, 1913 (reprinted London, 1986).

Oman, Charles (Sir), *Studies in Napoleonic Wars* (reprinted London, 1987).

Omnium, Jacob (Mathew Higgens), *Light Horse*, London, 1855.

von Ompteda, Baron Christian, *Memoirs of Baron Ompteda, Colonel in the King's German Legion During the Napoleonic Wars*, London, 1894 (reprinted London, 1987).

Paret, Peter, *Yorck and the Era of Prussian Reform 1807–1815*, Princeton, 1966.

Park, S.J., and Nafziger, George F., *The British Military: Its System and Organization 1803–1815*, Cambridge, Ontario, 1983.

Parkinson, Roger, *Clausewitz: A Biography*, New York, 1971.

Parquin, Charles (Capt.), *Napoleon's Victories: From the Personal Memoirs of Capt C. Parquin of the Imperial Guard 1803–1814*, Chicago, 1893.

Petit, Joseph, *Marengo or the Campaign of Italy, by the Army of the Reserve under the Command of the Chief Consul Bonaparte*, Philadelphia, 1801.

Petrie, F. Lorraine, *Napoleon & the Archduke Charles: A History Of The Franco-Austrian Campaign In The Valley Of The Danube In 1809*, London, 1909 (reprinted London, 1976).

Petrie, F. Lorraine, *Napoleon's Conquest of Prussia – 1806*, London, 1907 (reprinted London, 1977).

du Picq, Ardant (Colonel), *Battle Studies: Ancient and Modern Battle* (trans. Col. John N. Greely and Robert C. Cotton), Harrisburg, 1947.

de la Pierre, E.H. (Sous-Lieut.), *Simples éléments d'art militaire*, Paris, 1847.

Pirquet, Pierre-Martin, *Journal de campagne de Pierre-Martin Pirquet 1781–1861*, no place given, 2 vols, 1970.

Prussia – Kreigsministerium, *Regulations for the Prussian Infantry (1743)*, New York, 1968.

Prussia – Kreigsministerium, *Regulations for the Prussian Cavalry (1743)*, New York, 1968.

Puységur, Jacques Francoise de Chastenhat (Maréchal de France, Marquis de), *Art de la guerre par principes et par règles*, 2 vols, Paris, 1748.

Quimby, Robert S., *The Background of Napoleonic Warfare: The Theory of Military Tactics In Eighteenth-Century France*, New York, 1957.

Quincy, C.S. (Marquis de, Lt.-Gen.), *Maxims et instructions sur l'art militaire*, bound in vol. 7 of *Histoire de règne de Louis le grand* (7 vols), Paris, 1726.

Count Rapp, *Memoirs of General Count Rapp*, London, 1823 (reprinted 1985).

Reihn, Richard K., 'Linear Tactics and the Wargame', *The Courier*, vol. II, nos. 4, 5, Jan.–Apr. 1981.

Reihn, Richard K., *1812: Napoleon's Russian Campaign*, New York, 1990.

Renard, Jean Baptiste (General), *Considérations sur la tactique de l'infanterie en Europe*, Paris, 1857.

Roberts, Michael, *Gustavus Adolphus, A History of Sweden 1611–1632*, London, 1958.

Rochechouart (Comte de), *Memoirs of the Count de Rochechouart* (trans. Francis Lackson), New York, 1920.

Roemer, Jean, *Cavalry: Its History, Management, and Uses*, New York, 1863.

Rogers, H.C.B. (Colonel), *The British Army of the Eighteenth Century*, London, 1977.

Rolt, John, *On Moral Command*, 2nd ed., London, 1836.

Ross, Steven, *From Flintlock to Rifle: Infantry Tactics 1740–1866*, London, 1979.

Rothenberg, Gunther E., *The Art of Warfare in the Age of Napoleon*, Bloomington, Indiana, 1980.

Rothenberg, Gunther E., *Napoleon's Great Adversaries: The Archduke Charles and the Austrian Army 1792–1814*, Bloomington, Indiana, 1982.

Rouillon-Petit, F., *Campaigns mémorables des Français*, 2 vols, Paris, 1817.

de Saxe, Maurice (Comte de, Maréchal de France), *Mes rêveries*, 2 vols, Paris, 1757; *Reveries on the Art of War* (trans. Brigadier General Thomas R. Phillips), Harrisburg, Pa., 1944.

Shanahan, William O., *Prussian Military Reforms, 1786–1813*, New York, 1945.

Sicard, François, *Histoire des institutions militaires*, 5 vols, Paris, 1834.

Simes, Thomas, *A Military Guide for Young Officers*, London, 1781.

Skrine, Francis Henry, *Fontenoy and the War of the Austrian Succession*, London, 1906.

Smirke, Robert, *Smirke's Review of a Battalion of Infantry*, New York, 1811.

von Steuben, Frederick William (Baron), *Regulations for the Order and Discipline of the Troops of the United States (May 1792)*, Boston, 1794 (reprinted New York, 1985).

Stevenson, Roger, *Military Instructions for Officers Detached in the Field Containing a Scheme for Forming a Corps of a Partisan*, Philadelphia, 1775.

Stutterheim (Major-General), *A Detailed Account of the Battle of Austerlitz*, (trans. from French Major Pine Coffin), London, 1807.

Susane, Louis A. V. V., *Histoire de l'ancienne infanterie françoise*, 8 vols, Paris, 1849.

Suvarov, Aleksandr, *Nauka pobezhdat (The Art of Victory)*, Moscow, 1950.

Suvarov, Aleksandr, *Polkovoe uchrezhdenie*, Moscow, 1949.

Sweden, *Reglemente for Akunde Artilleriets Tjenstgoring Och Exercise*, Stockholm, 1808.

Sweden, *Forordning Och Reglemente for Regementerne Til Fot*, Stockholm, 1794.

Sweden, *Forordning Och Reglemente for Regementerne Til Fot*, Stockholm, 1813.

Taylor, Frank, *The Wars of Marlborough 1702–1709*, 2 vols, Oxford, 1921.

Ternaux-Compans, M., *Le général Compans*, Paris, 1912.

Thiébault, Paul Charles, *Mémoires du general Baron de Thiébault*, 5 vols, Paris, 1893–95.

Thiers, Adolphe, *History of the Consulate and Empire*, 12 vols, London, 1893.

Thomkinson, William (Lt.-Col.), *Diary of a Cavalry Officer in the Peninsular and Waterloo Campaigns 1809–1815*, London, 1894.

Tielke, J.G., *An Account of Some of the Most Remarkable Events of the War & A Treatise on Several Branches of the Military Art* (trans. Capt. C. Craufurd and Capt. R. Craufurd), 2 vols, London, 1787.

Tissot, Pierre François, *Trophées des armées françaises*, 6 vols, 1818–1821.

de Tousard, Louis, *American Artillerist's Companion on Elements of Artillery*, 2 vols, Philadelphia, 1809.

Turner, James, *Pallas Armata: Military Essays of the Grecian, Roman, and Modern Art of War*, London, 1683 (reprinted New York, 1968).

Turpin de Crispé, Lancelot (Count), *An Essay on the Art of War* (trans. Captain Joseph Otway), London, 1761 (originally published in French 1754).

d'Urban, Sir Benjamin (Major-Gen.), *The Peninsular Journal, 1808–1817*, London, 1930 (reprinted London, 1988).

d'Urtubie, Théodore, *Manuel de l'artillerie*, Paris, l'an XIII.

la Vallière (Chevalier de), François de la Baume le Blanc, *The Art of War Containing the Rules and Practice of the Greatest Generals in the Manoeuvres*, Philadelphia, 1776.

Vergnaud, Armand, Denis, *Nouveau manuel complet d'art militaire*, Paris, 1840.

Vertray, C.F.J.G., *L'armée française en Egypte 1798–1801 (Journal d'un officier de l'armée d'Egypt)*, ed. Henru Gallichet, Paris, 1883.

Viennet, Jean-Pons-Guillaume, *Souvenirs de la vie de Jean-Pons-Guillaume Viennet*, Moulins, 1929.

Von Schmidt, Carl (Major-General), *Instructions for Training, Employment, and Leading of Cavalry* (trans. Captain C.W. Bowdler Bell), London, 1881 (reprinted New York, 1968).

Warnery, Charles Emmanuel, (Major-General), *Remarks on Cavalry* (trans. Lt. Col. G.F.Koehler), Whitehall, 1805.

Weis, Karl, 'Skirmishing Light Cavalry of the Napoleonic Wars' (trans. Peter Hofschroer), *The Courier*, vol. IV, no. 4, Jan/Feb 1983, pp. 3–7.

Wilkinson, Henry C., 'The Lance in War', *The London Times*, 23 April 1903, p. 10.

Willyams, Cooper (Rev.), *A Voyage up the Mediterranean In His Majesty's Ship the Swiftsure*, London, 1802.

Wilson, Sir Robert, *The Life of General Robert Wilson*, 2 vols, London, 1862.

Wise, Terrance, *Artillery Equipment of the Napoleonic Wars*, London, 1979.

Wolfe, James (General), *General Wolfe's Instructions to Young Officers*, 2nd ed., London, 1780.

Wood, Sir Evelyn (General), *Achievements of Cavalry*, London, 1897.

Wood, Sir Evelyn (General), *Cavalry in the Waterloo Campaign*, London, 1895.

Wood, George (Captain), *The Subaltern Officer: A Narrative*, London 1826 (reprinted London, 1986).

Zuparko, ed., 'Charges, Firefights and Morale' (parts I–IV), March and July 1983; *Empire Eagles and Lions*, Cambridge, Ontario.

Glossary of Terms

à crémaillère: (a.k.a. Quincunx) a cumbersome type of square that from above looks like a cross; was employed, at least in theory, by the Prussians during the Silesian Wars.

appuy: To anchor. Usually used in reference to a flank; for example one appuys a flank on a pond or river.

Arquebus: An older type of firearm, similar to the musket except for its matchlock firing mechanism. It fired a heavier ball, weighing roughly 3½ ounces.

Battalion: An infantry organization usually commanded by the equivalent of a major (in the French army, a *chef de bataillon*; in the Austrian, an *oberstleutenent*), consisting of a varying number of companies. In 1791 a French battalion contained 9 companies; in 1809 it was reorganized into 6 companies. An Austrian battalion of the period contained 6 companies, while a battalion in the British army contained 10 companies.

Battalion Mass: The Austrian term for a battalion drawn up into a closed order column of manoeuvre. There appears to be much confusion among modern writers who have mistakenly elevated this to a separate type of formation, distinct from a closed order column.

Bricole Movement: The practice of advancing artillery while unlimbered.

Cadence: A uniform time and pace while marching, i.e. marching in step. The ability to march in cadence was the fundamental precondition for being able to perform any type of manoeuvre. Cadence was adopted by the French army during the 5 years preceding the outbreak of the Seven Years' War in 1756.

Caisson: A wagon or carriage used to transport artillery ammunition and projectiles.

Canister: Also called 'case shot'. This type of projectile consisted of a number of cast bullets housed in a tin canister. When fired these bullets would scatter over a large area, to maximize the number of casualties per round. Like round shot, it was fired at a low trajectory, but was used only at short range.

canon à la suédois: Small light cannons assigned directly to a regiment or battalion. These were first introduced by Gustavus Adolphus, hence the term 'Swedish cannons'.

Carbine: A short musket that was first designed to be used by horseman (in French: carabine).

Carabiniers: (1) Cavalry: Cavalry armed with short muskets, called carabines. In French service this was an élite unit, its troopers being chosen from the best marksmen in the cavalry. Although like dragoons they were also trained to fight on foot, this rarely, if ever, occurred in practice. They were usually used to engage enemy outposts. In French service by Napoleonic times many of these distinctions were lost, and carabiniers became heavy cavalry, and much to their chagrin in 1812 were forced to wear a cuirass.
(2) French Infantry: After 1792 the élite company in an infanterie légère regiment was known as the 'carabinier' company, and was the equivalent to the 'grenadier' company in a line regiment.

Case Shot: see CANISTER.

cavalerie légère: Meaning 'light cavalry'. Prior to 1749 this term was used in the French army to refer to all types of mounted troops other than the gendarmes and the chevaux-légers (both of which were heavier than the cuirassiers). Until this time in the French army, these latter two were the only two to be considered true 'cavalry'. The cavalerie légère included the cuirassiers, carabiniers and hussars. The dragoons were considered as a separate class.
In 1749 the term, cavalerie légère was abandoned and replaced by 'cavalerie', which referred to all mounted troops other than the dragoons.

Central Conversion: A formation changing the direction it faced by turning on its centre.

charge à la sauvage: An unbridled charge where the horseman gives full rein to the horse and attacks without any concern for order or cohesion among his squadron's ranks. This tactic was introduced gradually by Frederick the Great between 1741–1747 and was used only in the final years so that the trooper attacked his enemy with complete abandon, but was still perceived as being a part of a cohesive mass.

chasseur: Literally means 'hunter'. It was a popular term in the eighteenth century for referring to infantry or cavalry operating in extended order through the countryside.

chasseurs à cheval: A body of light cavalry, designed for service in advance or on the flanks of the army, corresponding most nearly to the Light Horse in the British service.

chasseurs à pied: Literally translated means 'hunters on foot'. As a light infantry force intended for detached service, it was loosely modelled on the German jaeger and was introduced into French service during the 1740s. Immediately prior to the French Revolution the term was applied to the light company in a line regiment's 2nd battalion or any company in a light infantry battalion. After 13 March 1803 it was exclusively reserved for the élite company in a light infantry battalion.

chevaulegers: The Austrian spelling for *chevaux-légers*.

chevaux-légers: Light cavalry first found in 15th century France. It was distinguished from the cavalry which was heavily encumbered by armour. The chevaux-légers regained popularity in the 1770s when one squadron (the 5th) was attached to each regiment of hussars. This experiment was short-lived and these squadrons were grouped together to form 6 regiments of chevaux-légers in 1779.

Closed Files: The distance between the files was brought close together. This was the normal mode before combat occurred.

Closed Order Column: See COLUMN AT QUARTER INTERVAL.

Closed Order Drill: The practice of limiting the soldier's activity in battle to a range of highly rigid and mechanical movements. Invariably, the adoption of closed order drill called for the arrangement of infantry and cavalry in massed formations where the men were positioned in a cross-hatched pattern of 'ranks' and 'files', see FILE and RANK.

Closed Ranks: Up until the second quarter of the 18th century it was common practice in many armies to have the infantry drawn up in both 'open' and 'closed' ranks, depending upon the tactical situation. 'Open' ranks referred to when there was a larger distance between each rank, usually around 4 paces, while when the troops were drawn up into 'closed ranks' this distance was reduced to around 1½ to 2 paces. Open ranks was used primarily as an intermediate formation prior to having the troops drawn up in closed order ranks, in which formation they would either advance towards or receive the enemy.

Closed Square: See SQUARES.

Column: A formation consisting of a series of platoons, companies, or divisions (of a battalion) in lines placed one behind another at pre-determined distances (intervals).

Column at Full Interval: A column where the distance separating each unit in the column equals the frontage of the first unit (also referred to as an 'open order column' or simply 'open column').

Column at Half Interval: A column where the distance separating each unit in the column equals half the width of the first unit in the column (also referred to as a 'half open column').

Column at Quarter Interval: A column where the distance between units is ¼ of the frontage of the first unit in the column.

Column of Attack: Starting in the early 1750s the French started to distinguish between closed order columns that were to be used for manoeuvring and those that were intended to assault the enemy. The exact differences between the two varied from regulation to regulation, and though the column of attack was officially sanctioned by the 1791 regulations, the tradition was continued up until the very end of the Napoleonic era.

Common Shell: This was a hollow cannon ball filled with gunpowder. It was fired using higher trajectories and consequently was mostly fired by howitzers or mortars.

Company: (1) Infantry: an organization of men, usually between 60 to 200 men, commanded by a captain.
(2) Cavalry: in the French imperial army half of a squadron (about 100 men in 1809), the equivalent of a British troop or a German 'flugel'.

corps de reserve: Literally, a 'reserve corps'.

Counter-Battery Fire: Artillery fire directed against enemy artillery.

coup d'oeil: Meaning literally 'a glance or blow of the eye', the term was used to refer to the ability of a commander accurately and quickly to assess the terrain for its use in tactical and grand tactical purposes. It was generally acknowledged that *coup d'oeil* consisted of two related talents: (1) the ability to judge how many troops a position could contain, e.g. how many battalions could be deployed in line between two points; and even more importantly (2) the ability to judge at first sight the advantages that could be derived from any given piece of terrain.

Cuirassiers:

Heavy cavalry wearing metal breast plates, called *cuirasses*, on the front and back and head plates. Out of favour in the mid eighteenth century, the cuirassier regained his position of prominence on the battlefield during the Napoleonic period.

en débandade:

'Helter skelter'; usually refers to the situation where an entire battalion is broken down into skirmishers without much regard to maintaining any type of closed order or reserve cadre.

Defile:

(1) [noun] A narrow pass that forces troops deployed in line temporarily to adopt a column. Example: a narrow clearing running through the woods or a pass between two hills.
(2) [verb] The process of moving through a narrow pass.
(3) [verb] To move to the left or the right, by marching by files (a flank march).

The Deploy:

A technique used by the Prussian army to have infantry manoeuvre from column to line, dating from the mid-1750s. The troops would oblique march (using the new lock step method) directly into line.

Deployment:

The process of manoeuvring from column to line. The opposite of 'ployment'.

Direct Fire:

(a.k.a. *feu à plein fouet*) Any aimed fire where the target was beyond the second point blank primitive but still within the effective range of the piece.

Division:

(1) In the early part of the 18th century this almost exclusively referred to a fraction of a battalion. The exact fraction of a battalion that made up a 'division' varied from army to army and period. However, for the most part battalions made up of 4 or 8 companies were divided into 4 'divisions', while battalions of 6 companies were organized into 3 'divisions'. The typical *infanterie française* battalion in 1749 consisted of 12 fusilier companies (plus 1 grenadier co) divided into 6 divisions.
(2) In the 1740s in the French army the word 'division'

began to acquire a second meaning. It gradually came also to refer to a 'division' of an army. By 1793 a division contained about 12 battalions, 2 cavalry squadrons and 22 cannons.

Double Shot: The practice of loading two pieces of round shot or one canister of case shot with one piece of round shot in a cannon to be fired at the same time. It was primarily a defensive technique used when the enemy advanced to close range.

Dragoons: Originally designed to serve as horse-mounted infantry, by the end of the 18th century dragoons came to be thought of and used as medium cavalry. Dragons were assigned the lion's share of housekeeping duties, such as outpost duties, etc.

Dressing: The process of straightening out the ranks in a line when they become disorganized, usually through movement.

en conversant: The pincer movements on either flank used in the *en tenaille* attack against the enemy artillery's infantry supports, see EN TENAILLE.

en crochet: This term literally means 'crocheted' and refers to a bent or crooked line. It was usually employed to 'refuse' a flank from an attacking enemy. Compare with POTENCE and REFUSED FLANK.

en fourrageur: See FORAGEUR.

en herse: A tactic used by infantry to attack artillery supported by cavalry. A line of skirmishers advanced followed by small reserves in closed column. Larger columns worked their way on either side of the enemy to outflank artillery and their supports.

en muraille: The practice of having the cavalrymen in each file riding knee to knee, with no or little spaces between each squadron.

en potence: In this formation, part of the line is thrown back 90° to the front, forming a right angle.

en tenaille: Artillery could defend itself by advancing its infantry supports in front of it. The attacking infantry then could use the following tactic. A line of skirmishers followed by their supports in the centre was held back. Other infantry formations attacked either flank, see EN CONVERSANT.

Echarpe: An older term for the oblique attack, for example: 'attacking in echarpe'.

echelon:

A series of companies, battalions, etc. that is staggered from left to right or right to left. In other words, each unit subsequent in the echelon is further to the flank and the rear than its preceding neighbour.

en échiquier:

The formations are placed in a 'checker board' pattern. In the 18th century and Napoleonic times, this meant that the battalions were deployed along two lines. There was a full interval between battalions. The battalions in the second line were directly behind the space left in the first line.

Evolution:

A mid-18th century term almost completely synonymous with 'manoeuvre'. See MANOEUVRE.

Extended Order:

A formation adopted by light infantry to create more space between files. During this period troops in extended order were usually drawn up into 2 ranks, each man separated by approximately a metre from his neighbour. It was also referred to as SKIRMISH ORDER.

feu de chasseur:

A form of volley fire, usually used by columns when treated by the enemy closely following behind. A rank or two fires and then proceeds to the rear, then the next rank fires. All the while the formation is slowly retiring in an orderly fashion.

File:

(1) [noun] The line of soldiers standing one behind another when in formation. Compare with RANK.
(2) [verb] To defile from line to form column.

Fire by Ranks:

Volley fire where one or more of the ranks in a formation fired in succession.

Fire by Files:

One of two files advances slightly in front of the line, aims and then fires. This is followed by the next one or two files. In this way, fire proceeds from one end of the formation until the other.

flanquer:

Troops deployed along either side of a large column to secure the flanks from enemy attack.

forageur:

Usually refers to cavalry fighting in a loose formation, typically 1 or 2 metres between each horse. It was generally used only in the day to day activities of a campaign and wasn't a common practice on a set-piece battlefield.

Fraising:

The process of deploying the pikemen in the centre of the battalion in one rank along the width of the battalion.

fusil:

In some armies, a variety of small musket usually carried by artillerymen, etc. In the French army, any type of musket.

Fusilier:

Originally, someone who carried a 'fusil'. In many armies,

the French, for example, this term gradually came to be applied to any common soldier who carried a musket.

Gendarmes: A body of cavalry formed by Henry IV upon his accession to the throne. It originally served as a type of body guard but by the late 17th century came to mean heavy cavalry. After the Revolution this term came to denote military police.

Grand Tactics: The principles, concepts and practices used to effect an advantage over the enemy at the next level higher than tactics. Grand tactics involves division and corps level considerations.

Grapeshot: Although canister was sometimes mistakenly referred to as grapeshot, strictly speaking this refers to a naval practice. Grapeshot consists of a bunch of large bullets quilted together and placed in a canvas bag. Owing to the damage it would cause to the guns, it was never fired from brass ordnance. Its tactical employment was similar to canister, SEE CANISTER.

Grenadiers: Selected from among the tallest and strongest men in the battalion, they were formed into special 'grenadier' companies. Grenadiers were at first equipped and trained to throw grenades. In most armies, the grenadier companies were removed from the parent regiments and converged into combined grenadier battalions. Although this was usually only done in time of war, the Prussians, for example, set up permanent grenadier battalions.

Half Open Column: See COLUMN AT HALF INTERVAL.

Hollow Shot: A hollow cannon ball that was filled either with gunpowder or molten lead, see COMMON SHELL.

Hollow Squares: See SQUARES.

Hussars: Hungarian in origin, these light troops were at first used as irregular cavalry delighting in raids, pursuit of disorganized enemy forces, etc. Starting in the mid-18th century, the trend was to use hussars increasingly as organized, if still light, cavalry.

Incline: To march obliquely to the left or right, see OBLIQUE MARCH.

infâmer cassation: The French term, used in the French and Prussian armies, for a dishonourable discharge.

infanterie légère: The French term for light infantry.

Intervals: A system of relative measurement used especially when creating a formation or performing a manoeuvre. The basic unit was the 'interval', which was equal to the frontage of a particular tactical unit, e.g. platoon, company, division (of a battalion), etc. All other distances were expressed either as a fraction or a multiple of this frontage. For example, if two companies were separated by half an interval the distance between them was equal to half the frontage of the company that was used as the standard.

Interline:	This refers to the practice of positioning troops between the first and second lines of battle.
Inverted Order:	The companies in a battalion were always positioned from right to left in a prescribed order, usually with the senior company on the right and the most junior in the middle or on the left. 'Inverted order' occurred when the companies were in the opposite arrangement.
Jäger:	The German term for 'skirmisher', literally it means 'hunter'. It is often also spelled 'jaeger'.
Light Dragoons:	The official title given to *chasseurs à cheval* when organized in the British army in late 1700's.
Light Troops:	The English term for *troupes légères*, it was mostly applied to organizations containing both infantry and cavalry which were to be used in the conduct of *petites guerres* (small wars) and trained in skirmisher tactics. In French service, such organizations were introduced during the first War Of Austrian Succession, and had become common during the Seven Years' War (1756–1763) and Revolutionary Wars.
Line:	The men in the battalion, regiment, etc. are placed along two or three ranks. This was the most common formation up until Napoleonic times.
Manoeuvre:	A predefined movement of troops used to change formation or position.
Marching by Files:	The men in the formation face left or right. Once they begin marching they follow the man that had been on the flank of that rank.
Marching by Lines:	A technique devised by Frederick the Great to attack quickly the enemy's right flank before the latter could effectively respond. All the units along an army line quarter wheel. The lengthy column thus formed moves rapidly to their right. Once they were extended sufficiently beyond the enemy's left flank they quarter wheeled. This was usually followed by an oblique attack.

499

Marching by Ranks:	This is the normal method. The formation marches, each man in a file following his leader at the front of the files.
Musketeer:	In the 17th century anyone who carried a musket. In the Prussian army (and the Russian army which emulated Frederick the Great) this term was applied to whoever was not a fusilier, light infantry or a grenadier.
Oblique Attack:	Devised by Frederick the Great during the Seven Years' War. One flank and the centre was 'refused', that is, held back. The other flank attacked in earnest. The Prussian army usually conducted its assault in echelons.
Oblique March:	A march diagonally to either the formation's left or right.
Open Column:	Same as 'open order column', see COLUMN AT FULL INTERVAL.
Open Files:	The spaces between files were opened up. This was more commonly done prior to the elimination of the matchlock.
Open Order Columns:	See COLUMN AT FULL INTERVAL.
Open Ranks:	The distance between individual ranks in the battalion is opened up (e.g. to 13 feet). This was necessary in the days before cadenced marching.
Pace:	A unit of measurement based on the average step of a soldier. It varied between countries. The English pace was equivalent to 30″; the French pace to 25.6″; and the German pace (called the 'Schritt'), 31.6.
Pandours:	Hungarian light infantry originally raised by Baron Trenck to combat robbers on and near the Turkish border. Skilled marksmen, they were adopted by the Austrian army during the Wars of Austrian Succession (the Silesian Wars).
Parallel Approach:	In the days before manoeuvres, an army would have to use the 'processional' method of forming line. This meant that the army had to approach the intended line advancing forward on the left side of the battlefield. Then it would have to march 'parallel' to the intended line, that is, across the battlefield. Line was then formed.
Parapet Fire:	A special form of volley fire that was originally used for troops stationed behind a parapet. Later, it was also used in the field when firing behind hedges, across bridges, etc.
pas de course:	The quickest allowable pace. The men were to move at a controlled run.
The Passage:	See THE DEPLOY.

peleton: The French term for 'platoon'.

Perpendicular
Approach: Once manoeuvres were introduced more efficient methods of deployment became possible. Battalions could march directly to where they were to form line and deploy. This meant their approach was literally 'perpendicular' to the intended line.

petite guerre: The French term for 'small war', i.e. the continuum of operations, petty skirmishes, etc. that went on continuously during the day-to-day operations of a military campaign, see SMALL WAR.

piquet: Literally, the 'pikeman'. Refers to the pikeman who served in outpost or guard duty to secure the company or battalion. After the disappearance of the pikeman, referred to anyone serving in this security function.

Platoon: Not an organizational unit. For example, in 1792 a French battalion consisted of 9 platoons, including grenadiers.

Platoon Fire: (In French *feu de peleton*). A system of regulating infantry fire by platoon. Ordinarily two platoons were made to fire at the same time and fire proceeded from each edge of the battalion towards the centre. During the time of Frederick the Great the Prussians would often perform this type of fire while slowly marching towards the enemy.

Ployment: The process of manoeuvring from line to column. The opposite of DEPLOYMENT.

point d'appui: Support, prop or fulcrum.

Point Blank: All artillery fire between the first and second point blank primitives. The first point blank primitive is the first point along the trajectory where the projectile crossed above the horizontal line between the barrel and the target. The second point blank primitive is where it crossed below this horizontal.

Positional Artillery: Artillery that was deployed to specific positions, rather than being assigned to a regiment. Positional artillery usually comprised the heavier pieces, 12-pounder or heavier.

Potence: The English term for *en potence*, see EN POTENCE.

Quincunx: See *à cremaillère*.

Random Fire: Any artillery fire conducted against targets further than the effective range.

Rank: A line of soldiers, positioned along the width of a platoon, company or battalion. See CLOSED RANKS, OPEN RANKS.

Rear Guard:

The portion of the army travelling in the rear to protect against an attack from this direction.

Refused Flank:

The condition of having a flank positioned so that it could not be immediately attacked by the enemy. Usually, a refused flank was formed by having the flank deploy obliquely or at right angles to the front line, so that it protected that flank.

Ricochet Fire:

(1) In a siege: the term refers to the practice of high trajectory fire used to dismount enemy cannons behind the parapets or other fortifications.
(2) Battlefield practice of aiming short so that the round shot would skip once or more along the ground in front of the target.

Round Shot:

Spherical solid shot, made out of cast iron fired out of cannons. It was usually fired at a low trajectory and its effect was confined to a narrow line of fire running between the gun and the target.

Shot:

(1) Men firing projectile arms, i.e. originally arbalists (crossbowmen), arquebusiers, etc.
(2) Solid shot ammunition for cannons.

Shrapnel:

See SPHERICAL CASE SHOT.

Skirmisher:

A soldier who 'skirmished', i.e. someone who fought in extended order (as opposed to closed order). See CHASSEUR, FLANQUER, LIGHT TROOPS, TIRAILLEUR and VOLTIGEUR.

Skirmish Order:

See EXTENDED ORDER.

Small War:

The English term for *petite guerre*.

Spherical Case Shot:

A hollow ball filled with smaller bullets. It would tear apart in mid air showering the enemy with multiple projectiles.

Squadron:

A low level cavalry organization approximating to the infantry company. Usually between 60 and 150 men.

Squares:

A variety of formations all with the distinguishing characteristic of being either rectangular or square in shape. These were defensive formations used to protect infantry from cavalry attacking the flank or rear. Although most drill booklets called for cavalry squares this was commonly recognized as being less than useless, and wasn't used in practice.
The three common versions found were as follows:
(1) the 'hollow' square, so-called because of the open ground in its centre. It was rectangular or square in shape

and was formed from either a battalion or a regiment. Occasionally, however, such as at the Battle of the Pyramids (21 July 1798) it was formed from a much larger body of troops.

(2) the 'closed' square, a more condensed variety, formed from a closed order column; the men in the third rank of each platoon or company in the column ran to the sides, so that each of the square's four sides offered a densely packed front.

(3) the 'small' square, used by small groups of isolated men standing back-to-back when suddenly caught in open ground and threatened by cavalry.

Swedish Pieces:
Gustavus Adolphus introduced light guns whose barrels were made of leather; these had much greater mobility and, unlike the heavy position pieces of the time, were able to follow the friendly troops around the battlefield. General de Brodarc introduced small light infantry pieces in 1741. Distributed among French infantry regiments they were known as 'Swedish pieces'.

Tactics:
The concept, principles and practices used to gain a local advantage over the enemy.

Threading:
The situation where the cavalry from both sides passed through one another.

tirailleur:
The French term for 'skirmisher' or 'rifleman'. Replaces concept of *chasseurs à pied* in late 18th century.

Troop:
A British cavalry organization equivalent to half a squadron.

Trooper:
A British term for cavalryman.

troupes légères:
See LIGHT TROOPS.

Vanguard:
The portion of an army that advanced or was positioned in front of the main body of troops. Its purpose was to secure the army's advance.

voltigeur:
Derives from the word meaning to flit about. The term was adopted in the French army in 1804 and referred to the men in a light battalion's skirmisher company. It was extended to a regular battalion's light company in 1805.

Wing:
(1) One half of an army when deployed in battle line, i.e. the left or right 'side'.
(2) One half of a battalion when deployed in line.

Zug:
A German term, used in the Prussian and Austrian armies for an organization equivalent to ½ of a 'half company', i.e. a ¼ of a company.

Index

Illustrations are indexed in *italic* type; **bold** type indicates a glossary definition or major treatment of the subject. Commentators who were active pre-1816 are indexed; for later ones, see the bibliography.